THE WORKS OF
SIR JOHN SUCKLING

The Non-Dramatic Works

SIR JOHN SUCKLING
By Sir Anthony Van Dyck

THE WORKS OF
Sir John Suckling

THE NON-DRAMATIC WORKS

Edited with
Introduction and Commentary by

THOMAS CLAYTON

OXFORD
AT THE CLARENDON PRESS
1971

Oxford University Press, Ely House, London W. 1

GLASGOW NEW YORK TORONTO MELBOURNE WELLINGTON
CAPE TOWN SALISBURY IBADAN NAIROBI DAR ES SALAAM LUSAKA ADDIS ABABA
BOMBAY CALCUTTA MADRAS KARACHI LAHORE DACCA
KUALA LUMPUR SINGAPORE HONG KONG TOKYO

FOREWORD

THIS edition of the works of Sir John Suckling is the result of the editors' close co-operation in a common pursuit lasting for several years, during which we have shared the labours of collating many copies of the early editions in libraries in the United Kingdom and the United States, have engaged in a continuing exchange of advice and information, and have criticized in detail the penultimate versions of each other's manuscripts; the history of our collaborative work is tangibly represented by an accumulated correspondence rather greater in volume than this edition. But the edition has been our end, and together we have attempted to present the best possible texts in a form as homogeneous as possible for the variety of materials and problems, and the works and days of the author and the editors, involved. We concede that, despite our co-operation, we are still unable to disclaim individual responsibility for any errors in the final form of the plays and the non-dramatic works, respectively, but we are convinced that, so far as our united lights allowed, Suckling has been the greater beneficiary for editorial collaboration.

We wish here also to make the acknowledgements of indebtedness that we can properly express with one voice. We are greatly indebted for the use of resources, but still more for the help and kindness of officials and assistants, to the Bodleian Library, the British Museum, the William Andrews Clark Library, the Folger Shakespeare Library, the Historical Manuscripts Commission, the Henry E. Huntington Library, the Kent County Archives Office, the Library Company of Philadelphia, the Library of Congress, the Newberry Library, the Oxford English Library, the Carl H. Pforzheimer Library, the Pierpont Morgan Library, the Public Record Office, the Rosenbach Collection, the Library of Trinity College, Dublin, and the National Library of Wales; and to the University Libraries of California (Los Angeles), Cambridge, Durham, Edinburgh, Harvard, Virginia, and Yale. And we are very grateful, for permission to reproduce materials in their collections, to the Chatsworth Settlement for the drawing by Inigo Jones, the William Andrews Clark Library and the Henry E. Huntington Library for title-pages and the engraving by William Marshall, the Henry Clay Frick Collection for the portrait of Suckling by Van Dyck, Mrs. Donald F. Hyde for a holograph letter, and Lord Sackville for a holograph letter and two manuscript poems.

We also share gratitude for the patience and care with which the readers for the Clarendon Press read our manuscripts and with wit as well as wisdom suggested improvements, and we owe a debt of magnitude to Dame Helen Gardner for her judicious and continuing assistance and advice. Finally, we are not Rosencrantz and Guildenstern nor, we hope, were meant to be, and we trust that it will be understood why we have written separate prefaces and made separate additional acknowledgements: even in collaborative work there are differences of applicable prefatory comment corresponding to divisions of primary labour, and we have, as persons, personal acknowledgements to make in our own ways.

L. A. B.
T. C.

PREFACE

I LIKE Suckling, and I have long thought him an unfortunately neglected poet and an interesting historical figure. But it would not have occurred to me to undertake a critical edition of his non-dramatic works without the suggestion of Dame Helen Gardner, made early during my graduate study at Wadham College, Oxford. To her I owe my greatest scholarly debt—for her concerned and intensive supervision, the example of her wisdom and exacting scholarship, and her unfailing kindness. The dissertation was, oddly enough, a pleasure to write, perhaps a little more so in retrospect than at the end of the writing. The present edition is very different from my dissertation and, I hope, in every way better, but that was done as scrupulously as I could have done it at the time, and Dame Helen went far to see that it was so. She is responsible for none of its faults, but I owe the relative best of this book to her, and it is properly so dedicated.

This is, in the strict sense, the first critical edition of Suckling's non-dramatic works. To W. C. Hazlitt's (1874 and 1892) and A. Hamilton Thompson's (1910) editions readers have long been indebted for modern collections of the known complete works, and I am especially indebted to them for first setting out in earnest and helping to point the way. But they had access to very limited textual and annotative resources, and it is not surprising that their editions were, for the most part, eclectic modernized reprints of the same works in the same order of the first and derivative editions of *Fragmenta Aurea* (1646) and *The Last Remains of Sir John Suckling* (1659) that contained some, not always beneficial, editorial emendations and were accompanied by general introductions and—in Thompson's edition, many and valuable—historical and explanatory notes. Many new resources have become available since 1910, however, and I have here attempted to integrate all of them to provide authoritative texts of a canon appreciably different in constitution and order from its earlier state, together with appropriate introductory matter, commentary, critical apparatus, and supplementary materials in two appendices.

On the arrangement of the works in this edition, the poems, the letters, the political polemic *To Mr. Henry German*, and the theological

Account of Religion are placed in that order, an obvious and logical one that is found in the early substantive editions. The poems and letters from *Fragmenta Aurea* (**1646**), *The Last Remains* (1659), and manuscript sources are inter-collected and printed, as far as the evidence permits, in approximate chronological order and, especially where evidence of chronology is equivocal or wanting, in groups of works closely related by stylistic and other internal affinities. Thus the poems are 'Juvenile Religious and Christmas-Seasonal Poems (*c.* 1626 or before)'; 'Secular Poems' of '(*c.* 1626–1632)', '(*c.* 1632–1637)', and '(1637–1641)'; 'Dubia'; and 'Poems Wrongly Printed as Suckling's in *The Last Remains*, 1659'. The letters are, first, those (Nos. 1–47) that are datable or can otherwise be helpfully and logically grouped, as, for example, by their inferential address to a person whose association with Suckling is terminally datable with reasonable certainty, such as Lady Mary Cranfield and Mary Bulkeley; and then 'Letters of Uncertain Date and Addressee' (Nos. 48–55, the last a letter doubtfully of Suckling's authorship). The order of the works is discussed in detail in the Textual Introduction (III. ii).

In addition to *To Mr. Henry German* and *An Account of Religion*, the present canon of seventy-eight poems and fifty-four letters includes, from manuscript, twelve previously uncollected poems and fourteen letters, and excludes seven traditionally canonical poems, four as dubious and three as certainly not by Suckling. For a seventy-ninth poem, 'To Mr. W. M. Against Absence', which is printed among the Dubia, arguments are advanced to support the probability of Suckling's authorship, and two other poems (Nos. 86–7) and a letter (No. 55) possibly by Suckling are here printed for the first time. The most important source of previously uncollected works is the collection of manuscripts of Lord Sackville, of Knole, Sevenoaks, Kent. All but one of the new poems and nine of the new letters—once the personal papers of the Earls of Dorset and of Suckling's uncle, Lionel Cranfield, first Earl of Middlesex—are found in this collection, and I am deeply indebted to Lord Sackville for permission to include them in this edition and to use facsimiles of three as illustrations. Of special interest among the previously uncollected works are the eleven juvenile religious and Christmas-seasonal poems from manuscript, which reveal a dimension of Suckling's writing and temperament that not even *An Account of Religion* much reveals or suggests, and the eleven letters, written over a period of eleven or twelve years, in Suckling's own hand. Finally, though not strictly part of the canon,

a number of poems and letters of great importance for the interpretation and placing in proper contexts of Suckling's works are included
in Appendix A, most of them collected and many of them printed
for the first time here. The canon is discussed in detail in the Textual
Introduction (II).

No manuscript collection of Suckling's works is extant, and probably none ever existed, but his works were obviously popular in his
day, since both substantive and derivative texts of one, two, or
several works are found in numerous manuscript and printed miscellanies—suggesting, by more than random groupings of some of
his poems, that the latter circulated often in 'papers of verses', in
which form some of the copy probably came to the printer. *Fragmenta
Aurea*, 1646, and *The Last Remains*, 1659, are sometimes more, sometimes less, reliable than early editions of the works of other seventeenth-century poets, and, like most, they were not published by
their author—in this case, because Suckling had been dead for some
years when they were printed. But even if Suckling had been alive
and had permitted publication it is doubtful whether he would have
had a direct supervising and proof-reader's hand in it. At any rate,
these books provide the sole substantive texts of many works and
copy-texts preferable on various grounds to a number for which there
are alternatives, and between them they provide a substantial
majority of the works in the canon. They are, however, far from
textually infallible, and it is indeed fortunate that there are a number
of extant variant texts of individual works, of which I have collated
all I could locate in a wide canvass of sources (see 'List of Sigla and
Textual Sources').

The text of the works in this edition can lay claim, I think, to
substantially greater authority than that of any earlier edition especially by virtue of the variant texts, which have sometimes provided
more authoritative copy-texts than are found in the substantive
editions; are the basis, through their variant readings, for editorial
inferences about the 'original' text that lies behind them; and are
the collective source of a number of readings more authoritative than
those of any one substantive text of a given work. Many of the new
authoritative readings might never have occurred to an editor's
unaided judgement as possible emendations and could only be supported by argument and speculation if they had, and on this account
alone the variant texts are invaluable, and they have contributed
extensive and significant changes in the texts of Suckling's relatively

major works, for example, 'The Wits', 'A Ballade. Upon a Wedding', *To Mr. Henry German,* and *An Account of Religion by Reason.* But I should like to hope that the editorial emendations, the only kind possible in the case of the unique substantive texts of two-thirds of the poems and all but a few of the letters, have also been appropriately informed by recent discoveries and have helped to bring the works to a more authoritative form. The matter of 'Copy-Text and Editorial Treatment' is discussed in the Textual Introduction (iii. i).

The rest of this edition exists chiefly for the direct illumination of Suckling's non-dramatic works. Some of the letters are apparently 'literary exercises', but most are addressed to particular persons and are otherwise 'historical' in the strict sense and therefore biographical as well as literary. Partly on this account, to obviate repetition in the Commentary, but also because a good deal about Suckling is known, is of interest, and has relevance to a study of his works, I have included in the General Introduction (i) a 'Life' of some length. The 'Life' provides much essential information not to be found in the *DNB* article on Suckling, and, though the discovery of some details is mine, I am so extensively indebted to the exhaustive researches of Herbert Berry, recorded in his dissertation, 'A Life of Sir John Suckling', University of Nebraska, 1953, and in *Sir John Suckling's Poems and Letters from Manuscript* (London, Ontario, Canada), 1960, that I have sometimes been at a loss when to allow an acknowledgement to pass as obvious and implicit. If I were thought to owe him little less than all, I should suppose justice done to both our houses; I am also indebted to him at many places in the Commentary. A note on the many portraits is appended to the 'Life' (i. i), and an essay on Suckling's 'Reputation' that emphasizes, and partly conveys by considerable quotation, his early eminence and later standing, completes the General Introduction (ii). Many editors also include an essay in literary criticism as part of their introductions, but it is my own view that, while this is a reasonably exercised option, it has no essential place in a critical edition. I have preferred to present the reader with reliable texts and essential supplementary and interpretative materials and to leave the specialized and agreeable offices of criticism to him and perhaps to myself in another place.

The Commentary is not intended to be exhaustive, but to be as selectively full as the individual work seems to warrant, consisting, first, in a general headnote on the subject, genre, antecedents, style, historical circumstances and date, close relationship to other works

by Suckling and others, and other matters of special interest, as
particular details are available and seem appropriate. Some of the
headnotes—as well as the notes on individual passages—may at first
seem to call to mind that '*Aretine*, in a Commedie of his, wittily com-
plaineth that ụpstart Commenters, with their Annotations and gloses,
had extorted that sense and Morall out of *Petrarch*, which if *Petrarch*
were aliue, a hundred Strappadoes might not make him confesse
or subscribe too' (Thomas Nashe, *Strange Newes, of the Intercepting
Certaine Letters, and a Conuoy of Verses, as They Were Going Priuilie to
Victuall the Lowe Countries*, 1592, sig. B1). But, *mutatis mutandis*, it has
seemed to me better to err on the side of extending *credit*—while
acknowledging that some affinities and felicities may well not have
been consciously intended—than 'timelessly' to pretend that it has
not by now been widely acknowledged that language itself and the
'unconscious minds' of authors have something of a life of their own
and make contributions to authorship beyond an author's immediate
awareness. To say, for example, that 'His Dream', a juvenile poem,
'belongs to a well-established tradition that probably had its formal
source in Ovid, *Amores* I. v', etc., is not to imply that Suckling, when
he wrote the poem, had his head full of Ovid and literary tradition,
but simply to note a fact about the relevant tradition, which did not
originate with Suckling (as the sub-genre of 'The Wits' probably did)
and to which he made a charming if slight original contribution.

In the Commentary notes on individual lines, which treat textual
problems, explain allusions, and provide aids to interpretation (but
generally exclude obsolete senses of words that may readily be found
in the *SOED*), attention is called to a number of parallels in Suckling's
works. Parallels of primary importance are quoted in full, and some
others are cited with accompanying key-words, but I have cited still
more in reference-form only. I am mindful of the possible abuses of
'the parallelographic school', as Greg called it, and the reasons for an
abbreviated citation are not always self-evident upon the pursuit;
but there is often a greater foundation for illuminating authorial and
critical inference in the correspondence between two passages than
is contained solely in a shared word or phrase, or paraphrase, and I
have noted them for that reason. For assistance with this task, I am
indebted to Messrs. Steven D. Crocker, who began, and Paul Page,
who completed, a computer-produced concordance for me.

If one's variously pertinent debts could be recorded *ab ovo*, summary
justice, at least, *might* be done to all to whom gratitude is genuinely

due, such as (for me), of the University of Minnesota, Professors Franz Montgomery, who brought me to the specialized study of English literature, and the late Norman J. DeWitt, who kept me actively at Latin and brought me to Greek; but one must chiefly acknowledge the immediate ones. I am especially indebted to Professors W. J. Cameron of McMaster University, Gwynne Blakemore Evans of Harvard University, and Mr. Edwin Wolf II, Curator of the Library Company of Philadelphia, for going to considerable trouble to give me information from their individual researches about poems in manuscript and printed miscellanies; to Mr. James M. Osborn of Yale University for assistance and kindnesses that pass count and specification; to Mr. D. G. Esplin, Acquisitions Librarian of the University of Toronto for wittily sharing some of his extraordinary bibliographical knowledge with me; to my friend Professor P. W. Thomas, of Cardiff College of the University of Wales, whose wry and rare good scholar- and fellowship enlightened my Oxford days both in and out of Bodley and the British Museum; and to Miss Margaret Weedon, Librarian of the Oxford English Library, for whom I worked as assistant for a time and who nevertheless allowed me to keep essential books on indefinite loan and gave me continuing cheerful and sagacious encouragement in my work (once, in gamesome mood, in the form of a Christmas greeting with a likeness of the bust of Sir John got up as Father Christmas).

I am greatly indebted to the *Times Literary Supplement* for publishing a request for 'Information, Please' and to those remarkably conscientious persons who of their great good will helpfully responded: Mr. Franklin M. Biebel, Director of the Frick Collection, New York, who called my attention to the presence in the Collection of the Van Dyck portrait of Suckling and made an inestimable contribution to my work in providing the master-link in the chain of portraits of which I had been investigating the genealogy; Professor R. J. Kaufmann, of the University of Rochester, New York; Mr. David Ramage, Librarian of Durham University; and Miss Lois Spencer, of London University. I have also to thank the Most Honourable the Marquis of Bath, for permission to print here Sir Henry Willoughby's letter to Charles I concerning Suckling's courtship of his daughter (MS. Longleat 114), and both his Lordship and Katherine, Mrs. Suckling, Lady of the Manors of Barsham and Shipmeadow, and her son, William Suckling, Esq., of Roos Hall, Beccles, Suffolk, for allowing manuscripts in their collection to be deposited in the Bodleian

Library for my use—and the last two for personal kindness and hospitality during a visit to Roos Hall. For financial assistance that enabled me to do much that I should not have been able to do without it, I am in more than the obvious way indebted to the American Council of Learned Societies, the Institute for the Humanities of the University of California, the Research Committee of the University of California (Los Angeles), the Research Committee of Oxford University, the Rhodes Scholarship Trust, and the Exhibition Fund of Wadham College, Oxford.

Special debts I must acknowledge with profound sadness as well as gratitude are those to the late Professors F. P. Wilson and, especially, Herbert Davis, who supervised my work for a time and helped me a great deal in Oxford and elsewhere, and J. B. Leishman, Esq., to whom, as one of my D.Phil. examiners, I am obliged for voluminous and helpful notes, which, he would not have been surprised to learn, also provided occasion for palaeographical exertions. The loss of such scholars to the profession of letters is the greater for their extraordinary humaneness.

Finally, in inadequate recognition of my wife's various and invaluable help and comfort, I should—with his joviality but without his irony—paraphrase Enobarbus: 'would you praise Ruth, say "Ruth"; go no further.'

T. C.

St. Paul, Minnesota

CONTENTS

LIST OF PLATES

REFERENCES AND ABBREVIATIONS

Reference is made to earlier selected or collected editions as

Suckling, *Selections*	*Selections from the Works of Sir John Suckling,* edited by the Rev. Alfred Inigo Suckling, 1836.
Hazlitt	*The Poems, Plays and Other Remains of Sir John Suckling,* edited by W. Carew Hazlitt, 2 vols., 1874, and 2nd ed. rev., 2 vols., 1892 (the second edition is intended except where otherwise specified).
Thompson	*The Works of Sir John Suckling in Prose and Verse,* edited by A. Hamilton Thompson, 1910.

Other references are

Aubrey, *Brief Lives*	'*Brief Lives*', *Chiefly of Contemporaries, Set Down between the Years 1669 & 1696,* edited by Andrew Clark, 2 vols., 1898.
Berry	*Sir John Suckling's Poems and Letters from Manuscript,* by Herbert Berry, London, Ontario, Canada, 1960.
Gardiner	*History of England from the Accession of James I to the Outbreak of the Civil War, 1603–1642,* by S. R. Gardiner, 10 vols., 1884–90.
Greg, *Bibliography*	*A Bibliography of the English Printed Drama to the Restoration,* by W. W. Greg, 4 vols., 1939–59.
Halkett and Laing	*A Dictionary of Anonymous and Pseudonymous Literature,* by Samuel Halkett and John Laing; edited by James Kennedy, W. A. Smith, and A. F. Johnson, 9 vols., 1926–62.
HMC . . . *Reports*	*Reports of the Historical Manuscripts Commission.*
Jonson, *Works*	*Ben Jonson,* edited by C. H. Herford and Percy and Evelyn Simpson, 11 vols., 1925–52.
Prestwich, *Cranfield*	*Cranfield: Politics and Profits under the Early Stuarts,* by Menna Prestwich, 1966.
Roberts	*Gustavus Adolphus,* by Michael Roberts, 2 vols., 1958.
Spence, *Anecdotes*	*Observations, Anecdotes, and Characters of Books and Men Collected from Conversation,* by Joseph Spence; edited by James M. Osborn, 2 vols., 1966.

Stationers' Registers	*A Transcript of the Registers of the Stationers of London, between 1554 and 1640 A.D.*, edited by Edward Arber, 5 vols., 1875–94.
Thomason	*Catalogue of the Pamphlets . . . Collected by George Thomason, 1640–1661*, 2 vols., 1908.
Tilley	*A Dictionary of the Proverbs in England in the Sixteenth and Seventeenth Centuries*, by Morris Palmer Tilley, Ann Arbor, Michigan, U.S.A., 1950.
Wing	*Short Title Catalogue of English Books, 1641–1700*, by Donald Wing, 3 vols., 1945–51.
CSPD	*Calendar of State Papers, Domestic Series.*
CSPV	*Calendar of State Papers . . . Relating to English Affairs, . . . Venice.*
DNB	*The Dictionary of National Biography.*
ELH	*ELH: A Journal of English Literary History.*
JWCI	*The Journal of the Warburg and Courtauld Institutes.*
MLN	*Modern Language Notes.*
MLQ	*Modern Language Quarterly.*
MLR	*Modern Language Review.*
N&Q	*Notes and Queries.*
OED	*Oxford English Dictionary.*
PBSA	*Publications of the Bibliographical Society of America.*
PMLA	*Publications of the Modern Language Association.*
PQ	*Philological Quarterly.*
P.R.O.	The Public Record Office.
RES	*The Review of English Studies.*
SB	*Studies in Bibliography.*
SP	*Studies in Philology.*
S.P.	State Papers.
TLS	*Times Literary Supplement.*

GENERAL INTRODUCTION

I. SUCKLING'S LIFE

IN the Court of Charles I, Sir John Suckling was the courtier's, soldier's, scholar's eye, tongue, sword, though not quite as Hamlet might have been and Richard Lovelace was.[1] But, if he sometimes had a soldier's eye and a scholar's sword, he also had the courtier's tongue, *in excelsis*, and he was the prototype and model of the Court Wits of the Restoration. Contemporary documents of state, records of civil proceedings and prosecutions in the courts, and his and others' correspondence confirm the likeness of Aubrey's exuberant miniature portrait of Suckling, in which he is epitomized as 'the greatest gallant of his time, and the greatest gamester, both for bowling and cards, so that no shop-keeper would trust him for 6*d*'. His years were few and strenuous, and it is appropriate that, having devoted most of his life to seizing the day, he took his leave of it by seizing the night, at thirty-two a martyr to his own financial, amatory, political, and military extravagance.

Suckling was born in his father's house, Goodfathers, Whitton, in the parish of Twickenham, Middlesex, shortly before 10 February 1608/9, when he was baptized in the parish church of St. Mary the Virgin.[2] He was descended from a Saxon family, resident in Norfolk and Suffolk for at least four centuries, which claimed a continuous line of descent from Thomas Esthawe, the Socling, who was 'admitted to certain copyholds of Langhall and Woodton', Norfolk, in 1348.[3] The name 'Suckling', denoting 'a person holding his estate by socage,

---

[1] The most detailed biography of Suckling prepared to date is the Ph.D. dissertation by Herbert Berry, 'A Life of Sir John Suckling', University of Nebraska, 1953, to which I am greatly indebted, especially for direction to uncatalogued documents in the Public Record Office. Although I have been able to supplement his work, especially from material in the Cranfield Papers, my indebtedness goes beyond the acknowledgement of his discoveries at important points; and my own biographical researches have depended very considerably on Mr. Berry's pioneer investigations in his dissertation and in his subsequent monograph, *Sir John Suckling's Poems and Letters from Manuscript*, London, Ontario, Canada, 1960 (hereafter cited as 'Berry').

[2] Daniel Lysons, *Environs of London*, 1792–6, iii. 588, and R. S. Cobbett, *Memorialls of Twickenham*, 1872, p. 47 (extract from the parish records).

[3] Alfred Inigo Suckling, *History and Antiquities of the County of Suffolk*, 1846, i. 39. In the Hundreds Rolls, two earlier Sucklings, Robert and Walter, are mentioned in 1274. For further genealogical information see Suckling's *History*, i. 29, 38–41; Joseph Muskett, *Suffolk Manorial Families*, ii (1902), 177–208; and Davy's 'Suffolk Collections', lxxiv (B.M. MS. Add. 19150), ff. 287–90.

or the tenure of the plough', replaced Esthawe as the family surname with the poet's great grandfather, Richard Suckling, who had been a Sheriff of Norwich. Suckling's grandfather, Robert, was also prominent in public affairs, as Sheriff (1564) and Mayor (1572) of Norwich, and as a Member of Parliament in 1571 and 1586.

Sir John Suckling, the poet's father, who was Robert Suckling's sixth and last son by his first wife, Elizabeth Berwick, was baptized in St. Andrew's Church, Norwich, on 29 March 1569. Having been at Gray's Inn,[1] he was by 1602 established as secretary to the Lord Treasurer, Thomas Lord Buckhurst and later first Earl of Dorset; he sat in the Parliaments of 1601 (Dunwich), 1614 (Reigate), 1623 (Middlesex), 1625 (Yarmouth), and 1626 (Norwich),[2] and was knighted at Theobald's by James I on 22 January 1615/16.[3] He became Receiver of Fines on Alienations in 1604, Master of Requests (by purchase) in 1619, and a Member of the Privy Council in 1622. In August 1622 he purchased for £7,000 the office of Comptroller of the King's Household, which he occupied until his death. He died on 27 March 1626/7 and was buried, with the poet's mother, in St. Andrew's Church, Norwich, on 4 April.[4]

On 14 October 1604 Sir John Suckling *père* married Martha Cranfield, the sister of an ambitious business associate, Lionel Cranfield, later first Earl of Middlesex and, until his impeachment in 1624, Lord Treasurer of England. Martha was born the daughter of Thomas Cranfield, a prosperous London merchant, by his first wife, Martha Randill, in 1578, and was twenty-six years old when she married. She died on 28 October 1613 and was buried in St. Andrew's Church, Norwich. Aubrey remarked—perhaps not altogether to the justice of Sir John *père*—that the poet's father 'was but a dull fellow . . . : the witt came by the mother' (ii. 240); and special tribute is paid to her wit in the inscription on her tomb.[5] Certainly verses were not Sir John *père*'s forte, for he 'wrote a few lines, even worse than [Lionel] Cranfield's', which 'are execrable', for *Coryats Crudities*, 1611 (p. 64; Prestwich, *Cranfield*, p. 97).

Suckling was the elder son and second of six children by this marriage. His elder sister Martha, who was born in 1605,[6] remained on

---

[1] *Gray's Inn Register*, ed. Joseph Foster, 1889, p. 77. He was admitted on 22 May 1590.
[2] *Members of Parliament*, 1878, i. 440, 458, 465, 470, 473, and ii (appendix), xl.
[3] Shaw, *Knights of England*, ii. 157.
[4] Davy's 'Suffolk Collections', loc. cit. (p. xxvii, n. 3).
[5] The inscription, which gives her age at the time of her death, is quoted in Francis Blomefield, *History of Norfolk*, iv (1806), 308–9.
[6] Her age was given as twenty-one when her father's will was contested in 1630 (P.R.O.

closer terms with Suckling throughout his life than his brother and other sisters did, and from her receiving a larger share than her sisters in her father's will[1] perhaps special paternal favour is to be inferred. Martha's first marriage, to Sir George Southcot, was terminated by his suicide, but she died the wife of her second husband, William Clagett, of Isleworth, Middlesex, on 29 June 1661.[2] Lionel Suckling, the younger son, was baptized at Twickenham in 1610, as was the youngest child, Elizabeth, in 1612.[3] Elizabeth died young and unmarried, but Lionel married twice and lived until September 1665, presumably on the estate of Newton, Norfolk, which he had inherited from his father.[4] The date of birth of Suckling's twin sisters, Anne and Mary, is unknown, but their father's will suggests that they were younger than the poet and probably were born in 1611. Anne married Sir John Davis, Lord of the Manor of Pangbourne, Berkshire, and died his wife on 24 July 1659.[5] Mary died unmarried on 17 October 1658, living in her early years perhaps with her sister Martha, and later with Martha and Anne together.[6]

Suckling's mother died in 1613, when he was four and a half years old, and two and a half years later his father married Jane Hawkins (*née* Reve or Reeve), widow of Charles Hawkins, on 2 March 1615/16.[7] Aubrey made a note to 'quaere Dr. Busby if he was not of Westminster schoole?', and, though 'so many seventeenth-century poets —of various stature—were Westminster boys',[8] the Westminster records do not show that Suckling was there, and he may have been educated entirely by tutors until he matriculated as a fellow-commoner at Cambridge from Trinity College in Easter Term, 1623.[9]

Chancery Proceedings, C. 2 Chas. I, S. 120/25), and as thirty when her marriage licence was issued (see p. xxxix, n. 1).

[1] P.C.C., 55 Skynner, 1627 (Somerset House), p. 1.

[2] Martha, Mary, and Anne Suckling lived together in the later years of their lives, and were buried in the same tomb in the parish church of St. James the Less, Pangbourne, Berkshire. The monumental inscription is quoted in Suckling, *History of Suffolk*, i. 38, n. 6, and in Muskett, ii. 189.

[3] Lysons, *Environs*, iii. 588. Elizabeth is referred to as the youngest child in her father's will.   [4] Muskett, ii. 193–4, 202, and his father's will, p. 1.

[5] It was through the marriage of her daughter, Anne Davis, to Sir Thomas Lee, Bt., that the Van Dyck portrait of Suckling came into the possession of the Lee family of Aylesbury, Buckinghamshire. See 'The Portraits of Suckling', pp. lxii–lxiv.

[6] Among the uncatalogued portions of the Cranfield Papers are two letters to Mary Cranfield, one signed 'M. S.', and the other subscribed with the names Martha and Mary Suckling and Phillip Willoughby (see Appendix A.iv, Nos. 1–2).

[7] *Registers of St. Olave, Hart Street, London, 1563–1700*, ed. W. Bruce Bannerman, 1916, p. 261.

[8] *The Poems of Henry King*, ed. Margaret Crum, 1965, p. 5.

[9] John and J. A. Venn, *Alumni Cantabrigienses*, i. iv (1927), 183. The *DNB* gives the date of matriculation as 3 July, but no authority is cited.

On the authority of Sir William Davenant, Aubrey says that Suckling 'studied three or four yeares (I thinke, four)' there; there is no indication that he took a degree, but he was apparently still associated with Trinity College in some manner on 3 March 1627/8 when *Paria*, a Latin comedy by Thomas Vincent, also of Trinity, was performed before the King. The prologue was spoken by a 'Mr. Suckline', carrying a snail in his hand and caressing it. The snail might well have served as an emblem for the performance, which lasted from eleven a.m. until five p.m.[1]

Suckling was admitted to Gray's Inn on 23 February 1626/7,[2] but he cannot have been much given to the study of law for he left the Inn almost immediately after his father's death on 27 March. His inheritance from his father consisted in

all my Mannors, Messuages, houses, Landes, Tenam^ts & hereditaments whatsoever within the Counties of Suffolke, Lincolne, and Middlesex with the lease of my house in Dorsett Court neere ffleetstreet London . . . At such time as he shall attaine vnto his age of ffive and Twentie yeares and not before. I alsoe give him all my Coppihould land houlden of the severall Lordshipps or Mannors of Istlworth, Sion of Istleworth Rectorie, and of Yorks hould within the Countie of Middlesex (Will, p. 1);

in short, all his father's estates, except the one to which his brother Lionel was heir and Roos Hall, Suffolk, which had been enfeoffed by contract before marriage to the use of his father's second wife (and widow), Jane. In addition, he received among other specified items two-thirds of his father's Latin books (Will, p. 4).

It is probable, though not certain, that later in 1627 Suckling accompanied the Duke of Buckingham's expedition to the Ile de Ré, for on 18 May 1627 Edward Lord Conway sent 'downe to Southampton to be received into yor [Lord Montjoy's] horse troope foure Gentlemen mounted vpon sufficient horses. The names . . . are Walley, Poultney, Suckling, and Egiocke. Their Armes are according to the dicipline and practise of Carebins a cheval. . . .'[3] Suckling is

1 This fact came to my attention in a letter from G. C. Moore Smith to Sir Walter Greg prefixed to sig. ᵖA1 of a copy of *Fragmenta Aurea*, 1646, formerly belonging to Greg and now in the Collection of Mr. James M. Osborn, of Yale University, to whom I am indebted for the use of the book. I am also very grateful to Mr. A. T. Stubbings, Librarian of Emmanuel College, Cambridge, for checking the manuscript and transcribing the relevant details. Emmanuel College MS. 68 (shelf-mark 1. 3. 16), f. 49, 'PARIA. Authore Thoma Vincent. Trin. Coll. Soc. Cant. Acta coram Sereniss. Rege Caro. Martij 3°. 1627. Ab hora undecima ad quintam'; and f. 49ᵛ, 'Proloquitur Mr. Suckline limacem in manu gerens & contrectans'.
2 *Register*, p. 180.
3 P.R.O., S.P. 16/73, No. 101 (catalogued in *CSPD 1627–8*, p. 182).

not specifically mentioned in Lord Herbert of Cherbury's *Expeditio in Insulam Ream*,[1] or in 'A true and exact Journal, or Diary, of the most material Passages, happening at, and after our Landing, at the Isle of Rhee, Anno 1627',[2] but only senior members of the expedition were mentioned by name in those accounts.[3]

On 22 October 1629 Suckling was licensed to proceed to the Low Countries to join Lord Wimbledon's regiment in the Dutch service.[4] In his farewell letter to Mary Cranfield, dated 30 October 1629 (No. 1), he implies that he was on the way to 'those countryes which I am now to visit' for the first time. He is listed among the 'Noble men, Vullunteirs, and Gentlemen of our Nation, which bore armes and trayled pikes at the Siege of the Busse [i.e. Bois-le-Duc, which fell on 7 September 1629]',[5] but it seems unlikely from the date of his licence and the contents of his letter to Mary that he had crossed over earlier with Lord Wimbledon or participated in active service. A letter written to William Wallis on 18 November (No. 9) is completely jocular and makes no reference to approaching action.

The holograph letter to Mary Cranfield identifies the addressee of some of the printed letters and provides probably a medial but perhaps an initial date for the letters written to her while she and Suckling apparently carried on a youthful love affair.[6] Suckling's relations with the immediate family of his uncle, the Earl of Middlesex, were close and lifelong, and with Mary, though comparatively brief, probably closest of all. Years later her half-sister Frances claimed to be 'the mistress and goddess in his poems', but Menna Prestwich is right to suggest that Suckling's 'Aglaura' is 'more likely to have been Mary' (Prestwich, *Cranfield*, p. 522). Though it is more probable that Aglaura was still another lady, Mary Bulkeley (a matter discussed further below), Mary Cranfield surely held a special place in Suckling's esteem.

Mary was born in 1610, the youngest daughter of Middlesex's

[1] 1656, translated as *The Expedition to the Isle of Rhé*, 1860. Alexander Brett and Edward Viscount Conway were also members of the expedition (*Expeditio*, pp. 15, 28; 'Mr. [Arthur] Brett' is mentioned in two of Suckling's letters, Nos. 9 and 11).

[2] This is the second of *Two Original Journals of Sir Richard Granville*, 1794. Granville may have been the 'Monsieur de *Granville*, commonly called Lieutenant *Strutt*', of one of Suckling's letters (No. 49).

[3] On this and the following military associations, see Berry, pp. 49–50.

[4] P.R.O., Exchequer Papers, E.157/14, f. 40ᵛ.

[5] H[enry] H[exham], *A Historicall Relation of the Famous Siege of the Busse, and the Suprising* [sic] *of Wesell*, Delft, 1630, sig. C6ʳ.

[6] See T. S. Clayton, 'Sir John Suckling and the Cranfields', *TLS*, 29 January 1960, p. 68. Seven of the printed letters (Nos. 2–8) were probably written to her, but only three can be more than approximately dated. Nos. 5, 6, and 7 were probably written from Germany.

first wife, Elizabeth Sheppard.[1] Even with other prospective suitors, apparently, 'marriage was out of the question, since Mary had no portion and Suckling was dissipating the fortune he had inherited', and she died unmarried shortly before 7 September 1635, when her brother-in-law, Henry Carey, Lord Lepington, wrote her father about the funeral arrangements (see Prestwich, *Cranfield*, pp. 511, 518, 522, and 539). Mary is a 'shadowy figure', but all of what little evidence there is suggests that she was a young woman of uncommon grace and charm. On 29 December 1634, William Hill, who managed Middlesex's estate at Forthampton, swore 'to forbear sack, unless it be to drink or pledge the health of your honour, your noble Countess or my Lady Mary', and her death 'caused great grief', not only to the family but also, for example, to Sir John Lawrence, who had built the Earl's waterworks at Wiston in 1630 (see 'Upon Sir John Laurence's bringing Water', text and Commentary, and Prestwich, *Cranfield*, pp. 509, 527). As late as 1640 Lord Sheffield 'said that he and his wife would prefer not to stay with Middlesex since Elizabeth could not bear the thought of the house without her sister' (Prestwich, *Cranfield*, p. 509, n. 1).

'Possibly Suckling was genuinely attracted to his cousin or he may only have been paying her mannered compliments' (Prestwich, *Cranfield*, p. 522), but Mary's close association with Suckling seems to have lasted for some time, though there is evidence from the cooler tone of Letter No. 8 that it was terminated by 1633, well before her death.[2] It was perhaps still active in 1632, however, when on 20 June Lord Sheffield wrote a very brief letter to her in which the only news concerns her father, her stepmother, and 'Sʳ John Sucklings quitting it [yᵉ Bath] to bowle at yᵉ spring garden'. Mary Cranfield may have been Suckling's first 'true' youthful love, and she appears to have been one of only two women to whom he was able to maintain an unmercenary devotion of some duration, but not even such devotion can be taken as convincing evidence of a deeply serious amorous relationship.

Suckling remained in Holland until a few days before 5 May 1630, when he wrote from Brussels that he had 'lately come out of a country' where most of the people 'would doe what Judas did for half the Money'.[3] During some of this time he was occupied with the study

---

[1] There is a genealogical tree in *HMC Sackville Report*, i. x.

[2] In both letters to Mary (q.v. in Appendix A.iv, Nos. 1–2) Martha Suckling seems to have been trying to interest her in Suckling's friend, Philip Willoughby, who may possibly have been the rival of Suckling's two poems 'To his Rival'.

[3] Letter No. 11. This description of the Dutch echoes that in his earlier letter to Wallis written at Leyden (No. 9).

of astrology, for he had been admitted 'in membrum Academiæ' at Leyden University as a 'matheseos studiosus' on 26 February 1629/30.[1] He probably remained at the University until he left Holland for Brussels. He may have remained on the Continent through much of the summer of 1630, but he had certainly returned to England by early September, for he was knighted at Theobald's on the 19th of that month;[2] moreover, his poem, 'Upon Sir John Laurence's bringing Water', refers to events of early September 1630.[3]

From early October 1631 Suckling was a member of the embassy of Sir Henry Vane, Charles I's Ambassador to Gustavus Adolphus. He remained in Germany in Vane's service until spring 1632, and a number of letters (Nos. 5 and 12–18) describe his travels and the progress of the war. Mr. Gifford, earlier a member of Lord Wimbledon's regiment in Holland,[4] was also a member of Vane's embassy; Suckling's letter of 9 November (No. 14) suggests that they were good friends, and it is probable that a printed letter (No. 18) was written to him in December, after Suckling had received news of his safe arrival at Court from Germany.

During his travels in Germany, Suckling was no doubt at times in danger,[5] but it is doubtful whether he had 'run the hazard of three battels, five sieges, and as many skirmishes', a tradition that derives from David Lloyd's fanciful biographical account, which is justly characterized by William Oldys as 'a Chaine of Hyperbolies'.[6] Suckling finally left Frankfurt in 1632 carrying Vane's dispatch of 30 March to the King. Having written briefly to Vane on his landing at Dover, he arrived in London on Tuesday, 10 April, and had a private audience with the King on Thursday. The details of events after his arrival and his interpretation of the attitudes of the Court are given in his letter to Vane of 2 May (No. 19).

Suckling's letter to Vane in effect initiated an abandonment of

---

[1] *Album Studiosorum Academiæ Lugdono Batauæ MDLXXV–MDCCCLXXV. Nomina Curatorum et Professorum per eadem Secula. Hagæ Comitum apud Martinum Nijhoff. MDCCCLXXV*, col. 225. Suckling's possible association with Sir Francis Fane at this time in Leyden and during the following year in Germany has some bearing on the authorship of the dubious translation, 'Foreknowledge' (see Commentary).

[2] In Metcalfe's *Book of Knights*, 1885, p. 191, this date is given. The date '19 December' is given in Thomas Walkley's *Catalogue of Dukes . . . with the Knights*, 1642, p. 144, but this is apparently a printer's error: the entries are arranged chronologically, and those immediately preceding and following Suckling's are dated 14 and 27 September, respectively.

[3] See Commentary, pp. 235–6.

[4] Hexham, *Historicall Relation*, sig. C5ᵛ.

[5] e.g. see Letter No. 16, ll. 4–10. For further details on 'The Expedition to Germany', see Berry, pp. 63–93.

[6] *Memoires*, 1668, pp. 157–62 (alleged military service under Gustavus, p. 159).

political and diplomatic affairs that lasted for some years. Almost immediately after he wrote he embarked heartily upon a course of dedicated prodigality and philandering, and only a month later Edmund Lord Sheffield wrote to Mary Cranfield that Suckling was moving from one gaming centre to another. In 1634 George Garrard referred to him as being 'famous for nothing before but that he was a great Gamester';[1] and, since he had spent so many months abroad between 1629 and 1632, Suckling must have devoted himself assiduously to gaming while he was in England, especially during 1633, to achieve such a reputation for it by the following year. Further evidence of his prodigality is the sale of some of his patrimony, technically not inheritable until nearly a year later, on 4 June 1633,[2] and his borrowing money 'from a wool merchant of London and agreeing to make a recognizance of twice the sum'.[3]

Aubrey does full justice to the reasons for Suckling's gambling notoriety:

He was the greatest gallant of his time, and the greatest gamester, both for bowling and cards, so that no shop-keeper would trust him for 6*d.*, as to-day, for instance, he might, by winning, be worth 200 *li.*, the next day he might not be worth half so much, or perhaps be sometimes *minus nihilo.* (ii. 240–1)

He was one of the best bowlers of his time in England. He playd at cards rarely well, and did use to practise by himselfe a bed, and there studyed how the best way of managing the cards could be. His sisters comeing to the Peccadillo-bowling-green crying for the feare he should loose all their portions. (Marginal note, ii. 241)

Aubrey adds that 'Suckling—from Mr. William Beeston—invented the game of cribbidge.[4] He sent his cards to all gameing places in the

[1] Letter to the Earl of Strafford, 10 November 1634 (*Strafforde's Letters*, ed. William Knowler, 1739, i. 336).

[2] The rectory and advowson at Fellesthorpe, Lincolnshire, were sold to Godfrey and James Carrington for £81 (P.R.O., Close Rolls, C. 54/2988).

[3] Berry, p. 94.

[4] This story is often thought to be apocryphal, but William Beeston, Aubrey's informant, was quite possibly acquainted with Suckling and may have been in a position to know. Beeston was working at the Cockpit Theatre, which his father had built, when Suckling's *Aglaura* was produced there on 3 April 1638 (see G. E. Bentley, *Jacobean and Caroline Stage*, ii (1941), 370); he may have been Aubrey's source for his report of the costumes that Suckling provided for the players (ii. 244). It is interesting to note that George Beeston played in a Restoration revival of *Brennoralt* (in Bodleian Library shelf-mark Vet. A. 3. f. 824, a copy of *Fragmenta Aurea*, 1658, *Brennoralt* is marked for prompting with the actors' names; see Commentary on *Brennoralt*, ii. 293–4).

The earliest reference to 'cribbage' noted in the *OED* occurs in Richard Brathwait, *The English Gentleman and Gentlewoman*, 1641, p. 126. In the same passage in the first and second editions of Brathwait's *English Gentleman*, 1630 and 1633, p. 226, there is no mention of cribbage, which suggests that the game was quite probably not invented before the 1630s, when Suckling could indeed have been its inventor. See further remarks in ii. ix and 238.

country, which were marked with private markes of his: he got 20,000 *li.* by this way' (ii. 245).[1]

In September or October 1633 Suckling began a mercenary courtship of Mistress Anne Willoughby, the third but eldest surviving marriageable one of five daughters of Sir Henry Willoughby, Bt., of Risley, Derbyshire, by his first wife, Elizabeth Knollys, and an heiress of high expectations.[2] Anne was not only heiress to her father's estate, since he had no sons, but also to the property of her mother.[3] Suckling was by this time well established at the Court, for his suit was supported by a letter of recommendation from the King, which gave him free access to Anne's company; the King's letter does not survive, but it is referred to in a long letter of complaint written to the King by Sir Henry on 31 October 1634.[4] The first stage of the courtship was quickly terminated, because (according to her father) 'she resolutelye declared her selfe that she could not affect him, nor would ever entertaine a thought of having him for a husband, although he were accompanied with never soe great advantages of estate or Freinds'; accordingly, she refused a letter from him carried by Phillip Willoughby. This letter is almost certainly No. 20 in this edition, first printed, without date or identification of the addressee, in *Fragmenta Aurea*, 1646.

Through reckless gambling and a somewhat surprising *naïveté*, Suckling lost a considerable amount of money in the summer of 1634. During July, August, and September, in a number of taverns and private houses,[5] he lent £2,600 in varying amounts to Sir John Morley, a fellow gambler of recent acquaintance. This amount and £600 more—he later complained in the Court of Chancery (February 1635)—was won from him by 'fraude fowle play & false dice and was wonne & lost vpon the Tickett'. Morley replied in a counter-suit for £1,600, which, because Morley had notes and securities and Suckling did not, the poet was obliged by judgement against him to pay; he finally turned the money over to the court between 4 and 11 May 1636.[6]

[1] That Suckling had used marked cards was also told Pope 'by the late Duke of Buckingham, and he had it from old Lady Dorset herself' (Spence, *Anecdotes*, No. 442, i. 189).

[2] This bizarre courtship is described in some detail in Berry, pp. 94–7.

[3] See George Ormerod, *History of Cheshire*, ed. Thomas Helsby, 1882, i. 724, 727.

[4] Quotations and many of the details of the courtship are taken from a manuscript fair-copy of Sir Henry's letter, which is given in full in Appendix A.iv, No. 3; that 'Anno Domini 1635' should be '1634' is clear from the externally datable events described in the letter. This copy is Longleat MS. 114, pp. 486–506, belonging to the Marquis of Bath and kept at Longleat, Wiltshire (catalogued in *HMC 3rd Report*, p. 185).

[5] One of the taverns was the Bear at the Bridge-foot, from which Suckling addressed one of his letters (No. 49).

[6] P.R.O., Chancery Proceedings, C.2 Chas. I, S.93/60, and Chancery Decrees and Orders, C.33/172, ff. 192ʳ, 226ᵛ (Berry's discovery).

Perhaps partly to compensate for these losses, Suckling renewed his courtship of Anne Willoughby, probably in late September or early October 1634. The course of the brief courtship was marked by extraordinary vicissitude, and some of its episodes are uncertain in detail or significance (there are doubtless many facts in Sir Henry Willoughby's letter to the King, but its obvious bias makes it suspect). Variously involved in its conduct were Charles I, the Earl of Northampton, Sir Henry Vane, Sir Gervase Clifton, Sir Thomas Hutchinson, and, again, Phillip Willoughby. The last three and Suckling himself, gaining access to the lady by order of the King (in a letter dated 16 October 1634),[1] reported to the King that she had signed a note in Suckling's favour to the effect that she 'doth love him to marry him'.[2] According to her father's letter, the note had been dictated by Phillip Willoughby and her signature obtained by duplicity or coercion.

A few days after Anne Willoughby had, for whatever reasons, yielded her signature, Suckling and Phillip Willoughby with three servants, 'on the King's business', had their coach stopped by Sir John Digby at Nottingham Bridge (which was eight miles from Sir Henry's seat at Risley), and 'a Rodomontado of such a Nature as is scarce credible' ensued.[3] Digby, the suitor preferred by Anne's father, demanded that Suckling sign an undertaking dictated by Anne in which he promised to 'disavow any Interest he hath in her either by Promise, or other Ways'. Suckling refused, and 'Mr. *Digby* then falls upon him with a Cudgel, which being a yard long, he beat out upon him almost to an handfull, he never offering to draw his Sword'. When Phillip Willoughby refused to avow by word of mouth that Suckling had no interest in her, Digby 'struck him three or four Blows on the Face with his Fist'; and 'one Affront he did them more, for finding them the next Day after he had so used them, in a great Chamber at Sir *Henry Willoughby*'s, he asked the young Gentlewoman, what she did with such baffled Fellows in her Company?' Suckling's failure to draw against Digby is less censurable than might at first

---

[1] The King's letter may be found in *HMC Various Collections*, vii. 405 (Additional MSS. of Sir Hervey Juckes Lloyd Bruce), and in *Letters . . . of King Charles I*, ed. Sir Charles Petrie, 1935, p. 82.

[2] Sir Gervase Clifton and Sir Thomas Hutchinson to the King, 22 October 1634 (ibid., p. 406).

[3] The quotations and many of the details following are taken from a full and colourful account of the episode given in a letter dated 10 November 1634 from George Garrard to the Earl of Strafford (*Strafforde's Letters*, i. 336–7; reprinted in Suckling, *Selections*, pp. 19–21, and Hazlitt, i. xxix–xxxi). Cf. Edward Walsingham, 'Hector Brittanicus, or The Life of Sir John Digby' [*c.* 1645], ed. Georges Bernard, in *Camden Miscellany*, xii (1910), 73.

appear, for he was 'but a slight timberd man, and of midling stature; Sir John Digby a proper person of great strength, and courage answerable, and yielded to be the best swordsman of his time' (Aubrey, ii. 241).

Sometime before 10 November, Sir Henry and his daughter arrived at Court in response to a royal summons prompted by reports of their conduct in the matter,[1] and 'the whole business of discerning the young woman's affection, is left to the discovery of my Lord of Holland, and the comptroller, Sir Henry Vane, who have been with her, and she will have none of Sutclin'.[2] This declaration terminated Suckling's marital aspirations.[3] Worse, in a violent sequel his loss of the heiress was compounded with further humiliation and a brief imprisonment.

Shortly after the encounter at Nottingham Bridge, Sir Kenelm Digby, the brother of Suckling's assailant, had spread about the Court 'every particle' of it,[4] and this may in part have provoked Suckling's attempt to take his revenge upon Sir John Digby in the '*actus secundus* plaid on Tusday last [18 November] at Blackfriars'.[5] Suckling and his associates, variously numbered from two to sixteen, assaulted Digby and his party outside the Theatre, but were put to flight after one of Suckling's men was killed.[6] Suckling and Digby, with their parties, were committed to the King's bench, though Suckling was released before 25 November, when he was seen in his coach about London. His letter to Sir Kenelm Digby (No. 21), probably written shortly after 18 November, refers both to Digby's tale-spreading and to the Blackfriars' brawl, in which, Suckling claimed, 'I haue switch[t] your brother, and hee hath run away vpon it'. No account supports Suckling's victory, however, and his reputed cowardice in this encounter provided ammunition for the lampoonists years after it took place.[7] ' 'Twas pitty', wrote Aubrey,

---

[1] See *Strafforde's Letters*, i. 337. [2] Ibid. i. 337.

[3] Suckling was not the only one to lose by this unsuccessful courtship. Sir Henry Willoughby's injudicious behaviour disqualified him from consideration for the office of Sheriff of Derby in 1638 (see *CSPD 1638–9*, p. 126). And his conduct may have been even less rational than it appeared, for in March 1640 he was legally adjudged a lunatic 'who hath been for divers months past visited with great distraction of mind and sense' (*CSPD 1640–1*, p. 239). [4] *Strafforde's Letters*, i. 336.

[5] Robert Leake to Sir Gervase Clifton, 25 November 1634 (*HMC Various Collections*, vii. 407).

[6] For the details see Leake's letter (ibid.); Aubrey, ii. 241; Walsingham, 'Life of Sir John Digby', p. 73; letter from Ambrose Randolf to Jane Lady Bacon, 21 November 1634 (*Private Correspondence of Jane Lady Cornwallis*, ed. Richard Lord Braybrooke, 1842, p. 197); and Anthony Mingay to Framlingham Gawdy, 29 November 1634 (*HMC Gawdy Report*, p. 150).

[7] See 'Upon Sir John Suckling's hundred horse', 1639 (Appendix A.v, No. 4); *Old Newes Newly Revived*, 1641; *Four Fugitives Meeting*, 1641; etc.

'that this accident brought the blemish of cowardise to such an ingeniose young sparke. Sir J. D. was such a hero that there were very few but he would have served in the like manner' (ii. 241).

As a 'Memorandum' from Mr. Snowdon, who 'tells me, that after Sir John's unluckie rencounter, or quarrell, with Sir John Digby, wherein he was baffled: 'twas strange to see the envie and ill nature of people to trample, and scoffe at, and deject one in disgrace; inhumane as well as un-christian' (ii. 244), Aubrey provides another anecdote, about Lady Moray's coming to Suckling's defence when he was being ridiculed for his Blackfriars' action at an entertainment she was giving at Ashley, Surrey.

The Lady Moray . . . seeing Sir John out of countenance, for whose worth she alwaies had a respect: 'Well', sayd shee, 'I am a merry wench, and will never forsake an old friend in disgrace, so [co]me sitt downe by me, Sir John' (said she), and seated him on her right hand, and countenanced him. This raysed Sir John's dejected spirites that he threw his reparties about the table with so much sparklingness and gentilenes of witt, to the admiration of them all. (ii. 244-5)

In 1635 Suckling was still in the financial straits where his injudicious dealings with Morley had placed him, and on 9 February he sold another large part of his patrimony.[1] Through much of this year he was occupied in the courts with suits and counter-actions, and he was gambling regularly, as usual, for he won nearly £2,000 in early September from Randall MacDonnell, Viscount Dunluce, at ninepins played at Tunbridge Wells.[2] But he also found time to attend to the interests of his family. Sometime before 15 May he assisted his cousin, Martha Lady Carey, in arranging an advantageous marriage for her daughter Anne. A letter to her father, the Earl of Middlesex, from Lady Carey describes the part Suckling played and almost certainly refers to one of Suckling's letters (No. 22).[3] The negotiations evidently had a favourable outcome, for the marriage articles were signed on 12 and 13 November, and Anne Carey was to marry James Hamilton (Earl of Clanbrassil, 1644), as she eventually did, though much later, in 1641.

On 2 July 1635 Suckling's sister Martha, at the age of thirty,

---

[1] The estate of Barsham, Suffolk, was sold to his uncle, Charles Suckling of Woodton, for £4,300 (P.R.O., Close Rolls, C.54/3031).

[2] *CSPD 1635*, p. 385.

[3] Suckling's letter was printed without date or identification of the addressee. Lady Carey's letter is printed in Appendix A.iv (No. 4), and this matter is further discussed in the Commentary.

married Sir George Southcot, of Shillingford St. George, Devon, who was sixty years old and had been four times widowed.[1] This was from the beginning a disastrous example of a May–December union, and, in a letter Suckling wrote Southcot on 9 September (No. 23), he accused Southcot of miserliness and, in effect, 'mental cruelty', and pointedly advised him that 'the Lure to which all stoop in this world, is either garnisht with pleasure or profit, and when you cannot throw her the one, you must be content to shew out the other'. Suckling's letter provoked Southcot to write on 18 November to the Earl of Middlesex, to complain about Suckling and renew objections to his wife's conduct inferentially made earlier to the Earl, who was apparently a kind of umpire in the domestic strife.[2] Martha's unfortunate marriage was punctuated by recurrent litigation, but she retained her brother's—and probably her uncle's—sympathies in the marital disputes until Southcot abruptly terminated the marriage by committing suicide, shortly after 9 October 1639.[3]

There are indications, particularly in letters found among the Cranfield Papers, that Suckling was capable of a degree of domesticity when he was away from the Court and that he was not unlike the Earl of Rochester, whose 'youthly spirit', according to Aubrey, 'did sometimes make him doe extravagant actions, but in the country he was generally civill enough. He was wont to say that when he came to Brentford the devill entred into him and never left him till he came into the country again' (ii. 304). It is interesting to note that Pope, too, in effect closely links the darker spirits of the two, remarking of Rochester that 'he was of a very bad turn of mind, as well as debauched' and of Suckling that he was 'an immoral man as well as debauched'.[4]

Suckling's acquaintance with 'Aglaura' probably dates from 1635. There is a well-established tradition that Frances Lady Buckhurst, Countess of Dorset, and Suckling's cousin, was this mysterious figure whose pseudonym is also the title of Suckling's first published play.

---

[1] The marriage is recorded in *Transcripts of the United Parishes of S. Mary Woolnoth and S. Mary Woolchurch haw 1538–1760*, ed. J. M. S. Brooke and A. W. C. Hallen, 1886, p. 148; Martha's age is given in *Allegations for Marriage Licences Issued by the Bishop of London, 1520–1828*, ed. J. L. Chester and G. J. Armytage, 1887, ii. 222.

[2] See Southcot's letter in Appendix A.iv, No. 5. Among the manuscript-catalogued portions of the Sackville MSS. in the Historical Manuscripts Commission are copies of 'ye first agreement' (No. 8929), in which 'Sir Gorge Southcote willbe contentt', etc., and 'Ladye SowthCott [is] to Call for her petition' (the Earl of Middlesex's hand; No. 8928).

[3] Suckling wrote a witty and irreverent letter of 'consolation' to his sister shortly after her husband's suicide (No. 44).

[4] Spence, *Anecdotes*, Nos. 442 and 470; i. 189, 201.

According to Pope, 'that lady took a very odd pride in boasting of her familiarities with Sir John. She is the mistress and goddess in his poems, and several of those pieces were given by herself to the printer. This the Duke of Buckingham [her nephew] used to give as one instance of the fondness she had to let the world know how well they were acquainted'; and Pope added (a decade later) that 'the witty Earl of Dorset [was] probably [a] son to Sir John Suckling'.[1] The Earl, who was born well over a year after Suckling had fled to France, could hardly have been his son, and the 'very odd pride' leading to such gossip is perhaps otherwise a well-founded phrase, since not until 1637 was Frances 'old enough to become a child-bride', as she did.[2] Moreover, except for her pride and Suckling's association with the whole family, there is no evidence whatever of a close association between her and Suckling like the one there had been between her elder sister Mary and him; but her remarks to her nephew prove that she was proud to have known and been related to the poet. That she was 'the mistress and goddess in his poems' is surely an affectionate boast of her declining years that may have owed something to a kind of 'unconscious identification' with her sister Mary, who died young and much beloved. Frances Cranfield was not Suckling's 'Aglaura', but it seems probable that some of the copy was indeed 'given by herself to the printer' of *Fragmenta Aurea*, 1646 (q.v. below, p. lxxxiv).

It has been convincingly argued by Mr. Berry that the 'Aglaura' and 'Dear[est] Princess' of Letters Nos. 25–35 was Mary Bulkeley, of Baron Hill, Beaumaris, Anglesey, one of 'the Two Excellent Sisters' addressed in Letter No. 24 (the other would have been her sister Anne [Bulkeley] Fawkenor).[3] None of the letters printed in the early editions mentions the name Bulkeley, but, on the basis of references to places in Letters No. 24 and 32, Hazlitt was able to suggest the family association (ii. 200 n.), which Thompson amplified by supplying further details about the geographical references and the family (pp. 405–6). Neither Hazlitt nor Thompson attempted to identify 'Aglaura', but Thompson, to whom the existence of Mary

---

[1] Spence, *Anecdotes*, Nos. 443 and 466; i. 190, 200.

[2] Frances continued to live with her parents until she and Lord Buckhurst started their married life together in 1641, but the marriage agreement was probably made early in 1637 (see Prestwich, *Cranfield*, pp. 541–2).

[3] The letters probably associated with 'Aglaura' are, with one exception, closely grouped (as here) in the early printed editions: No. 35 occurs alone in *The Last Remains*, 1659, sig. D6^v; in *Fragmenta Aurea*, 1646, Nos. 25–6 (sigg. E1^v–2) are separated from Nos. 27–34 and 24 (sigg. E4^v–8) by Nos. 51(a) and 51(b) (sigg. E2^v–4). See also 'Chronology, Genre, and the Order of the Works' below, pp. cxxii–cxxvii.

was unknown, did suggest that 'the Two Excellent Sisters' were Anne and (the youngest of three sisters) Margaret Bulkeley. He also reinforced the general association and enabled the letter's dating by suggesting the identity of the sisters' 'Cozen Dutchesse, [who] for the quenching of some foolish flames about her, has endured quietly the losse of much of the King's favour, of many of her houses, and most of her friends'. The 'Cozen Dutchesse' was probably Katherine Manners, widow of George Villiers, Duke of Buckingham, who incurred the King's displeasure when she married Viscount Dunluce—the same from whom Suckling won money at ninepins—in April 1635.[1] The closing lines make clear that the letter was written in winter.

Explicit evidence of Suckling's association with the Bulkeley family is to be found in Letter No. 43 (30 September 1639), which was not included in the early editions. In this letter Suckling wrote the Earl of Middlesex that he 'intend[ed] to kisse Mrs Buckleys hands' and that he would possibly see the Earl at Milcote, which was near one of the main routes to North Wales (see Berry, p. 104). Richard Bulkeley, Esq., the brother of the 'Excellent Sisters', had become head of his family in 1630 on the death of his father, Sir Richard Bulkeley,[2] and Suckling may have known him for some time and become acquainted with the rest of the family through him, since they were both at Gray's Inn at about the same time.[3] Of Richard's three sisters, two were married well before he wrote the Earl: Margaret had married Joseph Stockwell in 1638, and Anne took as her second husband Henry White in June or July 1639 (Berry, p. 104, n. 24). Mary Bulkeley must, therefore, have been Suckling's 'Aglaura'; but, except through his expressed devotion to her, she is a still more 'shadowy figure' than her earlier counterpart, Mary Cranfield.

Although their early acquaintance probably began at least in 1635, there is no mention of externally datable events in Suckling's letters to Mary Bulkeley, and only three may, by inference, be approximately dated, No. 33 perhaps in summer 1639 and Nos. 34–5 perhaps in winter 1639/40. The others (Nos. 25–32) are quite probably in chronological order, but there is no evidence to prove that they are;

[1] See *DNB*, s.v. 'MacDonnell, Randall'. The Duchess was related to the sisters through her niece, Dorothy Hill, who had married their brother Richard.

[2] For a detailed account of the Bulkeley family see 'History of the Bulkeley Family [by William Williams of (?) Beaumaris, 1674; National Library of Wales MS. 9080 E], ed. B. Dew Roberts, *Transactions of the Anglesey Antiquarian Society and Field Club*, 1948, pp. 1–99.

[3] Richard was admitted on 23 October 1626 (*Register*, p. 179).

nor is it possible to determine when the acquaintance developed into an amorous relationship. The affair possibly belongs chiefly to the years 1638 and 1639, as Mr. Berry suggests, and it may be that Suckling's constancy could stand no greater strain; but 'Aglaura' was apparently the first to withdraw, and there is some poignancy in the fact that Suckling was on the way to kiss her hands so shortly before she married a local squire, Richard Bodychen, in late 1639 (see Berry, p. 104).

Closely related to Suckling's letters to 'Aglaura', especially 'For the two Excellent Sisters' (No. 24), is a copy of a previously unpublished letter to 'Faire Mrs Anne & Mrs Mary' from 'Jo Mince', that is, Sir John Mennes.[1] According to Anthony Wood, Mennes helped Suckling with the composition of some of his poems and may have provided some of the copy for *Fragmenta Aurea*,[2] as Mr. Berry, calling attention to a proved connection between Mennes and 'Aglaura''s sister and brother-in-law in March 1644,[3] has very plausibly suggested. It seems quite likely that Suckling's and Mennes's addressees are the same, and that they are also the subjects of Suckling's poem, 'Upon two Sisters' (in which Mennes could—doubtfully—be the 'Yong Man' addressed in line 1), all three works possibly belonging to the early years of Suckling's association with the Bulkeleys, 1635-7. These associations also suggest the possibility that Suckling wrote to Mary Bulkeley the original of the copy of a love-letter preceding Mennes's in the manuscript ('A Doubtful Letter', No. 55), but the association is purely coincidental: no addressee is identified, and even the apparent subscript initials 'JS' may not be initials. The letter is doubtful on all, including stylistic, grounds.

The year 1637 was Suckling's literary *annus mirabilis*, and in it he probably gave more time to his writing than in any other single year of his life. Much of *Aglaura* was probably written in the first half of the year,[4] and *An Account of Religion by Reason* was written during a journey made by Suckling, Davenant, and Jack Young to

---

[1] It is printed, from Folger MS. V. a. 275, p. 125, in Appendix A.iv, No. 6, in this edition.

[2] See further comment in the Textual Introduction, p. lxxxviv.

[3] See B. Dew Roberts, ed. 'William Williams, "History"' (see p. xli, n. 2 above), p. 73, and *DNB*, s.v. 'Mennes, Sir John'. Suckling and Mennes were also associated—one cannot say how closely—on the expedition to the Ile de Ré in 1627 (Mennes was a captain, according to 'A Catalogue of all the Kinges Shippes' in Folger MS. V. a. 275, p. 55); and both were commissioned as captains of carabineers on 22 February 1639/40 (*CSPD 1639–40*, p. 481) and served at Newcastle during the Second Bishops' War.

[4] For further details on the date and composition of *Aglaura*, see Commentary, ii. 253-6.

Bath in August and September 1637. On the authority of Davenant himself, Aubrey gives a full account of this journey, including an amusing anecdote about Suckling's and Davenant's thwarting Jack Young's attempt to keep a midnight appointment with a maid (ii. 243–4):[1]

The second night they lay at Marlborough, and walking on the delicate fine downes at the backside of the towne, whilest supper was making ready, the maydes were drying of cloathes on the bushes. Jack Young had espied a very pretty young girle, and had gott her consent for an assignation, which was about midnight, which they happened to overheare on the other side of the hedge, and were resolved to frustrate his designe. They were wont every night to play at cards after supper a good while; but Jack Young pretended wearinesse, etc. and must needes goe to bed, not to be perswaded by any meanes to the contrary. They had their landlady at supper with them; said they to her, 'Observe this poor gentleman how he yawnes, now is his mad fit comeing uppon him. We beseech you that you make fast his dores, and gett somebody to watch and looke to him, for about midnight he will fall to be most outragious: gett the hostler, or some strong fellow, to stay-up, and we will well content him, for he is our worthy friend, and a very honest gentleman, only, perhaps, twice in a year he falls into these fitts.' Jack Young slept not, but was ready to goe out as the clock struck to the houre of appointment, and then goeing to open the dore he was disappointed, knocks, bounces, stampes, calls, 'Tapster! Chamberlayne! Hostler!' sweares and curses dreadfully; nobody would come to him. Sir John and W. Davenant were expectant all this time, and ready to dye with laughter. I know not how he happened to gett-open the dore, and was comeing downe stayres. The hostler, a huge lusty fellow, fell upon him, and held him, and cryed, 'Good sir, take God in your mind, you shall not goe out to destroy your selfe.' J. Young struggled and strived, insomuch that at last he was quite spent and dispirited, and faine to goe to bed to rest himselfe. In the morning the landlady of the house came to see how he did, and brought him a cawdle. 'Oh sir,' sayd she, 'you had a heavy fitt last night, pray, sir, be pleased to take some of this to comfort your heart.' Jack Young thought the woman had been mad, and being exceedingly vexed, flirted the porrenger of cawdle in her face. The next day his camerades told him all the plott, how they crosse-bitt him.

Parson Robert Davenant told Aubrey 'that that tract about Socinianisme was writt on the table in the parlour of the parsonage at

---

[1] According to Aubrey it was Jack Young who paid a stonecutter eighteen pence to inscribe the equivocal epitaph 'O RARE BENN IOHNSON' (ii. 13), on the serious tributary nature of which the company may be thought to cast some doubt.

West Kington', but according to Davenant's own account it was written at Bath. 'The Epistle' accompanying the *Account* was, at any rate, signed at '*Bath, Sept. 2.*', where it may have been completed if not entirely written.

'The Wits' (or 'A Sessions of the Poets', its title in *Fragmenta Aurea*) was written at about the same time as the *Account*.[1] In a letter to the Earl of Strafford (9 October) George Garrard refers to a 'Ballad made of the Wits sung to the King when he was in the *New Forest*, which I now send your Lordship'.[2] The King's party departed for Oatlands on a hunting expedition on 4 August, remaining in the New Forest for about a month; they left Lyndhurst to return to Oatlands on 4 September.[3] If Garrard is referring to Suckling's 'The Wits', it is quite likely that it was written in August or even July. Suckling was probably not a member of the hunting expedition—as Aubrey says, he left for Bath 'like a young prince for all manner of equipage and convenience, and . . . had a cartload of bookes carried downe' (ii. 242–3)—but there is no reason why he could not have made a journey from Bath to the New Forest (a distance of less than sixty miles) for the occasion.

Suckling's occupation with literary matters continued through the Christmas season of 1637 and into 1638. Sometime during that period he wrote commendatory poems for the second edition of *Malvezzi's Romulus and Tarquin*, translated by his cousin, Henry Carey, Lord Lepington, and for his friend William Davenant's *Madagascar; with Other Poems* (the imprimatur of the first is dated 22 January and of the second 26 February, 1637). Shortly before 7 February 1637/8 a lavish production of *Aglaura* was staged by the King's Company at Blackfriars. On that day Garrard wrote to Strafford:

Two of the King's Servants, Privy-Chamber Men both, have writ each of them a Play, Sir *John Sutlin* and *Will. Barclay*, which have been acted in Court, and at the *Black Friars*, with much Applause. *Sutlin's* Play cost three

---

[1] A copy among the Cranfield Papers (U269. F. 36, No. 46) is endorsed 'Rymes of som Poetts Of som Wittes About London Septemb[r] 1637' in the hand of the Earl of Middlesex, but this could be the date of the copy, the poem itself having been written earlier (see Commentary on 'The Wits').

[2] *Strafforde's Letters*, ii. 114. I know of no special musical setting, and 'The Wits' was probably sung to a familiar tune. J. D. Jones suggests, for example, that 'Falstaff's remark: "Let it thunder to the tune of Green Sleeves" (*The Merry Wives*, Act V, scene 5) is presumably a comment on the cult of making a well-known tune serve many sets of words' (see his letter on 'A Lost Poem by Queen Elizabeth I', *TLS*, 6 June 1968, p. 597).

[3] See *CSPD 1637*, pp. 355–6, 361–2, 367, 372, 374, and L.C. 5/134, in the P.R.O., which contains the Lord Chamberlain's itinerary of the party's progress.

or four hundred Pounds setting out, eight or ten Suits of new Cloaths he gave the Players; an unheard of Prodigality.[1]

Aubrey adds that Suckling 'bought all the cloathes himselfe, which were very rich; no tinsill, all the lace pure gold and silver'. Both Garrard's statement and a special prologue 'To the King' suggest that Charles was present at the Court production; and it is possible, as Greg suggests, that a manuscript copy, in the hand of a professional scribe, was prepared especially for presentation to the King in connection with this first performance.[2]

On 3 April *Aglaura* was produced again before the King and Queen, this time in the Cockpit Theatre, with new prologues and epilogues and a newly written alternative fifth act, which converted the play to a tragi-comedy.[3] The whole play, with all prologues and epilogues and both fifth acts, was probably printed shortly before, 'to present to the quality' when it was 'acted at Court', despite the date of the licence, 18 April.[4] The extravagant folio format of the book and its rarity suggest that Suckling had it printed at his own expense, and its comparative bibliographical magnificence did not escape criticism (see Appendix A.v, Nos. 1–3).

Suckling had perhaps already earned a reputation as a literary patron by the beginning of 1638, for two works were dedicated to him in that year: Wye Saltonstall's *Ovid de Ponto* (licensed 13 February, but not printed until 1639) and Thomas Nabbes's *Covent Garden* (licensed 18 May).[5] It is also possible that the production and publication of *Aglaura* in this year inspired the commendatory verses to Suckling to which he replied in his poem, 'An Answer to some Verses made in his Praise'. 'A Ballade. Upon a Wedding' may well have been written, as Hazlitt first suggested, in July, to celebrate the wedding of John Lord Lovelace, a suggestion based primarily upon a title in a manuscript text; certainly a terminal date, May 1639, can be confidently assigned to the poem, on the grounds that two lampoons on Suckling, written at about that time, are obvious burlesque of it.[6]

---

[1] *Strafforde's Letters*, ii. 150. As Berry has shown, Suckling did not in fact become a Gentleman of the Privy Chamber until 20 November 1638 (see below).

[2] See Greg's full description of the manuscript (B.M. MS. Royal 18 C. xxv) and its binding in *Dramatic Documents from the Elizabethan Playhouses*, 1931, p. 332; and Commentary on *Aglaura*, ii. 257–8.

[3] *Dramatic Documents of Sir Henry Herbert*, ed. Joseph Quincy Adams, 1917, p. 76.

[4] See Beaurline's remarks in ii. 261–2.

[5] *Stationers' Registers*, iv. 382, 385. The dedications are printed in Appendix A.iii, Nos. 1, 2.

[6] See these poems (Appendix A.v, Nos. 4, 5) and Commentary.

There is some evidence that another of Suckling's literary activities consisted in revising the works of others—in one way scarcely surprising, since deliberate or accidental revision is everywhere in evidence in variant texts of seventeenth-century poems, in several ways significantly in some of the poems printed as Dubia (q.v.) in this edition; but explicit mention of revision, in correspondence between two writers known to each other, suggests the more familiar formal process of friendly criticism. Sometime between 17 November 1638 and 19 March 1638/9 Dudley Lord North wrote a letter to Suckling, referring to Suckling's 'pretended conversion' by North's 'preface concerning Poetry', which North hoped would have 'some further vertue of operation' from Suckling.[1] With the same letter North enclosed his 'Corona. Alphabeticall, in imitation of the 119 Psalme', a 'peece of simple conversion' that he hoped Suckling would favour with 'friendly' as God with 'fatherly . . . correction'. It is possible that something of the final form of the 'Corona' and the 'preface' was due to Suckling's revision, but it is difficult if not impossible to determine with certainty how much (if any). The views and particularly the style are not uncharacteristic of Suckling and it is clear from North's heading, 'Concerning petty Poetry, made more generall in addresse then at first', that the essay had been expanded, but no specific credit is given to Suckling.

At about the same time, Mrs. Anne Merricke wrote in a letter, dated 21 January 1638/9 from Wrest, Bedfordshire, to Mrs. Lydall: 'I cu'd wish my selfe with you, to ease you of this trouble, and with all to see the Alchymist, which I heare [this *deleted in MS.*[2]] learne is reviv'd and the newe playe a ffreind of mine sent to Sr Iohn Sucklyn, and Tom: Carew (the best witts of the time) to correct'.[3] Suckling and Carew had been friends for some years, and on 20 November 1638 Suckling became a Gentleman of the Privy Chamber Extraordinary, as Carew already was.[4] Suckling, and Carew even more, had connections with Wrest through the Earl and Countess of Kent, and John Selden, who spent much of his time there and probably

---

[1] North's letter is printed in Appendix A.iii, No. 3. In North's *Forest of Varieties*, 1645, the letters are chronologically arranged, and the approximate date of this letter to Suckling (p. 216) may be inferred from the dated letters printed before and after it (pp. 193–5 and 216–17).

[2] The writer's original intention to write 'hear this day' was evidently changed to 'here learn'.

[3] P.R.O., S.P. 16/409, No. 167. In *CSPD 1638–9*, p. 342, where this letter is catalogued, it is said to be 'probably a presumed letter from a fashionable lady', which Rhodes Dunlap amplifies as 'apparently a literary exercise' (*The Poems of Thomas Carew*, 1949, p. xxxviii, n. 3).

[4] P.R.O., L.C. 5/134, f. 286.

married the Countess on the Earl's death.[1] Suckling's letter enquiring after Lady Kent's health (No. 45) was probably addressed to Selden and written later in 1639. Doubtfully, Anne Merricke may be the unidentified lady of Suckling's poem, 'Upon A. M.'.

When by 26 January 1638/9 conditions in Scotland had become serious enough for Charles I to recruit an army for a show of force in the north, Suckling was one of the first to volunteer, and 'within these three days has engaged himself to bring upon his own purse 100 horse to the rendezvous'.[2] As late as 28 February William Mountagu wrote that 'Sir John Succlin, who is the exactest and forwardest man in this service, hath as yet given his men nothing but colours for their hats, and as I am informed will give them nothing more',[3] but soon after that date Suckling fitted out his 'troope of 100 very handsome young proper men, whom he clad in white doubletts and scarlett breeches, and scarlet coates, hatts, and . . . feathers, well horsed, and armed. They say 'twas one of the finest sights in those days' (Aubrey, ii. 241–2). The equipment and pay of his men are said to have cost £12,000,[4] but even though this is probably a four-fold exaggeration Suckling's generosity is clear. Less vainglorious equipment would have served as well, however, and Suckling's extravagance afforded the lampoonists yet more material for their attacks on him.[5]

The King arrived in York on 31 March, the day before that appointed for the rendezvous. On 17 April he went to Selby, twelve miles from York, and reviewed seven troops of horse, of which Suckling's was the sixth.[6] It is very probable that Suckling wrote 'An Answer to a Gentleman in Norfolk that sent to enquire after the Scotish business' (Letter No. 38) at Selby or York sometime between the date of the rendezvous and 19 April, when the King's army began to march north.[7] The army was in Durham on 1 May, and on the 22nd Charles announced his decision to advance to Berwick. Arriving there

---

[1] For Carew's close acquaintance with Wrest see Dunlap, ed. *Poems of Thomas Carew*, pp. xxxviii–xxxix.

[2] The Earl of Northumberland to Edward Viscount Conway, 29 January 1638/9 (*CSPD 1638–9*, p. 378). Suckling's commitment was already noted on 25 January (see a letter to the Earl of Cork in *Lismore Papers*, ed. A. B. Grosart, 1886, 2nd ser., iv. 14).

[3] *HMC Buccleuch-Whitehall Report*, i. 280–1.   [4] Lloyd, *Memoires*, p. 159.

[5] See the lampoons in Appendix A.v, Nos. 4–7.

[6] Diary of the Duke of Rutland (*HMC Rutland Report*, i. 506–7). The Duke says that all the troops were armed with carbines except Suckling's, which had pole-axes, but he must have been mistaken. In *CSPD 1639–40* there are numerous references to Suckling's attempts to sell carbines, pistols, and light horse-armour, in 1640, in numbers which suggest that they must have been left over from the First Bishops' War.

[7] The letter is dated 'April 1639' in Bodleian MS. Dodsworth 61, f. 63.

on 30 May, the army moved on to set up camp at the Birks, three miles west of Berwick.[1]

In his letter to the Earl of Middlesex written on 6 June at the camp (No. 40) Suckling describes in detail the military fiasco that took the place of a battle between the English and Scots armies on Monday, 3 June, at Maxwellheugh, near Kelso. His description is corroborated by other accounts of the 'battle',[2] and on this occasion he was not guilty of the personal cowardice of which he was accused in the lampoons, 'Upon Sir John Sucklings Northern Discoverie' and 'Upon Sir John Sucklings most warlike preparations for the Scotish Warre' (q.v. in Appendix A.v, Nos. 6, 7). Suckling merely participated in a retreat ordered by the General of the Horse, the Earl of Holland; and even S. R. Gardiner, who considered the Earl a carpet knight, remarked that, 'finding the enemy too strong to be prudently attacked, he brought his men back in safety' (ix. 28). The inactivity of the troops massed on the border seems to have given Suckling time to write three of the letters which were printed without date or addressee. No. 39 was apparently written toward the last day of May or on 1 or 2 June, and Nos. 41 and 42 between 6 and 17 June, after the cessation of hostilities but before the signing of the Treaty of Berwick on 18 June.

About three months after the end of the First Bishops' War, Suckling wrote on 30 September 1639 to the Earl of Middlesex that he was about to leave London to kiss Mary Bulkeley's hands (Letter No. 43). He probably kissed her hands for the last time on that visit, for she was married in 1639, probably not long after Suckling came to see her, when he may have first learned of her plans to marry. Two letters, Nos. 34 and 35, appear to have been written after the visit, the first immediately after Suckling's departure from Mary, and the second some time later, when all hope was gone.

In November 1639 Suckling was helping to stand bail for another of the Earl of Middlesex's imprudent nephews, Vincent Cranfield. On 9 November Vincent wrote to Middlesex:

My lord
being in my lodging and in Physicke Mr. Alexander Bret[3] to whom I owe 120 *ll* hath done mee the favor as to arrest mee, doe mee the favor as to [see

---

[1] Gardiner, *History*, ix. 12–22.

[2] There is a lengthy description in Rushworth, *Historical Collections*, iii. 935–8, and another in B.M. MS. Sloane 650, ff. 104 ff., which was written from the camp on 5 June.

[3] Alexander Brett was related to Middlesex through the latter's marriage to Anne Brett, in 1620.

my Bayle, or *deleted in MS.*] send to Mr. Bret some boddy from you, within
[the *deleted*] a fortnight[.] I shall discharge your debt, and for ever remayne
for this Curtesy added to your former

your obliged servant and

From the Covent Kinnesman

garden V. Cranfeild[1]

9 November
1639

In response, Middlesex wrote to Sir Edmund Verney:

Sir,—

My unfortunate kynsman Vyncent Cranfeild is by his improvidence fallen
into troble, and is now in the custody of your officers. . . . The actions entered
against him are accordinge to this inclosd paper, amountinge in pryncipall
debtt to 3920 *l.*, besides the 1200 *l.* counterbond to Mr. Croocke and Mr.
Hofton, for savinge them, lesse the two hundred pounds, which is all for
one somm.

As for the 120 *l.* to Alexander Brett, which is the only dangerous action in
your courte, that I have satisfied and paid; as for the rest, I know formes must
be observed in all courts, and therfore sir John Suckling, my nephewe, and
Mr. Charles Treanche, esquire, are contented to be his bayle, and, for your
farther securetye and indemnitye, I do hereby bynd my selff. . . .[2]

This incident is of interest in throwing light on the character of one
of Suckling's lifelong friends, whose improvidence in financial matters
was less notorious but no less habitual than Suckling's. Vincent was
mentioned in Suckling's letter of 5 May 1630 to William Wallis
(No. 11), and a letter written at about the same time from Vincent
to the Earl of Middlesex reveals, in phrases very like those Suckling
might have used (or even supplied), that his acute susceptibility to
debt was already as well established as Suckling's:

My lord

Though concealment bee my best sanctuary, and retyre with what I have
reason most to affect, since excesse hath drawne an obscuring Curtayne 'twixt
mee and the world, yet I presume further to implore your sunlike favor to
disperse these clouds, and to preserve my horizon from absolute darknesse
as I have receivd many obligements and great ones, for what you voutsafe at
present makes my ingagments to your Lordship infinit; if your sale of the
houses depend on your resolve, your expedition of it (much conducing to my
benefit) wilbee a great favor, the sooner things dischargd, the lesse my

---

[1] Cranfield Papers, uncatalogued portions.
[2] *Letters and Papers of the Verney Family Down to the Year 1639*, ed. J. Bruce, 1853, p. 275.

charge; your writings, I am informd are ready, if you please that they may
bee seald withall convenient speed, to avoyd inconveniences that may happen
if it bee put off till the terme, I shall acknowledge it a favor, that obliges mee
to remayne

Your servant and Kinnesman
V. Cranfeild.[1]

As one of the defendants in the suit of Sir George Southcot *v.* Phillip
Willoughby *et al.*, he was also involved in the Southcot–Suckling
dispute.[2]

In early 1640 the activities of the Scots Covenanters provoked
the King to raise a force of 40,000 men for another expedition to the
North. Suckling was commissioned captain of a troop of carabineers,
'which . . . he is required to raise and have in readiness, duly exercised',[3] but he evidently had no intention this time of equipping men
at his own expense, for he began to try to sell arms, probably left
over from the earlier expedition, on 14 March. After much official
correspondence, Lord Montjoy finally agreed in April to buy this
equipment, which consisted of armour, pistols, and carbines.[4] Shortly
before Suckling was commissioned, letters were sent to the counties
directing their levies to be assembled most conveniently, within
their county borders, for a march to Newcastle on 20 May.[5] The
county rendezvous were later postponed and the march to Newcastle
ordered to be delayed until 10 June; still later the general rendezvous
was put off until 1 July.[6] Lord Conway, the General of the Horse,
was in Hull on 17 April, in York on the 20th, and in Newcastle by
the 22nd,[7] but most of the cavalry troops were still expected, and it
is probable that Suckling remained at Whitehall until some time after
the dissolution of the Short Parliament.

Shortly after Charles's declaration of his intention to summon a
new Parliament, Suckling had been recommended to Yarmouth as
a candidate by the Earl of Dorset.[8] Although he failed to be elected
Member for Yarmouth, the successful election of his cousin, James
Cranfield, in both Liverpool (for which Cranfield chose to sit) and

---

[1] Cranfield Papers, uncatalogued portions.
[2] P.R.O., Chancery Proceedings, C.3, 415/19, and C.S., 74/70.
[3] *CSPD 1639–40*, p. 481.
[4] Ibid., pp. 549, 552, 573 (*bis*), 586, 596, 605, 606; *CSPD 1640*, p. 17.
[5] Rushworth, *Historical Collections*, iii. 1089.
[6] Ibid. iii. 1170, and *CSPD 1640*, p. 219.
[7] *CSPD 1640*, pp. 43, 53, 64.
[8] Dorset first wrote in December 1639 and again on 27 February 1639/40 (*HMC 9th Report*, pt. i, pp. 311–12).

Bramber, Sussex, gave him a second opportunity when a writ was issued on 23 April for the Bramber by-election.[1] On the 30th, a little over a fortnight after the first meeting of the Parliament, Suckling was returned as Member for Bramber,[2] with some suspicion that chicanery rather than public favour had obtained his seat.[3] His victory was short-lived, however, for Charles dissolved the Parliament on Tuesday, 5 May. Some time shortly before or after his brief Membership in Parliament, Suckling was evidently summoned by Viscount Conway, Lord Deputy of the Army and General of the Horse, to repair to the North with his troop. His letter to Conway (No. 46), which cannot be precisely dated, gives illness as an excuse for his delay, but he is scarcely above suspicion of malingering, more likely for gaming purposes—or to seek his Membership—than out of cowardice, for he was at Newcastle when the battle took place.

The Second Bishops' War, which was scarcely less abortive than the First, was concluded by the battle fought at Newburn Ford, in the environs of Newcastle, on Friday, 28 August. The reports of the part Suckling's troop played are conflicting, but it is clear that it participated in the general retreat. The Scots army arrived within a mile of Newcastle on the night of Thursday, 27 August. On Friday morning Leslie, the Scots commander, marched his forces to Newburn Ford, which was guarded by 3,000 foot and 1,500 horse, and with artillery forced the English in the trenches and breastworks to abandon their positions. 'The raw troops, never having before seen a gun fired in anger, . . . threw down their arms and fled.'[4] The English cavalry was then driven off level ground by the Scots cavalry, which was personally led by Leslie. Having retreated, the English regrouped and attempted a counter-attack.

Bot our [Scots] troups doubling there resolutioun and courage, did mak good, not onlie there first attempt, bot also put Schir Johne Suckling bak with his horss troups, being the prime of all England (whiche ar oppositis) to the retreat, took sum of his horssis, whereof one (being most excelent) was presentit to our Generall . . . ; the rest were left to the takeris, to encourage everie brave gentilman to adventour.[5]

---

[1] For the writ see *Commons Journals*, ii. 9.

[2] *HMC 4th Report*, 'House of Lords Calendar', p. 25.

[3] Among the House of Lords Papers is a petition from Sir Edward Bishopp, Kt., who claims that Suckling achieved the election by 'undue means'. Allegedly, Suckling 'by threatening the better sort of Burgesses induced them to depart without giving any voices at all, and by offering money to the meaner sort persuaded them to vote for himself, and by those means obtained the election' (ibid.).

[4] Gardiner, ix. 194; the battle is fully described on pp. 192–5.

[5] 'Sure newis from Newcastell, and from the Scottish Army, 27th August, 1640', 'ane

The most persistent reports concerning Suckling were that some of
his horse were taken at Newburn and the best given to Leslie, or that
his coach was captured, with £300 and some clothing, and used by
Leslie; and rumours approximately contemporaneous with the events
also had it that Suckling had been killed and that he had not even
been at the place of the battle.[1] It is doubtful whether Suckling was
guilty of the special cowardice often attributed to him in this battle;
the general retreat of the English forces before the numerically
inferior Scots was almost certainly due to inexperience and dis-
organization.

Immediately after the retreat Suckling wrote two letters to his
cousin, Martha Carey, now Lady Monmouth,[2] which do not survive
but are mentioned in an undated letter from her to her father, the
Earl of Middlesex:

Sir

This night at sixe a clocke I receaved two letters from Sir John Sucklin
the longest which should have come sooner, has had some stopp, and so
against his will, not given your lordship that speedy notice he desired, he
desires your lordship pardon for not writing. it seems he write this before
he either eate or sleept, and was sufficiently tired, (the lord be praised that he
scaped with life). I have sent your lordship a coppie of all the newes in it as
he bid me, and should send another to Mr. Jermin but he is gone to the king;
There is so many flying false reports of him that I have sent the coppy of the
last, which came quicke, and gives me much satisfaction, Though I never
doubted but he would doe as bravely as any. I long much to se[e] your lordship and to receave your advise what course is to be taken this dangerous
time, for we are here mightily frighted. I beseech god to bringe him off in
safty (for our loose is so great already) in sweet honest Jacke. I humbly crave
your lordship blessing for

                                                      your lordships obedient loving daughter
my humble service   M. M.: Monmouth.[3] [*sic*]
to my lady I beseech
your lordship and my
love to my sister and
brothers

printed peice', in John Spalding, *Memorialls of the Trubles in Scotland and in England A.D
1624–A.D. 1645*, Aberdeen, 1850–1, i. 335–6.
    [1] See *CSPD 1640–1*, pp. 6, 178; *A Coppy of General Lesley's Letter to Sir Iohn Suckling*,
1641, p. 4; *HMC Westmoreland Report*, p. 393; *HMC Various Collections*, ii. 256; and *Camden
Society: Trevelyan Papers, Part III*, 1872, p. 192.
    [2] Henry Carey became second Earl of Monmouth on 12 April 1639 (see G.E.C., *Complete
Peerage*, ix. 59).
    [3] Cranfield Papers, uncatalogued portions. Were it not for the Earl of Middlesex's endorse-
ment, 'Daught[r] Monmouth 1640', and the fact that Suckling was never really in danger in

Suckling probably accompanied the army in its retreat to Yorkshire. Although his name is not listed among the names of officers on the muster-roll made after the retreat, his troop was probably one of Conway's '35. Troops already raised' that were not individually listed at the muster.[1] Furthermore, a tailor, Joseph Woodgate, of St. Bride's, Fleet Street, London, went to York on 13 September to speak with Suckling. He had still not seen him by the 25th, but Suckling was expected soon at Court there.[2]

Probably in December, shortly after the opening of the Long Parliament (3 November), Suckling wrote *To Mr. Henry German, in the beginning of Parliament, 1640*, in which he addressed general advice to the King on how he might deal with the widespread popular disquiet. The writing of this tract began Suckling's active involvement in the King's affairs that continued until his flight to France. At least until January 1641, however, he had by no means given up his usual course of life, for Sir William Uvedale mentions the loan of £50 to him and also a gaming debt of £100 owed to him by George Goring, colonel of the First Brigade in the Second Bishops' War.[3]

On 8 January—presumably 1641—Suckling wrote to the Earl of Newcastle inviting him to come to London but giving no specific reasons (Letter No. 47).[4] Suckling and Henry Jermyn may already have been contemplating means of bringing the army to the King's aid if what they considered the usurpation of the Royal power and prerogatives by Parliament continued to increase. And it may be, as Mr. Berry suggests, that the conspiracy which was later to be called the First Army Plot was already being planned, 'some two months earlier than is commonly believed' (Berry, p. 110). But perhaps Newcastle was only to be consulted about what assistance he would be willing to give should a crisis arise between Charles and his Parliament.[5]

In March 1641 two groups of Royalists were making independent plans to aid the King. One group was made up of Henry Percy

the First Bishops' War, this letter might be thought to have been written after the chief encounter of that war on 3 June 1639, for in his letter of 6 June (No. 42) Suckling refers to an earlier letter to Lady Carey in which he had asked her to pass on its news to Middlesex.

[1] See Rushworth, *Historical Collections*, iii. 1243–52.
[2] See *CSPD 1640–1*, pp. 177, 178.
[3] Ibid., pp. 414, 424, 456; 432, 452, 488.
[4] That this letter belongs to this year is not absolutely certain, but Berry (pp. 110–12) makes a reasonably strong case for it (see Commentary, p. 329).
[5] See the circumstantial account of the planning of the Army Plot and its political consequences in Gardiner, ix. 308–60.

(brother of the Earl of Northumberland), the Earl of Rochester, William Ashburnham, and Hugh Pollard, who were Members of Parliament as well as army officers. The offer of their services to the King —within the limits of constitutional law, as they interpreted it—was provoked by the vote of Commons on 6 March to transfer £10,000, originally allocated to the English army in Yorkshire, to the Scots army.

They proposed to induce the officers in the North to sign a declaration that they would stand by the King if Parliamentary pressure were put upon him to compel him to assent to the exclusion of the bishops from the House of Lords, or to force him to disband the Irish army before the Scots were disbanded, or if the full revenue which he had enjoyed for so many years were not placed in his hands.[1]

The original conspirators in the second group were Suckling and Henry Jermyn. Their purpose was similar, but they ignored constitutional considerations and set out first to secure the command of the army. The Earl of Newcastle was to replace the Earl of Northumberland, and George Goring, 'a man born to be the ruin of any cause which availed itself of his services', was to be his Lieutenant-General. At first Strafford's imprisonment and trial seem not to have been a central concern of either group, but, as Gardiner says, 'it may well have been that the effect of the outcry for what the House of Commons called justice inclined Charles to look to the army as a weapon which he might lawfully wield in order to secure Strafford as well as himself from irregular violence' (ix. 315). During the first week of Strafford's trial, the King was persuaded by Henry Percy to reject the plans of Suckling's group and accept those of his own, which provided for the army to be brought to the King's support by a petition. On 29 March Goring and Jermyn met the Parliamentary officers in Percy's lodgings in Whitehall to discuss the possibility of consolidating the two groups. Suckling was not admitted to the conference in spite of the pleading of Goring and Jermyn, and the attempt to combine efforts failed through disagreement over Suckling's participation and the command of the army. Jermyn and Percy were then commissioned to confer with the King for a decision between the two projects, but the King refused to entertain either.

The actions that led eventually to Suckling's flight were precipitated by the King's conviction that Strafford (against whom a

[1] Gardiner, ix. 309.

Bill of Attainder, passed in the Commons, was gradually gaining favour in the House of Lords) could only be saved by force. At nearly the same time that he was assuring the Members of both Houses that he meant in no way to abridge the law of England but hoped that the Members might find some way to spare Strafford's life, Charles was apparently authorizing an attack on the Tower, where Strafford was imprisoned. The Portuguese Ambassador, who had recently arrived to seek an English alliance against Spain, afforded an excuse for raising the necessary troops, in which Suckling and Captain Billingsley had been occupied for some days.[1] On Sunday, 2 May, Billingsley presented to Sir William Balfour, the Lieutenant in charge of the Tower, an order from the King for the admission of himself and a hundred men, but Balfour denied them entrance and communicated a report of the occurrence to the Parliamentary leaders.[2] In the accounts of Suckling's examination before the House of Commons on Monday, 3 May, it is not stated that he was at the Tower with Billingsley, and it appears probable from Pennington's testimony before the House that he was not. Pennington declared

from the lord maior that Sir John Suckling with 60 more in Cosse coats, swords and pistoles, were to the white horse taverne in Bread street upon friday last [30 April], and staid there all night, and are to meete againe this night, and that their was great multitudes of papist reported to the Spanish Embassadors house, which gives great discontent to the citty, and desyred the advise of this house[.] The commissary wilmot declared that Sir John Suckling was to get into Portiugall with armyes of horse . . . . their Sir John Clatworthy said that their was three regiments of foote, and one troope of horse to be raysed but for what ends he knoweth not, onely he saith that Sir John Sucklinge is to have a regiment and a troupe of horse. . . .[3]

The assembling of Suckling's company in the White Horse Tavern at such a time of general alarm in the city was sufficient to cast grave suspicion on his activities, whether he was at the Tower on Sunday or not. In a brief account written two days after his examination, Lady Monmouth also mentions the gathering in the tavern:

That daye [Monday] the house of Commons sent for Sir John Sucklin

---

[1] Although there is no evidence of an earlier close association between Suckling and Billingsley, they had probably been acquainted for some years, for Billingsley seems to have been a guest at the Earl of Middlesex's estate at Milcote. On 21 January 1636/7, Arthur Brett wrote to the Earl: 'If Collonel Billingsley bee at Millcott the warden would haue him repourt to London' (Cranfield Papers, uncatalogued portions).

[2] Gardiner, ix. 349.

[3] More's diary, entry for 3 May 1641 (B.M. MS. Harl. 477, ff. 26ᵛ–27ʳ).

and examined him strictly why he raised me[n], and at the same time my lord Maier write to my lord holland that many Captaines did assemble late in Cheapside, and in there Jollityes spoke high things. they nam'd him not, but t'was he and his company; he satisfied the house of Commons very well with his answere, but I heare the peeres meane to have a further saying to him[.] god send him well off.[1]

As he reveals in his own account, the Earl of Monmouth was no less concerned than his wife:

Sir John Suckling hath been examined before the Howse of Commons concerning his comission of raysing men for Portugall, and gave good satisfaction as some say, and yet there is a Committe apoynted for the further examinationne of him and Barce [i.e. Percy]. and certane whispers there are concerning Sir John, which I doe no ways like. I pray you Sir write nothing to him of this. and if you please say nothing of it to any other body; for if hee should heare of it, peradventure hee would take it ill at my hands.[2]

Since Suckling and his troop apparently did not approach the Tower with Billingsley, one cannot be certain of the real reason for his levying troops. It is clear, from the information in the letter quoted below, that he was not raising them for service in Portugal, but they may have been intended to protect the King and Queen if their persons were endangered. In a letter to his brother-in-law, the Earl of Middlesex, Arthur Brett summarized the events of Suckling's last days in England:

There is some light appeares of the plott concerning Fortefiing Portchmouth, and is putt in trust to 5 of the House of Commons: they doe not declare any particulars (cause they are commaunded secrecye[)] butt have informed they have discovered a dangerous plott, to bring the English army hiether, with a great Jealosye of the French: It is reported Franke Palmer gave the first notice of itt, from the Armye: Sir John Suckeling was examined by the Committie covering his desinge [i.e., 'design'], his answeare was, that hee hadd undertaken the profession of a shouldier and that his fortunes call'd him to itt; having gott Leave from his Majesty to rayse a Regiment, hee was For Portiugale; receaveing commicions from the Embassador whereupon hee was dismist; nottwithstanding they found him faulty in his answeare, yett tooke noe notice; They sent to the Embassadore, [to][3] know the certainty

---

[1] To the Earl of Middlesex, Wednesday, 5 May 1641 (Cranfield Papers, uncatalogued portions).

[2] To the Earl of Middlesex (Cranfield Papers, catalogued and summarized in *HMC 4th Report*, p. 295). The letter is dated 1 May, but it was probably written on the 4th or 5th. Suckling was examined on 3 May and due to appear before the Lords on the 6th. In further references to the apprehensions about the entry of soldiers into the Tower and the King's revocation of Billingsley's commission, Suckling's name is not mentioned.

[3] I have supplied words and letters where the manuscript is torn.

who returned answeare, hee neither hadd, nor expected any Commission to that end. The next morning being Thursday, hee was againe to appeare, Butt Harry Pearcye, Harry Jermaine William Davenant and him selfe all rann away. which augeres they weare the wise and active agents in this treacherous imployment. The House of Commons mooved the Lords, a letter might be drawne by them, with theire consent, and sent by 2 of theire House to the Armye, with some verball instructions, to informe them of theire wicked intent, which are allready gone. Likew[i]se to send one of the Lords with 2 of them to Portchmouth, to examine Collonell Goring, and to send him up to Lon[don] and with all to putt some of the Tray[tors] of that County into the Towne, for th[eir]e better securitie; For the Debuty, the bill is past the Lords, upon the opinion of all the Judges to bee Trea[son . . .]. the Debutye gives himselfe lost, and say[es] there is noe trust in Mann; the Queene Crys and take[s] onn extrea[m]ly: the T[ower] is guarded by the Lo [. . .¹] Companies; They have drawne a bill for the King, nott to dissolve [the] Parliament without the [consen]t of both Houses.

My Lorde, your Lordship is much happier with your fresh ayre att Millcott, then you could bee, att London in this troblesom time.²

Leaving London probably on the night of Wednesday, 5 May, after the last defences for their actions had been exposed, Suckling and Jermyn made their way to Portsmouth, where Goring was in command, and sailed for Dieppe in the royal pinnace, *Roebuck*, on Thursday, 6 May.³ Jermyn was in possession of the King's warrant licensing him to pass the sea.⁴ Davenant, whose part in the plot is uncertain, was captured at Faversham and brought back,⁵ and Percy was delayed in his escape, although he finally arrived safe but ill in Paris on 22 July. On the day that Suckling and Jermyn sailed, a writ for the arrest of Percy, Jermyn, Suckling, Davenant, and Billingsley, and their 'safe conduct into the howse', was issued and signed by the Earl of Northumberland.⁶ A formal proclamation against them was sent to the King on Friday, 7 May, and issued on the day after,⁷ but further action was suspended until 8 June.

Suckling arrived in Paris from Dieppe on Friday, 14 May, in

1 It is not clear what Brett wrote here, but Lords Essex, Saye, and Brooke were directed to provide for the admission of 500 men from the Tower hamlets to guard the fortress (Gardiner, ix. 355).

2 8 May 1641 (Cranfield Papers, catalogued and summarized in *HMC 4th Report*, p. 295).

3 More's diary, B.M. MSS. Harl. 477, f. 67; and 478, f. 636.

4 The warrant is printed in Rushworth, *Historical Collections*, iv. 274.

5 *Commons Journals*, ii. 147, 149; *Lords Journals*, iv. 250.

6 The writ may be found in National Library of Wales MS. Carreglwyd A. 794 (catalogued in *HMC 5th Report*, p. 413), and in John Nalson, *An Impartiall Collection of the Great Affairs of State*, 1682–3, ii. 245.

7 *Lords Journals*, iv. 238.

company with the Earl of Carnarvon. Jermyn had gone directly from
Dieppe to Rouen.[1] What Suckling did or how long he lived after his
arrival in Paris is uncertain. There is good evidence to show that
he was alive only as late as 23 July, when Sir Francis Windebank
wrote from Paris to his son Thomas: 'I feare my arreres in the Excheq^r
& the Household wilbe slowly paid, hauing heard that the House of
Com̃ons haue ordered that his M. shalbe moued for the stopping
of pen̄cons due to Mr Germain, S^r Io: Sucklin and my selfe. But Gods
will be done.'[2]

   The reports of the secret committee on the Army Plot began in the
House of Commons on 8 June. As a result of them, charges were
brought by the Commons against Suckling and the other conspirators
on 26 July. *In absentia*, Suckling, Jermyn, and Percy were found guilty
of high treason by a committee of seven on 13 August.[3] Suckling is
mentioned in the *Commons Journals* for 6, 14, and 17 December in
connection with the Commons' directions to a special committee
to consider 'in what Manner it is fit for this House to proceed upon
those Votes against those Gentlemen',[4] and in the same month or
before appeared *Newes from Sir John Sucklin Being a Relation of his Conversion from a Papist to a Protestant*, 1641,[5] according to which Suckling
fled from Paris to Spain with a 'Lady *Damaise* nigh kinswoman to the
Dutches of *Sheverey*, but a protestant', to escape from 'Lord *Lequeux*',
a rival for the lady's affections. Lequeux, repenting of his persecutions,
miraculously saved Suckling's life by confessing to officials of the
Inquisition that he had falsely accused Suckling and the lady of being
enemies of Rome who had come to Spain to conspire the death of
the King. The pamphlet concludes: 'Whereupon they were both
delivered, and the Lord *Lequeux* committed to tortures. Sir *John* and his
Lady are now living at the *Hague in Holland*, piously and religiously,
and grieves at nothing, but that he did the Kingdome of *England*
wrong.' This pamphlet may not be entirely fictitious, but there is
unfortunately nothing to substantiate any of its contents.

   In 1664 Suckling's family gave the date of his death as 7 May

[1] *CSPD 1640–1*, pp. 578, 585 (letters from Robert Reade to Thomas Windebank and
M. Battière to [Secretary Vane], respectively).
[2] P.R.O., S.P. 16/482, No. 73 (catalogued in *CSPD 1641–3*, p. 58). The discontinuance
of these pensions is mentioned in the *Commons Journals*, ii. 177, 183, 201, 212, and 232.
[3] Gardiner, x. 2; More's Diary, B.M. MS. Harl 479, f. 148ᵛ; *Commons Journals*, ii. 253.
[4] *Commons Journals*, ii. 333, 343, 346.
[5] Thomason, i. 52. This pamphlet purports to be news 'Sent in a Letter to the Lord
Conway, now being in Ireland'. As has been noted above, Suckling was intermittently
associated with Conway from 1627 at least until mid 1640.

1641,[1] which serves only to show how obscure his activities were after his flight from England on the day before that here given for his death. Notwithstanding the assurances of *Newes from Sir John Sucklin* that he 'lived in great honour' in Paris and later settled quietly at The Hague, it is probable that Suckling's reception in Paris, except by other fugitives, was cool. Those in Paris who did not wish to fall out of favour with Parliament would scarcely have associated freely with Suckling. The treatment of Percy, when he finally arrived in Paris on 22 July, is probably typical of that accorded to Suckling and Jermyn:

> Yesternight arrived here in Paris Mr. Percy very weake and indisposed. he made his adresses to mylady (the Countesse of Leycester) who receved him in her owne house, that he might be the better attended in his sicknes, but this morning one comming from my Lord, who landed yesterday at Diepe, brought letters by which his Lordship desires my lady not to receive him into her house, so that now he changes his lodging againe.[2]

The mentions of Suckling along with the other conspirators in the *Commons Journals* several months after his flight were probably a matter of form only, and should not be interpreted as evidence that he was still alive at the time. He was named in the *Journals* for the last time on 26 March 1642, when it was 'Ordered ... That a Time be prefixed for the Accusation of M. *Piercy*[,] *Jermyn*, and *Sucklyn*, &c. to the Lords, of High Treason, according to the Vote of the House' (ii. 499), but he was probably dead some time before this, for in February 1642 or earlier appeared *An Elegie Upon the Death of the Renowned Sir John Sutlin*.[3]

There are two different accounts of the means of Suckling's death. One, originating with the Earl of Roscommon and told to Dean Knightly Chetwood, was in turn given to Robert Harley, Earl of Oxford, who apparently passed it on separately to Pope and William Oldys. This sensational story has an apocryphal air, despite the circumstantiality—a trait of poetic as well as historical truth—of Pope's account:

> [Suckling] arrived late at Calais, and in the night his servant ran away with his portmanteau, in which was his money and papers. When he was

---

[1] *Visitation of Norfolk A.D. 1664*, ed. A. W. Hughes Clarke and Arthur Campling, 1933–4 ii. 209.

[2] M. Battière writing from Paris on 23 July 1641 (P.R.O., S.P. 78/111, f. 63).

[3] Thomason, i. 85. 'Printed in the Yeare, 1642' (title-page). From one of the ornaments used, this pamphlet appears to have been printed by Susan Islip, who printed *The Goblins* and *Brennoralt*, 1646.

told of this in the morning he immediately inquired which way his servant had taken, and ordered horses to be got ready instantly. In pulling on his boots [he] found one of them extremely uneasy to him, but as the horses were at the door he leaped into his saddle and forgot his pain. He pursued his servant so eagerly that he overtook him two or three posts off, recovered his portmanteau, and soon after complained of a vast pain in one of his feet, and fainted away with it. When they came to pull off his boots to fling him into bed, they found one of them full of blood. It seems his servant (who knew his master's temper well and was sure he would pursue him as soon as his villainy should be discovered) had driven a nail up into one of his boots in hopes of disabling him from pursuing him. Sir John's impetuosity made him regard the pain only just at first, and his pursuit hurried him from the thoughts of it for some time after. However, the wound was so bad and so much inflamed that it flung him into a violent fever which ended his life in a very few days.[1]

It is a matter of historical record that Suckling made his way from Dieppe, not Calais, to Paris and probably lived there for a time, and Aubrey's account of the less extravagant course of suicide has an inherently greater ring of truth to the circumstances:

Anno . . . [*sic*] he went into France, where after some time being come to the bottome of his fund that was left, reflecting on the miserable and despicable condition he should be reduced to, having nothing left to maintaine him, he (having a convenience for that purpose, lyeing at an apothecarie's house, in Paris) tooke poyson, which killed him miserably with vomiting. He was buryed in the Protestants church-yard. This was (to the best of my remembrance) 1646.[2]

In spite of the inaccuracy of Aubrey's 'best remembrance', the nature of the details in this account argues its substantial truth: for one 'that scornd to live by Almes or guifts', as the 'Epitaph on Sir John Suckling' has it (see Appendix A.ii, No. 3), suicide would seem to be the natural course. And Alfred Suckling states that 'family tradition confirms . . . [this] most revolting narration', adding that 'the destruction of all public records renders investigation on this point [of burial in the protestant church-yard] fruitless.'[3]

---

[1] Spence, *Anecdotes*, No. 444, i. 190–1. As Osborn notes, 'there are several versions of this gory tale, which substitute a razor or a pen-knife for the nail in the boot, but its truth is open to question. Aubrey's account of Suckling's death has now become generally accepted' (i. 191).

[2] ii. 242. The Earl of Oxford's and Aubrey's accounts may have become fused in Oldys's memory, for in his brief note on the story he said that Suckling's servant poisoned him as well as placed 'the blade of a pen knife' in his boot (see the manuscript notes in his copy of Langbaine's *Account of the English Dramatick Poets*, 1691, B.M. shelf-marks C.45.d.14, 15; his version is printed in *N&Q*, 2nd ser. i (1856), 172).

[3] *Selections*, p. 48.

In all three accounts—by Oldys, Pope, and Aubrey—Suckling's death is stated or implied to have taken place shortly after his arrival in France. Thomas May wrote that the conspirators fled on 6 May to France, 'where *Suckling* not long after dyed',[1] and there is no clear evidence to suggest that he remained alive as late as 1642.[2] References to him in satirical tracts printed throughout 1641 prove nothing. His notoriety in connection with the Army Plot would make his name indispensable, whether he were alive or not. He was condemned for high treason *in absentia*, and it is certain that he would have been so condemned with his co-conspirators even if the committee had knowledge that he was no longer living. Only one source, *Newes from Sir John Sucklin*, [December or earlier] 1641, states—with no confirmable details—that Suckling was alive, and its testimony is somewhat weakened by its conclusion, that he was living 'piously and religiously' with his lady at the Hague. On the other hand, *An Elegie upon the Death of the Renowned Sir John Sutlin*, [February or earlier] 1642, make it virtually certain that he was dead at the latest by January or early February 1642.

In the Cranfield Papers there is no further mention of Suckling after Arthur Brett's letter of 8 May 1641, which gave an account of the circumstances leading to his flight. This suggests either that the Cranfields, with whom Suckling was on closer terms than anyone except his sister Martha, had terminated all connections of affection or financial assistance with him, or that he is not mentioned for some other good reason, probably his early death. It is difficult to imagine that Suckling, ostracized by much of English society abroad and without income to support the life of extravagance to which he was habituated, could long survive the rigours of his exile. It seems probable, therefore, that he died in Paris by taking poison well before the end of 1641.

---

[1] *History of the Parliament of England*, 1647, p. 199 (sig. P2ʳ).

[2] Alfred Suckling, Hazlitt, Edward F. Rimbault (*N&Q*, 2nd ser. i (1856), 316), Thompson, and Thomas Seccombe (*DNB* article) place his death earlier or later in 1642, either without recorded authority or by inference from the appearance of the certainly posthumous pamphlets, *An Elegie*, [February] 1642 (Seccombe), and *A Copy of Two Remonstrances Brought over the River Stix in Caron's Ferry-boate by the Ghost of Sir John Suckling*, [20 February] 1643 (Alfred Suckling; Rimbault, who misdated this pamphlet '1642'; and Hazlitt, after Alfred Suckling). Thompson gives no authority (p. x). Lord Brooke's *The Nature of Truth*, 1640 (i.e. 1641), pp. 40–1 (cited in Commentary, ii. 267), supports Suckling's death in 1641.

THE PORTRAITS OF SUCKLING

The only authenticated original likeness of Suckling is the portrait painted by Sir Anthony Van Dyck, which forms the frontispiece to this volume. It is now in the Henry Clay Frick Collection in New York City. The details and colours of the portrait are as follows:

A slip of paper, which extends like a marker from between the leaves, bears the name SHAKSPERE in roman majuscules. Suckling is turning one of the leaves to a page on which the running-title, HAMLET, in roman majuscules, is dimly visible. He has very light curly brown hair, moustache, and *mouche*, and dark blue eyes. He wears a dark steely-blue doublet, with scalloped sleeves and lower edge. His collar and shirt-sleeves are white. His red mantle, which is fastened on his right shoulder with a gold brooch, is scalloped at the lower edge and on the sleeves. His girdle is brownish-rose, his hose white. His gold-buff boots, turned down at the top, are fastened in front with a brass button, and there is also a brass button on each instep. To the left, over the rocks, brown leaves and twigs of a plant. Above them, sunset sky and snowy mountains. The rock on the right is inscribed, in roman majuscules: NE TE QUÆSIVERIS EXTRA. Oil on canvas, $84\frac{1}{4} \times 50\frac{3}{8}$ in. ($2 \cdot 13 \times 1 \cdot 28$ m.).[1]

The portrait is not signed or dated, but the traditional attribution to Van Dyck dates from the mid seventeenth century,[2] and the portrait has been generally accepted as Van Dyck's work by art historians.[3] The date is difficult to establish, but from Suckling's appearance and the fact that Van Dyck was only in England for two periods —approximately April 1632 to March 1634, and late 1635 to September 1640—during the years of Suckling's maturity, it seems probable that the portrait was painted when Suckling was in his late twenties, that is, between 1636 and 1639. Van Dyck's portrait of Thomas Killigrew and—traditionally, though not certainly—Thomas Carew was signed and dated '1638', and it is interesting that both the natural scenery, especially the 'huge boulders, with bushes amongst them', and Suckling's costume are reminiscent of the drawings by Inigo Jones that Mr. Beaurline suggests are the original stage designs for the first production of *Aglaura*.[4] The pride Suckling otherwise

[1] *The Frick Collection: An Illustrated Catalogue*, introd. Sir Osbert Sitwell, 1949, i. 96–7.
[2] Aubrey first mentioned the portrait and described it as an original by Van Dyck (ii. 244).
[3] e.g. see John Smith, *Catalogue Raisonné*, 1829–42, iii. 197, No. 684; William Hookham Carpenter, *Pictorial Notices: Consisting of a Memoir of Sir Anthony Van Dyck*, 1844, p. 66, n. 1; Jules Guiffrey, *Sir Anthony Van Dyck*, trans. William Alison, 1896, p. 303, No. 874; Lionel Cust, *Anthony Van Dyck: An Historical Study of his Life and Works*, 1900, p. 135.
[4] The descriptive phrase is from *Designs by Inigo Jones for Masques & Plays at Court*, ed. Percy Simpson and C. F. Bell, 1924, p. 140. I am indebted to my wife for reminding me of the dated portrait and for suggesting the possible relationship between the portrait of

showed in the writing and production of *Aglaura*, through the extra-vagant folio printing (licensed 18 April 1638) and lavish stage pro-ductions (7 February and 3 April 1638) of the play, is by no means at odds with such a relationship; and, while the dated portrait and this possible relationship cannot prove a similar date for the portrait of Suckling, they strongly suggest early 1638 as a not unlikely date.

The portrait belonged originally to Suckling's sister, Martha Lady Southcot, and passed on her death to her niece, Anne Davis. Through Anne's marriage to Sir Thomas Lee, first Baronet, it came into the possession of the Lee family of Hartwell, near Aylesbury, Bucking-hamshire, with whom it remained until 1918, when it was purchased by the late Henry Clay Frick from the heirs of Colonel E. D. Lee, of Hartwell House.

All other authentic likenesses of Suckling derive at one or more removes from this portrait.[1] The chief derivative oils include: an anonymous seventeenth-century full-length copy, nearly identical with the original in size, at Knole House, Sevenoaks, Kent;[2] a seven-teenth-century bust-length copy attributed to Theodore Russel, probably from the original, in the National Portrait Gallery; an anony-mous seventeenth-century bust-length copy, probably from the 'Knole' copy, owned by Mr. William Suckling, of Roos Hall, Beccles, Suffolk; an anonymous later seventeenth-century portrait of the poet in classical attire, probably from the 'Roos Hall' copy, in the possession of Katherine, Mrs. Suckling, Lady of the Manors of Barsham and Shipmeadow, of Barsham House, Beccles, Suffolk.

The chief engravings are those by William Marshall (frontispiece to *Fragmenta Aurea*, 1646),[3] Michael Van der Gucht (frontispieces

Suckling and the stage setting for *Aglaura*. It is also interesting that Suckling is holding a copy of *Hamlet*, which may have influenced *Aglaura* as *The Tempest* did *The Goblins* (see ii. 274–5). On the Killigrew–Carew portrait, see *Poems of Thomas Carew*, ed. Rhodes Dunlap, 1949, frontispiece and pp. xliv–xlv; and, on the drawings by Inigo Jones, the Commentary on *Aglaura* in the present edition, ii. 261–2.

[1] The oils, miniatures, and engravings of Suckling, including doubtful and spurious like-nesses, are described, their relationships discussed, and some of them reproduced in Thomas Clayton, 'An Historical Study of the Portraits of Sir John Suckling', *JWCI*, 1960, xxiii. 105–26.

[2] This copy may have belonged to Lionel Cranfield, first Earl of Middlesex, if it was painted before 1645, when the Earl died, or to his daughter Frances, Lady Dorset. Either way it would have come into the possession of the Sackville family of Knole House through Charles Sackville, sixth Earl of Dorset, who was the heir both of his mother, Frances, and of his uncle, Lionel Cranfield, the third Earl of Middlesex.

[3] Marshall's engraving is a conflation probably of the 'Russel' copy (or another bust-length copy similar to it) with an engraving by Lucas Vorsterman of a portrait of the engraver Karel Van Mallery, generally attributed to Van Dyck (see p. 118 of ref. cited in n. 1). It is No. 97 of the engravings of William Marshall in Margery Corbett and Michael Norton,

to *Suckling's Works*, 1709, from the 'Roos Hall' copy, and 1719, from
the Marshall engraving), George Vertue (1744, from the 'Russel'
copy [?]), C. Rivers (1795, from the Vertue engraving), James Hop-
wood (*c.* 1790–1810, from the Vertue engraving), James Thomson
(frontispiece to Suckling, *Selections*, 1836, from the 'Roos Hall' copy),
and Annan and Swan (frontispiece to *Suckling's Works*, 1892, from the
Thomson engraving).

One of the best-known works said to represent Suckling is the
portrait of a boy in the Ashmolean Museum, Oxford, which was
formerly attributed to W. Dobson but is now attributed to Cornelius
de Neve. The only authority for the identification of the subject as
Suckling is the inscription, 'SIR JOHN SUCKLING', which was painted
on the canvas *c.* 1720 by John Whiteside, whose own authority is not
known. By comparison with the Van Dyck portrait, this seems very
unlikely to be a representation of the poet. It was engraved by
R. Newton in 1820, and a copy of the Newton engraving was used
as the frontispiece to *Suckling's Works*, 1874.

II. SUCKLING'S REPUTATION

Suckling's literary reputation was established by 1638, when he was
twenty-nine years old. 'The Wits' had been sung to the King the
year before,[1] and *Aglaura*, also completed in 1637, was 'acted in
the Court, and at the *Black Friars*, with much Applause', during the
Christmas season of 1637/8. Immediately after its first production, it
was eulogized by an anonymous admirer:

> If learning will beseem a Courtier well,
> If honour waite on those who dare excell,
> Then let not Poets envy but admire,
> The eager flames of thy poetique fire;
> For whilst the world loves wit, *Aglaura* shall,
> Phœnix-like live after her funerall.[2]

Again, after the second production in April 1638, an anonymous
encomium was addressed to Suckling,[3] and by 1640 one of the highest

*Engraving in England in the Sixteenth and Seventeenth Centuries, Part III: The Reign of
Charles I*, 1964; it is described on p. 132 and reproduced as plate 67*b*.
  [1] See the 'Life' above, p. xliv.
  [2] *Witts Recreations*, 1640, sig. B3ᵛ. The poem must have been written after the first
production, for in the second—made a tragi-comedy by the alternative fifth act—Aglaura lived.
  [3] 'To Sir *John Sutlin* upon his *Aglaura*: First a bloody Tragædy, then by the said Sir
John, turn'd to a *COMEDIE*' (q.v. in Appendix A.ii, No. 2).

compliments that could be paid to a play, so it would seem, was that it would 'out-blaze bright *Aglaura's* shining robe'.[1]

Although in literary matters he was primarily famous as a poet and playwright, Suckling was apparently also well known as a discerning critic and as a patron of other writers. In the winter of 1638/9 Dudley Lord North sent him some verses to correct,[2] and on 21 January 1638/9 a Mrs. Anne Merricke wrote in a letter that she wished she could see the 'newe playe a ffreind of mine sent to Sʳ Iohn Sucklyn, and Tom: Carew (the best witts of the time) to correct'.[3] Wye Saltonstall dedicated his *Ovid de Ponto* to Suckling in 1638 or 1639, expressing to Suckling the hope that, 'since you have honoured the Muses with a famous Poeme, you would express your noble mind in defending [Ovid's 'youngest daughter'] from the censure of the world'.[4] And Thomas Nabbes, in dedicating his *Covent Garden* (1638) to Suckling, compared Suckling's muse to Pindar and his own to Bacchylides, praising Suckling for both his writing of *Aglaura* and his literary patronage: 'As you are a *Patron* to all good endeavours, you merit to be the subject of many *Encomiums*: But your selfe by your selfe in making the world (which can never be sufficiently gratefull for it) happy in the publication of your late worthy labour, have prevented the intentions of many to dignifie that in you which is so farr above them.'[5]

Suckling gave most of his time to the extravagant social life of the Court, and his reputation for conversational brilliance probably outshone that he had won by his writings. He 'grew famous at court for his readie sparkling witt which was envyed, and he was (Sir William [Davenant] sayd) the bull that was bayted. He was incomparably readie at repartyng, and his witt most sparkling when most sett-upon and provoked' (Aubrey, ii. 240). It is regrettable that social repartee not only loses in translation but is frequently lost altogether except by reputation. Aubrey's remarks constitute the best testimonial to Suckling's wit, and his own works offer the best evidence of it. What

---

[1] See the commendatory verses by S. Hall before S[amuel] H[arding], *Sicily and Naples*, 1640, sig. A4ʳ.
[2] See North's letter in Appendix A.iii, No. 3.
[3] P.R.O., S.P. 16/409, No. 167. In *CSPD 1638–9*, p. 342, where this letter is catalogued, it is said to be 'probably a presumed letter from a fashionable lady', to which Rhodes Dunlap adds that it is 'apparently a literary exercise' (*Poems of Thomas Carew*, 1949, p. xxxviii, n. 3).
[4] The dedications are printed in full in Appendix A.iii, Nos. 1–2. It is not certain when the dedication was written. *Ovid de Ponto* was licensed on 13 February 1638 (*Stationers' Registers*, iv. 382) but not printed until 1639.
[5] See the full dedication in Appendix A.iii, No. 2). *Covent Garden* was licensed on 28 May 1638 (*Stationers' Registers*, iv. 385), shortly after the publication of *Aglaura*.

little other testimony there is is confined to such scattered anecdotal squibs as 'Jack Suckling comeing into a house with a great fair pair of Stairs and little rascally chambers said that the Chambers might come hand in hand down stayres',[1] which does, however, suggest a gift for the easy, unreflecting leaps of imagination that illuminate ordinary talk with the flash of wit.

As flagrant as Suckling's public behaviour was, most of his con-temporaries were unable to see his works in isolation from his life. Until his involvement in the army plot he doubtless remained for many, as Aubrey described him, 'the greatest gallant of his time, and the greatest gamester'. And immediately after his flight to France in May 1641, which inevitably followed the exposure of his plot, he became one of the chief objects of vilification for the Roundhead pamphleteers. With his literary accomplishments either denigrated or completely ignored, he is referred to in 1641 alone in at least six-teen anti-Royalist tracts, some devoted exclusively to him.[2] To the Puritans he was a gambler, a rake-hell, a writer of licentious verses, a coward, a traitor, and—in a grand and characteristic hyperbole—'a scum of ungodliness from the seething pot of iniquity'.[3] But to the Royalists, in proportional reaction, he became an even greater gallant, wit, and writer of brilliance, and was—to David Lloyd, as to many—a martyr in the King's cause. His poems appeared regularly in printed miscellanies and song-books until long after the Restoration,[4] and his literary reputation, far from fading, increased rapidly.

---

[1] Folger MS. V. a. 180, f. 81ᵛ, the commonplace-book of Mildmay Fane, second Earl of Westmorland, compiled, on the evidence of the opening and closing letters, between 1655 and 1663; it contains, in addition to anecdotal Characters of various countries, transcripts of letters written in 1628–31 by Mary, Countess of Westmorland, to her son, Sir Francis Fane, whose travels during that time closely paralleled Suckling's, with whom he may have been in company.

[2] *A Conspiracy Discovered*, *A Letter Sent by Sir John Suckling from France*, *A Bloody Masacre Plotted by the Papists*, *Four Fugitives Meeting*, *A Coppy of General Lesley's Letter to Sir John Suckling*, *The Liar*, *Newes from Rome*, *A Mappe of Mischiefe*, *The Stage-Players Complaint*, *Time's Alteration*, *Old Newes Newly Revived*, *The Sucklington Faction*, *A Letter from Rhoan in France*, *The Country-Mans Care*, *The Copie of a Letter Sent from the Roaring Boys in Elyzium*, and *Newes from Sir John Sucklin*. There are undoubtedly others.

[3] *A Mappe of Mischiefe*, 1641, p. 5.

[4] Poems by Suckling appear in the following collections: *The Academy of Complements*, 1646, 1650, etc.; *A Musicall Banquet*, 1651; *Catch that Catch Can*, 1652, 1658, 1663; *Select Musicall Ayres, and Dialogues*, 1652; *Select Musicall Ayres and Dialogues, in Three Bookes*, 1653; *Wits Interpreter*, 1655, 1662, and 1671; *Sportive Wit*, 1656; *Wit and Drollery*, 1656, 1661, 1682; Henry Lawes, *Ayres and Dialogues*, 1658; *Select Ayres and Dialogues*, 1659; *Select Ayres and Dialogues for One, Two, and Three Voices*, 1659, 1669; *An Antidote Against Melancholy*, 1661; *Merry Drollery* [1661], 1670, 1691; *Recreations for Ingenious Head-Peeces*, 1663 (also issued with the title *Wits Recreations Refin'd*); *Musick's Delight on the Cithren*, 1666; *Catch that Catch Can*, 1667; *The New Academy of Complements*, 1669; *Oxford Drol-lery*, 1671; *Windsor Drollery*, 1671; *The Musical Companion*, 1673; *Synopsis of Vocal Musick*,

Perhaps not long after his death, since the manuscript collection appears to date from the early and mid 1640s, one of the longest eulogies, an 'Epitaph upon Sir John Suckling', was written by James Paulin, who praised Suckling both as poet and as man, and concluded that 'if man could bee, | Or ere was perfect, this was hee: | Twas Suckling, hee who, though his ashes have, | His honoured name shall never find a grave' (printed in full in Appendix A.ii, No. 3). And in 1646 the publisher Humphrey Moseley was at pains to keep Suckling's name alive (and doubtless his own business flourishing) by publishing a collection. For the first edition of *Fragmenta Aurea*, Thomas Stanley specially wrote a poem to accompany the engraved frontispiece:

> *SUCKLIN* whose numbers could invite
> Alike to wonder and delight
> And with new spirit did inspire
> The *Thespian* Scene and *Delphick* Lyre;
> Is thus exprest in either part
> Above the humble reach of art;
> Drawne by the Pencill here you find
> His Forme, by his owne Pen his mind.[1]

The book evidently proved very popular, for it was followed two years later, in 1648, by a second edition.

The beheading of Charles I provided George Daniel an occasion to unite the Martyr-King and the Martyr-Poet in an elegy on Charles in which he laments his own inability to treat so tragic a subject but concludes Suckling equal to the task:

> but what Stile
> Carries a Buskin deep enough to Sing
> Royal Distresses and lament a King?
> Call *Suckling* from his Ashes, reinspir'd
> With an Elizian Trance; soe fitly fir'd
> To sing a Royall orgie. There Soules move
> Without their Passions, how to feare or Love;
> Enraptur'd with divine Beatitude,
> Beyond our Earth. Hee, while he liv'd, pursu'd

1680; *Wit and Mirth*, 1682, 1684; *The Academy of Complements*, 1684 (later edition of *Windsor Drollery*); Henry Bold, *Latine Songs*, 1685; *Catch that Catch Can: Or, the Second Part of the Musical Companion*, 1685; *The Second Book of the Pleasant Musical Companion*, 1686; *Wit and Mirth: Or, Pills to Purge Melancholy*, 1706, 1707, 1709, 1720.
[1] The poem is printed anonymously in *Fragmenta Aurea* but appears in Stanley's *Poems and Translations* ('Printed for the Author, and his Friends'), 1647, sig. ²A3ʳ, and *Poems*, 1651, p. 77. See also Lord Brooke's related allusion to Suckling (1641) cited in ii. 267.

> Those noble flights, as might become the name
> Of Maiestye; made greater in his flame.
> Now, might he rise, earth-freed! His only Quill
> May write of this. . . .[1]

And sometime before 1650, when he completed *The Faerie King* (though he went on revising for another four years), Samuel Sheppard paid homage to Suckling in his writers' 'Hall of Fame' (Book v, Canto vi):

> SUCLIN the next, who (like that silver Swan
> but now I mentiond) lost the earth in's prime
> and yet hee dy'de, a very old, old man
> such is the power of wit, & force of Rime,
> "though Death's uncertaine, life bee but a span
> "wise men command the Starres, & vanquish Time,
> were his AGLAURA, only, extant hee
> might claime the height of Immortallitie.[2]

And in his *Epigrams, Theological, Philosophical, and Romantick*, 1651, he extended his praise in the 'Third Pastoral' of the *Mausolean Monument* that concludes the book. Making Suckling the rival of Fletcher, Beaumont, Jonson, and Shakespeare, he continues:

> SUCKLIN, whose neat superior phrase
> At once delights, and doth amaze,
> Serene, sententious, of such worth,
> I want fit words to set it forth,
> Exactly excellent, I think,
> He us'd *Nepenthe* stead of Inke,
> In this he all else doth out-do,
> At once hee's grave and sportive too.[3]

At about the same time Robert Baron was at work in Suckling's praise in 'Doubts and Feares', a title that Suckling might have used himself:

> Yet may I ere on Earth I quit my room
> Bespeak a better in Elizium.
>   Sweet *Suckling* then, the glory of the Bower
> Wherein I've wanton'd many a geniall hower,

---

[1] 'An Eclogue: Spoken by Hilas and Strephon', in *Poems of George Daniel Esq. of Beswick*, ed. A. B. Grosart, 1878, ii. 195–6 (the manuscript of Daniel's poems was first printed by Grosart).

[2] *The Faerie King* is described and quoted from extensively in Hyder E. Rollins, 'Samuel Sheppard and his Praise of Poets', *SP*, 1927, xxiv. 509–55 (esp. 538–55). The text is here quoted from the manuscript (Bodleian Library, MS. Rawl. Poet. 28, f. 67^r).

[3] Quoted from Rollins, ibid. p. 533.

> Fair Plant! whom I have seen *Minerva* wear
> An ornament to her well-plaited hair
> On highest daies, remove a little from
> Thy excellent *Carew*, and thou dearest *Tom*,
> Loves Oracle, lay thee a little off
> Thy flourishing *Suckling*, that between you both
> I may find room: then, strike when will my fate,
> I'l proudly hast to such a Princely seat.

In another poem on Suckling alone Baron's enthusiasm is further vitiated by the excesses of his horticultural imagery:

> *On Sir* John Suckling

> The Rose (the Splendor of *Flora's* Treasurie)
>   *Smells sweeter* when tis *pluckt* than on the *Tree.*
> So odorous *Suckling* (when he liv'd a *Flower*
>   Able alone to make the Nine a *Bower*)
> Is held since he by Times *Sith mow'd* has been
>   The *Sweetest Plant* in the *Pierian green.*
> Nor envious *Fate*, nor *Northern blasts* together,
>   Though he was *nipt i'th' bud* can make him *wither.*[1]

Suckling is praised in three of the commendatory poems before William Cartwright's *Comedies, Tragi-Comedies, with Other Poems, 1651,*[2] and three years later he and Carew together were placed in the company of Petrarch and Sidney among the shades:

> There (purged of the folly of disdayning)
> *Laura* walk'd hand in hand with *Petrarch* joind.
> No more of Tyrant Goblin *Honour* plaining.
> There *Sidney* in rich *Stella's* arms lay twind,
> *Carew* and *Suckling* there mine eye did find,
> And thousands who my *song* with silence covers
> 'Privacy pleaseth best enjoying Lovers.'[3]

And in a play written in 1655 Suckling is placed alone in the ultimate company, when Mrs. Love-wit says to Crisis: 'Sometimes to your wife you may read a piece of *Shak-speare, Suckling,* and *Ben. Johnson* too, if you can understand him.[4]

---

[1] R[obert] B[aron], *Pocula Castalia,* 1650, pp. 102, 126–7. In his 'BALLADE Vpon the Wedding', pp. 66–72, which parallels Suckling's 'Ballade' stanza for stanza, Baron implicitly pays further homage.
[2] By William Barker, sig. b7ʳ; John Leigh, sig. *1ʳ; and William Bell, sig. ***2ᵛ.
[3] *Stipendariæ Lacrymæ, or, A Tribute of Teares,* The Hague, 1654, p. 15.
[4] [Edmund Prestwich], *The Hectors, or the False Challenge* (III. iii), 1656, p. 50 (according to the title-page the play was written in the preceding year).

Certainly these encomia, despite their frequent extravagance, establish Suckling's high contemporary reputation, but it must be noted at the same time that there is little direct evidence that Suckling was so highly admired by all, including the most prominent, poets of his time: Jonson, Herrick, King, Milton, and surprisingly even Carew, have nothing to say about him, and Waller's approval can only be inferred from his having written an answer to a poem by Suckling. On the other hand, there is evidence that some of his contemporaries held him in appreciably lower regard than his encomiasts (envy probably being part of the cause), as Brome's contemptuous 'Upon Aglaura in Folio' and other lampoons on Suckling show (q.v. in Appendix A.v).

With the Restoration and the reopening of the playhouses, Suckling came into the full glory to be expected for one who had not only suffered in the Royalist cause but also fortuitously anticipated the tastes of the Court wits of Charles II's reign. His three completed plays were frequently revived with success, as many entries in Pepys's diary show—though Pepys himself did not always think well of them (he consistently thought *Aglaura* 'a mean play; nothing of design in it', but liked *Brennoralt* more often than not).[1] The references to Suckling in Congreve's *Way of the World* (IV. i) suggest that admiration for his poetry was far more widespread than it had been in his own day, and it is, of course, there that Millamant conferred upon him that most durable character of 'natural, easy Suckling'. He had become enshrined as a lyric poet—the last age could 'produce nothing so courtly writ, or which expresses so much the Conversation of a Gentleman, as Sir John Suckling', according to Eugenius, in the *Essay of Dramatick Poesie*—and Dryden further saw him, as a dramatist, as one who had followed Shakespeare, Fletcher, and Jonson, and 'refin'd upon them'.[2]

Since Suckling was now firmly established on Parnassus by informed opinion, it is not surprising that his poems were widely imitated, as they had, of course, begun to be much earlier. In an introductory stanza to one of many imitations of 'A Ballade. Upon a Wedding', the author apologizes for his presumption:

> As an attendant on Sir *John*
> I wait without comparison,

---

[1] The relevant entries are given in G. E. Bentley, *The Jacobean and Caroline Stage*, v 1956), 1204–5, 1208, and 1210–11.
[2] *Defense of the Epilogue*, following *The Conquest of Granada*, 1672, p. 169.

> Great difference is in our pen
> And something in the Maids and Men,
> I do not write to get a name
> At best, this is but Ballad-fame,
> And *Suckling* hath shut up that door,
> To all hereafter as before.[1]

Beginning his imitation, 'Now *Tom* if *Suckling* were alive, | And knew who *Harry* were to wive, | He'd shift his scæne I trow', he further apologizes in the second stanza: 'But since his wit hath left no heir | Ile sing my song of such a pair.'

In a rather startling parallel, the Hon. Edward Howard, author of the anonymously printed *Poems and Essays* . . . *by a Gentleman of Quality*, shows how highly Suckling was thought of in 1674 (pp. 48–9):

Of all the Pens of the Ancients, I judge that of *Petronius Arbiter* to be in all kindes the most polite and ingenious, it being so familiarly applicable to the Natures and converse of men, as is not to be parallel'd in Antiquity: wherefore I cannot raise his commendation higher, than to allow him their best general Writer, or Essayist. And with us, I know of none so near his parallel as the late Sir *John Suckling*, whose wit was every way at his command, proper and useful in Verse and Prose, equally gentile and pleasant: And I believe he has not too partial an esteem and memory, if allow'd the *Petronius* of his Age.

Only two years later Edward Phillips wrote that Suckling's poems 'have a pretty touch of a gentile Spirit, and seem to savour more of the Grape then Lamp, and still keep up their reputation equal with any Writ so long ago; his Plays also still bring audience to the Theater'.[2]

In 1685 Suckling was ranked among poets of enduring fame— Chaucer, Sidney, Cowley, Dryden, Jonson, Shakespeare, Spenser, and, less happily, Lee and Creech—by an anonymous judge whose enthusiasm for him is clear:

> From East to West *Sucklings* soft Muse shall run,
> Swift as the Light, and glorious as the Sun;
> Each Pole shall eccho his Eternal Fame,
> And the bright Mistress, he vouchsafes to name.[3]

To William Winstanley Suckling was 'one so filled with *Phœbean* fire, as for excellency of his wit, was worthy to be Crowned with a Wreath

---

[1] '*A Ballad on a Friends wedding, to the Tune of Sir* John Sucklings *Ballad*', in [John Raymund], *Folly in Print, or A Book of Rhymes*, 1667, p. 116.
[2] *Theatrum Poetarum*, 1675, p. ²116.
[3] *Miscellany Poems and Translations by Oxford Hands*, 1685, p. 157.

of Stars', who made poetry 'his Recreation, not his Study, and did not so much seek fame as it was put upon him'. The best character of Suckling, he thought, was that given by the poet himself in 'The Wits' (ll. 79–86).[1] Gerard Langbaine, writing in 1691, subscribed to Lloyd's character of Suckling's works, '*viz.* That his Poems are Clean, Sprightly, and Natural; his Discourses Full and Convincing; his Plays well humor'd and Taking; his Letters Fragrant and Sparking: only his Thoughts were not so loose as his Expression, witness his excellent Discourse to my Lord *Dorset*, about Religion'.[2]

By the end of the seventeenth century, Cowley had far eclipsed most of the poets of Suckling's period in critical esteem. In the preface to *Letters and Poems Amourous and Gallant*, for example, the author asserts that there is 'nothing more gay or sprightly than those [poems] of Sir *John Suckling*', but he reserves his highest praise: 'we must allow Dr. *Donne* to have been a very great Wit; Mr. *Waller* a very gallant Writer; Sir *John Suckling* a very gay one, and Mr. *Cowley* a great genius'.[3] At about the same time John Dennis wrote in a letter to Dryden that 'Suckling, Cowley and Denham, who formerly Ravish'd me in ev'ry part of them, now appear tastless to me in most',[4] implicitly discrediting the whole group.

But if Suckling was in the process of being embalmed by the critics and literary historians, his works seem still to have had a popular following, which was probably due to the musical settings of many of his poems that continued to be printed, and his continuing influence on later poets. 'The Wits' had introduced to English poetry one genre, and 'A Ballade. Upon a Wedding' another, that many imitators found irresistible.[5] Although no musical setting survives for the 'Ballade', its melody, whether specially composed or of earlier origin, was so closely associated with it and so widely known that even songs that were not imitations were specified to be sung to the tune of 'I tell thee *Dick*'.[6]

---

[1] *Lives of the Most Famous English Poets*, 1687, p. 154.

[2] *An Account of the English Dramatick Poets*, 1691, ii. 498–9.

[3] [By William Walsh], 1692, sig. A4ᵛ. It was also the author's view that among all these poets 'that Softness, Tenderness, and Violence of Passion, which the Ancients thought most proper for Love-Verses, is wanting', and that none of them would have been a 'very great Lover'.

[4] 3 March 1693, *Letters upon Several Occasions*, 1696, p. 50 (reprinted in *Letters of John Dryden*, ed. Charles E. Ward, Durham, N.C.: Duke University Press, 1942, p. 68).

[5] Dr. Johnson once mentions 'some stanzas . . . on the choice of a laureat; a mode of satire by which, since it was first introduced by Suckling, perhaps every generation of poets has been teazed' (*Lives of the English Poets*, ed. George Birkbeck Hill, 1905, i. 15).

[6] e.g. see N[athaniel] T[hompson], *A Choice Collection of 120 Loyal Songs*, 1684, p. 243.

In three articles Arthur H. Nethercot has surveyed the changing reputations of the Metaphysical poets: in the seventeenth century, during the age of Pope, and during the age of Johnson and the 'Romantic Revival'.[1] He does not specifically include Suckling, but the vicissitudes of Suckling's reputation followed with fewer extremes the pattern of the others', as one would expect. In *The Tatler*, in 1709 and 1710, Steele three times appreciatively refers to and quotes from Suckling, but Addison, in characterizing a 'male coquet' through the description of an imaginary visit to his bedroom, unflatteringly speaks of 'Suckling's Poems, with a little heap of black patches on it', on a bedside table.[2] Doubtless to many of Addison's contemporaries Suckling's works were merely part of the impedimenta of successors to the Sir Fopling Flutters of the Restoration, but the author of *A Miscellaneous Poem, Inscribed to the Earl of Oxford* (1712, p. 86) places Suckling in a clearer perspective than we should perhaps expect in the age of Pope:

> What *Suckling* writes, the Gentleman displays,
> And gay *Ideas* gives of former Days.
> Derives the Poets, and the Pleasures past,
> And unconstrain'd like him, his wit we taste.
> And whilst we there no intricasies find,
> 'I'll tell thee, *Dick*' revives th'enliven'd mind.
> Let then familiar Lines of hasty Birth,
> Produc'd by Accidents of wine or mirth,
> Uncensur'd pass; nor Pedants there pretend
> To find those Faults which they want wit to mend.

Although he did not explicitly do so, one supposes that Pope would have classed Suckling with 'the mob of gentlemen who wrote with ease'; but his opinion was only once implied, in a somewhat inscrutable remark made to the Rev. Joseph Spence: 'Carew (a bad Waller), Waller himself, and Lord Lansdowne, are all of one school, as Sir John Suckling, Sir John Mennes, and Prior are of another.'[3] There is rather less ambiguity in Spence's anecdote of Lockier, who remarked that, 'considering the manner of writing then in fashion, the purity of Sir John Suckling is quite surprising' (No. 663, 1730), which 'may be compared with Spence's statement in his little History of English Poetry, written in French: "Mais le Chevalier *Suckling* fut le seul

---

[1] *JEGP*, 1924, xxiii. 173–98; *SP*, 1925, iv. 161–79; and *PQ*, 1925, xxii. 81–132.
[2] *The Tatler*, ed. George A. Aitkin, 1898–9, i. 329; ii. 69, 256; and iv. 240.
[3] *Anecdotes*, No. 455; i. 196.

Genie tout pur; & qui par sa pureté ne se laissa pas infecter de la contagion generale" ' (*Anecdotes*, i. 274 n.).

John Oldmixon's judgement on Cowley indicates to what low Donne's reputation had sunk, and at the same time shows that neither Suckling nor Waller had fallen far from critical grace in his day: 'it seems strange to me, that after *Suckling* and *Waller* had written, whose Genius's were so fine and just, Mr. *Cowley* should imitate Dr. *Donne*; in whom there's hardly anything that's agreeable, or any Stroke which has any Likeness to Nature'.[1] As for Samuel Johnson's opinion of the Cavalier poets, 'Suckling he knew first and liked best; he quotes from Suckling, not very frequently, but steadily throughout the first edition of the *Dictionary*, and of the whole group it is only on Suckling that he ever passes any critical judgement.'[2] Johnson's judgement, however, that 'Suckling neither improved versification nor abounded in conceits' and could not reach the 'fashionable style [that] remained chiefly with Cowley',[3] does not favour Suckling, even as the best of his group.

If Suckling's reputation was destined to fade in the eighteenth century, he nevertheless remained more popular than the other two important poets of the 'Cavalier' group, Herrick and Carew. While there was no edition of Herrick's poems and only one of Carew's (except for his poems in *A Complete Edition of the Poets of Great Britain*, 1792–5) in the eighteenth century, Suckling's complete works were printed four times, in 1709, 1719, 1766, and 1770, and his poems also appeared in *A Complete Edition*.[4] In the nineteenth century there was little vacillation in Suckling's reputation as a sportive and wittily amorous Court poet. Although in 1798 Nathan Drake, in reprinting a table evaluating earlier poets, dismissed all others except Shakespeare and Milton as 'unable to support the contest even with the poets of the last forty or fifty years', he had clearly changed his mind six years later, for he mentions Suckling specifically as one of the beneficiaries of a 'new partiality for the whole body of our elder poetry'.[5] Two more complete editions and a comprehensive selection of his works were published in 1836, 1874, and 1892.

---

[1] *The Art of Logick and Rhetorick*, 1728, p. xviii.

[2] W. B. C. Watkins, *Johnson and English Poetry before 1660*, Princeton, N.J., 1936, p. 83. The author notes that there are sixteen quotations from Suckling in the *Dictionary* under A, B, and C alone.

[3] 'Life of Cowley', *Lives*, ed. Hill, i. 22.

[4] For the editions of Herrick and Carew see *Poetical Works of Robert Herrick*, ed. L. C. Martin, 1956, pp. xix, xxxiv–xxxv, and *Poems of Thomas Carew*, ed. Rhodes Dunlap, 1949, pp. lxxvi–lxxviii.

[5] *Literary Hours, or Sketches Critical and Narrative*, 1798, p. 446; cf. 3rd ed., 1804, iii. 25.

In the 1850s David Masson remarked that 'For one who now reads anything of Carew there are twenty who know by heart some verses of his friend and brother-courtier, Sir John Suckling'.[1] Since that time, while Carew's stock has risen along with that of the Metaphysical poets whose work some of his own best poetry resembles, Suckling's has remained comparatively steady. He has never ranked so high in popular estimation as he did in his own time and during the Restoration, but, while his position is now far humbler than it once was, it is likely to remain fixed as that of one of the more interesting as well as influential lyric poets of his century.[2] He is perhaps not least interesting in eluding the kind of stereotypy to which even Lovelace, who deserves and often receives better, lends himself as the prototype of the Cavalier poets. Arthur H. Nethercot did not include Suckling among the Metaphysical poets in his extensive study of their reputation, A. C. Partridge has not included him in *The Tribe of Ben* at least as a writer of—as his sub-title clarifies—*Pre-Augustan Classical Verse in English* (1966), he is clearly no 'post-Spenserian', Pope plainly misclassified him in his opaque remark, and such terms as 'Baroque' could do little to define his characteristic manner. In relation to the 'Schools' of Donne, Johnson, and Spenser, Suckling cannot be placed more accurately than in a *schola*—or *ludus*—*sui generis*: at its best, his work is of uncommon fluency, graceful force, and witty lucidity, and his is a rare *sprezzatura*.

[1] *Life of John Milton*, 1881–94, i. 503 (the first edition was printed in 1859–80).
[2] Perhaps the extra-academic references to a poet are as much a measure of his currency as the amount of space devoted to him in scholarly publications. It is in any case interesting to note, among recent mentions of Suckling, a light poem about him by Ogden Nash ('Brief Lives in not so Brief—III', *The New Yorker*, 2 January 1960, p. 50).

TEXTUAL INTRODUCTION

I. THE MAJOR EDITIONS OF SUCKLING'S WORKS

THE following list contains all editions of the complete works of Suckling and substantial selections of special interest and importance. To clarify references to signatures made in both volumes of this edition, collations are given for the two fully substantive early editions, *Fragmenta Aurea*, 1646, and *The Last Remains*, 1659. Except for '(1661?)', the marginal identifications are essentially those of Greg's *Bibliography*, to which the reader is referred for formal title-page transcriptions, full bibliographical descriptions, and discussion (iii. 1130–6, iv. 1705). For information about the states of the general title-page and the frontispiece of *Fragmenta Aurea*, 1646, and the surreptitious reprint of *Fragmenta Aurea*, 1658, here identified as '(1661?)', see L. A. Beaurline and Thomas Clayton, 'Notes on Early Editions of *Fragmenta Aurea*' (*SB*, 1970, xxiii. 165–70), which supplements Greg's studies.

i. SEVENTEENTH-CENTURY EDITIONS (ALL 8°)

1646 *Fragmenta Aurea. A Collection of All the Incomparable Peeces, Written by Sir John Suckling. And Published by a Friend to Perpetuate His Memory. Printed by His Owne Copies. London, Printed for Humphrey Moseley, and Are To Be Sold at His Shop, at the Signe of the Princes Armes in St Pauls Churchyard. MDCXLVI.*

Collation: πA⁴ (A1+1), A–G⁸ H⁴, ²A–E⁸ F⁴, ³A–D⁸, ⁴A–C⁸ D⁴; 169 leaves, paged (A2) 3–119, (²A4) 1–82, (³A2) 3–64, (⁴A3ᵛ) 2–52.

Notes. The first edition (Greg, iii. 1130–1). The general title-page is found in three states, which are, in terms of their most salient characteristics and in the order of their printing, '(A) FRAGMENTA AVREA | . . . Churchyard. | MCDXLVI.', '(B) Fragmenta Aurea. | . . . Churchyard | MDCXLVI', and '(C) Fragmenta Aurea. | . . . Churchyard. | MDCXLVI.' Greg identified two states, his '1646(*¹)' corresponding with (A), and his '1646(†¹)' corresponding with (B) and (C) together. The demonstrable order of printing is the reverse of what he—quite reasonably—thought it to be.

See 'Notes on Early Editions of *Fragments Aurea*' (*SB*, 1970, xxiii), where the previously undifferentiated two states of the portrait engraved by William Marshall as frontispiece for this edition are also discussed.

1648 *Fragmenta Aurea. A Collection of All the Incomparable Peeces Written by Sir John Suckling and Published by a Friend to Perpetuate His Memory. Printed by His Owne Copies. London, Prinred* [sic] *for Humphrey Moseley, and Are to Be Sold at His Shop at the Signe of the Princes Arms in S. Pauls Church-Yard. 1648.*

Notes. The second edition, reprinted from the first but contains some significant substantive alterations, which are discussed on pp. xcvi–xcvii below (Greg, iii. 1132).

1658–9 [WORKS consisting of—]

1658 *Fragmenta Aurea: A Collection of All the Incomparable Peices, Written by Sir John Suckling. And Published by a Friend to Perpetuate His Memory. The Third Edition, with Some New Additionals. Printed by His Own Copies. London: Printed for Humphrey Moseley at the Prince's Arms in St. Paul's Churchyard. 1658.*

[Together with—]

1659 *The Last Remains of Sr John Suckling. Being a Full Collection of All His Poems and Letters Which Have Been So Long Expected, and Never Till Now Published. With the Licence and Approbation of His Noble and Dearest Friends. London: Printed for Humphrey Moseley at the Prince's Arms in St. Pauls Churchyard. 1659.*

Collation: (²)[π1] A⁸ (A1+a⁴) B–G⁸; 60 [or 61] leaves, paged (A4) 1–37, (C8) 3–19, (E4) 1–41.

Notes. The third edition (a reprint of the first edition) of *Fragmenta Aurea*, and the first edition of *The Last Remains*, which apparently constitutes the 'New Additionals' mentioned on the title-page of *Fragmenta Aurea*, 1658 (Greg, iii. 1132–4). The publication of *The Last Remains* appears to have been delayed, as Greg notes, adding: 'Whether copies of the *Fragmenta* were issued before the *Remains* were ready is uncertain, but it seems likely, since copies certainly occur alone. There is no doubt that copies of the *Remains* were issued separately, as was to be expected, since they would be needed to supplement the *Fragmenta Aurea* of 1646 and 1648' (n. 2).

(1661?) *Fragmenta Aurea: A Collection of All the Incomparable Peices, Written by Sir John Suckling. And Published by a Friend to Perpetuate His Memory*[.] *The Third Edition, with Some New Additionals. Printed by His Own Copy. London, Printed for Humphrey Moseley at the Prince's Arms in St. Paul's Churchyard. 1658.*

Notes. A surreptitious reprint of *Fragmenta Aurea*, 1658, and in bibliographical fact the fourth edition. Greg identified this edition, as '1658' from an imperfect copy in the Bodleian Library that wants all before sig. N1 (iii. 1134). From the complete copy in the Houghton Library of Harvard University (shelf-mark EC. Su185. 646fe), which was unknown to Greg, it is possible to suggest an approximate date, to identify the printer as probably T. Johnson, and to assign the responsibility for the piracy to Francis Kirkman. See 'Notes on Early Editions of *Fragmenta Aurea*' (*SB*, 1970, xxiii). The Houghton Library copy contains an anonymous engraved portrait after Marshall's that is as rare as recorded copies of this edition and was very likely engraved for it.[1]

(1672?) [WORKS consisting of—]

Fragmenta Aurea. A Collection of All the Incomparable Pieces Written by Sir John Suckling and Published by a Friend to Perpetuate His Memory. Printed by His Own Copies. London, Printed for Humphrey Moseley, and Are To Be Sold at His Shop at the Sign of the Princes Arms in S. Pauls Church-Yard. 1648. [sic] ['1648.']

[Together with—]

The Last Remains of Sir John Suckling. Being a Full Collection of All His Poems and Letters Which Have Been So Long Expected, and Never Till Now Published. With the License and Approbation of His Noble and Dearest Friends. London: Printed for Humphrey Moseley, at the Princes Arms in St. Pauls Church-Yard. 1659. ['1659.']

Notes. This is apparently a surreptitious 'reprint of an imperfect copy of the 1658–9 volume in which the loss of the first quire A had been made good by prefixing πA2–4 and A1–5 from the *Fragmenta Aurea* of 1648' (Greg, iii. 1134–5).

1676 (reissue). *The Works of Sir John Suckling. Containing All His Poems, Plays, Letters, &c. Published by His Friends (From His Own Copies) To Perpetuate His Memory. London, Printed for Henry Herringman at the Anchor in the Lower Walk of the New Exchange. 1676.*

Notes. Another issue of (1672?), 'in which a cancel (verso blank) replaces the general title to the *Fragmenta* (A1)' (Greg, iii. 1135–6).

---

[1] Besides the one in the Houghton copy, I know of only one other print, that in the British Museum's Department of Prints and Drawings, which is reproduced and the engraving discussed in Thomas Clayton, 'An Historical Study of the Portraits of Sir John Suckling', *JWCI*, 1960, xxiii. 118–19 and pl. 15a.

1696 *The Works of Sir John Suckling, Containing All His Poems, Love-Verses, Songs, Letters, and His Tragedies and Comedies. Never Before Printed in One Volume. London, Printed for H. H. and Sold by R. Bentley in Covent-Garden, J. Tonson in Fleet-Street, T. Bennet in St. Paul's Churchyard, and F. Saunders in the New-Exchange, 1696.*

Notes. This edition 'was based on the *Fragmenta Aurea* of 1648, but the additions published in *The Last Remains* of 1659 were incorporated at the end of each section' (Greg, iii. 1136).

ii. POST-SEVENTEENTH-CENTURY EDITIONS

1709 *The Works of Sir John Suckling. Containing His Poems, Letters and Plays. London: Printed for Jacob Tonson, within Grays-Inn Gate, next Grays-Inn Lane. MDCCIX.* [8°]

1719 *The Works of Sir John Suckling. Containing His Poems, Letters, and Plays. London: Printed for Jacob Tonson, at Shakespeare's Head, over against Katharine-Street in the Strand. 1719.* [12°]

—— *London: Printed for J. Tonson; and Sold by W. Taylor at the Ship in Pater-Noster-Row. MDCCXIX.* [12°]

1766 *The Works of Sir John Suckling. Containing His Poems, Letters, and Plays. Dublin: Printed by Oli. Nelson, at Milton's Head, in Skinner Row. MDCCLXVI.* [8°]

1770 *The Works of Sir John Suckling. Containing, His Poems, Letters, and Plays. London: Printed for T. Davies, in Russel-Street, Covent-Garden. MDCCLXX. 2 vols.* [8°]

1792–5 Robert Anderson, M.D., ed. *The Poetical Works of Sir John Suckling . . . Edinburgh: Printed by Mundell and Son, Royal Bank Close. Anno 1793.* [In] *A Complete Edition of the Poets of Great Britain . . . London: Printed for Iohn & Arthur Arch, 23 Gracechurch Street. And for Bell & Bradfule and I. Mundell & Cº Edinburgh,* 1792–5, iii. 725–50. [Contains only the poems from *FA46* and *LR*.]

1810 Alexander Chalmers, ed. *The Works of the English Poets, from Chaucer to Cowper . . . in Twenty-One Volumes,* London, 1810, vi. 483–508. [Contains the poems from *FA46* and *LR*, and the lampoon, 'Sir John got him on an Ambling Nag'.]

1836 The Rev. Alfred Inigo Suckling, ed. *Selections from the Works of Sir John Suckling. To Which is Prefixed a Life of the Author, with Critical Remarks on His Writings and Genius*, London and Norwich, 1836. [This is the first edition to contain a memoir of Suckling that adds substantially to the brief accounts of his life in Lloyd and Langbaine.]

1874 W. Carew Hazlitt, ed. *The Poems, Plays and Other Remains of Sir John Suckling. A New Edition with a Copious Account of the Author, Notes, and an Appendix of Illustrative Pieces*, 2 vols., London, 1874. [The first scholarly edition. The text is modernized, eclectic (although only the early printed editions were collated), and not always accurate. Alfred Suckling's memoir is reprinted and supplemented with references to the Calendars of State Papers, etc. New poems, all doubtful or spurious, and two letters, one previously unprinted and the other uncollected, are added from manuscript. *To Mr. Henry German* is printed from the 1641 4° pamphlet. An appendix contains five of the pamphlets lampooning Suckling that were printed after his flight to France.]

1892 —— *Second Edition Revised*, 2 vols., 1892 (The Library of Old Authors). ['The "Additional Notes" [by "W. W.", supposedly Wordsworth, printed all together in the 1874 edition] have now been transferred to their proper places; certain corrections and other improvements have been introduced. . .' (i. ix–x).]

1886, etc. Frederick A. Stokes, ed. *The Poems of Sir John Suckling. With Preface and Notes*, New York, 1886 and later ('Third Edition', 1891; 'Fourth Edition', n.d.) [Contains 85 poems, including prologues, epilogues, and songs from the plays; arranged according to topic or verse-form.]

1896 John Gray, ed. [A decorative edition without title-page. Colophon:] *Here Ends This Edition of the Poems & Songs of Sir John Suckling, Edited by John Gray*, London: Ballantyne Press, 1896. [Contains the songs from the plays in addition to the poems from *FA46* and *LR*.]

1910 A. Hamilton Thompson, ed. *The Works of Sir John Suckling in Prose and Verse. Edited, with Introduction and Notes*, London, 1910. [Critical introduction only. Modernized text based on a collation of the early editions. Contains all uncollected works added to the canon by Hazlitt (except one letter, No. 9 in the present edition), but no new ones. There is a fairly long, useful, and generally dependable commentary that is especially valuable for its references to parallel passages in contemporary and earlier authors.]

1933 R. G. Howarth, ed. *Minor Poets of the Seventeenth Century*, London, 1933. [Contains a general critical introduction on Lord Herbert, Carew, Suckling, and Lovelace, and a modernized text of the poems from *FA46* and *LR*, songs from the plays, and 'Inconstancy in Love', 'Upon Sir John Sucklings hundred horse' with 'The Answer', and 'On King Richard the third, who lies buried under Leicester bridge'.]

1953 —— 2nd ed. rev. and enl., London, 1953. [Contains the same introduction and text as above but adds 'To Celia. An Ode'.]

II. SOURCES AND CANON

The posthumous *Fragmenta Aurea*, 1646, and *The Last Remains of Sir John Suckling*, 1659, contain nearly all of Suckling's works and provide the only substantive texts of many of them. *Aglaura* (with its two songs, Poems Nos. 65–6), three commendatory poems, and a political tract were printed during his lifetime, but *Aglaura* is the only one of which Suckling is likely to have had much to do with the publication,[1] though the printing of the commendatory poems was certainly authorized. From other sources fourteen letters, eleven juvenile poems from family papers, and another poem of commonplace-book origin may with confidence be added to the canon. Other works ascribed to Suckling are either doubtful or demonstrably not of his authorship.[2]

i. THE SUBSTANTIVE EDITIONS

a. *Fragmenta Aurea*, 1646

For the first edition of Suckling's works, 'a booke called Poems and Letters &c. by Sir John Sucklyn' and *The Goblins* were entered to

---

[1] See Commentary, ii. 257.
[2] I have derived considerable benefit from L. A. Beaurline's article, 'The Canon of Sir John Suckling's Poems' (*SP*, 1960, lvii. 492–518), and I shall have occasion to refer to it below (as 'Canon').

Humphrey Moseley in the Stationers' Register on 24 July 1646.[1] The other two plays in the volume, *Brennoralt* (as *The Discontented Colonell*) and *Aglaura*, had already been printed for other booksellers, and Moseley acquired his rights in the former from Francis Eglesfield and Henry Twiford on 1 August 1646, but those in the latter from Thomas Walkley not until 22 February 1648.[2] The preliminaries of *FA46* came from the shop of Susan Islip, on the evidence of ornaments and, on the general title, the recurrence of the imprint used on the special titles of *The Goblins* and *Brennoralt*, which she also printed; *Aglaura* was apparently printed by Thomas Warren.[3] The *Poems, &c.*, that is, all the non-dramatic works in *FA46* (sigg. A–H4, pp. 1–119), were printed in Ruth Raworth's shop.[4] The text was evidently set and corrected with considerable care, for only two trivial press-variants affect it (both errors corrected very early in the run); the uncorrected misprints 'Aud' for 'And' (sig. B6ᵛ [o], p. 28), and

---

[1] Greg, *Bibliography*, iii. 1130. For full bibliographical descriptions of the first and subsequent seventeenth-century editions, see *Bibliography*, iii. 1130–6. Four later editions appeared legitimately in the seventeenth century, in 1648, 1658, 1676, and 1696. Two surreptitious editions, referred to by Greg as '(1658?)' and '(1672?)' (of which the legitimate edition of 1676 was in fact a reissue with a cancel title-page), appeared between 1658 and 1676. An annotated list of these editions is given in Section 1 above.

[2] Greg, *Bibliography*, ii. 541, 621.

[3] Ibid. iii. 1131, n. 6. The preliminaries were printed by half-sheet imposition with sigg. 4D–D4ᵛ, the final pages of *Brennoralt*.

[4] The placing and condition of parentheses and numerals used in the top-centred pagination (there are no running-titles) makes certain that two skeleton-formes were used, one for inner A, B, E, F, and G, outer C and D, and the half-sheet H; and a second for the other formes of sheets A–G.

On the somewhat ambiguous evidence of recurrent spelling variations, two compositors would seem to have been involved: one compositor apparently set the inner formes of sheets A–F, another the outer formes of those sheets, all of G, and the half-sheet H. In general, but not without anomalies, the compositors of the inner and outer formes show preferences, for example, respectively for the following alternative spellings: doubled consonants/single consonants, e.g. 'hugge', 'legg'; *-ea-*/*-ee-*, e.g., 'clearly', '[in]stead', 'near'; *-ie-*/*-ee-*, e.g. 'believe', 'relieve'; *-e*/ no *e*, e.g., 'adde', 'borne', 'custome'; *-u-*/*-h-*, e.g. 'guesse'; *-y-*/*-i-*, e.g. 'ayre', 'dyet'; and *-o-*/*-ou-*, e.g. 'favor'. Different authorial spellings occur in about equal numbers in text set by the two compositors, some doubtless by the coincidence of habit, others probably by coincidence in spite of the compositor's usual practice or because he had none.

According to Beaurline's study of the evidence (see *SB.* 1963, xvi. 47), a single compositor set the section containing the poems; Beaurline identifies him as also having worked, in Ruth Raworth's shop, on *Poems of Mr. John Milton*, 1645, and other books, concluding from the evidence of his inferred habits that the copy for 'The Wits' must not have been holograph. I take this to be the compositor—if there were two—who set the inner formes of *Poems, &c.*, on the basis of the alterations made in text set from printed copy, i.e. the two songs from *Aglaura* and the three commendatory poems (sigg. B1ᵛ–B2, B3ᵛ–B4, and C7ᵛ), the strongest evidence that the same compositor worked on both Milton's *Poems* and Suckling's *Poems, &c.* The differences between the spellings of works set from printed and those from manuscript copy strongly suggest that compositors more freely exercised their preferences on the former, following the accidentals of the latter more closely—less out of reverence, probably, than out of the necessity for closer attention.

'Chnrch Ceremonis' for 'Church Ceremonies' (sig. C1 [o] p. 33), are the only remaining errors that are certainly not traceable to copy.

The *Poems, &c.* consist of thirty-two poems (including the two songs previously printed in *Aglaura*), twenty-nine letters, *To Mr. Henry German, in the Beginning of Parliament, 1640,* and *An Account of Religion by Reason,* with its preliminary 'Epistle'. They provide the only substantive texts of sixteen poems and twenty-seven letters, and, although a preponderance of authorial spellings is to be found nowhere in *FA46*, the general excellence of the copy is attested by the over-all soundness of the texts. There are serious deficiencies only in 'Upon my Lady Carliles walking' (omission of last stanza, probably editorial), 'The Wits' (corruption, omission of words between stanzas, and the probably editorial omission of ll. 69–72, which are indecent and insulting to the Queen), 'A Ballade. Upon a Wedding' (transposition of stanzas and of lines within a stanza), and 'Upon my Lord Brohalls Wedding' (omission of speech-prefixes). And only the texts of 'The Wits' and 'A Ballade. Upon a Wedding' suggest setting from defective and therefore perhaps in some sense 'unauthorized' copy (although 'foul papers' might be expected to show not very different characteristics); the errors in these poems fortunately can be corrected from other substantive texts.

On the general title of *FA46* it is stated that the 'Collection of all the Incomparable Peeces, WRITTEN By Sir JOHN SVCKLING', was *'published by a Friend to perpetuate his memory'* and 'Printed by his owne Copies'—the latter a false claim with respect to *Aglaura*, its songs, and the commendatory poems. Indeed, all such publishers' claims are suspect (cf. Moseley's for *The Last Remains*), but the texts of the non-dramatic works are prima facie authoritative, and any statement about their provenance deserves further consideration. Three persons have been identified as the 'Friend': Basil Fielding, second Earl of Denbigh; Sir John Mennes; and Frances Lady Dorset, wife of Richard Sackville, fifth Earl of Dorset.

In 1729 Elijah Fenton wrote that Suckling's 'Poems and Letters were published by his friend the Earl of Denbigh, after his death; from such imperfect copies as his Lordship could hastily collect: and therefore it is not strange if many of them still retain their Corruption'.[1] His statement is not supported by external evidence, and it is made improbable by the general reliability of the *Fragmenta* texts and

[1] *The Works of Edmund Waller Esq.r in Verse and Prose. Published by Mr Fenton,* 1729, p. xix.

the unlikelihood of a close relationship between Suckling and the Earl.[1] On the basis of likely associations between Suckling and Sir John Mennes,[2] Mr. Berry has very plausibly suggested that Mennes provided Moseley with at least the letters to 'Aglaura'; it is also possible that he gave the letters to the 'Friend' rather than directly to the printer, or that the text of these letters was set from copies already in the 'Friend's' possession.

The third suggested identification of the 'Friend'—if there was a single or chief one—as Lady Dorset best fits the facts. Lady Dorset was Suckling's first cousin, *née* Frances Cranfield, and her nephew, John Sheffield, first Duke of Buckingham and Normanby, 'used to give as one instance of the fondness she had to let the world know how well they were acquainted' that 'she is the mistress and goddess in his poems, and several of those pieces were given by herself to the printer'.[3] Suckling was closely associated with the Cranfield family and a frequent visitor at the houses of his uncle (Frances's father) the Earl of Middlesex throughout his life, and Frances was living with her parents until she married, in January 1641.[4] But there is no evidence and little likelihood of an amorous association between Suckling and her, although there apparently had been such an association between him and her sister, Mary, to whom a number of the letters are addressed (all or most of Nos. 1–8). In support of the strong possibility of Lady Dorset's having provided some of the copy for *Fragmenta Aurea*, it is perhaps worth noting that 'she had been educated more elegantly than her stepsisters'; she 'had been given French governesses and wrote stylized letters in French to her father . . . in a copperplate hand'.[5]

Copies of some of Suckling's poems survive among the Cranfield Papers, and it is not unreasonable to suppose that others were collected and saved by Lady Dorset. The *Account of Religion* was addressed to her father-in-law, Edward Sackville, fourth Earl of Dorset, and the superiority of the *FA46* text of that work to other extant texts, including a seventeenth-century copy still in the possession of the Suckling family, suggests that its copy must have been very close to the original presented to the Earl, if not the original itself.

---

[1] The possibility of the 'Friend''s being the Earl of Denbigh is discussed in more detail in T. S. Clayton, 'Thorn-Drury's Marginalia on Sir John Suckling', *N&Q*, N.S. (1959), vi. 148–50.   [2] See 'Life' above, p. xlii.

[3] Spence, *Anecdotes*, No. 443; i. 190.

[4] This association is further discussed in T. S. Clayton, 'Sir John Suckling and the *Cranfields*', *TLS*, 29 January 1960, p. 68; and see 'Life' above, pp. xxxix–xl.

[5] Prestwich, *Cranfield*, p. 541.

It is not difficult to explain why the unpublished holograph letters were not included with the papers given to the printer, for they were, with two exceptions (one letter each to Mary Cranfield and William Wallis, Nos. 1 and 11), addressed to her father, none of whose property passed to Lady Dorset on his death.[1] Her own personal papers have unfortunately not survived, and the holograph letters and texts of poems are all among her father's papers. If, as seems likely, Lady Dorset provided most of Moseley's copy for the *Poems, &c.*, it may well be that she approached Moseley herself and suggested the publication of Suckling's works, and that the *Fragmenta Aurea* were indeed '*published by a Friend to perpetuate his memory*'.

The spellings in *Fragmenta Aurea* do not afford clear evidence that Moseley's copy consisted of holograph papers, as his claim on the title-page would suggest. In 'The Stationer to the Reader' in *The Last Remains*, 1659, Moseley explicitly refers to transcriptions, and, though no such reference is made in *Fragmenta Aurea*, it is doubtful whether holograph papers, as some could well have been, or even unique copies would have been given to the printer, and therefore probable that transcriptions were used. Moreover, since no literary works certainly in Suckling's hand survive (but see comments on the juvenile poems under 'Manuscript Sources' below), there is little reason to suppose that Suckling kept his holograph papers, and it is likely that 'his owne Copies' means, at most, no more than fair copies made for him by a professional scribe.

Five of the poems in *Fragmenta Aurea* are almost certainly reprinted from the texts previously printed, and the existence and identity of the 'Friend' remains uncertain; but there is considerable evidence to support the substantial truth of Moseley's title-page claims and, in general, to establish Suckling's authorship of the works. This evidence includes close association of some works with Suckling during his lifetime; external ascription in substantive texts, correspondence, and the like; copies found among or references made to his works in family papers; extensive parallel passages in two or more of his works; homogeneity of attitude and style; and finally the over-all reliability of *FA46*'s texts where variant texts exist for comparison.[2] The

---

[1] It has generally been thought that Lady Dorset, as the Earl's last surviving child, inherited his estate, but late in 1673, Lionel, the third Earl, changed his will in favour of his nephew, Charles, and all she received by it was 'the full sume of ten pounds' (Brice Harris, *Charles Sackville, Sixth Earl of Dorset*, Urbana, Illinois, 1940, p. 64).

[2] This evidence is set forth in the edition *passim*, according to its kind and the work to which it applies (some individual examples are summarized in Beaurline, 'Canon', pp. 493–6).

negative evidence is equally impressive—in the lack of conflicting ascriptions, the anonymity of variant texts not explicitly ascribed to Suckling, and, in combination with these circumstances, the presence of unique substantive texts.

The authorship of only one poem is disputed, and of one letter otherwise questionable, both involving Suckling and Thomas Carew. 'Upon my Lady Carliles walking'—a dialogue between 'T. C.' and 'J. S.'—is subscribed 'T: C:' in Bodleian MS. Rawl. Poet. 199; but among other considerations 'J. S.''s decisive last word and the poem's final stanza in the manuscript, which is wanting in *FA46* (probably omitted deliberately because it is libellous as well as indecent), argues Suckling's rather than Carew's authorship.[1] Letter No. 51(*b*), 'An Answer' by 'Tom' to 'Jack''s 'Letter to a Friend to diswade him from marrying a Widow' (51(*a*)), is traditionally ascribed to Thomas Carew.[2] One of two variant texts (the other anonymous) supports Suckling's authorship of 51(*a*); the text of 'An Answer' (51(*b*)) in *FA46* is unique. The three letters by Carew that have been printed (*Poems*, ed. Dunlap, pp. 202–6) show him to be a not ineffective epistolary ironist, but they are so different in kind and address from 'An Answer' that they afford no stylistic evidence of Carew's authorship. On the other hand, 'An Answer' is very much in Suckling's otherwise well-established idiom—the one he uses not only in 'A Letter' itself but in other witty exercises in the often 'depersonalized' art of letter-writing[3]—and contains striking and subtle parallels with other works of his; it seems probable, therefore, that 'An Answer' is also by Suckling.[4]

It may fairly be said that the *Poems, &c.* of 1646 constitute a collection that is on the whole both canonically and textually reliable.

b. The Last Remains of Sir John Suckling, 1659

According to its general title, *Fragmenta Aurea*, 1658, was 'The Third Edition, with some New Additionals', implying that 'the *Remains*

---

[1] See further discussion in Commentary, p. 238.

[2] Rhodes Dunlap prints the two letters in Appendix D, 'Poems and Letters Addressed to Carew', only implying Carew's authorship in the phrase ' "Tom" 's answer' (*Poems of Thomas Carew*, 1949, pp. 211–12, 288).

[3] Cf. Letters Nos. 9, 11, 36–9, 48–50, and 52–3. For the generic source of this two-part exercise (which Suckling may echo), see Commentary on Letter No. 51(*a*).

[4] 'Tom''s having the last word here is no strong argument against his authorship, partly on the grounds that Suckling's capacity for mild self-satire (and the yielding of the last word here is not even that) is well established in the often-quoted stanzas from 'The Wits', ll. 73–80. 'The constant Lover' and 'The Answer' (headed 'Sir J. S.' and 'Sir Toby Matthews', respectively) are a parallel pair, and this matter is further discussed below, pp. xc–xcii.

were intended to form part of the collection', either by assimilation with the *Fragmenta* or as a separate supplement.[1] The date of the imprint of *The Last Remains*, 1659,[2] suggests difficulty in assembling the 'New Additionals' or some other delay that forced Humphrey Moseley to have them printed separately; but probably he had from the first intended them to be so, since, as Greg remarks, they would be required to supplement the *Fragmenta Aurea* of 1646 and 1648. The copies of *Fragmenta*, 1658, that are found separately suggest that Moseley had stocks of this book and sold some copies before the *Remains* were completed, but in spite of almost certain delay the *Remains* were published well before Moseley acquired his rights in them, for the title was not entered to him in the Stationers' Register until 29 June 1660.[3] *The Last Remains* were printed in the shop of Thomas Newcombe (who had married Ruth Raworth, the printer of the *Poems, &c.* for the first edition of *Fragmenta Aurea*, in 1648 or 1649).[4] Some carelessness or more probably haste in the printing is suggested by the number of press corrections (the variants, affecting the text on five pages, are listed under 'Copy-Text and Editorial Treatment' below), the presence of an errata leaf (sig. a⁴), and the survival of the error 'alace' for 'place' (sig. A6ᵛ). Most of the 'corrections' on the errata leaf were necessary but were almost certainly

[1] Greg, *Bibliography*, iii. 1133, n. 1. For full bibliographical descriptions of *Fragmenta Aurea*, 1658, and *The Last Remains* see iii. 1132–4, but Greg errs in the printer, who was not *Newman* but *Newcombe* (see *Pforzheimer Catalogue*, iii. 1037, and below).

[2] In the Thomason copy 'June' is written next to the date on the title-page, and this, as Greg notes, is confirmed by Thomason's manuscript catalogue. *The Last Remains* could, of course, have been printed several months before Thomason acquired it, and *Fragmenta Aurea* may have been printed late in 1658.

[3] Greg, *Bibliography*, iii. 1134.

[4] All ornaments except the peacock on sig. C7 (*Letters* title) are found in C. William Miller, 'Thomas Newcombe: A Restoration Printer's Ornament Stock', *SB*, 1950, iii. 155–70. One ornament (Miller No. 8) that Ruth Raworth used for the *Poems, &c.*, 1646, was also used in the 1658 edition of *Fragmenta Aurea* and in the *Remains*, 1659.

Two skeleton-formes were used throughout—for the inner and outer formes, respectively, throughout—in the printing of the non-dramatic works (sigg. A–D8), as is proved by the placement and condition of the parentheses and numerals in the top-centred pagination (there are no running-titles) and by the locations of recurrent rules. And two compositors, with quite distinct spelling practices, set the text apparently *seriatim*. Compositor 'X' appears to have set sigg. A8–B2, C8–D1ᵛ, and D4ᵛ–D8 (Poems, pp. 9–13; Letters, pp. 3–6 and 12–19); and compositor 'Y' the greater part of the text, sigg. A4–A7ᵛ, B2ᵛ–C6, and D2–D4 (Poems, pp. 1–8, 14–29, and 30–7; Letters, pp. 7–11). There are no certain differential spellings on sig. B3ʳ⁺ᵛ (part of which consists in the text of the French poem, 'Desdain'), but they are generally modern and were probably also set by 'Y'. Some examples of the compositors' respective preferences are ('X' 's given first): *again/agen*; *-e/no e*, e.g. 'finde'; *-e-/-ea-*, e.g. 'brest'; *-ey/-y*, e.g., 'countrey'; *-es/-s*, e.g. 'destroyes'; *-oor/-ore*, e.g. 'door' ('Y' also uses 'rore'); *-u-/-h-*, e.g. 'guest' (i.e. 'guessed'); *-e-/no e*, e.g. 'onely'; *-th-/-d-*, e.g. 'murther'; *-ei-/-ie-*, e.g. 'peirce'; and *-ie-/-ee-*, e.g. 'yield'. There is a higher ratio of authorial spellings in the work of the compositor who set the smaller number of pages ('X'), but this may be due only to the fact that his practices are in general more archaic, those of the other compositor comparatively modern.

made without reference to copy, as, for example, in the alteration to
'*King Gorbuduke*' from '*Queen Gorbuduke*' (Letter No. 48, l. 3), and to
'loos'd' from 'lost' ('Detraction execrated', l. 36), which may have
been so written in the copy and is in any case—though it makes no
sense—closer to the obviously intended 'los[e]'t'.

The 'Epistle Dedicatory' prefixed to *The Last Remains* (sig. a1ʳ⁺ᵛ) is
addressed to 'The Lady Southcot', Suckling's sister, who is somewhat
ambiguously credited with providing the copy for the book.[1] Before
leaving the country, Moseley says in 'The Stationer to the Reader'
(sigg. A2–3ᵛ), Suckling

> first took care to secure the dearest and choisest of his Papers in the several
> Cabinets of his Noble and faithful Friends; and among other Testimonies of
> his worth, these elegant and florid Peeces of his Fancie were preserved in the
> custody of his truly honorable and vertuous Sister, with whose free per-
> mission they were transcribed, and now published exactly according to the
> Originals.

This must be taken to mean—though it need not be true—that most
if not all *The Last Remains* were supplied by Lady Southcot. About
the authenticity of the collection evidently Moseley himself, and
perhaps Lady Southcot, too, entertained doubts, for he insists upon
it in 'The Stationer to the Reader', and in the 'Epistle' adds that
'here are nothing else but his, not a line but what at first flow'd from
him, and will soon approve it self to be too much his to be alter'd or
supplied by any other hand; and sure he were a bold man had thoughts
to attempt it'.

The Last Remains consist of forty-three poems,[2] twelve letters (at
least three of which—Nos. 36–8—are epistolary political tracts), and
the unfinished play, *The Sad One*. For twenty-seven of the poems, all
but one of the letters (No. 38, 'An Answer to a Gentleman', with
manuscript attributions to Suckling), and the play, it provides the
only substantive texts. On the same grounds as are available to
authenticate the works in *Fragmenta Aurea*, 1646 (see pp. lxxxv–lxxxvi
above), the authorship of the letters and the play is not in doubt. But,
of the sixteen poems for which there are variant texts, only three—

---

[1] The prefatory matter is printed between the list of 'Sigla and Sources' and the beginning
of the text below.

[2] This number includes the three translations (discussed below), 'A Song to a Lute' (printed
both with the Poems and in *The Sad One*, which also contains a brief drinking song that is
omitted here), and 'Song' (beginning 'If you refuse me once') as two poems, of which it is
in fact composed.

'The constant Lover', 'The Answer', and 'To a Lady that forbidd to love before Company'—are elsewhere attributed to Suckling (though 'A Song to a Lute' occurs also in *The Sad One*). Five are anonymous: 'Love and Debt alike troublesom', 'Song' ('The crafty Boy'), 'The deformed Mistress', 'Upon A. M.', and 'Foreknowledge'. The remaining seven are attributed to other authors.

As Mr. Beaurline has epitomized the problem of the canon in *The Last Remains*, 'the questionable tone of Moseley's prefaces, the unknown sources of his information and the seven rival claims cause the entire [poetical] contents of the book to be in doubt. In these circumstances, each poem must present some positive evidence of genuineness before it can be admitted to the canon' ('Canon', p. 501). Among the reasons he gives for the doubtfulness of the collection is the subscription of the initials 'J. S.' to all but a few of the poems, a point well taken, owing to the oddity of the phenomenon in seventeenth-century printed collections of poems by a single poet. The origin of these initials—editorial or from commonplace-books, or both —is uncertain, but the apparent intention of their use is to communicate conviction of the works' authenticity. It is also important to note that the play and most of the canonical poems in *The Last Remains* are demonstrably or inferentially of early composition (whereas most of the works in *Fragmenta Aurea* belong to Suckling's 'later' years, that is *c.* 1633–41), a factor that contributes considerably to the apparent dubiousness of the collection and also partly explains why there are variant texts of so few of the works.

Of the seven disputed poems, three are certainly not by Suckling: 'Song' ('If you refuse me once') is by Lord Herbert of Cherbury, and 'Song' ('Oh, that I were all soul'), printed in *LR* as though it were part of Lord Herbert's poem, is by Sir Robert Ayton; the 'Song' beginning 'When Deare I doe but thinke on thee' is by Owen Felltham.[1] The other four, although of uncertain authorship, are probably not by Suckling. 'Love turn'd to Hatred' is ascribed in a manuscript text to 'Capt. Tyrell', who is too nearly anonymous to attract attributions by the power of his name. The 'Song' beginning 'I prethee send me back my heart' (printed attribution to Dr. Henry Hughes and an ambiguous manuscript attribution to Lady Alice Egerton) has a feminine delicacy that is altogether alien to Suckling (in 'The Expostulation I' Suckling uses an explicitly female speaker

---

[1] On the authorship of these poems, see Commentary.

whose utterances are not especially feminine).[1] 'The guiltless Inconstant' was printed as Carew's in _Poems_, 1640, but all the manuscript attributions but one (which is dual: to 'T. C.', of later addition, in the title and 'W. P.' at the end) support the authorship of Walton Poole. The _LR_ text of this poem is very corrupt, and, despite a few rather striking parallel phrases and a doubtful biographical speculation (the effects of Suckling's loss of 'Aglaura'), there is little in its style to support Suckling's authorship. In this poem, which is redundant, 'helical' in structure, and arbitrary in organization, a self-pitying speaker soliloquizes about the loss of one great love and his consequent attempts to 'find in many what I lost in one', a species of undramatic and sentimental maundering normally uncharacteristic of Suckling, who also does not trouble to rationalize inconstancy.[2] In rhythm, cadence, and tone (given the differences in subject and situation), the poem is not unlike 'If shadows be a picture's excellence' and is probably also by Walton Poole.[3] 'To the Lady Desmond' (as 'Upon the Black Spots worn by my Lady D. E.') was printed as 'Of another Author' in Dudley Lord North's _A Forest of Varieties_, 1645, which has some connection with Suckling. It is stylistically not uncharacteristic, but its textual corruption in _LR_, the lack of external support for Suckling's authorship, and the intrinsic authority of a manuscript text subscribed 'P[eter]. Apsley' supports the likelihood of the latter's authorship.

Five other poems require discussion here. In my view, four and perhaps all five are by Suckling, but for only three of them does the evidence seem strong enough to warrant their inclusion in the canon. In _LR_, where these poems are otherwise untitled, the headings 'Sir J. S.' and 'Sir Toby Matthews'—of 'The constant Lover' and 'The Answer', respectively—seem to support Mathew's authorship of 'The Answer'; but the same two poems in the earlier-printed and superior texts in _Wit and Drollery_, 1656, are titled, 'A Song by Sir John Suckling' and 'The Answer by the same Author', which I take to be the truth of the matter.[4] That the poems were intended to

---

[1] As Beaurline points out, Norman Ault, who first discovered the attribution to Hughes, still believes that internal evidence makes the poem Suckling's (see _Seventeenth Century Lyrics_, 1950, n. to p. 162).

[2] Chiefly on the basis of parallel passages, Beaurline concluded that 'it is either Suckling's work or a very close imitation of him' ('Canon', p. 505); or, it might be added, one in which he had a revising hand or that he found interesting enough to imitate.

[3] See Edwin Wolf II, ' "If shadows be a picture's excellence" : An Experiment in Critical Bibliography', _PMLA_, 1948, lxiii. 831–57.

[4] Beaurline remarks that the title of 'The Answer' in _Wit and Drollery_ is 'no doubt' in error ('Canon', p. 503).

constitute a kind of unit, as dramatic assertion and refutation, seems
well established by the fact that 'The Answer' accompanies six of the
seven substantive texts of 'The constant Lover'.[1] Sir Tobie Mathew
is mentioned in 'The Wits' (ll. 57–64) and there is other (slight)
evidence of association between him and Suckling,[2] but there is
certainly nothing in the works undoubtedly written by him to confirm or even suggest the possibility of his authorship of 'The Answer'.[3]
If Mathew didn't write it, then it seems probable that Suckling did,
intending the two poems as a kind of dialogue, with 'Sir J. S.' and
'Sir Toby Matthews' as, in effect, speech-headings (which need not,
of course, be his: the second could have been an unauthorized accre-
tion of later origin).

Suckling's authorship of 'The Answer' is consistent with his general
predilection for poetical dialogues, dramatic monologues, and the use
of 'depersonalized' fictional speakers;[4] and the light raillery to which
he subjects himself here is not very different from that in 'The Wits'
(ll. 73–80). In 'The constant Lover' the speaker's utterance is not
unlike that of 'The careless Lover' (which follows 'The Answer' in
LR); he regards three days' constancy as unparalleled, attributing it,
however, not to his own restraint but to 'that very very Face', with-
out which 'There had been at least ere this | A dozen dozen in her
place'. The speaker of 'The Answer' is a sententious and railing
'philosopher', the rhetorical speaker 'Sir Toby Matthews', who utters
sentiments quite consonant, however, with those expressed by 'The
constant Lover'.[5] He jocosely and somewhat hyperbolically rebukes
'The constant Lover' in terms of passion and reason, and ridicules
him for a fool's dotage: 'She to whom you were so true, | And that
very very Face, | Puts each minute such as you | A dozen dozen to

---

[1] The seventh is the Henry Lawes autograph song-book (*HL*), from which it is not
surprising that 'The Answer', as an individual poem inferior to 'The constant Lover' and not
required to supplement it as song, is missing (both poems appear in *Dx4*, another seventeenth-
century manuscript song-book).

[2] The mention in 'The Wits' is depreciative, but see Commentary.

[3] The well-known ability of so many men of the time to produce creditable 'papers of
verses' on a variety of subjects can scarcely be used to convey much individual conviction.

[4] See, for example, his poetical first-person Characters ('A Pedler of Small-wares', 'A
Barber', 'A Soldier'), 'Upon my Lady Carliles walking in Hampton-Court garden' (dialogue),
'A Ballade. Upon a Wedding' (dramatic monologue spoken by a West Country rustic), and
'Upon my Lord Brohalls Wedding' (dialogue); the polemical exchange of letters between
a 'London Alderman' and a 'Scottish Lord' (Nos. 36–7); and the 'Letter to a Friend to dis-
wade him from marrying a Widow' with the 'Answer' (on which see p. lxxxvi above).

[5] 'Sir Toby' 's 'more Fool then Lover' (l. 8), and indeed the whole stanza, also has something
of a parallel in 'The careless Lover' 's lines, 'Who does not thus in *Cupids* school, | He makes
not Love, but plays the Fool' (ll. 38–9). All three poems are closely related in subject and
tone, and the antitheses are more rhetorical than real.

disgrace.' In the inclusive unity of the two poems, inconstancy is universal except when, occasionally, the attractive power of an object and the self-deceit of a subject combine; and even then the resulting constancy is a one-way Terentian 'universum triduum' with a libertine cast.

Of the three translations ('Foreknowledge' is the third), only 'Profer'd Love rejected' and 'Disdain' are almost certainly by Suckling. These are translations respectively of 'A Phillis' and 'Desdain', printed in *Les Satyres et Autre Oevvres du Sr Regnier*, of which there were at least ten editions between 1614 and 1638. H. E. Berthon has made the doubtful suggestion that two other poems in the same collection served as Suckling's models for 'Song' ('Why so pale and wan fond Lover') and 'Loves Siege',[1] but the circumstantial evidence of association in a source-book binds at least these two translations together and supplements the stylistic evidence for Suckling's authorship. The two are further suggestively bound by the title 'Profer'd Love rejected' and the 'proffer'd services' of 'Disdain' (l. 3): the title of the former is almost certainly editorial, but the parallel nevertheless suggests a possible physical relationship between the two and perhaps their identity of authorship. That the theme, rhetorical situation, and attitude of 'Profer'd Love rejected' are characteristic of Suckling has of course been noticed before and is obvious from a reading of his other poems;[2] 'Disdain', in which a faithful and disdainful woman rejects a would-be lover, resembles 'Perjury disdain'd' in theme and attitude. Both translations share the ballad stanza with 'The constant Lover', 'The Answer', and 'Loves Siege', as all these poems share the fairly frequent use of feminine rhymes in the second and fourth lines and the sparing but strategic use of acephalous lines ('The constant Lover' and 'The Answer', however, would properly be described as catalectic-trochaic ballad stanzas). Finally, 'Disdain' contains a collocation of figures that Suckling uses in a similar way elsewhere: 'For things that may be, rack your brain, | Then lose not thus your labor' (ll. 19–20) is reminiscent of 'What Rack can Fancy find so high? | Here we must Court, and here ingage, | Though in the other place we die' ('Loving and Beloved', ll. 13–15; cf. Letter No. 29, ll. 7–8).

[1] *MLR*, 1911, vi. 221–3. The suggested models are, respectively, 'Pourquoi perdez-vous la parole' and 'Amour, héraut de la beauté'.

[2] Remarked pejoratively by L. E. Kastner: 'there is ground apparently for the belief that the poem in question does not belong to Suckling, but that it was included among his works at a later date because its subject and substance are in keeping with much of his erotic verse'; the 'ground apparently' must be the late date and exaggerated dubiousness of *The Last Remains* (see *MLR*, 1910, v. 497, and 1911, vi. 223–4).

A consideration of alternative authors—a known author writing in a comparatively alien idiom or an anonymous author writing in Suckling's—adds support to the stylistic evidence that these two poems are indeed by Suckling and should be included in the canon.[1]

'Foreknowledge'—a translation of (presumably) a Greek original poem and a Latin verse-translation of that—is not unlike Suckling's juvenile poems, but it has little individuality (as such a poem could scarcely have); and the Henry Fane commonplace-book, in which there is an anonymous variant text, affords no real additional evidence.[2] In my view, the poem is probably Suckling's, but there is insufficient evidence to allow it to be admitted to the canon.

'Love and Debt alike troublesom' has a number of parallels of image and idea in other poems (q.v. in Commentary), and the epigrammatic turn of thought and phrase in the concluding couplet, 'Nor sigh for love of Lady fair; for this each wise man knows: | As good stuff under Flanel lies, as under Silken clothes', is eminently characteristic of Suckling. But these doggerel fourteeners are unlike anything else he wrote, including the canonical poems of his youth, and even the parallels can be counted for little enough, because they are traditional and commonplace. This poem cannot be regarded as very certainly Suckling's, and it is undoubtedly a very early poem if it is his.

Rejecting the seven disputed poems as dubious or not of Suckling's authorship, and finding 'positive arguments of some sort' to support Suckling's authorship of only twelve poems in *The Last Remains*, Mr. Beaurline concluded that 'in the absence of any argument, we must consider the remaining twenty-four as doubtful poems' ('Canon', p. 506). But I have found that there is reasonable support, in most of the same kinds of evidence that substantiate Suckling's authorship of the *Fragmenta Aurea*, for thirty-four of the poems, and I have included these in the canon. The evidence for Suckling's authorship of individual works—in addition to those discussed here —is given in the Commentary, often implicitly, in references to significant parallel passages and comments on historical associations. There is another kind of evidence of identity of authorship in the variously definable homogeneity of a corpus of works that speaks

---

[1] Another translation, 'Epigramme de Monsieur des-Portes', beginning 'Some four years, ago I made Phillis an offer', was printed as Charles Cotton's in *Poems on Several Occasions* 1689, p. 195 (the poem is not in *Cotton's Poems*, ed. John Beresford, 1923, or ed. John Buxton, 1958); it is printed in the Commentary on 'Profer'd Love Rejected'.

[2] Folger MS. V. a. 180 (DeRicci 1085. 1); see Commentary, p. 296.

better for itself than explicit parallels or categorical distributions of abstracted characteristics. This homogeneity is certainly to be found in the majority of Suckling's canonical poems, and it is more easily apprehended upon a reading of the works as ordered in this edition than as unhelpfully arranged in *Fragmenta Aurea* and *The Last Remains* (see 'Chronology, Genre, and the Order of the Works' below).

In many respects, *The Last Remains* is a collection inferior to *Fragmenta Aurea*, but a close examination of it argues that, despite the suspicions occasioned by Moseley's apparently strenuous efforts to convince the reader of its authenticity, his claims in the prefatory addresses are not so very far from the truth. The presence of works not by Suckling is almost certainly to be accounted for by the fact that 'the dearest and choisest of his Papers' were indeed his but not necessarily of his authorship; that some were memorial and defective transcriptions of poems by others; and that some were poems by others that he was tentatively revising, with or without solicitation. An editor's scrutiny of the individual works in such a collection as *The Last Remains* must be more exacting, perhaps, than that demanded by the *Fragmenta Aurea*, but it is not different in kind; if the methods and judgement are sound, the results should be comparable.

ii. OTHER PRINTED SOURCES

Five poems by Suckling were printed with his authorization during his lifetime; the texts of these in *Fragmenta Aurea*, 1646, are unauthoritative reprints. The two songs, 'No, no faire Heretique' and 'Why so pale and wan fond Lover', were first printed in *Aglaura*, 1638.[1] The commendatory poems were first printed in:

1. ROMVLVS AND TARQUIN *First Written in Italian* By the *Marques Virgilio Malvezzi*: And now *taught English*, by H: L.ᵈ Cary. of Lepingtō the second Edition. LONDON Printed *by I. H. for* Iohn Benson . . . 1638. ['To his much honoured, the Lord *Lepington*, upon his Translation of *Malvezzi* his *Romulus & Tarquin*', signed 'Jo. Suckling.', sig. A4ʳ⁺ᵛ.]

2. Madagascar; WITH OTHER Poems. By W. DAVENANT. LONDON, Printed by *John Haviland* for *Thomas Walkly* . . . 1638. ['To MY FRIEND *Will. Davenant*; upon his Poem of *Madagascar*', sig. A7ʳ⁺ᵛ, and 'On his other Poems', sig. A8ʳ, both signed 'I. Suckling.']

[1] For full bibliographical description see Greg, *Bibliography*, ii. 540; and see Commentary, ii. 257.

A sixth work, '*To Mr,* Henry German *in the beginning of* PARLIA-
MENT, 1640', was printed as 'A COPPY OF A LETTER FOVND
IN THE PRIVY LODGEINGS AT WHITEHALL. Printed in the
yeare, 1641.'[1] This pamphlet may have been published after Suckling's flight on 6 May, but even if it had been printed earlier
the omission of the names of the printer, the place of printing, and the
author suggests surreptitious publication; and it is probable that the
printer did not even know who the author was, for the use of Suckling's name could probably be expected to sell many copies. The text,
probably representing an earlier version of the work than is found in
Fragmenta Aurea (see Commentary), is very corrupt, which argues
that the pamphlet cannot have had a direct association with the poet.[2]

Although it has never been included in a collection of his works,
one other work requires discussion here. Probably soon after his
flight to France appeared the anonymous 4° pamphlet, 'THE
COPPY OF A LETTER WRITTEN TO THE LOWER HOVSE
OF PARLIAMENT TOUCHING DIVERS GRIEVANCES AND
INCONVENIENCES OF THE STATE &C. *LONDON* Printed by
Iohn Dawson for *Thomas Walkley,* 1641.'[3] This pamphlet has been
ignored in previous specialized work on Suckling, but his authorship
continues to be generally accepted.[4] It was first attributed to him,
without authority, in the first edition of the *Somers Tracts.*[5] In his
prefatory statement in the second edition, Sir Walter Scott observed
that the pamphlet referred to the third Parliament of Charles I, but
he nevertheless accepted Suckling's authorship.[6]

The pamphlet appears to have been written immediately after the

---

[1] *A Coppy* is grouped among pamphlets acquired in May 1641 in Thomason, i. 14. The
place of printing as London, and the printer as John Dawson, have been identified by John
Cook Wyllie, on the basis of similarities in shop practice between this pamphlet and *The
Coppy of a Letter to the Lower House* etc., which carries Dawson's imprint (see 'The Printer
of a 1641 Suckling Pamphlet', *PBSA*, 1953, xlvii. 70). An ornament used for this printing
(which I have been unable to find used in any other book in the Bodleian Library printed by
him between the years 1641 and 1646) is identical in size and design, but greatly superior in
execution, to that (probably a copy) used by Susan Islip in *The Goblins,* 1646, sig. A2, and
Brennoralt, 1646, sig. A3.

[2] Regarding the text of the pamphlet as the 'original one', Hazlitt used it as copy-text,
correcting occasionally from the *Fragmenta* text (ii. 227–34).

[3] It is grouped with pamphlets acquired in August in Thomason, i. 26.

[4] The pamphlet is attributed to Suckling in Halkett and Laing, i. 433, and included with
his works in Wing (S 6124).

[5] 1748–52, iv. iii (1951), 436: '*A Letter written to the Lower House of Parliament. By Sir
John Suckling.*'

[6] *Somers Tracts,* 1809–15, iv. 105 (Scott's note is echoed in the ascription to Suckling
of an anonymous manuscript text of this work in the *Catalogue of Manuscripts in the Cambridge
University Library,* 1856–67, iv. 312). The third Parliament sat from 17 March 1628 to
11 March 1629.

parliamentary elections in 1628,[1] for it begins: 'If my Country had held me worthy to have served in this Parliament, I had now beene made a member of your lower house as formerly I have beene in sundry other Parliaments . . .' (p. 1). At that time Suckling was barely nineteen and the poems he wrote at that age would scarcely suggest an ability so convincingly to conceal his age and identity. And, in decrying the wastefulness of the expedition to the Ile de Ré (which Suckling had been sent to accompany), the writer of the pamphlet goes on to avow that 'My experience in Discipline of Warres by Land and Sea, can say no more then referre it to others, for it is a course I never was bred to in my youth, and now to late in my age to practise' (p. 14). The attribution of this pamphlet to Suckling probably derives from an impressionable inscription on a copy of the pamphlet made by someone who read it long after his death.[2] It was apparently printed for the first time in 1641, but the bookseller, Thomas Walkley, must have felt that the general topicality of its complaints—even fourteen years after the events which gave rise to them—would make it saleable following the opening of a new Parliament. The title is ambiguous enough to have allowed its printing and sale upon the calling of any Parliament, but the Long Parliament of 1640 was the first to be called (except for the abortive Short Parliament) after the dissolution of the Parliament of 1628.

The second edition of *Fragmenta Aurea*, of 1648, might be regarded as something of a source (as it occasionally was for Hazlitt and Thompson), because, while it is otherwise a reprint, it contains substantial and significant alterations in the texts of three poems. Most of these could not be editorial and (with the possible exception of the restoration of four lines of 'The Wits' that are wanting in *FA46*) could not be explained as resulting from reconsultation of the copy used by the printer of *FA46*.[3] A number are certainly authoritative corrections (for which there are other witnesses), and it seems likely that those which are not—and are not editorial—gained admission to *FA48* not only by editorial concurrence in the 'superiority' of the

---

[1] The latest event mentioned is the expedition to the Ile de Ré, which took place between 27 June and 8 November 1627 (Gardiner, iv. 171, 198).

[2] It is also impossible that it could have been written by Sir John Suckling *père*, who died in 1627 before the Ré expedition took place.

[3] This would presuppose extensive compositorial or editorial departures from copy in the *FA46* texts of at least these three poems and, improbably, Moseley's retention (or resolicitation) of the copy after the book had been printed.

Besides those in the non-dramatic works, there are approximately 150 substantive and semi-substantive alterations in the *FA48* text of *The Goblins* and a few improvements in the punctuation of *Brennoralt* (see Commentary and critical apparatus for these plays).

readings but by the supposed authority of the source(s), as is perhaps supported by the anomalous 'scribal' spellings of the four lines restored to 'The Wits' (ll. 69–72).

In the text of 'The Wits', *FA48* has twenty-two substantive departures from *FA46*: nine are shared with all other substantive witnesses and are undoubtedly authoritative; seven are unique and are probably editorial; in six others *FA48* agrees twice with two or more other witnesses, twice with *Cran6*, and once each with *Harv7* and *M3*. No known extant text, therefore, can have served as sole source for its corrections (unless, of course, some conflicting agreements are fortuitous). The alterations were apparently made from a marked-up copy of *FA46* containing readings from one or more sources or by a somewhat careless consultation of (probably) a single manuscript, since a number of erroneous readings in *FA46* are uncorrected in *FA48* (see critical apparatus). Of the eight alterations in 'A Ballade. Upon a Wedding', two are unique and probably editorial; the other six are found in other variant witnesses. As in 'The Wits', errors remain, the most serious being the transposition of ll. 61–6 and 67–72, which occur in the correct order in *Ash3* and *RP3* (*H17* omits ll. 61–6); the evidence is insufficient to decide whether this agreement with *FA46* is due to a defective source, spasmodic alteration, or editorial rejection of a transposition in the source. In 'Womans Constancy' three of *FA48*'s substantive departures are inferior in sense or rhythm to the readings in *FA46* (the one improvement, in l. 14, could have been editorial). There are no other known variant texts of the poem, but whatever their source these three readings are manifestly corrupt.

The interest of these substantive variants in *FA48* consists chiefly in their demonstrating genuine if casual editorial concern in the publication of the second edition of *Fragmenta Aurea* and their manifesting contemporary editorial judgement, both in 'emending' (apparently) and in choosing between alternative readings; the unique readings are almost certainly editorial corruptions, however, and since there are extant substantive texts of the entire poem none of its other readings has much value.

Variant texts of Suckling's poems appeared in numerous seventeenth-century printed miscellanies and song-books. These are indicated by sigla in the apparatus for individual poems, and the books in which they occur are given in the list of 'Sigla and Textual Sources'.

iii. MANUSCRIPT SOURCES

No manuscript collection of Suckling's non-dramatic works is extant and probably none ever existed. The arrangement of the works in the substantive printed editions is neither chronological nor otherwise systematic. Although the placing of some poems and letters can be explained as deliberate, or as probably resulting from physical association with other works in the copy, one can only infer that the copy consisted in miscellaneous 'papers of verses' containing one or several poems, single letters and groups of letters, and the like. Given the conduct, pace, and brevity of Suckling's life, and what is known of his temperament, it would indeed be surprising if there were an ordered manuscript collection of his works. Lacking such a collection, which might otherwise replace as copy-text or at any rate serve as a source of systematic comparison and correction for a printed collection of uncertain provenance and some imperfection, an editor is bound to pay greater attention than might otherwise be necessary to miscellaneous variant texts. Indeed, where they are the only means, besides the editor's own judgement, of evaluating, supplementing, and correcting a printed collection, they are indispensable, and often invaluable.

Of the canonical non-dramatic works printed in the substantive editions, only *An Account of Religion, To Mr. Henry German*, three letters, and less than a third of the poems circulated in manuscript copies that are still extant; by comparison, there are extant copies of all the dubious poems printed in *The Last Remains*. These facts suggest—if the *Remains* were printed entirely or for the most part from Suckling's own papers (see p. xciv above)—that Suckling was more interested in the random accumulation of others' poems he liked (or had been asked to correct) than in either circulating or making collected fair copies of his own. The variant texts of the dubious poems provide the external evidence that they are dubious, and those of the canonical poems that they either are by Suckling, or probably are or could be; texts of both, of course, are sources of almost certainly authentic readings missing or corrupt in the printed texts.

Fourteen letters and twelve poems certainly by Suckling failed to find their way into the substantive editions. The source of all but five of the letters and one of the poems, and the only manuscript source of major importance, is the collection of Cranfield Papers, which were originally the personal papers of Suckling's uncle, Lionel

PLATE I

SIR JOHN SUCKLING
Engraving by William Marshall (State A)

PLATE 2

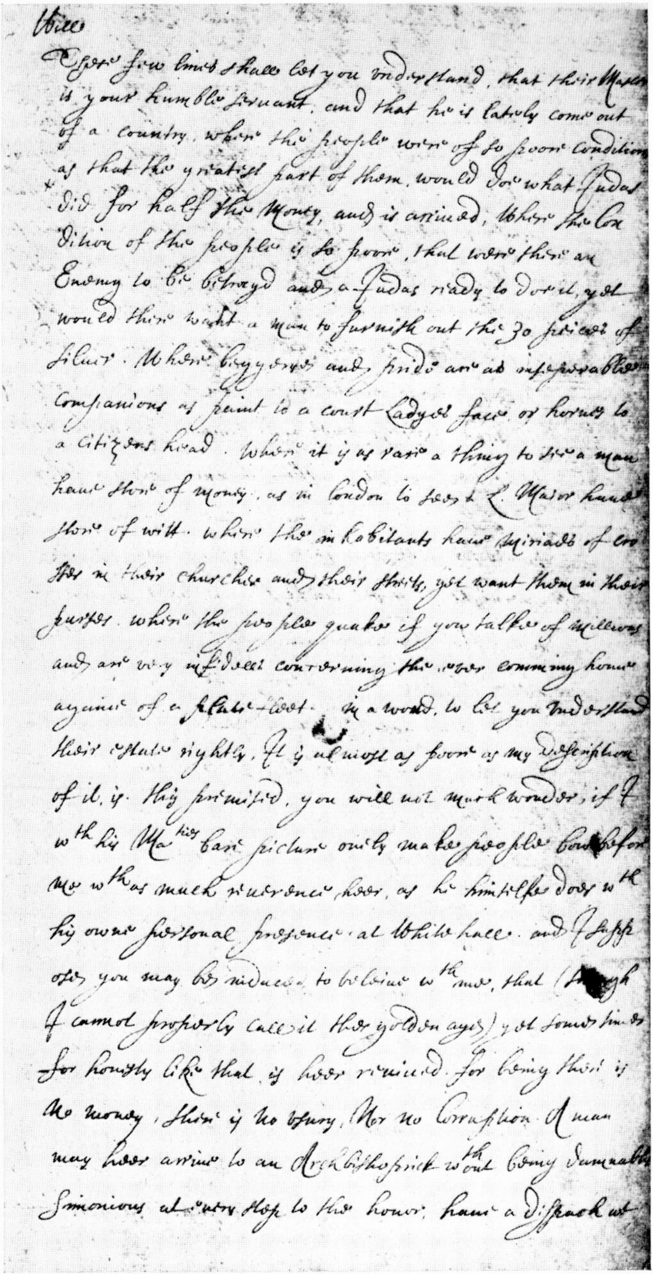

Holograph Letter, 5 May 1630 (page 1), No. 11

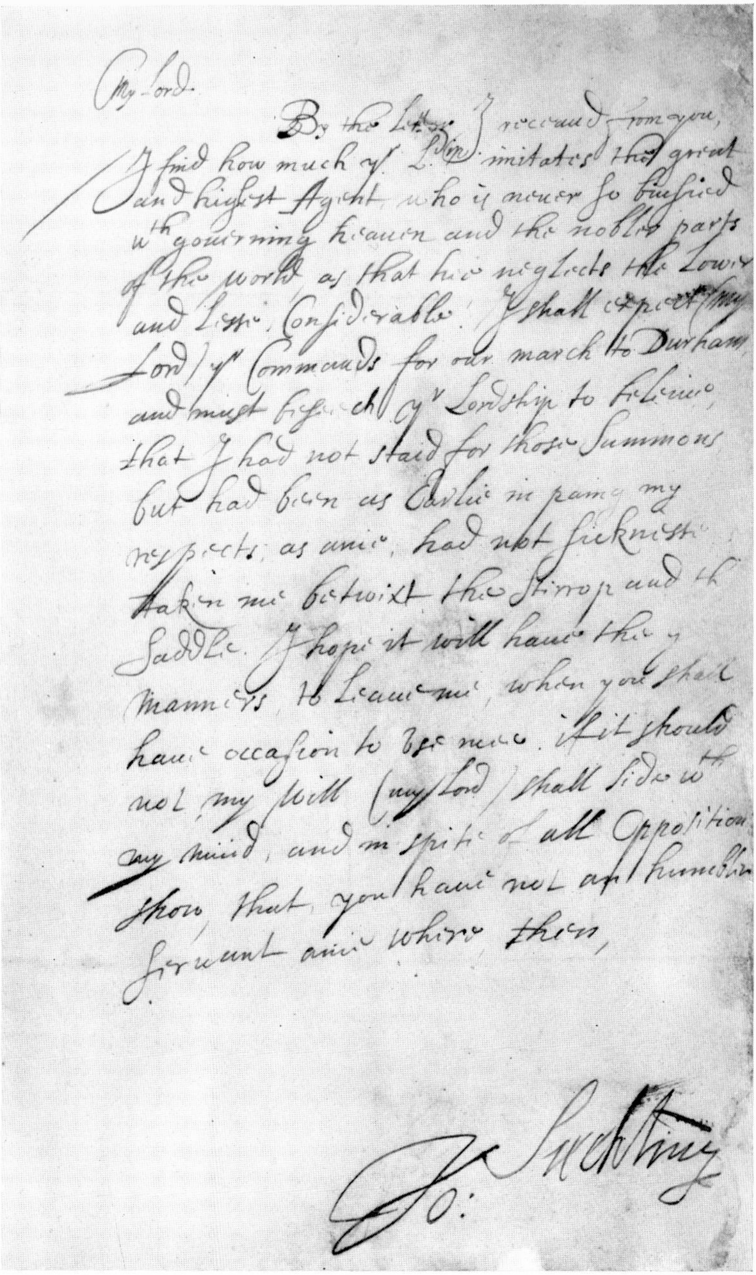

PLATE 3

My Lord.

By the Letter I received from you,
I find how much of yr Lordp imitates that great
and highest Agent, who is never so busied
wth governing heaven and the nobler parts
of the world as that hee neglects the lower
and lesse Considerable. I shall expect my
Lord, yr Commands for our march to Durham,
and must beseech yr Lordship to believe,
that I had not staid for those Summons
but had been as earlie in paing my
respects, as anie, had not sickness
taken mee betwixt the stirrop and th
Saddle. I hope it will have the y
Manners, to leave mee, when you shall
have occasion to use mee. if it should
not, my will (my Lord) shall side wth
my mind, and in spite of all Opposition
show, that you have not a humbler
servant anie where, then,

Jo: Suckling

Holograph Letter, April–May 1640, No. 46

PLATE 4

Vpon Christmas

Haile welcome time, whose long expected date
The pensive hearts of men doth elevate
Who from their toile cessations now require,
And live in warme Elysiums by the fire
Vpon whose sunny banks the take delight
To see the winged, and foure-footed fight,
And charge each other in the flaming fields
With spitts for speares, & dripping-pans for shields
Some better friends doe turne about, & play
Till scorcht w'th heat become to men a prey.
And schollers too prison-schoole set free
Proclaime aloud a goale deliverie,
Invoke the Gods of sports, nor feare y maine
By Plough-day writs to bee attackt againe.
Well did o'r fathers then by Christ set free
Elect us thus to their fraternitie.
But shall those impious mouths by new-fond lights
Inspird revile, & loath these sacred rites,
Whose festivalls w'th prayer, & almes allayd
A time of Charitie, and gladnesse made
Shall they w'th poison-bearing slaunder staine
This time, and it abolish as profane?
Noe Noe: lets keepe it still whilst them wee see
With Christmas pull downe Christ Nativitie

a. 'Upon Christmas'
Cranfield Papers (U. 269. F. 36, No. 37, f. 2ʳ)

A Dreame.

Scarce had I slept my wonted rowsd
But that meethought I heard the last Trompe's sorond.
And in a Moment, Earth's faire Frame did passe
The Heav'ns did melt and All confusion was:
My thoughts straight gave mee Earth's great daie was come
And that I was nowe to receive my Doome.
Twixt Hope & Feare whilst I thus trembling stood
Heaving the Bad, and yet expecting Good.
Summon'd I was to shewe howe I had spent
That Span-long tyme wch God on earth mee lent.
Cold Feares possest mee, for I knewe not Lyes
(Though guilded ore) could blynd th' Eternall's Eye.
Besides my Bosome frend my Conscience mee accus'd,
That I too much this little Tyme abus'd.
And nowe nor summes of gould nor bribes (alasse)
Could mee reprive, Sentence must straight waie passe.
Great frends could nothing doe nor lustfull Peere
Nor smooth fac'd _Buckingham_ was Favourite heere.
Theire helpes were vaine, what could I then saie more
I had done ill, and death lay at the dore.
But yet meethought it was too much to dy
To die a while much lesse eternally
And therefore streight I did my Sinnes unmaske
And in _Christ's_ name a Pardon there did aske
wch God then granted, And god grant hee may
Make this my dreame proove true ith' latter day.

Bucklyn.

Cranfield, the first Earl of Middlesex.[1] These Papers also contain unique texts of two new poems possibly by Suckling, 'A New-years Gift' and 'Gnomics'; important variant texts of five printed poems, a letter (No. 23), and *To Mr. Henry German*; a superior variant text of a poem printed in 1673 as Davenant's that may be Suckling's ('To Mr. W. M. Against Absence'); and family papers that are directly associated with Suckling and some of his works. Of primary importance in the collection are the letters, all nine of which are in Suckling's own hand.[2] Seven of these were written to the Earl of Middlesex in 1630–1 (Nos. 10, 12, 14, 16, 17) and 1639 (Nos. 40 and 43), and one each was written to Mary Cranfield in 1629 (No. 1) and William Wallis in 1630 (No. 11).

Eleven juvenile poems (Nos. 1–11), first discovered and printed by Mr. Beaurline,[3] are of scarcely less importance and of considerable interest: all but one are religious, as none of Suckling's mature poems is (but cf. *An Account of Religion*, written in 1637), and they were written before he was twenty years old, most of them several years earlier, it would appear. These poems occur in two separate groups. The first (but perhaps later composed) contains 'Faith and Doubt' (f. 1, untitled in manuscript) and 'A Dreame' (f. 2), written in an elegant primarily italic hand on the leaves of a single sheet folded to make a folio.[4] Both poems are subscribed 'J: Sucklyn Esq', and there is ample internal evidence of Suckling's authorship in over-all style,

---

[1] The Cranfield Papers are now part of the collection of manuscripts of Lord Sackville of Knole, Sevenoaks, Kent. They came into the Sackville family through Charles Sackville, first Earl of Middlesex (by a re-creation) and sixth Earl of Dorset, whose mother was Frances, Lady Dorset, the daughter of the first Earl of Middlesex (and possibly the 'Friend' responsible for the publication of *Fragmenta Aurea*, 1646; see pp. lxxxiv–lxxxv above). Charles Sackville was the heir of his uncle, Lionel Cranfield, the third Earl of Middlesex (who died in 1675), as well as of his mother.

Some of the Cranfield Papers have been summarized and catalogued in *Manuscripts of Lord Sackville, Vol. I: Cranfield Papers, 1551–1612*, 1942, but the papers from 1613 to 1645, including the Suckling letters, have not yet been fully catalogued. The papers are further described in Felix Hull, *Guide to the Kent County Archives Office*, Maidstone, 1958, pp. 150–6; they are at present kept in the care of the Historical Manuscripts Commission.

[2] Letters Nos. 10, 11, 14, 16, 17, 40, and 43 (this edition) were catalogued and briefly summarized in *HMC 4th Report*, pp. 290, 293–4, and 300; transcriptions of them, with detailed annotation and historical commentary, have been printed by Berry, who first discovered No. 12, which was uncatalogued (pp. 56–62, 64–5, 68–72, 74–6, 78–9, 100–3, 105–7). No. 1 (uncatalogued) was first noticed and printed in T. S. Clayton, 'Sir John Suckling and the Cranfields', *TLS*, 29 January 1960, p. 68. Facsimiles of an early and a late letter, Nos. 11 (p. 1 only) and 46 (not from the Cranfield Papers), both of which were written with some care, are given between pp. xcviii–xcix.

[3] Nos. 1–9 in 'New Poems by Sir John Suckling', *SP*, 1962, lix. 653–5, and Nos. 10–11 in 'Canon', 512–13. I am especially indebted to him for calling them to my attention well before they were in print.

[4] Cranfield Papers, MS. U. 269. F. 36, No. 38. A facsimile of 'A Dreame' is given between pp. xcviii–xcix.

significant parallel passages, and attitudes expressed elsewhere in his works (see citations for individual poems in Commentary). From internal evidence, 'A Dreame' is datable with some conviction in 1624–6 (see Commentary).

The second group, which may have been written at about the same time or somewhat earlier,[1] consists of the first nine poems in this edition. The poems occupy three sides of a single folio, the paper of which bears a watermark different from the paper in the first group, as Mr. Beaurline notes ('New Poems', p. 652). This group is written in a primarily italic hand that is in many respects similar to the first but is far less assured and elegant and is apparently that of a young person; it is probably not the same hand, and, though it is possibly holograph, it is probable that neither is.[2] Since Mr. Beaurline has argued the case for Suckling's authorship at some length in 'New Poems' (pp. 651–7), it is sufficient here to comment that the poems are stylistically very similar to those of the first group and share significant parallel passages with those and other canonical works (cited for individual poems in the Commentary).

Two orthographical features of these fair copies are of special interest. The first is that they show a 'wide divergence' from Suck-

---

[1] Cranfield Papers, MS. U. 269 F. 36, No. 37. A facsimile of 'Upon Christmas' is given between pp. xcviii–xcix.

[2] It is not always easy to be certain of the identity of examples of Stuart handwriting, especially when there are as many variables involved as there are here: both groups of poems are painstakingly written fair-copies; for comparison, there are only the holograph letters, most of them obviously written in great haste in a mixed hand that favours secretarial forms in approximate proportion to the speed of composition (cf. Berry, p. 5). Most carefully written are Letters Nos. 10, 11 (both 1630), and 47 (1641?); the one closest in date to the poems is Letter No. 1 (1629), which despite a number of (not very graceful) flourishes has none of the apparently professional skill of the first group of poems. I once believed—and in my dissertation wrote—that the two groups were probably in the same hand (the second having been written earlier), possibly holograph, in spite of the fact that they appeared (superficially, I thought) unlike even the earliest of the holograph letters. Arguing on palaeographical and orthographical grounds, Beaurline has expressed his belief 'that the same person wrote both. However the hand is probably not Suckling's; it is predominantly Italian, while Suckling, in his letters, writes in the secretary hand' ('New Poems', p. 652).

Citing a number of significant supporting details, Mr. P. J. Croft, of Messrs. Sotheby and Co., has communicated to me privately that in his view the hand of the first group is 'altogether too scribal in character to support the idea of its being autograph' and that the second group is 'clearly in an immature hand . . . of rather poor quality (probably that of a relatively uneducated person), and this is supported by the quality of the text itself', notably in the metrical defects of 'Upon the Epiphanie', l. 4, and 'Upon Christmas', l. 11, examples of 'certain kinds of error which one hardly expects to find in an autograph manuscript . . . I find it hard to believe that this hand can be the poet's either.' My own present view is that the hand of the first group is certainly professional, that of the second a different one belonging to a young person, possibly Suckling: there seem to be more than fortuitous resemblances between this hand and Suckling's in his letter of 1641 (?), No. 47, but an assertion stronger than 'possibly holograph' would, I think, misrepresent the weight of the evidence, and even that may be unduly hopeful.

ling's spellings in the holograph letters (see 'New Poems', p. 652). The second is that far greater care has been taken to homogeneate the spellings of the rhyme-words than is the case with either *Fragmenta Aurea* or *The Last Remains*. This is a characteristic of *Aglaura*, 1638, and the agreement of the two groups of poems with the songs in this matter suggests that Suckling was rather more concerned with some aspects of the formal presentation of his poems than one might have expected.

The uncatalogued Cranfield manuscript of *To Mr. Henry German* is an untitled and unsubscribed professional fair-copy of very high associational and intrinsic authority. It is written in a shaded secretary hand on all four sides of the folios of two folded sheets and contains catchwords. Both the accidentals and the substantives of the text support its authority. It is very carefully punctuated, containing a number of Suckling's characteristic parentheses; and, though it has few authorial spellings (the comparatively individual 'beleive', 'Cavaleir', and 'ffeild' are exceptions), its 'display orthography' is very similar to that of the manuscript juvenile poems. This manuscript must be virtually identical with the copy used by the compositor of the text in *Fragmenta Aurea*, for the length of this work makes it highly improbable that two texts could be so similar unless one were derived from the other or both from the same source (*FA46*'s unique readings are such that the manuscript could not have been copied from it). Except for the title, *FA46* differs from it only in omissions, unauthoritative unique readings, and a few trivial variants shared with other witnesses that could have arisen fortuitously; it shares two otherwise unique readings with the manuscript, while the manuscript has only three unique readings, all trivial and easily corrected by conjecture (see apparatus, ll. 78, 97, 137). Because of its greater presumptive authority and its over-all superiority, the manuscript has replaced *Fragmenta Aurea* as copy-text for this work in the present edition.

Also of considerable interest among the uncatalogued Papers is 'The Coppy of Sr I^n Suckline his lettr to Sr Georg SowthCot' (No. 23), so endorsed by the Earl of Middlesex, which identifies the addressee, his and Suckling's address at the time of writing, and the precise date, none of which is given in the *Fragmenta* text (a letter from Southcot to the Earl—q.v. in Appendix A.iv, No. 5—concerning Suckling's letter is equally interesting). This copy is written on ff. 1^r and 2^r of a single folded sheet in a non-professional secretary hand;

it is divided into (mostly) sentence-length paragraphs, is scantly punctuated, and contains a number of obvious errors, a few of them —clearly due to eye-slips—corrected (see Commentary). The substantive differences between this and the *Fragmenta* text are extensive and rather puzzling, but it would appear that the manuscript is a transcription of Suckling's uncorrected draft and the *Fragmenta* text (which contains a few errors and probably sophisticated readings) a near descendant of a lost fair copy, possibly the original or an accurate transcription of it. The latter is strongly suggested by the fact that in *Fragmenta Aurea* this letter immediately follows a jocular consolatory letter on her husband's suicide written by Suckling to his sister, Lady Southcot, from whom the printer's copy for these letters may have come, though not necessarily directly, as it did for *The Last Remains* (see 'The Substantive Editions' above).

The remaining Cranfield Papers of particular interest here are the variant texts of canonical poems, especially that of 'The Wits', the contents and terminal date of which are given as 'Rymes | Of som Poetts | Of som Wittes | About London | Septemb^r 1637' (f. 2^v) in the Earl of Middlesex's endorsement; it is unsubscribed and otherwise untitled.[1] This manuscript is written, on ff. 1–2 of a single folded sheet, in a bold, mixed, primarily secretary hand leaning toward cursive italic (proper names are fully italic); it has a good deal in common with the italic hand of the group of poems discussed below.

This text of 'The Wits' is puzzling in several respects. It is uncertain whether 'About London' refers to 'Poetts' and 'Wittes', as in 'men about town', or to the work itself and the time of its circulation. The closeness of its association with Suckling is also uncertain: Mr. Beaurline comments that the 'document . . . was once folded into a small square suitable for enclosing with a letter' ('Experiment', p. 46), and the words 'About London' may point to its having been posted to the Earl as an unauthoritative copy of a version circulating in the capital. The text does not have spaces between stanzas, but division into octaves is indicated by marginal lines; it also lacks the suspension of monosyllables between ll. 4 and 5 of each stanza (see text and Commentary) and some of the suspended words themselves (in intrinsically better texts), suggesting that either its model or at any

---

[1] MS. U. 269. F. 36, No. 46, catalogued in *HMC 4th Report*, p. 278. It is discussed in L. A. Beaurline, 'An Editorial Experiment: Suckling's *A Sessions of the Poets*', *SB*, 1963, xvi. 43–60 (esp. pp. 46, 49–50, 53–4).

rate its ultimate ancestor had the suspensions. It contains more unique variants than any other text, which suggests that 'it is another version (i.e. an early draft or later revision) or a very corrupt transcription' ('Experiment', p. 49). Even if it were a corrupt transcription of an early draft, as is possible, its value as evidence of Suckling's revision is appreciably diminished by its corruption, since it is often impossible to distinguish between weak readings later improved and corruptions.[1] In this case, the corrupt state and questionable authority of the text in turn cast doubt upon the nature of the family association rather than the latter conferring a kind of authority upon the text, and the chief textual value of the manuscript lies in the distribution of its readings with those of other variant texts of the poem.

Finally, the Cranfield Papers contain, in a sheet folded and sewn into a quarto booklet, a handsome fair copy of four canonical poems and a fifth of uncertain authorship that is an answer to the poem that precedes it (it is discussed in the following section).[2] These are 'Against Absence', f. 1r+v; 'Song', beginning 'I prethee spare me, gentle Boy', f. 2; 'Against Fruition I', ff. 2v–3 (titled 'Against Fruition'); 'To Mr. W. M. Against Absence', f. 3; and 'To Mr. Davenant for Absence', f. 4 (ff. 3v and 4v blank). Only the third poem has a title, and none identifies the author. The poems are written in a graceful, shaded, cursive italic hand, the same as that in which letters from John Langley, tutor to the Earl of Middlesex's sons,[3] are written, and one very similar to and possibly the same as the primarily secretary hand of the manuscript of 'The Wits'. The poems are generally well if sparingly punctuated and textually reliable, having authoritative readings in several places where *Fragmenta Aurea* has not, but containing obvious sophistications in others (see critical apparatus and Commentary). There are fewer authorial spellings and homogeneated rhyme-words than in the manuscripts of the juvenile poems, and one or two corrections are certainly not authoritative. Nevertheless, this manuscript's certain family association and textual reliability give it high authority, and its variant readings must be given very serious consideration.

One other manuscript is important because of its family associations. This is a seventeenth-century copy of *An Account of Religion by Reason* (*S*) now in the possession of Mr. William Suckling, of Roos

---

[1] The text of 'The Wits' is further discussed in the Commentary.
[2] MS. U. 269. F. 36, No. 42; catalogued in *HMC 4th Report*, p. 306, and described by Beaurline in 'Canon', pp. 515–16.
[3] Prestwich, *Cranfield*, p. 540; Langley also acted as a bailiff.

Hall, Beccles, Suffolk. It probably belonged originally to Suckling's
uncle, Charles Suckling of Woodton, to whose second son he may
have addressed advice to marry (Letter No. 53) and from whom the
present owner is descended. It occupies nine folio pages, the first two
written in a neat, non-professional, primarily italic hand, the remaining seven, apparently in haste by the same person, in secretary hand.
The last seven pages, especially, contain a great number of manifest
errors. This text, another text of the work in Bodleian MS. Arch.
Seld. B. 8, and the *Fragmenta* text present a typical example of the
genetic 'ambiguity of three texts' so named by Greg; but, to the
extent that judgement may be allowed to intrude upon a logically
insoluble ambiguity, it would appear that the three texts are genuinely substantive and collateral. There are errors and omissions in
the *Fragmenta* text that must be supplied from the others, but there
are no strong extrinsic or intrinsic reasons for abandoning it as copy-
text.

The Cranfield Papers are the only source of major importance, as
source, for an edition of Suckling's works, but any source of new
canonical works, especially in the author's holograph, or of substantive texts of known works is of the highest value. Two holograph
letters besides those in the Cranfield Papers come from, respectively,
the Hyde Collection (No. 46)[1] and the collection of manuscripts of
the Duke of Portland (No. 47),[2] and there are manuscript copies of
three lost originals in the Ashmolean Collection in the Bodleian
Library (No. 9),[3] the Public Record Office (No. 19),[4] and the Henry
E. Huntington Library (No. 21).[5]

Besides the holograph letters and the Cranfield juvenile poems,
only one poem not printed in *Fragmenta Aurea* and *The Last Remains*

---

[1] Modernized text printed in the catalogue of *The R. B. Adam Library Relating to Dr.
Samuel Johnson and his Era*, 1929, iii. 232; transcription in Berry, p. 109.

[2] The manuscript volume containing it is 'Vere Papers 1614–1626, Cavendish Papers
1602–1659' (f. 161ʳ⁺ᵛ), which is on loan to the British Museum as MS. 29/235. 619. E.
The letter was catalogued and partly transcribed in *HMC Portland Report*, ii. 133, and
reprinted from there in [T. Longueville], *The First Duke and Duchess of Newcastle-upon-
Tyne*, New York, 1910, p. 47; full transcription in Berry, p. 113. A facsimile of the reverse
side of this letter is given in Berry, p. 114.

[3] Ashmole MS. 826, ff. 101–2. As Berry notes (p. 51), this letter was first noticed by
Oldys and first printed (in a bowdlerized version) in the *Gentleman's Magazine*, 1796, lxvi.
16–17; Hazlitt first printed it in full in modern spelling, and Berry gives a diplomatic transcription (pp. 52–4).

[4] S.P. 16/216, No. 6, catalogued and summarized in *CSPD 1631–3*, p. 322; modernized
texts printed from separate transcriptions by both Hazlitt and Thompson, and a diplomatic
transcription including the cipher and interlinear deciphering by Berry, pp. 87–93.

[5] MS. Letter HA 12760, catalogued and printed in modern spelling in *HMC Hastings
Report II*, i. 76; diplomatic transcription in Berry, p. 96.

CORRIGENDA

Page cv, l. 5, *omit* printed

Page cxvii, l. 12, *for* xcix–xci *read* xcix–ci

Page 49 (Text), l. 23, *for* Sophonisha *read* Sophonisba

Page 64 (Apparatus), l. 8, *for* LS: *read* not LS:

Page 224, l. 2, *for* c–cli *read* xcix–c

Page 225, l. 9, *for* i. 71 *read* i. 171

Page 238, l. 8, *for* ii.   ). *read* ii. 251).

Page 262, *last line should read*: Goblins, IV. iii. 26–8; and *Brennovalt,*
       III. i. 27–30 and III. iii. 1–11; there are

Page 263, l. 23, *for* 'Epithalamion *read* 'Ecclogne

Page 267, l. 23, *for* viii *read* vii

Page 296, l. 14, *for* 1665 *read* 1663

has a strong enough claim to be admitted to the canon, and that is 'On King Richard the third, who lies buried under Leicester bridge', first discovered in British Museum MSS. Harleian 6917, f. 50ᵛ (anonymous, but it immediately follows a lampoon on Suckling's *Aglaura*, 'Upon Aglaura printed in Folio I'), and Additional 11,811, ff. 2ᵛ–3 (subscribed 'Sʳ John Suckling'), and printed by R. G. Howarth.[1] This poem is in the genre of imprecation, as are the poems with which it is grouped in the present edition, 'Upon L. M. weeping' (with which it shares a strong similarity of cadence, tone, and expression) and 'Detraction execrated'. Suckling refers to Richard III as 'the worst of our Kings' in *To Mr. Henry German* (see ll. 46–9); and the rather odd periphrases, 'streaming vapours' and 'scaly frye' (ll. 2, 7), have a formal parallel in 'watry store' ('To my Lady E. C. at her going out of England', l. 22) and 'soft feathered Queristers' (*Goblins*, III. vii. 101, collocated with Suckling's only other use of 'canop[y]', l. 101, and with 'Silver purling streams', l. 109), which is echoed in the 'featherd Travellers' or 'Choristers' of the two substantive texts of 'To a Lady that forbidd to love before Company' (l. 12). Unlike the purely conjectural attributions (see 'Dubious Works' below), which are based on a narrow conception of Suckling's work as almost exclusively 'natural, easy', and amatory, this one is likely to have authority. The subscription is firmly supported by internal evidence, and I have accordingly included it in the canon without reservations.

iv. DUBIOUS WORKS NOT IN THE SUBSTANTIVE EDITIONS

In addition to the pamphlet discussed above (pp. xcv–xcvi), six spurious and seven doubtful works not included in *Fragmenta Aurea*, 1646, or *The Last Remains*, 1659, have been attributed to Suckling, printed in collections of his works, or considered for admission to the canon.[2]

---

[1] Ed. *Minor Poets of the Seventeenth Century*, 2nd ed., 1953, p. 244 (modernized text); the poem is presented, without discussion, as Suckling's. Beaurline briefly discusses this poem in 'Canon', pp. 510–11, where he notes that the attribution is 'by the same hand as the body of the poem' but expresses some doubts about Suckling's authorship; Berry, who prints the Harleian text collated with the Additional MS., remarks that 'it must be admitted to the canon with reservations' (pp. 25–6).

[2] Hazlitt, Thompson, and Howarth included several poems from this group in their editions, and Berry discusses and reprints one of them (as only very tentatively Suckling's) in his *Poems and Letters from Manuscript*. Beaurline discusses seven of the poems at some length, and, though I have added a few details, I have condensed my own remarks accordingly, referring the reader to 'Canon' for further discussion.

Attributions that are not based on coincidental association or faulty recollection, or both, seem to be founded in a very limited conception of Suckling's literary mode. The six works discussed immediately below (Nos. 1–6) are certainly spurious.

1. *A Sermon on Malt* (prose)

This work was printed from manuscript as Suckling's, without authority for the ascription, by R. P. T. Coffin and A. M. Witherspoon, in *A Book of Seventeenth-Century Prose*, New York, 1929, and again in revised and expanded versions of that anthology in 1946 and 1957.[1] George Williamson pointed out that several seventeenth-century printed texts of the work are textually superior but made no further suggestions about its authorship, though he implicitly questioned Suckling's.[2] The grounds for the ascription are clearly that in the source, Bodleian MS. Ashmole 826, f. 102ᵛ, the 'Sermon' (there anonymous) falls immediately between Suckling's letter to 'Will' (No. 9), signed 'I. Suckling', ff. 101–2, and 'An Answer to a Gentleman in Norfolk' (No. 39), signed 'I. S. or A. C.', f. 103ʳ⁺ᵛ. In the *Catalogue of Ashmole Manuscripts*, 1845, col. 476, however, the author is given as 'Mr. Dod', i.e. John Dod (1549?–1645), to whom the work is usually assigned (see *DNB*); and *A Sermon upon the word Malt . . . by the Rev. J. D. author of the Remarkable and Approved Sayings*, 1777, was followed by a number of other editions in the eighteenth and nineteenth centuries. Outside this anthology, the 'Sermon' has never been printed as Suckling's.

2. [*Winifreda*] ('Away, let nought to love displeasing')

In reply to a question about the authorship of this poem, which was first printed in *Miscellaneous Poems by Several Hands*, 1726, Richard Lord Braybrooke wrote in January 1851 that it was 'usually entitled "Winifreda", [and] has been attributed to Sir John Suckling, but with what justice I am unable to say'.[3] In further correspondence, other possible authors were suggested and later printed occurrences noted,[4] but Suckling was not mentioned again and the poem's authorship was not finally settled. The poem, probably of eighteenth-century authorship, is certainly not by Suckling and has never been printed as his.

---

[1] *Seventeenth-Century Prose and Poetry*, ed. Alexander M. Witherspoon and Frank J. Warnke, 2nd ed., 1957 (reprinted 1963), pp. 436–7.
[2] *MLN*, 1935, l. 463–4.   [3] *N&Q*, 1st ser., iii. 27 (cf. ii. 519).
[4] Ibid. iii, 108–9, 155; iv. 196, 238; v. 38.

3. *On a Fart in the Parliament House* ('Down came grave, ancient Sir John [Serjeant] Crook')

This work is ascribed to Suckling in the 1699 and 1707 editions of *Wit and Mirth: Or, Pills to Purge Melancholy*, from which the ascription in the *Catalogue of* [Sloane] *Manuscripts in the British Museum* probably derives (1782, ii. 827). In its numerous manuscript occurrences (at least twenty-two in the Bodleian Library and the British Museum alone), it is frequently dated 1607 and ascribed to John Hoskins. Aubrey gives Hoskins as the author, apparently on good authority, for he implies in the same paragraph that he had communicated with Hoskins's son about a collection of his father's poems (i. 418). As Mr. Beaurline suggests ('Canon', p. 509), the poem was perhaps already notorious by 1610, for Jonson seems to refer to it in *The Alchemist* (II. ii. 63–4), which was printed in that year, the year after Suckling was born.

4. *Cantilena Politica-Jocunda Facta post Principis Discessum in Hispaniam, 1623*; or *De Gallico Itinere* ('I come from England into France'[1])

This poem was first printed as Suckling's by Hazlitt in 1874 from British Museum MS. Harleian 367, on the authority of the manuscript's probably conjectural ascription to Suckling in the handwriting of Sir Henry Ellis. It was printed several times in the seventeenth century and occurs in numerous manuscript miscellanies, where it is attributed to both Richard Corbet and Thomas Goodwin, but nowhere to Suckling, although it is sometimes coincidentally associated with him, as in a title-suggestion that it be sung 'to the Tune of Sir John Sucklings Ballad'.[2] It was printed in Corbet's *Certain Elegant Poems*, 1647, and *Poems*, 1672 (though not in *Poetica Stromata*, 1648, edited by the younger John Donne), but George Thorn-Drury suggested, with great probability, that the reason for its ascription to Corbet was the similarity of its frequent title, 'De Gallico Itinere', to the title of Corbet's poem, 'Iter Boreale';[3] it has been dismissed

---

[1] And for 'come', in variant texts, 'came', 'go', 'rode', 'went', and the like.

[2] 'Three Merry Boyes of Kent' in *Folly in Print*, 1667, as Beaurline points out ('Canon', p. 508), also suggesting the probability that Ellis faultily recalled a coincidental association of this poem with Suckling in the 1699 and 1707 editions of *Wit and Mirth: Or, Pills to Purge Melancholy*, where it is headed 'John Dory, made upon his expedition into France' and followed by 'A Second part of John Dory, to the same Tune. Upon Sir John S—— Expedition into Scotland, 1639' ('Sir John got him on an Ambling Nag').

[3] Ed. *Parnassus Biceps*, 1927, p. 171, n. on p. 24.

as spurious by Corbet's most recent editors.[1] Aubrey was convinced
of Goodwin's authorship: 'The *Journey into France*, crept in Bishop
Corbet's poems, was made by him. . . . The *Journey into France* was
made by Mr. Thomas Goodwyn, of Ludlowe, . . .; [*sic*] certaine' (i.
270). The early date, manuscript attributions, and internal evidence
of its satirical attack on Roman Catholicism all support the authorship
of Thomas Goodwin, an Independent divine.

5. *Sir John Sucklings Answer* ('I tell thee foole, who e're thou be')

This lampoon, written in 1639, was first included among Suckling's works in 1874, by Hazlitt, who printed it from Bodleian MS.
Ashmole 36–7, f. 54, unfortunately omitting the provocation, 'Upon
Sir John Sucklings hundred horse', without which the 'Answer' makes
appreciably less sense. R. G. Howarth first printed the two together,
commenting that the author of the first is unknown and referring
to the second as 'Suckling's "*Answer*" '. The two poems occur in
numerous manuscript miscellanies and at least two seventeenth-
century printed books; they are almost invariably found together
and were very likely written at the same time.[2] Both poems effectively
ridicule Suckling, with whose life and works the author(s) must have
been very familiar, for, besides containing allusions to specific events
and at least one individual work, the lampoons are in the stanza-form
of Suckling's 'Ballade. Upon a Wedding'.[3] The poems have been
doubtfully ascribed to Sir John Mennes, probably on the grounds of
his association with the two printed books in which they appear.
It is possible (though doubtful, I think) that the two poems were
written by different persons, but Suckling can hardly have written
the 'Answer', which damns not only the Scots but the English
Royalists and the speaker himself.[4] The 'Answer' is not a repudiation
but an ironical confirmation of the charges of 'Upon Sir John Sucklings
hundred horse', and both are accordingly included with the lampoons
on Suckling in this edition.

[1] *Poems of Richard Corbet*, ed. J. A. W. Bennett and H. R. Trevor-Roper, 1955, p. 168.
[2] The 'Answer' is wanting in only two of sixteen texts known to me, and one has the first
line of the 'Answer'. The two printed books are *Wit and Drollery*, 1656 (p. 44), and *Le
Prince d'Amour*, 1660 (p. 148).
[3] For the apparent allusion to a work by Suckling, cf. ll. 31–6 with Letters Nos. 37,
ll. 33–9, and 38, ll. 17–21. The observation about the stanza-form was made independently
by Beaurline, Berry, and the present editor.
[4] As Beaurline points out ('Canon', pp. 510–11), J. W. Ebsworth was the first to comment
that 'it certainly is not Suckling's', adding that it 'has a smack of Cleveland about it' (ed. *Choice
Drollery 1656*, 1876, p. 393).

6. *A Relation of a Quaker, that to the Shame of his Profession, Attempted to . Bugger a Mare near Colchester* ('All in the Land of Essex')

This poem has not previously been considered for admission to the canon, and it is certainly not by Suckling, despite the conjectural modern ascription, 'by Suckling or Denham', noted in pencil on the broadside in the Thomason Collection.[1] Two stanzas will suffice to represent the character of all seventeen:

> All in the Land of *Essex*
> Near *Colchester* the zealous,
>   On the side of a bank,
>   Was play'd such a prank,
> As would make a Stone-horse jealous.
>
> Help *Woodcock*, *Fox*, and *Nailor*.
> For Brother *Green's* a Stalion[.]
>   Now Alas what hope,
>   Of converting the Pope,
> When a Quaker turns Italian.

The *Thomason Catalogue* suggests only that the work is 'By Sir John Denham?' (ii. 234). The pencilled suggestion of Suckling's authorship is quite possibly based on the superficial resemblance to 'Sir John Suckling's Answer', but quite aside from the fact that this piece bears no resemblance to Suckling's canonical works, it cannot have been written much less than a decade after he died. Among the persons referred to in the poem, George Fox (1624–91) founded the Society of Friends in 1648–50, and James Nayler (1617?–60) became a Quaker in 1651; the term 'Quaker' itself did not come into currency until 1650 (*DNB*, s.v. 'Fox, George') or 1653 (*OED*).

Seven less certainly spurious but still doubtful works have been or are here for the first time considered for admission to the canon. The first four (Nos. 7–10) have been discussed in detail by Mr. Beaurline, and the first also by Mr. Berry.

7. *To Celia. An Ode. By Sir John Suckling* ('Youth and Beauty now are thine')

Norman Ault discovered this poem in *The Grove: Or, a Collection of*

---

[1] Professor Ernest Sirluck, of the University of Toronto, with whose permission I include this work here, called to Beaurline's attention the ascription to Suckling pencilled on the manuscript, Thomason 669. f. 21 (35), dated 20 May (1659) by Thomason.

Original Poems, Translations, &c., 1721 (p. 269; reissued in 1732 with Theobald's name as editor, as Mr. Beaurline notes), and printed it in his *Treasury of Unfamiliar Lyrics*, 1938 (p. 179); it was subsequently included among Suckling's poems by Howarth. Mr. Beaurline has made the interesting suggestion that the poem may be 'the lost song that Orsames sang' in *Aglaura*, but both he and Mr. Berry are also doubtful of Suckling's authorship.[1] The poem has little stylistically in common with Suckling's certainly canonical works (it would appear to be of Restoration or eighteenth-century composition), and *The Grove* itself lacks the over-all authority that might otherwise inspire confidence in the attribution.[2] There remains a remote possibility that the poem is Suckling's, but there is no evidence to justify its inclusion in the canon.

8. *In Brennoralt* ('Thy love is chaste, they tell thee so')

Mr. Beaurline discovered this poem in British Museum MS. Harleian 3991, f. 83. Though the heading was added by the scribe, the manuscript text was evidently copied from *The New Academy of Complements*, 1669 (p. 150), the textual source of much of the Harleian manuscript.[3] Except for a loose parallel chiefly of situation in *The Sad One* (IV. iv. 45–71), there is no real evidence that this poem is by Suckling, and Mr. Beaurline, remarking that 'there is no evidence of a lost song in the printed text' of *Brennoralt*, is very likely right in suggesting that it was probably written for a Restoration revival of the play (see 'Canon', p. 517). There is no evidence to prove that the poem could not be by Suckling, but very little that it is.

9. *Inconstancie in Woman* ('I am confirm'd a woman can')

This poem, headed 'Sir John Suckling's Verses', was first printed as Suckling's in *Notes and Queries* (1st ser., 1849–50, i. 72) by 'A[lexander] D[yce?]', from 'a small quarto MS. Collection of English Poetry, in the hand-writing of the time of Charles I', which is now

---

[1] See 'Canon', p. 511, and Berry, p. 11.

[2] Certainly 'Shun the Folly of Disdain, | Pride affords a short-liv'd Reign, | Full of Pain' is very far from such thematically related lines as 'I hate a fool that starves her Love | Onely to feed her pride', in 'Loves Siege' (ll. 39–40). As Beaurline shows, some of Theobald's attributions are erroneous and his claim to have printed all the works included for the first time is demonstrably false ('Canon', p. 511).

[3] I am indebted to Professor W. J. Cameron, of McMaster University, for pointing out to me the close connection between the manuscript and printed miscellany.

Folger MS. V. a. 162;[1] it was retained as Suckling's by Hazlitt, Thompson, and Howarth. The poem occurs anonymously in numerous seventeenth-century printed books and manuscripts, including the Henry Lawes autograph manuscript (*HL*), which suggests the possibility, at least, that it may be by Dr. Henry Hughes, who wrote thirty-five of the songs in that volume and to whom the 'Song', 'I prethee send me back my heart', is (elsewhere) ascribed.[2] Mr. Beaurline remarks on the 'authoritative air' of two lines that express sentiments paralleled in two canonical poems but adds, 'the difficulty is that the majority of Suckling's contemporaries had very similar ideas'.[3] The attribution is unique and unauthoritative, the internal evidence is slight and unconvincing, and this poem can be regarded as doubtful at best.

10. *To Mr. W. M. Against Absence* ('Pedlar in love, that with the common Art')

This poem was first printed, in a section of new poems, in *The Works of Sr William Davenant K^t*, 1673 (p. 294), 'Consisting of Those which were formerly Printed, and Those which he design'd for the Press: Now Published out of the Authors Originall Copies', the dedication of which is signed by 'Mary D'avenant'. Mr. Beaurline first considered it as possibly Suckling's and printed the manuscript text in *Cran2*, concluding that 'either Suckling wrote the two copies of verses as an exercise, or, more likely, Davenant wrote the first poem and Suckling replied with the second. What keeps one in doubt of Davenant's authorship is the total lack of other poems of the same type in Davenant's work'.[4]

The manuscript text occurs as the fourth in a group of five otherwise unquestionably authentic poems in a booklet found among the papers of Suckling's uncle, the Earl of Middlesex (see Introduction, p. ciii). The fifth poem, 'To Mr. Davenant for Absence' (*Fragmenta Aurea* title; untitled in manuscript), as an answer to this one, serves to date it as certainly written early enough—in the early

---

[1] As Beaurline and I discovered independently. The manuscript is actually headed, in a hand much later than but in imitation of that of the body of the text, 'Sr Iohn Suckling verses' (f. 23^v).

[2] See E. F. Hart, 'Caroline Lyrics and Contemporary Song-Books', *The Library*, 5th ser., 1935, viii. 91–2; the 'Song' is ascribed to Hughes in Henry Lawes, *Ayres and Dialogues . . . Third Book*, 1658, p. 6.

[3] 'Canon, p. 507; cf. Commentary, n. on ll. 19–20.

[4] 'Canon', p. 517; although I have given my own judgement and added a number of details here and in the Commentary, my discussion of this work is considerably indebted to Beaurline's.

1630s—to be included in Davenant's *Madagascar; with Other Poems*,
1638, and, though the shorter poems in that volume are commendatory or otherwise occasional, the contents are not so limited in
kind as absolutely to exclude this poem on principle. The external
evidence of authorship is equivocal: though the manuscript *group*
has high authority by external confirmation and family association,
there is no reason why a poem by another author could not be
included, especially when it is the antecedent to an answer poem;
on the other hand, Davenant's *Works* were published five years after
his death, and the identity of 'Mary D'Avenant', the publisher's
claims, and the authenticity of the 'new poems', in general, are
questionable.

The internal evidence strongly favours Suckling's authorship: virtually all the variant readings of the manuscript text are superior
(see note on Text); Suckling shows a fondness for a pedlar as fictional
speaker elsewhere ('Upon Newyeares day' and 'A Pedler of Small-
wares'); there is direct address and a comparatively pronounced
quasi-dramatic situation (cf. the 'Songs', 'Why so pale and wan fond
Lover' and 'No, no, faire Heretique'); there are several striking
parallels of phrase, image, and idea in certainly authentic works (see
Commentary); and there is an epigrammatic turn on a proverb at
the end. There is little positive internal evidence to support the
authorship of Davenant, who, though he is capable of epigrammatic
closing couplets, does not share Suckling's fondness for proverbs, and
who almost always more closely resembles Waller than Suckling ever
does. That Suckling's answer to 'To Mr. W. M. Against Absence',
in heroic couplets, is directly addressed to Davenant (in the *Fragmenta* text) and is in octosyllabic couplets is largely indifferent, and
Suckling could certainly have written an answer to his own poem,
as reference to 'Against Absence' and the two poems 'Against
Fruition', and Letters Nos. 36–7, not to mention 'The constant Lover'
and 'The Answer', and Letters Nos. 51(*a*) and 51(*b*), will readily
suggest; indeed, both pro and con positions are represented by
canonical works in this manuscript group. The manuscript text of
'To Mr. W. M. Against Absence' could be Suckling's touched-up
version of a poem by Davenant, but in general the evidence for
Suckling's authorship is stronger than that for Davenant's, and the
evidence against it weaker than that against Davenant's. Two
awkward facts, however, prevent confident assignment of this poem
to Suckling: the printing of the poem as Davenant's, and a title in

the printed text that is at odds with Suckling's address of his answer to 'Mr. Davenant'.[1]

11. *A New-years Gift* ('The Phenix dyes, yet still remaine')

This and the following poem are found anonymously on individual loose leaves among the Cranfield Papers.[2] Both are written in shaded, comparatively non-cursive italic hands, almost certainly those of a young person but probably not the same hand. This poem is datable in 1626/7, from the reference in line 5 to the 5,630 'yeare | Time hath turn'd round this wheely spheare' (calculating from the date of the Creation, according to Bishop Ussher, 4004 B.C.), about the time when Suckling wrote the juvenile religious poems and 'A Barley-break'. It is a 'gift' to the writer's mother—if Suckling's, his step-mother (see p. xxix above). Most of the first twenty lines are in octosyllabic couplets (ll. 1–4 a rhyming quatrain) but with the number of syllables in individual lines varying from 8 to 11 (in metrical poems—as distinct from 'The Wits', which is in four-stress verse—Suckling frequently employs catalexis or initial truncation but he rarely omits, or adds, more than a single syllable); the last four lines are a separate iambic-pentameter quatrain sharing the same rhyme as the first four lines. The poem makes extensive use of classical deities, which is not characteristic of Suckling, and lacks the skill even of his juvenile religious poems. On the other hand, the sentiments are consonant with those of the religious poems (though not very individual) and the concluding four lines bear a fairly strong similarity in metre, cadence, and phrase to the last four lines of 'Upon Richard the third'. And the 'here in heaven on earth' in the last line but one has something in common with 'Milcot walks' as 'the blessed shades' (Letter No. 4, ll. 2–3). But there are insufficient grounds for admitting this poem to the canon, and it remains certainly a juvenile and doubtful poem at best.

12. *Gnomics* ('Revenge is swate, and reck'ned as cleare gaine')

This manuscript poem occurs, on a single leaf, in the same collection as 'A New-years Gift', and the handwriting, especially in

---

[1] It seems to me possible—but utterly conjectural—that Suckling wrote both poems, originally with general descriptive titles or none, and sent copies to Davenant (of an early draft; see note on *Text* in Commentary) and probably Walter Montagu ('Mr. W. M.'), the addressees perhaps to be accounted for by their participation with Suckling in a running poetical 'debate' or a sociable 'academic' argument in person ('To Mr. W. M.' sounds as if it could itself be an 'answer'). And if both poems, with titles, were found among the papers used as printer's copy for Davenant's *Works*, it is obvious why the title 'To Mr. Davenant for Absence' would have been omitted. [2] MS. U. 269. F. 36, not individually numbered.

description, is very similar. The poem itself—ten lines of primarily iambic decasyllabic lines, with feminine endings in ll. 8 and 10, rhyming *ababccdede*—is a series of pious and ethical sentiments expressed in personified abstractions. 'Esteeme of pieti's growne out of season' (l. 10) is faintly reminiscent of ll. 17–24 of 'Upon Christmas', but the parallel is not striking and the idea, especially as expressed in 'Gnomics', is commonplace. This, too, is certainly a juvenile poem and, on the available evidence, doubtfully of Suckling's authorship.

13. *A doubtful letter* (perhaps to Mary Bulkeley from Suckling or Sir John Mennes)

This letter, subscribed with either the initials 'JS' or a terminal flourish that looks very much like them, is found in Folger MS. V.a.275, f. 125, just above the transcription of a brief letter to 'Faire Mrs Anne & Mrs Mary' (Bulkeley, presumably; see p. xlii above) from 'Jo Mince', that is, Sir John Mennes. The external evidence for its association with Suckling is both scant and circumstantial, the connection with the Bulkeley sisters (itself inferential) being the major grounds. The two letters are in secretary and italic hand, respectively, each apparently written by a different person. The solemnness, uninventive expansiveness, extravagant diplomacy, and gratuitous circumlocution of this letter make it quite unlike Suckling's other letters to ladies, but it was obviously written as a kind of initial declaration of affection exceeding friendship, and none of the canonical letters is comparable with it. There are, however, a few (commonplace and not very striking) parallels—in 'smoothered long in silence', 'Loves firebrand' (not verbatim but by periphrasis in canonical works), 'my proffered service', and the like (see Commentary)—that make it worth printing as possibly though not very probably by Suckling. If it is by Suckling and to Mary Bulkeley, it was probably written between 1636 and 1638.

III. THE TEXT OF THE PRESENT EDITION
i. COPY-TEXT AND EDITORIAL TREATMENT

The canon of Suckling's non-dramatic works in this edition consists of seventy-eight poems, fifty-five letters (including 51(*a*) and 51(*b*) as two), *To Mr. Henry German, in the Beginning of Parliament, 1640*, and *An Account of Religion by Reason. Fragmenta Aurea* (1646), *The Last Remains of Sir John Suckling* (1659), and manuscripts provide unique substantive texts, and therefore the copy-texts, of fifty-four of the poems and all but three of the letters they contain. The texts of five of the poems from *Fragmenta Aurea* are reprints (Nos. 65–6, 72–4), and 'A Song to a Lute' (No. 31), in *The Last Remains*, was almost certainly printed from a separate transcription of the text in the play, *The Sad One*, which formed part of the same collection. For these six derivative poems I have, of course, rejected the collections as copy-text in favour of their sources (see critical apparatus and Commentary).

No manuscript collections of Suckling's poems are extant, and no single source contains more than a few poems, but there are variant substantive texts of twenty-one—nearly a third—of the canonical poems, three of the letters, *To Mr. Henry German*, and *An Account of Religion*. Despite a wide disparity in provenance and external or intrinsic authority, these variant texts provide invaluable evidence for establishing critical texts nearer Suckling's originals than those of the early editions or the more recent editions of Hazlitt and Thompson almost exclusively based upon them. They also provide an array of hypothetical copy-texts.

Since all critical editions aim at a text as authoritative and as near the author's original as possible, one may be inclined to choose as copy-text the one 'nearest the archetype' or the one most resembling the author's in orthography—that is, spelling, for the most part. This seems to me theoretically sound, but it has seemed to me unwise, in practice, to substitute individual manuscript copy-texts, of widely differing provenance and character, for those of the substantive editions in quest of 'something of the character of the original' when that consists chiefly in archaic spelling or inadequate or misleading punctuation (to which Suckling was prone in the holograph letters). On the other hand, characteristics more significantly authorial than these, such as Suckling's demonstrably favoured dashes and parentheses, and the inferentially original graphic pattern of 'The Wits' most fully realized in manuscript texts, demand special consideration; and in some cases a high degree and comprehensiveness of authority may recommend adoption. Practically speaking, there are generally fewer dashes and parentheses in manuscript than in printed texts, and there have seemed to me sufficiently cogent reasons to reject the substantive editions as copy-text—except as noted above—only for 'To a Lady that forbidd to love before Company' (Poem No. 46) and *To Mr. Henry German*. The manuscript texts of these are intrinsically more authoritative than the printed texts in both substantives and accidentals, and the manuscript of *To Mr. Henry German* also has the external authority of family association (see Introduction above, p. ci, and Commentary); moreover, both are quasi-archetypal. In the text of 'The Wits' I have, of course, incorporated the inferentially original graphic pattern (see Commentary).

Except in isolated instances, the substantive editions alone provide accidentals that, though not flawless, are generally consistent with sound seventeenth-century usage and fit for the demands of a critical edition, as certainly more nearly representing the fulfilment of the author's intention than those of most manuscript texts. And the substantive editions are not far, in this respect, from the Royal manuscript and the 1638 printed folio of *Aglaura*; both of these were probably produced for Suckling and are less 'modern' and contain more of his spellings, but they by no means follow his practice closely as it is shown in the holograph letters.[1] The punctuation and spelling of the copy-texts have been emended sparingly, for the most part, and all departures are recorded in Appendix B, 'Alterations of Copy-Text Accidentals'. Most of the emendations are consistent with the system in the individual work, but they have been made on my own judgement, so I have normally recorded them without citing an authority. Where the pointing is seriously in question I have discussed it in a note, citing earlier editions and editors where appropriate.

A certain number of silent alterations have also been made in the text, in eliminating the long 'ſ', the ligature 'œ', and the vagaries of both minuscule, or lower-case, and majuscule, or capital, forms of 'I/J' and 'U/V', and in expanding contractions.[2] I have retained the fount-distinctions of printed copy-texts and supplied them, in accordance with contemporary printer's practice, for proper names and the like in works here printed from manuscript; but I have uniformly given such opening and closing addresses as 'Madam' and 'Your humble servant' in the main fount, for which I have always used roman type regardless of the fount of the original.[3] I give titles in bold face roman type with terminal periods silently eliminated. I

---

[1] And, as Beaurline notes, some of the correspondences in the Royal manuscript are apparently due to the coincidence of Suckling's habits with the scribe's (see ii. 258). In the notes on *Text* in the Commentary for individual poems, I have often commented on the relative copy-text claims of the witnesses and the reasons for my choice.

[2] The only ambiguous contractions in the holograph letters are those for 'honorable', and Suckling consistently spells 'honor' without 'u'. Since faithful transcriptions of all the extant holograph letters have been recently printed, there is little point in repeating their scribal peculiarities here. All but one of the letters are in Berry; No. 1 is in *TLS*, 29 January 1960, p. 68.

[3] Exceptions are the Greek original and the italicized Latin text of 'Foreknowledge' (Poem No. 84).

have also silently modified three rather more important characteristics of some of the copy-texts: I have eliminated the subscription 'J. S.' from the texts of the poems from *The Last Remains*, where all but three have them;[1] I have supplied stanza-numbers in the minority of poems that do not have them in the substantive editions;[2] and I have dropped 'This' from the addresses of the six holograph letters in which it occurs (Nos. 1, 10, 11, 14, 16, and 17).

All the poems in *The Last Remains* have titles or headings, some of them obviously supplied by an editor (e.g. No. 56, 'English'd thus by the Author'), as do ten of eleven juvenile poems found in manuscript fair-copies closely associated with the author (see Introduction above, pp. xcix–xci); seven of the poems in *Fragmenta Aurea* are without titles. Many of the titles in both books are such helpful commonplaces as 'His Dream' and 'Against Fruition', and some are authorial and others are doubtless editorial, since treatments of conventional themes are bound later to attract as well as originally to be given conventional titles. Titles serve the very useful purposes of facilitating reference and indicating poetical subject and treatment, and I have been prompted to adopt or supply them where they are wanting in the copy-text and to modify a few others. These titles have been supplied by analogy with those of the manuscripts and substantive editions, and I have in all cases noted the source of the title in the critical apparatus and commented on its adoption in the Commentary. In fact, all variant titles are recorded in the critical apparatus or, as noted there, in the Commentary.[3] Supplied titles, titles adopted in

---

[1] The three poems wanting initials are Nos. 58–9, which are headed 'Sir J. S.' and 'Sir Toby Matthews', respectively, and 'The careless Lover' (No. 60) immediately following them (see Introduction above, pp. xc–xcii).

[2] Stanza-numbers have been supplied to the following poems from *Fragmenta Aurea* (in their order in this edition): 'Loves World' (21), 'Against Fruition I' (40), 'Song' ('Why so pale and wan' (66), from *Aglaura*, 1638, where the stanzas are also without numbers), 'The Wits'(71), and 'A Ballade. Upon a Wedding' (76); and to the following from *The Last Remains*: 'Detraction execrated' (38), 'The Invocation' (47), 'The Expostulation I' and 'II' (48–9), 'Profer'd Love rejected' (57), 'The careless Lover' (60), and four dubious 'Songs' (81, 91–3). Periods have been silently dropped from the numbers of the printed texts.

[3] For the poems in *Fragmenta Aurea* I have adopted or supplied titles for 'A Barley-break' (15, title from manuscript), 'To his Rival I' (44), 'Loves Offence' (55), 'Womans Constancy' (63), 'Loves Clock' (64), 'Loves Siege' (67), and 'A Summons to Town' (70). I have also rejected the unhelpful 'Song' in favour of 'Loves Feast' (54), replaced 'A Sessions of the Poets' by the demonstrably original 'The Wits' (71), and made such necessary additional modifications as supplying distinctive roman numerals to the two poems 'Against Fruition' ('I' to 40, 'II' to 41). For the poems in *The Last Remains* I have expanded 'Song' to 'A Song to a Lute' (32), the probably authorial title in *The Sad One*, and substituted other titles as follows: 'The Expostulation II' for 'Song' (49), 'Love's Sanctuary' for 'Song' (53), and 'Disdain' for 'English'd thus by the Author' (56). I have also added 'The constant Lover' and 'The Answer' to the headings of the exchange between 'Sir J. S.' and 'Sir Toby Matthews' (58–9), and again I have made minor modifications in the supplying of roman numerals where

place of the traditional titles in the early editions, and modifications in traditional titles are given in square brackets in the Contents, the text, the head-titles in the Commentary, the critical apparatus, and the index, but not in general discussion in the Introduction and Commentary.

The substantives of the text are the heart and soul of a critical edition, and it is in the establishment of these, in a more authoritative form than any single copy-text could provide, that the variant texts have proved most useful. Greg remarks that 'in a critical edition the text rightly chosen as copy may not by any means be the one that supplies most substantive readings in cases of variation' ('The Rationale of Copy-Text', *SB*, 1950–1, iii. 26); and, when textual evidence and critical judgement show the higher authority of readings in variant texts or errata, or the need for editorial emendations, they have been adopted, and the reasons for emending, when these are not self-evident, are given in the Commentary.[1]

I have found infrequent occasion to emend readings in unique substantive texts, but in a few cases I have, I think, either restored original readings or more closely approximated the original form or design of the work, including the stanza-form or 'graphic structure'.[2] In the treatment of variant substantive texts, I have initially undertaken distributional and directional study, and genealogical analysis, or 'stemmatics', in order to apply what could be learned of the transmission of the text to the deliberation between individual variants,[3] and I have put hypotheses based on these kinds of study to practical use wherever possible; but I have also found myself very much in agreement with George Kane, that an editor 'can neither evade the responsibility for decisions about originality by referring them to a

necessary. Editorial alterations have also been made in the titles of seven dubious poems or poems wrongly printed as Suckling's (see text, critical apparatus, and Commentary for Nos. 83, 85–8, and 92–3). Finally, I have supplied 'Faith and Doubt' to the one untitled poem in the group of juvenile religious poems (10).

1 Only *The Last Remains* has an errata leaf. Its comparatively few 'corrections' were apparently made without reference to copy (see Introduction above, p. lxxxvii), but a few have been adopted as necessary emendations, and all are recorded in the critical apparatus and some discussed in the Commentary.

2 Editorial emendations have been made, for example, in the following poems for which there is a single substantive witness: 8, 9, 13, 14, 17, 20, 24, 28, 38, 44, 47, 48, 68, and 78.

3 In this kind of study I have taken guidance especially from W. W. Greg, *The Calculus of Variants: An Essay on Textual Criticism*, Oxford, 1927; Paul Maas, *Textual Criticism*, trans. Barbara Flower, Oxford, 1958; and Vinton Dearing, *A Manual of Textual Analysis*, Berkeley and Los Angeles, California, U.S.A., 1959. I have also been considerably influenced by George B. Kane's closely reasoned comments on the limitations of such analysis, in relation to certain kinds of texts, in the Introduction to his edition of *Piers Plowman: The A Version*, 1960.

genealogy, nor put his text beyond criticism by calling it "critical" '.[1]
The evidence and conclusions of textual study are summarized in a
note on *Text* normally placed immediately after the headnote (if any)
in the Commentary on individual works.

The critical apparatus records for each work the source, the sigla or
titles of substantive and other significant variant texts, all departures
from the substantives and 'semi-substantives' of the copy-text,
and all substantive variants of editorial importance and some of
special interest. For a few works substantive variants have been
recorded in full—as explicitly indicated in the apparatus—where they
are relatively few, where there are only two or three texts, or where
the state of the text demands; but in general the variants recorded
are (generously) representative. All variants are 'significant', but some
are more significant than others: a selection is justified by its ability
economically and more or less accurately to represent the textual
problems posed by variant witnesses, which are in fact the readings
cited themselves, in many cases. Such problems may be buried in a
full record of variants, which at the same time inevitably obscures
minutiæ of transmission that sometimes have a directional significance inversely proportional to their textual importance for a critical
reader. I have tried to strike a balance by providing an ample selection. Individual readings seriously in question are discussed either in
the general notes on *Text*, or in separate notes on individual lines, in
the Commentary.

The form of the critical apparatus is generally conventional, but it
might be noted that the symbol 'Σ' is used, by analogy with Greg's
use of it in *The Calculus of Variants*, to stand for 'the sum of unspecified
witnesses', always a majority, that share the reading cited. Variants
are recorded in order of their closeness to the reading of the present
text, with the sigla of witnesses given, after their reading, in alphabetical and numerical order. The accidentals of substantive variants
shared by Σ or by more than one specified witness are normalized,
as, of course, are readings introduced into the copy-text from other

---

[1] *Piers Plowman*, p. 114. And it may be added, as applicable here, *mutatis mutandis*, that
'each crux is unique, and often several considerations must be weighed in its solution. It will
then be evident that the authority of a text of this kind must vary from line to line; the assurance with which originality is determinable, and, indeed, has been determined by its editor,
must depend on the arguments available in any given case and his ability to perceive them. It
has seemed to me right in honesty to make this clear. If a "critical" text is one in which the
editor has compared the variant readings, then mine is critical, but it is not critical in any
Lachmannian sense of being invested with a mysterious authority that sets it beyond question
by its users' (p. 165).

witnesses; the variants of single witnesses, when recorded, are given as they stand in the source.

Full identification of the sigla used in the critical apparatus and textual notes is given in the list of Sigla and Textual Sources. This list, as its heading indicates, also serves as a list of sources, alphabetized by sigla and thus bringing together witnesses belonging to the same collection, such as the Rawlinson Poetical manuscripts in the Bodleian Library, but not all the manuscripts in individual repositories. The works that are found in each manuscript or printed book are indicated by serial numbers given in parentheses after the identification of the witness, with '*P*' standing for 'Poem', '*L*' for 'Letter', and '*App*' for 'Appendix'. The separate series of serial numbers supplied for the poems, letters, and Appendix A are given in numerical order along with the works to which they apply in the list of Contents. They are elsewhere used, besides in the list of Sigla and Textual Sources, in the text, critical apparatus, Commentary, and Appendix B.

Note on Press-Variants. Mr. Beaurline and I collated twenty-six copies of *Fragmenta Aurea*, 1646, and fifteen copies of *The Last Remains*, 1659 (a somewhat rarer book), on a Hinman Collator, and checked the variants found against a number of other copies. The few press-variants we found are of bibliographical interest, but only three are of very direct textual importance, all occurring in the inner forme of sheet B in *The Last Remains* (only one copy—Library Company of Philadelphia, shelf-mark 66908.o—has the uncorrected state): sig. B1ᵛ, 'To the Lady Desmond', l. 13, 'grace' and 'allow'd' (*c*) for 'Graces' and 'allowed' (*u*); and sig. B2, 'Upon Platonic Love', l. 12, 'quintessence' (*c*) for 'quintescence' (*u*) (the titles given here are those of this edition; in *The Last Remains* the first is titled 'Upon the Black Spots worn by my Lady D. E.' and the second is part of the 'Song' beginning 'If you refuse me once, and think again'). I have adopted the corrected readings here, because they are manifestly 'right', if only as necessary editorial emendations: 'quintescence' is as likely to be a compositor's slip as a copy-spelling; the metre demands 'grace', and 'allow'd' accords with 'crown'd' in l. 10 of the same poem. 'Graces' could have stood in the printer's copy, for it is shared by one of the substantive variant texts, but it is doubtful that it is strictly 'original' (see Poem No. 83, critical apparatus and Commentary).[1]

---

[1] The variants in the preliminaries of *Fragmenta Aurea*, including the Marshall engraving, the general title-page, and the publisher's preface, are discussed in 'Notes on Early Editions of *Fragmenta Aurea*' (*SB*, 1970, xxiii). The others are (numbers of uncorrected

ii. CHRONOLOGY, GENRE, AND THE ORDER OF THE WORKS

Suckling's non-dramatic works are grouped by type in the early editions, each type being set off by a divisional title-page in *Fragmenta Aurea*, 1646: *Poems, &c.*, pp. 1–49 (sigg. A1–D1); *Letters to divers Eminent Personages*, pp. 51–96 (sigg. D2–F8ᵛ), with the tract, 'To Mr. Henry German, in the beginning of Parliament, 1640', placed last; and *An Account of Religion by Reason*, pp. 97–119 (sigg. G1–H4). *The Last Remains of Sir John Suckling*, 1659, contains, without divisional title-page, poems, pp. 1–37 (sigg. A4–C6), and *Letters to Several Persons of Honor*, pp. 1–19 (sigg. C7–D8). The order of individual works within groups is not altogether random in either book, but it is neither conspicuously chronological nor otherwise based upon a consistent principle that recommends it as an order to be adopted in a critical edition. The 'integrity of sequence', therefore, is hardly worth preserving for the works in either book, and if it were preserved there would be no editorial alternative to presenting separate collections of poems and of letters from each copy-text, an unsatisfactory arrangement.

Fortunately, a number of the poems and letters are exactly, closely, or approximately datable, and the close resemblances in subject, genre, style, and historical reference between these and many of the undatable works provide practical principles for the more helpful, approximately chronological order I have adopted in this edition. The order of the works in the early editions is not without interest, however, and I shall briefly discuss that before taking up the order in the present edition.

copies in parentheses): Sig. A1(o), the special title-page of *Poems, &c.*, 'Sir' (*c*) for '*Sir*' (*u*) in 'Sir JOHN SUCKLING' (four copies). (2) Sig. B2(i), 'again.' (*c*) for 'again‚' (*u*) in 'To his much honoured, the Lord Lepington', l. 26 (one copy). (3) Sig. B1(o), 'nimbler' (*c*) for 'nimblea' (*u*) in 'A Barley-break', l. 6 (one copy); and, at a second stage of correction in the same forme, (4) sig. B4ᵛ(o), top rule alligned with left margin and spaced 9½ × 11 mm. between page-numerals and stanza-number '1' (*c*), for placement 2 mm. to right of left margin and 7½ × 13 mm. between page-numerals and '1' (*u*), which was not corrected with 'nimblea' (nine copies only have the final stage of correction). (5) Sig. G2(i), decorative initial 'I' rightside up (*c*) for inverted initial (*u*, two copies).

In *The Last Remains* the remaining press variants are: (1) Sig. A4ᵛ(o), catchword 'Truth' (*c*) for 'But' (*u*, four copies). (2) A considerable number of variants on sigg. B3(o) and B3ᵛ(i) in the text of the French poem, '*Desdain*', which are recorded in the critical apparatus (Appendix A.vi.1). (3 and 4) Sig. C4ᵛ(o), two stages of correction in 'The Expostulation I': in the first, l. 18, 'Though' (*c*, four copies) for 'Tough' (*u*); in the second, l. 17, 'my' (*c*, two copies) for 'ɯy' with turned 'm' (*u*; the majority of copies have the uncorrected state of both variants).

a. The Order of the Non-Dramatic Works in *Fragmenta Aurea* and *The Last Remains*

For general reference and to make the discussion below easier to follow, I tabulate here the poems and letters in the order in which they occur in the substantive editions by title or first words (for letters), page numbers, signatures, and formes, adding their serial number in the present edition. The evidence on which the summary remarks are made is set forth in detail in the Introduction above and in the Commentary.

Fragmenta Aurea: Poems

Order		Title or first words (*Letters*)	Pages	Sigg.	Formes
77	1	On New-years day 1640	3–4	A2^{r+v}	i/o
62	2	Loving and Beloved	5–6	A3^{r+v}	o/i
55	3	[Loves Offence]	6	A3^v	i
71	4	A Sessions of the Poets [The Wits]	7–11	A4–6	i/oo/ii
21	5	Loves World	11–13	A6–7	i/oo
66	6	Song (Why so pale)	14	A7^v	i
50	7	Sonnet I	14–15	A7^v–8	ii
51	8	Sonnet II	15–16	A8^{r+v}	i/o
52	9	Sonnet III	16–17	A8^v–B1	o–o
72	10	To his much honoured, the Lord Lepington	18–19	B1^v–2	ii
40	11	Against Fruition [I]	19–20	B2^{r+v}	i/o
63	12	[Womans Constancy]	20–1	B2^v–3	oo
65	13	Song (No, no, faire Heretique)	22	B3^v	i
73	14	To my Friend Will. Davenant	23	B4	i
74	15	On his other Poems	23	B4	i
15	16	[A Barley-break]	24	B4^v	o
54	17	Song [Loves Feast]	25	B5	o
32	18	Upon my Lady Carliles walking	26–7	B5^v–6	ii
42	19	To Mr. Davenant for Absence	27–8	B6^{r+v}	i/o
43	20	Against Absence	28–9	B6^v–7	oo
13	21	A Supplement of an imperfect Copy	29–30	B7^{r+v}	o/i
64	22	[Loves Clock]	30–1	B7^v–8	ii
67	23	[Loves Siege]	31–3	B8–C1	i/o–o
78	24	Upon my Lord Brohalls Wedding	33–4	C1^{r+v}	o/i
70	25	[A Summons to Town]	34–5	C1^v–2	ii
41	26	Against Fruition [II]	36	C2^v	o
76	27	A Ballade. Upon a Wedding	37–41	C3–5	o/ii/oo
44	28	[To his Rival I]	41–2	C5^{r+v}	o/i
61	29	Song (Honest Lover whosoever)	43–4	C6^{r+v}	i/o
69	30	Upon two Sisters	45	C7	o
45	31	To his Rival [II]	46–7	C7^v–8	ii
68	32	Farewel to Love	47–9	C8–D1	i/o–o

Fragmenta Aurea: Letters

2	1	Fortune and Love	53–4	D3^{r+v}	o/i
52	2	'A disswasion from Love'	54–7	D3^v–5	ii/oo
3	3	Though (Madam) I have ever	57–8	D5^{r+v}	o/i

Fragmenta Aurea: Letters. Of the prose works in *Fragmenta Aurea*, *An Account of Religion*, and 'To Mr. Henry German' are placed last because they are the most substantial. *An Account*, as by far the longest of the prose pieces and as a 'Discourse' so-called in its earlier-circulating form in manuscript copies is intrinsically distinct from

⋆ Dubious.　　　† Poems wrongly printed as Suckling's.

and more important than the others; it is therefore placed last of all, preceded by a special title-page suggested by its headings in manuscript (see critical apparatus). 'To Mr. Henry German' is an epistolary political tract of greater length and importance than the remaining pieces, is alone dated by year (1640), and concerns events antecedent to the civil war, all of which considerations may account for its being placed last in the group of letters.

The principle determining the order of the remaining twenty-nine letters is apparently the origin of the copy, in the main, though for some letters that cannot be determined. The first seven and the last six letters appear to have come from one or more members of the family of Suckling's uncle, Lionel Cranfield, first Earl of Middlesex: he is directly addressed in the last (No. 15), a kind of Character, and a lady at his estate at Milcote is addressed in the fourth (No. 4); The Earl of Dorset, Suckling's cousin-by-marriage to the Earl of Middlesex's daughter, Frances, is jocularly referred to in the second letter (No. 52, undatable). The fifth and sixth letters (Nos. 44 and 23) are written to Suckling's sister Martha, Lady Southcot, and her husband Sir George, respectively, and while she may have been the source of the copy for these it is just as likely that they came from one of the Cranfields, since the Earl of Middlesex was involved in their marital dispute and there is a manuscript of one of these letters (No. 23) among the collection of Cranfield Papers. The seventh letter in the first group (No. 13), and, in the last group, the first (No. 5), third (No. 7), fifth (No. 18), and sixth (No. 15), were written from Germany in 1631 and 1632 during Suckling's employment in the embassy to Gustavus Adolphus, as a number of the holograph letters to the Earl of Middlesex were (these, Nos. 12, 14, 16, and 17, were not included in the early editions). Close connections between these and the holograph letters to the Earl (see especially Letter No. 18, text and Commentary) suggest a more intimate relationship than simply that of their being sent from Germany by Suckling. Four of the last six letters were demonstrably written from Germany in 1631–2 (Nos. 5, 7, 15, and 18), and a fifth (No. 6) almost certainly was. This group, then, is closely related in time and place of writing, and apparently also in the persons addressed. The first group covers a wider period of time: three are certainly datable (No. 13, 1631; No. 23, 1635; No. 44, 1639), the other four are not; but Letters Nos. 2, 3, and 4, in the first group, and Nos. 5, 6, and 8 in the last, were addressed to a lady; their similarities, in relation to a holograph letter to

Mary Cranfield (No. 1), suggest that they too were written to her (see Introduction above, pp. xxxi–xxxii).

The reason for the separation of these two groups in *Fragmenta Aurea* is not clear, but it may well be that the first was available to the printer before the second. It seems likely that the first two letters, like the last 'letter' ('To Mr. Henry German'), were deliberately so placed for special reasons: the first letter dramatically and characteristically begins, 'Fortune and Love have ever been so incompatible, that it is no wonder (Madam)', etc., and the second is the witty and ironical 'A disswasion from Love'.

A second group of related letters are those to Suckling's 'Aglaura' and 'dear Princess', Nos. 24–34. These apparently occur in chronological order, except that the one inferentially earliest, No. 24 ('For the two Excellent Sisters'), is given last, and between the second and third occurs the rhetorical exchange of correspondence on marrying a widow (No. 51). There is no apparent reason for this odd interruption, which could be due either to following the order of a group of letters from the same source or to the printer's receipt of the letters to Aglaura in two parts. The latter seems a more likely explanation, which may also account for the presence of three more somewhat miscellaneous letters between the second group to Aglaura and the last group of the *Letters*, one of the two associated with the Cranfields. This miscellaneous group, the twenty-first through twenty-third in *Fragmenta Aurea*, consists of a letter inferentially written to Anne Willoughby in 1633 (No. 20, q.v. in Commentary, and see Introduction, p. xxxv), preceded and followed by two undatable letters of unknown addressee, one probably a literary exercise (No. 53).

It is clear from this brief survey that the order of the letters in *Fragmenta Aurea*, though it can be in general accounted for, affords no sufficient organizing principle for a critical edition. The first group of letters in *Fragmenta Aurea* consists of seven probably provided by the family of Lionel Cranfield: the first, third, and fourth letters were probably written to Mary Cranfield *c.* 1629–32; the second letter is an undatable literary exercise (No. 52); the fifth and sixth letters (1639, 1635) concern the marital problems of Suckling's sister; the seventh letter was written in 1631, perhaps to Suckling's cousin-by-marriage, Henry Carey, Lord Lepington (see Commentary, Letter No. 13). The second group consists of thirteen letters, eleven associated with Suckling's Aglaura, perhaps provided in two parts; the letter with reply (No. 51) that stands between the second and third of these letters may or may not have come from the same source. This general group is followed by three miscellaneous letters of uncertain source (Nos. 20, 53, and 5), and the third and last major group consists of six letters probably provided by the Cranfield family (four probably to Mary Cranfield, one to her father the Earl of Middlesex, and one perhaps to a friend and fellow-courier of Suckling's in Germany).

The Last Remains: Letters. There are only twelve letters in *The Last Remains* of 1659, all of which may have been supplied to the printer by Suckling's sister, Lady Southcot (see Introduction above, p. lxxxviii). The first seven are apparently in chronological order and were written between Summer 1638 and December 1639, and all but the last concern the 'Scottish business' (Nos. 36–9, 41–2). The first three are epistolary political-tracts, the second three witty newsletters written from the North during the First Bishops' War in May and June 1639; their addressees ('Sir' and 'My Lord') are not identifiable. The seventh (No. 45), is a probably ironical consolatory letter to John Selden on the death of his employer and rival for the Countess's affections, the Earl of Kent. The next four letters (Nos. 48, 54, 35, and 50) are undatable letters that have the stamp of literary exercises, and the last is a letter apparently written to Martha Lady Carey in 1635. All these letters could well have come from the same source, and they *are* coherently ordered as far as they could be. The last letter (No. 22) could have been an undated draft-copy of a letter sent to Lady Carey (cf. the manuscript copy of No. 23). The four preceding it are too vague in reference to be certainly datable but are unified by their conspicuous rhetoric (the one 'To T. C.' may well have been 'sent'). The datable letters must have been either dated or otherwise kept or put in order by Lady Southcot, or whoever provided them, because it is unlikely that they could or would have been accurately ordered editorially by the publisher twenty years after the events. *The Last Remains*, in short, has its letters in nearly the best possible order.

Fragmenta Aurea: Poems. The first and last of the thirty-two poems in *Fragmenta Aurea* are plainly placed as they are for 'patriotic' and dramatic reasons: 'On New-years day 1640. To the King' is first and 'Farewel to Love' last. The inversion of the dramatic openings and closings in the poems and in the letters is not without interest: the poems begin with a loyal subject's address to the King in 1640, and the letters end with a royalist's address to Parliament in 1640; the non-dramatic works conclude with *An Account of Religion*, and there is even an appropriate transition between the last poem, 'A Farewel to Love', and the first letter, beginning 'Fortune and Love have ever been so incompatible'.

The rest of the *Poems, &c.*, however, are not so logically ordered. Some are probably grouped because they were grouped in the printer's copy, notably 'Sonnets I–III' (sigg. A7ᵛ–B1), 'To Mr. Davenant for Absence' and 'Against Absence' (sigg. B6–7), 'Upon my Lord Brohalls Wedding' and 'A Summons to Town' (sigg. C1–2), which may both concern Jack Bond; and perhaps 'Loves Clock' and 'Loves Siege' (sigg. B7–C1). And the first and third almost certainly constituted copy-groups. The 'Sonnets' alone have roman-numeral-headed titles of the type 'Sonnet I', 'Sonnet II', etc.; titles of this or any other kind were not commonly supplied in *Fragmenta Aurea*, in which seven poems, nearly one-quarter, had no titles (Nos. 15, 44, 55, 63, 64, 67, and 70), though they could easily have been supplied in several instances (e.g. No. 44, 'To his Rival I' in the present edition). Moreover, it seems more than coincidental that 'Jack Bond' is mentioned in 'A Summons to Town' and 'B' is one of the participants in the 'Dialogue' of 'Upon my Lord Brohalls Wedding' immediately preceding. 'Loves Clock' and 'Loves Siege', on the other hand, could have come together chiefly because they employ extended conceits in the same way.

But, except for these conjunctions, no over-all ordering principle is in evidence, and the poems seem to have been placed almost at haphazard, although 'Loving and Beloved' ('There never yet was honest man That ever drove the trade of Love') was almost certainly placed second deliberately, after the expression of duty to the King in 'Upon New-years day 1640'. Perhaps the most curious arrangement is that of the two 'Songs' from *Aglaura*, which, though apparently both set from *Aglaura*, 1638, do not occur together as one would expect; and, while the first, 'Why so pale and wan fond Lover?', is related in sense to 'Sonnet I', which follows it, 'No, no, faire Heretique' has little to do with 'Womans Constancy' (untitled) preceding, and nothing to do with the commendatory poem to Lord Lepington following. I cannot explain why the two songs from *Aglaura* are not together, but it may be significant that all five poems from printed copy are found on pages of the inner formes of their respective sheets: 'Why so pale' is on A7ᵛ, 'To his much honoured' on B1ᵛ–2, 'No, no, faire Heretique' on B3ᵛ, and 'To my Friend Will. Davenant' and 'On his other Poems' on B4. It appears that these poems are where they are because the text was composed by formes and the poems from printed copy were composed at about the same time and placed where they would best fit the space rather than the sense of surrounding poems. It is at any rate apparent that length of poem was a primary determinant of placing. 'On New-years day 1640', the first page of which has a large ornament at the top, takes exactly two pages; the second, 'Loving and Beloved', probably placed second deliberately as the tribute 'To the King' was first, awkwardly has the last two lines of its final stanza on a second page; below it, 'Loves Offence' neatly fills the page, with the assistance of generous whites and a bottom rule; 'The Wits' occupies the following four pages and part of a fifth, and 'Loves World', which has no relation but proximity to 'The Wits', completes that page and the following two. 'Song' and 'Sonnets I–III' occupy the following four pages.

Another consideration that may have influenced the placing in different formes is economy of type and composition, because the title-types of 'Against Fruition [I]' (B2) are used again for 'Against Fruition [II]' (C2ᵛ),[1] and those of 'Upon my L[ady Carliles] . . . Dialogue . . . . [I.] S.' (B5ᵛ) are used again in 'Upon my L[ord Brohalls Wedding.] Dialogue. S.' (C1). The over-all impression made by the order of poems in *Fragmenta Aurea* is that there is no systematic principle at work, but that a few poems were deliberately placed— first and last, or in juxtaposition with poems to which they are obviously closely related and may have been physically related in the copy. The rest seem to have fallen where they must to suit the printer's convenience or economy.

The Last Remains: Poems. Not counting '*Desdain*', and the Greek and Latin originals of No. 84, which precede the translations of them, there are forty-three poems in *The Last Remains*, and, except for the placing of a few poems, there is no more systematic arrangement here than there was in *Fragmenta Aurea*. 'The Invocation'—an appropriate beginning—is placed first, and, since the title is not apt, it may well have been supplied to accompany and justify the placing. Immediately following is one of Suckling's best-known poems, 'The constant Lover', with 'The Answer'. Curiously placed last in the collection is

---

[1] It should be noted that the skeleton-forme used for the inner formes of sheets A and B was used for the outer formes of sheets C and D, and vice versa.

'A Prologue of the Author's to a Masque at Witten' which may have been held out in the hope that the masque itself might be forthcoming. It is perhaps noteworthy that of the nine dubious or erroneously attributed English poems, seven occur among the first fourteen in the book; in addition, 'The Answer' to 'The constant Lover', headed 'Sir Toby Matthews', occurs third, and following the fourteen are two translations, 'Profer'd Love rejected' and 'Disdain', that might be questioned. Eleven of these poems occur in extant variant texts (which support Suckling's authorship of three). The inference is that the source of most of these is mixed and miscellaneous copy, consisting either of papers once belonging to Suckling and supplied to the printer by Lady Southcot (probably the source of the remaining twenty-nine poems), or miscellaneous texts attributed to him and masquerading in the preliminary address of 'The Stationer to the Reader' as 'the dearest and choisest of his Papers in the several Cabinets of his Noble and faithful Friends' (sig. A2ᵛ).

The list, and the serial numbers attached to individual poems, graphically point out the fact that the great majority of the remaining twenty-nine poems are of early composition, and that a few of them may have been together in papers of verses that were transcribed for printer's copy, notably 'Profer'd Love rejected' and 'Disdain', 'The Metamorphosis' and 'To B. C.', 'A Barber' and 'A Soldier', and 'Love's Burning-glass' and 'The Miracle'; it is possible that even these were brought together by the printer on account of their similarity, but since other potential juxtapositions of the same kind were not made, it would seem that these pairings are those of the source of the printer's transcriptions.

b. The Order of the Non-Dramatic Works in the Present Edition

If *Fragmenta Aurea* and *The Last Remains* were systematically ordered, the non-dramatic works would pose no problem of arrangement or combination. They were not, and the only advantage their arrangement of works within a genre affords is that of a 'convenient' but otherwise unhelpful model, which would serve rather to obscure and confuse than to clarify and emphasize literary and historical relationships. I have therefore adopted an arrangement that seems to me superior in coherence and, in the main, chronology, and is justified by stylistic similarities and historical evidence and inferences, generally bringing together poems and prose works from the two substantive editions and from manuscript. The canonical poems are given first (Nos. 1–78), followed by the dubious poems (Nos. 79–90) and the poems wrongly printed as Suckling's in *The Last Remains* (Nos. 91–3). The letters, including the shorter epistolary tracts and a dubious letter (Nos. 1–54, 55), follow, in approximate chronological order through No. 47. The 'serious' and longer prose works are placed last (as they are in *Fragmenta Aurea*), *To Mr. Henry German* followed by *An Account of Religion*. Since the over-all arrangement within genres is chronological, the skeletal outline is inevitably based upon 'touchstone' works whose placing is certain. The dates of dated works and the evidence for the dates of other datable works are presented in detail elsewhere, and I shall simply summarize these matters here.

The Prose Works. To Mr. Henry German is datable on external and internal evidence as approximately contemporaneous with the opening of the Long Parliament on 3 November 1640; the 'Epistle' that forms part of *An Account of Religion* is dated 2 September, and Aubrey gives the year as 1637. Of the letters, eleven—ten holographs and a manuscript copy—are dated in full, and two others are dated in part or are datable by explicit references (Nos. 43 and 47). The addressees, dates, subjects, historical references, attitudes, and varying styles of these letters allow inferences to be made about many of the printed letters with varying degrees of certainty.

Least certain in date (and to a lesser extent addressee) are those to Mary Cranfield, certainly No. 1, a dated holograph (30 October 1629), and probably Nos. 2–8, two or three of which are datable in 1631; the rest can be placed only in '1629–1635', but, since the letters do seem to have been written to the same person and are more personal or amatory than 'factual', it seemed most useful to place them together. Of Letters Nos. 9–19, most of them to the Earl of Middlesex, seven holographs and a manuscript copy are dated in full, and the other three (Nos. 13, 15, and 18) can be placed with reasonable certainty with the help of the dated ones. No. 21, and to a lesser extent Nos. 20 and 22, are also datable on internal and external evidence by season, at least, and year (1633–5). No. 23 is fully dated in a manuscript copy. Nos. 24–35, all printed without date or identification of addressee, are related by their address to 'Aglaura' and 'dear Princess' and in other ways; the addressee is identifiable from a holograph (No. 43), and by various kinds of inference they can be placed very approximately *c.* 1636–9. As with the letters to Mary

Cranfield, and for the same reason, it seems best to group these letters together, even though they may overlap in chronology with a few that follow. Letters Nos. 36–9, all from *The Last Remains*, are closely datable on the basis of their references to historical events between Summer 1638 and April 1639; No. 40 is a holograph dated 6 June (demonstrably 1639), and Nos. 41 and 42 are datable on the basis of their references to approximately contemporaneous events. No. 43, a holograph, is exactly datable by a reference to 'St. Georges feast, which is on Munday next'. Nos. 44 and 45 are inferentially datable in relation to mentioned events, as are Nos. 46 (an undated holograph concerned with military preparations of known occasion) and —less certainly—47, dated only 8 January.

It is possible that a few of the letters mentioned above might be placed elsewhere if they were strictly datable, especially those presumably to Mary Cranfield and Mary Bulkeley, but they are few, and there is some compensation in the collective effect and ease of comparison attending their present placing. Of undatable letters (Nos. 48–54), I have placed first what seems stylistically to be the earliest, and last a letter that is probably a literary exercise and affords little evidence for placing (as a 'railing letter' it might be either a youthful fiction or a historical adult-writing resembling one; cf. the letter to Sir Kenelm Digby, No. 21, written in late 1634). Letters Nos. 51(*a*) and 51(*b*) are a fictional interchange between 'Jack' and 'Tom', presumably Carew, that seems a little more polished than 'To T. C.' (No. 50), which I have placed before it, as I have placed 'The Wine-drinkers to the Water-drinkers', not addressed specifically to 'T. C.' or 'Tom', before that because it is similar in idiom. Also related—by opposition—are 'A disswasion from Love' (No. 52), which echoes the preceding exchange, and the persuasion to marry addressed 'To a Cosin' (No. 53). This arrangement seems to me the best for these miscellaneous letters, but it is not to be understood as having significance beyond that of the judgement exercised in the placing.

The Poems. The poems pose a far more difficult problem, not only because few are certainly datable but because even 'lyric' poems are intrinsically less homogeneous as a genre than letters; less likely, unless explicitly occasional, to be historically circumstantial; and stylistically elusive. A handful of poems are datable with some certainty, either in 1632 or before, or in 1637 or after (especially Nos.

71–4 and 76–8). But because most of these, especially those written in 1637 or after, are commendatory verses in heroic couplets or are otherwise highly specialized in form, such as 'The Wits', 'A Ballade. Upon a Wedding', and the dialogue, 'Upon my Lord Brohalls Wedding', they are of limited value as touchstones. The plays, however, constitute an invaluable supplementary group. All four are datable within a fairly narrow range of years or months, and Suckling had a habit of quoting himself *in extenso* in them. It is possible, of course, that flights of lyric fancy loosed in the plays might later have been developed into independent poems, but it is far more likely, where there are close parallels between finished poems and passages in plays, that the latter have been adapted from the former, and so I have practically assumed. *The Sad One* was probably written in 1630–2, most actively, perhaps, in 1632, since Suckling was out of the country much of the time between October 1629 and April 1632, and there are several striking parallels between *The Sad One* and Suckling's letter to Sir Henry Vane of 2 May 1632. *Aglaura* was completed by July 1637, *The Goblins* after September 1637, and *Brennoralt* probably in 1639–40. The very dates of the plays, and the external record of Suckling's active and continuous involvement in political and military affairs from 1638 until his flight to France in 1641 (and his continued gaming), though they prove nothing, suggest that such time as he had for writing was increasingly given to drama, or to quasi-dramatic works: 'The Wits' is narrative, but dramatic in event and prominently visual; 'A Ballade. Upon a Wedding' employs a 'depersonalized' rustic speaker; and 'Upon my Lord Brohalls Wedding' is a 'dialogue' in which the varying verse is metrically almost as loose as it is in the plays. Stronger evidence is the fact that *Aglaura* is virtually an anthology of Suckling's poetry, whereas the later *The Goblins* and *Brennoralt* show relatively little evidence of incorporating poems—and even some of the ones they do incorporate were certainly composed before *Aglaura*, because they figure prominently there.

The evidence of the plays other than *The Sad One* strongly supports the division made here between poems written before and poems written in or after 1637. Of the nine 'SECULAR POEMS (1637–1641)', seven were certainly written within that period, but it is possible that 'A Summons to Town' (No. 70) and 'An Answer to some Verses' (No. 75) were written earlier; they are placed here chiefly because 'An Answer' has a generic kinship to Suckling's commendatory poems that precede it, and 'A Summons to Town' has close parallels with 'Upon two Sisters' immediately preceding (and perhaps written in 1637 or after) and also some associations that ally it both with 'The Wits' (John Hales is the addressee) and *An Account of Religion* ('leave Socinus and the Schoolmen', l. 9). It follows, however, from lyric materials translated into dialogue in the plays, that if these two poems were not written in 1637 or after, most of the other poems were very likely written before, on the evidence of *Aglaura*.

Of the first group, the 'JUVENILE RELIGIOUS AND CHRIST-MAS-SEASONAL POEMS (*c.* 1626 or before)', the unifying principle is subject and theme, style, inferential date, and physical association in the two manuscripts in which all eleven are found (see Introduction, pp. xcix–ci). These are reasonably certainly datable in 1626 or before, and that they belong together on virtually all accounts can hardly be doubted. The second and third groups, 'SECULAR POEMS (*c.* 1626–1632)' and 'SECULAR POEMS (*c.* 1632–1637)', are so defined, as a class, because unlike the first group they are non-religious; they are divided chronologically, in general, with the help of the touchstones of *The Sad One*, *Aglaura*, and individual datable poems. The earlier group is made up of poems that either are prominently 'quoted' or adapted in *The Sad One* or are very similar in subject or style to datable poems that fall within the period, and that do not figure in *Aglaura*. The later group is made up of poems that do not closely resemble the datable poems in the earlier group and do not figure prominently in *The Sad One*, and that either do figure prominently in *Aglaura* or closely resemble those that do (numerous substantiating parallels are noted in the Commentary). This analogical and eliminative scheme does not purport to be scientific, but to be practical. Claims can by no means be made for its absolute 'accuracy', but it is approximately chronological, and where it is not the works are grouped in terms of generic, thematic, or otherwise stylistic affinities.

If the '*c.*' is allowed its intended weight, the groupings will not be misunderstood as implying any kind of absolute chronological demarcation. Some of the poems grouped with those of 1632–7 were quite possibly written before 1632 (e.g. 'The Invocation', 'The Expostulation I', etc.), but they profit, I think, from their present grouping. And some of the last in the earlier group may actually have been written later, though with the exception of 'Upon my Lady Carliles walking' (No. 32) I think this rather doubtful, on stylistic grounds.

In the group of 'SECULAR POEMS (*c.* 1626–1632)', six of the

twenty-eight poems (Nos. 12–39) are at least terminally datable with
reasonable accuracy: 'A Barley-break' (No. 15), *c.* 1626; 'A Barber'
(No. 19), 1632 or before; 'Lutea Allison' (No. 24), 1629–30; 'Upon Sir
John Laurence's bringing Water' (No. 28), *September 1630*; 'To my
Lady E. C.' (No. 30), before April 1631; and 'A Song to a Lute' (No.
31), 1631–2. The terminal dates are, then, 1626, 1629–30, 1631, and
1632. The other poems in this group have been arranged in relation
to these, to those of the earlier group of religious poems, to *The
Sad One*, and to the poems in the later group. 'A Barley-break' is
almost as early as the religious poems, but the juxtaposition of the
manifestly early 'His Dream' with the last of the earlier group 'A
Dreame' seems to me to have much to commend it, and there is no
proof that it post-dates 'A Barley-break'. And 'A Supplement of an
imperfect Copy' and 'Love's Representation' have more than enough
stylistically in common with 'His Dream' to recommend their placing soon after it. The nature of the corpus is such that there is no
other poem in this group of poems that is similar enough to benefit
from juxtaposition with 'Love's Representation', so the demonstrably early 'A Barley-break' follows, itself followed by four poems
(Nos. 16–19) that are in some respects similar both to it and to the
religious poems: all four are narrative or quasi-dramatic Characters,
playing a rhetorical game analogous to that of the real game, used
expressively, in 'A Barley-break'; and one, 'A Pedler of Small-wares'
(No. 17), has parallels of image and significance in one of the Christmas-seasonal poems, 'Upon Newyeares day' (No. 7). The ordering
of the rest of the poems in the group is in general based on the same
kind of flexible relationship between datable poems and others that
closely resemble them.

It is unnecessary here to comment in detail on the placings of all
the rest of the group, but it might be noted that Nos. 24–7 are
closely and explicitly associated with Wiston, an estate of Suckling's
uncle, the Earl of Middlesex, and with one of the Earl's daughters.
Poems Nos. 33–5 impersonally—despite 'Upon T. C.'—and briefly
exploit conceits, and Poems Nos. 36–9 are generically, tonally, and
otherwise stylistically related as paradoxical encomium and imprecation (there are also more specific parallels between them). Poems
Nos. 31 and 32 are so placed partly by default: 'A Song to a Lute',
a song in *The Sad One* parodying one of Jonson's in *The Devil is an Ass*
(produced in 1616 but first printed in 1631) is presumably close
in date to the preceding poem, 'To my Lady E. C.'; and 'Upon

my Lady Carliles walking' is related to 'Upon T. C. having the P.'
by 'T. C.', the antagonist in the dialogue on Lady Carlile, whom 'J. S.'
attacks and 'T. C.' defends (there is also a certain irony in the juxtaposition, but the intention was not sinister).

The most miscellaneous class of all is that of the thirty 'SECULAR
POEMS (*c.* 1632–1637)', Nos. 40–69, which are in the main more
mature in style than the majority of the poems in the earlier group,
but are quite without the guidance of terminal dates except as provided by adaptation in *Aglaura*. The last five are so placed for the
most obvious reasons: the last, 'Upon two Sisters' (No. 69), presumably concerns Suckling's Aglaura and her sister, and the romance
apparently flourished in the years from 1636 or even later to 1639;
and the poem has several close parallels with 'A Summons to Town',
the first in the next group, which would seem to have been written
in 1637. The preceding two poems, 'Loves Siege' and 'Farewel to
Love' (Nos. 67 and 68), may very well have been written earlier;
I have put them together because they are very similar stylistically,
and placed them here last for peripheral 'dramatic' reasons and because
they are quite different from the other amatory poems and do not
properly fit anywhere else. The two 'Songs' before them (Nos. 65
and 66) were first printed in *Aglaura*, and while one of them *may*
have been written some years earlier (see Commentary on 'Why so
pale and wan', pp. 260–1), both are eminently mature literary com-
positions and probably do not long antedate the play; 'Why so pale
and wan' is placed second because it is closer in its ironical spirit
and expression to 'Loves Siege'. No. 64, 'Loves Clock', is tonally and
otherwise similar to 'No, no, faire Heretique', with which it shares
a complicated stanza-form and a preoccupation with time, which,
however, is exploited to quite different and therefore instructive ends
in the two.

The poems placed first in the group are, like the last poems in the
preceding group, literary exercises in sub-genres, the paradoxical
encomium and imprecation there, the expression of various Caroline
positions in the debate and philosophy of love here. The first two,
'Against Fruition I' and 'II' (Nos. 40–1) are also, like the preceding,
in heroic couplets; the next two, 'To Mr. Davenant for Absence' and
'Against Absence', are in octosyllabic couplets, with numerous
catalectic lines, as are the following two 'To his Rival'. The next
poem, 'To a Lady that forbidd to love before Company' (No. 46),
in heroic couplets, reconciles some of the assertions of the preceding

poems and addresses itself directly to the lady (it also develops, in much the same way, some of the images used in the preceding poem, 'To his Rival II'). The following three poems (Nos. 47–9) are all expostulations, although the first is titled 'The Invocation' and the third was called simply 'Song' in *The Last Remains*; all are impassioned soliloquies by tormented lovers, and the first and third are also in complex stanza-forms (the second is in octaves of octosyllabic couplets). The three 'Sonnets' (Nos. 50–2) were apparently linked in manuscript and by authorial design, and they are also intimately related in tone, attitude, rhetorical situation, and complexity of stanza-form. And the second, in particular, suggests, in its direct address to Cupid ('Of thee (kind boy) I ask no red and white'), that the other playful 'Cupid' poems might properly follow it, as they do in the present edition, in 'Love's Sanctuary', 'Loves Feast', and 'Loves Offence' (Nos. 53–5), in order of increasing condensation, complexity, and wit. 'Disdain' and 'Profer'd Love rejected' (Nos. 56 and 57) are both translations in ballad stanzas expressing rejection in love, the first rather solemnly, the second with a telling irony that loses something in Suckling's translation (see another in the Commentary on 'Profer'd Love rejected'); these two are related in form, theme, and expression to 'The constant Lover' and 'The Answer' to it, which follow (Nos. 58 and 59). The next poem, 'The careless Lover', is in a more complex stanza-form than that of the ballads preceding, and it has a refrain; but it shares a number of formal and thematic similarities, as well as explicit parallels, with the immediately preceding poems. And this, beginning 'Never believe me if I love', is followed by 'Song' ('Honest Lover Whosoever'), 'Loving and Beloved' ('There never yet was honest man'), and 'Womans Constancy' ('There never yet was woman made'; Nos. 60–3); the first lines are sufficient to indicate the affinities that suggested the placing.

The arrangement of the works in the present edition can hardly pretend to absolute authority, but it is generally consistent with most of the kinds of evidence available for the placing of the works according to literary and historical criteria, which inevitably fall at odds, at times, but not, I hope, without the compensation of suggestive juxtaposition. At the least, this is a more helpful and instructive arrangement for the reader and student of Suckling's poetry than that of the early printed editions.

SIGLA AND TEXTUAL SOURCES

Individual works found in the manuscripts or printed books are specified in parentheses by *P*[*oem*], *L*[*etter*], or *App*[*endix*], etc., followed by the serial number or other identification given in the Table of Contents.

SPECIAL SYMBOLS AND ABBREVIATIONS

(*c*)	corrected state
(*u*)	uncorrected state
Ed.	the present editor
MS(*S*).	manuscript(s); in addition to the usual uses, 'MS.' is used in the critical apparatus in place of the siglum at the head of the notes on the work when a manuscript copy-text is the sole witness
Σ	all printed and manuscript witnesses except those individually specified by their sigla
~	the hyphen-level tilde takes the place, in a collated reading, of the sole substantive, or the substantive in the analogous position, in the lemma (e.g. 'wit, / it;] ~; ~:')
∧	the inferior caret indicates the absence of a character, normally a punctuation-point or the like (e.g. 'minde.] ~ₐ')
+	the plus sign (1) precedes interpolated matter in a collated text (which may be the copy-text) that has not been incorporated in the present text (e.g. 'anye]+other *N&Q*'), and (2) indicates the agreement, in a shared reading, of a witness whose readings are normally unspecified (e.g. 'Σ+FA48')

EARLY EDITIONS

FA46	*Fragmenta Aurea*, 1646 (the first edition)
FA48	*Fragmenta Aurea*, 1648 (the second edition, substantive in part)
FA58	*Fragmenta Aurea*, 1658 (the third edition, from *FA46*)
LR	*The Last Remains of Sir John Suckling*, 1659 (the first and only substantive edition)

MANUSCRIPTS, PRINTED MISCELLANIES, OTHER EARLY
PRINTED BOOKS, AND MODERN EDITIONS

*A*4	British Museum, Add. MS. 4968 (*P* 79)
*A*10	10308 (*P* 92)
*A*11	11811 (*P* 39, 83, 92)
*A*23	23229 (*P* 53, 80)
*A*25	25707 (*P* 93)
*A*29	29492 (*P* 15)
*A*31	31432 (*P* 50)
*A*33	33998 (*P* 82)
*A*37	37157 (*P* 91)
*A*47	47111 (*P* 66)
Ag	*Aglaura*, 1638 (*P* 65, 66)
Ag-c	*Aglaura*, 1638, the tragi-comic version of Act v
Ag-t	*Aglaura*, 1638, the tragic version of Act v
*Ash*3	Bodleian Library, Ashmole MS. 36–7 (*P* 43, 54, 76 [twice]; *L* 38; *App* A.v.4–5 [twice])
*Ash*4	Bodleian Library, Ashmole MS. 47 (*P* 40)
*Ash*8	826 (*L* 9, 38)
AAM	*An Antidote Against Melancholy*, 1661 (*P* 76)
AC	*The Academy of Complements*, 1646 (*P* 50, 66, 88; *L* 51[a])
*AC*84	*The Academy of Complements*, 1684 (later edition of *Wind-D*; *P* 58, 59, 66, 88)
AD	Henry Lawes, *Ayres and Dialogues ... Third Book*, 1658 (*P* 81)
AS	Bodleian Library, MS. Arch. Seld. B. 8 (*Account of Religion*)
B	Bodleian Library, MS. Ballard 29 (*P* 74)
Bold	Henry Bold, *Poems Lyrique, Macaronique, Heroique, &c.*, 1664 (*App* A.i.2–4); cf. *LS*
Brome	Richard Brome, *The Weeding of the Covent-Garden*, 1658 (*App* A.v.1)
[B.M. Loan]	British Museum, Loan MS. 29/235.619.E (MSS. of the Duke of Portland, 'Vere Papers 1614–1626, Cavendish Papers 1604–1659'; *L* 47)
C	Cambridge University Library, Add. MS. 22 (*L* 38; *App* A.v.4–5)
Car	Thomas Carew, *Poems*, 1640 (*P* 82)
Cor	Cornell University Library, MS. E 7003 (*P* 71)

Cran	Kent County Archives Office, Cranfield Papers (uncatalogued, or catalogued in *HMC 4th Report*, and unnumbered; *P* 86, 87; *L* 1, 10–12, 14, 16, 17, 23, 40, 43; *To Mr. Henry German*; *App* A.iv.1–2, 4–5)
Cran2	Kent County Archives Office, Cranfield Papers, MS. U.269.F.36, No. 42 (*P* 40, 42, 43, 54, 85)
Cran6	Cranfield Papers, MS. U.269.F.36, No. 46 (*P* 71)
Cran7	No. 37 (*P* 1–9)
Cran8	No. 38 (*P* 10, 11)
D	Bodleian Library, Dodsworth MS. 61 (*L* 38)
Dav	*The Works of Sir William Davenant Kt*, 1673 (*P* 85)
Don	Bodleian Library, MS. Don. c. 57 (*P* 27)
DonD	Don. d. 55 (*P* 40; *App* A.i.1)
Du	Durham University Library, Mickleton and Spearman MS. 9 (*App* A.v.4–5)
Dx4	New York Public Library, Drexel MS. 4041 (*P* 50, 51, 58, 59, 65, 66, 88)
Dx42	New York Public Library, Drexel MS. 4257 ('John Gamble Commonplace Book'; *P* 50, 51, 65, 76, 88; *App* A.v.4)
Eg9	British Museum, Egerton MS. 923 (*P* 58, 59, 66; *App* A.v.4–5)
Eg27	2725 (*P* 82; *L* 38)
[Elegie]	*An Elegie upon the Death of the Renowned Sir John Sutlin*, 1642 (*App* A.ii.2)
EP2	Bodleian Library, MS. Eng. Poet. f. 24 (*P* 50)
EP5	c. 50 (*P* 93)
EP9	e. 97 (*P* 66)
EP53	c. 53 (*P* 71; *App* A.v.1–4)
F7	Folger Shakespeare Library, MS. V.a.97 (*P* 82)
F24	V.a.124 (*P* 66, 83, 88; *App* A.i.5)
F25	V.a.125 (*P* 92)
F60	V.a.160 (*L* 51[a]; *App* A.v.1, 4–5)
F62	V. a. 162 (*P* 88; *App* A. i. 10)
F69	V.a.169 (*P* 81)
F80	V.a.180 ('Henry Fane Commonplace-Book'; *P* 84)

F92	Folger Shakespeare Library, MS. V.a.192 (*P* 76)
F275	V.a.275 (*L* 55; *App* A.iv.6)
F308	V.a.308 (*P* 66, 88)
F339	V.a.339 (*P* 58, 59, 88)
FA46	Sir John Suckling, *Fragmenta Aurea*, 1646 (the first edition)
FA48	Sir John Suckling, *Fragmenta Aurea*, 1648 (the second edition)
FA58	Sir John Suckling, *Fragmenta Aurea*, 1658 (the third edition)
H17	British Museum, Harleian MS. 6917 (*P* 39, 46, 76, 92; *App* A.v.1, 4–5)
H18	6918 (*P* 93; *App* A.ii.3)
H35	3511 (*P* 81)
H38	3889 (*P* 81)
H39	3991 (*P* 81, 88, 90; *App* A.v.4–5, 7)
H63	6383 (*App* A.v.4–5)
H69	6396 (*P* 88; *App* A.v.4–5)
Harv6	Harvard University Library, MS. Eng. 626F (*P* 93)
Harv7	703 (*P* 58, 59, 71)
Haz, Haz²	W. Carew Hazlitt, ed. *The Poems, Plays and Other Remains of Sir John Suckling*, 1874, 1892 (*Haz* indicates identity of readings in the two editions; *Haz²* indicates that the reading is that of the second edition only)
Hunt	Henry E. Huntington Library, MS. 198 ('Haslewood-Kingsborough Manuscript'; *P* 71; *App* A.v.4–5)
[Huntington]	Henry E. Huntington Library, MS. HA 12760 (*L* 21)
[Hyde]	Donald F. Hyde Collection, Four Oaks Farm, Somerville, New Jersey (*L* 46)
HL	A manuscript song-book in the autograph of Henry Lawes, in the possession of Miss Naomi D. Church, Beaconsfield (*P* 58, 65, 81, 88)
JG	*The Jovial Garland* [*c.* 1672] (*P* 81)
L	Edinburgh University Library, Laing MS. iii. 436 (*P* 27, 92)
Longleat	MSS. of the Marquis of Bath; Longleat MS. 114 (*App* A.iv.3)
Ltr41	*A Coppy of a Letter Found in the Privy Lodgeings at Whitehall*, 1641 (*To Mr. Henry German*)
Ltr43	*A True Copie of a Letter Found in the Kings Army*, 1643 (*To Mr. Henry German*)
Lu	Owen Felltham, *Lusoria*, 1661 (*P* 93)

LR	*The Last Remains of Sir John Suckling*, 1659
LS	Henry Bold, *Latine Songs*, 1685 (*P* 66); cf. *Bold*
Mad	Sir William Davenant, *Madagascar; with Other Poems*, 1638 (*P* 73, 74)
M3	Bodleian Library, Malone MS. 13 (*P* 71, 83)
M6	16 (*P* 82 [twice])
MusD	*Musarum Deliciæ*, 1655 (*App* A.v.1, 7)
MD	*Merry Drollery*, 1661 (*P* 71, 76)
MDC	*Musicks Delight on the Cithren*, 1666 (*P* 81, 88)
[*Nabbes*]	Thomas Nabbes, *Covent Garden*, 1638 (*App* A.iii.2)
North	Dudley 3rd Baron North, *A Forest of Varieties*, 1645 (*P* 83; *App* A.i.9, A.iii.3)
NAC	*The New Academy of Complements*, 1669 (*P* 90)
O2	James M. Osborn Collection, New Haven, Connecticut (housed in the Yale University Library), MS. Chest II, No. 21 (*P* 50, 55, 58, 59, 66, 81, 91-3)
O5	Osborn Collection, MS. Chest II, No. 25 (*App* A.v.7)
OD	*Oxford Drollery*, 1671 (*P* 58, 59)
OV	Edward Lord Herbert of Cherbury, *Occasional Verses*, 1665 (*P* 91)
P	Rosenbach Collection, Philadelphia, Phillipps MS. 9500 (*P* 13, 40, 44, 51, 55, 61, 64-7, 71)
PB	*Parnassus Biceps*, 1656 (*App* A.v.1)
PD	*Le Prince d'Amour*, 1660 (*App* A.v.4-5)
[*P.R.O.*]	Public Record Office, State Papers, 16/216, No. 6 (*L* 19)
R	British Museum, Royal MS. 18 C xxv (a scribal copy of the tragic version of *Aglaura*, c. 1637; *P* 65, 66)
Ros2	Rosenbach Collection, Philadelphia, MS. 240/2 (Catalogue, *English Poetry to 1700*, Philadelphia: the Rosenbach Company, 1941, No. 195; *P* 82)
Ros4	Rosenbach Collection, MS. 243/4 (Catalogue, No. 190; *P* 82, 93; *App* A.i.8)
R&T	Henry Carey, Lord Lepington, *Malvezzi's Romulus and Tarquin*, 2nd ed., 1638 (*P* 72)
RD7	Bodleian Library, Rawlinson MS. D. 737 (*P* 93)
RP1	Bodleian Library, Rawlinson Poet. MS. 16 (*App* A.i.7)
RP3	37 (*P* 76)
RP6	65 (*P* 81)
RP11	116 (*P* 43)

RP14	Bodleian Library, Rawlinson Poet. MS. 147 (*P* 79; *App* A.i.6)
RP16	160 (*P* 40; *App* A.i.1)
RP19	199 (*P* 32)
S	A manuscript in the possession of Mr. William Suckling of Roos Hall, Beccles, Suffolk (*Account of Religion*)
[Saltonstall]	Wye Saltonstall, *Ovid de Ponto*, 1639 (*App* A.iii.3)
[Satyres]	*Les Satyres et Autre Oeuvres Folastres du Sr Regnier*, 1614 (*App* A.vi.1-2, of which *P* 56 and 57 are translations)
St	British Museum, Stowe MS. 180 (*To Mr. Henry German*)
SMA	*Select Musicall Ayres and Dialogues*, 1652 (*P* 51, 65, 88)
SMA53	*Select Musicall Ayres and Dialogues in Three Bookes*, 1653 (*P* 51, 65, 81, 88)
SO	*The Sad One*, in *The Last Remains of Sir John Suckling*, 1659 (*P* 31)
SW	*Sportive Wit: The Muses Merriment*, 1656 (*P* 40)
T4	Bodleian Library, Tanner MS. 465 (*App* A.v.4-5)
T6	65 (*To Mr. Henry German*)
T8	88 (*L* 38)
Th	A. Hamilton Thompson, ed. *The Works of Sir John Suckling in Prose and Verse*, 1910
TC	British Museum, Thomason Collection, MS. bound with Tract No. 669 (*To Mr. Henry German*)
TCD	Trinity College, Dublin, MS. G.2.21 (*P* 82; *App* A.i.8 [twice])
VB	*Vox Borealis: or The Northern Discoverie*, 1641 (*App* A.v.6)
W	National Library of Wales, Carreglwyd MS. 340 (*App* A.v.4-5)
W3	Bodleian Library, Wood 397, a manuscript bound in a printed book (*SMA 3*; *P* 66)
Waller	Edmund Waller, *Poems, &c.*, 3rd ed. ('Printed by I. N. for H. Mosleys'), 1645 (*P* 40; *App* A.i.1)
W&D	*Wit and Drollery*, 1656 (*P* 58, 59; *App* A.v.4-5)
W&D61	*Wit and Drollery*, 1661 (*P* 50)
West-D	*Westminster Drollery*, 1671 (*P* 82)
Wind-D	*Windsor Drollery*, 1671, 1672 (*P* 58, 59, 66, 88)
[Witts Rec]	*Witts Recreations*, 1640 (*App* A.ii.1)

WI	*Wits Interpreter*, 1655 (P 36, 50, 51, 88; *App* A.i.10)
WI62	*Wits Interpreter*, 1662 (P 36, 51 [twice], 81, 88)
WR	*Wits Recreations*, 1650 (P 68)
T	Yale University Library, MS. Vault 10, Drawer 3 (Phillipps MS. 9621; *Account of Religion*)

FRAGMENTA AVREA.

A Collection of all

THE

Incomparable Peeces,

WRITTEN

By Sir JOHN SVCKLING.

And publiſhed by a Friend to perpetuate his memory.

Printed by his owne Copies.

LONDON,
Printed for *Humphrey Moſeley*, and are to be
ſold at his ſhop, at the Signe of the Princes Armes in St *Pauls* Churchyard.
MDCXLVI.

Fragmenta Aurea.

A Collection of all

THE

Incomparable Peeces,

WRITTEN

By Sir JOHN SVCKLING.

And published by a Friend to perpetuate his memory.

Printed by his owne Copies.

LONDON,
Printed for *Humphrey Moseley,* and are to be sold at his shop, at the Signe of the Princes Armes in S.t *Pauls* Churchyard.
MDCXLVI.

To the READER

WHILE *Sucklins* name is in the forehead of this Booke, these *Poems* can want no preparation: It had been a prejudice to Posterity they should have slept longer, and an injury to his own ashes. They that convers'd with him alive, and truly, (under which notion I comprehend only knowing Gentlemen, his soule being 5 transcendent, and incommunicable to others, but by reflection) will honour these posthume Idæa's of their friend: And if any have liv'd in so much darknesse, as not to have knowne so great an Ornament of our Age, by looking upon these Remaines with Civility and Understanding, they may timely yet repent, and be forgiven. 10

In this Age of Paper-prostitutions, a man may buy the reputation of some Authors into the price of their Volume; but know, the Name that leadeth into this Elysium, is sacred to *Art* and *Honour*, and no man that is not excellent in both, is qualified a *Competent Judge*: For when Knowledge is allowed, yet Education in the Censure of 15 a Gentleman, requires as many descents, as goes to make one; And he that is bold upon his unequall Stock, to traduce this Name, or Learning, will deserve to be condemned againe into Ignorance his Originall sinne, and dye in it.

But I keep backe the Ingenuous Reader, by my unworthy Preface: 20 The gate is open, and thy soule invited to a Garden of ravishing variety: admire his wit, that created these for thy delight, while I withdraw into a shade, and contemplate who must follow.

To the Reader. *FA46, sigg. πA3–4*

THE LAST
REMAINS

O F

Sᵗ *JOHN SUCKLING.*

Being a Full

COLLECTION

Of all his

P O E M S and L E T T E R S

which have been fo long expeȻed,
and never till now Publifhed.

W I T H

The *Licence* and *Approbation* of his

Noble and Dearest

F R I E N D S.

LONDON:

Printed for *Humphrey Moſeley* at the Prince's
Arms in St. *Pauls* Churchyard. 1659.

The General Title-Page of the First Edition of *The Last Remains of Sir John
Suckling*, 1659 (Henry E. Huntington Library, shelf-mark 147908)

To The
MOST HONORED
AND HIGHLY DESERVING,
THE
Lady Southcot

THOUGH I approach with all humility in presenting these Poems
to your *Ladiship*, yet dare I not despair of their acceptation,
since it were a kind of Felony to offer them to any other. They come
to you at so many capacities, that they seem rather to return and
rebound back to you, as the famous ARCADIA was sent to that excel- 5
lent *Lady*, who was Sister to that great *Author*. Your *Ladiship* best
knows, that I now bring the Last REMAINS of your Incomparable
Brother, Sir JOHN SUCKLING: And as here are all the World must
ever hope for, so here are nothing else but his, not a line but what at
first flow'd from him, and will soon approve it self to be too much his 10
to be alter'd or supplied by any other hand; and sure he were a bold
man had thoughts to attempt it. After which 'twould be high presumption in me to say more, but that I am

(Madam)
Your Ladiships most obliged, and 15
Most obedient humble Servant,
HUM: MOSELEY.

To the Most Honored *etc. LR, sig.* a1^{r+v} ($A1 + a^4$)

THE STATIONER
TO THE
READER

AMONG the highest and most refin'd Wits of the Nation, this
Gentile and Princely Poet took his generous rise from the Court;
where having flourish'd with splendor and reputation, he liv'd only
long enough to see the Sun-set of that Majesty from whose auspicious
5 beams he derived his lustre, and with whose declining state his own
loyal Fortunes were obscured. But after the several changes of those
times, being sequestred from the more serene Contentments of his
native Country, He first took care to secure the dearest and choisest
of his Papers in the several Cabinets of his Noble and faithful Friends;
10 and among other Testimonies of his worth, these elegant and florid
Peeces of his Fancie were preserved in the custody of his truly honorable and vertuous Sister, with whose free permission they were
transcribed, and now published exactly according to the Originals.

This might be sufficient to make you acknowledge that these are
15 the real and genuine Works of Sir *John Suckling*. But if you can yet
doubt, let any Judicious soul seriously consider the Freedom of the
Fancie, Richness of the Conceipt, proper Expression, with that air
and spirit diffus'd through every part, and he will find such a perfect
resemblance with what hath been formerly known, that he cannot
20 with modestie doubt them to be his.

I could tell you further, (for I my self am the best witness of it)
what a thirst and general enquiry hath been after what I here present
you, by all that have either seen, or heard of them. And by that time
you have read them, you will believe me, who have (now for many
25 years) annually published the Productions of the best Wits of our own,
and Forein Nations.

H. M.

The Stationer to the Reader. *LR, sigg. A2–3^v*

POEMS

JUVENILE RELIGIOUS AND CHRISTMAS-SEASONAL POEMS

(*c.* 1626 or before)

1. Upon St. Thomas his unbeliefe

FAITH comes by heare-say, love by sight: then hee
   May well beleive, and love whom hee doth see:
But since men leave both hope, and charitie,
And faith is made the greatest of the three,
All doctrine goes for truth: then say I thus,   5
More goes to heaven with *Thomas Didymus.*

2. Upon Christmas Eve

VAILE cobwebs from the white-ned floore
   And let *Arachne* spin noe more;
With holly-bushes all adorne
Untill the comeing of the morne,
And fancy then the Lord of Light is there   5
As he did once in *Moses*-bush appeare.

3. Upon Christ his birth

STRANGE news! a Cittie full? will none give way
   To lodge a guest that comes not every day?
Noe inne, nor taverne void? yet I descry
One empty place alone, where wee may ly:

POEMS. *FA46, LR, other printed texts, MSS. For the arrangement of the poems in this edition,* see *Introduction, pp. cxxxiii–cxxxviii.*

JUVENILE RELIGIOUS AND CHRISTMAS-SEASONAL POEMS. *Cran7 and Cran8 (MS., possibly holograph) Italics supplied, except in* [Faith and Doubt] *and* A Dreame
     1. Upon St. Thomas his unbeliefe. *Cran7*
     2. Upon Christmas Eve. *Cran7*
     3. Upon Christ his birth. *Cran7*

In too much fullnesse is some want: but where? 5
Mens empty hearts: let's aske for lodgeing there.
But if they not admit us, then wee'le say
Their hearts, as well as inn's, are made of clay.

4. Upon Stephen stoned

U<small>NDER</small> this heape of stones interred lies
  No holocaust, but stoned sacrifice
Burnt not by altar-coales, but by the fire
    Of Jewish ire,
Whoes softest wordes in their hard hearts alone 5
    Congeal'd to stone,
Nor peirceing them recoild in him againe,
    Whoe beeing slaine
As not forgetfull, whence they once did come,
Now beeing stones hee found in them a tombe. 10

5. Upon St. Johns-day comeing after Christmas day

L<small>ET</small> the Divines dispute the case, and try
  The dubiousnesse of that great mystery
That *John* should live untill the day of doome:
This may suffice, he stayes till *Christ* is come.

6. Upon Innocents day

W<small>HAT</small> treason can there in an infant lurke?
  Or in an innocent what hurtfull worke?
Yet must you, suckeing infants, dy for these,
White as your milke who have your consciences?
Noe 'tis not strange: soe should all martyres dy 5
Drinkeing the new-milk of sincerity.

     4. Upon Stephen stoned. *Cran*7
     5. Upon St. Johns-day *etc. Cran*7
     6. Upon Innocents day. *Cran*7

7. Upon Newyeares day

Arise my Muse, a Newyear's-gift præpare,
 Noe thing of too much cost, nor yet soe rare,
But fitt for Ladyes dresses, and rehearse
A Pedlar's pack of fancy's in thy verse,
That if thy fancies have a prosperous fate   5
They may with favours thee retaliate.

8. Upon the Epiphanie
Or starr that appear'd to the wisemen

Astrologers, from hence you may devise
 Peripatetick orders in the skies:
Sith here a Philosophick wakeing starr
Hath taught the Magi comeing from afarr
The *summum bonum* in a trice to find   5
Not in high roofes, but oxen-stalls inshrin'd.
O calculate this starr, and surely then
You'l find it does præsage good health to men.

9. Upon Christmas

Haile wellcome time, whoes long expected date
 The proner hearts of men doth elevate
Who from their toile cessations now require,
And live in warme *Elysiums* by the fire
Upon whoes sunny bank's they take delight   5
To see the winged, and foure-footed fight,
And charge each other in the flameing field's
With spitts for speares, and dripping-pans for sheilds;
Some better freinds doe turne about, and play
Till scorcht with heat become to men a prey.   10
And schollers too, from prison-schoole set free
Proclaime aloud a gaole deliverie,

7. Upon Newyeares day. *Cran7*
8. Upon the Epiphanie *etc. Cran7*   4 afarr *Ed.*: farr *MS.*; *see note*
9. Upon Christmas. *Cran7*   11 too, from *Ed.*: too *MS.*; *see note*
12 gaole *Ed.*: goale *MS.*

Invoke the Gods of sports, nor feare the maine
By Plough-day writs to bee attach't againe.
Well did our fathers then by *Christ* set free   15
Elect us thus to their fraternitie!
But shall those impious mouth's by new-fond lights
Inspir'd revile, and loath these sacred rites,
Whoes festivalls with prayer, and almes allay'd,
A time of Charitie, and gladnesse made,   20
Shall they with poison-beareing slaunder staine
This time, and it abolish as profane?
Noe Noe: let's keepe it still whilst them wee see
With Christmas pull downe *Christ* Nativitie.

10. [Faith and Doubt]

T HAT *Heaven* should visitt *Earth* and come to see
   Poore wretched *Man*, rich but in Miserie,
That *Hee* whom all the *Heavens* could not contayne
Should in a Virgin-wombe soe long remayne,
Is such a wonder and soe great! that heere   5
Our *Faith* not *Reason* must us steere.
But that the *God* of life, should come to dy
And dye for us, O there's the howe, and why!
Each *Man* is *Thomas* heere, and faine would see
Something to helpe his Infidellitie,   10
But I beleive; *Lord* helpe my faithlesse mynd
And with Sainct *Thomas* lett mee *Pardon* find.

11. A Dreame

S CARCE had I slept my wonted rownd
   But that meethoughts I heard the last *Trompe* sownd:
And in a Moment *Earth*'s faire *Frame* did passe,
The *Heav'ns* did melt, and all confus'on was.
My thoughts straight gave mee, *Earth*'s great daie was come, 5
And that I was nowe to receive my doome.

---

10. [Faith and Doubt.] *Cran8 (subscribed* J: Sucklyn Esq.) *Title supplied*
11. A Dreame. *Cran8 (subscribed* J Sucklyn. Esq)

'Twixt Hope and Feare, whil'st I thus trembling stood
Feareing the Bad, and yet expecting Good:
Summon'd I was, to showe howe I had spent,
That span-long tyme which *God* on earth mee lent.   10
Cold Feares possest mee; for I knewe noe Lyes
(Though guilded o're) could blynd th' Eternall's Eyes.
Besides my Bosome frend my Conscience mee accus'd,
That I too much this little Tyme abus'd.
And nowe noe summes of gould, noe bribes (alasse)   15
Could mee repreive, Sentence must straight waie passe.
Great Frends could nothing doe, noe lustfull Peere,
Noe smooth-fac'd *Buckingham*, was *Favourite* heere.
Theis helpes were vaine; what could I then saie more?
I had done ill, and death lay at the dore.   20
But yet meethoughts it was too much to dy,
To die a while, much lesse eternally:
And therefore streight I did my Sinnes unmaske
And in *Christ's* name, a *Pardon* there did aske
Which *God* then granted; and *God* grant hee may   25
Make this my dreame proove true i'th' latter day.

POEMS,

&c.

Written by
Sir JOHN SUCKLING.

Printed by his owne Copy.

The Lyrick Poems were set in
Musick by Mr. *Henry Lawes*, Gent.
of the Kings Chappel, and one of
His Majesties Private Musick.

LONDON,

Printed by *Ruth Raworth* for *Humphrey Moseley*, and
are to be sold at his shop at the signe of the
Princes Arms in S. *Pauls* Church-yard. 1646,

SECULAR POEMS

(*c.* 1626–1632)

12. His Dream

O N a still silent night, scarce could I number
One of the clock, but that a golden slumber
Had lockt my senses fast, and carried me
Into a world of blest felicitie,
I know not how: First to a Garden where   5
The Apricock, the Cherry, and the Peare,
The Strawberry, and Plumb, were fairer far
Then that eye-pleasing Fruit that caus'd the jar
Betwixt the Goddesses, and tempted more
Then fair *Atlanta's* Ball, though gilded ore.   10
I gaz'd a while on these, and presently
A Silver-stream ran softly gliding by,
Upon whose banks, Lillies more white then snow
New faln from heaven, with Violets mixt, did grow;
Whose scent so chaf'd the neighbor air, that you   15
Would surely swear Arabick spices grew
Not far from thence, or that the place had been
With Musk prepar'd, to entertain Loves Queen.
Whilst I admir'd, the River past away,
And up a Grove did spring, green as in *May*,   20
When *April* had been moist; upon whose bushes
The pretty Robins, Nightingals, and Thrushes
Warbled their Notes so sweetly, that my ears
Did judge at least the musick of the Sphears.
But here my gentle Dream conveyed me   25
Into the place which I most long'd to see,
My Mistress bed; who, some few blushes past,
And smiling frowns, contented was at last
To let me touch her neck; I not content
With that, slipt to her breast, thence lower went,   30
And then——I awak'd.

ᵇECULAR POEMS. *FA46, LR, and MSS.*
   12. His Dream. *LR*   16 surely *LR (Errata)*: softly *Haᶻ, LR (Text), Th; see note*
wear] + that *Haᶻ, Th*

13. A Supplement of an imperfect Copy of Verses of Mr. Will. Shakespears, By the Author

1

ONE of her hands, one of her cheeks lay under,
  Cozening the pillow of a lawful kisse,
Which therefore swel'd, and seem'd to part asunder,
  As angry to be rob'd of such a blisse:
    The one lookt pale, and for revenge did long,   5
    While t'other blusht, 'cause it had done the wrong.

2

Out of the bed the other fair hand was
  On a green sattin quilt, whose perfect white
Lookt like a Dazie in a field of grasse,   9
  *And shew'd like unmelt snow unto the sight: Thus far
  There lay this pretty perdue, safe to keep   *Shakespear*
  The rest oth' body that lay fast asleep.

3

Her eyes (and therefore it was night) close laid,
  Strove to imprison beauty till the morn;
But yet the doors were of such fine stuffe made,   15
  That it broke through, and shew'd it self in scorn,
    Throwing a kind of light about the place,
    Which turn'd to smiles still as't came near her face.

4

Her beams (which some dull men call'd hair) divided:
  Part with her cheeks, part with her lips did sport,   20
But these, as rude, her breath put by; some guided
  Wiselyer downwards sought, but falling short,
    Curl'd back in rings, and seem'd to turn agen
    To bite the part so unkindly held them in.

---

13. A Supplement *etc. FA46 (ll. 1–9 are a corrupt version of Shakespeare's* Lucrece, *ll. 386–95; see Commentary) MS.: P (from FA46)*   21 by; some guided *Ed.*: by still; some *FA46; see note*

14. Love's Representation

LEANING her head upon my Brest,
   There on Loves Bed she lay to rest;
My panting heart rock'd her asleep,
My heedful eyes the watch did keep:
Then Love by me being harbored there,   5
(No hope to be his Harbinger)
Desire his rival, kept the door;
For this of him I begg'd no more,
But that, our Mistress to entertain,
Some pretty fancy he would frame,   10
And represent it in a dream,
Of which my self should give the Theam.
Then first these thoughts I bid him show,
Which onely he and I did know,
Arrayed in duty and respect,   15
And not in Fancies that reflect:
Then those of value next present,
Approv'd by all the World's consent;
But to distinguish mine asunder,
Apparell'd they must be in wonder.   20
Such a device then I would have,
As Service not reward should crave,
Attir'd in spotless Innocence,
Not self-respect, nor no pretence:
Then such a Faith I would have shown,   25
As heretofore was never known,
Cloth'd with a constant clear intent,
Professing always as it meant.
And if Love no such Garments have,
My minde a Wardrobe is so brave,   30
That there sufficient he may see
To cloath Impossibility.
There beamy Fetters he shall finde,
By admiration subt'ly twin'd,
That will keep fast the wanton'st thought,   35
That ere Imagination wrought:

---

14. Love's Representation. *LR*   1 head *Haz*, *Th*: hand *LR*   6 (No . . .
Harbinger)] *omit parentheses LR* (Harbinger,)   No] In *Haz*   33 There *Ed.*: Then *LR*

There he shall finde of Joy a chain,
Fram'd by despair of her disdain,
So curiously that it can tie
The smallest hopes that Thoughts now spie.   40
There acts as glorious as the Sun,
Are by her veneration spun,
In one of which I would have brought
A pure unspotted abstract thought,
Considering her as she is good,   45
Not in her frame of Flesh and Blood.
These Attoms then, all in her sight
I bad him joyn, that so she might
Discern between true Loves Creation,
And that Loves form that's now in fashion.   50
Love granting unto my request
Began to labor in my Brest;
But with this motion he did make,
It heav'd so high that she did wake,
Blush'd at the favor she had done,   55
Then smil'd, and then away did run.

15. [A Barley-break]

I

LOVE, Reason, Hate, did once bespeak
  Three mates to play at barley-break;
Love, Folly took; and Reason, Fancy;
And Hate consorts with Pride; so dance they:
Love coupled last, and so it fell   5
That Love and Folly were in hell.

2

They break, and Love would Reason meet,
But Hate was nimbler on her feet;
Fancy looks for Pride, and thither
Hyes, and they two hugge together: 10
Yet this new coupling still doth tell
That Love and Folly were in hell.

14. 39 can *Ed.*: can't *LR*   48 she *Ed.*: he *LR*   53 this] the *LR (Errata); see note*
15. [A Barley-break.] *FA46 Title from MS. MS.: A29*   6 were] are *MS.(u)*
12 were] are *MS.*

3

The rest do break again, and Pride
Hath now got Reason on her side;
Hate and Fancy meet, and stand   15
Untoucht by Love in Folly's hand:
Folly was dull, but Love ran well,
So Love and Folly were in hell.

16. A Candle

THERE is a thing which in the Light
   Is seldom us'd, but in the Night
It serves the Maiden Female crew,
The Ladies, and the Good-wives too:
They use to take it in their hand,   5
And then it will uprightly stand;
And to a hole they it apply,
Where by its good will it would dye:
It spends, goes out, and still within
It leaves its moisture thick and thin.   10

17. A Pedler of Small-Wares

1

A PEDLER I am, that take great care
  And mickle pains for to sell Small-ware:
I had need do so, when women do buy,
That in small wares trade so unwillingly.

2

L. W.

A Looking-glass, wilt please you Madam buy?   5
A rare one 'tis indeed; for in it I
Can shew what all the world besides can't do,
A Face like to your own, so fair, so true.

15. 14 on] by *MS.*   18 So] Yet *MS.*   were] are *MS.*
16. A Candle. *LR*
17. A Pedler of Small-wares. *LR*

3
L. E.

For you a Girdle, Madam? but I doubt me
Nature hath order'd there's no Waste about ye:　　　　　10
Pray therefore be but pleas'd to search my Pack,
There's no ware that I have that you shall lack.

4
L. E.　L. M.

You Ladies, want you Pins? if that you do,
I have those will enter, and that stiffly too:
It's time you choose in troth; you will bemone　　　　15
Too late your tarrying, when my Pack's once gone.

5
L. B.　L. A.

As for you Ladies, there are those behind
Whose ware perchance may better take your mind:
One cannot please ye all; the Pedler will draw back,
And wish against himself, that they may have the knack.　　20

18. A Soldier

I AM a man of war and might,
　And know thus much, that I can fight,
Whether I am i'th' wrong or right,
　　　　　　　devoutly.

No woman under heaven I fear,　　　　　5
New Oaths I can exactly swear,
And forty Healths my brain will bear
　　　　　　　most stoutly.

I cannot speak, but I can doe
As much as any of our crew;　　　　　10
And if you doubt it, some of you
　　　　　　　may prove me.

17. 10 Waste] waist *Haz, Th; see note*　　　20 they *Ed.* : you *LR; see note*
18. A Soldier. *LR*

I dare be bold thus much to say,
If that my bullets do but play,
You would be hurt so night and day,   15
                         Yet love me.

19. A Barber

I AM a Barber, and I'de have you know,
  A Shaver too, sometimes no mad one though:
The reason why you see me now thus bare,
Is 'cause I always trade against the haire.
But yet I keep a state; Who comes to me,   5
Whos'ere he is, he must uncover'd be.
When I'm at work, I'm bound to find discourse
To no great purpose, of great *Swedens* force,
Of *Witel*, and the Burse, and what 'twill cost
To get that back which was this Summer lost.   10
So fall to praising of his Lordships haire,
Ne'r so deform'd, I swear 'tis *sans* compare:
I tell him that the Kings doth sit no fuller,
And yet his is not half so good a color:
Then reach a pleasing Glass, that's made to lye   15
Like to its Master, most notoriously:
And if he must his Mistress see that day,
I with a Powder send him strait away.

20. Perjury [disdain'd]

A LAS it is too late! I can no more
  Love now, then I have lov'd before:
My *Flora*, 'tis my Fate, not I;
And what you call Contempt, is Destiny.
I am no Monster sure, I cannot show   5
Two hearts; one I already ow:
And I have bound my self with oaths, and vowed
Oftner I fear then Heaven hath ere allowed,

---

19. A Barber. *LR*
20. Perjury [disdain'd.] *LR*   disdain'd *Ed.*: excus'd *LR; see note*

That Faces now should work no more on me,
Then if they could not charm, or I not see.   10
And shall I break them? shall I think you can
Love, if I could, so foul a perjur'd man?
Oh no, 'tis equally impossible that I
Should love again, or you love Perjury.

21. Loves World

1

IN each mans heart that doth begin
  To Love, there's ever fram'd within
A little world, for so I found,
When first my passion reason drown'd.

2

Instead of *Earth* unto this frame,   *Earth*   5
I had a faith was still the same,
For to be right it doth behoove
It be as that, fixt and not move;

3

Yet as the Earth may sometime shake
(For winds shut up will cause a quake)   10
So, often jealousie, and fear,
Stolne into mine, cause tremblings there.

4

My *Flora* was my *Sun*, for as   *Sunne*
One *Sun*, so but one *Flora* was:
All other faces borrowed hence   15
Their light and grace, as stars do thence.

21. Loves World. *FA46*

5

My hopes I call my *Moon*; for they   *Moon*
Inconstant still, were at no stay;
But as my Sun inclin'd to me,
Or more or lesse were sure to be: 20

6

Sometimes it would be full, and then
Oh! too too soon decrease agen;
Eclip'st sometimes, that 't would so fall
There would appear no hope at all.

7

My thoughts 'cause infinite they be   25
Must be those many *Stars* we see;   *Starres*
Of which some wandred at their will,
But most on her were *fixed* still.   *Fixed Planets*

8

My burning flame and hot desire   *Element*
Must be the *Element of Fire*,   *of Fire*
Which hath as yet so secret been   30
That it as that was never seen:

9

No Kitching fire, nor eating flame,
But innocent, hot but in name;
A fire that's starv'd when fed, and gone   35
When too much fewel is laid on.

10

But as it plainly doth appear,
That fire subsists by being near
The Moons bright Orbe, so I beleeve
Ours doth, for hope keeps love alive.   40

11

My fancy was the *Ayre*, most free   *Ayre*
And full of mutability,
Big with Chimera's, vapours here
Innumerable hatcht as there.

12

The *Sea*'s my mind, which calm would be   *Sea*   45
Were it from winds (my passions) free;
But out alas! no *Sea* I find
Is troubled like a Lovers mind.

13

Within it Rocks and Shallows be,
Despair and fond credulity.   50

14

But in this World it were good reason
We did distinguish Time and Season;
Her presence then did make the *Day*,   *Day*
And *Night* shall come when shee's away.   *Night*

15

Long absence in far distant place   55
Creates the *Winter*, and the space   *Winter*
She tarryed with me; well I might
Call it my *Summer* of delight.   *Summer*

16

Diversity of weather came
From what she did, and thence had name;   60
Somtimes sh'would smile, that made it fair;
And when she laught, the Sun shin'd clear.

17

Sometimes sh'would frown, and sometimes weep,
So Clouds and Rain their turns do keep;
Sometimes again sh'would be all ice,   65
Extreamly cold, extreamly nice.

18

But soft my Muse, the world is wide,
And all at once was not describe:
It may fall out some honest Lover
The rest hereafter will discover.   70

21. 53 [*Margin*] Day *supplied*   54 [*Margin*] Night *supplied*

22. The Metamorphosis

THE little Boy, to shew his might and power,
   Turn'd *Io* to a Cow, *Narcissus* to a Flower;
Transform'd *Apollo* to a homely Swain,
And *Jove* himself into a Golden Rain.
   These shapes were tolerable, but by th' Mass   5
   H'as metamorphos'd me into an Ass!

23. To B. C.

WHEN first, fair Mistress, I did see your face,
   I brought, but carried no eyes from the place:
And since that time God *Cupid* hath me led,
In hope that once I shall enjoy your bed.
   But I despair; for now alas I find,   5
   Too late for me, The blind does lead the blind.

24. *Lutea Allison:* *Si sola es, nulla es*

THOUGH you *Diana*-like have liv'd still chast,
   Yet must you not (Fair) die a Maid at last:
The roses on your cheeks were never made
To bless the eye alone, and so to fade;
Nor had the cherries on your lips their being   5
To please no other sense then that of seeing:
You were not made to look on, though that be
A bliss too great for poor mortalitie:
In that alone those rarer parts you have,
To better uses sure wise Nature gave   10
Then that you put them to; to love, to wed,
For *Hymens* rites, and for the Marriage-bed
You were ordain'd, and not to lie alone;
One is no number, till that two be one.

To keep a maidenhead but till fifteen,   15
Is worse then murder, and a greater sin
Then to have lost it in the lawful sheets
With one that should want skill to reap those sweets:
But not to lose't at all, by *Venus*, this,
And by her son, inexpiable is;   20
And should each Female guilty be o'th' crime,
The world would have its end before its time.

25. Upon the first sight of my Lady Seimor

WONDER not much, if thus amaz'd I look,
Since I saw you, I have been Planet-strook:
A Beauty, and so rare I did descrie,
As should I set her forth, you all as I
Would lose your hearts; for he that can   5
Know her and live, he must be more then man.
An apparition of so sweet a Creature,
That credit me, she had not any feature
That did not speak her Angel. But no more
Such heavenly things as these we must adore,   10
Nor prattle of; lest when we do but touch,
Or strive to know, we wrong her too too much.

26. *Non est mortale quod opto:* Upon Mrs. A. L.

THOU thinkst I flatter when thy praise I tell,
But thou dost all Hyperboles excell:
For I am sure thou art no Mortal creature,
But a Divine one thron'd in humane feature.
Thy piety is such, that heaven by merit,   5
If ever any did, thou shouldst inherit:

24. 15 but till] till but *Haz*²
25. Upon the first sight *etc. LR*
26. *Non est mortale etc. LR*

Thy modesty is such, that hadst thou bin
Tempted as *Eve*, thou wouldst have shunn'd her sin:
So lovely fair thou art, that sure Dame Nature
Meant thee the pattern of the Female creature: 10
Besides all this, thy flowing Wit is such,
That were it not in thee, 't had bin too much
For Woman-kind: should Envy look thee ore,
It would confess thus much, if not much more.
I love thee well, yet wish some bad in thee,   15
For sure I am thou art too good for me.

27. Upon A. M.

YEELD not, my Love; but be as coy,
    As if thou knew'st not how to toy:
The Fort resign'd with ease, men Cowards prove
And lazie grow. Let me besiege thy Love,
Let me despair at least three times a day,   5
And take repulses upon each assay:
If I but ask a kiss, straight blush as red
As if I tempted for thy maidenhead:
Contract thy smiles, if that they go too far,
And frown as much as if you meant to mar   10
That Face, which Nature sure intended
Should ne'r be marr'd, because't could ne'r be mended.
Take no corruption from thy Grandame *Eve*;
Rather want faith to save thee, then believe
Too soon: For credit me 'tis true,   15
Men most enjoy, when least they doe.

---

27. Upon A.M. *LR. MSS. (substantive variants recorded in full): Don (a distinct version), L; see note*   Upon A. M.] Sonnet *L: omit Don*   1 not *Σ*: all *LR*   1–2 as coy | . . . toy *Σ*: withall as coy | . . . sport and toy *LR*   2 thou knew'st] ye knew *L*
4 thy *Σ*: my *LR*   6 take repulses] be repuls'd *Don*   8 I] I'd *Don*   9 thy] yoᵣ *L*   go] grow *Don*   10 frown as much as if you meant to mar *Don*: frowne some-tymes as if ye mean't to Marr *L*: let thy frowns be such as threaten war. *LR*   11–12 sure . . . | Should ne'r *Σ*: sure never . . . | Should ere *LR*
13–16 *sic*]   Still quicken my desires, and let them still
                Rather oft hope to have, then have their fill;
                For Love most perfect is when yet it grows,
                And Love pays best which paying ever owes.
                        Don (spelling normalized and punctuation supplied)
14 thee] *omit L*   15 'tis] it's *L*   16 most *L*: most of all *LR*

28. Upon Sir John Laurence's bringing Water over the hills to my Lord Middlesex his House at Wiston

AND is the Water come? sure't cannot be,
It runs too much against Philosophie;
For heavy bodies to the Centre bend,
Light bodies only naturally ascend.
How comes this then to pass? The good Knights skill   5
Could nothing do without the Waters will:
    Then 'twas the Waters love that made it flow,
    For Love will creep where well it cannot go.

29. A Prologue of the Author's to a Masque at Wiston

EXPECT not here a curious River fine,
Our wits are short of that: alas the time!
The neat refined language of the Court
We know not; if we did, our Country sport
Must not be too ambitious: 'tis for Kings,   5
Not for their Subjects, to have such rare things.
Besides though, I confess, *Parnassus* hardly,
Yet *Helicon* this Summer-time is dry:
Our wits were at an ebbe or very low,
And, to say troth, I think they cannot flow.   10
But yet a gracious influence from you
May alter Nature in our Brow-fick crew.
Have patience then, we pray, and sit a while;
And, if a laugh be too much, lend a smile.

28. Upon Sir John Laurence's bringing Water *etc. LR*   Wiston *Ed.*: Witten *LR; see note*
29. A Prologue *etc. LR*   Wiston *Ed.*: Witten *LR; see note*

30. To my Lady E. C. at her going out of England

I MUST confess, when I did part from you,
  I could not force an artificial dew
Upon my cheeks, nor with a gilded phrase
Express how many hundred several ways
My heart was tortur'd, nor with arms across   5
In discontented garbs set forth my loss:
Such loud expressions many times do come
From lightest hearts, great griefs are always dumb;
The shallow Rivers rore, the deep are still.
Numbers of painted words may shew much skill,   10
But little anguish; and a cloudy face
Is oft put on, to serve both time and place:
The blazing wood may to the eye seem great,
But 'tis the fire rak'd up that has the heat,
And keeps it long: True sorrow's like to wine,   15
That which is good does never need a signe.
My eyes were channels far too small to be
Conveyers of such floods of miserie:
And so pray think; or if you'd entertain
A thought more charitable, suppose some strain   20
Of sad repentance had, not long before,
Quite emptied for my sins, that watry store.
So shall you him oblige that still will be
Your servant to his best abilitie.

31. A Song to a Lute

HAST thou seen the Doun ith' air
  when wanton blasts have tost it;
Or the Ship on the Sea,
    when ruder winds have crost it?
Hast thou markt the Crocodiles weeping,   5
  or the Foxes sleeping?

30. To my Lady E. C. *etc. LR*
  31. A Song to a Lute. *The Sad One,* 1659 (*SO*) *Variant printed text:* **LR** (*Poems*)
A Song to a Lute] A Song *LR* (*Poems*)   1 Doun] Down *Haz, LR* (*Poems*), **T**h: dawn
Haz (in *SO*)   1 ith'] in the *LR* (*Poems*)   4 winds] *LR* (*Poems*); waves *LR*
(*SO*); *see note*

Or hast view'd the Peacock in his pride,
   or the Dove by his Bride,
    when he courts for his leachery?
Oh so fickle, oh so vain, oh so false, so false is she!   10

32. Upon my Lady Carliles walking in Hampton-Court garden

Dialogue

T. C.   J. S.

Thom.

Dɪᴅsᴛ thou not find the place inspir'd,
  And flow'rs, as if they had desir'd
No other Sun, start from their beds,
And for a sight steal out their heads?
Heardst thou not musick when she talk't?   5
And didst not find that as she walkt
She threw rare perfumes all about
Such as bean-blossoms newly out,
Or chafed spices give?——

J. S.

I must confesse those perfumes (*Tom*)   10
I did not smell; nor found that from
Her passing by, ought sprung up new:
The flow'rs had all their birth from you;
For I pass't o're the self same walk,
And did not find one single stalk   15
Of any thing that was to bring
This unknown after after-spring.

31. 7 view'd] viewed *LR (Poems)*
    32. Upon my Lady Carliles walking *etc. FA46. MS.: RP19 (subscribed* T. C.; *substantive variants recorded in full)*   Upon . . . J. S.] A Dialogue betw: T: C: and Sʳ: J: S: *MS. Speech-headings throughout* Thom. . . . J. S.] C: . . . S: *MS.*   2 if] though *MS.* 5 when] as *MS.*   6 And didst not] Didst thou not *MS.*   7–8 all about | . . . bean-blossoms newly out] ev'ry where | . . . Arabian gumtrees beare *MS.; see note*   12 sprung] sprang *MS.*   13 had all their birth from] were wholly made by *MS.*   14 For I pass't o're] I'me sure I past *MS.*   15 And did not] Nor could I *MS.*   16–17 was . . . | This unknown after after-spring] came . . . | Newes of this unknowne after=spring *MS; see note*

Thom.

Dull and insensible, could'st see
A thing so near a Deity
Move up and down, and feel no change?   20

J. S.

None, and so great, were alike strange;
I had my Thoughts, but not your way,
All are not born (Sir) to the Bay;
Alas! *Tom*, I am flesh and blood,
And was consulting how I could   25
In spite of masks and hoods descry
The parts deni'd unto the eye;
I was undoing all she wore,
And had she walkt but one turn more,
Eve in her first state had not been   30
More naked, or more plainly seen.

Thom.

'T was well for thee she left the place,
For there's great danger in that face;
But had'st thou view'd her legg and thigh,
And upon that discovery   35
Search't after parts that are more dear,
(As Fancy seldom stops so near)
No time or age had ever seen
So lost a thing as thou hadst been.

J. S.

'Troth in her face I could descry   40
No danger, no divinity.
But since the pillars were so good
On which the lovely fountain stood,
Being once come so near, I think
I should have ventur'd hard to drink.   45

32. 18–20 could'st . . . change?] to . . . change! *MS.*   22–3 way | . . . Bay] wayes
| . . . bayes *MS.; see note*   26 masks and hoods] silkes and lawn *MS.; see note*   31 or]
and *MS.*   32 'T was] 'T is *MS.*   33 For there's *MS.*: There is *FA46; see note*
that] the *MS.*   34 view'd] seene *MS.*   35 upon] after *MS.*   36 Search't
after] Prest on to *MS.*   37 seldom] hardly *MS.*   stops] stepps *MS.*   38 No time
or age] Noe age, noe time *MS.*   39 So lost a thing] A thing soe lost *MS.*
40–9 *from MS.* (*accidentals normalized*): omit *FA46; see headnote in commentary*

What ever fool like me had been
If I'd not done as well as seen?
There to be lost why should I doubt,
Where fools with ease go in and out?

33. Upon T. C. having the P.

TROTH, *Tom*, I must confess I much admire
   Thy water should find passage through the fire:
For fire and water never could agree;
These now by nature have some sympathie:
Sure then his way he forces; for all know   5
The *French* ne'r grants a passage to his foe.
If it be so, his valor I must praise,
That being the weaker, yet can force his ways;
And wish that to his valor he had strength,
That he might drive the fire quite out at length: 10
For (troth) as yet the fire gets the day,
For evermore the water runs away.

34. Love's Burning-glass

WONDERING long how I could harmless see
   Men gazing on those beams that fired me,
At last I found, it was the Chrystal Love
Before my heart, that did the heat improve:
Which by contracting of those scatter'd rayes   5
Into it self, did so produce my blaze.
Now lighted by my Love, I see the same
Beams dazle those, that me are wont t'inflame,
And now I bless my Love, when I do think
By how much I had rather burn then wink.   10
But how much happier were it thus to burn,
If I had liberty to choose my urn!
But since those beams do promise only fire,
This flame shall purge me of the dross, Desire.

33. Upon T. C. having the P. *LR*   Upon T. C. having the P.] Upon T[homas] C[arew]
Having the Pox *Ha*ꝝ², *Th; see note*
34. Love's Burning-glass. *LR*

35. The Miracle

IF thou bee'st Ice, I do admire
How thou couldst set my heart on fire;
Or how thy fire could kindle me,
Thou being Ice, and not melt thee;
But even my flames, light at thy own,   5
Have hardned thee into a stone!
Wonder of Love, that canst fulfill,
Inverting nature thus, thy will;
Making ice another burn,
Whilst it self doth harder turn!   10

36. The deformed Mistress

I KNOW there are some Fools that care
Not for the body, so the face be faire:
Some others too that in a female creature
Respect not beauty, but a comely feature:
And others too, that for those parts in sight   5
Care not so much, so that the rest be right.
Each man his humor hath; and faith 'tis mine
To love that woman which I now define.
First I would have her Wainscot Face and Hand
More wrincled far then any pleited band,   10
That in those furrows, if I'de take the pains,
I might both sow and reap all sorts of grains:
Her Nose I'de have a foot long, not above,
With pimples embroder'd, for those I love;
And at the end a comely Pearl of Snot,   15
Considering whether it should fall or not:
Provided next that half her Teeth be out,
I do not care much if her pretty Snout
Meet with her furrow'd Chin, and both together
Hem in her Lips, as dry as good whit-leather: 20

35. The Miracle. *LR*   5 at] as *Haz, Th*   9 another *Ed.*: one another *LR; see note*

36. The deformed Mistress. *LR.*   *Variant printed text: WI*   deformed] choice of a *WI*
3 others] asses *WI*   6 rest] C *WI; cf. l. 28*   9 Face *WI*: Foot *LR*   11–12 pains
| . . . all sorts of grains] pain | . . . great store of grain *WI*   14 embroder'd] rubied ore
WI; see note   18 I do not care much *Ed.*: Nor do I care much *LR*: I care not *WI*
(*wanting foot in ll. 17–18*)   20 whit- *LR* (*Errata*): white *LR* (*Text*)

One Wall-Eye she shall have; for that's a signe
In other Beasts the best, why not in mine?
Her Neck I'le have to be pure Jet at least,
With yellow Spots enammell'd; and her Breast
Like a Grashoppers wing both thin and lean,　　25
Not to be toucht for dirt, unless swept clean:
As for her Belly, 'tis no matter, so
There be a Belly, and a Cunt below;
Yet if you will, let it be somthing high,
And always let there be a timpanie.　　30
But soft, where am I now! here I should stride,
Lest I fall in, the place must be so wide;
And pass unto her Thighs, which shall be just
Like to an Ants that's scraping in the dust:
Into her Legs I'de have Loves issues fall,　　35
And all her Calf into a gouty Small:
Her Feet both thick, and Eagle like displaid,
The symptoms of a comely handsom Maid.
As for her parts behind, I ask no more,
If they but answer those that are before,　　40
I have my utmost wish; and having so,
Judge whether I am happy, yea or no.

37. Upon L. M. weeping

WHOEVER was the cause your tears were shed,
May these my curses light upon his head:
May he be first in love, and let it be
With a most known and black Deformitie,
Nay far surpass all Witches that have been　　5
Since our first parents taught us how to sin!
Then let this Hag be coy, and he run mad
For that which no man else would ere have had:
And in this fit may he commit the thing
May him impenitent to th' gallows bring!　　10

36. 28 a Cunt below *Ed.* and *WI* (a thing below): A C— also *Haz*: ────── *LR, Th*
37. Upon L. M. weeping. *LR*　　L. M.] L[ady] M[iddlesex] *Haz*

Then might he for one tear his pardon have,
But want that single grief his life to save!
And being dead, may he at heaven venter,
But for the guilt of this one fact ne'r enter.

38. Detraction execrated

1

THOU vermin Slander, bred in abject minds
  Of thoughts impure, by vile tongues animate,
Canker of conversation! couldst thou find
Nought but our Love, whereon to shew thy hate?
Thou never wert, when we two were alone;   5
What canst thou witness then? thy base dull aid
Was useless in our conversation,
Where each meant more, then could by both be said.

2

Whence hadst thou thy intelligence, from earth?
That part of us ne'r knew that we did love: 10
Or from the air? Our gentle sighs had birth
From such sweet raptures as to joy did move:
Our thoughts, as pure as the chaste Mornings breath,
When from the Nights cold arms it creeps away,
Were cloth'd in words, and Maidens blush that hath   15
More purity, more innocence then they.

3

Nor from the water couldst thou have this tale;
No briny tear hath furrowed her smooth cheek;
And I was pleas'd: I pray what should he aile
That had her Love, for what else could he seek?   20
We shortned days to moments by Loves art,
Whilst our two souls in amorous extasie
Perceiv'd no passing time, as if a part
Our Love had been of still Eternity.

38. Detraction execrated. *LR. Division into octaves supplied*

4

Much less couldst have it from the purer fire: 25
Our heat exhales no vapor from course sense,
Such as are hopes, or fears, or fond desires;
Our mutual Love it self did recompence.
Thou hast no correspondencie in heaven,
And th'elemental world thou seest is free: 30
Whence hadst thou then this talking, Monster? even
From hell, a harbor fit for it and thee.

5

Curst be th'officious Tongue that did address
Thee to her ears, to ruine my content:
May it one minute taste such happiness,   35
Deserving lose't, unpittied it lament!
I must forbear her sight, and so repay
In grief, those hours Joy shortned to a dram:
Each minute I will lengthen to a day,
And in one year outlive *Methusalem*.   40

39. On King Richard the third, who lies buried under Leicester bridge

WHAT meanes this watry Canop' bout thy bed,
    These streaming vapours o're thy sinfull head,
Are they thy teares? alasse in vaine they're spilt,
'Tis now too late to wash away thy guilt:
Thou still art bloudy *Richard*, and 'tis much,   5
The water should not from thy very touch,
Turne quite *Egyptian*, and the scaly frye
Feare to be kild, and so thy carkise flye.
Bathe, bathe thy fill, and take thy pleasure now
In this cold bed, yet guilty *Richard* know   10
Judgement must come, and water then will be
A Heaven to thee in hellish miserye.

38. 25 couldst *Ed.*: could *LR*   29 correspondencie] correspondence *Haz*
36 lose't *Haz, Th*: lost *LR (Text)*: loos'd *LR (Errata)*
    39. On King Richard the third, *etc. A11 (subscribed* Sʳ John Suckling). *Variant MS.:*
H17 (substantive variants recorded in full)   who . . . bridge] supposed to be buried under the
bridge at Leycester *H17*   1 Canop'] Canopy *H17*   thy] this *H17*   2 thy *H17*:
they *A11*   sinfull *A11 (margin)*, *H17*: guilty *A11 (text)*   3 they're] th'are *H17*
4 too *H17*: to *A11*   11 will] would *H17*   12 in] middst *H17*

SECULAR POEMS

(c. 1632–1637)

40. Against Fruition [I]

1

Stay here fond youth and ask no more, be wise,
Knowing too much long since lost Paradise;
The vertuous joyes thou hast, thou would'st should still
Last in their pride; and would'st not take it ill
If rudely from sweet dreams (and for a toy) 5
Th'wert wak't? he wakes himself that does enjoy.

2

Fruition adds no new wealth, but destroyes,
And while it pleases much the palate, cloyes;
Who thinks he shall be happyer for that,
As reasonably might hope he should grow fat 10
By eating to a Surfet: this once past,
What relishes? even kisses loose their tast.

3

Urge not 'tis necessary, alas! we know
The homeliest thing which mankind does is so;
The World is of a vast extent we see, 15
And must be peopled; Children then must be;
So must bread too; but since there are enough
Born to the drudgery, what need we plough?

4

Women enjoy'd (what s'ere before th'ave been)
Are like Romances read, or sights once seen: 20

40. Against Fruition [I.] *FA46. MSS.: Ash4, Cran2, DonD (from Waller), P (from FA46), RP16 (ll. 1–19 only). Variant Printed Texts: SW (from Ash4), Waller, DonD, RP16, and Waller contain alternating stanzas 'for fruition' by Waller (q.v. in Appendix A.i.1)* I *Ed.:* omit *FA46* 6 Th'wert *Σ (Cran2 corrected from* Th'art): Tho'wert *FA46*: Thou wert *Waller* (omit wert *eds. 1–2; see Commentary*): Thou not [awak't] *DonD* 8 pleases *Ash4, Cran2, SW*: pleaseth *Σ* 10 should *Ash4, Cran2, SW*: might *Σ* 16 then *Ash4, Cran2, RP16, SW*: there *DonD, FA46, P, Waller; see note* 19 what s'ere *Ash4, Cran2*: whatsoe're *RP16, SW*: what e're *DonD, FA46, Waller* (what e're[tofore] *DonD, Waller*) th'have *Cran2, SW*: t'have *Ash4, FA46*: they have *DonD, P, Waller*: hath *RP16* 20 sights] Plays *Ash4, P, SW*: Scenes *DonD, Waller*

Fruition's dull, and spoils the Play much more
Than if one read or knew the plot before;
'Tis expectation makes a blessing dear:
It were not heaven, if we knew what it were.

5

And as in Prospects we are there pleas'd most   25
Where somthing keeps the eye from being lost,
And leaves us room to guesse, so here restraint
Holds up delight, that with excesse would faint.
They who know all the wealth they have, are poor,
Hee's onely rich that cannot tell his store.   30

41. Against Fruition [II]

FYE upon hearts that burn with mutual fire;
    I hate two minds that breath but one desire;
Were I to curse th'unhallow'd sort of men,
I'de wish them to love, and be lov'd agen.
Love's a *Camelion*, that lives on meer ayre,   5
And surfets when it comes to grosser fare:
'Tis petty Jealousies, and little fears,
Hopes joyn'd with doubts, and joyes with *April* tears,
That crowns our Love with pleasures: these are gone
When once we come to full *Fruition*;   10
Like waking in a morning, when all night
Our fancy hath been fed with true delight.
Oh! what a stroke 'twould be! Sure I should die,
Should I but hear my mistresse once say, I.
That monster Expectation feeds too high   15
For any Woman e're to satisfie:
And no brave Spirit ever car'd for that
Which in Down-beds with ease he could come at.
Shee's but an honest whore that yeelds, although
She be as cold as ice, as pure as snow: 20
He that enjoys her hath no more to say
But keep us Fasting if you'l have us pray.

40. 24 It *Ash4, Cran2, SW*: Heaven *Σ*
41. Against Fruition [II.] *FA46*   II *Ed.: omit FA46*

Then fairest Mistresse, hold the power you have,
By still denying what we still do crave:
In keeping us in hopes strange things to see   25
That never were, nor are, nor e're shall be.

42. To Mr. Davenant for Absence

WONDER not if I stay not here,
    Hurt Lovers (like to wounded Deer)
Must shift the place; for standing still
Leaves too much time to know our ill.
Where there is a Traytor eye   5
That lets in from th'enemy
All that may supplant an heart,
'Tis time the Chief should use some Art:
Who parts the object from the sence,
Wisely cuts off intelligence.   10
O how quickly must men die,
Should they stand all Loves Battery!
Persinda's eyes great mischief do,
So does (we know) the Canon too;
But men are safe at distance still: 15
Where they reach not, they cannot kill.
Love is a fit, and soon is past,
Ill dyet onely makes it last;
Who is still looking, gazing ever,
Drinks wine i'th' very height o'th' Fever.   20

43. Against Absence

MY whining Lover, what needs all
    These vows of life Monastical?
Despairs, retirements, jealousies,
And subtile sealing up of eyes?

---

42. To Mr. Davenant for Absence. *FA46. MS.: Cran2 (substantive variants recorded in full)* To ... Absence] *omit Cran2*   5 Traytor] traitors *Cran2*   6 th'enemy] the Enemy *Cran2*   11 must men *Cran2* (Men): men must *FA46*   14 does *Cran2*: do *FA46; see note*   20 o'th'] of *Cran2*

43. Against Absence. *FA46. MSS.: Ash3, Cran2, RP11*   Against Absence] *omit Ash3, Cran2*

Come, come, be wise, return again,   5
A finger burnt's as great a pain;
And the same Physick, self same art
Cures that, would cure a flaming heart,
Would'st thou whiles yet the fire is in
But hold it to the fire again.   10
If you (Dear Sir) the plague have got,
What matter is't whether or not
They let you in the same house lie,
Or carry you abroad to die?
He whom the plague, or Love once takes,   15
Every Room a Pest-House makes.
Absence were good if't were but sence
That onely held th'Intelligence:
Pure love alone no hurt would do.
But love is love, and magick too;   20
Brings a mistresse thousand miles,
And the sleight of locks beguiles,
Makes her entertain thee there,
And the same time your Rival here;
And (oh! the divel) that she should   25
Say finer things now then she would;
So nobly Fancy doth supply
What the dull sence lets fall and die.
Beauty like mans old enemy's known
To tempt him most when hee's alone: 30
The ayre of some wild o'regrown wood
Or pathlesse Grove is the Boyes food.
Return then back, and feed thine eye,
Feed all thy sences, and feast high.
Spare dyet is the cause Love lasts,   35
For Surfets sooner kill than Fasts.

43. 9 whiles *Ash3, Cran2* : whilst *FA46, RP11*   18 held *Cran2, RP11* : holds *Ash3,*
FA46; see note   21 thousand *Σ* : a thousand *FA46*   22 locks *Σ* : looks *FA46*

44. [To his Rival I]

M Y dearest Rival, least our Love
   Should with excentrique motion move,
Before it learn to go astray,
Wee'l teach and set it in a way,
And such directions give unto't,   5
That it shall never wander foot.
Know first then, we will serve as true
For one poor smile, as we would do
If we had what our higher flame,
Or our vainer wish could frame.   10
Impossible shall be our hope;
And Love shall onely have his scope
To joyn with Fancy now and then,
And think what Reason would condemn:
And on these grounds wee'l love as true,   15
As if they were most sure t'ensue;
And chastly for these things wee'l stay,
As if to morrow were the day.
Mean time we two will teach our hearts
In Lovers burdens bear their parts: 20
Thou first shalt sigh, and say shee's fair,
And I'le still answer, past compare;
Thou shalt set out each part o'th' face,
While I extol each little grace;
Thou shalt be ravisht at her wit,   25
And I, that she so governs it;
Thou shalt like well that hand, that eye,
That lip, that look, that majesty;
And in good language them adore:
While I want words, and do it more.   30
Yea we will sit and sigh a while,
And with soft thoughts some time beguil;
But straight again break out and praise
All we had done before, new-waies.
Thus will we do till paler death   35
Come with a warrant for our breath;

44. [To his Rival I.] *FA46. Title supplied; see note. MS.: P* (*from FA46*)   5 direc-
tions] instructions *P*   19 time] while *P*   20 Lovers *Ed.*: Loves *FA46*

And then whose fate shall be to die
First of us two, by Legacy
Shall all his store bequeath, and give
His love to him that shall survive;   40
For no one stock can ever serve
To love so much as shee'l deserve.

45. To his Rival [II]

Now we have taught our Love to know
    That it must creep where't cannot go,
And be for once content to live,
Since here it cannot have to thrive;
It will not be amisse t'enquire   5
What fuel should maintain this fire:
For fires do either flame too high,
Or where they cannot flame, they die.
First then (my half but better heart)
Know this must wholy be her part: 10
(For thou and I, like Clocks, are wound
Up to the height, and must move round;)
She then by still denying what
We fondly crave, shall such a rate
Set on each trifle, that a kisse   15
Shall come to be the utmost blisse.
Where sparks and fire do meet with tinder,
Those sparks meer fire will still engender:
To make this good, no debt shall be
From service or fidelity;   20
For she shall ever pay that score,
By onely bidding us do more:
So (though she still a niggard be)
In graceing, where none's due, shee's free.
The favors she shall cast on us,   25
(Least we should grow presumptuous)
Shall not with too much love be shown,
Nor yet the common way still done;

45. To his Rival [II.] *FA46*   II *Ed.: omit FA46*

But ev'ry smile and little glance
Shall look half lent, and half by chance: 30
The Ribbon, Fan, or Muffe that she
Would should be kept by thee or me,
Should not be giv'n before too many,
But neither thrown to's when there's any;
So that her self should doubtful be   35
Whether 'twere fortune flung't, or she.
She shall not like the thing we do
Sometimes, and yet shall like it too;
Nor any notice take at all
Of what, we gone, she would extol: 40
Love she shall feed, but fear to nourish,
For where fear is, love cannot flourish;
Yet live it must, nay must and shall,
While *Desdemona* is at all:
But when shee's gone, then Love shall die,   45
And in her grave buried lie.

46. To a Lady that forbidd to love before Company

WHAT noe more favours, not A Ribbon more,
       Noe fanne, nor muffe to hold as heretofore?
Must all those little blisses then be left,
And every kisse wee have become a theft?
May we not looke our selves into a Traunce,   5
Let our soules parly at our eyes, not glaunce,
Not touch the hand, nor by soft wringing there
Whisper a love that none but eyes can heare?
Not free a sighe, A sighe that's there for you,
Deare must I love you, yet not love you too?   10
Bee not so nice Faire, sooner shall they Trace
The featherd Travellers from place to place,

45. 33 too] to *FA46*

46. To a Lady *etc. H17* (*subscribed* S^r J: Suckling). *Variant printed text: LR* (*substantive variants recorded in full*)   2 Noe] Not *LR*   3 those] the *LR*   4 every kisse wee have become a] what was once Loves gift, become our *LR*   6 Let] Teach *LR*   7 nor] not *LR*   8 none but eyes] only yes *LR*   10 yet] and *LR*   11 Bee not so nice Faire,] Be wise, nice, fair; For *LR*   12 Travellers] Choristers *LR; see note*

By prints they leave i'th' Ayre, and sooner say
By what right line the last starre made his way
That fledd from heaven to us, then guesse or know   15
How our loves first did spring, or how they grow;
Love is all spirit, fayries sooner may
Bee taken Tardy when they night-tricks play
Then wee; we are too safe I feare, that rather
Would they could finde us both in bedd together!   20

47. The Invocation

1

Y E juster Powers of Love and Fate,
 Give me the reason why
  A Lover crost
  And all hopes lost
 May not have leave to dye.   5

2

It is but just, and Love needs must
Confess it is his part,
  When he doth spie
  One wounded lie,
 To pierce the others heart.   10

3

But yet if he so cruel be
To leave one breast to hate,
  If I must live
  And thus survive,
 How far more cruel's Fate?   15

---

46. 13 By *LR*: The *H17* leave] make *LR* i'th' Ayre] In th'air *LR* 15 us]
earth *LR; see note* or] to *LR* 19 safe I feare, that] dull and lumpish *LR*
 47. The Invocation. *LR* 8 he *Ed.*: she *LR* 12 leave *Ed.*: have *LR; see note*

4

In this same state I find too late
I am; and here's the grief:
    Cupid can cure,
    Death heal I'm sure,
  Yet neither sends relief.   20

5

To love, or die, beg onely I,
Just Powers some end me give;
    And Traitor-like
    Thus force me not
  Without a heart to live.   25

48. The Expostulation [I]

1

TELL me ye juster Deities,
  That pitty Lovers miseries,
Why should my own unworthiness
Fright me to seek my happiness?
It is as natural, as just,   5
Him for to love, whom needs I must:
All men confess that Love's a fire,
Then who denies it to aspire?

2

Tell me, if thou wert Fortunes thrall,
Wouldst thou not raise thee from the fall?   10
Seek only to orelook thy state
Whereto thou art condemn'd by Fate?
Then let me love my *Coridon*,
And by Love's leave, him love alone:
For I have read of Stories oft,   15
That Love hath wings and soars aloft.

47. 21 love *Ed.*: live *LR*
48. The Expostulation [I.] *LR*   I *Ed.: omit LR*

3

Then let me grow in my desire,
Though I be martyr'd in that fire:
For grace it is enough for me
But only to love such as he: 20
And never shall my thoughts be base,
Though luckless, yet without disgrace:
Then let him that my Love shall blame,
Or clip Loves wings, or quench Loves flame.

49. [The Expostulation II]

1

UNJUST Decrees! that do at once exact,
From such a Love as worthy hearts should own,
So wild a passion,
And yet so tame a presence
As holding no proportion   5
Changes into impossible obedience:

2

Let it suffice, that neither I do love
In such a calm observance, as to weigh
Each word I say,
And each examin'd look t'approve   10
That towards her doth move,
Without so much of fire
As might in time kindle into desire;

3

Or give me leave to burst into a flame,
And at the scope of my unbounded will   15
Love her my fill;
No superscriptions of Fame,
Of honor, or good name,
No thought but to improve
The gentle and quick approaches of my Love.   20

48. 21 And *Ed.*: For *LR*
49. [The Expostulation II.] *LR. Title supplied* (Song *LR: see note*)

4

But thus to throng and overlade a soul
With Love, and then to leave a room for fear,
    That shall all that controll,
    What is it but to rear
  Our passions and our hopes on high,   25
    That thence they may descrie
The noblest way how to despair and die?

50. Sonnet I

1

D O'ST see how unregarded now
    that piece of beauty passes?
There was a time when I did vow
    to that alone;
    but mark the fate of faces: 5
That red and white works now no more on me
Then if it could not charm or I not see.

2

And yet the face continues good,
    and I have still desires,
Am still the self same flesh and blood,   10
    as apt to melt
    and suffer from those fires;
Oh! some kind power unriddle where it lies,
Whether my heart be faulty, or her eyes?

3

She every day her Man doth kill,   15
    and I as often die;

---

50. Sonnet I. *FA46. MSS.: A31, Dx4, Dx42, EP2, O2. Variant* printed texts: *AC,*
W&D61, WI
    Sonnet I] Sonnet by Sir John Suckling *Dx4 (later hand)*: A Song *WI*: An Amorous Catch
W&D: Loves Ne plus Ultra *EP2*: Upon the withered Roses of his quondam Mistresses
cheeks *AC*: *omit A31, Dx42, O2*   1 Do'st] Look *WI*: To *EP2*: I *W&D61*   14 my
heart be faulty, or her eyes] her face be guilty, or my eyes *A31, Dx4*   15 doth *Σ*: does
A31, FA46

Neither her power then, nor my will
　　　　can question'd be,
　　　what is the mystery?
Sure Beauties Empires, like to greater States　　　　20
Have certain periods set, and hidden fates.

51. Sonnet II

1

O F thee (kind boy) I ask no red and white
　　　　to make up my delight,
　　　no odd becomming graces,
Black eyes, or little know-not-whats, in faces;
Make me but mad enough, give me good store　　　　5
Of Love, for her I Court,
　　　　　　　I ask no more,
'Tis love in love that makes the sport.

2

There's no such thing as that we beauty call,
　　　　it is meer cousenage all;　　　　10
　　　for though some long ago
Like't certain colours mingled so and so,
That doth not tie me now from chusing new;
If I a fancy take
　　　　　　　To black and blue,　　　　15
That fancy doth it beauty make.

3

'Tis not the meat, but 'tis the appetite
　　　　makes eating a delight,
　　　and if I like one dish
More then another, that a Pheasant is;　　　　20

51. Sonnet II. *FA46. MSS.: Dx4, Dx42 (subscribed* Sr John Suckling*), P (from FA46).
Variant printed texts: SMA, WI, WI62a (from WI55), WI62b (see note)*
　　Sonnet II] Sonnet by Sir John Suckling *Dx4 (later hand)*: A Song *WI55*: Beauty deny'd
WI62a: No Beauty in Women *WI62b*　　1 thee] the *SMA, WI, WI62b*

What in our watches, that in us is found,
So to the height and nick
                    We up be wound,
No matter by what hand or trick.

52. Sonnet III

1

OH! for some honest Lovers ghost,
    Some kind unbodied post
    Sent from the shades below.
    I strangely long to know
Whether the nobler Chaplets wear,   5
Those that their mistresse scorn did bear,
    Or those that were us'd kindly.

2

For what-so-e're they tell us here
    To make those sufferings dear,
    'Twill there I fear be found,   10
    That to the being crown'd,
T'have lov'd alone will not suffice,
Unlesse we also have been wise,
    And have our Loves enjoy'd.

3

What posture can we think him in,   15
    That here unlov'd agen
    Departs, and's thither gone
    Where each sits by his own?
Or how can that *Elizium* be
Where I my Mistresse still must see   20
    Circled in others Armes?

4

For there the Judges all are just,
    And *Sophonisba* must
    Be his whom she held dear;
    Not his who lov'd her here: 25

51. 21 watches, that . . . found] Matches, may . . . bound *SMA*
52. Sonnet III. *FA46*

The sweet *Philoclea* since she dy'de
Lies by her *Pirocles* his side,
     Not by *Amphialus*.

5

Some Bayes (perchance) or Myrtle bough
     For difference crowns the brow   30
     Of those kind souls that were
     The noble Martyrs here;
And if that be the onely odds,
(As who can tell) ye kinder Gods,
     Give me the Woman here.   35

53. [Love's Sanctuary]

1

THE crafty Boy that had full oft assay'd
     To peirce my stubborn and resisting Brest,
(But still the bluntness of his Darts betrayed)
Resolv'd at last of setting up his rest
     Either my wilde unruly heart to tame,   5
     Or quit his Godhead, and his Bow disclaim.

2

So all his lovely Looks, his pleasing Fires;
All his sweet Motions, all his taking Smiles;
All that awakes, all that inflames Desires;
All that by force Commands, all that beguiles: 10
     He does into one pair of Eyes convey,
     And there begs leave that he himself may stay.

3

And then he brings me, where his ambush lay,
Secure and careless to a stranger Land;
And never warning me, which was foul play,   15
Does make me close by all this Beauty stand,

---

53. [Love's Sanctuary.] *LR. MS.: A23 (substantive variants recorded in full)*
Love's Sanctuary *Ed.*: Song *LR*: omit *MS.*   10 by force *MS.*: by sweet *LR (Text)*:
sweetly *LR (Errata); see note*   11 into] omit *MS.*   13 then *MS.*: there *LR*
his] this *MS.*

Where first struck dead, I did at last recover,
To know that I might onely live to love her.

4

So I'll be sworn I do, and do confess
The blinde Lads power, whilst he inhabits there;   20
But I'll be even with him neretheless,
If ere I chance to meet with him elswhere.
    If other eyes invite the Boy to tarry,
    I'll flie to hers as to a Sanctuary.

54. [Loves Feast]

1

I PRAY thee spare me, gentle Boy,
Presse me no more for that slight toy,
That foolish trifle of an heart;
I swear it will not do its part,
Though thou dost thine, employ'st thy power and art.   5

2

For through long custom it has known
The little secrets, and is grown
Sullen and wise, will have its will,
And like old Hawks pursues that still
That makes least sport, flies onely where't can kill.   10

53. 21 him]+ fort *MS.*   neretheless *LR (Errata), MS.:* nevertheless *LR (Text)*   23–4
If . . . | I'll flie to hers] All . . . | To hers he flys *MS.; see note*
24+ *Two additional stanzas in A23*:
                    Alas god knows I feard no forraine face
                    But hauing all the lookes at home wth stood
                    Thought I might safely haue presumed to go
                    Where no eys language could be understood
                        But when my heart did wth her eys confer.
                        I found there needed no Interpreter

                    full soon shee lookt; and full as soon my heart
                    Did make her offer of it selfe and mee
                    And in a silent conference Impart
                    How mu^ch I would her humble servant bee
                        My life or death depends on her reply
                        Happy that shee must bidd me liue or die
54. [Loves Feast.] *FA46. MSS.: Ash3, Cran2*
Loves Feast *Ed.:* Song *FA46: omit MSS.*

3

Some youth that has not made his story,
Will think perchance the pain's the glory,
And mannerly sit out Loves Feast;
I shall be carving of the best,
Rudely call for the last course 'fore the rest.   15

4

And oh! when once that course is past,
How short a time the Feast doth last!
Men rise away, and scarce say grace,
Or civilly once thank the face
That did invite, but seek another place.   20

55. [Loves Offence]

1

I F when Don *Cupids* dart
  Doth wound a heart,
      we hide our grief
      and shun relief,
The smart increaseth on that score;   5
For wounds unsearcht but ranckle more.

2

Then if we whine, look pale,
And tell our tale,
      men are in pain
      for us again;   10
So, neither speaking doth become
The Lovers state, nor being dumb.

---

54. 13 sit] fit *Hax, Th*
55. [Loves Offence.] *FA46. Title supplied. MSS.: O2, P (from FA46*   5 smart
increaseth on that score] paine increaseth of that lore *O2*

3

When this I do descry,
Then thus think I,
    love is the fart   15
    of every heart:
It pains a man when 'tis kept close,
And others doth offend, when 'tis let loose.

56. [Disdain]

1

To what end serve the promises
    And oaths lost in the air?
Since all your proffer'd services
    To me but tortures are.

2

Another now enjoys my Love,   5
    Set you your heart at rest:
Think not me from my faith to move,
    Because you faith protest.

3

The man that doth possess my heart,
    Has twice as much perfection,   10
And does excell you in desert,
    As much as in affection.

4

I cannot break so sweet a bond,
    Unless I prove untrue:
Nor can I ever be so fond,   15
    To prove untrue for you.

56. [Disdain.] *LR (a translation of* Desdain, *q.v. in Appendix A.vi.1). Title and indentation of ll. 2, 4 of each stanza supplied*
Disdain *Ed.*: English'd thus by the Author *LR*

5

Your attempts are but in vain,
  (To tell you is a favor:)
For things that may be, rack your brain;
  Then lose not thus your labor.   20

57. Profer'd Love rejected

1

I T is not four years ago,
    I offered Forty crowns
To lie with her a night or so:
    She answer'd me in frowns.

2

Not two years since, she meeting me   5
    Did whisper in my eare,
That she would at my service be
    If I contented were.

3

I told her I was cold as snow
    And had no great desire;   10
But should be well content to go
    To Twenty, but no higher.

4

Some three moneths since or thereabout,
    She that so coy had bin,
Bethought herself and found me out,   15
    And was content to sin.

5

I smil'd at that, and told her I
    Did think it something late,
And that I'de not repentance buy
    At above half the rate.   20

57. Profer'd Love rejected. *LR (a translation of* A Phillis, *q.v. in Appendix A.vi.2).
Indentation of ll. 2, 4 of each stanza supplied*

6

This present morning early she
 Forsooth came to my bed,
And *gratis* there she offered me
 Her high-priz'd maidenhead.

7

I told her that I thought it then   25
 Far dearer then I did,
When I at first the Forty crowns
 For one nights lodging bid.

58. [The constant Lover]

Sir J. S.

1

O<small>UT</small> upon it, I have lov'd
 Three whole days together;
And am like to love three more,
 If it hold fair weather.

2

Time shall moult away his wings   5
 Ere he shall discover
In the whole wide world agen
 Such a constant Lover.

---

58. [The constant Lover.] *LR. Title supplied. MSS.: Dx4, Eg9, F339, Harv7, HL, O2 (generally corrected to agree with LR; only uncorrected readings are noted). Variant printed texts: AC84 (later ed. of Wind-D), OD, Wind-D, W&D*

The constant Lover *Ed.*: A Song by Sir John Suckling *W&D*: A Song with the Answer *OD*: Song *AC84, Wind-D*: Sonetto *Eg9: omit Σ* (*LR headed* Sir J. S., *as here*) 2 + And though I never lov'd before, *AC84, Wind-D* 3 am like to] perchance might *W&D*: I thinke shall *O2* 4 hold *Σ*: prove *LR* 5 moult] melt *F339, Harv7, O2, W&D* away his wings] his wings away *Harv7, O2, W&D* (wing) 6 shall] (*Dx4, F339, HL, LR*): can *AC84, Eg9, Harv7, O2, OD, Wind-D, W&D; see note* 6 + Among an hundred thousand men, *AC84, Wind-D* 7 In] Nay in *AC84, Wind-D*: Through *Dx4, Eg9, F339* agen] about *Dx4, F339: omit Eg9*

3

But a pox upon't, no praise
    There is due at all to me: 10
Love with me had made no stay,
    Had it any been but she.

4

Had it any been but she
    And that very very Face,
There had been at least ere this   15
    A dozen dozen in her place.

59. [The Answer]

Sir Toby Matthews

1

S AY, but did you love so long?
    In troth I needs must blame you:
Passion did your Judgment wrong,
    And want of Reason shame you.

58. 9 But] Yet *F339, OD*   a pox *Σ*: the spite *HL, LR*: out *AC84, Wind-D*: now
I think *OD; see note on Text*   upon't *Σ*: upont's *HL*: upon all *Eg9*: on't is *LR*
10 There is due at all *Σ*: Here . . . *HL*: omit There or Here *LR*: none at all is due *Eg9*: can
at all be due *AC84, OD, Wind-D*   11 Love with me had made no stay] For I had not
loued an houre *Harv7*   stay *Σ*: staies *LR*   11+ But had quickly fled away *AC84,
Wind-D*   13 Had it any been but she] Had it not been she alone *Harv7, HL; see note*
14 very very *Σ*: very *LR; see note*   15 There had been] I had had *Eg9*   at least] long
time *O2, W&D*: omit *AC84, Eg9, OD, Wind-D*   ere] by *Dx4, F339, HL*   this] this with
me *AC84, OD, Wind-D*: now *Eg9*   15+ For to court my company, *AC84, Wind-D*
    59. [The Answer.] *LR. MSS. and variant printed texts: as for* The constant Lover, *but
HL omits*
    The Answer *Eg9, Harv7, OD*: The Answer by the same Author *W&D*: An Answer *O2*:
An Answer to this *Dx4*: Her Answer *AC84, Wind-D*: responsus *F339*: omit *LR* (headed
Sir Toby Matthews, *as here*)   2 In] omit *Dx4, F339, Harv7, OD*   troth] truth *AC84,
OD, Wind-D*: sooth *O2, W&D*: fayth *Eg9, Harv7*   2, 4 you] yee *F339, W&D*
3 Passion] patience *Dx4, F339*   Judgment] beauty *OD*   3+ Nay, betray'd your
flattering Tongue, *AC84*   4 And *Σ*: Or *Eg9, LR*: As [want of wit doth shame you]
AC84, Wind-D

2

Truth, Times fair and witty Daughter,   5
    Quickly did discover,
You were a Subject fit for laughter,
    And more Fool then Lover.

3

Yet you needs must merit praise
    For your constant Folly,   10
Since you doted three whole dayes:
    Were you not melancholy?

4

She to whom you were so true,
    And that very very Face,
Puts each minute such as you   15
    A dozen dozen to disgrace.

60. The careless Lover

1

NEVER believe me if I love,
    Or know what 'tis or mean to prove;
And yet in faith I lye, I do,
And she's extremely handsom too:
    She's fair, she's wondrous fair,   5
    But I care not who know it,
    Ere I'le die for love, I'le fairly forgo it.

59. 6 Quickly did *Σ*: Quickly can *Eg9* : Shortly shall *LR*   7 You *Σ*: Y' *LR*   were *Σ*: are *Eg9, LR*   7 + Seeing your brains are now grown softer *AC84, Wind-D*   9 Yet *Σ*: But *LR*   you needs must *Dx4, F339, O2, W&D*: I grant you *AC84, Eg9, Harv7* (doe I), *LR, OD, Wind-D; see note*   11 Since you doted] Since that you lov'd *O2, W&D*: Since you loved *Dx4, F339*: Pray, since that you did [love so long] *Eg9*   11 + As your learned Legend says, *AC84, Wind-D*   12 + She to whome you were soe trew | With her witt and power | Scornes and Laughs at such as you | A Thousand in one houer *Harv7*   13 were *Σ*: are *Eg9*: prov'd *LR*: lov'd *O2, W&D*   14 very very] very *AC84, Wind-D*   14 + Gives you truly all your due *AC84, Wind-D*   15 minute] moment *O2*   16 to] in *Harv7*
    60. The careless Lover. *LR. Refrain condensed to* She's fair, *etc. in stanzas 2–6 of LR*
6 *etc.* know *Ed.* : knows *LR; see note*

2

This heat of hope, or cold of fear,
My foolish heart could never bear:
One sigh imprison'd ruines more   10
Then earthquakes have done heretofore:
   She's fair, she's wondrous fair,
   But I care not who know it,
   Ere I'le die for love, I'le fairly forgo it.

3

When I am hungry I do eat,   15
And cut no fingers 'stead of meat;
Nor with much gazing on her face
Do ere rise hungry from the place:
   She's fair, she's wondrous fair,
   But I care not who know it,   20
   Ere I'le die for love, I'le fairly forgo it.

4

A gentle round fill'd to the brink
To this and t'other Friend I drink;
And when 'tis nam'd anothers health,
I never make it hers by stealth: 25
   She's fair, she's wondrous fair,
   But I care not who know it,
   Ere I'le die for love, I'le fairly forgo it.

5

Black-Friars to me, and old *Whitehall*,
Is even as much as is the fall   30
Of fountains or a pathless grove,
And nourishes as much my love:
   She's fair, she's wondrous fair,
   But I care not who know it,
   Ere I'le die for love, I'le fairly forgo it.   35

6

I visit, talk, do business, play,
And for a need laugh out a day:

60. 31 or *Ed.*: on *LR*

Who does not thus in *Cupids* school,
He makes not Love, but plays the Fool:
    She's fair, she's wondrous fair,   40
    But I care not who know it,
    Ere I'le die for love, I'le fairly forgo it.

61. Song

1

HONEST Lover whosoever,
  If in all thy love there ever
Was one wav'ring thought, if thy flame
Were not still even, still the same:
      Know this,   5
    Thou lov'st amisse,
    And to love true,
Thou must begin again, and love anew.

2

If when she appears i'th' room,
Thou dost not quake, and art struck dumb,   10
And in striving this to cover
Dost not speak thy words twice over,
      Know this,
    Thou lov'st amisse,
    And to love true,   15
Thou must begin again, and love anew.

3

If fondly thou dost not mistake,
And all defects for graces take,
Perswad'st thy self that jeasts are broken,
When she hath little or nothing spoken,   20
      Know this,
    Thou lov'st amisse,
    And to love true,
Thou must begin again, and love anew.

61. Song. *FA46. MS.: P (from FA46)*   9 appears i'th'] comes into the *P*

4

If when thou appear'st to be within,   25
Thou lett'st not men ask and ask agen,
And when thou answer'st, if it be
To what was askt thee, properly,
   Know this,
    Thou lov'st amisse,   30
   And to love true,
Thou must begin again, and love anew.

5

If when thy stomack calls to eat,
Thou cutt'st not fingers 'steed of meat,
And with much gazing on her face   35
Dost not rise hungry from the place,
   Know this,
    Thou lov'st amisse,
   And to love true,
Thou must begin again, and love anew.   40

6

If by this thou dost discover
That thou art no perfect Lover,
And desiring to love true,
Thou dost begin to love anew:
   Know this,   45
    Thou lov'st amisse,
   And to love true,
Thou must begin again, and love anew.

62. Loving and Beloved

1

THERE never yet was honest man
  That ever drove the trade of love;
 It is impossible, nor can
 Integrity our ends promove:
For Kings and Lovers are alike in this   5
That their chief art in reigne dissembling is.

61. 41–8 *omit* P   **62.** Loving and Beloved. *FA46*

2

Here we are lov'd, and there we love:
 Good nature now and passion strive
Which of the two should be above,
 And laws unto the other give.   10
So we false fire with art sometimes discover,
And the true fire with the same art do cover.

3

What Rack can Fancy find so high?
 Here we must Court, and here ingage,
Though in the other place we die.   15
 Oh! 'tis tortue all, and cozenage;
And which the harder is I cannot tell,
To hide true love, or make false love look well.

4

Since it is thus, God of desire,
 Give me my honesty again,   20
And take thy brands back, and thy fire;
 I'me weary of the State I'me in:
Since (if the very best should now befal)
Loves Triumph, must be Honours Funeral.

63. [Womans Constancy]

1

THERE never yet was woman made,
 nor shall, but to be curst;
And oh! that I (fond I) should first
 of any Lover
This truth at my own charge to other fools discover. 5

2

You that have promis'd to your selves
 propriety in love,
Know womens hearts like straws do move,
 and what we call
Their sympathy, is but love to jett in general. 10

---

63. [Womans Constancy.] *FA46. Title supplied. Variant printed text: FA48 (generally from FA46 but contains substantive variants as noted in the critical apparatus)*

3

All mankind are alike to them;
 and though we iron find
That never with a Loadstone joyn'd,
  'tis not its fault:
It is because the loadstone yet was never brought.   15

4

If where a gentle Bee hath fall'n
 and laboured to his power,
A new succeeds not to that Flower,
  but passes by;
'Tis to be thought, the gallant else-where loads his thigh.   20

5

For still the flowers ready stand:
 one buzzes round about,
One lights, one tasts, gets in, gets out;
  all, all waies use them,
Till all their sweets are gone, and all again refuse them.   25

64. [Loves Clock]

1

THAT none beguiled be by times quick flowing,
 Lovers have in their hearts a clock still going;
For though Time be nimble, his motions
  are quicker
  and thicker   5
 where Love hath his notions:

63. 11 are] is *FA48*   12–13 iron . . . | That never with a Loadstone] seldome . . . | The Loadstone with the Iron *FA48*   14 its *FA48*: the irons *FA46*   15 the loadstone yet] neere the Loadstone it *FA48*, *Haz* (*but* yet *for* it), *Th*; *see note*
  64. [Loves Clock.] *FA46*. *Title* (The Lover's Clock *Th*) *and stanza divisions supplied.* MS.: P (*from FA46*)

2

Hope is the main spring on which moves desire,
And these do the lesse wheels, fear, joy, inspire;
     The ballance is thought, evermore
                    clicking   .   10
                    and striking,
                    and ne're giving ore;

3

Occasion's the hand which still's moving round,
Till by it the Critical hour may be found,
     And when that falls out, it will strike   15
                    kisses,
                    strange blisses,
          and what you best like.

65. Song

1

No, no, faire Heretique, it needs must bee
                    But an ill Love in mee,
                    And worse for thee.
For were it in my Power,
To love thee now this hower,   5
                    More than I did the last;
'Twould then so fall,
I might not Love at all;
     Love that can flow, and can admit increase,
     Admits as well an Ebb, and may grow lesse.   10

2

True Love is still the same; the torrid Zones,
                    And those more frigid ones,
                    It must not know:

65. Song. *Aglaura*, 1638 (IV. iv. 4–23). *Symmetrical line-arrangement supplied (see note).*
MSS.: Dx4, Dx42 (ll. 1–10 only), HL, P (from FA46), R. Variant printed texts: FA46,
FA48, SMA. Substantive variants recorded in full
     Song] *omit HL, SMA*   1 needs must] cannot *HL*   7 'Twould Σ + *FA48*
(Aglaura), Th: It would *Dx42, P*: I would *Ag, FA46, FA48 (Poems), Haz*   11–20 *omit*
Dx42   13 It] Yett *Dx4*

For Love growne cold or hot,
Is Lust, or Friendship, not   15
                    The thing wee have;
For that's a flame would die,
Held downe, or up too high:
          Then thinke I love more than I can expresse,
          And would love more, could I but love thee lesse.   20

66. Song

1

W HY so pale and wan fond Lover?
                    Prithee why so pale?
Will, when looking well can't move her,
                    Looking ill prevaile?
                    Prithee why so pale?   5

2

Why so dull and mute young Sinner?
                    Prithee why so mute?
Will, when speaking well can't win her,
                    Saying nothing doo't?
                    Prithee why so mute?   10

3

Quit, quit, for shame, this will not move,
                    This cannot take her;
If of her selfe shee will not Love,
                    Nothing can make her,
                    The Devill take her.   15

65. 17 would] will *Dx4*   18 too] to *Ag*

66. Song. *Aglaura*, 1638 (IV. ii. 14–28). *MSS.: A47, Dx4, Eg9, EP9, F24, F308, O2,*
P(from FA46), R, W3. Variant printed texts: AC, AC84 (later ed. of Wind-D), FA46, LS,
Wind-D

Song] A Song by S^r Jo. Suckling *Eg9*: A gent: having repulse from a gent=woeman,
A freind gives him counsell. A Song *F24*   1 and] *omit F24*   3–4 Will, when look-
ing well can't move her, | Looking] If looking well, it will not [can never *F308*: thou canst
LS: can't *O2*: cannot *F24*] move her, | Can [Will *F24, LS, O2*] looking *AC, AC84, Wind-D*
6 and] *omit F24*   Sinner] seegnior *F24*   8–9 Will, when speaking well can't win her, |
Saying] If speaking well it cannot [thou canst not *LS*: cann't *O2*: cannot *Eg9, F24*] win her, |
Can [Will *F24, O2*] saying *AC, AC84, F308, Wind-D*   8 well] faire *W3*   11 will
not] cannot *Eg9, W3*: woon't *R: omit EP9*   move,] (~_∧ *Ag, Dx4, R, W3*): move her *AC,*
AC84, F308, LS, Wind-D: doe it *F24*   12 This cannot take] This can no ways take
F308: Thou must forsake *F24*   14 Nothing] No man *F24*: I know not what *F308*
15 The] Then let the *F308*

67. [Loves Siege]

1

Tis now since I sate down before
    That foolish Fort, a heart,
(Time strangely spent) a Year, and more,
    And still I did my part:

2

Made my approaches, from her hand   5
    Unto her lip did rise,
And did already understand
    The language of her eyes;

3

Proceeded on with no lesse Art,
    My Tongue was Engineer: 10
I thought to undermine the heart
    By whispering in the ear.

4

When this did nothing, I brought down
    Great Canon-oaths, and shot
A thousand thousand to the Town,   15
    And still it yeelded not.

5

I then resolv'd to starve the place
    By cutting off all kisses,
Praysing and gazing on her face,
    And all such little blisses.   20

6

To draw her out, and from her strength,
    I drew all batteries in:
And brought my self to lie at length
    As if no siege had been.

67. [Loves Siege.] *FA46. Title from Th. MS.: P (from FA46)*   12 the] her *P*
811849   F

7

When I had done what man could do,   25
   And thought the place mine owne,
The Enemy lay quiet too,
   And smil'd at all was done.

8

I sent to know from whence, and where,
   These hopes, and this relief?   30
A Spie inform'd, Honour was there,
   And did command in chief.

9

March, march, (quoth I) the word straight give,
   Lets lose no time, but leave her:
That Giant upon ayre will live,   35
   And hold it out for ever.

10

To such a place our Camp remove
   As will no siege abide;
I hate a fool that starves her Love
   Onely to feed her pride.   40

68. Farewel to Love

1

WELL shadow'd Landskip, fare-ye-well:
   How I have lov'd you, none can tell,
     At least so well
    As he that now hates more
    Then e're he lov'd before.   5

2

But my dear nothings, take your leave,
No longer must you me deceive,
     Since I perceive
    All the deceit, and know
    Whence the mistake did grow.   10

68. Farewel to Love. *FA46. Derivative printed text*: Wits Recreations, *1650* (*WR*)

3

As he whose quicker eye doth trace
A false star shot to a mark't place,
    Do's run apace,
    And thinking it to catch,
    A gelly up do's snatch: 15

4

So our dull souls, tasting delight
Far off, by sence, and appetite,
    Think that is right
    And real good; when yet
    'Tis but the Counterfeit.   20

5

Oh! how I glory now! that I
Have made this new discovery!
    Each wanton eye
    Enflam'd before: no more
    Will I encrease that score.   25

6

If I gaze now, 'tis but to see
What manner of deaths-head 'twill be,
    When it is free
    From that fresh upper skin,
    The gazers Joy, and sin.   30

7

The Gum and glist'ning which with art
And studi'd method in each part
    Hangs down the heart,
    Looks (just) as if, that day
    Snails there had crawl'd the *Hay*.   35

8

The Locks, that curl'd o're each eare be,
Hang like two Master-worms to me,
    That (as we see)

68. 12 mark't] Market *WR*   31 Gum *Haz, Th*: Gun *FA46*   33 heart] hair,
't *Th*: hair *Haz; see note*

Have tasted to the rest
Two holes, where they lik't best.   40

9

A quick corse me-thinks I spy
In ev'ry woman; and mine eye,
    At passing by,
Checks, and is troubled, just
As if it rose from Dust.   45

10

They mortifie, not heighten me:
These of my sins the Glasses be:
    And here I see
How I have lov'd before.
And so I love no more.   50

69. Upon two Sisters

BELEEV'T yong Man, I can as eas'ly tell
How many yards and inches 'tis to hell;
Unriddle all predestination,
As the nice points we now dispute upon!
Had the three Goddesses been just as fair,   5

.   .   .   .   .   .

It had not been so easily decided,
And sure the apple must have been divided:
It must, it must; hee's impudent, dares say
Which is the handsomer till one's away.   10
And it was necessary it should be so;
Wise Nature did foresee it, and did know
When she had fram'd the Eldest, that each heart
Must at the first sight feel the blind-god's dart:
And sure as can be, had she made but one,   15
No plague had been more sure destruction;
For we had lik't, lov'd, burnt to ashes too,

68. 41 me-thinks] methink *Haz, Th*   44 Checks *Haz, Th*: Check *FA46*
69. Upon two Sisters. *FA46*   4 As *Th (suggestion)*: Or *FA46*   6 *wanting in
all editions. Hazlitt suggested* As ... and Aglaura are; *see note*   12 Wise] While *Haz*

In half the time that we are chusing now.
Variety, and equal objects make
The busie eye still doubtful which to take: 20
This lip, this hand, this foot, this eye, this face,
The others body, gesture, or her grace;
And whilst we thus dispute which of the two,
We unresolv'd go out, and nothing do.
He sure is happy'st that has hopes of either,   25
Next him is he that sees them both together.

70. [A Summons to Town]

SIR,
Whether these lines do find you out,
Putting or clearing of a doubt;
(Whether Predestination,
Or reconciling three in one,
Or the unriddling how men die,   5
And live at once eternally,
Now take you up) know 'tis decreed
You straight bestride the Colledge Steed:
Leave *Socinus* and the Schoolmen,
(Which *Jack Bond* swears do but fool men)   10
And come to Town; 'tis fit you show
Your self abroad, that men may know
(What e're some learned men have guest)
That Oracles are not yet ceas't:
There you shall find the wit, and wine   15
Flowing alike, and both divine;
Dishes, with names not known in books,
And lesse amongst the Colledge-Cooks,
With sauce so pregnant that you need
Not stay till hunger bids you feed.   20
The sweat of learned *Johnsons* brain,
And gentle *Shakespear*'s eas'er strain,
A hackney-coach conveys you to,
In spite of all that rain can do:
And for your eighteen pence you sit   25
The Lord and Judge of all fresh wit.
News in one day as much w'have here
As serves all *Windsor* for a year,
And which the Carrier brings to you,
After 't has here been found not true.   30

70. [A Summons to Town.] *FA46. Title supplied*

Then think what Company's design'd
To meet you here, men so refin'd,
Their very common talk at boord,
Makes wise, or mad a young Court-Lord,
And makes him capable to be   35
Umpire in's Fathers Company.
Where no disputes nor forc't defence
Of a mans person for his sence
Take up the time, all strive to be
Masters of truth, as victory: 40
And where you come, I'de boldly swear
A Synod might as eas'ly erre.

71. [The Wits]

(A Sessions of the Poets)

1

A SESSIONS was held the other day,
   And *Apollo* himself was at it (they say;)
The Laurel that had been so long reserv'd,
Was now to be given to him best deserv'd.
            And
Therefore the wits of the Town came thither,   5
'Twas strange to see how they flocked together;
Each strongly confident of his own way,
Thought to carry the Laurel away that day.

2

There was *Selden*, and he sate hard by the chair;
Wenman not far off, which was very fair;   10

71. [The Wits.] *FA46. Title from MSS. MSS.: Cor, Cran6, EP53, Harv7, Hunt, M3,
P (ll. 95–102 only; from FA46). Variant printed texts: FA48, MD (FA48 generally from
FA46 and MD from FA48, but both contain significant substantive variants as noted in the
critical apparatus); see note. (Beaurline) = a critical edition of 'The Wits' alone by L. A.
Beaurline; differences from present text noted (see note). Arrangement of stanzas and suspensions:
see note*
   The Wits *Harv7, Hunt, M3*: A Sessions of Wit *MD*: A Sessions of the Poets *FA46:
omit Cor, Cran6 (endorsed* Rymes of som Poetts Of som Wittes About London Septemb^r
1637 *by Suckling's uncle, the Earl of Middlesex), EP53; see note*   1 Sessions *Σ*: Session
FA46 (Sessions in title), Cran6   8 Thought . . . away that day] (*omit* away *EP53: omit
that day Hunt*): That day thought . . . away *FA48*   carry *Σ+FA48*: gain *FA46*   9 was
Σ+FA48: omit FA46   hard] close *FA48*

Sands with *Townsend*, for they kept no order;
Digby and *Chillingworth* a little further:
> And

There was *Lucans* Translator too, and he
That makes God speak so bigge in's Poetry;
Selwin and *Waller*, and *Berkeleys* both the brothers;   15
Jack Vaughan and *Porter*, with divers others.

3

The first that broke silence was good old *Ben*,
Prepar'd before with Canary wine,
And he told them plainly he deserv'd the Bayes,
For his were call'd Works, where others were but Plaies;   20
> And

Bid them remember how he had purg'd the Stage
Of errors, that had lasted many an Age,
And he hop'd they did think the *silent Woman*,
The Fox, and the *Alchymist* out done by no man.

4

Apollo stopt him there, and bid him not go on,   25
'Twas merit, he said, and not presumption
Must carry it; at which *Ben* turned about,
And in great choler offer'd to go out:
> But

Those that were there thought it not fit
To discontent so ancient a wit;   30
And therefore *Apollo* call'd him back agen,
And made him mine host of his own new Inne.

5

Tom Carew was next, but he had a fault
That would not well stand with a Laureat;

71. 11 Townsend] Johnson *Harv7*   12 Chillingworth *Harv7*: Shillingworth
Σ+MD: Shillingsworth *EP53*, *FA46*: Sellengworth *Cor*   15 Berkeleys *M3*: Bark-
leyes *EP53*: Bartlets *Σ+FA48* (Bartlett *Hunt*)   16 and ... with *Σ*: with ... and
EP53, *Hunt*: and ... and *FA46*   17 broke] brake *Cor*, *Cran6*, *Harv7* (*Beaurline*)
20 where] whereas *Cor*: when *Hunt*: the *Cran6*: omit *M3*   others] other *M3*: theirs *Hunt*
but] call'd *Cor*: omit *EP53*, *Hunt*   23 hop'd *Σ+FA48*, *Haz*, *Th*: hopes *FA46*   did
Σ+MD: + not *FA46*   25 stopt] stops *FA48*   there] here *Cran6*, *Harv7*, *M3*   bid
Σ (*cf. l. 21*): bade *Cran6*, *FA46* (bad)   27 [carry] it *Σ*: 't *FA46*: the Bayes *Cran6*
29 thought it not]+so *Hunt*, *M3* (*Beaurline*): did not think *Cor*, *Cran6*   33 Carew]
Carey *Cor*, *M3*: Cary *Cran6*, *EP53*, *Harv7*

His Muse was hard bound, and th'issue of's brain   35
Was seldom brought forth but with trouble and pain.
And
All that were present there did agree,
A Laureats Muse should be easie and free;
Yet sure 'twas not that, but 'twas thought that his Grace
Consider'd he was well he had a Cup-bearers place.   40

6

Will. *Davenant* asham'd of a foolish mischance
That he had got lately travelling in *France*,
Modestly hoped the handsomnesse of's Muse
Might any deformity about him excuse.
And
Surely the Company would have been content,   45
If they could have found any President;
But in all their Records either in Verse or Prose,
There was not one Laureat without a nose.

7

To *Will Berkeley* sure all the wits meant well,
But first they would see how his snow would sell: 50
Will smil'd and swore in their judgements they went lesse,
That concluded of merit upon successe.
So
Sullenly taking his place agen,
He gave way to *Selwin*, that streight stept in;
But alas! he had been so lately a wit,   55
That *Apollo* himself hardly knew him yet.

8

Toby Mathew (pox on 't! how came he there?)
Was busily whispering some-body i'th'ear,

71. 35 hard] hyde *FA48*   th'[issue]] the *Cor, Harv7, M3, MD* (*Beaurline*)   of's] of his
Cor, Cran6   38 Laureats *Σ*: Laureat *FA46*   39 that his Grace] the disgrace *Cor*
40 Cup-bearers] Sewers *Cran6*   43 the handsomnesse of's] (of his *Hunt*: that the
. . . of his *Cor, EP53*): that his handsome *Cran6*   46 could] + but *Harv7* (*Beaurline*)
47 [either] in] *omit Cran6, Harv7* (*Beaurline*)   49 Berkeley *EP53, M3*: barcklett
Hunt: Bartlet *Σ* + *FA48*   52 + So *Σ*: And *Cran6*: *omit FA46*   53 Sullenly
Cran6, Harv7, M3: Suddenly *EP53, FA46, Hunt*: Silently *Cor; see note*   54 that *Cor,
EP53, Hunt, M3*: who *Cran6, FA46, Harv7*   56 himself *Σ* + *FA48*: *omit FA46*
hardly] scarce *Cran6, FA48*   57 Mathew *Cran6, Harv7, M3*: Mathews *Σ*   on 't
[!] *Σ*: on him *FA46*   how came] what made *FA48*   58 busily whispering *Σ*: busie
whispering with *EP53*: whispering nothing *Cran6, FA46, FA48*   some-body i'th' *Σ* (some
lady *Harv7*: i'the *EP53, M3*: in the *Cor*): in some-bodies *Cran6, FA46, FA48*

When he had the honour to be nam'd i'the Court:
But Sir, you may thank my Lady *Carlile* for't;   60
   For
Had not her Character furnisht you out
With something of handsome, without all doubt
You and your sorry Lady Muse had been
In the number of those that were not to come in.

     9

In haste two or three from the Court came in,   65
And they brought letters (forsooth) from the Queen;
'Twas discreetly done too, for if they had come
Without them, they had scarce been let into the room.
   This
Made a dispute; for 'twas plain to be seen
Each man had a mind to gratify the Queen: 70
But *Apollo* himself could not think it fit;
There was difference, he said, 'twixt fooling and wit.

     10

Suckling next was call'd, but did not appear,
And strait one whisperd *Apollo* in's ear,
That of all men living he cared not for't,   75
He loved not the Muses so well as his sport;
   And
Prized black eyes, or a lucky hit
At bowls, above all the Trophies of wit;
But *Apollo* was angry, and publiquely said
'Twere fit that a fine were set on his head.   80

     11

Wat Montague now stood forth to his tryal,
And did not so much as suspect a denial;

71. 59 i'the *EP53, M3*: in the *Cran6*: i'th' *Harv7, Hunt*: in *FA46*: at *Cor* 61 For
had *FA46* Character *Σ + FA48*: care *FA46* 64 to come *Σ (omit* to *EP53)*: let *FA46*
65 two or three from the Court *Σ*: from the Court two or three *FA46* 67 too] *omit*
Cor, Cran6, Hunt, MD they had *Σ*: th'had *FA46, Harv7* ('t had) 68 they had *Σ*:
th'had *FA46, Harv7* (th'ad; *Beaurline*) 69–72 *Σ (text from FA48; spelling normalized)*:
omit FA46; see note 69 This made *FA48* 72 'twixt *Σ*: betwixt *FA48, Harv7*
74 And *Σ*: But *FA46* in's *EP53, Harv7, M3*: i'th' *FA46, Hunt*: in th' *Cran2* in the
Cor, MD 76 well] much *Cor, Harv7, Hunt (Beaurline)* 77 And prized *FA46*
or] and *Cor, Cran6, M3* 80 on his *Σ*: upon's *FA46*: upon his *EP53, Harv7*

Wise *Apollo* then asked him first of all
If he understood his own Pastoral.

For

If he could do it, 'twould plainly appear   85
He understood more than any man there,
And did merit the Bayes above all the rest,
But the Mounsier was modest, and silence confest.

12

During these troubles, in the Crowd was hid
One that *Apollo* soon mist, little *Sid*;   90
And having spied him, call'd him out of the throng,
And advis'd him in his ear not to write so strong.

Then

Murrey was summon'd, but 'twas urg'd that he
Was Chief already of another Company.

13

Hales set by himself most gravely did smile   95
To see them about nothing keep such a coil;
Apollo had spied him, but knowing his mind
Past by, and call'd *Faulkland* that sate just behind:

But

He was of late so gone with Divinity,
That he had almost forgot his Poetry,   100
Though to say the truth (and *Apollo* did know it)
He might have been both his Priest and his Poet.

14

At length who but an Alderman did appear,
At which *Will. Davenant* began to swear;
But wiser *Apollo* bid him draw nigher,   105
And when he was mounted a little higher

71. 83 Wise *Σ*: But wise *FA48*: But witty *FA46*   then *Σ*: *omit FA46* (But witty *Apollo* asked)   85 For if *FA46*   could do it, 'twould] (do't *Harv7*, *M3*, *MD*: it would *Harv7*): did, it would *Cran6*   88 silence] silent *Cor*, *Cran6*, *Harv7* (*Beaurline*): silene *M3*; *see note*   89 Crowd *Σ+FA48*: Court *Cor*, *FA46*: Troupe *Cran6* 90 Sid *Σ+FA48*: Cid *FA46*, *MD*   92 in his] in's *Cran6*, *EP53*   92+ Then *Cor*, *EP53*, *FA48*, *Harv7*: Next *Cran6*: *omit FA46*, *Hunt*, *M3*   93 Murrey] Murray *Cor*, *M3*: Murry *Hunt*: Murre *MD*   105 wiser] wise *M3* (*Beaurline*)   bid *Σ* (did bid *EP53*): bade *Cran6*, *FA46* (bad)

He
Openly declared that 'twas the best signe
Of good store of wit to have good store of coyn,
And without a Syllable more or lesse said,
He put the Laurel on the Aldermans head.   110

15

At this all the wits were in such a maze
That for a good while they did nothing but gaze
One upon another, not a man in the place
But had discontent writ in great in his face.
Onely
The small Poets clear'd up again,   115
Out of hope (as 'twas thought) of borrowing;
But sure they were out, for he forfeits his Crown
When he lends any Poet about the Town.

72. To his much honoured, the Lord Lepington, upon his Translation of Malvezzi his Romulus and Tarquin

IT is so rare and new a thing to see
Ought that belongs to young Nobility
In print, (but their owne clothes) that we must praise
You as we would doe those first shew the wayes
To Arts or to new Worlds: You have begun: 5
Taught travell'd youth what 'tis it should have done:

71. 106+ He Σ+*FA48*: omit *FA46*   107–8 that 'twas . . . wit Σ+
FA48 (*but cf. following note*): that [the best signe | Of good store of] wit's *FA46*; *see
note*   107 that 'twas *Harv7*, *M3*: that it was *FA48*, *Hunt*: it was *Cor*, *Cran6*, *EP53*
114 writ in great] Σ+*Harv7* (*u*): written great *Cran6*, *Harv7* (*c*; writen) (*Beaurline*): writ
Hunt: writ at large *FA48*   115 Onely the *FA46*   Poets] ones *FA48*: covey *M3*:
omit *EP53* (smalls)   clear'd] cheer'd *EP53*, *FA48*, *Haz*, *Hunt*, *Th*   118 any] to
any *Cran6*, *FA48*, *Haz*   Poet Σ+*FA48*: Poets *FA46*
72. To his much honoured, *etc. Henry Carey, Lord Lepington,* Malvezzi's Romulus and
Tarquin, *2nd ed., 1638* (*R & T*). *Variant printed text: FA46* (*accidental variants only; probably
a direct descendant*)

For't has indeed too strong a custome bin
To carry out more wit than we bring in.
You have done otherwise, brought home (my Lord)
The choicest things fam'd Countreyes doe afford: 10
Malvezzi by your meanes is English growne,
And speaks our tongue as well now as his owne.
Malvezzi, he: whom 'tis as hard to praise
To merit, as to imitate his wayes.
He does not shew us *Rome* great suddenly,   15
As if the Empire were a Tympany,
But gives it naturall growth, tels how, and why
The little body grew so large and high;
Describes each thing so lively, that we are
Concern'd our selves before we are aware: 20
And at the warres they and their neighbours wag'd
Each man is present still, and still engag'd.
Like a good prospective he strangely brings
Things distant to us: and in these two Kings
We see what made greatnesse. And what 't has beene   25
Made that greatnesse contemptible againe.
And all this not tediously deriv'd,
But like to Worlds in little Maps contriv'd.
'Tis he that doth the Roman Dame restore,
Makes *Lucrece* chaster for her being whore;   30
Gives her a kinde Revenge for *Tarquins* sinne,
For ravish't first, she ravisheth againe.
She sayes such fine things after't, that we must
In spite of vertue thanke foule Rape and Lust,
Since 'twas the cause no woman would have had,   35
Though she's of *Lucrece* side, *Tarquin* lesse bad.
       But stay: like one that thinks to bring his friend
A mile or two, and sees the journeyes end,
I straggle on too farre: long graces do
But keepe good stomacks off that would fall to.   40

72. 40 to] too *FA46*

73. To my Friend Will. Davenant; upon his Poem of Madagascar

WHAT mighty Princes Poets are? those things
  The great ones stick at, and our very Kings
Lay downe, they venter on; and with great ease,
Discover, conquer, what, and where they please.
Some Flegmatick Sea-Captaine would have staid   5
For money now, or Victualls; not have waid
Anchor without 'em; Thou (*Will*) do'st not stay
So much as for a Wind, but go'st away,
Land'st, View'st the Country; fight'st, put'st all to rout,
Before another cou'd be putting out!   10
And now the newes in towne is, *Dav'nant's* come
From *Madagascar*, Fraught with Laurell home,
And welcome (*Will*) for the first time, but prithee
In thy next Voyage, bring the Gold too with thee.

74. On his other Poems

THOU has redeem'd us, *Will*; and future Times
  Shall not account unto the Age's crimes
Dearth of pure Wit: since the great Lord of it
(*Donne*) parted hence, no Man has ever writ
So neere him, in's owne way: I would commend   5
Particulars, but then, how should I end
Without a Volume? Ev'ry Line of thine
Would aske (to praise it right) Twenty of mine.

75. An Answer to some Verses made in his praise

THE antient Poets, and their learned rimes,
  We still admire in these our later times,
And celebrate their fames: Thus though they die,
Their names can never taste mortalitie:

73–4. To my Friend, *etc., and* On his other Poems. *William Davenant*, Madagascar, *1638*
(**Mad**; *both poems subscribed* I. Suckling). *Variant printed text:* FA46 (*accidental variants
only; probably direct descendants*)
75. An Answer to some Verses *etc. LR*

Blind *Homer's* Muse, and *Virgil's* stately Verse, 5
While any live, shall never need a herse.
Since then to these such praise was justly due
For what they did, what shall be said to you?
These had their helps; they writ of Gods and Kings,
Of Temples, Battels, and such gallant things: 10
But you of Nothing; how could you have writ,
Had you but chose a Subject to your Wit?
To praise *Achilles*, or the Trojan crew,
Shewed little art, for praise was but their due.
To say she's fair that's fair, this is no pains: 15
He shews himself most Poet, that most feigns:
To find out vertues strangely hid in me,
I, there's the art and learned Poetrie;
To make one striding of a Barbed Steed,
Prancing a stately round: (I use indeed 20
To ride *Bat Jewels* Jade;) this is the skill,
This shews the Poet wants not wit at will.
　　I must admire aloof, and for my part
　　Be well contented, since you do't with art.

76. A Ballade.
Upon a Wedding

I

I TELL thee *Dick*, where I have been,
Where I the rarest things have seen,
　　Oh things beyond compare!
Such sights again cannot be found
In any part of English ground, 5
　　Be it at Wake, or Fair.

75. 10 such *LR* (*Errata*): of such *LR* (*Text*)
　　76. A Ballade. Upon a Wedding. *FA46*. MSS.: *Ash3*, *Dx42* (*ll. 1–4* [... cannot] *only*),
H17 (*subscribed* Sr John Suckling), *RP3*. *Variant printed text: FA48 (generally from FA46
but contains significant substantive variants as noted in the critical apparatus). Derivative MSS.
and printed texts: see Commentary. On omissions and transpositions of stanzas see note*
　　A Ballade. Upon a Wedding *FA46*: The Wedding *RP3*: A Ballad, or Parly, between two
West-Country men on sight of a Wedding *AAM*: On the Marriage of the Lord Lovelace
H17: *omit Ash3, Dx42; see note* 1 I ... where] I ... that *Dx42, H17*: I'le ... where
Ash3, RP3; see note 2 Where I the rarest ...] The rarest ... that I *Ash3* 2, 3, 4
things | things | sights] things | things | things *Dx42*: sights | sights | sights *Ash3*: sights |
sights | things *H17; see note* 3 beyond *Σ+FA48*: without *FA46* 5 In any part
Σ (On *Ash3*): In any place on *FA46*

2

At *Charing-Crosse*, hard by the way
Where we (thou know'st) do sell our Hay,
  There is a house with stairs;
And there did I see comming down   10
Such folk as are not in our Town,
  Forty at least, in Pairs.

3

Amongst the rest, one Pest'lent fine,
(His beard no bigger though then thine)
  Walkt on before the rest: 15
Our Landlord looks like nothing to him:
The King, (God blesse him) 'twould undo him,
  Should he go still so drest.

4

At Course-a-Park, without all doubt,
He should have first been taken out   20
  By all the Maids i'th' Town:
Though lusty *Roger* there had been,
Or little *George* upon the Green,
  Or *Vincent* of the Crown.

5

But wot you what? the youth was going   25
To make an end of all his woing;
  The Parson for him staid:
Yet by his leave (for all his haste)
He did not wish so much all past,
  (Perchance) as did the maid.   30

6

The maid, (and thereby hangs a tale,
For such a maid no Whitson-ale
  Could ever yet produce)
No Grape that's kindly ripe, could be
So round, so plump, so soft as she,   3[5]
  Nor half so full of Juyce.

76. 12 Forty *Σ*: Vorty *FA46* (*cf.* folk, *l. 11*); *see note* 21 i'th'] inth' *Ash3*: o'th'
RP3 24 Vincent] Vincent *Ash3(a)* (Davenant *deleted*) 28 Yet] Bu[t]
Ash3, RP3 29 wish so much *Σ* (soe much *Ash3[a]* [for *deleted*]): so much wis[
FA46 33 Could] Can *RP3*: Did *Ash3*

7

Her fingers were so small, the Ring
Would not stay on which they did bring,
    It was too wide a Peck:
And to say truth (for out it must)   40
It lookt like the great Collar (just)
    About our young Colts neck.

8

Her feet beneath her Petticoat,
Like little mice stole in and out,
    As if they fear'd the light: 45
But oh! she dances such a way!
No Sun upon an Easter day
    Is half so fine a sight.

9

He would have kist her once or twice,
But she would not, she was so nice,   50
    She would not do't in sight;
And then she lookt as who should say
I will do what I list to day;
    And you shall do't at night.

10

Her Cheeks so rare a white was on,   55
No Dazy makes comparison,
    (Who sees them is undone)
For streaks of red were mingled there,
Such as are on a Katherine Pear,
    (The side that's next the Sun.)   60

11

Her mouth so small when she doth speak,
Thou'dst swear her teeth her words did break,
    That they might passage get;

76. 37–42 *sic*] *after l. 72 in Ash3*   37 fingers were *H17, RP3* : finger was *Ash3, FA46;*
see note   38 they] he *FA48*   43–8 *sic*] *after l. 72 in H17*   46 oh!] *Dick FA48*
49–54 *omit Ash3, H17*   50 so *RP3: omit FA46 (stanza omitted Ash3, H17); see note*
52 should] would *RP3*   55 was] had *Ash3, H17*   58 were] are *Ash3, H17*
59 Katherine *H17* : Katherin *RP3* : Katherne *FA46* : Kathrins *Ash3*   60 The] That
H17, RP3   61–72 *sic Ash3, RP3:* 61–6 *and* 67–72 *transposed FA46: omit* 61–6 *H17;*
see note   61 doth *Ash3, RP3: does FA46*

But she so handles still the matter,
They come as good as ours, or better,   65
   And are not spoil'd one whit.

12

Her lips were red, and one was thin,
Compar'd to that was next her chin;
   (Some Bee had stung it newly.)
But (*Dick*) her eyes so guard her face;   70
I durst no more upon her gaze,
   Then on the Sun in *July*.

13

If wishing should be any sin,
The Parson self had guilty bin,
   (She lookt that day so purely;)   75
And did the youth so oft the feat
At night, as some did in conceit,
   It would have spoil'd him, surely.

14

Passion oh me! how I run on!
There's that that would be thought upon,   80
   (I trow) besides the Bride:
The bus'nesse of the Kitchin great;
For it is fit that men should eat,
   Nor was it there deni'd.

15

Just in the nick the Cook knockt thrice,   85
And all the waiters in a trice
   His summons did obey:
Each serving man with dish in hand,
Marcht boldly up, like our Train Band,
   Presented, and away.   90

76. 64 she so . . . still] o she . . . so *RP3*   64–5 handles . . . come *Ash4, RP3*:
handled . . . came *FA46*   66 spoil'd one *Ash3, RP3*: spent a *FA46*   71 her *Σ*: them
FA46; see note   73 should be] might be *H17*: had been *Ash3, RP3; see note*
74 Parson self *Ed.*: Parson himself *FA46*: Parson's self *H17, RP3*: Parson sure *Ash3; see
note*   77 At] That *Ash3, H17*   79–114 *omit Ash3*   79–84 *sic FA48, H17,*
RP3: after l. 96, with first and last three lines transposed, FA46   82 bus'nesse] business *H17, RP3*   Kitchin *H17, RP3*: Kitchin's *FA46*   89 Train [Traine] *H17, RP3*:
Train'd *FA46*

16

When all the meat was on the Table,
What man of knife, or teeth, was able
    To stay to be intreated?
And this the very reason was,
Before the Parson could say Grace,   95
    The Company was seated.

17

Now hatts fly off, and youths carrouse;
Healths first go round, and then the house,
    The Brides came thick and thick:
And when 'twas nam'd anothers health,   100
Perhaps he made it hers by stealth.
    (And who could help it? *Dick*)

18

O'th' sodain up they rise and dance,
Then sit again and sigh, and glance;
    Then dance again and kisse: 105
Thus sev'ral waies the time did passe,
Whilst ev'ry Woman wisht her place,
    And ev'ry Man wisht his.

19

By this time all were stoln aside
To counsel and undresse the Bride;   110
    But that he must not know:
But yet 'twas thought he ghest her mind,
And did not mean to stay behind
    Above an hour or so.

20

When in he came (*Dick*) there she lay   115
Like new-faln snow melting away;
    ('Twas time I trow to part)

76. 91–6 *omit RP3*   95 Before] why ere *H17*   97–102 *omit H17*
100 anothers] another *RP3*   107 Whilst *FA48, H17, Haz, RP3, Th:* Till *FA46*
115 in he came] he came in *Ash3, H17; see note*

Kisses were now the onely stay,
Which soon she gave, as who should say,
    Good b'w'y'! with all my heart.   120

21

But just as Heav'ns would have to crosse it,
In came the Bridemaids with the Posset:
    The Bridegroom eat in spight;
For had he left the Women to't
It would have cost two hours to do't,   125
    Which were too much that night.

22

At length the candles out, and now
All that they had not done, they do:
    What that is, who can tell?
But I beleeve it was no more   130
Then thou and I have done before
    With *Bridget*, and with *Nell*.

77. On New-years day 1640.
To the King

I

A W A K E (great Sir) the Sun shines heer,
    Gives all Your Subjects a New-yeer,
Onely we stay till You appear,
For thus by us Your Power is understood:
He may make fair days, You must make them good.   5
      Awake, awake,
        and take

---

76. 119 should *Ash3, H17* : would *FA46, RP3* (*cf. l. 52*)   120 Good b'w'y' *RP3* (b'wy) :
God b'w'y' *H17* (bu'y), *FA48* (B'w'y'), *Haz, Th*: Good Boy *Ash3* (God *Ash3[b]*), *FA46*;
see note   121–6 *omit Ash3*   127–8 now . . . do *Σ+FA48, Haz, Th*: out . . .
do't *FA46* (*cf. l. 125*) : Candles are out and all must go | And then what was not done they
do *Ash3*   128 had not done] might not doe *H17*   129–30 is . . . was] was . . . was
H17 : was . . . is *Ash3*
    77. On New-years day 1640. *etc. FA46. Refrain condensed to* Awake, awake, &c. *in
stanzas 2–4 in FA46*

Such Presents as poor men can make,
They can adde little unto blisse
    who cannot wish.   10

2

May no ill vapour cloud the skie,
Bold storms invade the Soveraigntie,
But gales of joy, so fresh, so high,
That You may think Heav'n sent to try this year
What sayl, or burthen, a Kings mind could bear.   15
    Awake, awake,
    and take
Such Presents as poor men can make,
They can adde little unto blisse
    who cannot wish.   20

3

May all the discords in Your State
(Like those in Musick we create)
Be govern'd at so wise a rate,
That what would of it self sound harsh, or fright,
May be so temper'd that it may delight.   25
    Awake, awake,
    and take
Such Presents as poor men can make,
They can adde little unto blisse
    who cannot wish.   30

4

What Conquerors from battels find,
Or Lovers when their Doves are kind,
Take up henceforth our Masters mind,
Make such strange Rapes upon the place, 't may be
No longer joy there, but an extasie.   35
    Awake, awake,
    and take
Such Presents as poor men can make,
They can adde little unto blisse
    who cannot wish.   40

5

May every pleasure and delight
That has or does your sence invite
Double this year, save those o'th' night:
For such a Marriage-bed must know no more
Then repetition of what was before.   45
      Awake, awake,
      and take
Such Presents as poor men can make,
They can adde little unto blisse
     who cannot wish.   50

78. Upon my Lord Brohalls Wedding

Dialogue

S.   B.

S.   In bed dull man?
When *Love* and *Hymens* Revels are begun,
And the Church Ceremonies past and done?

B.   Why who's gone mad to day?

S.   Dull Heretick, thou wouldst say,   5
He that is gone to Heaven's gone astray;
     Brohall our gallant friend
Is gone to Church as Martyrs to the fire.

B.   Who marry differ but i'th' end,
      Since both do take   10
The hardest way to what they most desire.

S.   Nor staid he till the formal Priest had done,
But ere that part was finisht, his begun.

B.   Which did reveal
The hast and eagernesse men have to seal   15
     That long to tell the money.

78. Upon my Lord Brohalls Wedding. *etc. FA46. Speech headings: as here at ll. 1, 4, 5 in FA46, others supplied; Haz and Th follow FA46 but supply additional headings at ll. 29 (B.) and 33 (S.); see Commentary. Space between speeches supplied (FA46 has space between ll. 28–9 only), and punctuation modified as necessary (see Appendix B: Altered Accidentals)*

S.   A sprigg of Willow in his hat he wore,—

B.   The loosers badge and liv'ry heretofore.

S.   But now so ordered that it might be taken
      By lookers on, forsaking as forsaken.   20
                  And now and then
      A carelesse smile broke forth, which spoke his mind,—

B.   And seem'd to say she might have been more kind.

S.   When this (dear *Jack*) I saw,
                        Thought I   25
                  How weak is Lovers Law?

B.   The bonds made there (like gypsies knots) with ease
      Are fast and loose, as they that hold them please.

S.   But was the fair Nymphs praise or power lesse
      That led him captive now to happinesse,   30
      'Cause she did not a forreign aid despise,
      But enterr'd breaches made by others eyes?
                  The Gods forbid!
      There must be some to shoot and batter down,
      Others to force and to take in the Town.   35
                  To Hawkes (good *Jack*) and hearts
                        There may
                  Be sev'ral waies and Arts:
      One watches them perchance, and makes them tame;
      Another, when they're ready, shews them game.   40

  78. 29 S.] B. *Haz, Th*   33 *Haz and Th assign to* S. (*continuing from l. 29 in present*
text)

DUBIA

79. Love turn'd to Hatred

I WILL not love one minute more I swear,
No not a minute; not a sigh or tear
Thou getst from me, or one kind look agen,
Though thou shouldst court me to't and wouldst begin.
I will not think of thee but as men do   5
Of debts and sins, and then I'le curse thee too:
For thy sake women shall be now to me
Less welcom, then at midnight ghosts should be:
Ile hate so perfectly, that it shall be
Treason to love that man that loves a she;   10
Nay I will hate the very good, I swear,
That's in thy sex, because it doth lie there;
Their very vertue, grace, discourse, and wit,
And all for thee; what, wilt thou love me yet?

80. Love and Debt alike troublesom

THIS one request I make to him that sits the clouds above,
That I were freely out of debt, as I am out of love:
Then for to dance, to drink and sing, I should be very willing;
I should not ow one Lass a kiss, nor ne'r a Knave a shilling.
'Tis only being in Love and Debt, that breaks us of our rest;   5
And he that is quite out of both, of all the world is blest:
He sees the golden age wherein all things were free and common;
He eats, he drinks, he takes his rest, he fears no man nor woman.
Though *Crœsus* compassed great wealth, yet he still craved more,
He was as needy a beggar still, as goes from dore to dore.   10

DUBIA. *LR and MSS.*
   79. Love turn'd to Hatred. *LR. MSS.: A4, RP14.* Love turn'd to Hatred] Capt. Tyrell.
Of Mrs Winchcombe *RP14: omit A4*   4 to't ... wouldst] (would *A4*): to it ... *omit
RP14*   5 I will not] I'le never *RP14*   7 women *MSS.*: woman *LR*   now to]
unto *RP14*: to *A4*   8 should *RP14*: shall *A4, LR; see note*
   80. Love and Debt alike troublesom. *LR. MS.: A23 (lines divided as common metre
rather than as fourteeners)*   2 That I were freely] weare I as truly *MS.*   9 compassed great] was Composed of *MS.*

Though *Ovid* were a merry man, Love ever kept him sad;
He was as far from happiness, as one that is stark mad.
Our Merchant he in goods is rich, and full of gold and treasure;
But when he thinks upon his Debts, that thought destroys his
    pleasure.
Our Courtier thinks that he's preferr'd, whom every man envies; 15
When Love so rumbles in his pate, no sleep comes in his eyes.
Our Gallants case is worst of all, he lies so just betwixt them;
For he's in Love, and he's in Debt, and knows not which most vex't
    him.
But he that can eat Beef, and feed on bread which is so brown,
May satisfie his appetite, and owe no man a crown: 20
And he that is content with Lasses clothed in plain woollen,
May cool his heat in every place, he needs not to be sullen,
Nor sigh for love of Lady fair; for this each wise man knows:
As good stuff under Flanel lies, as under Silken clothes.

81. Song

[Probably by Dr. Henry Hughes]

I

I PRETHEE send me back my heart,
  Since I cannot have thine:
For if from yours you will not part,
  Why then should you keep mine?

2

Yet now I think on't, let it lie, 5
  To send it me were vain,
For th' hast a thief in either eye
  Will steal it back again.

80. 13 Our... treasure] Hou^r Marchant he Comes Rich | from Endea full of treashure *MS*.
15 thinks that he's preferr'd] he is perfumed in state *MS*. 17 Our . . . case] The . . .
Cause *MS*. he lies so] for he is *MS*. 18 vex't *Ed.*: vex *LR*, *MS*. 22 needs *MS*.:
need *LR* 23 sigh for love of Lady fair] sight for losse of lady gay *MS*. 24 lies] is *MS*.
  81. Song. *LR*. MSS.: *H35*, *H38* (*ll. 1–12 only; for association with Suckling, see note*), *HL*,
RP6. *Variant printed texts*: *JG* (*ll. 1–16 only; obviously conflated*), *SMA53*. *Derivative
MSS. and printed texts* (*readings ignored in critical apparatus*): *AD* (*from SMA53*), *F69* (*from
SMA53*), *H39* (*from W162*), *MDC* (*from AD*), *O2* (*from LR*), *W162* (*from AD*) 4 should
you *Σ*: shouldst thou *JG* (+ then), *LR* keep *Σ*: have *H35*, *JG*, *LR* 5 Yet] But
H35, *JG*, *RP6* 6 send *Σ*: find *LR* me were *Σ*: were in *H38*, *LR*: me 'twere in *JG*
7 For th'hast] For thou hast *H38*, *JG*: She hath *RP6* 8 Will *Σ*: Would *LR*

3

Why should two hearts in one breast lie,
And yet not lodge together?   10
Oh Love, where is thy sympathie,
If thus our hearts thou sever!

4

But Love is such a mysterie,
I cannot find it out:
For when I think I'm best resolv'd,   15
I then am most in doubt.

5

Then farewel care, and farewel woe,
I will no longer pine:
For I'le believe I have her heart,
As much as she hath mine.   20

82. The guiltless Inconstant

[Probably by Walton Poole]

M Y first Love whom all beauty did adorn,
Firing my heart, supprest it with her scorn;
Since like to tinder in my breast it lies,
By every sparkle made a sacrifice.
Each wanton eye now kindleth my desire,   5
And that is free to all which was entire;
Desiring more by the desire I lost,
As those that have Consumptions hunger most.

---

81. 11 Oh] Ah *H35, HL, RP6*   12 hearts *Σ*: breasts *LR*   thou] do *F69, H38,*
JG, RP6   13–20 *omit H38*   16 most in *Σ*: in most *LR*   17–20 *omit JG*
17 Then] but *HL*   19 For] But *F69, H39, HL, MDC, W162*
82. The guiltless Inconstant. *LR. MSS.: A33, Dobell MS. (title and subscription only
known; see note), Eg27, F7, M6a, M6b (ll. 1–19 only; from M6a), Ros2, Ros4, TCD. Variant
printed texts:* Thomas Carew, *Poems,* 1640 *(Car); West-D (from F7)*
    The guiltless Inconstant] The Sparke *Car, Eg27:* Upon his Loves Vicissitude *A33:* On
his first Love *F7:* My first Love burnt my hart to tynder, | since, every sparklinge eye doth
Kindle fire *Ros2:* On the 2 first verses of the former Copye for the Lady Denham *TCD:* The
answer to it *Ros4 (see note): omit M6*   1 beauty *Σ*: beauties *Car, LR*   3 Since]
And since *A33, F7:* Sun-[like] *Car*   to *Σ*: the *LR*   5 now kindleth *Σ*: now kindles
Car, M6, Ros2: can kindle *LR*   7–8 *omit A33, F7, Ros2*   8 have . . . hunger *Σ*:
in . . . hunger *Car*: in . . . linger *LR*

And now my wandring thoughts are not confin'd
Unto one woman, but to womankind: 10
This for her shape I love, that for her face,
This for her gesture, or some other grace:
And sometimes where that none of these I find,
I chuse there by the kernel, not the rind:
And so may hope since my first hope is gone,   15
To find in many what I lost in one;
And like to Merchants after some great loss
Trade by retail, that cannot do in gross.
The fault is hers who made me go astray,
He needs must wander that hath lost his way: 20
Guiltless I am; she did this change provoke,
Which made that Charcoal, which to her was Oak.
And as a Looking glass from the Aspect
Whilst it is whole, doth but one face reflect;
But crackt, or broke in pieces there are shown   25
Many less faces, where was first but one:
So Love unto my heart did first prefer
Her image, and there planted none but her;
But since 'twas broke and martyr'd by her scorn,
Many less faces in her place are born.   30
Thus like to tinder am I prone to catch
Each falling sparkle, fit for any match.

82. 9 And] For *A33, F7, Ros2*   13 sometimes ... of these [I/do] *Σ* (those *Ros2*): *omit*
... of all these things [I] *LR: omit* ... of these [do] use to *Car*   that ... I] I ... do *A33,
Car, F7, M6*   14 there by *Σ* (thereby *Car, Ros2, Ros4*): therein *M6*: her by *LR*
15 may *Eg27, M6, Ros2, TCD*: I *Car, LR, Ros4*: do *A33, F7*   first] chief *A33, F7, Ros2,
Ros4, TCD*   hope is] hope be *A33, F7, Ros2*: hopes are *Car*: love is *Eg27* (hope *deleted*)
18 do] trade *M6*: deale *A33*: now [ingrosse] *Car*   19 The fault is hers] She is in fault
A33, F7, Ros2 (She was), *Ros4, TCD*   who *Σ*: that *Car, LR, Ros4*   made me go] caused
me first *A33, F7, Ros2*: caused me *Ros4, TCD*   21 did *Σ*: doth *LR*   22 Which
Σ: Who *M6, Ros4, TCD*: And *Car, LR*   to her] at first *A33, F7, Ros2*: before *Ros4,
TCD*   23 And] For *A33, F7, Ros2*   from] to *A33, F7, M6, Ros2*   25 crackt,
or broke in pieces *Σ* (broke or crackt in peices *TCD*): being crackt or broken *Car, LR*
shown *Σ*: grown *LR*   26 less] more *M6* (lesse *deleted*): halfe *Car*   was first but *Σ*
(were *M6*): there was but *LR*: at first were *Car*   28 planted *Σ*: placed *A33, F7, Ros2*:
LR, Ros4   29 since] when *A33, F7, Ros2*   broke] crackt *A33, F7, Ros2, Ros4, TCD*
30 faces] beauties *Eg27, M6, Ros4, TCD*   place] seat *A33, F7, Ros2*: face *Car*: roome
Ros4, TCD   31-2 *Σ* (*text from Car, spelling normalized*): *omit LR*   31 am I] I am
A33, F7

83. [To the Lady Desmond]
(Upon the Black Spots worn by my Lady D. E.)

[Probably by Peter Apsley]

MADAM,
I know your heart cannot so guilty be,
That you should wear those spots for vanity;
Or as your Beauties Trophies, put on one
For every murther that your eyes have done:
No, th'are your Mourning-weeds for Hearts forlorn,   5
Which though you must not love, you could not scorn;
To whom since cruel Honor doth deny
Those joyes could onely cure their misery,
Yet you this noble way to grace them found,
Whilst thus your grief their martyrdom hath crown'd.   10
Of which take heed you prove not prodigal,
For if to every common Funeral
Of your eyes martyrs, such grace were allow'd,
Your Face would wear no Patches, but a Cloud.

---

83. [To the Lady Desmond.] *LR. MSS.: A11, M3 (the textual archetype: see note on Text), F24. Variant printed text:* Dudley Lord North, *A Forest of Varieties*, 1645 *(North)*
To yᵉ Lady Desmonde *M3:* Upon the Black Spots worn by my Lady D. E. *LR:* The reason of a Gentlewomans wearing small blacke patches. Of another Author *North:* On his Mʳˢ beauty spotts *F24: omit A11; see note on Text*   Madam] *omit A11 (but* Madam *to* wear, *l. 11), North*   3–4 *omitted here, placed after l. 14 in F24*   4 that *Σ:* which *LR*   5 th'are *M3:* they're *Σ:* they are *North; see note on Text*   6 must not . . . could] cannot . . . must *A11:* could not . . . would *F24*   7–10 *omit A11*   7–8 *omit F24*   11 Of which take heed you prove not] But yet take heed be not too *F24:* but take heed Madam, bee not too *A11*   13 Of your eyes martyrs *Σ:* By your eyes martyr'd *LR:* caus'd by your eyes *F24*   grace] Graces *F24* (graces), *LR(u):* favour *A11*   13–14 were . . . would] be . . . will *A11, North*   14 no *Σ:* not *LR*

84. [Foreknowledge]

Εἰ μὲν ἦν μαθεῖν
Ἅ δεῖ παθεῖν
Καὶ μὴ παθεῖν
Καλὸν ἦν τὸ μαθεῖν
Εἰ δὲ δεῖ παθεῖν
Ἅ δεῖ μαθεῖν
Τὶ δεῖ μαθεῖν
Χρῆ γὰρ παθεῖν.

5

Scire si liceret quæ debes subire,
Et non subire, pulchrum est scire:
Sed si subire debes quæ debes scire,
Quorsum vis scire, nam debes subire?

Englished thus

IF man might know
   The ill he must undergo,
And shun it so,
   Then it were good to know:
But if he undergo it,
   Though he know it,
What boots him know it?
   He must undergo it.

5

---

84. [Foreknowledge.] *LR* (*a translation of* Εἰ μὲν ἦν μαθεῖν *and* Scire si liceret *etc.*). *Title supplied* (Englished thus *in LR*). *MS.:* F80 (*substantive variants in English; recorded in full*) *see Commentary*   2 The ill] What *MS.*   4 it were] were it *MS.*   5–6 But . . . it] But if hee know it | And must undergoe it *MS.*

85. To Mr. W. M. Against Absence

[Perhaps by Sir William Davenant]

PEDLAR in love, that with the common Art
    Of traffiquers dost fly from Mart to Mart,
Thinking thy passions (false as their false ware)
Will, if not here, vent in another fare,
As if thy subtle threatning to remove   5
From hence would raise the price of thy poore love.
Thou know'st the deere being shot, the hunter may
Securely trust him, though he run away.
For fleeing with his Wound, the arrow more
Doth gal and vexe him then it did before.   10
Absence from her you love, that love being true,
Is but a thin cloud 'twixt the Sun and you,
Takes not the too-strong object from your Eye
But makes you fit and abler to descry.
Then know (my loving smal Philosopher)   15
You vainely take the Paynes to fly from her
On whom in absence you doe ever thinke,
For that's a kind of seeing when you winke.

86. [A New-years Gift]

THE Phenix dyes, yet still remaine
    The Eagles youth, renew'th Againe;
Bright *Thetis* her Horned Waine
Is Remade, Refin'd, Reset Againe.
Five thousand Six Hundred Thirty yeare   5
Time hath turn'd rownd this wheely spheare,
Yet still that yeare is called New
That Circulair the Rest Insew,

85. To Mr. W. M. Against Absence. *Cran2. Title from* Dav. *Variant printed text*: The
Works of Sr William Davenant K^t, *1673, p. 294* (Dav; *substantive variants recorded in full*)
    To Mr. W. M. Against Absence] (Mr, *Dav*): omit *Cran2*   1 that] thou *Dav*
6 would] could *Dav*   9 fleeing] flying *Dav*   10 doth] does *Dav*   12 but . . .
'twixt] (t'wixt *Cran2*): omit . . . between *Dav*   13 Takes not the too-strong] It does
not take the *Dav*   14 makes you fit and] rather makes you *Dav*   15 loving smal]
wandring weake *Dav*   17 doe] must *Dav*   18 that's] (thats *Cran2*): 'tis *Dav*
    86. [A New-years Gift.] *Cran. Title, punctuation, and italics supplied*

On which new day, this new-years gift
Your Tribute is, and my poore Shift   10
Apollos braine, *Minnervas* hand is wanting,
Orpheus straine, riche-treashewred *Juno* vanting.
May I with-out all these Present
In rude Lin'd paper my intent,
A *satisfactus* or summe Duty rather   15
Which nature bindes me to, a mother,
Rewishing that your yeares may last
My Summer, Autumne and my Blast,
Yester day, to day, so still the same
In Vertu, Beauty and your name.   20

Long may you wish and yet Long wish in vaine
Hence to depart, and yet that wish Obtaine;
Long may you here in heaven on earth Remaine
And yet a heaven in heaven here affter gaine.

87. [Gnomics]

REVENGE is swate, and reck'ned as cleare gaine,
Aboundance breedes contempte, in baser mindes,
Chance, and wisdome, ne'r march in selfsame train,
Hope, (to sustein it) somethinge ever findes.
Envie pines, at welfare of another,   5
Love laboureth alwaies, to good his brother.
Fortitude defies pævishe fortunes frowne,
Anger devesteth us, of al reason,
Nobilitie from vertue, hath hir crowne,
Esteeme of pieti's growne out of season.   10

87. [Gnomics.] *Cran. Title supplied*

88. Inconstancie in Woman

1

I AM confirm'd a woman can,
Love this or that or anye man.
This daye her love is meltinge hott,
To morrow sweares she knowes you not!
Let her but a new Object finde,   5
And she is of an Other Mynde!
  Then hange me Ladyes at your doore,
  If e're I doate uppon you more!

2

Yet still I'le love the faire ones, whye?
For nothinge but to please myne Eye.   10
And soe the fatt and softe-skinn'd dame
I'le flatter to Appeas my flame.
For her that's musicall I'le longe
When I am sad, to singe a songe.
  But hange me Ladyes at your doore,   15
  If e're I doate uppon you more!

3

I'le give my fancy leave to range
Through Ev'ry face to finde out change.
The black, the browne, the faire shall be
But Objects of varietye.   20

88. Inconstancie in Woman. *HL (first words in each line capitalized, terminal punctuation in stanzas 2–3 supplied, and contractions and the refrain in ll. 15–16 and 23–4 expanded). Variant MSS.: Dx4, Dx42, F24 (ll. 1–8 only), F62, F308, F339, H39, H69. Variant printed texts: AC, MDC (2 stanzas only), SMA, Wind-D, WI. Except as noted, Haz and Th agree with N&Q, 1st ser., 1849, i. 72, and the latter with F62, from which the poem was first printed in N&Q*
Inconstancie in Woman *SMA*: vpon a womans inconstancy *F24*: Womens Inconstancie *WI (1662 & 1671)*: Sᵣ Iohn Suckling verses *[later hand than text] F62*: Song *Wind-D, WI*: A Song *AC*: omit Σ 2 anye] +other *N&Q* 3 This] *(Dx4, F62, H39, HL, MDC, SMA)*: To *AC, Dx42, F24, F308, F339, H69, Wind-D, WI; see note* her love is] she's *F62* 4 you not] not what *AC, F308, Wind-D* 5–6 omit *H39* 5 Let her] If she *F62, H69* 6 And] Then *H69*: and streight *Dx42*: Then straite *F62* she is] she's *N&Q* 9–24 omit *F24* 9 Yet still] But yet *F339*: But still *H69, WI*: And yet *F308*: And if *AC, Wind-D* I'le] *(F62, HL [Ile], SMA)*: I Σ+*N&Q* ones] *(Dx4, Dx42, HL)*: one Σ: and *WI*: [fair]some *N&Q; see note* 10 myne] my *AC, F62, Wind-D, WI* 11–12, 13–14 *transposed AC, F308, Wind-D* 12 I'le] I *AC, F308, F339, Wind-D, WI* 13 her] she *F62* I'le] *(Dx42, F62, H69, HL, N&Q)*: I Σ 15 But] Then *AC, Dx42, F62, F308, H69, Wind-D* 17–24 omit *MDC* 18 face] where *F62* out] a *AC, Dx4, F308, H69, Wind-D, WI*

I'le court you all to serve my turne,
But with such flames as shall not burne.
For hange me Ladyes at your doore,
If e're I doate uppon you more!

89. To Celia, an Ode

By Sir John Suckling

YOUTH and Beauty now are thine,
O let Pleasure, *Celia*, join;
                    Be Divine.

Shun the Folly of Disdain,
Pride affords a short-liv'd Reign,   5
                    Full of Pain.

All the Graces court the Kind,
Beauty by a tender Mind
                    Is refin'd.

90. In Brennoralt

THY love is chaste, they tell thee so,
But how young Souldier shalt thou know?
Do by her,
As by thy Sword,
Take no friends word,   5
But try her;
'Twill raise her Honor one step higher.
Fame has her tryal at Loves bar,
Deify'd *Venus* from a Star,
Shoots her lustre;   10
She had never been Goddess't,
If *Mars* had been modest:
Try and trust her.

88. 21 serve] (+*N&Q*): please *F62*   23 For] (*Dx4*, *HL*, *SMA*, *WI*): Then *AC*,
Dx42, *F62*, *F308*, *F339*, *H69*, *Wind-D*
  89. To Celia, an Ode. *The Grove; or, A Collection of Original Poems, Translations, etc.*,
1721
  90. In Brennoralt. *NAC. Title from H39. MS.: H39 (from NAC)*   1 they tell]
shee tells *MS.; see note*

91. Song

1

IF you refuse me once, and think again,
 I will complain.
You are deceiv'd, Love is no work of Art,
  It must be got and born,
  Not made and worn,   5
By every one that hath a heart.

2

Or do you think they more then once can dye,
 Whom you deny?
Who tell you of a thousand deaths a day,
  Like the old Poets feign   10
  And tell the pain
They met, but in the common way.

3

Or do you think't too soon to yield,
 And quit the field?
Nor is that right; they yield that first intreat;   15
  Once one may crave for Love,
  But more would prove
This heart too little, that too great.

---

91. Song. *LR* (*printed with* Song ['Oh that I were all Soul, that I might prove'], *following,
as a single poem*). *MSS.*: *A37, O2* (*from LR, also presenting two poems as one*). *Variant printed
text*: Lord Herbert of Cherbury, *Occasional Verses,* 1665 (*OV*). *Substantive variants recorded
in full*
 Song] Ditty *A37, OV: omit O2; see note*   2–3 complain. . . . deceiv'd,]~, . . .~: *OV*
4 got and] freely *A37*   6 By every one that hath a heart] Or such wherein you have no
part *A37, OV*   8 Whom] When *A37*   10 feign₍ₐ₎] fain, *OV*   12 met,]
~₍ₐ₎ *OV*   13 [think]'t] it is *A37, OV*   15 Nor is that right₍ₐ₎ [; *Ed.*]] You are
deceiv'd, *A37, OV*   that] who *A37, OV*   19–36 *three stanzas omit A37, LR: present
in OV* (*q.v. in Commentary*)

92. [Upon Platonic Love]

[By Sir Robert Ayton]

1

OH that I were all Soul, that I might prove
    For you as fit a Love,
As you are for an Angel; for I vow
None but pure spirits are fit loves for you.

2

You're all Etherial, there's in you no dross,   5
    Nor any part that's gross.
Your coursest part is like a curious Lawn,
O're Vestal Relicks for a covering drawn.

3

Your other part, part of the purest fire
    That ere Heaven did inspire,   10
Makes every thought that is refined by it,
A quintessence of goodness and of wit.

4

Thus have your Raptures reach'd to that degree
    In Love's Philosophy,
That you can figure to your self a fire   15
Void of all heat, a Love without desire.

---

92. [Upon Platonic Love.] *LR. Title from A10x. MSS.: A10, A10x (alterations in the hand of Sir John Ayton; see note), A11, F25, H17, L, O2 (from LR, though sophisticated, and like it presented as a continuation of* Song ['If you refuse me once, and think again']). *Gullans = The English and Latin Poems of Sir Robert Ayton, 1963, ed. Charles B. Gullans (see note)*
vpon platonik loue *A10x, L (later hand; omit* vpon): To C. C. maide of honour *A11*: To Mrs Cicely Crofts *H17*: Vpon Platonick Love: To Mistress Cicely Crofts, Maide of Honor *Gullans:* omit *Σ (headed* Song *as part of* 'If you refuse me once, and think again' *LR); see note*
3 vow *Σ*: know *LR*: dare avow *A10*   5 You're *A10 (+A10x), F25, Gullans*: Y'are *A11, H17*: You are *L, LR*   there's] there is *A10, Gullans, Haz, L*   7 part] half *A11, F25, L*   a] the *A10x, Gullans*   8 O're... drawn *Σ* (The *LR*: By *L*): To Vestall relicks for a curtain drawn *O2*: To cover Vestall Relecks *A10*   covering] curtain, *L, O2* 9 [other] part *Σ*: parts *A11, L, LR*   11 thought] thing *A11, H17*   13 have... reach'd] (hath *A10x, A11*): do... reach *A10, Gullans*   Raptures] rapture *A10x*

5

Nor in Divinity do you go less;
    You think, and you profess,
That Souls may have a plenitude of Joy,
Although their Bodies never meet t'enjoy.   20

6

But I must needs confess, I do not finde
    The motions of my minde
So purified as yet, but at their best
My Body claims in them some interest.

7

I hold that perfect joy makes all our parts   25
    As joyful as our hearts.
Our senses tell us, if we please not them,
Our Love is but a dotage or a dream.

8

How shall we then agree? You may descend,
    But will not, to my end.   30
I fain would tune my fancy to your Key,
But cannot reach to that abstracted way.

9

There rests but this, that while we sojourne here,
    Our bodies may draw neer:
And when they can their joys no more extend,   35
Then let our souls begin where they did end.

92. 20 never meet t'[enjoy] *Σ* (to *L*): meet not to *A10, LR*   enjoy *Σ*: employ *LR*
21 But] Now *A11, H17, L*   23 their *Σ*: the *A10x, F25, LR*   24 some*Σ*: an *LR*
25–32 *omit H17*   25–6 *omit L*   25 I hold that . . . parts] (hold a *A10x, Gullans*): I hold
my Ioyes not perfyt if each part *A10* : I thinke my Ioyes not full if any parte *A11*   27–8 Our
. . . us . . . we . . . | Our] My . . . me . . . I . . . | My *A10, A10x(2), A11, Gullans; see note*
31 tune] turn *O2*   32 abstracted *Σ*: abstract *A10* (+*A10x*): obstructed *LR*   33 while
Σ+*O2*: whilst *F25, LR*   sojourne *Σ*+*O2*: sorrow *LR*   35 they can their joys no
more *A10* (there love), *A11, H17* (our Joyes): no more their joys they can *LR*: our joys
they can noe more *A10x, Gullans, L* (that here *for* our joys): their joyes noe more they can
F25   36 begin] go on *O2*

93. Song

[By Owen Felltham]

1

W HEN Deare I doe but thinke on thee
   Mee thinkes all things that lovely bee
Are present, and my soule delighted:
For beauties that from worth arise
Are like the grace of Deities   5
Still present with us, though unsighted.

2

Soe while I sitt, and sighe the daye
With all his borrowed lights awaye
Till nights blacke wings doe overtake mee,
Thinking on thee thy beauties then,   10
As suddaine lights doe sleeping men,
Soe they by their bright rayes awake mee.

3

Thus Absence dies, and dyeing proves
No absence can subsist with loves
That doe partake of faire perfection;   15
Since in the darkest night they maie
By their close motions find a waye
To light each other by reflection.

---

93. *Song. Harv6. Variant MSS.:* A25 (*from* Ros4), EP5, H18, O2 (*from* LR), RD7
(*from* Lu), Ros4. *Variant printed texts:* LR; Owen Felltham, *Lusoria: Or Occasional Pieces,*
1661 (*Lu*). *Substantive variants recorded in full*
   Song LR : To his Mistrisse H18 : To his loue Ros4: omit Σ   1 Deare I doe] Dearest,
I Lu, LR, O2, RD7   on] of EP5, LR   7 Soe] Thus Lu, LR, O2, RD7   while] whilst
LR, O2, Ros4   8 his] her EP5   borrowed] spreading Lu, RD7   lights] light A25,
Ros4   9 doe] doth EP5   11 sleeping] sleepy A25, Ros4   14 absence] absent
A25   subsist] consist Lu, RD7   15 doe] to RD7   of] with EP5   16 night]
nights A25   17 their] Loves LR, O2   close motions] quick motion Lu, LR, O2,
RD7   18 light] see Lu, LR, O2, RD7   18–19 each . . . each] such . . . each Lu :
each . . . such RD7

4

The waving Sea can with each floud
Bathe some highe Promont that hath stood 20
Farre from the maine upp in the River:
O thinke not then but love can doe
As much; for that's an Ocean too
Which flowes not every daie, but ever.

93. 20 Promont] Palace *Lu, RD7* 22 O] I *RD7* 24 Which] That *Lu, RD7*

LETTERS

LETTERS

To divers Eminent

PERSONAGES:

Written on several Occasions,

By

Sir JOHN SUCKLING.

Printed by his owne Copy.

LONDON,

Printed by *Ruth Raworth* for *Humphrey Moseley*, and
are to be sold at his shop at the signe of the
Princes Arms in S. *Pauls* Church-yard. 1646.

LETTERS

TO

SEVERAL PERSONS

OF

HONOR.

BY

Sᵗ *JOHN SUCKLING.*

LONDON:

Printed for *Humphrey Moseley* at the Prince's
Arms in St. *Pauls* Churchyard. 1659,

Special Title-Page from the First Edition of *The Last Remains of Sir John Suckling,*
1659 (Henry E. Huntington Library, shelf-mark 110162)

LETTERS

1. To Mary Cranfield, 30 October 1629

The Lady
Mary Cranfeild

Madam

I SHOUD heere set forth the discontent and deepe melancholy I
now entertaine, for the great loss of such a world of goodnes at 5
once, as your selfe is! But to shew my sorrow by barren Expressions,
were but to let you see daylight through courtaines, or at the best,
with him that was to paint *Æneas* parting from his *Troy*, but draw
a vayle before it! Let it suffice, that those countryes which I am now to
visit, are but soe many faire roomes in a prison, The whole world 10
it self, not yealding halfe that pleasure which your blest company
can give! I would say more, but I have already trespas'd both upon
time and tide to let you see I am

Gravesend.
October 30th.
   1629

Yours more then his owne 15

J. Suckling.

2. [To Mary Cranfield, 1629–1635 (?)]

FORTUNE and Love have ever been so incompatible, that it is
no wonder (Madam) if having had so much of the one for you,
I have ever found so little of the other for my self; Comming to Town
(and having rid as if I had brought intelligence of a new-landed
Enemy to the State) I find you gone the day before, and with you 5
(Madam) all that is considerable upon the place; for though you have
left behind you, faces whose beauties might well excuse perjury in
others, yet in me they cannot, since to the making that no sin, Loves

LETTERS. *FA46, LR, and MSS. For the arrangement of the letters in this edition, see Introduction, pp. cxxxi–cxxxiii. The name of the person addressed and the date are given, wherever
possible, at the head of each letter*
  1. *Cran (holograph)*
  2. *FA46.* [*To Mary Cranfield, 1629–1635(?)*]: *see note*   3 to Town] *to the town Haz*

Casuists have most rationally resolved, that she for whom we forsake,
10 ought to be handsomer then the forsaken, which would be here
impossible: So that now a gallerie hung with *Titians* or *Vandikes* hand,
and a chamber filled with living Excellence, are the same things to
me; and the use that I shall make of that Sex now, will be no other
then that which the wiser sort of Catholiques do of Pictures; at the
15 highest, they but serve to raise my devotion to you: Should a great
Beauty now resolve to take me in (as that is all they think belongs
to it) with the Artillery of her eyes, it would be as vain, as for a
Thief to set upon a new robb'd passenger; You (Madam) have my
heart already, nor can you use it unkindly but with some injustice,
20 since (besides that it left a good service to wait on you) it was never
known to stay so long, or so willingly before with any; After all, the
wages will not be high; for it hath been brought up under Platonicks,
and knows no other way of being paid for service, then by being
commanded more; which truth when you doubt, you have but to
25 send to its master and

> Your humble Servant,
> *J. S.*

3. [To Mary Cranfield, 1629–1635]

THOUGH (Madam) I have ever hitherto beleeved play to be a
thing in it self as meerly indifferent as Religion to a States-man,
or love made in a privie-chamber; yet hearing you have resolved
it otherwise for me, my faith shall alter without becomming more
5 learned upon it, or once knowing why it should do so; so great and
just a Soveraignty is that your reason hath above all others, that mine
must be a Rebel to it self, should it not obey thus easily; and indeed
all the infallibility of judgement we poor Protestants have, is at this
time wholy in your hands.
10   The losse of a Mistris (which kills men onely in Romances, and is
still digested with the first meat we eat after it) had yet in me raised
up so much passion, and so just a quarrel (as I thought) to Fortune
for it, that I could not but tempt her to do me right upon the first
occasion: yet (Madam) has it not made me so desperate but that I
15 can sit down a loser both of that time and money too, when there shall
be the least fear of losing you.

3. *FA46*

And now, since I know your Ladyship is too wise to suppose to your self impossibilities, and therefore cannot think of such a thing, as of making me absolutely good; it will not be without some impatience that I shall attend to know what sin you will be pleased 20 to assigne me in the room of this: something that has lesse danger about it (I conceive it would be) and therefore if you please (Madam) let it not be Women: for to say truth, it is a dyet I cannot yet rellish, otherwise then men do that on which they surfetted last.

Your humblest Servant, 25

J. S.

4. [To Mary Cranfield, 1629–1635 (?)]

Madam,

BEFORE this instant I did not beleeve *Warwickshire* the other world, or that *Milcot* walks had been the blessed shades. At my arrival here I am saluted by all as risen from the dead, and have had joy given me as preposterously and as impertinently as they give it 5 to men who marry where they do not love. If I should now die in earnest, my friends have nothing to pay me, for they have discharged the Rites of Funeral sorrow before hand. Nor do I take it ill, that report which made *Richard* the second alive so often after he was dead, should kill me as often when I am alive; The advantage is 10 on my side: The onely quarrel I have, is that they have made use of the whole Book of Martyrs upon me; and without all question the first Christians under the great persecutions suffered not in five hundred years, so many several waies as I have done in six daies in this lewd Town. This (Madam) may seem strange unto you now, 15 who know the Company I was in; and certainly if at that time I had departed this transitory World, it had been a way they had never thought on; and this Epitaph of the Spaniards (changing the names) would better have become my Grave-stone, then any other my friends the Poets would have found out for me: 20

Epitaph.

Here lies Don Alonzo,
Slain by a wound received under
His left Pappe,

4. *FA46*   5 as [preposterously]] *omit Haz, Th*

25   *The Orifice of which was so*
                               Small, no Chirurgion could
                                      Discover it.
                                       Reader,
                              If thou wouldst avoid so strange
30   *A Death,*
                              Look not upon Lucinda's *eyes.*

   Now all this discourse of dying (Madam) is but to let you know
how dangerous a thing it is to be long from *London*, especially
in a place which is concluded out of the World. If you are not to
35 be frighted hither, I hope you are to be perswaded; and if good
Sermons, or good Playes, new Braveries, or fresh Wit, Revells,
(Madam) Masks that are to be, have any Rhetorique about them,
here they are I assure you in perfection; without asking leave of the
Provinces beyond Seas, or the assent of ———. I write not this that
40 you should think I value these pleasures above those of *Milcot*: for
I must here protest, I preferre the single Tabor and Pipe in the great
Hall, far above them: and were there no more belonging to a journey
then riding so many miles, (would my affairs conspire with my desires)
your Ladyship should find there not at the bottom of a Letter
45   Madam,
                                   Your humble Servant.

5. [To Mary Cranfield, 5–10 October 1631]

Madam,

To tell you that neither my misfortunes nor my sins did draw
   from me ever so many sighs as my departure from you has done,
and that there are yet tears in mine eyes left undryed for it; or that
5 melancholy has so deeply seized me, that colds and diseases hereafter
shall not need above half their force to destroy me, would be I know
superfluous and vain, since so great a goodnesse as yours, cannot but
have out-beleeved already what I can write.
   He never knew you that will not think the losse of your Company,
10 greater then the Imperialists can at this time the losse of all their
Companies; and he shall never know you that can think it greater

---

4. 35 frighted] frightened *Haz, Th*
5. *FA46*   10 at *Ed.*: all *FA46; see note*

then I, who though I never had neither wisdom nor wit enough to admire you to your worth, yet had my Judgement ever so much right in it, as to admire you above all. And thus he saies that dares swear he is   15

Your most devoted servant.

6. [To Mary Cranfield, 1631 (?)]

Madam,

THE distrust I have had of not being able to write to you any thing which might pay the charge of reading, has perswaded me to forbear kissing your hands at this distance: So, like Women that grow proud, because they are chaste; I thought I might be 5 negligent, because I was not troublesom. And, were I not safe in your goodnes, I should be (Madam) in your judgement; which is too just to value little observances, or think them necessary to the right honouring my Lady.

Your Ladyship I make no doubt, will take into consideration, that 10 superstition hath ever been fuller of Ceremony then the true worship. When it shall concern any part of your real service, and I not throw by all respects whatsoever to manifest my devotion, take what revenge you please. Undo me Madam: Resume my best Place and Title; and let me be no longer   15

Your humble servant.

7. [To Mary Cranfield, Winter 1631/2]

Madam,

BY the same reason the Ancients made no sacrifice to death, should your Ladyship send me no Letters; since there has been no return on my side. But the truth is, the place affords nothing: all our dayes are (as the Women here) alike: and the difference of *Fair*, does rarely 5 shew it selfe; Such great State do Beauty and the Sun keep in these parts. I keep company with my own Horses (Madam) to avoid that of the men; and by this you may guesse how great an enemy to my living contentedly my Lady is, whose conversation has brought me to so fine a diet, that, wheresoever I go, I must starve: all daies are 10

5. 12 neither] any *FA48, Haz*   **6.** *FA46*   **7.** *FA46*

tedious, companies troublesom, and Books themselves (Feasts heretofore) no relish in them. Finding you to be the cause of all this,
Excuse me (Madam) if I resent: and continue peremptory in the
resolution I have taken to be

15   Madam, during life,
                                          Your humblest Servant.

8. [To Mary Cranfield, after 10 April 1632 (?)]

Madam,

BUT that I know your goodnes is not mercinary, and that you
receive thanks, either with as much trouble as men ill news, or
with as much wonder as Virgins unexpected Love, this letter should
5 be full of them. A strange proud return you may think I make you
(Madam) when I tell you, it is not from every body I would be thus
obliged; and that if I thought you did me not these favours because
you love me, I should not love you because you do me these favours.
This is not language for one in Affliction, I confesse, and upon whom
10 it may be at this present, a cloud is breaking; but finding not within
my self I have deserv'd that storm, I will not make it greater by
apprehending it.
        After all, least (Madam) you should think I take your favours as
Tribute; to my great grief, I here declare, that the services I shall be
15 able to render you, will be no longer Presents, but payments of Debts;
since I can do nothing for you hereafter, which I was not obliged to
do before.

                              Madam,
                                   Your most humble and faithful servant.

9. [To William Wallis], 18 November 1629

Will:

IT is reported here a Shipboard, that the winde is as weomen are,
for the most parte bad! That it altogether takes parte with the
water, for it crosses him continually that crosses the Seas. That it is
5 not good for a state reserv'd Polititian to come to sea, for he is subject
to lay forth his minde, in very plaine tearmes. That it is an ill gaming

place, for foure dayes together here has byne very bad casting of all sides, and I thinke if we had tarryed longer, it would have byne worse. That soe much Rope is a needeles thinge in a Ship, for they drowne here altogether, not hange. That if a Wench at Land, or a Ship at Sea, spring a leake, tis fit and necessary they should be pumpt. That *Dunkirke* is the Papists Purgatorie, for men are faine to pay money to be free'd out of it! Or to speake more like a true Protestant, it is the water-hell; for if a man scape this, tis ten to one he shalbe saved. That lying foure nights a shipboard, is almost as bad as sitting up, to loose money at threepenny Gleeke, and soe pray tell Mr. *Brett*; and thus much for Sea newes.

   Since my coming a shoare, I finde, that the people of this Cuntry, are a kinde of Infidells, not beleiving in the Scripture! for though it be there promist, there shall never be another Deluge; yet they doe feare it daily, and fortifie against it. That they are Natures youngest Children, and soe consequently have the least portion of Witt, and Mannors! or rather that they are her Bastards, and soe inherite none at all. And sure their auncestors when they begott them thought on nothing but Munkeys, and Bores, and Asses, and such like ill favor'd creatures; for their Phisnomyes are soe wide from the rules of pro-portion, that I should spoyle my prose to let in the discription of them. In a word, they are almost as bad as those of *Leicestershire*. Their habits are as monstrous as themselves, to all strangers, but by my troath to speake the naked truth of them; the difference betwixt the dressing of their weomen and ours, is only this; theis bumbast their tailes, and ours their Armes. As for the Cuntry: the water, and the King of *France*, beleagre it round; sometymes the *Hollander* getts ground upon them, sometymes they upon him; it is soe even a Level, that a man must have more then the quantity of a graine of Mustard-seede in faith, to remove a Mountaine here, for there is none in the Cuntry; their owne Turfe is their fyring altogether, and it is to be feared, that they will burne up their Cuntry before Doomesday. The Ayre what with their breathing in it and its owne naturall Corrup-tion, is soe unwholesome, that a man must resolve to be at the Charge of an ague once a Moneth: The plague is here constantly, I mean Excise; and in soe greate a manner, that the whole Cuntry is sick on't. Our very Farts stands us in I know not how much Excise to the States, before we let them. To be learnd here is Capitall Treason of them, beleiving that *Fortuna favet fatuis*; and therefore that they may

10

15

20

25

30

35

40

45

9. 26 Phisnomyes] physiognomies *Ha*ʒ   43 stands] stand *Ha*ʒ

have the better successe in their Warrs, they chuse Burgomasters,
and Burgers, as we doe our Maiors, and Aldermen, by their greate
Bellyes, little witts, and full Purses. Religion they use as a stuff
Cloake in summer, more for shew then any thing else; their *summum*
50 *bonum* being altogether wealth. They wholly busie themselves about
it, not a man here but would doe that which *Judas* did, for halfe the
money. To be short! the Cuntry is stark nought, and yet too good
for the inhabitants; but being our Allyes, I will forbeare their
Character, and rest

55　*Leydon　November* 18th　　　　　　　　Your humble servant
　　　1629.　　　　　　　　　　　　　　　　　　*J: Suckling.*

10. To the Earl of Middlesex, 3 May 1630

To the right honorable
the Earle of
Middlesex

Right honorable

5　　THOUGH there be nothing that I can write, that can deserve
　　　your Lordships patience in the reading, yet (since the Neglect
of my duty cannot but prove a greater sinn then that of being troublesome) the presentation of my devotions shall find I trust though not
your acceptation yet your pardon, and the boldnesse of your humble
10 servant be held excused, if he shall now disturb your greater and
better affaires, with a rude relation of the occurrences in these parts,
which at this present are most of all unworthy your sight, in respect
that the preparations unto the warr (the Onely news the season of
the yeare affords) are now but meane and poore! The Prince of *Orange*,
15 with a farr less force then the last years was, is upon going or sending
up to his Rendezvous at *Wesell*, and is thought (though the common
voice runs for a seidge at *Antwerp* and *Linge*, or an Onslight upon the
Country of *Mast*) to intend nothing but the defence of the Frontiers
and the offence of the Enemy as Occasion shall serve. The Arch-
20 duchesse seemes rather to be busied about the punishing the last yeares
Commanders, then in providing any for this, and the forces she has

10. *Cran (holograph)*　　　18 Mast *Ed.*: Wast *MS.; see note*

to bring into the feild this summer are onely those which are expected
dayly from *Germany* under the Command of *John* of *Nassaw*, who to
that purpose was sent from *Brussells* to the Emperour not more then
three weeks since. The cause of these so small Levies is thought to 25
bee the generall want of money, which to the *Hollander* proceeds from
his great gettings; (*Shertogenbosck* and *Fernanbuc* having as yet beene
onely places of charge) to the *Brabanter*, his great losses and little
trading. And the poverty of the latter is supposd to be farr greater
then that of the former; for heer the private purses are drawne dry, 30
there, onely the publique. Such an ebb of fortune as now is, was never
heard of in this countrey: the Captaines in some places are not
ashamd to begg, and the common souldiers of late are growne
insolent, though for five years together they have exprest more then
a Catholique obedience in forbearing their pay, through the Natural 35
love they beare to Superstition and the Infanta. The Fountaine of
all this Miserye they make the Ambition of the *Spanish* and the
faction betwixt them and the Nobles of the Country, Not leaving
altogether unblamd the Cardinall, that is heere, who (they say) has
perswaded the King of *Spain*, that this Country is of it self able to 40
mantaine warr against the other. To incourage the Souldier at this
present, a hot rumor is spread abroad of the Landing of the plate
fleet in *Spain*, and of three Millions to bee sent hether with all speed,
but their Expectation of them has beene so long and often frustrated,
that they can hardly now be induced to beleive any such thing. The 45
Generalls place is taken from *Henry Vandenberg* and his Command of
horse disposd of already, to Marquis *Francisco di Sapata*: he has been
lately sent for into *Spain* by the King, but has refusd to goe, knowing
the danger in respect of his many enemyes to be certaine there, and
his security as certaine heere in respect of his great power and the 50
love the people bears him. *Granendonc* (having offered to the Infanta
to make his defence before the King) is now retired into the Country,
where he has increasd the hatred of the people upon him, by finding
money for the Purchase of some great possessions there, which he
could not be intreated to find for the bying of Powder in *Bolduc*. 55
The Governour of *Wesell* is now in *Antwerp* Castle, and expected
shortly too be brought forth to execution, for it is more then three
weeks since his process was first taken out against him. This last
commander is by many bitterly rayld against, by some excusd, by
most pityed, in that he does now by one onely misfortune loose not 60
onely his estate (which he had 50 yeares laboured for under the King)

but also his honour and Life. Your Lordship has now what the barrennes of the time affords. If I have trespassed upon your patience, and you be pleasd to forgive it, It is a favor far above the desert of

65   *Brussels.   May.* 3th.   Your Lordships
        1630   devoted servant.
                                                        J. Suckling

11. To William Wallis, 5 May 1630

To his very much respected
Freind Mr. *William Wallis*
at the house of the right
honorable the Earle of
5   *Middlesex*

Will

THESE few lines shall let you understand, that their Master is your humble servant, and that he is lately come out of a country, where the people were of so poore conditions as that the greatest part
10 of them, would doe what *Judas* did for half the Money, and is arrived, Where the Condition of the people is so poore, that were there an Enemy to be betrayd and a *Judas* ready to doe it, yet would there want a man to furnish out the 30 peices of silver. Where beggerye and pride are as inseperable companions as paint to a court Ladyes
15 face or hornes to a citizens head. Where it is as rare a thing to see a man have store of money, as in *London* to see a Lord Maior have store of witt. Where the inhabitants have miriads of crosses in their churches and their streets, yet want them in their purses. Where the people quake if you talke of millions and are very infidells concerning
20 the ever comming home againe of a plate fleet. In a word, to let you understand their estate rightly, It is almost as poore as my description of it, is. This premised, you will not much wonder, if I with his Majesties bare picture onely make people bow before me with as much reverence heer, as he himselfe does with his owne personal
25 presence at *Whitehall.* And I suppose you may be induced to beleive with me, that (though I cannot properly call it the golden age) yet some time for honesty like that, is heer revived; for being there is

11. *Cran (holograph)*

no money, there is no usury, Nor no Corruption. A man may heer arrive to an Archbishoprick without being damnably Simonious at every step to the honor, have a dispach at Court without greasing 30 my Lord and his Secretary too. No man goes to law with unjust titles, for that which out-ballances right in other places is heere not to be found. No man couzens the poore country he is set to governe, for that which shoud beare him out afterwards at court, is heere wanting. Coyning is an Art forgotten Amongst them. My Lord of 35 *Holland* his patent for minting the light gold of the country would have found nothing to doe heere after a day, though there had been added to it, minting the heavy. And were Sir *Randal Cranfeild* Master of the Mint in this place, he would not be angry I am perswaded if a Sir *Robert Harlo* should couzen him of it. In a word, Necessity has 40 made their goodnes and humanity unquestionable. As for their Religion, it is a thing I cannot say much of, as having not yet sufficiently dived into it. Yet as far as I conceive of it, it would suit well enough with us young men. If a man be drunke overnight, it is but Confessing it next morning or when he is sober, and the matter 45 proves not Mortal. To the liing with ones Sister, there is no more required then the telling the truth of it to a ghostly father. And you may jumble as many wenches as you please upon bedds, provided you wil but mumble as many *Avemaries* upon beads. For their honoring the Lady *Mary* above al, I must confes (though some count it 50 Superstition and sinn) for my owne part I doe not. And to speak the plain truth, I esteeme of the Religion, as a good, and a Joviall one. For whatsoever is reported of the Austerity of their Monks and friers, beleive me, that have beine in their Company, and have seen their Capuches of, They are the maddest shavers in the world. The onely 55 thing to be dislikt is, that (notwithstanding the *Hollander* crosses them sufficiently abroad) they wil so superfluously and to little purpose crosse themselves at home. That, in their visitation of the sick a fryer carryes the host upon his shoulders, when in the new testament we never find amongst al the sick that our savior visited, that he 60 ever rode upon an Ass to any one of them. That they wil offer to assevere their church Visible at al times, when to my knowledge at certaine howres tis shut upp and not to be seene by any. Lastly, That they wil be so foolish as to have a Purgatory when without it they might goe directly to heaven. 65

11. 49 For] and *deleted MS.*   50 al] + why, tis a point, *deleted MS.*   57 superfluously] + crosse *deleted MS.*

I should now send you the news of the Country, but my time and paper wil give me onely leave to write my self

Brussels   Mai. 5th.   Yours as his owne
    1630.   *J. Suckling*

70 Sir

If you please to cloth my humble service and my devotions in good language and present them to my Lord *Middlesex* and the yong Ladyes you shal for ever oblige a poore wandring traveller and make him rest

                                  Your humble debtor
75   *J. Suckling.*
            My service to Mr. *Brett.*

12. [To the Earl of Middlesex], 10 October 1631

Right honorable

Y O U R Lordship in my last had more of truth, then I conceivd then or imagind, for I can add nothing now, unles I should set the battaile afresh in order, and the second time discomfitt it, which
5 would be to particularize into a volume. Onely *Rostac* is taken since, and the king getts ground dayly, being at this present in *Bamberg.* *Rostac* was not supprisd or beseidgd but delivered by the garrison, being 2500, who straitway marcht to the duke of *Micleberg,* from whom it was first taken away by the Emperour by force and unjustly.
10 Indeed the very pretence of al these warrs, he being couzen to the King of *Sweden.* There is nothing els presents it self worth your reading; when any does, my pen shal not be idle. This morning we receivd news that the Bishops of *Bamberg* and *Witzberg* are come in to the King and have payd 30000 sterling composition, and that the Duke
15 of *Bavaria* has lately leveld a good army for his owne defence as tis thought and not for the ayd of the Imperialist. We are now upon our journey to the Camp from whence I suppose news wil be more certaine, which he wil not fayle to send over that is

October 10th.   Your Lordships humble servant
20   1631.   *J. Suckling.*
Hamborough.

11. 71 and my] + best *deleted MS.*
12. *Cran (holograph): MS. torn; letters, etc., supplied as indicated in Appendix B: Altered Accidentals* 13 Bishops *Ed.*: Bishop *MS.* 15 as tis] as it [tis] *added in margin and superscript MS.*

There are forces to the number of 8000 comming out of *Lorraine* to the assistance of *Tilley.*

13. To an Unidentified Lord [October 1631]

My Noble Lord,

Y O U R humble Servant had the honour to receive from your hand a Letter, and had the grace upon the sight of it to blush. I but then found my owne negligence, and but now could have the opportunity to ask pardon for it. We have ever since been upon a March, 5 and the places we are come to, have afforded rather blood than Inke: and of all things, Sheets have been the hardest to come by, specially those of Paper. If these few lines shall have the happines to kisse your hand, they can assure, that he that sent them knows none to whom he owes more obligation then to your Lordship, and to whom he 10 would more willingly pay it: and that it must be no lesse than necessity it self that can hinder him from often presenting it. *Germany* hath no whit altered me, I am still the humble servant of my Lord [   ] that I was, and when I cease to be so, I must cease to be

John Suckling.   15

14. To the Earl of Middlesex, 9 November 1631

To the right honorable the
Earle of *Middlesex*
at his house in great
St. *Bartholmews*

Right honorable   5

H A V I N G overcome a journey dangerous and troublesome both in respect wee have past through onely the ruines of countryes and also that partyes of horse and foot were every where abroad, at length wee are arrived at *Wirtzberg,* where the Embassador had Audience on *Sunday* last. Since the battayle of *Leipswick* the king has 10 continued victorious, entring still farther into *Germanye* and at this time being in the very heart of it. *Erford, Kenings-hoff,* and *Sweinsford* as Master of the feild are since come into his hands; *Witzberg,* by

13. *FA46 (on addressee, see note)*   14. *Cran (holograph)*

Composition, and the Castle by assault he took the seventh of *October*,
15 where the Souldier found such pillage, that it is ordinary for the
lower ranke of them now to loose 300 Duckats upon a drums head.
On *Wensday* last *Hannow* a towne of great Consequence and strong
was taken in, not without private intelligence had with the Counts
mother her self as some think. On *Munday* wee had a fliing report that
20 *Prage* was taken by the Heyre of *Wallesten* and yesterday the king
receivd it for certaine by 4 severall lettres. The Duke of *Sax.* is there
too by this time. *Nodimberg* has Contributed 200000 rextallars and
Francfort 150000. This morning his Majesty is marcht with al his
armye on that side of the *Rhen* that looks toward the Palatinate, and
25 told my Lord Embassadour that the next news he should heare
would be that he was in *Francfort*. *Tyllye* not withstanding his last
losses is in rumor noe lesse then a hundred thousand, and by certaine
intelligence had from prisoners that Coronell *Hebron* latelye brought
in, he is betweene 40 and 50 thousand strong. On *Thursday* last he
30 tooke *Rotenberg* and *Wintzem* and so marcht up to *Nodimberg*. But
upon the news that the king is going for *Francfort*, tis thought he
wil alter his course and meet him. The Coronells say, that the king
is resolvd for a second battel, and without al doubt your Lordshipp
shal erelong heare of Mischeife. Last night I went to supp with my
35 Lord Marquis and wishing that some occasion might present it self
wherein I might serve him, he was pleasd to tell me, that he was now
going to beseidge *Magdeburg*, and that his army would be there
before him. He is between 7 and 8000 strong but they are most of
them *Duch* and given him by the king, for his owne are al dead of the
40 plage to 1200. The king esteems much of him, and the Souldier
honors him, and he himself takes al the ways to become a brave
souldier, and to doe some act worthy of himself. While all the world
is thus in action, pardon me (my Lord) if I must hope your Lordshipp
will not long be idle. Since you cannot now sett downe with satisfac-
45 tion of your owne conscience, The Christian world never more needing able men then at this present. It is a thing (my Lord) that al those
that truly honor and serve you, have long since askt of heaven, and
I more particularly cease not stil to demand it, as being more especially obliged to be,

50 *Witzberg.*   *November* 9th.   Your Lordships in his best service
        1631.   *J. Suckling.*

14. 21 Duke *Ed.*: Di *MS.*; *see note*   23 Majesty] + his *deleted MS.*

The gentleman that shal present these lettres, if your Lordship know him not already, wil deserve a more special taking notice of, having made himself well knowne to my Lord of *Arrundel* and most of the court, and who I make no doubt wil give your Lordship occasion to 55 desire his better acquaintance. His name is Mr. *Gifford*.

15. [To the Earl of Middlesex, a Character: November 1631(?); perhaps 1637]

My Lord,

To perswade one that has newly ship-wrackt upon a Coast to imbarque sodainly for the same place again, or your Lordship to seek that content you now enjoy in the innocence of a solitude, among the disorders and troubles of a Court, were I think a thing the 5 King himself (and Majesty is no ill Orator) would find some difficulty to do. And yet when I consider that great soul of yours, like a Spider, working all inwards, and sending forth nothing, but like the Cloister'd Schoolmens Divinity, threads fine and unprofitable: if I thought you would not suspect my being serious all this while, for what I should 10 now say, I would tell you that I cannot but be as bold with you as your Ague is, and for a little time, whether you will or not, entertain you scurvily.

When I consider you look (to me) like —— I cannot but think it as odd a thing, as if I should see *Van Dike* with all his fine colours and 15 Pensills about him, his Frame, and right Light, and every thing in order, and yet his hands tyed behind him: and your Lordship must excuse me if upon it I be as bold.

The wisest men, and greatest States have made no scruple to make use of brave men whom they had laid by with some disgrace: nor 20 have those brave men so laid by, made scruple, or thought it a disgrace to serve again, when they were called to it afterwards.

These general motives of the State and Common good, I will not so much as once offer up to your Lordships consideration, though (as 'tis fit) they have still the upper end: yet, like great *Oleoes*, they 25 rather make a shew then provoke Appetite. There are two things which I shall not be ashamed to propound to you, as ends; since the greater part of the wise men of the world have not been ashamed to make them theirs: and if any has been found to contemn them, it hath

15. *FA46*   25 Oleoes] olios *Th*: aloes *Haz*; *see note*

30 been strongly to be suspected that either they could not easily attain
to them, or else that the readiest way to attain to them was to contemn them. These two are *Honour* and *Wealth*: and though you stand
possest of both of them, yet is the first in your hands like a sword,
which, if not through negligence, by mischance hath taken rust, and
35 needs a little clearing; and it would be much handsomer a present to
posterity, if you your self in your life time wipe it off.

For your *Estate* (which it may be had been more had it not been
too much) though it is true that it is so far from being contemptible,
that it is Nobly competent, yet must it be content to undergo the
40 same fate greater states (Common-wealths themselves) have been and
are subject to: which is, when it comes to be divided in it self, not to
be considerable. Both *Honour* and *Estate* are too fair and sweet *Flowers*,
to be without *Prickles*, or to be gathered without some scratches.

And now (my Lord) I know you have nothing to urge but a kind
45 of incapability in your self to the service of this State; when indeed
you have made the onely bar you have, by imagining you have
one.

I confesse (though) had *vice* so large an Empire in the Court, as
heretofore it has had, or were the times so dangerous that to the living
50 well there, wise *conduct* were more necessary then *vertue* it self; Your
Lordship would have reason (with *Æsops* countrey-mouse) to under-
value all change of condition; since a quiet mediocrity is still to be
preferred before a troubled superfluity: but these things are now no
more: and if at any time they have threatned that Horizon, like great
55 clouds, either they are fallen of themselves to the ground, or else,
upon the appearing of the Sunne (such a Prince as ours is) they have
vanished, and left behind them clear and fair daies. To descend to
parts, envie is so lessen'd, that it is almost lost into vertuous emula-
tion, every man trusting the Kings judgement so far, that he knows
60 no better measure of his own merit, then his reward. The little word
behind the back, and undoing whisper, which, like pulling of a sheat-
rope at Sea, slackens the sail, and makes the gallantest ship stand still;
that that heretofore made the faulty and the innocent alike guilty, is
a thing, I beleeve, now so forgot, or at least so unpractiz'd, that those
65 that are the worst, have leisure to grow good, before any will take
notice they have been otherwise, or at least divulge it.

'Tis true, *Faction* there is, but 'tis as true, that it is as winds are,
to clear, and keep places free from corruption; the oppositions being

15. 38 too] so *Haz*   63 that that] that *Haz*

as harmlesse, as that of the meeting-tides under the bridge, whose
encounter makes it but more easie for him that is to passe. To be 70
a little pleasant in my instances; The very women have suffered
reformation, and wear through the whole Court their faces as little
disguised now, as an honest mans actions should be, and if there
be any have suffer'd themselves to be gained by their servants, their
ignorance of what they granted may well excuse them from the shame 75
of what they did. So that it is more then possible to be great and
good: and we may safely conclude, if there be some that are not so
exact, as much as they fall short of it, just so much they have gone
from the great Original, God; and from the best Copies of him on
earth, the King and the Queen.   80

To conclude, If those accidents or disasters which make men grow
lesse in the world (as some such, my Lord, have happened to you)
were inevitable as death, or, when they were once entered upon us,
there were no cure for them, examples of others would satisfie me for
yours; but since there have been that have delivered themselves from 85
their ills, either by their good *Fortune*, or *Vertue*, 'twould trouble me
that my friends should not be found in that number, as much as if
one should bring me a Catalogue of those that truly honoured my
Lord of *Middlesex* and I should not find among the first,

Your humble Servant.   90

16. To the Earl of Middlesex, 29 November 1631

To the right honorable the Earle
of *Middlesex* at his house
in great St. *Bartlomews*.

Right honorable

IN my last you had (though then not so certainely knowne) most 5
certaine news. For *Francefurt* was taken and a slight garrison of
600 men put into it. The passages are not as yet any of them cutt off,
but it is every day expected. Our Journey betwixt *Wirtzberg* and
Francfort confirmd it, for besides the miserye of liing in straw foure
nights together, wee had continuall Alarums, and the governours of 10
all the townes wee stayd in had intelligence that the enemye would

---

15. 69 meeting-tides] meeting tides *Haz, Th*   89 Middlesex *Ed.*: —— *FA46*
16. *Cran (holograph)*

bee with them that very night and were especially commanded to
stand upon their guard. *Nodimberg* is at length beseidgd by the Enemy
and news of it past to the king three days since, who now is before
15 *Mentz* on this side of the river, upon passing his army over. The kings
horse and some of his foot are so nigh that the canon plays upon them
night and day from the towne. The Electors *Colen* and *Mentz* are at
consultation in a strong fort a little below *Coblens*; the bishop of *Wirtzberg* is with them and some say *Bamberg*. 2000 *Spaniards* are in *Mentz*
20 besides what were in it before and the last news is, that *John* of
Nassaw himself is there within, resolute to hold it out to the last.
The Palatinists are impatient and would faine see their prince in
armes; the receivd opinion that 6000 men would now recover all,
makes them storme at the Palsgraves backwardnes, and they have
25 much adoe to forbeare the state of *England*, in which they thinke the
fault to be of his not comming up. At *Hanno* the news was hot, that
the prince was comming with 10000 *Hollanders*, and heere at *Francfort*
there was some small buz of it, but as yet it is not beleivd. The king
of *Suede* takes it not altogether so well, that his Majesty wil not
30 declare himself, nor in such an opportunity, send men or money.
I have some things of secret (so great a statesman am I growne on the
suddain) which I could wish your Lordship had, but all our lettres
goe in great danger of intercepting and there are other respects,
greater then that, which makes me not dare to send them but in
35 Cyphre; I was once to day so boldly resolute as to determine to send
your lordship inclosd a Character, but the Consideration, that I am
troublesome enough in this way of intelligence, and that I shal erelong
wayt upon you in person, smootherd that motion as soone as it was
borne. Two little pamphlets your lordshipp shal receave with this
40 lettre, which though they may seeme at first veiw to be but Pamphlets and foolish ones, yet there is something more in them then
ordinary and we cal them rarityes heere, because they are something
hard to come by. If these or any thing els I shal doe, can give your
lordshipp the least content, I shal count it none of the smallest for-
45 tunes that have befalne mee, it being my utmost study and Ambition
how to deserve the honor of being thought

November 29th.   Your lordshipps humble servant
   1631.   *J. Suckling.*
Francfort.

16. 27 comming] + up *deleted MS.*   39 borne.] + I haue put vp heere *deleted MS.*
43 els I] + can *deleted MS.*

17. To the Earl of Middlesex, 4 December 1631

To the right honorable
the Earle of *Middlesex*
at his house in great
St. *Bartlomews*.

Right honorable   5

SINCE my last, heere has beene a sudden change, the greatest that
has been in so short a time. For the king left *Mentz* and went to
Releive *Nodinberg*, and before he had marcht a league above *Francfort*,
certaine intelligence came that the Enemy had quitted the seidge
in three days. So that the king on *Friday* went directly up to *Heydle-*   10
berg, and he will not tis thought find any great resistance, for those
of the Palatinate shal noe sooner see him, but they wil rise with him.
Tilley is in some disgrace and there is a rumor that these crosses have
crazd him. My Lord Embassador has dispacht away this post with
such secrecy again and speed, that I can not enlarge my lettre with   15
the news of the taking of *Maidenburg* and of the intents supposed of
the Enemy, but am constrained to write my self in al hast

September 4th   Your Lordshipps most humble servant
    1631.   *J. Suckling.*
Francfort.
                                                                          20

18. [To Mr. Gifford, December 1631]

My Noble Friend.

THAT you have overcome the danger of the Land and of the Sea,
is news most welcom to us, and with no lesse joy receiv'd
amongst us than if the King of *Sweden* had the second time overcome
Tilley, and again past the *Meine* and the *Rhine*. Nor do we in this look   5
more upon our selves and private interests, then on the publike, since
in your safety both were comprised. And though you had not had
about you the affairs and secrets of State, yet to have left your own
person upon the way, had been half to undoe our poor Iland, and the
losse must have been lamented with the tears of a whole Kingdom.   10
    But you are now beyond all our fears, and have nothing to take

17. *Cran* (*holograph*)   10 days.] + Since *deleted MS.*   Friday] + is gone *deleted*
MS.   18 September] Septemb. *MS.*, *in error for* December: *see note*
    18. *FA46*

heed on your self, but fair Ladies. A pretty point of security; and such a one as all *Germany* cannot afford. We here converse with Northern Beauties, that had never heat enough to kindle a spark in any mans

15 breast, where heaven had been first so merciful, as to put in a reasonable soul.

There is nothing either fair or good in this part of the world; and I cannot name the thing can give me any content, but the thought that you enjoy enough otherwhere: I having ever been since I had

20 the first honour to know you,

Yours, more then his owne.

19. [To Sir Henry Vane], 2 May 1632

Right honorable

WHAT my journey through *France* afforded your Lordship had in hast from *Dover* by the way of *Antwerp*. On *Tuesday* I arrived at Court and came soone enough to find the face of it extreamely

5 changed, lookinge asquint upon you in *Germany*, as well as upon all us that were sent from thence. The fault at first I layd upon the night and my owne bad eys, but the next day made it cleare and plaine. The pacquett to my Lord Treasurer I presented first and the takinge of *Donawart*, who both to the bearer and the news seemd alike indif-

10 ferent! Somethinge coole if not cold! Perchance his garb. From thence I went to the king, and made my way by *Maxfeild*, *Murrey* being not there. His Majesty was well content the king was still victorious, but tooke it not so hot as those of *France*, nor did he at first conceive of it of so great importance. The bedchamber men were most of them

15 there, and the king spoke lowd; that little therfore I had to say to him from Sir *Isaack Wake*, and your Lordship, I reservd for a more private Audience, that I might see something more into the kings mind. Mr. *Murrey* would have had it beene the next morning, but I deferd it a day, and having seene my Lord of *Middlesex*, and spoken

20 with your sonn, I found as I conceivd the reason of what I soe much wonderd at, and a better way, then otherwise perchance I had taken. Before therfore I went to the king, I attended my Lord Treasurer,

19. *P.R.O., S.P. 16/216, No. 6 (MS., probably in a scrivener's hand; see note). In the critical apparatus, italicized readings without lemma indicate passages in a numeric cipher in the MS.; MS. (d) indicates deciphered readings written superscript in the MS.; see note* 9–10 *who . . . Perchance MS.* 9 seemd] shewed *MS. (d)* and told him that by more particular command I was more specially to wayt upon his Lordship; that I was to speake to the king that Morning, but was come before to kisse his Lordships hands. And having in a manner repeated what I was to say (because I knew that which I had both from you and Sir *Isaack Wake*, was somethinge too much *Sweden* and monarchy) I mingled with it the noyse of the *Spaniards* passinge the *Mosell*, the Confirmation of the Landgrave of *Hessens* defeat and the voted forces of *Wallesten* (of which I conceyvd by Circumstance you writt nothing) all which more specially hee commanded mee to represent to his Majesty! In the Conclusion I told him, that if there were anythinge in what I had sayd, that could seeme lesse fitt to his Lordship or anythinge besides that his Lordship could thinke more fitt, I stood there ready to be disposd of by him. Upon which he imbraced me, thankt your Lordship more especially for that Addresse, promised to send away presently to you, and wild me to attend while he came to the king, that he might present me, which he did. The king was very well pleasd and satisfyed, much better then he was at my first appearinge; he questioned me much and about many things, resolvd for a dispach but seemd to referr it to my Lord Treasurer! He conceyvd you had blanks already, but yet should have more, since you required them. Thus things have past in show well in this last act. By the dispach it selfe you will easily judge, whether reality bee intended or no? If, after all this delay, it bee full and without reserves, the feares of all those that honor you and serve you, are at an end. Howsoever though there bee some, yet the next from you, (I conceyve) will take them all away. The disposall of the Coferers place after this manner, makes the world thinke, that there is some staggering in the freindship betwixt my Lord Treasurer and you, if not a breach. And those that are of Sir *Thomas Roes* cabinet, would perswade, that you were sent over, to undoe the affaires of the king of *Swede* and your owne! Many that really wish you well, begin to imagine, that you shall bee kept there longer then you would. If there be any such thing, the causes certainely will be these. First, your greatnes with my Lord Marquis and

19. 25–7 *And . . . both* MS. 27–8 *was . . . it the* MS. 31–2 *all . . . Majesty* MS. 33–4 *anythinge . . . that his Lordship* MS. 35 *more fitt* MS. 41–2 *but . . . Treasurer* MS. 42 *blanks* MS.: blanks MS. (*d*): . . . *Th* 44–7 *By . . . are* MS. 45 reality] really MS. (*d*), *Th* 46 [honor] you] + at an end *deleted* MS. 48 *next from you* MS. 49–51 *this . . . breach* MS. 50 some] some some MS. 51–2 *Sir . . . cabinet* MS. 52–3 *sent . . . owne* MS. 54 *really . . . well* MS. 54–5 *bee . . . would* MS. 55 certainely] + must *deleted* MS. 56–7 *your . . . intelligence* MS.

your too strict intelligence one with another, which is heere represented to the full. And howsoever your Lordshipp thinkes thinges
are reconciled betwixt my Lord Treasurer and him, yet they say
60 otherwise heere and the effects speake no lesse. No man dares thinke
well of him heere and by what your sonn and I have observd, it is
easy to beleive, the kinges eares himselfe has beene a little to open
to the reports. I doe him all the service I can, where I find it may
doe any good, though I know *Jacob Ashley* has lost himselfe about the
65 same thing! That which may in a second place bee considerable, will
bee, your too lively representations, making the king of *Swede* to
outway the Emperor, more then they will allow him heere to doe.
And indeed your Lordships Case in this is not much unlike that of
Sharneses, for, where you are they thought you to much a *Spaniard*, and
70 heere they thinke you all much a *Spaniard*. Then againe the weomen
take it ill, that your son should bee a states-man before theirs, and
my Lady *Weston* has lett fall in a manner so much to my Lady *Dane*.
Besides which I conceive has more importance, larger instructions
were by him carried to the king, then to my Lord Treasurer, and
75 sooner. Last of all, whether your Lordships Clearks have in your
absence, followed your directions or no, or whether they have
behaved themselves ill or well, in the issuing out and disposing of
moneys, I cannot tell, but, I suspect, a sinister report has beene made
of all. Your person would certainly bee necessary heere, and I make
80 no doubt, your wisedome will find out the quickest and best way for
it, unles you yourself (as it well may be after all this) know, that all
the world on this side of the seas are in errors. That which makes
me any way stagger in my hopes of your suddain comming home, is,
That the king of *Swede* knows too well, that *England* satisfyed in the
85 demands of the Palatinate, and things at a full point concerning that
particular, this crowne will no longer make court to him, and after
it hee must expect no great matters from hence. Besides, *France* which
in show pretends to goe along with us, really perchance intends
nothing lesse, since there is nothing but that of the Palatinate, that
90 can keepe *Spain* and us from tying a more strict knot together, and
nothing but that that has kept us so long asunder. And the ill will

19. 57–8 *heere . . . full MS.*   58–9 *thinkes . . . him MS.*   60–1 *No . . . heere MS.*
62–3 *the . . . can MS.*   64–5 *has . . . thing MS.*   66–7 *your . . . Emperor MS.*
69 Sharneses] Pharneses *Th   where . . . Spaniard MS.*   71–2 *take . . . Weston MS.*
71 Lady Dane] L. Dane *MS.*: Lord Vane *Th; see note*   73–5 *larger . . . sooner MS.*
78 *sinister report MS.*   84 *of Swede MS.*   85 *Palatinate MS.*   86–7 *this
. . . hence MS.*   89–90 *that can . . . together MS.*   91 *kept . . . asunder MS.*

bee, that if his Majesty of *Swede* make larger progresses and bee more fortunat, wee shall heere feare him as too great or hee himselfe will bee more difficult. If hee bee lesse successfull, wee shall not conclude with him, as too weake. And now my Lord, your Lordship has what 95 wee talke heere; I am not peremptory that things are so, as I have heere represented them, but I am certaine, they are thought to be soe. Your Lordships better Judgment will resolve it, and I am more then Confident, will yet bring every thing to its right place; you have many heere that can doe more towards it, but none that more sin- 100 cerely wishes it, then

May 2d. 1632.   Your humble servant
Whitehall.   *Jo. Sucklinge.*

If your Lordship would please to thinke it fitt to send at random and by any messengers rather then none the news, it would not cer- 105 tainely be amisse.

20. [To Anne Willoughby, Autumn 1633]

SINCE Joy (the thing we all so Court) is but our hopes stript of our fears, pardon me if I be still pressing at it, and like those that are curious to know their fortunes aforehand, desire to be satisfied, though it displeases me afterward. To this Gentleman (who has as much in-sight as the t'other wanted Ey-sight) I have committed the 5 particulars, which would too much swell a Letter: if they shall not please you, 'tis but fresh subject still for Repentance; nor ever did that make me quarrel with any thing but my owne starres. To swear new oaths from this place, were but to weaken the credit of those I have sworn in another: if heaven be to forgive you now for not beleeving of 10 them then, (as sure as it was a sin) heaven forgive me now for swearing of them then (for that was double sin.) More then I am I cannot be, nor list,

                                                   Yours,
                                                   J. S.   15

I am not so ill a Protestant as to beleeve in merit, yet if you please to give answer under your owne hand, such as I shall for ever rely upon: if I have not deserv'd it already, it is not impossible but I may.

---

19. 92–3 *Majesty ... fortunat MS.*   92 *progresses MS.*: *progresse MS.* (*d*)   93 *him ... great MS.*   93–5 *hee ... weake MS.*
20. *FA46*

21. To Sir Kenelm Digby [18–30 November 1634]

THE common report tells mee, that you have bine a large talker in my affaires; doing becomes a man better; Know then (Sir) that I have switcht your brother, and hee hath run away upon it; You have profest to maintaine your Brothers actions, and I, to maintaine
5 myne owne; And I may thinke, til I know the contrarie, You dare not question any of them.

J. Sucklyn

For Sir *Kelham Digby.*

22. [To Martha Lady Carey, Spring 1635]

IT is none of the least discourtesies money hath done us Mortals, the making things easie in themselves, and natural, difficult: Yong and handsome people would have come together without half this trouble, if that had never been: This would tell you, Madam, that
5 the offer having nothing about it of new, begot in our yong Lover very little of any thing else but Melancholy, which notwithstanding (I could easily perceive) grew rather from a fear of his Fathers minde, then a care of satisfying his own: that perswaded me to throw in all, and adde the last reserve which fortunately turned the Scale, the
10 Cavalier setting a greater rate, and truly, upon the kindness of it, then upon the thing; and in that shewed the courtesie of his Judgment, as well as his Ability; the Uncle is no less satisfied then the Nephew, and both are confident to draw —— to the same thoughts, to whom, as it was fit, I have left the office.
15   And now, Madam, you may safely conclude the cause to be removed out of *Pluto's* Court into *Cupids*; from the God of Moneys, to the God of Loves; who if he break not off old Customers, will quickly dispatch them, since he seldom delays those that have past their tryals in the other place.
20   Your humble Servant

J. S.

---

21. *Huntington Library, MS. HA 12760 (MS. copy)*   3 switcht *Ed.*: switch *MS.*
22. *LR*   16 Pluto's] *i.e.* Plutus'; *see note*   17 Loves *Ed.*: Love *LR*; *see note*

23. To Sir George Southcot, 9 September 1635

For his Much Respected Brother
Sir *George Southcoate*
at his Lodging in *Fleete*-streete

Sir,

S INCE the setling of your Family would certainly much conduce 5
to the setling of your mind (the care of the one being the trouble
of the other) I cannot but reckon it in the number of my misfortunes,
that my affairs deny me the content I should take to serve you in it.

It would be too late now for me (I suppose) to say any thing to
advance or confirm you in those good resolutions I left you in, being 10
confident your own reason hath been so just to you, as long before
this to have represented a necessity of redeeming time and fame, and
of taking an handsome revenge upon your self for the injuries you
would have done your self.

Change I confesse (to them that think all at once) must needs be 15
strange, and to you hateful, whom first your owne nature, and then
custome, another nature, have brought to delight in those narrow
and uncouth waies we found you in. You must therefore consider
that you have entred into one of those neer conjunctions of which
death is the onely honourable divorce; and that you have now to 20
please another as well as your self; who though she be a Woman, and
by the patent she hath from nature, hath liberty to do simply; yet can
she never be so strongly bribed against her self, as to betray at once
all her hopes and ends, and for your sake resolve to live miserably.
Examples of such loving folly our times afford but few; and in those 25
there are, you shall find the stock of Love to have been greater, and
their strengths richer to maintain it, than is to be feared yours can be.

Woman (besides the trouble) has ever been thought a Rent-charge,
and though through the vain curiosity of man it has often been
inclosed, yet has it seldom been brought to improve or become pro- 30
fitable; It faring with marryed men for the most part, as with those
that at great charges wall in grounds and plant, who cheaper might
have eaten Mellons elsewhere then in their owne Gardens Cucumbers.

23. *FA46. MS.: Cran (copy); see note*   1–3 For . . . Fleete-streete *MS.: omit FA46*
9 to say any thing *MS.: omit FA46*   16 you] + certainely *MS.*   27 than] + it
Haz   be] + & besides necessity & an impossibility of liuing togetherwise allwayes
attending it wᵗʰ, & to thanke heauen for it you cannot pleade. *MS.*   32 charges] chardge
MS.

The ruines that either time, sicknesse, or the melancholy you give
35 her shall bring, must all be made up at your cost: for that thing a
husband is but Tenant for life in what he holds, and is bound to
leave the place Tenantable to the next that shall take it. To conclude,
a young Woman is a Hawk upon her wings; and if she be handsome,
she is the more subject to go out at check; Faulkners that can but
40 seldom spring right game, should still have something about them
to take them down with. The Lure to which all stoop in this world,
is either garnisht with pleasure or profit, and when you cannot throw
her the one, you must be content to shew out the other. This I speak
not out of a desire to increase your fears which are already but too
45 many, but out of a hope that when you know the worst, you will at
once leap into the River, and swim through handsomly, and not
(weather-beaten with the divers blasts of irresolution) stand shivering
upon the brink.

Doubts and fears are of all the sharpest passions, and are still
50 turning distempers to diseases; through these false Opticks 'tis, that
all you see is like evening shaddows, disproportionable to the right,
and strangely longer then the true substance: These (when a handsome way of living and expence suitable to your Fortune is represented
to you) makes you in their stead see want and beggery: thrusting
55 upon your judgement impossibilities for likelyhoods, which they with
ease may do, since (as the wise man saith) they betray the succors
that reason offers.

'Tis true, that all here below is but diversified folly, and that the
little things we laugh at Children for, we do but act our selves in
60 great; yet is there difference of Lunacy, and of the two, I had much
rather be mad with him, that (when he had nothing) thought all
the Ships that came into the Haven his; Than with you, who (when
you have so much comming in) think you have nothing; This fear
of losing all in you, is the ill issue of a worse Parent, desire of getting

23. 34 you *MS.*: + shall *FA46*   39–41 Faulkners . . . game, should still have
something about them to take them down with] Since therefore it is impossible for you
allwayes to please her with yᵉ right game you must haue something by you to take her doune
wᵗʰ vpon occasion *MS.*   42 pleasure . . . profit *MS.*: profit . . . pleasure *FA46*
42–3 you cannot throw her the one] it is bare one [*sic*] yᵉ one side *MS.*   43 to shew out]
still to be shewing her *MS.*   45 worst] ill & yᵗ this ill is Joynd wᵗʰ A worse necessity
MS.   46 through] *omit MS.*   49–50 are still turning] doe often turne *MS.*
50 Opticks] lights *MS.*   50–1 that all *MS.*: all that *FA46*   51 right *MS.*: truth
FA46 (*cf. No. 32, ll. 6–8*)   52, 54 These (when . . .) makes you] These make you
when *MS.*   53 expence . . . is] an expence . . . are *MS.*   54 makes] make *MS.*
56 the wise man *MS.*: Solomon *FA46*; *see note*   59–60 do but act our selves in great]
act but in greate our selves *MS.*   60 is there difference] are there degrees *MS.*
64 getting] gathering *MS.*

in you; So that if you would not be passion-rent, you must cease to 65
be covetous: Money in your hands is like the Conjurers Divel, which,
while you think you have that, has you.

The rich Talent that God hath given, or rather lent you, you have
hid up in a napkin, and Man knows no difference betwixt that and
Treasures kept by ill Spirits, but that yours is the harder to come by. 70
To the guarding of these golden Apples, of necessity must be kept
those never-sleeping Dragons, Fear, Jealousie, Distrust, and the like;
so that you are come to moralize *Æsop*, and his fables of beasts are
become prophecies of you; for while you have catcht at the shadow,
uncertain riches, you have lost the substance, true content. 75

The desire I have ye should be yet your self, and that your friends
should have occasion to blesse the providence of misfortune, has made
me take the boldnes to give you your own Character; and to shew
you your self out of your own glasse: And though all this tells you
but where you are, yet it is some part of a cure to have searcht the 80
wound. And for this time we must be content to do like Travellers,
who first find out the place, and then the neerest way.

Wiston   Your humble Servant
September the 9th 1635   *John Suckling*

24. [To Mary and Anne Bulkeley, Winter 1635 (?)]

For the Two Excellent Sisters

T HOUGH I conceive you (Ladies) so much at leisure that you
may read any thing, yet since the stories of the Town are meerly
amorous, and sound nothing but Love, I cannot without betraying
my owne judgement make them news for *Wales*. Nor can it be lesse
improper to transport them to you, then for the King to send my 5
Lord of *C*. over Ambassador this winter into *Green-land*.

It would want faith in so cold a Countrey as *Anglesey*, to say that
your Cozen Dutchesse, for the quenching of some foolish flames

23. 66 hands *MS*.: hand *FA46; see note*   67 have that,] have∧ yᵗ, *MS*.: have, that *FA46*
69 hid up in a napkin] hetherto wrapt vp in A napkin *MS*.   70—1 kept . . . guarding]
garded . . . keeping *MS*.   71—2 must be kept . . . Distrust] are placed those too too watche-
full serpents Jelousie Care feare mistrust *MS*.   72 never-sleeping] never sleeping *FA46*
74—5 have catcht . . . have lost] catch . . . loose *MS*.   75 uncertain riches] vnnecessary
wealth *MS*.   76 be yet] yet be *MS*.   79 own] + flattering *MS*.   80 are,]
are hurt, *Haz*   81 for this time] *omit MS*.   83—4 Wiston . . . Suckling *MS*.
(*accidentals normalized*): omit *FA46*   83 Wiston *Ed*.: Westenn *MS*.
  24. *FA46*. [*To Mary and Anne Bulkeley, Winter 1635 (?)*]: *see Commentary*

about her, has endured quietly the losse of much of the Kings favour,
10 of many of her houses, and of most of her friends.

Whether the disfigurement that Travel or sicknes has bestowed
upon *B. W.* be thought so great by the Lady of the Isle, as 'tis by
others, and whether the alteration of his face has bred a change in her
mind—it never troubles you—Ladies. What old Loves are decay'd,
15 or what new ones are sprung up in their room; Whether this Lady
be too discreet, or that Cavalier not secret enough; are things that
concern the inhabitants of *Anglesey* not at all. A fair day is better
welcom and more news, then all that can be said in this kind. And
for all that I know now, the Divels Chimney is on fire, or his pot
20 seething over, and all *North-Wales* not able to stay the fury of it. Perchance while I write this, a great black cloud is sayling from Mistris
Thomasses bleak Mountains over to *Baron-hill*, there to disgorge it
self with what the Sea or worse places fed it with before.

It may be the honest banks about you turn bankrupt too, and
25 break; and the Sea like an angry Creditor seizes upon all, and hath
no pitty, because he has been put off so long from time to time. For
variety (and it is not impossible) some boysterous wind flings up the
hangings; and thinking to do as much to your cloths, finds a resistance, and so departs, but first breaks all the windows about the house
30 for it in revenge.

These things now we that live in *London* cannot help, and they are
as great news to men that sit in Boxes at *Black-Fryars*, as the affairs of
Love to Flannel-Weavers.

For my own part, I think I have made a great complement, when
35 I have wisht my self with you, and more then I dare make good in
Winter: and yet there is none would venture farther for such a happines then

Your humble servant.

25. [To Mary Bulkeley, 1636–1639]

SINCE you can breath no one desire that was not mine before
it was yours,—or full as soon, (for hearts united never knew
divided wishes) I must chide you (dear Princesse) not thank you, for
your Present: and (if at least I knew how) be angry with you for
5 sending him a blush, who needs must blush because you sent him

one. If you are conscious of much, what am I then? who guilty am of
all you can pretend to, and somthing more—unworthinesse. But why
should you at all (Heart of my heart) disturb the happines you have
so newly given me? or make love feed on doubts, that never yet
could thrive on such a diet? *If I have granted your request*——Oh!——   10
Why will you ever say that you have studied me, and give so great
an instance to the contrary? That wretched *If*—speaks as if I would
refuse what you desire, or could: both which are equally impossible.
My dear Princesse, There needs no new Approaches where the
Breach is made already; nor must you ever ask any where, but of your   15
fair self, for any thing that shall concern

Your humble Servant.

26. [To Mary Bulkeley, 1636–1639]

My Dearest Princesse,

B UT that I know I love you more then ever any did any, and that
yet I hate my self because I can love you no more, I should now
most unsatisfied dispatch away this messenger.

The little that I can write to what I would, makes me think writing   5
a dull commerce, and then—how can I chuse but wish my self with
you—to say the rest. My Dear Dear, think what merit, vertue,
beauty, what and how far *Aglaura* with all her charmes can oblige,
and so far and something more I am

Your humble Servant.   10

27. [To Mary Bulkeley, 1636–1639]

W HEN I receive your lines (my Dear Princesse) and find there
expressions of a Passion; though reason and my own immerit
tell me, it must not be for me, yet is the Cozenage so pleasing to me,
that I (bribed by my own desires) beleeve them still before the other.
Then do I glory that my Virgin-Love has staid for such an object to   5
fixe upon, and think how good the Stars were to me that kept me
from quenching those flames (Youth **or** wild Love furnished me
withall) in common and ordinary Waters, and reserved me a Sacrifice

25. 12 instance] interest *Haz, Th*
26. *FA46*   **27.** *FA46*

for your eyes;—While thought thus smiles and solaces himself within
10 me, cruel Remembrance breaks in upon our retirements, and tells
so sad a Story, that (trust me) I forget all that pleased Fancy said
before, and turnes my thoughts to where I left you. Then I consider
that stormes neither know Courtship, nor Pittie, and that those rude
blasts will often make you a Prisoner this Winter, if they doe no
15 worse.

While I here enjoy fresh diversion, you make the sufferings more,
by having leisure to consider them; nor have I now any way left me
to make mine equal with them, but by often considering that they
are not so: for the thought that I cannot be with you to bear my
20 share, is more intolerable to me, then if I had borne more———but
I was onely born to number houres, and not enjoy them———yet can
I never think my selfe unfortunate, while I can write my selfe

Aglaura,
Her humble Servant.

28. [To Mary Bulkeley, 1636–1639]

WHEN I consider (my Dear Princesse) that I have no other
pretence to your favours, then that which all men have to the
Original of Beauty, Light: which we enjoy not that it is the inheritance of our eyes, but because things most excellent cannot restrain
5 themselves, but are ours, as they are diffusively good; Then doe I find
the justnesse of your quarrel, and cannot but blush to think what
I doe owe, but much more to thinke what I doe pay, Since I have
made the Principal so great, by sending in so little Interest———
When you have received this humble confession, you will not I hope,
10 conceive me one that would (though upon your bidding) enjoy my
selfe, while there is such a thing in the world, as———

Aglaura———
Her humble Servant.
J. S.

29. [To Mary Bulkeley, 1636–1639]

SO much (Dear *Mary*) was I ever yours since I had first the honour
to know you, and consequently so little my self since I had the
unhappines to part with you, that you your self (Dear) without what

28. *FA46*   3 it is] 'tis *Ha2*   **29.** *FA46.* 1 Mary *Ed.:* — *FA46*

I would say, cannot but have been so just as to have imagined the
welcom of your own letters; though indeed they have but removed
me from one Rack, to set me on another; from fears and doubts
I had about me of your welfare, to an unquietnesse within my self,
till I have deserv'd this Intelligence.

How pleasingly troublesome thought and remembrance have been
to me since I left you, I am no more able now to expresse, then another
to have them so. You onely could make every place you came in
worth the thinking of, and I do think those places worthy my
thought onely, because you made them so. But I am to leave them,
and I shall do't the willinger, because the Gamester still is so much
in me, as that I love not to be told too often of my losses: Yet every
place will be alike, since every good object will do the same. Variety
of Beauty and of Faces (quick underminers of Constancy to others)
to me will be but pillars to support it; Since when they please me
most, I most shall think of you.

In spite of all Philosophy, it will be hottest in my Climate, when
my Sun is farthest off; and in spite of all reason, I proclaim, that I am
not my self but when I am

Yours wholy.

30. [To Mary Bulkeley, 1636–1639]

THOUGH desire in those that love be still like too much sail in
a storm, and man cannot so easily strike, or take all in when he
pleases: Yet (Dearest Princesse) be it never so hard, when you shall
think it dangerous, I shall not make it difficult, though——Well; Love
is Love, and Aire is Aire; and (though you are a Miracle your self)
yet do not I believe that you can work any; without it I am confident
you can never make these two thus different in themselves, one and
the self same thing; when you shall, it will be some small furtherance
towards it, that you have

Your humble servant.   10
J. S.

Who so truly loves the fair *Aglaura*, that he will never know
desire, at least not entertain it, that brings not letters of recommendation from her, or first a fair Pasport.

30. *FA46*

31. [To Mary Bulkeley, 1636–1639]

My Dear Dear,

THINK I have kist your Letter to nothing, and now know not
what to answer. Or that now I am answering, I am kissing you
to nothing, and know not how to go on! For you must pardon, I must
5 hate all I send you here, because it expresses nothing in respect of
what it leaves behind with me. And oh! Why should I write then?
Why should I not come my self? Those Tyrants, businesse, honour,
and necessity, what have they to do with you and I? Why should we
not do Loves commands before theirs whose Soveraignty is but
10 usurped upon us? Shall we not smell to Roses 'cause others do look
on? or gather them, 'cause there are prickles, and something that
would hinder us? Dear—I fain would—and know no hindrance—but
what must come from you—and—why should any come? since 'tis
not I, but you must be sensible how much time we lose, It being long
15 since I was not my self, but

                                                    Yours.

32. [To Mary Bulkeley, 1636–1639]

Dear Princesse,

FINDING the date of your Letter so young, and having an
assurance from [   ] who at the same time heard from Mr. [   ]
that all our Letters have been delivered at [B] I cannot but imagine
5 some ill mistake, and that you have not received any at all. Faith I
have none in Welch man; and though Fear and Suspition look often
so far that they oversee the right, yet when Love holds the Candle,
they seldom do mistake so much. My Dearest Princesse, I shall long,
next hearing you are well, to hear that they are safe: for though I can
10 never be ashamed to be found an Idolater to such a shrine as yours,
yet since the world is full of profane eyes, the best way, sure, is to
keep all mysteries from them, and to let privacy be (what indeed it
is) the best part of devotion. So thinks

                                        My D. D. P.
15   Your humble Servant.

---

31. *FA46*
32. *FA46*   6 Welch man *Ed.*, *Haz* (Welsh): Welch, man *FA46*: Welshman *Th;*
see note

33. [To Mary Bulkeley, Summer 1639 (?)]

SINCE the inferiour Orbes move but by the first, without all question desires and hopes in me are to be govern'd still by you, as they by it. What mean these fears then? Dear Princesse.

Though Planets wander, yet is the Sphere that carries them the same still; and though wishes in me may be extravagant, yet he in 5 whom they make their motion is, you know, my dear Princesse,

Yours, and wholy to be disposed of by you.

And till we hear from you, though (according to the form of concluding a Letter) we should now rest, we cannot.

34. [To Mary Bulkeley, October 1639 (?)]

Fair Princesse,

IF parting be a sin (as sure it is) what then to part from you? if to extenuate an ill be to increase it, what then now to excuse it by a letter? That which we would alledge to lessen it, with you perchance has added to the guilt already, which is our sodain leaving 5 you. Abruptnesse is an eloquence in parting, when Spinning out of time, is but the weaving of new sorrow. And thus we thought; yet not being able to distinguish of our owne Acts, the fear we may have sinn'd farther then we think of, has made us send to you, to know whether it be Mortal or not. 10

35. [To Mary Bulkeley, Winter 1639/40 (?)]

THERE was (O seldom happy word of was!) a time when I was not *Mountferrat*, and sure there was a time too, when all was handsome in my heart; for you were there (Dear Princess) and filled the place alone. Were there—Oh wretched word again, and should you leave that lodging, more wretched then *Mountferrat* needs must be 5

Your humble Servant

J. S.

33. *FA46*   34. *FA46*   35. *LR*

36–7. An Exchange of Purported Letters between a London Alderman and a Scottish Lord, Summer–Autumn 1638

36. To a 'Scottish Lord' from a 'London Alderman', Summer–Autumn 1638

My Lord,

BUT that you do and say things in *Scotland* now (my Lord) unfit for a good Subject to hear, I should have hoped your Lordship by a true relation of the passages there, would have disabused your humble Servant here. Distance and mens fears have so enlarged the truth, and so disproportioned every thing about the Town, that we have made the little Troop of Discontents a gallant Army, and already measure no *Scotchman* but by his evening shadow.

We hear say you have taken *Livery* and *Seisin* of *Northumberland*, and there are that have given in *Cumberland* for quietness sake, and are content to think it part of *Scotland*, because it is so barren. *London* Scriveners begin to wish they had St. *Michael-Mounts* Mens security for the Borderers they have standing-bound in their Shops; and the *Witheringtons* and *Howards* Estates are already freely disposed to the needier Rebels. Much of this part of the World is in Agues, but not all my Lord: There are that have read the Chronicles, and they finde the *English* oftner march'd into *Edenburgh*, then the *Scots* into *London*.

Your old Friend Alderman [   ] (a learned Bard, and a great In-seer into times) saith, It is a Byle broken out in the Breech of the Kingdom, and that when it is ripe, it will heal of it self: Others use a handsomer Similitude, and compare *Scotland* to a Hive of swarming Bees, which they say the King watches to reduce them for the better. There is a sawcy kinde of intelligence about the Town, of Ten thousand pounds that should be sent by my Lord *M.* for redemption of affairs there: But this the wiser sort suspects; for besides that his Majesty buyes his own again, they say none but the King would give so much for it.

Some are scandalized at the word of *Union*, and protest they finde no resemblance betwixt this New Covenant and our *Saviours*. Others wonder why they would make use of Religion, rather than their Poverty, for the cause of their mutining, since the one is ever suspected, and the other none would have disputed.

36–7. An Exchange of Purported Letters *etc. LR: see note*
36. *LR*   10 have given] give *Haz, Th*

In short, while one part of the Town is in whisper, and serious, the other part smiles. I therefore desire your Lordship to send me word in what state things stand there, that I may know of which side to be: 35 But I beseech you think it not any inbred love to mischief, that I now send to enquire how Rebellion prospers; but impute it to a certain foolish and greedy curiosity in mans nature of news, and remember that he that hath this disease about him, is

Your humble Servant. 40

37. An Answer from the 'Scottish Lord' to the 'London Alderman', Summer–Autumn 1638

Good Mr. Alderman,

IT is most true (I confess) that we do say things here unfit for you to hear there, and for this very reason I will forbear particulars: But this I do (Mr. Alderman) not so much out of fear for my self, as care for you; for though you write in the *Present-tense*, and use the 5 *particle* (*now*) which is a kinde of an exclusive word, yet it is well enough known a *Scotchman* at all times might speak what an *English-man* durst not hear. It seems (Sir) strange to me, that in the beginning of your Letter you give us the name of Rebels, when none are more his Majesties most humble Subjects than we, as in the front of our 10 Petitions and Messages most plainly appears: True it is, that in case the King will not do what we would have him, we have provided Arms; and have perswaded those here, and sent to others abroad to assist us: But that we have at any time denied our selves to be his most faithful Subjects (by your favor Mr. Alderman) I think will 15 hardly appear. For the taking of *Livery* and *Seisin* of *Northumberland* (if there be any such thing) neither you nor my Lord [ ] ought to be troubled at it, for that is a business belongs to the Law, and upon a tryal had here in *Edenburgh* before any of the Covenant, no question but there will be a speedy end of it. The thing I most wonder at, is, 20 that our old Friend should be so much mistaken, as to call *Scotland* the breech of the Kingdom, since you know that is a part of all the rest most subject, and is still put to endure the lash; so that in all likelihood it should rather be your Countrey than ours.

For your Simily of the Bees, and reducing us to the better, you 25 may assure his Majesty from me, that it will not quit cost: For both

37. *LR*

his Predecessors and himself have found sufficiently, that hived or
unhived, we yield not much Honey.

Now Sir, for our new Covenants having relation to the other, you
30 must know, That though it is not absolutely alike in all, yet in some
things it doth not disagree; and in this especially it suits, That there
is but little care taken for setling High Commission Courts in either.

The last scruple that troubles you is, why in this case we have
made use of Religion (which every one is apt to doubt) rather than
35 Poverty (which no man would have disputed;) and to say truth in
this, I was something unsatisfied my self, until I had spoken with one
of the Learneder of the Covenant, who told me, That he had observed
very few to thrive by publishing their poverty, but a great many
by pretending Religion. And now I doubt not, but I have in part
40 satisfied your curiosity; there remains onely that I give you my
opinion, concerning which party you ought to be of; and according
to the friendship that is betwixt us, I will deal plainly with you, that
if you had no more to lose then some of us have, this would be no ill
side, (for you see how God hath blest the *Hollanders*.) But as you are,
45 *London* is no ill place; for should you bring your money hither, the
Temptation would be too strong for the men: And like a hungry
man brought to a strange Table, we should fall to, without much
enquiring whose the meat was.

38. Epistolary Tract, April 1639

An Answer to a Gentleman in Norfolk that sent to
enquire after the Scotish business

Sir,

THAT you may receive an account of the Scotish business, and
why there hath been such irresolution and alteration about the
Levies lately; it is fit you know that this Northern storm (like a new
5 Disease) hath so far pos'd the Doctors of State, that as yet they have
not given it a name; though perchance they all firmly believe it to be
Rebellion: And therefore (Sir) it is no wonder, if these do here as the
learned in Physick, who when they know not certainly the grief,

　　38. An Answer to a Gentleman *etc. LR.* MSS.: *Ash3, Ash8, C, D, Eg27, T8*
　　An Answer . . . business] (in Norfolke who *Ash8: omit* in Norfolk *LR*): A letter, sent by
Sʳ John Suckling to a freind of his in Norfolke, concerning the Scottish businesse *T8*: Sʳ John
Sucklings Lr̃e out of Scotland April. 1639 *D*: Sʳ John Sucklings Letter to a friend of his.
Anno: Dom: 1640 *Eg27*: Sʳ John Sucklings Letter to his freind *Ash3*　　　　8 certainly]
omit Ash3, D, Eg27, T8

prescribe medicines sometimes too strong, sometimes too weak. The truth is, we here consider the Scotish affairs much after the rate that Mortals do the Moon: the simpler think it no bigger then a Bushel, and some (too wise) imagine it a vast World, with strange things undiscovered in it; two ill ways certainly of casting it up, since the first would make us too secure, the other too fearful. I confess I know not how to meet it in the middle, or set it right, nor do I think you have: since I should believe the question to be rather *A King or no King*, then *A Bishop or no Bishop*. In great Mutinies and Insurrections of this nature, Pretences speciously conscionable were never wanting, and indeed are necessary; for Rebellion it self is so ugly, that did it not put on the vizard of Religion, it would fright rather then draw people to it; and being drawn, it could not hold them without it. Imaginary cords that seem to fasten Man to Heaven, such as this Covenant, have tied things here below surer together then any other obligation. If it be Liberty of Conscience they ask, 'tis a foolish request, since they have it already, and must have it in despight of power: For as *Theoderic* the Goth said to the Jews, *Nemo cogitur credere invitus*. If the exercise of Liberty, 'tis dangerous: For scarce three men are of the same opinion in all, and then each family must have a war within it self. Look upon their long preparations, (and consider withall that Prophecies are ceas'd, and that they could not foretell that this Book should be sent them) and you will easily conclude they rather employed Conscience, then Conscience employed them. Enquire after their Leaders, and you will hardly find them Apostles, or men of such high sanctity, that they should order Religion in the world. *Lesly* himself (if his story were search'd) would certainly be found one, who because he could not live well here, took up a

---

38. 10 affairs *Σ*: affair *LR*   that *Σ*+*LR* (*Errata*): the *LR* (*Text*): as *Ash3* (*omit* after the rate *preceding*), *C*   11 the simpler] (+ sort *Ash3*): the simple *D*, *T8*: some *Ash8*   13 two ill ways certainly *Σ*: certainly two ill ways *Ash8*, *LR*   16 have] can *Ash3*, *C*   or] and *Ash8*, *D*; *see note*   17 then *Σ*: there, then *LR*   and *Σ*: or *LR*   18 Pretences *Σ*: Pretensions *LR*   19 it self is *D*, *Eg27*, *T8*: of it selfe is *Ash3*: is it self *LR*: is of it self *Ash8*, *C*   20 fright] affright *C*, *D*, *Eg27*   21 to it] unto it *Ash3*, *Eg27*, *T8*: *omit C*   and] + if *Ash3*, *D*, *Eg27*   22 Imaginary *Σ*: *new paragraph LR*   Man] men *Ash8*, *D*, *T8*   22–3 such as this Covenant, have *Σ* (the Covenant *Eg27*: hath *D*: such is . . . wᶜʰ hath *T8*): have *LR*: whenas they [tye them] *Ash8*   24 'tis] it is *C*, *D*, *T8*   27 Liberty *Σ*: that Liberty *Ash8*, *C*, *LR*; *see note*   scarce *Σ*: not *Ash8*, *C*, *LR*   30 [withall] that *Σ*: *omit LR*   Prophecies are . . . that *Σ* (*omit* that *Ash3*): Prophecie is . . . therefore *Ash8*, *C* (yᵉ gift of prophecy), *LR*; *see note*   ceas'd *Σ*+*Haz* (*after Ash8*): seal'd *LR*   31 that *Σ*: *omit LR*   sent *Σ*: + unto *Ash8*, *C*, *LR*   easily *D*, *Eg27*, *T8*: readily *Ash3*: *omit Ash8*, *C*, *LR*   32 employed . . . employed] employed . . . *omit Ash8*: employ . . . employed *Ash3*: employ . . . employs *Eg27*: employ . . . *omit D*   34 high *Σ*: *omit Eg27*, *LR*   34–5 in the world *Σ* (in the worke *Eg27*): *omit Ash8*, *C*, *LR*   36 here *Σ*: there *Ash8*, *C*, *LR*; *see note*

trade of killing men abroad, and now is return'd for Christs sake to kill men at home. If you will have my opinion, I think their quarrel to the King is, that which they may have to the Sun: He doth not
40 warm and visit them, as much as others. God and Nature have placed them in the shade, and they are angry with the King of *England* for it. To conclude, this is the case: The great and wise Husbandman hath placed the Beasts in the Outfields, and they would break hedges to come into the Garden. This is the belief of

45   Your humble Servant.

39. To an Unknown Correspondent, late
May or 1–2 June 1639

Sir,

W E are at length arrived at that River, about the uneven running of which, my Friend Mr. *William Shakespear* makes *Henry Hotspur* quarrel so highly with his Fellow-Rebels; and for his sake I have
5 been something curious to consider the scantlet of ground that angry Monsieur would have had in, but cannot find it could deserve his choler, nor any of the other side ours, did not the King think it did. The account I shall now give you of the war will be but imperfect, since I conceive it to be in the state that part of the Four and twenty
10 hours is in, which we can neither call night nor day: I should judge it dawning towards earnest, did not the Lords Covenanters Letters to our Lords here something divide me. So (Sir) you may now imagine us walking up and down the banks of *Tweed* like the Tower-Lyons in their Cages, leaving the people to think what we would do if we were
15 let loose. The Enemy is not yet much visible, (It may be it is the fault of the Climate, which brings Men as slowly forwards as Plants:) But it gives us fears that the Men of Peace will draw all this to a dumb shew, and so destroy a handsom opportunity which was now offered, of producing glorious matter for future Chronicle.
20   These are but Conjectures, Sir: The last part of my Letter I reserve for a great and known Truth, which is, That I am (Sir)

                                   Your most humble Servant, &c.

38   39 which] that *D: omit Ash8, T8*   40 as [much]] so *Ash3, C, T8*   have] hath *C, D, Eg27, T8*   40, 43 placed . . . placed *Σ*: placed . . . planted *T8* : planted . . . placed *D*: planted . . . planted *LR; see note*   41 with] at *Ash3, Eg27, T8*   England] the land *D, T8*   43 the *Σ*: *omit C, Eg27, LR*   44–5 This . . . Servant] (And this *Ash3, Ash8*): *omit T8* : ec. *D*   45 Your humble Servant] (+ written by Sr John Sucklin as 'tis said *C*): Yo^r most humble servant J. S. or A. C. *Ash8*: Yo^~ *Ash3, Eg27: omit D, T8*
    39. *LR*

40. To the Earl of Middlesex, 6 June 1639

For the right honorable
the Earle of
Middlesex

Camp: *June* the 6th.

My Lord.

EVERIE daie is now so big with noveltie that you must be Contented to receave a Journall instead of a letter. On *Mundaie* the
horse had order to take in *Kelsey* or dislodge the Enemie who was
newlie then intrencht there. Wee had 3000 foot allowd to the Action
and some Ordinance, our selves being 1600. The first that appeard
was (if our prospective glasses lied not) my Lord *Car* with a Troop
of Lanciers, who hastilie retir'd, our forlorne hopes pressing something too close upon him. When wee came upon the Top of the hill
wee consulted how and where wee should Charg, and as yet our foot
were not come up to us, besides both horse and man gaspt for breath,
the weather and long being in Armes causing it. During this Time the
Enemie advanct from their works and suddenlie an incontemptible
number were visible. This Causd a message from our Generall (my
Lord *Holland*) who sent a Trumpetter to let them know that they
had broken the Common faith in Assembling arm'd within 10 miles of
the *Twede*, and that therefore they must Expect he should endeavor
to force them to retreat. They returnd, that wee had first broken it,
in Comming thether and that if wee would not retire they would
endeavor to force us. And now the word was given to Charg; but by
this Time wee discoverd dust, and out of that dust grew a greater
bodie then all the right and left hand forces were together. It was
now time to think of Retreat—but wee receavd a second message
Civiller then the first to this purpose. That the king was informd (as
indeed he was) that they were a Contemptible number, but wee
should see they were not, yet they would not begin, but were there
to defend themselves. My Lord *Diall* tells me since, that we ow our
quiet retreat to the Lord *Lowden*, who told those that were earnest
to Charg, that if they should doe so, he stood readie to charge them,
adding that wee were Cavaleirs that studied not the Cause but came
for honor and love to the king. Wee guest these to be about 8000.
On *Tuesdaie* the rest of their forces came up to them and undiscovered,
to the amazement of all and to the no great Creditt of the horse, sat

40. *Cran (holograph)*   22 them to] + return *deleted MS.*

downe within veiw of the kings Camp, and there entrencht. That night in great hast the horse was sent for. This Causd no smal
40 apprehensions, onelie the king remain as fixt as inconcernd and when it was hastilie told him, that *Lesley* was within foure miles of him, said, why then I am within foure miles of *Lesley*. This daie being *Wensdaie* my Lord *Donfermelin* is come from the Covenanters with a petition, promising all humble allegeance, if the king would by his lords
45 (*English*, for they protest the other have abusd both sides.) heare their greivances; and after Councell had, The Knight Marshall is sent with an Answer to this purpose, that if they will Remove the Armie out of his sight and suffer his last Proclamation to be read, that then he will heare and redress. (The last part (it maie be) will unravell all.)
50 Our horse are much harast by Continuall Alarums and hard marches, and our men, manie sick of Loosnesses and Plurisies, which wee ascribe to their violent drinking of *Twede* water that daie wee went to *Kelsey*. The first of the diseases I sufferd my share in through the same cause. My lord it is now one of the Clock and sleep is precious,
55 for wee have tasted little of it this week; and the truth is, should my bodie sue my mind for the losse it has drawne it into, I know not what reparation it would be able to make. That, (which will be left of me) shall ever be much at your service

My lord when you please to
60   Command your humble servant
                        Jo: Suckling.

My Lord.

By the illnesse of the hand your Lordship sees the straitness of Time. I must therefore beg the same favor from you, that in my letter before
65 I have from my lady *Carey* to you, which is that you would be pleasd having read this letter to inclose it and send it to *More-park* to your Daughter, that shee may see though scurvilie I acquitt my self of my obligation I have made to her.

41. [To the Earl of Middlesex (?), 7–17 June 1639]

My Lord,

AT this instant it is grown a Calm greater then the Storm, and if you will believe the Soldier, worse: Good Arms and Horses are already cheap, and there is nothing risen in value but a *Scotchman.*

40. 38 entrencht *Ed.*: entrench *MS.*   50 by *Ed.*: *omit MS.* (*torn*)   march[es,]
MS. (*torn*)   **41.** *LR*

Whether it be (my Lord) the word *Native*, or the Kings good nature, 5
we know not; but we find, they really have that mercy on Earth,
which we do but hope for from heaven; nor can they sin so fast, as
they are forgiven.

Some (and not unreasonably) perchance will imagine that this
may invite good Subjects to be ill; and that as the Sun melts Ice, but 10
hardens Clay, Majesty, when it softens Rebellion, may make Allegi-
ance stubborn. If (my Lord) they shall more straitly now besiege the
Kings ear, and more boldly ingross suits; Posterity must tell this
miracle, That there went an Army from the South, of which there
was not one man lost, nor any man taken prisoner but the King. 15

All we have to raise the present joys above the future fears, is, That
we know Majesty hath not swallowed down so severe Pills, as it was
thought Necessity would prescribe for the purging and setting it self
right.

Your humble Servant. 20

42. To an Unknown Correspondent
[Before 18 June 1639]

Sir,

T HE little stops or progresses which either love of the Publick,
private Fears, Niceties of Honor, or Jealousie have caused in the
Treaty now on foot, arrive at me so slowly, that unless I had one of
Mr. *Davenants* Barbary-Pigeons, (and he now employs them all, he 5
says, himself for the Queens use) I durst not venture to send them,
Sir, to you; lest coming to your hands so late, you should call for the
Map to see whether my Quarters were in *England* or in *Barbary*. The
truth is, I am no first Favorite to any Lord of Secrets at this time;
but when they come from Council, attend the short turn with those 10
that are; and as in discharge of Peeces, see a whisper go off some good
space of time before I hear it; so satisfie my thirst of Novelty from the
stream, not from the fountain.

Our very thoughts are hardly news; and while I now intend to
write you other mens (for my own are not worthy of knowledge) it 15
is not without some fear that they have already sent them to *Whitehal*
themselves.

There are, Sir, here that have an opinion, Necessity, not good
nature produc'd this Treaty; and that the same Necessity which

42. *LR*

20 made them thus wise for Peace, will make them as desperate for War, if it succeed not suddenly.

Some conceive little distrusts among themselves will facilitate the work, and that the danger now grown nearer, will divide the Body, by perswading each man to look to his own particular safety: So we
25 see Men in Ships, while there is hope, assist each other; but when the wrack grows visible, leave the common care, and consult onely their own escape.

There are some imagine, this Treaty of either side is not so much to beget a good Peace as a good Cause; and that the Subject could
30 do no less than humbly petition, not to appear a Rebel; nor the King no less then graciously to hear those Petitions, not to appear a Tyrant; and that when one party shall be found unreasonable, the other will be thought excusable.

J. S.

43. To the Earl of Middlesex [30 September 1639]

For the Earle of
Middlesex
at *Melcott*

> I have procurd you your
> 5 choice of horsses, and D.
> *Cadimans* you may have, but
> at a great rate.

My Lord.

THE noise and fame of this fleet has alreadie fild *Warwickshire*;
10   all that can be news is this days fresh Intelligence, and that is, the *Hollander* is augmented to 73 and the *Spaniard* 56, but if you would reckon Tons off ship they are equall number. My Lord *Northumberland* goes not at all, and the next wind carries forth the *Spaniard*, who stays but for a mast or two and a faire and Constant gale. My Lord
15 *Holland* remembers himself to you, and is verie gladd you are Embarque't in the fishing. They expect you everie howre, but I shall bee absent to my greif, who want much half an howres discourse with you. The Scotch biusnes is in ill Termes, and that which they have now sent the King to Confirme, is worse, then their former unreasonable-
20 nes.

43. *Cran (holograph)*

The particulars are too long. *Roben Lesley* goes this night away with an Answer, but what I know not. If you come not up before St. *Georges* feast, which is on *Munday* next, I shall see you possiblie, because I intend to kisse Mrs. *Buckleys* hands, if I bee not gone away with these shipps, and set downe in *France.*   25

Whitehall.   Your humble servant
Munday.   *Jo: Suckling.*

44. [To Martha Lady Southcot, October 1639]

Madam,

I THANK Heaven we live in an Age in which the Widdows wear Coulers, and in a Country where the Women that lose their Husbands may be trusted with poison, knives, and all the burning coals in *Europe*, notwithstanding the president of *Sophonisba* and 5 *Portia*: Considering the estate you are in now, I should reasonably imagine meaner Physitians then *Seneca* or *Cicero* might administer comfort. It is so far from me to imagine this accident should surprize you, that in my opinion it should not make you wonder; it being not strange at all that a man who hath lived ill all his time in a house, 10 should break a Window, or steal away in the night through an unusual Postern: you are now free, and what matter is it to a Prisoner whether the fetters be taken off the ordinary way or not? If insteed of putting off handsomly the chain of Matrimony, he hath rudely broke it, 'tis at his owne charge, nor should it cost you a tear; Nothing (Madam) 15 has worse Mine than counterfet sorrow, and you must have the height of Womans Art to make yours appear other, especially when the spectators shall consider all the story.

The sword that is placed betwixt a contracted Princesse and an Ambassador, was as much a Husband, and the onely difference was, 20 that that sword laid in the bed, allowed one to supply its place; this Husband denied all, like a false Crow set up in a Garden, which keeps others from the fruit it cannot taste it self: I would not have you so much as enquire whether it were with his garters or his Cloak-bag strings, nor ingage your self to fresh sighs by hearing new relations. 25

The Spanish Princesse *Leonina* (whom *Balzac* delivers the Ornament of the last Age) was wise; who hearing a Post was sent to tell her her Husband was dead, and knowing the Secretary was in the way

for that purpose, sent to stay the Post till the arrival of the Secretary,
30 that she might not be obliged to shed tears twice. Of ill things the
lesse we know, the better. Curiosity would here be as vain, as if a
Cuckold should enquire whether it were upon the Couch or a Bed,
and whether the Cavalier pull'd off his Spurrs first or not. I must
confesse it is a just subject for our sorrow to hear of any that does quit
35 his station without his leave that placed him there; and yet as ill a
Mine as this Act has: 'twas *a-la-Romansci*, as you may see by a line
of Mr. *Shakespears*, who bringing in *Titinius* after a lost battel, speaking
to his sword, and bidding it find out his heart, adds

> *By your leave Gods, this is a Romanes part.*

40   'Tis true, I think Cloak-bag strings were not then so much in
fashion; but to those that are not Sword-men, the way is not so
despicable; and for my owne part, I assure you Christianity highly
governs me in the minute in which I do not wish with all my heart
that all the discontents in his Majesties three Kingdoms would find
45 out this very way of satisfying themselves and the world.

                                                              J. S.

45. [To John Selden, November–December 1639 (?)]

Sir,

I SEND to you now to know how we do here; for in my Lady *Kents*
well-being, much of ours consists: If I am the last, you must
impute it to the tenderness of my fears, which durst not enquire into
5 so great a misfortune; or to the coming of bad news, which ever
comes latest thither, whither it knows it shall be most unwelcome.
For I confess, the report of so great a sickness as my Lady *Kents*,
would give me more trouble then half the Sex, although amongst the
rest a Mistress or two took their Fortunes: And though such excel-
10 lence cannot change but for the better, yet you must excuse us that
enjoy the benefit of her conversation here, if we are content Heaven
should onely give her the blessing of the Old Testament, and for a
while defer those of the New. The onely comfort I have had in the
midst of variety of reports hath been, that I have seen nothing of
15 extraordinary in the Elements of late; and I conceived it but reasonable, that so general an ill as my Lady *Kents* death would be, should

be proclaimed by no less then what foretels the evil of great Princes, or the beginning of great Plagues; when so unlucky a minute shall arive, I would conclude, the virtuous and better sort of people have lost some of their Power and credit above; and that the sins are more 20 Particularly punished of him that is

Her much obliged,
And Sir
your most humble Servant
J. S. 25

46. To Edward Viscount Conway [April–May 1640]

For the right honorable
the Lord Viscount *Conoway*
Lord Deputie of his Majesties
Armie and Generall
of the horse. 5

My Lord.

By the letter I receavd from you, I find how much your Lordship imitates the great and highest Agent, who is never so biusied with governing heaven and the nobler parts of the world, as that hee neglects the lower and lesse Considerable! I shall expect (my Lord) 10 your Commands for our march to *Durham*, and must beseech your Lordship to beleive, that I had not staid for those Summons, but had been as Earlie in paiing my respects as anie, had not Sicknesse taken me betwixt the Stirrop and the Saddle. I hope it will have the manners, to leave me, when you shall have occasion to use mee. If it 15 should not, my Will (my Lord) shall side with my mind, and in spite of all Opposition show, that you have not an humbler Servant anie where, then,

Jo: Suckling

46. *Hyde Collection MS. (holograph)*   1 5 manners] g manners *MS.; see note*

47. To the Earl of Newcastle, 8 January [1641 (?)]

For the much honored
the Earle
of
Newcastle.

5 My Lord.

Are the small buds of the White and Red rose more delightful then the roses themselves? And Cannot the King and Queen invite as stronglie as the roiall Issue? Or has your Lordship taken up your freinds Opinion of you to your owne use, so that when you are in my
10 Lord of *Newcastles* Companie, you cannot think of anie other. Excuse me (my lord) I know it is a pleasure to enjoy a priveledge due to the highest Excelence, (which is to be Extreamlie honor'd and never seen) but withall I beleive the goodnesse of your nature so great, that you will not think your self dearelie borrowed, when your presence shall
15 concerne the fortune of an humble servant. I write not this (my Lord) that you should take a Journey on purpose; that were as Extravagant, as if a man should desire (the Universall Benefactor) the Sun to come a moenth or two before his time, Onelie to make a spring in his garden. I will, as men doe his, wait (my lord) your Comming and in the mean
20 time promise my self good howres without the help of an Astrologer, Since I suddenlie hope to see the noblest Planett of our Orb in Conjunction with your Lordship for the good of

January 8th.   Your humblest Servant
London   *Jo: Suckling*

47. *B.M. Loan MS. 29/235.619.E, f. 161 (holograph)*

LETTERS OF UNCERTAIN DATE
AND ADDRESSEE

48.

Ladies,

THE opinion of things, is the measure of their value, as was wisely said of a Neece of Queen *Gorbudukes*. Know then, that if another then the Coronet had received this Script, he would not perchance have valued it so highly. The *Sybil* Leaves had not so much 5 consultation about them, nor were they half so chargeable as these are like to be. We have first sent them to Secretary *Cook*, imagining nothing but a State-key could unlock those Mysteries. Now we are in quest of an *Arabick* Figure-Caster, for as much of it as we conceive is *Chaldee* or *Syriack*: The Coronet believes there are noble things in it; 10 but what *Beaumont* said of worth wrapt up in rivelled skin, he saith of this, Who would go in to fetch it out? Indeed the opinions about it have been different: some thought it a little against the State; others a Ballad with the Pictures the wrong way; and the most discreet have guest it to be a collection of Charms and Spells, and have adventured 15 to cut it into Bracelets, to be distributed and worn by poor people, as remedies against Cramps and Tooth-aches; onely we will preserve the Faces. And for Mistress *Delana's*, we do not despair but *Vandike* may be able to Copy it; Threescore pounds we have offered, and I think Fourscore will tempt him. For Mistress *T.* there are in that, 20 certaine *je ne scay quoys*, which none but those that have studied it can discover, and Sir *Anthony* shall hold his hand till Mr. *H.* comes to Town. This is all the favor can be done in this business by

Your humble Servant

J. S. 25

49.

The Wine-drinkers to the Water-drinkers, greeting.

WHEREAS by your Ambassador two daies since sent unto us, we understand that you have lately had a plot to surprize or (to speak more properly) to take the waters; and in it have not onely a little miscarryed, but also met with such difficulties, that unlesse 5

you be speedily relieved, you are like to suffer in the adventure;
We as well out of pitty to you, as out of care to our State and Common-Wealth (knowing that Women have ever been held necessary,
and that nothing relisheth so well after Wine) have so far taken it
10 into our consideration, that we have neglected no means since we
heard of it first, that might be for your contents, or the good of the
cause; and therefore to that purpose we have had divers meetings at
the *Bear* at the *Bridge*-foot, and now at length have resolv'd to dispatch to you one of our Cabinet-Councel, Colonel *Young*, with some
15 slight Forces of Canary, and some few of Sherry, which no doubt
will stand you in good steed, if they do not mutiny and grow too
headstrong for their Commander; him Captain *Puffe* of *Barton* shall
follow with all expedition, with two or three Regiments of *Claret*;
Monsieur de *Granville*, commonly called Lieutenant *Strutt*, shall lead
20 up the Reer of Rhenish and White. These succors thus timely sent,
we are confident will be sufficient to hold the Enemy in Play; and
till we hear from you again, we shall not think of a fresh supply: For
the Waters (though perchance they have driven you into some
extremities, and divers times forc't their passages through some of
25 your best guarded places) yet have they, if our intelligence fail us not,
hitherto had the worst of it still, and evermore at length plainly run
away from you.

    Given under our hands at the *Bear*,
      this fourth of *July*.

50. [To Thomas Carew]
To T. C.

THOUGH writing be as tedious to me, as no doubt reading will
be to thee, yet considering that I shall drive that trade thou
speak'st of to the *Indies*, and for my Beads and Rattles have a return
of Gold and Pearl; I am content for thy sake, and in private thus to
5 do penance in a sheet.

    Know then, Dear *Carew*, that at Eleven last night, flowing as much
with Love as thou hast ebbed, thy Letter found me out. I read, considered, and admired, and did conclude at last, That *Horseley* Air
did excel the Waters of the *Bath*; just so much as Love is a more noble
10 disease then the Pox.

    50. *LR*   To T. C.] To T[homas] C[arew] *Haz, Th*

No wonder if the Countesses think time lost, till they be there: Who would not be where such Cures flow! The care thou hast of me, that I should traffick right, draws me by way of Gratitude to perswade thee to bottle up some of that, and send it hither to Town; thy returns will be quicker then those to the *Indies*, nor need'st thou 15 fear a vent, since the disease is Epidemical.

One thing more, who knows (wouldst thou be curious in the search) but thou maist finde an Air of contrary Virtue about thy House, which may, as this destroyes, so that create Affection; if thou couldst, 20

> *The Lady of* High-gate *then should embrace*
> *The disease of the Stomach, and the word of disgrace.*
> Gredeline *and* Grass-green
> *Shall sometimes be seen*
> *Its Arms to in-twine* 25
> *About the* Woodbine.

In honest Prose thus: We would carry our selves first, and then our Friends, manage all the little Loves at Court, make more *Tower* work, and be the Duke of *B.* of our Age, which without it, we shall never be. Think on't therefore, and be assured, That if thou joyn'st me in the 30 Patent with thee, in the height of all my greatness I will be thine, all but what belongs to *Desdemonna*, which is just, as I mean to venture at thy Horse-race *Saturday* come seven-night.

J. S.

51(*a*).

A Letter to a Friend to diswade him from marrying a Widow which he formerly had been in Love with, and quitted

AT this time when no hot Planet fires the blood, and when the Lunaticks of *Bedlam* themselves are trusted abroad; that you should run mad, is (Sir) not so much a subject for your friends *pitty*, as their *wonder*. 'Tis true, *Love* is a *natural distemper*, a kind of *Small Pocks*: Every one either hath had it, or is to expect it, and the sooner 5 the better.

50. 14 up] us *Haz, Th*   16 Epidemical *LR* (*Errata*): Epedemical *LR* (*Text*); *see note* 29   B.] B[uckingham] *Haz*   31 of *Ed.: omit LR*
    51(a) and **51(b)**. *FA46* (*printed in parallel columns: see note*), etc.
    51(a). *FA46. MS.: F60. Variant printed text: AC*
    A Letter . . . quitted] (had formerly been *Th*): A Letter of Sir *J. S. to T. C.* disswading him from marrying of a Widdow *AC*: Written by one to his freind that woed a widow, to whome he had formerly bin a suitor when she was a maide *F60*

Thus far you are excused: But having been well cured of a *Fever*, to court a *Relapse*, to make *Love* the *second time* in the *same Place*, is (not to flatter you) neither better nor worse then to fall into a *Quag-* 10 *mire* by *chance*, and ride into it afterwards on *purpose*.

'Tis not *Love* (*Tom*) that doth the mischief, but *constancy*, for *Love* is of the nature of a *burning-glasse*, which kept still to one place, *fires*; changed often, doth *nothing*: a kind of *glowing-Coal*, which with shifting from hand to hand a man may easily endure. But then to *marry*! 15 (*Tom*) Why thou hadst better live *honest*. *Love* thou knowst is *blind*: what will he do when he hath *Fetters* on thinkest thou?

Dost thou know what *marriage* is? 'Tis *curing* of *Love* the *dearest way*; a waking a *loosing Gamester* out of a *winning dream*; after a long expectation of a strange *banquet*, a presentation of a *homely meal*. Alas! 20 (*Tom*) *Love seeds* when it runs into Matrimony, and is good for nothing. Like some *Fruit-trees*, it must be transplanted if thou wouldst have it active, and bring forth any thing.

Thou now perchance hast vowed all that can be vowed to any *one face*, and thinkst thou hast not left any thing unsaid to it: do but make 25 *love* to *another*, and if thou art not suddenly furnisht with *new language*, and *fresh oathes*, I will conclude *Cupid* hath used thee worse then ever he did any of his train.

After all this, to marry a *Widow*, a kind of *chew'd-meat*! What a fantastical stomack hast thou, that canst not eat of a dish til another 30 man hath cut of it? Who would wash after another, when he might have fresh water enough for asking?

Life is sometimes a long journey: to be tyed to ride upon one beast still, and that half-tyr'd to thy hand too! Think upon that (*Tom*.)

Well; if thou must needs *marry* (as who can tell to what height thou 35 hast sinned?) Let it be a Maid, and no *Widow*: for (as a modern Author hath wittily resolved in this case) 'tis better (if a man must be in Prison) to lie in a private room then in the hole.

51(a). 11 that Σ+*FA48*, *Haz*, *Th*: that that *FA46*   12 to Σ: in *FA46* (*cf.* 51[*b*], *l.* 9)   12 fires Σ: fireth *FA46*   13 often Σ: + it *FA46*   14 may easily endure Σ: easily endures *FA46*   15 better Σ: + to *FA46*   17 curing] the curing *F60*: a curing *AC*   18 a [waking] *AC*: A kinde of *F60*: or *FA46*   dream Σ: + and *FA46*   20 Love seeds] Love-seeds *FA46*   into Σ: up to *FA46* (*cf.* 51[*b*], *l.* 20) 24 not left any thing Σ: left nothing *FA46*   25 new language Σ: new-language *FA46* 26 I will conclude] it is to be concluded. &c. *F60*   26–37 Cupid . . . hole] *omit F60* 28 a [Widow] *AC*, *Haz*, *Th*: *omit FA46*   29 eat] taste *AC*   til] untill *AC* 31 asking] calling for *AC*   32–4 Life . . . Well] *omit AC*   32 long journey] long-journey *FA46*   35–6 for . . . case] *omit AC*   37 room] chamber *AC*   hole.] + Yours. *AC*

51(*b*).
An Answer to the Letter

CEASE to *wonder* (honest *Jack*) and give me leave to *pitty thee*, who labourest to condemn that which thou confessest *natural*, and the *sooner had*, the *better*.

Thus far there needs no *excuse*, unlesse it be on *thy* behalf, who stilest *second thoughts* (which are by all allowed the *Best*) a *relapse*, and 5 talkest of a *quagmire* where no man ever stuck fast, and accusest *constancy* of *mischief* in what is *natural*, and *advisedly undertaken*.

'Tis confest that *Love* changed often doth nothing; nay 'tis nothing; for *Love* and *change* are incompatible: but where it is kept fixt to its first object, though it *burn* not, yet it *warms* and *cherisheth*, so as it 10 needs no *transplantation*, or *change* of *soyl* to make it fruitful: and certainly if *Love* be *natural*, to *marry* is the best *Recipe* for living honest.

Yes, I know what *marriage* is, and know you know it not, by terming it the *dearest way* of *curing Love*: for certainly there goes more charge to the keeping of a *Stable full* of *horses*, then *one* onely *Steed*; 15 and much of vanity is therein besides, when, be the errand what it will, this *one Steed* shall serve your turn as well as twenty more. Oh! if you could serve your *Steed* so! *Marriage* turns pleasing *Dreams* to ravishing *Realities* which out-doe what *Fancy* or *expectation* can frame unto themselves. That *Love* doth *seed* when it runs into *Matrimony*, 20 is undoubted truth; how else should it *increase* and *multiply*, which is its greatest *blessing*?

'Tis not the want of *Love*, nor *Cupids* fault, if every day afford not *new language*, and *new waies* of expressing affection: it rather may be caused through an *excesse* of *joy*, which oftentimes strikes *dumb*. 25

These things considered I will *marry*; nay, and to prove the second *Paradox* false, I'le marry a *Widow*, who is rather the *chewer*, then *thing chewed*. How strangely fantastical is he who will be an hour in plucking on a *strait-boot*, when he may be forthwith furnisht with enough that will come on easily, and do him as much credit, and better 30 service? *Wine* when *first broacht*, drinks not half so well as after a while *drawing*. Would you not think him a mad man who whilst he might fair and easily ride on the *beaten road-way*, should trouble himself with *breaking up of gaps*? A well-wayed horse will safely convay

51(*b*). *FA46* (*on the authorship of* An Answer *see Introduction, pp. lxxxvi–lxxxvii*) 6 accusest]
accuseth *FA48, Haz, Th*   24 new language] new-language *FA46*   new waies] new-waies
FA46   31 first broacht] first-broacht *FA46*   33 beaten road-way] beaten-road-way *FA46*

35 thee to thy journeys end, when an *unbackt Filly* may by chance give
thee a fall. 'Tis *Prince*-like to marry a *Widow*, for 'tis to have a *Taster*.

'Tis true, *life* may prove a *long journey*; and so believe me it must
do, A *very long one* too, before the *Beast* you talke of prove *tyr'd*. Think
you upon that (*Jack*.)

40   Thus (*Jack*) thou seest my wel-tane resolution of *marrying*, and
that a *Widow*, not a *maid*; to which I am much induced out of what
Pythagoras saith, (in his *2da Sect. cuniculorum*) that *it is better lying in
the hole, then sitting in the Stocks*.

52.

A disswasion from Love

Jack,

THOUGH your disease be in the number of those that are better
cured with time then precept, yet since it is lawful for every man
to practise upon them that are forsaken and given over (which I take
5 to be your state) I will adventure to prescribe to you; and of the
innocence of the Physick you shall not need to doubt, since I can
assure you I take it daily my self.

To begin Methodically, I should enjoyn you Travel; for Absence
doth in a kind remove the cause (removing the object) and answers
10 the Physitians first Recipez, vomiting and purging; but this would
be too harsh, and indeed not agreeing to my way. I therefore advise
you to see her as often as you can, for (besides that the rarity of visits
endears them) this may bring you to surprise her, and to discover
little defects, which though they cure not absolutely, yet they
15 qualifie the fury of the Feaver: As neer as you can let it be unseason-
ably, when she is in sicknes, and disorder; for that will let you know
she is mortal, and a Woman, and the last would be enough to a wise
man: If you could draw her to discourse of things she understands not,
it would not be amisse.

20   Contrive your self often into the Company of the cryed-up Beauties;
for if you read but one book, it will be no wonder if you speak or
write that stile; variety will breed distraction, and that will be a
kind of diverting the humour.

I would not have you deny your self the little things (for these

Agues are easier cured with Surfets than abstinence;) rather (if you 25
can) tast all: for that (as an old Author saith) will let you see

> *That the thing for which we wooe,*
> *Is not worth so much ado.*

But since that here would be impossible, you must be content to
take it where you can get it. And this for your comfort I must tell 30
you (*Jack*) that Mistresse and Woman differ no otherwise then
Frontiniack and ordinary Grapes: which though a man loves never
so well, yet if he surfet of the last, he will care but little for the first.

I would have you leave that foolish humour (*Jack*) of saying you
are not in love with her, and pretending you care not for her; for 35
smothered fires are dangerous, and malicious humors are best and
safest vented and breathed out. Continue your affection to your Rival
still; that will secure you from one way of loving, which is in spite;
and preserve your friendship with her woman; for who knows but
she may help you to the remedy. 40

A jolly glasse and right Company would much conduce to the
cure; for though in the Scripture (by the way it is but *Apocrypha*)
Woman is resolved stronger than Wine, yet whether it will be so or
not, when wit is joyned to it, may prove a fresh question.

Marrying (as our friend the late Ambassador hath wittily observed) 45
would certainly cure it; but that is a kind of live Pigeons laid to the
soals of the feet, a last remedy, and (to say truth) worse than the
disease.

But (*Jack*) I remember I promised you a letter, not a Treaty;
I now expect you should be just, and as I have shewed you how to 50
get out of love, so you (according to our bargain) should teach me
how to get into it. I know you have but one way, and will prescribe
me now to look upon Mistris *Howard*; but for that I must tell you
aforehand, that it is in love as in Antipathy: The Capers which will
make my Lord of *Dorset* go from the Table, another man will eat 55
up. And (*Jack*) if you would make a visit to *Bedlam*, you shall find,
that there are rarely two there mad for the same thing.

Your humble Servant.

---

52. 53 now] not *Haz, Th*   54 in [love] *FA48, Haz, Th: omit FA46*

53. [Perhaps to Charles Suckling of Bracondale]

To a Cosin (who still loved young Girles, and when they came to be mariageable, quitted them, and fell in love with fresh) at his fathers request, who desired he might be perswaded out of the humour, and marry

Honest *Charles*,

WERE there not fooles enow before in the Common-Wealth of Lovers, but that thou must bring up a new Sect? Why delighted with the first knots of roses, and when they come to blow (can
5 satisfie the sence, and do the end of their Creation) dost not care for them? Is there nothing in this foolish transitory world that thou canst find out to set thy heart upon, but that which has newly left off making of dirt-pyes, and is but preparing it self for loam, and a green-sicknes? Seriously (*Charles*) and without ceremony, 'tis very
10 foolish, and to love widdows is as tolerable an humour, and as justifiable as thine—for beasts that have been ridd off their legges are as much for a mans use, as Colts that are un-way'd, and will not go at all:—Why the divel such yong things? before these understand what thou wouldst have, others would have granted. Thou dost not marry
15 them neither, nor any thing else. 'Sfoot it is the story of the Jack-anapes and the Partridges: thou starest after a beauty till it is lost to thee, and then let'st out another, and starest after that till it is gone too; Never considering that it is here as in the *Thames*, and that while it runs up in the middle, it runnes down on the sides; while thou
20 contemplat'st the comming-in-tide and flow of Beauty, that it ebbes with thee, and that thy youth goes out at the same time: After all this too, She thou now art cast upon will have much ado to avoid being ugly. Pox on't, Men will say thou wert benighted, and wert glad of any Inne. Well! (*Charles*) there is another way if you could find
25 it out. Women are like Melons: too green, or too ripe, are worth nothing; you must try till you find a right one. Tast all, but hark you— (*Charles*) you shall not need to eat of all, for one is sufficient for a surfet.

Your most humble servant.

30 I should have perswaded you to marriage, but to deal ingenuously,

53. *FA46*　11 off *FA48, Haz, Th*: of *FA46*　20 comming-in-tide] (+*FA48, Haz*): coming-in tide *Th*　30 ingenuously *FA48, Haz, Th*: ingeniously *FA46*

I am a little out of arguments that way at this present: 'Tis honourable, there's no question on't; but what more, in good faith I cannot
readily tell.

54.

Sir,

L EAST you think I had not as perfectly forgot you, as you glory
to have done me: Let these Lines assure you, That if at any time
I think of you, it is with as much scorn, as you vainly hitherto may
have supposed 't has been with affection. A certain general Com- 5
passion in me, and Pity of poor follies, of which number I take this to
be one, A Triumph where there has been no Conquest, has perswaded
me to let you know thus much.

And now if that you have had so much Faith, as that you could
believe a thing so impossible as that of my loving of you, would you 10
but reduce your self to believe a thing so reasonable, as that there
never was any such matter, you would make me step into a belief,
that you never yet had the good thoughts of

J. S.

55. [Perhaps to Mary Bulkeley from Suckling or Sir John Mennes, date unknown]

I HAVINGE (moste fayre and courteous Ladye) in my tyme seene
many exquisite and worthy gentillwoemen in all perfection whose
splendent graces might astonish the sences and inthrall the affection
to love, yet not any one of all those would I chouse were the choyce
of free election really and wholye in myne owne power, to electe one 5
to possess to live together in Nuptiall rights untill *Atropos* should
break yt in sunder. Why I was ever soe farr from prevailinge with the
verye secrete affectiones of my hearte that I could not obteyne, no
not soe much as one thought to affect to love: Debatinge thus with
my selfe and seeinge I could not affect any of those peereless Parra- 10
gons, neyther any which ever my eye beheld, I resolved with my
selfe ever constantlie to remaine in freedom, which I have performed
everye waie untill now with a free and constant minde. But no sooner
had myne eye veiwed your sacred selfe and sawe how you were

54. *LR*
55. *F275 (MS. copy)*

811849   M

15 endowed with all perfection not onely in the Anexments of the body
but allso in the graces of the minde, wherein both art and nature
strove to excell each other in preeminence, I stoode amazed and my
sences kept all silence; yet my eye veiwed you with great content
but my minde with greater admiration. Thus have I smoothered long
20 in silence soe that now I am deeper plunged in desyer then before
I was wrapped in Admiration: Soe that desyre animated by resolution
willed mee to manifeste my affection, which I beinge no sooner
resolved to doe, but presentlye bashfulnes and unworthines stayed
my speech in disclosinge my affection; yet Desyre (Loves fyrebrand)
25 by his restles instigation hath now emboldned me by this my writing
to prostrate unto your sacred person and most gracious and favourable
protection to accept my ever loyall, secret, trew, faithfull, and obedient
service which my heart hath ever vowed faythfullie to performe,
which yf your courteous disposition kindle acceptance, and favourable
30 graunt of this my proffered service to give me entertainment, I doe
moste lovingelie intreat If tyme will not affoord you to write me an
answere, neyther modestye suffer you to utter yt in words, yet I
praye you lett the lovelye splendour of your modest and Christall
eyes present unto my veiwe some hope of your future entertainement.
35 Thus fearinge my over boldnes in withdrawinge you from your
serious employments and zealous cogitations should importune you
too longe, wishinge all honour to your person, prosperitye in all your
actions, content to all your desyres, with all internall and externall
happines and eternal blessednes, I rest your and no more his owne
40 ever to command,

                                                    J S

TO MR. HENRY GERMAN,
IN THE BEGINNING OF PARLIAMENT,
1640

Sir,

THAT it is fitt for the Kinge to doe somethinge extraordinary
att this present, is not onely the opinion of the wise, but their
expectation. Men observe him more now than att other tymes, for
Majestie in an Ecclypse, (like the Sun) drawes eies that would not 5
soe much as have look'd towards it, if it had shin'd out, and appear'd
like it selfe. To lie still now would att the best shewe but a calmnes of
minde, not a magnanimitie: Since in matter of government, to thinke
well (att any tyme, much lesse in a very Active) is little better than
to dreame well. Nor must hee stay to Act till his people desire, 10
because 'tis thought nothinge rellishes with them else: For therefore
hath nothinge rellish'd with them, because the King hath for the
most part staid till they have desir'd, done nothinge, but what they
have, or were petitioninge for.

But *that* the King should doe, will not bee soe much the question, 15
as *what* hee should doe.

And certainly for a King to have right Counsell given him, is att
all tymes strange, and att this present almost impossible; his Partie
for the most part (I would that were modestlie said and it were not
all) have so much to doe for their owne preservation, that they cannot 20
without breakeing a lawe in Nature intend anothers. Those that
have courage have not perchance Innocence, and soe dare not shewe
themselves in the Kings businesse: and if they have innocence, they
want parts to make themselves considerable; So consequently the
thinges they undertake. Then in the Court they give much Counsell, 25
as they beleive the King inclyn'd, determine of his good by his
desires, which is a kinde of Settinge the Sun by the Diall, Interest that
cannot erre, by Passions which may.

To Mr. Henry German, *etc. Cran. Variant MSS.: St, T6, TC. Variant printed texts:*
FA46, Ltr41, Ltr43
To . . . 1640 *FA46*: Sr John Sucklings letter to Mr Hen: Jermin *T6*: A Coppy of a
Letter Found in the Privy Lodgeings at Whitehall *Ltr41*: A Letter Concerninge these
tymes. 1643 *TC*: A True Copie *etc. (as with Ltr41) Ltr43*: omit *Cran, St*   9 (att
any tyme, much *FA46*: ʌatt any tyme (much *Cran* 17 certainly] surely *Ltr41, St, TC*
17–18 is att all tymes] at all times is *Ltr41, St, TC*   18 present] time *Ltr41, St, TC*
27–8 that . . . which] which . . . that *T6*: which . . . which *FA46*   28–9 may. [*new
paragraph*] In *Σ*: may in *Cran, Ltr41*

In goinge about to Shewe the King a cure nowe, a Man should
30 first plainly shewe him the disease. But to Kings as to some kinde of
Patients it is not alwaies proper to tell how ill they are. And it is too
much like a Countrey-Clowne, not to shew the way, unlesse hee know
from whence, and discourse of things before.

Kings may bee mistaken and Counsellors corrupted, but true
35 interest alone (saies *Mounsieur de Rohan*) cannot erre; It were not
amisse then to finde out this interest, for settinge downe right Principles before conclusions, is weighing the Scales, before wee deale out
the Comoditie.

Certainly the great Interest of the King is a union with his people,
40 and whosoever hath told him otherwise (as the Scripture saies of the
Devill) was a seducer from the first. If there ever had beene any one
Prince in the whole world, that made a felicity in this life, and left
faire fame after death, without the love of his Subjects, there were
some colour to despise it.

45 There was not amonge all our Princes a greater Courter of the
People, than *Richard* the third, not soe much out of feare, as out of
wisedome. And shall the worst of our Kings have striven for that,
and shall not the best? (it being an Angelicke thinge to gaine Love.)

There are two things in which the People expect to bee satisfied:
50 Religion and Justice; Nor can this bee done by any little Arts, but
by reall and Kingly resolutions.

If any shall thinke that by dividing the factions (a good rule att
other tymes) hee shall master the rest now, hee will bee strangely
deceiv'd; for in the beginning of things that would doe much, but
55 not when whole Kingdomes are resolv'd. Of those now that lead
those parties, if you could take off the major number, the lesser would
governe, and doe the same things still; Nay if you could take off all,
they would sett upp one and followe him. It will cleerely appeare that
neither the persons of the Scottish, nor English Actors upon the Stage,

---

29 cure‸ now,] Cure, now‸ *FA46* : cure, but *Ltr41* : Cure, Ha℈, *Th*   31 are] be *FA46* :
fare *Ltr43*   33 from whence] + you come *Ltr41*, *T6*, *TC*   35 saies] saith *FA46* :
said *Ltr41*   Mounsieur de] the Duke de *TC*: the Duke of *Ltr41*, *St*   39 a] an
St: the *Ltr41*, *T6*   40 saies] saith *FA46*, *Ltr41*   41 ever] *omit Ltr41*, *St*,
T6, *TC*   45 amonge] amongst *St*, *T6*, *TC*   Courter] Courtier *FA46*, *T6*, *TC*; *see note*
48 Angelicke] Angelical *FA46*, *Ltr41*, *TC*   50 this] it *Ltr41*, *St*, *TC*   Arts] art *T6*,
TC: acts *FA46*, *Ltr41*, *St*   51 reall] Royal *FA46*   53 now] *omit Ltr41*, *St*, *TC*
54 the Σ: *omit Cran*, *Ltr41*   58 him.] + For as *Cato* said of the *Romans*, [+ that *St*,
TC] they were like sheep, and [+ that *Ltr41*] the way to drive them was in a flock [fold
TC], for if [+ any *St*] one would be extravagant [lead well *for* would be extravagant *TC*]
all the rest would [will *TC*] follow; so it would [will *St*] be here. *Ltr41*, *St*, *TC*; *see note*
58–63 It . . . value] *omit FA46*   59 nor] and *Ltr41*, *TC*

are a considerable number to the great bodie of *England*, but the things 60
they undertake. Which done by another hand, (and soe done, that
there remaine no jelousie) leaves them where they were, and not
much risen in value. And of how great consequence it is for the King
to resume this right, and bee the Author himselfe, lett any body
Judge: since as *Cumenes* said, those that have the Art to please the 65
people, have comonly the power to raise them.

To doe things so, that there shall remaine no jelousie, is very
necessary, and is no more than really reforminge (that is, pleasing)
them. For to doe things that shall greive heereafter and yet pretend
love (amongst lovers themselves, where there is the easiest faith) 70
will not be accepted. It will not bee enough for the King to doe what
they desire, but hee must doe something more. I meane by doing
more, doing something of his owne: as throwing away things they
call not for, or giving things they expected not. And when they see
the King doing the same things with them, it will take away all 75
thought and apprehension that hee thinkes the things they have
done alreadie, ill.

Now if the King ends the differences, and takes away suspect for
the future, the case will fall out to bee no worse than when two
Duellists enter the Feild (where the worsted Partie, the other having 80
no ill opinion of him, hath his sword given him again without further
hurt, after he is in the others power.) But otherwise it is not safe to
imagine what may followe: For the People are naturally not valiant,
and not much Cavaleir. Nowe it is the nature of Cowards to hurt,
when they can receive none: they will not bee content (while they 85
feare, and have the upper hand) to fetter onely royaltie, but perchance
(as timorous Spirritts use) will not thinke themselves safe, whiles
that is att all, and possibly this may bee the present state of things.

In this great worke (att least to make it appeare perfect and lasting
to the Kingdome) it is necessary the Queene really joyne. For if shee 90
stand aloofe, there will still bee suspitions: it being a receiv'd opinion
in the world, that shee hath a great interest in the Kings favour, and
power. And to invite her, shee is to consider with herselfe, whether

60 a considerable number] considerable *Ltr41*, *St*, *TC*; *see note*   62 remaine] remains
Ltr41, *St*, *TC*   65 Cumenes] Eumenes *T6*: Comines *Ltr41*: Commines *St*:
Cominus *Ltr43*, *TC*: Comneus *FA46*   said] saies *St*, *TC*: saith *Ltr41*   66 comonly] *omit*
Ltr41, *St*, *T6*   70 amongst Σ: amonge *Cran*   72 something more] + for that will
shew the heartinesse *Ltr41*, *St*, *TC*   78 differences] difference *Ltr41*, *St*, *TC*
suspect] the suspect *Ltr41*: suspicion *T6*   for Σ: from *Cran*   85 none] + and wound
even the dead *Ltr41*, *St*, *TC* (*omit* even)   88 may bee] is *FA46*, *Ltr41*, *St*, *TC*
90 necessary] + that *Ltr41*, *T6*   91 suspitions] suspition *Ltr41*, *St*, *T6*, *TC*

such great vertues and eminent Excellencies (though they bee highly
95 admir'd and valued by those that know her and are about her) ought
to rest satisfied with so narrowe a payment, as the estimation of a
few: and whether it bee not more proper for a great Queen to arrive
att universall honor, and love, than private esteeme and value. Then
how becomeing a worke for the sweetnesse and softnesse of her Sex
100 is composing differences, and uniting hearts; and how proper for
a Queene, reconciling King and people.

There is but one thing remaines, which whisper'd abroade, busies
the Kings minde much, if not disturbes it, in the midst of these great
resolutions, and that is the preservation of some servants which hee
105 thinkes somewhat hardly torne from him of late, which is of soe tender
a nature, I shall rather propound something about it, than resolve it.

The first *Quære* wilbee, whether as things now stand (Kingdomes
in the ballance) the King is not to follow Nature, where the conserva-
tion of the more generall still comaunds and governes the lesse; As
110 Iron in particular sympathie stickes to the Load-stone, but yet if
it bee joyn'd with a great bodie of Iron, it quitts those particular
affections to the Load-stone, and moves with the other, to the greater,
the Comon-Countrey.

The second will bee whether if hee could preserve these Ministers
115 they can bee of any use to him heereafter: since no man is serv'd
with a greater prejudice, than hee that employs suspected Instru-
ments, or not belov'd, though Able, and deserving in themselves.

The third is whether to preserve them, there bee any other way
than for the King to bee first right with his people: Since the rule in
120 Philosophie must ever hold good. *Nihil dat, quod non habet*: before the
King hath power to preserve, hee must have power.

Lastly whether the way to preserve this power bee not to give
it away; For the people of *England* have ever beene like wantons,
which pull and tugge as long as the Princes have pull'd with them,
125 as you may see in *Henry* the third, King *John*, *Edward* the second,
and indeed all the troublesome and unfortunate Raignes; but when
they have lett it goe they come and putt it into their hands againe
that they may play on, as you may see in Queene *Elizabeth*.

97 few *Σ*: Iew *Cran*   99 Sex] Love *Ltr41*, *St*, *TC*   100 composing] + of *FA46* :
compounding *St* : compounding of *Ltr41*, *TC*   104 which] whom *FA46*, *St*   105 is] +
a thing *Ltr41*, *St*, *TC*   109 more] *omit Ltr41*, *St*, *TC*   still] will *TC* : wills *St* : weale
Ltr41   112 other, to] *omit* to *Ltr41*, *St*, *TC*   113 Countrey] Center *T6*, *TC*
114 these] those *FA46*, *TC*   116 a] *omit Ltr41*, *St*, *TC*   120 Nihil] nil *FA48*,
Th : nemo *Ltr41*   121 hath] have *FA46*, *Ltr41*, *TC*   preserve] save *FA46*

I will conclude with a Prayer (not that I thinke it needs att the present: Prayers are to keepe us from what may bee, as well as pre- 130 serve us from what is) That the King bee neither too insensible, of what is without him, nor too resolv'd from what is within him. To bee sicke in a dangerous sicknesse, and finde noe paine, cannot bee but with losse of understanding. 'Tis an Aphorisme of *Hippocrates*: And on the other side, *Opiniastrie* is a sullen Porter and (as it was 135 wittily said of *Constancie*) shutts out oftentymes better things, than it letts in.

131 bee neither] may [not *deleted*] be neither *St*: be not *T6*: may be not *TC*: may not be *Ltr41* 133 in] of *Cran* (in *written over*), *FA46, Ltr41* 135 Opiniastrie] Opinionastry *TC*: Opinionaster *St*: Opinionist *Ltr41* 136 wittily said] witnessed *Ltr41*, *St: omit TC* 137 in *Σ*: it *Cran* + Finis *FA46, Ltr41, St, TC*

A N
ACCOVNT
OF
RELIGION
BY
REASON.

A Difcourfe upon Occafion pre-
fented to the Earl of *Dorfet*.

By
Sir JOHN SUCKLING.

Printed by his owne Copy.

Lucret. pag.227. *Tentat enim dubiam mentem rationis egeſtas*.

LONDON,
Printed by *Ruth Raworth* for *Humphrey Moſeley*, and
are to be fold at his fhop at the figne of the
Princes Arms in S. *Pauls* Church-yard. 1646.

To Edward Sackville, fourth Earl of Dorset; 2 September 1637

AN ACCOUNT OF RELIGION BY REASON

The Epistle

I SEND you here (my Lord) that Discourse enlarged, which frighted the Lady into a cold sweat, and which had like to have made me an *Atheist* at Court, and your Lordship no very good Christian. I am not ignorant that the fear of *Socinianisme* at this time, renders every man that offers to give an account of Religion by 5 Reason, suspected to have none at all: yet I have made no scruple to run that hazard, not knowing why a man should not use the best Weapon his Creator hath given him in his defence. That *Faith* was by the Apostles both highly exalted, and severely enjoyned, is known to every man, and this upon excellent grounds; for it was both 10 the easiest and best way of converting: the other being tedious, and almost uselesse; for but few among thousands are capable of it, and those few not capable at all times of their life, Judgement being required. Yet the best servant our Saviour ever had upon Earth, was so far from neglecting or contemning Reason, that his Epistles were 15 admired, even by those that embraced not the Truthes he delivered. And indeed, had the *Fathers* of the *Church* only bid men *beleeve*, and not told them *why*, they had slept now un-Sainted in their Graves, and as much benighted with Oblivion, as the ordinary *Parish-Priests* of their owne Age. 20

That man is deceivable, is true; but what part within him is not likelyer to deceive him then his Reason? For as *Manilius* said,

> *Neque enim decipitur ratio neque decipit unquam.*

And how unlikely is it that that which gives us the Prerogative above other Creatures, and wholy entitles us to future happinesse, 25 should be laid aside, and not be used to the acquiring of it?

An Account of Religion by Reason. *FA46. MSS.: AS, S, Υ (from FA58: readings specified only when different from those of FA46; Σ = AS, S)*

The Epistle.   8 hath] has *Σ*   in *Σ*: for *FA46*   22 to deceive him *Σ: omit FA46*   23 Neque enim ... neque *Σ*: Nam neque ... nec *FA46; see note*   26 [not] be *S*: to be *AS; omit FA46*

But by this time (my Lord) you finde how apt those which have nothing to do themselves are, to give others trouble. I shall onely therefore let you know that your Commands to my Lord of *Middlesex* 30 are performed; and that when you have fresh ones, you cannot place them where they will be more willingly received, then by

Bath, Sept. 2.   Your humble Servant,
                                                John Suckling.

A Discourse written by Sir John Suckling, Knight, to the Earl of Dorset

AMONG the truths (my Lord) which we receive, none more reasonably commands our belief, then those which by *all* men, at *all* times have been assented to. In this number and highest I place this great one, that there is a *Deity*; which the whole world hath been 5 so eager to embrace, that rather then it would have none at all, it hath too often been contented with a very mean one.

That there should be a great Disposer and Orderer of things, a wise Rewarder and Punisher of good and evil, hath appeared so equitable to men, that by instinct they have concluded it necessary; 10 Nature (which doth nothing in vain) having so far imprinted it in us all, that should the envie of Predecessors deny the secret to Succeeders, they yet would find it out. Of all those little ladders with which we scale heaven, and climb up to our Maker, that seems to me not the worst, of which man is himself the first step. For but by 15 examining how I, that could contribute nothing to mine owne being, should be here, I come to ask the same question for my Father, and so am led in a direct line to a last Producer, that must be more then man. For *if man made man, Why died not I when my Father died*? Since according to that great *Maxime* of the Philosophers, *the cause taken* 20 *away, the effect does not remain.* Or if the first man gave himself being, why hath he it not still? Since it were unreasonable to imagine any thing could have power to give it self life, that had no power to continue it. That there is then a God, will not be so much the

A Discourse *etc.*

A Discourse written by Sir John Suckling, Knight, to the Earl of Dorset *Σ* (*precedes* Epistle *in AS*): A Discourse by Sir John Suckling, Knight *FA46* (*see title-page*): A Discourse of Religion *Haz, Th*   1 receive] + and *Σ*   4 hath] had *Haz*   10 doth] does *Σ*   11 of] + the *Haz*   14 himself *Σ*: *omit FA46*   15 that] which *Σ* 19 great *Σ*: *omit FA46*   21 hath] has *Σ*

dispute: what this God is, or how to be worshipped, is that which
hath troubled poor mortals from the first, nor are they yet in quiet. 25
So great has been the diversity, that some have almost thought God
was no lesse delighted with variety in his service, then he was
pleased with it in his works. It would not be amisse to take a survey
of the world from its cradle; and with *Varro*, divide it into three
Ages: the *Unknown*, the *Fabulous*, and the *Historical*. 30

The first was a black *night*, and discovered *nothing*: the second was
a weak and glimmering *light*, representing things imperfectly and
falsely: the last (*more clear*) left handsom monuments to posterity.
The *unknown* I place in the age before the Flood, for that Deluge swept
away things as well as men, and left not so much as footsteps to trace 35
them by. The *fabulous* began after the Flood; in this time Godheads
were cheap, and men not knowing where to choose better, made
Deities one of another. Where this ended, the *historical* took beginning: for men began to ingrave in pillars, and to commit to Letters,
as it were by joynt consent: for the three great *Epoches* or Termes of 40
Accompt were all established within the space of thirty yeers: The
Grecians reckoning from their *Olympicks*: The *Romans* from the building
of their City: and the *Babilonians* from their King *Salmonassar*. To bring
into the scale with Christian Religion any thing out of the first Age,
we cannot; because we know nothing of it. 45

And the second was so *fabulous*, that those which took it up afterwards, smil'd at it as ridiculous and false (which though was easier
for them to do then to shew a true.) In the *historical*, it improved, and
grew more refined: but here the *Fathers* have entred the field, and
so cleerly gained the victory, that I should say nothing in it, did I 50
not know it still to be the opinion of good wits, that the particular
Religion of Christians has added little to the general Religion of the
World. Let us take it then in its *perfecter estate*, and look upon it in
that age which was made glorious by the bringing forth of so many
admirable spirits, and this was about the eightieth *Olympiad*, in 55
the year of the world 3480; for in the space of an hundred yeers,
flourished almost all that *Greece* could boast of: *Socrates, Plato, Aristotle,
Architas, Isocrates, Pythagoras, Epicurus, Heraclitus, Xenophon, Zeno,
Anaxagoras, Democritus, Demosthenes, Parmenides, Zenocrates, Theophrastus,*

24 dispute[: *Ed.*] *Σ*: ~[,] as *FA46*   worshipped, is] worshipped—this is *Haʓ*
42 Olympicks *Σ*: Olympiades *FA46; see note*   43 Salmonassar] Psalmanasar *Haʓ*
49 have *Σ*: omit *FA46*   53 its] our *Σ*   perfecter] perfect *Haʓ*   55 eightieth
Σ+*FA48, Haʓ, Th*: 80. *FA46*   56 an] a *Σ*   58 Zeno] Zene *Σ*   59 Theophrastus
Σ+*Υ*: Theophrastes *FA46, FA58*

60 *Empedocles*, *Tymæus*, with divers others, Orators and Poets. Or
rather (for they had their Religion one from another, and not
much different) let us take a view of it in that Century in which
Nature (as it were to oppose the *Grecian* insolence) brought forth
that happy birth of *Roman* wits: *Varro*, *Cicero*, *Cæsar*, *Livie*, *Salust*,
65 *Virgil*, *Horace*, *Vitruvius*, *Ovid*, *Pliny*, *Cato*, *Marcus Brutus*; and this
was from *Quintus Servilius* Consulship to that of *Augustus*, two hundred seventy yeers after the other. And to say truth, a great part of
our Religion, either directly or indirectly hath been professed by
Heathens; which I conceive not so much an exprobation to it, as a
70 confirmation; it being no derogating from truth, to be warranted by
general consent.

First then, the Creation of the world is delivered almost the same
in the *Phœnician* stories with that in *Moses*; from this the *Grecians* had
their *Chaos*, and *Ovid* the beginning of his *Metamorphosis*. That *All*
75 *things were made by God*, was held by *Plato*, and others; that *darknes*
was before night, by *Thales*; that *the Stars were made by God*, by *Aratus*;
that *life was infused into things by the breath of God*, *Virgil*; that *Man was*
made out of dust, *Hesiod*, and *Homer*; that *the first life of man was in sim-*
plicity and nakednes, the *Ægyptians* taught: and from thence the Poets
80 had their *Golden Age*. That *in the first times mens lives lasted a thousand*
yeers, *Berosus*, and others: that *somthing divine was seen amongst men, till*
the greatnes of our sins gave them cause of remove, *Catullus*: and this he
that writes the story of *Columbus*, reports from the *Indians* of *a great*
Deluge, almost all. But to the main, they held *one God*, and though
85 *multiplicity* hath been laid to their charge, yet certainly the clearer
spirits understood these petty Gods as things, not Deities; second
causes, and several vertues of the great power: by *Neptune*, water;
Juno, aire; by *Dispater*, earth; by *Vulcan*, fire; and sometimes one God
signified many things, as *Jupiter* the whole world, the whole heaven;
90 and sometimes many gods, one thing, as *Ceres*, *Juno*, *Magna Mater*,
the earth. They concluded those to be vices which we do; nor was
there much difference in their vertues; onely Christians have made
ready beleef the highest, which they would hardly allow to be any.
They held rewards for the good, and punishments for the ill; had

60 Tymæus] Tymens *Σ*   others,] other∧ *Σ* ([other]s *deleted S*)   65 Vitruvius]
Vitrurius *S*: Victurius *AS*   66 Servilius *Σ*: + his *FA46* (*cf. ll.* 99, *100*)   71 general
Σ: common *FA46*   76 night *S*: might *AS*: light *FA46*; *see note*   78 out
Σ: *omit FA46*   81 till *Σ*: + that *FA46*   82 [cause] of *Σ*: to *FA46*   84 held
Σ: hold *FA46*   85 hath] has *S*: had *AS*   86 not *Σ*: + as *FA46*   90 Juno,]
∼∧ *FA46*, *Σ*   Magna Mater[, *Ed*.] *Σ* (mater *AS*: Water *S*): magna, *FA46*

their *Elizium*, and their *hell*; and that they thought the pains *eternal* 95
there, is evident, in that they beleev'd from thence was no return.
They proportion'd sufferings hereafter, to offences here; as in *Tan-*
talus, *Sisyphus*, and others, among which that of Conscience (the worm
that never dies) was one, as in the Vultures gnawing of *Prometheus*
heart, and *Virgils* ugliest of the Furies thundring in *Pirithous* ear, was 100
not obscurely shown; and yet neerer us, they held the number of the
Elect to be but small, and that there should be a last day in which the
World should perish by fire. Lastly they had their Priests, Temples,
Altars.

We have seen now the *Parallel*; let us enquire whether those things 105
they seem to have in common with us, we have not in a more excellent manner, and whether the rest in which we differ from all the
world, we take not up with reason. To begin then with their *Jupiter*
(for all before were but little stealthes from *Moses* workes) how much
more like a Deity are the actions our stories declare our God to have 110
done, then what the Ethnick Authors deliver of theirs? How excel-
lently elevated are our descriptions of him? Theirs looking as if they
knew that power onely by their fears, as their Statues erected to him
declare: for when he was *Capitolinus*, he appear'd with thunder; when
Latiaris, besmear'd with blood; when *Feretrius*, yet more terrible: We 115
may ghesse what their conceptions were, by the worship they gave
him: How full of cruelty were their sacrifices? it being received almost
through the whole world, *that gods were pleased with the blood of men*: and
this custom neither the *Grecian* Wisdom, nor *Roman* Civility abolished,
as appears by sacrifices to *Bacchus Onesta*, and *Jupiter Latiaris*. 120

Then the ceremonies of *Liber Pater*, and *Ceres*, how obscene? and
those daies which were set apart for the honour of the gods, celebrated with such shews as *Cato* himself was ashamed to be present at.
On the contrary, our services are such as not only *Cato*, but God himself may be there: we worship him that is the purest Spirit, in purity 125
of spirit; and did we not beleeve what the Scriptures deliver from
himself, yet would our reason perswade us that such an Essence could
not be pleased with the blood of beasts, or delighted with the steam
of fat: and in this particular, Christians have gone beyond all others
except the Mahometans; besides whom there has been no Nation 130
that had not sacrifice, and was not guilty of this pious cruelty.

100 the *Σ*: *omit FA46*   Pirithous] Pirythous's *AS*   113 that] what *Th*
120 by] + the *Haz*   Bacchus Onesta, and Jupiter Latiaris. *Σ* (Bacchus, *S*): Bacchus.
FA46   122 which were] *omit Haz*   123 as] that *Σ*   130 besides whom]
omit Σ   has] had *S*: haue *AS*

That we have the same vertues with them is very true; but who can deny that those vertues have received additions from Christianity, conducing to mens better living together? revenge of injuries *Moses*
135 both took himself, and allowed by the Law to others; *Cicero* and *Aristotle* placed it in vertues quarter, and made it part of fortitude: We extol patient bearing of injuries; and what quiet the one, and what trouble the other would give the world, let the indifferent judge. Their justice took only care that men should not do wrong: ours that
140 they should not think it, the very coveting severely forbidden: and this held too in chastity, desire of a woman unlawfully being as much a breach of the commandement, as the enjoying, which shew'd not only the Christians care, but wisdom to prevent ill, who provided to destroy it where it was weakest, in the Cradle, and declared, He was
145 no lesse then a God which gave them these Laws; for had he been but man, he never would have provided or taken care for what he could not look into, the hearts of Men, and what he could not punish, their thoughts. What Charity can be produced answerable to that of Christians? Look upon the Primitive times, and you shall find that
150 (as if the whole World had been but a private Family) they sent from Province to Province, and from Places farre distant, to Releeve them they never saw nor knew.

Now for the happinesse which they proposed: if they take it as the Heathens understood it, it was an *Elizium*, a place of blessed
155 shades, at best but a handsom retirement from the troubles of this World: if according to the duller Jewes, Feastings and Banquettings; (for it is evident that the *Sadduces*, who were great observers of the Mosaical Law, had but faint thoughts of any thing to come) there being in *Moses* books no promises but of Temporal blessings, and
160 (if any) an obscure mention of eternity. The Mahometans are no lesse sensual, making the renewing of youth, high Feasts, a woman with great eyes, and drest up with a little more fancie, the last and best good.

Then the hell; How gentle with the Heathens? but the rowling of
165 a stone, filling of a sieve with water, sitting before Banquets and not daring to touch them, exercising the trades and businesse they had on earth; with the Mahometans, but a Purgatory acted in the grave, some pains inflicted by a bad Angel, and those qualified and mitigated

136 quarter, and made it part of fortitude: Σ: quarter: *FA46*   137 [one,] and Σ: *omit*
FA46   139 took only Σ: only took *FA46*   141 held Σ: holds *FA46*   142 [as]
the Σ+*Haz*: their *FA46*   166 trades . . . businesse Σ: trade . . . businesses *FA46*

too, by an assisting good one. Now for the Jewes, as they had no
hopes, so they had no fears; so that if we consider it rightly, neither   170
their punishments were great enough to deter them from doing ill,
nor their rewards high enough to invite men to strictnes of life; for
since every man is able to make as good a heaven of his own, it were
unreasonable to perswade him to quit that certain happines for an
incertain: whereas Christians with a much more noble consideration   175
both in their heaven and hell took care not onely for the body but the
soul, and for both above mans apprehension.

    The strangest, though the most Epidemical disease of all Religions,
has been an imagination men have had, that the imposing painful and
difficult things upon themselves, was the best way to appease the   180
Deity, grossly thinking the chief service and delight of the Creator
to consist in the tortures and sufferings of the Creature. How laden
with chargeable and unnecessary Ceremonies the Jews were, their
feasts, circumcisions, sacrifices, great Sabbaths, and little Sabbaths,
fasts, burials, indeed almost all their worship, sufficiently declare: 185
and that the Mahometans are much more infected, appears by the
cutting of their *Præpuces*, wearing iron rings in the skins of their
Fore parts, launcing themselves with knives, putting out their eyes
upon the sight of their Prophets Tombe, and the like. Of these last
we can shew no patterns amongst us: for though there be such a   190
thing as whipping of the body, yet it is but in some parts of Christen-
dom, and there perchance too, more smil'd at then practis'd. Our
Religion teacheth us to bear afflictions patiently when they fall upon
us, but not to force them upon our selves: for we beleeve the God we
serve, wise enough to chuse his owne service, and therefore presume   195
not to adde to his commands. With the Jews it is true we have somthing in common, but rather the names then thinges: Our Fasts
being more the medicines of the body, then the punishments of it,
spiritual, as our Sabbaths; both good mens delight, not their trouble.

    But least this discourse should swell into a greatnesse, such as   200
would make it look rather like a defence which I had labour'd to get,
then an accompt which I carry alwaies about me; I will now briefly
examine, whether we beleeve not with reason those things we have
different from the rest of the world. First then, for the perswasion of
the truth of them in general, let us consider what they were that   205

170 so that] *omit FA58, Haz, Y*
FA46; see note   a *Σ*: as *FA46*   178 the *Σ*: *omit FA46*   187 their [Præpuces]
Σ: the *FA46*   skins *Σ*: skin *FA46*   193 teacheth] teaches *Haz, Th, Y*   202
carry alwaies *Σ*: alwaies carry *FA46*
175 incertain[e] *S*: uncertaine *AS*: uncertainty

conveigh'd them to us: men (of all the world) the most unlikely to plot the cozenage of others, being themselves but simple people, without ends, without designes, seeking neither honour, riches, nor pleasure, but suffering (under the contrary) ignominy, poverty, and
210 misery; enduring death it self, nay courting it: all which are things distasteful to nature, and such as none, but men strangely assured, would have undergone. Had they feigned a story, certainly they would not in it have registred their owne faults, nor deliver'd him whom they propounded as a God, ignominiously crucified: add to
215 this the progresse their doctrine made abroad, miraculous above all other before or since: other Religions were brought in with the sword, power forcing a custom, which by degrees usurp'd the place of truth: this even power it self opposing. For the *Romans* (contrary to their custome which entertained all Religions kindly) persecuted this:
220 which by its owne strength so possessed the hearts of men, that no age, sex, or condition, refused to lay down life for it. A thing so rare in other Religions, that among the Heathens, *Socrates* was the sole martyr: and the Jews (unlesse of some few under *Manasses* and *Antiochus*) have not to boast of any. If we cast our eyes upon the
225 healing of the blind, curing the lame, redeeming from the grave, and but with a touch or word, we must conclude them done by more then humane power, and if by any other, by no ill; These busie not themselves so much about the good of man: and this Religion not only forbids by precept the worship of wicked spirits, but in fact destroys
230 it wheresoever it comes. Now as it is clear by Authors impartial (as being no Christians) that strange things were done, so it is plain they were done without imposture. Delusions shun the light; These were all acted openly, the very enemies both of the master and disciples daily looking on. But let us descend to those more principal
235 particulars, which so much trouble the curious wits: these I take to be the *Incarnation*, *Passion*, *Resurrection*, and *Trinity*.

For the first, That man should be made without man, why should we wonder more in that time of the world, then in the beginning? much easier, certainly, it was here, because neerer the natural way;
240 Woman being a more prepared matter then earth. Those great truths, and mysteries of salvation would never have been received without miracles; and where could they more opportunely be shown, then at his entrance into the world, where they might give credit to his

216 other *AS*, *FA46* (+ either): *omit S*   217–18 truth: this] truth, in this *Ha*
238 more *Σ*: + at it *FA46*

following actions and doctrine? So far it is from being against my reason to think him thus borne, that it would be against it to beleeve 245 him otherwise; it being not fit that the Son of God should be produced like the race of men. That humane nature may be assumed by a Deity, the enemy of Christians, *Julian*, confirms; and instances (himself) in *Æsculapius*, whom he will have descend from heaven in mortal shape, to teach us here below the Art of Physick. Lastly, 250 That God has liv'd with men, has been the general fancy of all Nations: every particular having this tradition; that the Deity at some time or other conversed amongst men. Nor is it contrary to reason to beleeve him residing in glory above, and yet incarnate here: So in man himself, the soul is in heaven when it remains in flesh, for 255 it reacheth with its eye the Sun; why may not God then being in heaven, be at the same time with us in flesh? since the soul without the body would be able to do much more then with it, and God much more then the soul, being the soul of the soul. But it may be urged as more abstruse, how all in heaven, and all in earth at once? Observe 260 man speaking (as you have done seeing:) Is not the same speech, at the instant it is uttered, all in every place? Receives not each particular ear, alike, the whole? and shall not God be much more Ubiquitary then the voice of man?

For the *Passion* (to let alone the necessity of satisfying divine 265 Justice this way, which whosoever reads more particularly our Divines, shall find rationally enforced) we find: the Heathen had something neer to this (though, as in the rest, imperfect) for they sacrificed single men for the sins of a whole City or Countrey. *Porphyrius* having laid this foundation, *That the supreme happines of the soul is to see God*, and 270 that it cannot see him unpurified, concludes, That there must be a way for the *cleansing of Mankind*; and proceeding to find it out, he tells that Arts and Sciences serve but to set our wits right in the knowledge of things, and cleanse us not enough to come to God: the like judgment he gives of purging by *Theurgie*, and by the mysteries 275 of the Sun; because those things extended but to some few, whereas this cleansing ought to be universal for the benefit of all mankind: in the end resolves that this cannot be done, but by one of the three *In-beings*, which is the word they use to expresse the Trinity. Let us

255 [remains] in Σ: + the *FA46*   257 in Σ: + the *FA46*   260 at once Σ: *omit FA46*   263 alike] like Σ 267 Heathen] Heathens Σ; *see note*   269 a Σ: the *FA46*   271 unpurified] purified Σ; *see note*   272 to] *omit* Σ 276 extended Σ: extend *FA46*   279 In-beings] In-beginnings *FA58*, *Haz*, *Y*   Trinity Σ: + by *FA46*

280 see what the divinest of the Heathens (and his Master *Plato*) delivers,
to admiration, and as it were *Prophetically*, to this purpose. *That a*
truly just man be shewn (saith he) *it is necessary he be spoil'd of all his Orna-*
ments, so that he must be accounted by others a wicked man, be scoffed at, put
in prison, beaten, nay be crucified: and certainly for him that was to
285 appear the highest example of patience, it was requisite to undergo
the highest tryal of it, which was an *undeserved death*.

Concerning the *Resurrection*, I conceive the difficulty to lie not so
much upon our Lord, as us; it being with easie Reason imagined, that
he which can make a body, can lay it down, and take it up again.
290 There is somthing more that urges and presses us: for since in our
estate we promise our selves hereafter, there will be no need of Food,
Copulation, or Excrement, to what purpose should we have a mouth,
belly, or lesse comely parts? it being strange to imagine God to have
created man, for a moment of time, a body consisting of particulars,
295 which should be uselesse to all eternity. Besides, Why should we desire
to carry that along with us which we are ashamed of here, and which
we find so great a trouble, that every wise man (were it not forbidden)
would throw it off before it were worn out? To this I should answer,
that as the body is partner in good or ill doing, so it is but just it should
300 share in the rewards or punishments hereafter: and though by reason
of sin we blush at it here, yet when that shall cease to be, why we
should be more ashamed then our first Parents were, or some in the
less discover'd parts of the World are now, I cannot understand.
Who knowes not but these unsightly parts shall remain for good use,
305 and that putting us in mind of our imperfect estate here, they shall
serve to increase our content and happines there? What kind of thing
a glorified body shall be, how chang'd, how refin'd, who knowes?
Nor is it the meanest invitement to me now, to think that my estate
there, is above my capacity here. There remains that which does not
310 onely quarrel with the likelyhood of a Resurrection, but with the
possibility; alleadging, that man corrupted into dust, is scattered
almost into infinite, or devoured by an irrational creature, goes into
aliment, and so grows part of it, then that creature perchance made
like food to another: And truly did we doubt of Gods power, or not
315 think him omnipotent, this were a *Labyrinth* we should be lost in:
but it were hard, when we see every petty Chymick in his little shop

bring into one body things of the same kind, though scatter'd and disorder'd, that we should not allow the great Maker of all things to do
the same in his owne Universe.

There remains onely the mistery of the *Trinity*; to the difficulty 320
of which, the poverty and narrownesse of words have made no small
addition.

St. *Austin* plainly saies the word *Person* was taken up by the Church
for want of a better; *Nature, Substance, Essence, Hypostasis, Suppositum,*
and *Persona,* have caused sharp disputes amongst the Doctors: at 325
length they are contented to let the three first and three last signifie
the same thing. By all of them is understood somthing *Compleat,*
Perfect, and *Singular*: in this onely they differ, that *Nature, Substance,*
Essence are communicable *ad quid,* and *ut quo,* (as they call it) The
other are not at all: but enough of this; Those that were trusted with 330
this secret, and were the immediate Conveighers of it to us, wrapt
it not up in any of these terms. We then hold God to be one, and but
one, it being grosse to imagine two omnipotents, for then neither
could be so; yet since this God is perfectly good, and perfect goodnes
cannot be without perfect love, nor perfect love without communica- 335
tion, nor to an unequal or created, for then it must be inordinate; We
conclude a Second increated *Coeternal* though *Begotten*: nor are these
contrary (though they seem to be so) even in created substances, that
one thing may come from another, and yet that from whence it comes,
not be before that which comes from it; as in the *Sun* and *Light*. But 340
in these high mysteries, similitudes (it may be) will be the best
Arguments. In Metaphysicks they tell us, that to the constituting
of every being, there is a *Posse sui esse,* from whence there is a *Sapientia*
sui esse, and from these two proceedeth an *Amor sui esse*: and though
these three be distinct, yet they make up one perfect being. Again, 345
and more familiarly; There is a hidden Original of waters in the earth,
from this a spring flows up, and of these proceeds a stream: this is
but one essence, which knows neither a before, nor after, but in
order, and (that too) according to our considering of it: the Head of
the Spring is not a Head, but in respect of the Spring; for if somthing 350
flow'd not from it, it were no Original, Nor the Spring a Spring if it

319 Universe] University *FA58*, *ϒ*   330–1 trusted with this secret, and were *Σ*: *omit*
FA46   331 wrapt] wrap *FA58*, *ϒ*   334 could *Σ*: would *FA46*   God *Σ*
god *S*): good *FA46*   337 increated *S*: intreated *AS*: *omit FA46*   341 (it may
be) will be *Σ* (*parentheses supplied*): may be *FA46*   344 proceedeth] proceeded *S*:
proceed *AS*   345 they] + may *FA58, Haz, S, ϒ*   348 nor *Σ*: + an *FA46*
350 [of] the *Σ*: a *FA46*

did not flow from somthing, nor the Stream a Stream but in respect
of both: Now all these three are but one Water, and though one is
not the other, yet they can hardly be considered one without the
355 other. Now, though I know this is so far from demonstration, that
it is but imperfect instance (perfect being impossible of infinite by
finite things) yet there is a resemblance great enough to let us see the
possibility. And here the eye of Reason needed no more the spectacles
of Faith, then for these things of which we make sympathy the cause,
360 as in the Load-stone; or antipathy, of which every man almost gives
instance from his owne nature: nor is it here so great a wonder that
we should be ignorant; for this is distant and removed from sence,
these neer and subject to it; and it were stranger for me to conclude
that God did not work *ad extra*, thus one and distinct within himself,
365 because I cannot conceive how begotten, how proceeding; then if
a Clown should say the hand of a Watch did not move, because he
could not give an account of the wheels within. So far it is from being
unreasonable, because I do not understand it, that it would be
unreasonable I should: For why should a created substance compre-
370 hend an uncreated, A circumscribed and limited, an uncircumscrib'd
and unlimited? And this I observe in those great Lovers and Lords of
Reason, quoted by the Fathers, *Zoroastres, Trismegistus, Plato, Numenius
Plotinus, Proclus, Amelius,* and *Avicen,* that when they spoke for this
mystery of the Trinity, of which all writ something, and some almost
375 as plainly as Christians themselves, that they discussed it not as they
did other things, but delivered them as Oracles which they had
received themselves, without dispute.

Thus much of Christian Profession compared with others: I should
now shew which (compar'd within it self) ought to be preferred
380 but this is the work of every pen, perchance to the prejudice of Religion it self. This excuse (though) it has, that (like the chief Empire
having nothing to conquer, no other Religion to oppose or dispute
against it, It hath been forced to admit of Civil wars, and suffer under
its owne excellency.

385   *FINIS*

355–6 from . . . but Σ: from a . . . but an *FA46*   363 stranger] as strange
364 distinct] distinctly *FA58*, *Υ*   367 it is Σ+*Υ*: is it *FA46*, *FA58*   370 A
omit Σ   372 Zoroastres] Zoroastes *FA48*, *Haʒ*   373 for Σ: of *FA46*   380 per
chance Σ: perhaps *FA46*   383 against it, It Σ: against, it *FA46*   hath] has
385 FINIS] *omit AS*

APPENDIX A

POEMS AND LETTERS CLOSELY ASSOCIATED WITH SUCKLING

I. ANSWERS AND AN ANTECEDENT TO THE FOLLOWING POEMS BY OR ASCRIBED TO SUCKLING

1. Against Fruition I

In answer of Sir John Sucklins Verses

[By EDMUND WALLER]

Con.

Stay here fond Youth, and ask no more, be wise,
Knowing too much long since lost Paradise.

Pro.

And by your knowledge we should be bereft
Of all that Paradise which yet is left.

Con.

The vertuous joyes thou hast, thou wouldst, should still   5
Last in their pride, and wouldst not take it ill,
If rudely from sweet Dreams, and for a toy
Thou awak't? he wakes himselfe that does enjoy.

Pro.

How can the joy or hope which you allow,
Be stiled vertuous, and the end not so?   10
Talke in your sleep, and shadows still admire;
'Tis true, he wakes that feeles this reall fire,
But to sleep better; for who ere drinks deep
Of this Nepenthe, rocks himselfe asleep.

A.i.1. In Answer of Sir John Sucklins Verses. *Waller (3rd ed.).* *MSS.: DonD (from Waller, 1st or 2nd ed.), RP16 (ll. 1–39 only). Substantive variants in Suckling's part ('Con') not recorded here (see Poem No. 40); others recorded in full*
In Answer of Sir John Sucklins Verses] (to *for* of *DonD*): Against & For Fruition *RP16*
3 should be] shalbe *RP16*   9 which] that *RP16*

Con.

Fruition adds no new wealth, but destroyes,   15
And while it pleaseth much, yet still it cloyes;
Who thinkes he shall be happier made for that,
As reasonably might hope, he might grow fat
By eating to a Surfeit, this once past
What relishes? even kisses lose their tast.   20

Pro.

Blessings may be repeated while they cloy;
But shall we starve, 'cause Surfeitings destroy?
And if fruition did the taste impaire
Of kisses, why should yonder happy Paire,
Where joyes just *Hymen* warrants all the night,   25
Consume the day too in this less delight?

Con.

Urge not 'tis necessary, alas! we know
The homeliest thing that Man-kind does is so;
The World is of a large extent we see,
And must be peopled, Children there must bee,   30
So must Bread too: but since there are enough
Borne to that drudgery, what need we plough?

Pro.

I need not plough, since what the stooping Hine
Gets of my pregnant Land, must all be mine;
But in this nobler Tillage 'tis not so,   35
For when *Anchises* did faire *Venus* know,
What intrest had poore *Vulcan* in the Boy,
Great-soul'd *Æneas*, or the present joy?

Con.

Women enjoy'd, what eretofore they have been,
Are like Romances read, or Scenes once seen: 40
Fruition dulls or spoyles the Play much more,
Then if one read, or knew the Plot before.

Pro.

Playes and Romances read and seen doe fall
In our Opinions, yet not seen at all
Whom would they please? to an Heroick tale   45
Would you not listen, lest it should grow stale?

A.i.1. 21 while] till *RP16*   24 kisses] kissing *RP16*   25 Where joyes] whose
joy *RP16*   26 this] the *RP16*   35 nobler] noble *RP16*   38 soul'd] (sold
DonD) : fa‸nd *RP16*

Con.

'Tis Expectation makes a Blessing deare:
Heaven were not Heaven, if we knew what it were.

Pro.

If't were not Heaven, if we knew what it were,
'Twould not be Heaven to them that now are there.   50

Con.

As in prospects we are there pleased most,
Where something keeps the eie from being lost,
And leaves roome to guess: so here restraint
Holds up delight, that with excess would faint.

Pro.

Restraint preserves the pleasure we have got,   55
But he ne'r has it that enjoyes it not.
In goodly prospects, who contracts the space,
Or takes not all the bounty of the place?
We wish remov'd what standeth in our light,
And Nature blame for limiting our sight,   60
Where you stand wisely winking, that the view
Of the faire prospect may be alwaies new.

Con.

They who know all the wealth they have are poore,
Hee's onely Rich that cannot tell his store.

Pro.

Not he that knows the wealth he has is poore,   65
But he that dares not touch, nor use his store.

2. Against Fruition I

Another for Fruition,
In Answer to Sir John Suckling

[By HENRY BOLD]

Go on! *Bold Boy*! and put her to't, *be wise*!
Not knowing how to *keep lost paradise.*
The *wicked plagues* thou hast, wouldst ne're have *cease*?
But reign, at *height*! and would it not thee *please*
If, gently from night frights, for *real joy*,   5
Thou wert awakt? who *sleeps*, can ne're *enjoy.*

A.i.2. Another for Fruition, *etc. Bold*

Not to enjoy, is *worse*, then *not* to *have*:
And that ne're *cloyd*, for which we stil do *crave*;
Who holds himself less *happy*, by that mean
Might hope, with as much *reason*, to wax *lean*   10
By *feeding* to the *full*; they purchas'd, once,
Oh how we relish it! and *kiss* for th'nonce!

'Tis *more* then *requisite*, upon this *score*
The choicest thing that man *does*, is not *more*:
The *world* is *wide*; of blessings it is *one*   15
To *Multiply*, Come! Come! it must be *done*!
As sure as *Drink*! Each one's oblig'd unto't,
"He that ne're *Occupyes*, wil ne're have *fruit*.

Women *enjoy'd* (for they are *none* before)
Are like a fine *Romance*, read o're and o're: 20
Fruitions *sprightful*, and the *play's* not known,
What 'tis or is *not* till that *act*, be *done*:
To *save* our *longing*, that a *blessing* is,
"Heaven *unknown*, is a *Fools Paradice*.

And as in *prospects*, where the scrutinous *eye*   25
Unrandom'd can it self ne're *satisfie*,
And will not be *confin'd*, so *Liberty*
Quickens that *pleasure*, which *restrain'd* would *dye*.
He that hath *store* to tell must needs be *rich*,
He's only *poor*, that know's not, *which* is *which*.   30

3. Against Fruition II

For Fruition,
In Answer to Sir John Suckling

[By Henry Bold]

Pox on those *hearts* that *singly freeze* with *cold*,
I *Love* two *minds*, that one *opinion* hold:
Were I to *bless the better sort* of men,
I'de wish them *Loving*, to be *Lov'd agen*.
Love *Cormorant-like*, on every *pray* doth fall: 5
And's *hunger-starv'd*, where there is *none* at all.

A.i.3. For Fruition, *etc. Bold*

'Tis the *Grand confidence*, and *mighty hope*,
Unsheath'd of *fear*, with winter *tears* dry'd up,
That *Love*, takes *pleasure* in; That can be *none*,
That only dwels, in *Contemplation*:   10
Like drowsie *Dreams* at *midnight*, when all *day*,
Our *Bodies* have been *weary'd*, some strange way.
Oh! how 'twould irke me! sure I *madd* should go
Did I but hear my *mistress* twice say no!
No thought our *Expectation screw's* so *high*,   15
But single! *Woman* soon can *satisfie*.
And what *low-spirit*, won't *aspire*, to *that*,
Which may be *purchas'd*, at so *cheap* a *rate*?
She's *honest*, that does *yeild* although Poor Fooll,
She be as *hot* as *Summer*, *warm* as *Wooll*.   20
He that hath *mist* her, has to say, at last,
E'en *pray* whos' will, if I must *ever fast*.
Then (fairest Ladies) use what *nature* gave,
Never *denying*, what we ever *Crave*,
Confirming us that *that's* not *strange* at all,   25
Our *Fathers did*, we *do*, and *Children shall*.

4. Sonnet II. Of thee (kind boy) I ask no red and white

Answer to Sir *J. S.*

[By HENRY BOLD]

1.

Give me (*dear Lad!*) the pure *white* and *red*
    When I court *Maiden-head*,
        Such even (unequall'd) *Grace*,
    Of *Aires* and other, *you know whats* in *face*,
Enough to make one *mad*! let me but have   5
    A *Beauty*, that will *move*,
        'Tis all I crave;
    Unhansome dulls the *Edge* of *Love*.

2.

We know there are *such things*, as *foul* and *fair*,
    They no impostures are;   10
        For though *some youth* (of late)
    Lik't *certain colour*, at *uncertain* rate,

A.i.4. Answer to Sir J. S. *Bold*   2 Maiden-head *Ed.*: Meaden-bead *Bold*

That does not warrant me, from chusing right;
  If *Black* and *Blew* I vy
    With *Red* and *White*,   15
  That *Fancy*, is meer *Fantasie*.

3.

What boots an *Appetite*, if there's no *meat*,
  That we can *Love* or *Eat*;
    But if I view a *Dish*,
  Well *garnisht*, and set *forth*, tis as I'de *wish*;   20
As with our *Watches*, where the *inside's* made
  Perhaps of *Steel* or *Brass*,
    Our *Value's* laid,
Upon the Gold or Silver Case.

5. Song. Why so pale and wan fond Lover?

Answer

[Perhaps by JOHN EGERTON, second Earl of Bridgewater]

Why so fierce and grime proud railer?
  Prithee, why so grime?
Thou didst looke as pale or paler,
  When thou wast foold like him.
    Prithee, why so grime?   5

Why so stout thou bold adviser?
  Prithee, why so stout?
If men would be somewhat wiser,
  Women would not flout.
    Prithee, why so stout?   10

A Foole he came so let him goe,
  As he came hither,
The windes to *Gotham* freely blow,
  To carry thither,
    Two Fooles together.   15

A.i.5. Answer. *MS. notation in* Aglaura, *1638, p. 23 (Huntington Library copy; see Commentary).* *MS.:* F24 *(substantive variants recorded in full)*

  Answer] Her Answer *F24*   1 fierce and grime proud] bold grim young *F24*
4 thou wast foold] as thou lov'dst *F24*   8 be somewhat] once grow *F24*   11 he
came so let him] you came so shall you *F24*   12 As he came] since you come *F24*
13 windes . . . blow] wind . . . blowes *F24*   Gotham] Goatum *F24*

6. Love turn'd to Hatred

An Answer to the former Paper

by Mr. Womack

Love thee! No shouldst thou fall into a trance
That nothing would awake thee but a glance
From me, shouldst thou grow mad and rave
And pester nature, so that not the grave
Could silent be in these thy frantick fits   5
And nothing could reduce thee to thy witts
But some prevailing charme of mine, I vowe it,
I'ld not bestow the poorest frowne to do it.
No not a scorne should my compassion give thee
Nor yet the least contempt wold that releive thee.   10
I'le never think on thee but as men do
On Hell with horror and to shun thee too;
And yet to shew dislike I will enjoyne
My self a penance for this thought of mine:
My hatred shall be rays'd to that degree   15
That I'le reserve no hatred but for thee;
Those deare affections thou hast beene denyde
Both sexes and all men shall share beside.
Their very view and folly I'll adore,
All, all, but thee! Way foole and tempt no more.   20

7. I prethee send me back my heart

An answeare to my Lady Alice Edgertons Songe
Of I prethy send mee back my Hart

[By JANE CAVENDISH or ELIZABETH BRACKLEY]

I cannot send you back my hart
   For I have but my owne,
And that as Centry stands apart
   Soe Watchman is alone.

A.i.6. An Answer to the former Paper *etc.* RP14   18 beside *Ed.*: besides RP14
A.i.7. An answeare to my Lady Alice Edgertons Songe *etc.* RP1 *(punctuation supplied)*

Now I doe leave you for to spy   5
Where I my Campe will place,
And if your Scouts doe bringe alye
May bee your selfe will face.

Then if you challenge mee the feild
And would mee batle sett,   10
I then as Maister of the feild
Perhaps may prove your nett.

8. The guiltless Inconstant [Antecedent]

The fervency of his affection

[By JOHN GILL]

My love hath burnt my heart to tinder.
Since every sparkeling Eye doth kindle fire
Consume att length it must into a cinder,
If *Cupids* mercy grant not my desire;
  Whoe onely for this blessed favour cries,   5
  Harden my heart, or else putt out those eyes.

9. To the Lady Desmond

[Upon the Black Spots worn by my Lady D. E.]

Occasioned partly by the Verses above, partly by a faire
Ladies keeping on her Mask in the house on a hot day

[By DUDLEY LORD NORTH]

The incompa-   I ne're till now thought patches ornaments;
rable Lady   Gentile and happy was your Authors muse,
Carlile.   As gently cruell are her faire intents
                 Who kills and mournes: but why doe you refuse

A.i.8. The fervency of his affection. *TCD(a)* (*p. 452; punctuation supplied*). *Variant MSS.*: *Ros4*, *TCD(b)* (*p. 346*). *Subscribed* John Gill *in Ros4*, *TCD(a)*
  The fervency of his affection] To his love *Ros4* : *omit TCD(b)*   1 love hath] first love *TCD(b)* (+ *title of Ros2 text of* The guiltless Inconstant, *consisting of the first two lines of this poem*)   3 Consume] And burne *TCD(b)*   att length it must] it must at length *Ros4* : I must att last *TCD(b)*   5 Whoe onely] which daylie *TCD(b)*   this] his *Ros4*
6 my] this *Ros4*   those *Σ*: myne *TCD(a)*
  A.i.9. Occasioned partly by the Verses above, *etc. North*

Their names, who so much wit and fairenesse owne?   5
I met that very day you shew'd those lines
A beautie such as if it would have shone
Would have out pierc'd the parching'st Sun that shines,
But chamber maskt shee was, close mourner to
The funerall solemnitie shee wore,   10
Innocent guilty, sweetly sad, as who
Resolv'd to intombe her selfe to kill no more.
It may be also, shee did apprehend
Another scorching Summer would undoe us,
And soe her selfe o'reclouded to befriend   15
Mortalitie; 'twas double favour to us.
But Sun-like beautie, know great mischiefes flow
From great Eclipses, well as blazing Stars;
Wee die as well, except your selfe you show
As by your beames, or our intestine wars: 20
Shine then and triumph still; better some die
Then this Sphere want its second quickning eye.

10. Inconstancie in Woman

The Answer

His witts infirm'd that thinkes wee can
Love this or that in inconstant man:
To daie the love that melts in heate
To morrow wee would faine repeate,
Did wee not in this object find   5
What tells us yesterdaie was blind.
Then hang that servant for a signe
That could so well his doome devine.

He that still loves and knowes not why
But fatt and soft and faire to th'eie   10
May easily injoye such Dames
If flattery will appease his flames,

A.i.10. The Answer. *F62 (punctuation supplied and headwords capitalized). Variant printed text: WI (substantive variants recorded in full)* 1 infirm'd] infirm *WI* that] who *WI* 2 in inconstant] or any *WI* 3 To [daie]] This *WI* that melts in] that's melting *WI* 5 wee not] not you *WI* this] the *WI* 6 blind] winde *WI* 7 for] on *WI* 8 doome devine] doings define *WI* 9 He that still] And he that *WI* not *WI*: no *F62* 10 th' *WI*: the *F62* 12 flattery] flattering *WI* will *WI*: well *F62*

And she whose musick love can breed
Sure for a song maye buy his Creed.
Then hang that servant for a signe   15
That leaves the Goddesse, loves the shrine.

The Fancy that takes leave to range
Finds little truth in often change,
Since all those various sweets that hee
Makes objects of inconstancy   20
Are royall forts, and needs no charme
'Gainst him that burnes and's scarce luke warme.
Then hange him Ladies at your doore
That doats on Outsides, knowes no more.

II. COMMENDATORY POEMS AND AN EPITAPH

1. To Sr. John Suckling

If learning will beseem a Courtier well,
If honour waite on those who dare excell,
Then let not Poets envy but admire,
The eager flames of thy poetique fire;
For whilst the world loves wit, *Aglaura* shall,   5
Phœnix-like live after her funerall.

2. To Sr. John Sutlin upon his *Aglaura*: First, a bloody Tragædy, then by the said Sir John, turn'd to a Comedie

When first I read thy Book, me thought each word
Seem'd a short Dagger, and each line a Sword.
Where Women, Men, Good, Bad, Rich, Poore, all dy;
That needs must prove a fatall Tragedy.
But when I finde, whom I so late saw slaine,   5
In thy first Booke, in this revive againe:

A.i.10. 13 whose *WI*: whoe *F62*   14 Sure for a song maye buy his] This ever then shall be my *WI*   15 Then] To *WI*   16 That leaves . . . loves] Love's not . . . but *WI*   Goddesse *WI*: Goddist *F62*   17–24 *omit WI*   22 and's *Ed.*: and *F62*
A.ii.1. To Sr. John Suckling. *Witts Recreations*, 1640, Epigram 16 (*anonymous*)
A.ii.2. To Sir John Sutlin upon his Aglaura: *etc.* [*William Norris,*] An Elegie upon the Death of the Renowned Sir John Sutlin, *1642*

I cannot but with others much admire,
In humane shape a more then earthly Fire:
So when *Prometheus* did informe this Clay,
He stole his Fire from heaven. What shall I say?　　10
First for to kill, and then to life restore,
This *Sutlin* did, the Gods can doe no more.

3. Epitaph upon Sir John Suckling

I pitty thee, dull soule, who ere thou art,
yet needs must pardon thy unwitting fault
who carelesly treads ore this sacred vault
nere minding who lyes here, but dost depart;
Stay passenger, and make a gentle halt,　　5
With new conceptions fill thy pregnant heart:
Know of more goodnesse these the Reliques are
Then thou canst comprehend, or I declare;

Thinke on a soule enricht with Arts
And seasoned with the choicest parts,　　10
Compleately choice in every kinde
Of ornament to decke the minde,
His minde as highe as was his merit,
Heroyck, active, full of spirit:

Thinke on a bounty free as ayre　　15
To whom who ever did repaire
Sad or unfurnish'd never parted
From his sweet presence heavy harted;
Kindnesse received he nere forgott,
Kindnesse bestowed he minded not:　　20

Thinke who securely can withstand
The love and envy of a land;
Envyed he was else pitty twere,
Of envy worth nere lost her share,
He that lackes enemies is poore,　　25
And begging lyes at pittys doore:

Thinke on a Courtier void of shifts,
That scornd to live by Almes or guifts,

A.ii.3. Epitaph upon Sir John Suckling. *H18 (subscribed* J. Paulin)

Whose language could dissolve at once
A nunnery of Virgin Zones: 30
Yet in his courtshipp still thought fitt
To exercise more grace then witt:

Thinke on a schollar without pride,
A Souldier with much bloud un-dyed,
A Statesman, yet noe whit ambitious,   35
A Libertine, and yet not vitious,
Thinke to the heigh, if man could bee,
Or ere was perfect, this was hee:

'Twas *Suckling*, hee who, though his ashes have,
His honoured name shall never finde a grave.   40

III. DEDICATIONS, ETC.

1. To the Right Worshipfull
Sir John Suckling
Knight

Sir,

    Ovids youngest daughter drest in blacke, and like a mourner drownd all
in teares, doth come to desire your favour, that since you have honoured the
Muses with a famous Poeme, you would expresse your noble mind in defend-
5 ing her from the censure of the world. She doth not mourne like some dissembling heire in formall blacke, but doth shew unfained griefe for *Ovid's*
sorrow: And though vertue doth not alwayes runne in a blood, yet I hope shee
will not disgrace him from whom she did derive her birth, but rather merit
that my service in wayting on her to so noble a Patron may be accepted, that
10 while she is entertained, I for her sake may be acknowledged,

The servant of your
worthy vertues,
Wye Saltonstall.

A.iii.1. To the Right Worshipfull *etc. Wye Saltonstall*, Ovid de Ponto, Containing foure
books of Elegies, *1639* (*licensed 13 February 1637/8*)

2. To the Right Worthy of his Honours Sir John Suckling, Knight

Sir

There is no excuse for this my presumption, but a presumption upon your φιλανθρωπία.

It is likewise an error in my weaknesse, to put so meane a piece to a second tryall; when in your perusall it will meet with a more piercing judgement, 5 then the *Stages*, that gave it some partiall allowance. For the stile, 'tis humble:

Serpit humi tutus nimium, timidusque procellæ.

Your owne is *Pindarus*, mine *Bacchylides*. Yet I would have endeavour'd to make the persons speake better, had it been proper to their condition. As 10 you are a *Patron* to all good endeavours, you merit to be the subject of many *Encomiums*: But your selfe by your selfe in making the world (which can never be sufficiently gratefull for it) happy in the publication of your late worthy labour, have prevented the intentions of many to dignifie that in you which is so farr above them. My hope is, that by your favourable acceptance 15 of this, I may gaine some opinion with others; to whom I have and always do declare my selfe in my desires ambitious to be knowne by you at the becoming distance of

Your honourer and humble Servant
Thomas Nabbes.

3. For Sir John Suckling upon the preface concerning Poetry and the Corona

Noble Sir,

Your late request, which was to me an obliging command, makes me send you that peece which you honored with your pretended conversion; I never thought it any thing til now, and now I make it yours that it may receive some further vertue of operation from you; and seeing I finde you a proposi- 5 tion convertible, I presume to lend you another peece of simple conversion. It consists of a few begging verses; if you find them blind, impute it to their hasty and zealous production. They beg a hand from God, a favorable eye from you; from him fatherly, from you friendly correction; they need it from you, and the lesse you need from them, the more your happinesse, and 10 their obligation. I submit them and my selfe to you as

Your faithful servant.

A.iii.2. To the Right Worthy of his Honours *etc. Thomas Nabbes*, Covent Garden: A Pleasant Comedie, *1638 (licensed 28 May 1638)*

A.iii.3. For Sir John Suckling *etc. Dudley 3rd Baron North*, A Forest of Varieties, *1645, p. 216 (printed between pieces dated 17 November 1638 and 19 March 1638/9)*

IV. LETTERS

1. To Mary Cranfield from Martha and Mary Suckling and Phillip Willoughby, 27 August 1633

[See Letters Nos. 1–8]

To the adventurous Reader

Madame

When you know, what strange disasters, your not comming hath caused, (as know you must) Then will you either wish your selves here, in pitty to
5 releive your distressed creatures, or else repent, that you have cast awaye, those which thirsted to see you at London; for by your promiss made, life did abide, in

London 27°   your most devoted, (troubled) servants
August 1633   Martha Suckling   Mary Suckling
10   and most unfortunate
                                            Philip Willughby

2. To Mary Cranfield from Martha or Mary Suckling, late 1633 (?)

[See Letters Nos. 1–8]

To the faire hands of the Lady Marye Cranfeild

Madame

If I did not intirely honner you I should take itt harshly to be so palpably Feared: espetially when all I thought and sayde was reall truth: in ernest
5 Mr. Wilughby intended to be courted for his company: he knows his one worth so well that he expected somthing in a parswading winning way, not a Fearing: and had your Ladyship used your power I am confident he had stayd: dearest my Lady Mary assure your self the uttmost indevor has not binn omitted by her that constantly is

10   your voued humble
                                            servant   MS

A.iv.1. *Cran*   3 hath] + made *deleted MS.*   6 London;] + and *deleted MS.*
A.iv.2. *Cran* (*MS. torn: letters supplied as indicated by square brackets within text; some punctuation and capitalization supplied*)   5 one *probably* = own

To my Lady Shefeald my true servis. If you had not gon to More-park sure
Mr. Wilughby would have come when his ocations had binn over: he goes
not till to morrow after diner: in a lyne yett try what may be done for stay at
least for coming. Agayne doubt nott   15
    your faithfull servant   thatts serious   MS

Pray madam burn this and sale not tomorrow. We shall all think els[e] you
care not for seeing us.

My Lady Shefeald your compliment staggers him. Doe not think I jest when
I say your Ladysh[ips . . . ow]n comand [will not] be denyed. Hast hast: 20

3. To Charles I from Sir Henry Willoughby, 31 October 1634

[See Letters Nos. 20 and 21]

Sir Henrye Willoughbyes Letter to his Majesty
Concerning his daughters Marriage with Sir John Sucklinge &c.
Anno Domini 1635

May it please your Majesty

Being interrupted in my journey to wait upon your Majesty by some
Indisposition that hath seized upon me, (occasioned by my late travell which
hath bin some thing greivous to me by reason of severall Infirmities that
accompanye me, and have made of late to Stirr little abroad out of mine 5
owne house) I presume with all humilitye to present these lines unto your
Majesty to the end that they may on my behalfe give your Majesty an
accompt of the Dutifullnesse of my hart towards your Majesty, together
with a true Relation of the state of the Businesse concerning my daughter
which by your Majesties last Royall and gracious letter to me bearing date 10
the 16th of October I feare hath bin much misreported to your Majesty.

I beseech your Majesty therefore in the First place to receive my humble
and bounden thankes for the great honour your Majesty did me by your
first letter dated ~ ~ ~ ~ ~ ~ which I received by the Earle of Northampton,
according to the tennor of which I gave Sir John Suckling free accesse to my 15
daughter, being confident that your Majesty would not use your sacred hand
to recommend any for a suitor to her, but such as your Majesty either knewe
or were crediblye informed to be in every regard a fitt and proportionable
Match for her, or that if his estate should fall short of what her fortune
would in reason require, your Majesty would by your illimited bountye 20

A.iv.3 *Longleat*   Anno Domini 1635] *actually 1634; see Introduction, p. xxxv and
n. 4)*   10 Royall] + letter *deleted MS.*

supplye for him, haveing once taken him and his suit into your Royall
Breast. And he being in soe eminent a place of your Majesties particuler
esteeme and favour, as Sir John Suckling was reported to me to be in. But
Sir Johns Negotiation with my daughter had such successe as I had not
25 occasion att that time to inquire further into the particulers of his estate and
qualitye for she resolutelye declared her selfe that she could not affect him,
nor would ever entertaine a thought of having him for a husband, although
he were accompanied with never soe great advantages of estate or Freinds.
Hereupon I conceived Sir John Sucklings pretences had bin att an end untill
30 about a yeare after, I discovered by chance some secrett practises that he
had sett on foote with some servants of my owne, and some neere about my
daughter, whom I perceived he had Corrupted to abuse me and to betraye
her unto him: And yett by his owne letters to these Agents of his (which
were intercepted) I was sattisfyed that he had noe incouragements from my
35 daughter to pursue his suite and as small hopes of gaining her affection, but
Condoled himselfe that he must be soe unhappye to leave the kingdome
(upon the occasion of a waightye Embassage that he wrote your Majesty
Employd him in.) without being admitted by her to come to my house to
kisse her hands before he went, for he said that soe he might have her assent
40 to come; he valewed not any prohibition of mine to the Contrarye. I confesse
unto your Majesty that this wakened me in thinking of bestowing my
daughter in a fitting place. And being assured by her, of her Conformitye,
to what I should direct in this occasion, soe as her likeing might Concurre
in the person of the man whom I should propose unto her, I entertained a
45 Treatye with Mr. John Digbye att whose mothers house I now am. Of which
it seemeth Sir John Sucklings Agents did gett him notice and advertised him
of it. Whereupon he seeing his hopes to be reduced into a very straight issue,
And that a very little time longer was likelye to put an absolute end unto
them, Did then applye all his strength to Compasse his desire. And by meanes
50 of one Mr. Phillipp Willoughbye, that upon pretence of being my kinseman
assured unto him selfe the Freer accesse unto my house sought all the wayes
he could to enveagle my daughters affections unto him, which untill then
she was the opposite unto. Mr. Willoughbye did not Carrye his Negotiation
soe privatelye but I had knowledge of his purpose and therewith Taxed him,
55 as the basest and unworthiest breach of hospitalitye. But he with the greatest
oaths and execrations upon him selfe that may be, did utterlye denye it
and assured me that Sir John Suckling never after my daughters refusing him
had harboured thought of that match, and swore to me that since her peremptory refusing of receivinge a letter from Sir John which was about a
60 yeere agoe he would have delivered in private from him, he never soe much
as mentioned his name unto her, or moved her att all in his behalfe. Upon
my thus taxing Mr. Willoughbye with this unworthy Comportment towards

A.iv.3. 34 were *Ed.: omit MS.*

me and my daughter, and thereupon forbidding him my house, he held me
in hand that he would but stay till he had cleered himselfe of those unjust
aspertions to which purpose he dispatched away a servant pretending to　65
send for another man, from whose mouth I received knowledge of what I
called to accompt for, soe that in his presence he might Justefye himselfe
unto me. But in stead of Cleering that, this messengers Journey brought
downe Sir John Suckling (whom he acknowledged after that he had sent for.)
and with him came Mr. Controller. Concerning whose Carriage towards　70
me I will not now trouble your Majesty with any longer relation, reserving
the particulars of that untill I have the honour to come in person unto your
Majesties presence. But I shall humblye represent unto your Majesty that
after Sir John Suckling had claimed my daughter to his wife (and by his
manner of proceeding would have had it thought she was att least contracted　75
to him) she utterlye denyed any engagement to have passed betweene them,
and with great dislike of those asseverations of his, urged him if he could
produce any testimonies of what he would have to be beleived in his behalfe.
Soe that Mr. Comptroller upon his goeing awaye did confesse himselfe to be
sorrye for the Journey he had undertaken, and ingaged his honour to me　80
that now he sawe that Sir John had not that Interest which he was perswaded before that he had, he should from thenceforward whollye desist
from his suite, and I should never more be troubled with any sollicitations
in his behalfe. Neverthelesse, within three dayes after the Earle of Northampton came to my house, using such language to me, and afterwards to　85
my daughter in your Majesties name, and with such Comportment towards
me upon occasion of what passed in Mr. Comptrollers presence, as it would
have much greived me and afflicted me to have soe farr incurred your Majesties displeasure, by seekeinge in a dutyfull manner to preserve my daughter
from that Ruine that I apprehended, if I had not bin crediblye enformed,　90
that he had not bin att Court to receive those Commands that his lordshipp
pretended from your Majesty, since Mr. Comptrollers being att my house.
Whereupon I confesse I gave his lordshipp Colder entertainment, then otherwise I should gladlye have afforded a person of his qualitye, and he had soe
little discourse with my daughter, (for it exceeded not the ordinary words of　95
salutation and in my brothers presence) that his lordshipp could not take
any ground from thence to relate any thing to your Majesty of her affection
to Sir John Suckling. So that I was much amased, when I received your
Majesties last letter by Mr. Willoughbye wherein your Majesty taketh
notice of relations made by my lord of Northampton and Mr. Comptroller　100
much differing from that I have heere sett downe, and which is the truth.
Of which Sir John Suckling made such advantage, as that he and Mr. Willoughbye under the title of your Majesties sacred Name and Command
tooke my daughter out of my hands and deteined her some howers in private

A.iv.3. 78 be *Ed.: omit MS.*

105 Conference by themselves alone first one after another, and afterwards both
together, admitting none other to be in the Roome, and with a hye hand
keeping me her Father from comming in to speake with her. Untill by these
indirect proceedings and undue suggestions, they had wrested from my
daughter somewhat that by noe meanes they would suffer me to be ac-
110 quainted withall. And then they called in Sir Jervis Clifton and Sir Thomas
Huttchinson to attest her owning of what I am Confident Mr. Willoughbye
dictated unto her. Whereunto she was most drawne by a letter that was
delivered her from Mr. Comptroller, which whether it came from him or noe
I am in much doubt of, for it seemeth the Contents of it were such as would
115 not endure the light but they conjured my daughter to secrecye, And would
not lett her keepe the letter (though it were written to her) saying that Mr.
Comptroller had ingaged them to bring it back unto himselfe.

Upon this strange proceeding of theires with me, and upon sight of your
Majesties letters to me, whereby I perceive how your Majesty hath bin mis-
120 informed by them that would make a pray of my daughter to her Ruine and
my great discomfort, And upon Sir Jervis Clifton telling me how highlye
your Majesty was displeased with me which he sayd your Majesty expressed
very apparentlye, by your Majesties conveying your Commands to me by
a letter without any seale or superscription on the outside, I tooke a Resolu-
125 tion to come and prostrate my selfe att your Majesties feete, And humblye
to laye hold of that parte of your Majesties last letter, wherein most gracious-
lye your Majesty was pleased, to allowe me that liberty which your Majesty
is too just to denye to any of your subjects which is to represent humblye
unto your Majesty the reasons why I will not give my Consent that Sir John
130 Suckling should marrye with my daughter. And then to Dispose of her in
such sort as with the advice of her neerest and best Frends will appeare unto
me most for her advantage. I beseech your Majesty therefore be pleased to
weigh in your Royall brest what I have allreadye said concerning Sir John
Sucklings unworthy procedings in seekeing to deceive me of my Child,
135 after he had received a small Answer from her, and me. His proud and dis-
dainfull Carriage towards me in my owne person when he was att my house
with Mr. Controller. His sending a Challenge (to be delivered by Sir Francis
Darcye Justice of Peace) to fight in Duell with my brother, from whom my
daughter hopeth to inheritt noe small portion or estate, if she deserve not
140 the Contrarye. His being as I am crediblye informed noe gentleman by birth,
otherwise then by being sonne to one that from a most obscure and lowe
begining had the honour to be imployed in your Majesties service. His haveing a Meane estate in noe degree proportionable to the fortune my daughter
may bring with her, which alsoe I understand is much incumbred, and
145 weakened by his owne Rioutous liveing, his unlimited gameing and profuse
expences which with a much greater estate then all mine is in probabilitye
likelye to last but a small time. Finallye his haveing soe unluckye a Reputation

with all persons of honour that knowe him, that that woman must be
most unfortunate that shall be his wife. And when your Majesty shall have
Considered maturelye these reasons to diswade me from matching my   150
daughter with Sir John Suckling, I am Confident that that princely hart of
yours which harboureth nothing but Justice and Royall vertues, will not be
offended, that now upon better information of particulers Concerning Sir
John I use the Industrye and authoritye belonginge to all parents, to preserve
my Child from Ruine. Although she should have bin soe unfortunate and   155
indiscreete to have bin wrought upon by deceipt and Cunning to expresse
any likeing to this person, against whom I have soe just exceptions. But much
more when my Daughter with all the obedience of a dutifull and good Child
assures that she will never thinke of bestoweing her selfe in any Match
without my Consent and likeing. It remaineth that I humblye Crave your   160
Majesties pardon for presuming to trouble your Majesty with soe manye,
and soe rude lines which I make bold to doe that your Majesty may not
remaine unsattisfyed of my dutifullnesse and observance to your Majesties
Commands in any the least particuler. And soe praying God dayelye to blesse
your Majesty with all happinesse and Contentment I humbly take my   165
leave and rest

From Gothurst the   your Majesties most loyall
   last of October   subject and most humble
                           servant:
                           Henrye Willoughbye   170

4. To the Earl of Middlesex from Martha Lady Carey, 15 May [1635]

[See Letter No. 22]

Sir

    Though I have a great desire to see your lordship and discourse with you
more at large then I can by writing, yet I wish it might rather be here if you
please to doe us the favour, then at London, since tis so dangerous for the
small poxe, and besides I am in a diet of steele that I can hardly stire from   5
hence. I desired Sir Jhon Sucklin to informe your lordship howe farre I had
proceeded in the match I acquainted you with when I was last to waite one
your lordship and this daye he writes to me, that your lordship approves of
it which much satisfies me, yet me thinkes the conditions are hard for us to
performe and accept, and I hope yet for better. I pray Sir thanke Sir Jhon for   10
the care and paines he has taken in it for me, in the treaty he put me in minde
of. Your lordship by the resemblance there is betwixt you in these affaires,

so that in your lordships absence, I was obliged to him for taking it upon him. For what remaines of survaying of lands and drawing assurances I hope
15 your lordship will advise me, and what else is to be done, which I shall humbly crave when all is ripe for it, and in the meane time I beseech your blessing for

Moore this 15th of Maye   Your lordships obedient dearly
                                                 loving daughter
                                                 Martha Cary

5. To the Earl of Middlesex from Sir George Southcot, 18 November 1635

[See Letter No. 23]

Right honourable

Your faire and lovinge respect in patient heeringe of me hath imboldned me to present unto your farther consideration these my ensueinge greifes that I take it under correction that your neece my wife pretendinge mourninge
5 doth not well in offeringe to be a howsekeeper in givinge entertainement to all that comes, but that it would be more fitt for her to live with her speciall friends where shee might have better counsell and consolations then shee can have in this place. Neither can indifferent men as well as my selfe thinke that these expences wilbe imposed uppon me to defray. For I doe utterly
10 disclaime them and the company that shee entertaines which are as fearefull to me as those evill spirits which her brother lately wrote unto me that men could sooner gett money of then from me, but my Lord you well know that your Lordships love as well as myne cannot but looke unto it that these troublous spirits bringe not this Ladyes fortunes to a wofull successe. And
15 wherras your Lordship att my beinge with you found fault with my sparinge expences and yet I have heard it spoken that Kinge James, for your commendation in that way when you were in his great favour called you his good husband, when you had saved him so many thousands in his expence about the Navy that then by your meanes was reformed[.] Thus referringe all to
20 god and your Lordships wisedome I rest

Dated this 18th of   your Lordships in all humblenes
November 1635   to be commanded
                                                 George Southcote

A.iv.5. *Cran*   12 money] + from *deleted MS.*

6. To Anne and Mary [Bulkeley] from Sir John Mennes, 1634–8 (?)

[See Letters Nos. 24–35, 43, 55]

Faire Mrs. Anne and Mrs. Mary

My sudden and unexpected departure for the university would not admit any other retribution for our Christmas entertainement but paper thankes. Lett yt therefore excuse my personall honors one with your personall con- 5
veying of my commendations to Mrs. Rose and your littell sister. Impute brevity to the shortness of tyme, this being a midnight letter, for which imputation I shall thanke you much. Your truest honorer

Jo Mince

V. LAMPOONS

1. Upon Aglaura in Folio [I]

[By RICHARD BROME]

By this large Margent did the Poet meane
To have a Comment writ upon the Scene?
Or is it that the Ladyes (who ne're look
In any, but a Poem or Play-book)
May in each Page, have space to scribble down   5
When such a Lord or Fashion came to town?
As *Swaines* in *Almanacks* accompt doe keep
When their Cow calv'd, and when they bought their Sheep.
Ink is the life of Paper, 'tis meet then
That this, which scap'd the *Press*, should feel the *Pen*.   10
A Room with one side furnish'd, or a Face
Painted half way is but a foule disgrace.

A.iv.6. *F275*
 A.v.1. Upon Aglaura in Folio [I.] *MusD. MSS.: EP53 (subscribed* R:W :, *but see Commentary), F60, H17 (also Bodleian MS. Sancroft 53, transcribed from Brome). Variant printed texts: Brome, PB*
  Upon Aglaura in Folio [I *Ed.*]] Upon Aglaura printed in Folio *Brome, F60, PB:* omit *EP53* 2 the] each *H17 :* his *Brome* 4 In] On *Brome :* But in [a Poem or in a Play-book] *PB* 6 came] comes *Brome* 7–8, 11–16 *omit F60* 12 foule] faire *Brome*

This great Voluminous Pamphlet may be said
To be like one that hath more haire then head,
More excrement than body; Trees that sprout   15
With broadest leaves, have still the smallest fruit.
When I saw so much white, I did begin
To think *Aglaura* either did lye in,
Or else did Penance, never did I see
(Unlesse in Bills dash'd in the Chancery)   20
So little in so much, as if the feet
Of Poetry, like Law, were sold by th' sheet.
If this new fashion should but last one year,
Poets, as Clerks, would make our Paper deare.
Doth not that Artist erre, and blast his fame,   25
Who sets out pictures lesser than the frame?
Was ever Chamberlain so mad, to dare,
To lodge a child in the great bed at *Ware*?
Aglaura would please better, did she lie
I'th' narrow bounds of an Epitome;   30
Pieces that are weaved of the finest twist,
As Silk and Plush, have still more stuff than list.
She that in *Persian* habits, made great brags,
Degenerates in this excesse of rags,
Who by her Gyant bulk, this onely gaines,   35
Perchance in Libraries to hang in chains.
'Tis not in Books, as Cloath; we never say,
Make *London* measure, when we buy a Play;
But rather have them par'd; those leaves be fair
To the judicious, which more spotted are.   40
Give me the sociable pocket books,
These empty Folio's onely please the looks.

A.v.1.   15 that] which *Brome, EP53, F60, PB*   19 did] tooke *Brome, EP53*
20 *omit H17*   21 feet] fleete *EP53*   23 should Σ (Should this new fashion last
but one halfe year *PB*): doe *H17, MusD*   25 that] the *Brome*   26 Who] That
Brome, EP53, PB   30 I'th' Σ: In th' *H17, MusD*: in the *EP53*   31–2 *omit F60*
33 habits] habit *Brome, F60*   great] such *F60, PB*   37 Books] Book *Brome*
39 be] are *F60, PB*   fair] *defaced EP53*   40 more *Brome, F60*: much *H17, MusD*:
most *PB*: nere *EP53; see note*   41–2 books . . . looks] booke . . . Cooke *F60*
42 looks] Cooks *Brome, EP53 (apparently, but defaced), F60 (Cooke), PB; see note*

2. [Upon Aglaura in Folio II]

[By THOMAS MAY?]

You poore sonnes of the Muses Nyne
This wast of paper hath undone:
See this wonder, there mett in one
Pactolus streames and *Helicon*!
Well, it has beene some plaies doome   5
To have bin acted in lesse roome
Then thou art: sure thie sceane
Was *London* thou greate *Persian Queene*.
For marke the Margent, faith tis pritty,
The suburbs bigger then the Citty.   10
Th'art like a Cheese, whose paring greate
Is more by three parts then the meate;
Or an homely simile in troth,
Like bottle beere the most is froth.
But though such roome thou takest now, had   15
All that is Drosse binn purged, and badd,
The quintiscence might have been putt
With *Homers Illiads* in a Nutt.

3. [Upon Aglaura in Folio III]

The old Poett *Arrius*, a man
Of the last print in Amsterdam,
Whose body thrice repeated scerce
Could meeter out three foote in verse,
Yet would him in a Statue vaunt   5
Which might have fitted *John a Gaunt*:
Soe stands in this great volume he
Thats but a Dwarfe in Poetry.

A.v.2. [Upon Aglaura in Folio II.] *EP53 (subscribed* T: M:**;** *headwords capitalized).*
Title supplied
    A.v.3. [Upon Aglaura in Folio III.] *EP53 (subscribed* W: D:**;** *headwords capitalized and*
punctuation supplied). Title supplied

4. Upon Sir John Suckling's hundred horse

I tell thee *Jack* thou'st given the King,
So rare a present as no thing
　　　Would welcomer have been;
A hundred horse, beshrew my heart!
It was a Noble, Gallant part,　　　　　　　　　　5
　　　The like will scarce be seen.

For every Horse shall have on's back
A Man as valiant as Sir *Jack*,
　　　Although not halfe so witty;
Yet I did hear the other day,　　　　　　　　　10
Two Tailors made seaven run away,
　　　Good faith the more's the pitty.

Nay more then that, thy selfe dost goe,
In person to affront the foe,
　　　And kill the Lord knows whom:　　　　　15
But faith were all men of my minde,
I thinke thou'dst rather stay behinde,
　　　'Tis safer being at home.

But yet methinkes I see thee charge,
Thy selfe with freedome to enlarge,　　　　　20
　　　'Gainst foes that make a salley;
Courage brave heart, courage brave *John*,
I wish thou gost more bravely on,
　　　Then in *Black-Friers* Alley.

A.v.4. Upon Sir John Suckling's hundred horse. *W&D. MSS.: Ash3(a) (f. 53), Ash3(b)*
(f. 130), C, Du, Dx42, Eg9, EP53, F60, H17, H39 (from PD), H69, Hunt, T4, W. Variant
printed text: PD
　Upon Sir John Suckling's hundred horse *Ash3(a), F60 (Suckling and his), H39, PD:* Upon
Sir John Suckling *W&D: Σ see Commentary*　　I I *Σ:* I'le *W&D*　　Thou'st given]
th'hast given *Eg9, F60, H17, Hunt, W:* thou gav'st *Ash3(b), EP53, H39, H69*　　2 as *Σ:*
that *Dx42, F60, H39, H69, Hunt, PD, W&D*　　no thing] nothing *C, Dx42, F60, H17, H39,*
H69, Hunt, T4: noe nothing *W*　　3 Would *Σ:* Could *Dx42, F60, H39, H69, PD, W&D*
4 A *Σ:* An *Ash3(b), C, Du, Dx42, H69, W&D*　　5 Gallant *Σ:* Gent[i]le *Dx42, F60,*
H69, W&D　　7–12 *Σ: as last stanza, W&D: omit Dx42, EP53, F60, H69*　　7 For
Σ: And *Ash3(b), W&D*　　11 Two *Σ:* Three *W&D*　　13 that *Σ:* this *Ash3(b):*
so *W&D*　　14 the *Dx42, Eg9, EP53, H17, H69, W:* thy *Σ; see note*　　16 my *Σ:*
thy *C, W&D*　　17 thou'dst *C, Du, EP53, Hunt, T4:* th'hadst *F60, H17, H69:* thou
hadst *Ash3(b), Dx42, H39, PD, W&D:* thou dost *W:* thou doth *Eg9:* And rather for to
stay behind *Ash3(a)*　　rather] better *Ash3(b), H39, H69, PD*　　18 'Tis] It's *Ash3(a),*
C, Du, H39, PD, T4　　19 But yet *Σ:* And yet *H69:* And now *F60, W&D:* For why
Ash3(a)　　22 brave [heart] *Σ:* my *F60, H39, H69, PD, W&D*　　brave [John] *Σ:*
my *F60, W&D*　　23 thou gost] thou now goest *C:* thou'ldst go *Du, H69:* thou now
goe *T4:* thou maist go *H39, PD:* thee goe *Ash3(b), Dx42, H17*

I would advise thee take a course,   25
That thou maist mount the swiftest horse,
   Of all the troop thou givest:
That when the Battailes once begun,
Thou swiftly then away maist run,
   And shew us that thou livest.   30

Thou shalt be entertained here,
By Ladies that doe hold thee deare,
   By day and eke by night:
They'l make thee doe as Love commands,
Pull off Warres Gantlets from thy hands,   35
   Were never made to fight.

Since under *Mars* thou wert not borne,
To *Venus* fly and thinke no scorne,
   Let it be my advice,
Leave Warres and thankfull be to Fate,   40
Recovered hath thy lost Estate,
   By Carding and by Dice.

5. Sir John Suckling's Answer

I tell thee foole who e're thou be,
That made this fine sing song of me,
   Thou art a riming Sot;
These very lines doe thee betray,
Thy barren wit makes all men say,   5
   'Twas some rebellious Scot.

But 'tis no wonder if you sing,
Such songs of me that am no King,
   When every Blew-cap swears,

A.v.4. 25 a *Σ*: this *Ash3(b)*, *Dx42*, *F60*, *H39*, *H69*, *PD*, *W&D*   26 That thou maist mount *Σ* (That thou should'st mount *Dx42*, *F60*): To mount thee on *H39*, *PD*: Be sure to mount *W&D*: Troth even to take *H69*   31–6 *as last stanza in Du*   35 Pull off [Warres] *Σ*: Pull [Warres] fierce *F60*, *W&D*: Plucke *Dx42*: Leave *H69*   from] for *Ash3(a)*, *Du*, *H17*, *H39*, *H69*, *W*; *see note*   thy *Σ*: those *Ash3(b)*, *Dx42*, *Eg9*, *EP53*, *F60*, *W*, *W&D*   40 Warres] Warre *Ash3(b)*, *Dx42*, *EP53*, *H17*, *H69*: Mars *Du*, *Hunt*, *H39*, *PD*

A.v.5. Sir John Suckling's Answer. *W&D*. *MSS. and variant printed texts: as for A.v.4, except Dx42 (first line only) and EP53 (omit)*
Sir John Suckling's Answer] *Sucklin's answear H69*: The Answer *F60*, *H39*, *PD*: his Answere *C* (*his of later addition*): The Reply *H17*: omit *Ash3(b)*, *Dx42*, *Hunt*; *see note*   1 I *Σ*: I'le *Eg9*, *H17*, *W*, *W&D*   2 made *Σ*: mad'st *F60*, *T4*, *W&D* this] a *Ash3(b)*, *C*, *Eg9*, *H17*, *H69*, *Hunt*, *T4*, *W*   sing *Σ*: omit *W&D*   5 Thy *Σ*: This *Ash3(a)*, *H39*, *PD*: Their *F60*, *W&D*   8 that] who *Ash3(a)*, *C*, *H39*, *H69*, *Hunt*, *PD*

Hee'l not obey King *James* his barne,   10
That hugs a Bishop under his Arm,
    And hangs him in his Ears.

Had I been of your Covenant,
You'd call me Son of *John of Gaunt*,
    And give me great renown: 15
But now I am *John* for the King,
You say I am but a poor *Suckling*,
    And thus you cry me down.

Well, 'tis no matter what you say,
Of me, or mine, that ran away,   20
    I hold it no good fashion,
A Loyall Subjects blood to spill,
When we have knaves enough to kill,
    By force of Proclamation.

Commend me unto *Lashly* stout,   25
And his fellow Pedlars round about,
    Tell them without remorse,
That I will plunder all their packs,
Which they have got with stolne knick knacks,
    With these my hundred horse.   30

This holy Warre, this zealous firk,
Against the Bishops and the Kirk,
    Is a pretended bravery:
Religion all the world can tell,
Amongst Highlanders ne'r did dwell,   35
    'Tis but to cloak their knavery.

Such desperate gamesters as you be,
I cannot blame for tutoring me,
    Since all you have is down:
And every boor forsakes his Plow,   40
And swears that hee'l turn gamester now,
    To venture for a Crowne.

A.v.5   11 under his] under's *C*, *H17*, *H39*, *H69*, *Hunt*, *PD*, *T4*   14 of Gaunt *Σ*
a Gaunt *C*, *Hunt*, *PD*, *T4*: Agant *Du*, *W&D*   17 but *Σ*: omit *Du*, *F60*, *H17*, *Hunt*,
W&D   20 ran] runn *Ash3(a+b)*, *C*, *Du*, *H69*, *Hunt*, *T4*   21 good] great
Ash3(b), *C*, *Du*, *H69*, *Hunt*   25 Lashly] Leshley *C*, *F60*: Lesly *T4*: Lesley *H39*, *PD*:
Leisly *Hunt*: Leisley *Ash3(b)*, *Eg9*, *W*; *see note*   26 And his fellow] (*C*, *H39*, *PD*,
W&D): And's fellow *F60*, *H17*, *H69*: And fellow *Ash3(b)*, *Du*, *Eg9*, *Hunt*, *T4*, *W*: And al
his *Ash3(a)*   28 their *Σ*: the *W&D*   29 got] gotten *Ash3(a, b)*: stuff'd *Eg9*
H69, *W*: [the which they] stuffe *H17*: stollen [with knicks and knacks] *Hunt*: And ride
myself upon their backs *T4*   32 Bishops *Σ*: Bishop *Du*, *H69*, *W&D*   36 'Tis *Σ*
It's *Ash3(a)*, *H39*, *Hunt*, *PD*, *W&D*

6. [Upon Sir John Sucklings Northern Discoverie]

Sir *John* got on a bonny browne Beast
  To *Scotland* for to ride a,
A brave Buffe Coat upon his back,
  A short Sword by his side a.
Alas young man, we *Sucklings* can   5
  Pull down the Scottish pride a.

He danc'd and pranc'd, and pranckt about
  'Till people him espide a;
With pyeball'd apparrell he did so quarrell,
  As none durst come him nye a.   10
But soft, Sir *John*, ere you come home,
  You will not look so high a.

Both Wife, and Maid, and Widow, pray'd
  To the Scots he would be kind a;
He storm'd the more, and deeply swore   15
  They should no favour find a.
But if you had been at *Barwick* and seen,
  He was in another ruff a.

His men and he in their jollitie
  Did drinke, quarrell, and quaffe a,   20
'Till away he went like a *Jack of Lent*:
  But it would have made you to laugh a,
How away they did creep, like so many Sheep,
  And he like an Essex Calfe a.

When he came to the Camp, he was in a damp   25
  To see the *Scots* in sight a,
And all his brave Troops like so many droops,
  To fight they had no heart a.
And when the Allarme cal'd all to arme,
  Sir *John* he went to shite a.   30

They prayd him to mount, and ryde in the Front
  To try his Courage good a:
He told them the *Scots* had dangerous plots,
  As he well understood a.
Which they denyed, but he replyed   35
  It's sinne for to shed blood a.

A.v.6. [Upon Sir John Sucklings Northern Discoverie.] *Vox Borealis: Or the Northern Discoverie,* 1641 (*VB*). *Title supplied*

He did repent the money he spent,
   Got by unlawfull Game a;
His curled locks could endure no knocks,
   Then let none goe againe a: 40
Such a Carpet Knight as durst not fight,
   For feare he should be slaine a.

7. Upon Sir John Sucklings most warlike preparations for the Scotish Warre

[Perhaps by SIR JOHN MENNES]

Sir *John* got him on an Ambling Nag,
   To *Scotland* for to ride a,
With a hundred horse more, all his own he swore,
   To guard him on every side a.

No Errant Knight ever went to fight   5
   With halfe so gay a Bravado;
Had you seen but his look, you'ld have sworn on a book
   Hee'ld have conquer'd a whole Armado.

The Ladyes ran all to the windowes to see
   So gallant and warlike a sight a,   10
And as he pass'd by, they began to cry,
   Sir *John*, why will you go fight a?

But he like a cruel Knight, spurr'd on,
   His heart did not relent a,
For, till he came there he shew'd no fear,   15
   Till then, why should he repent a?

The King (God bless him) had singular hopes
   Of him and all his Troop a;
The Borderers they, as they met him on the way,
   For joy did hollow and whoop a.   20

None lik'd him so well as his own Colonel,
   Who toke him for *John de Weart* a,
But when there were shows of gunning and blows
   My gallant was nothing so peart a.

A.v.7. Upon Sir John Sucklings most warlike preparations *etc.* Sir *J*[*ohn*] *M*[*ennes*] *and Ja*[*mes*] *S*[*mith*], Musarum Deliciæ, *1655, pp. 82–3 (MusD). MSS.: H39, O5 (both from MusD). Substantive variants recorded in full*   most] *omit* H39   1 on] *omit* O5
22 de] a O5   24 nothing] not *H39*

For when the *Scots* Army came within sight   25
   And all men prepar'd to fight a,
He ran to his Tent, they ask'd what he meant,
   He swore he must needs go shite a.

The Colonel sent for him back agen
   To quarter him in the Van a,   30
But Sir *John* did swear he came not there
   To be kill'd the very first man a.

To cure his fear he was sent to the Rere,
   Some ten miles back, and more a,
Where he did play at Tre trip for Hay   35
   And nere saw the enemy more a.

But now there is peace, he's return'd to increase
   His money, which lately he spent a,
But his lost honour must still ly in the dust,
   At *Barwick* away it went a.   40

VI. TWO FRENCH POEMS TRANSLATED
BY SUCKLING

1. Desdain

A quoy servent tant d'artifices
Et des sermens au vent jettez
Si vos amours et vos services
Me sont des importunitez.

L'amour à d'autres vœux m'appelle   5
N'attendez jamais rien de moy,
Me pensez vous rendre infidelle
En me tesmoignant vostre foy.

A.v.7. 28 needs] need *O5: omit H39*   shite a] —— *O5*
A.vi.1. Desdain. *Les Satyres . . . du Sr Regnier,* 1614, f. 125. *Variant printed text: LR (two states: substantive variants recorded in full; LR (c) agrees with* Les Satyres *except where otherwise specified)*
   Desdain] Disdain *LR (u)*   1 d'] de *LR (u)*   2 des] *omit LR*   au] aux *LR*
vent] nent *LR (u)*   4 Me] Mi *LR (u)*   5 L'] Le *LR (u)*   a d'] al *LR (u)*
m'] mi *LR*   appelle] Appelle *LR (u)*   6 N'attendez] N'tendez *LR*   de] du *LR (u)*
7 Me] Ne *LR*   pensez vous] pensez nous *LR (c)*: peusez nous *LR (u)*   8 En] A *LR*
(c): Au *LR (u)*   me] mi *LR*   vostre] nostre *LR (u)*

L'amant qui mon amour possede
Est trop plain de perfection: 10
Car doublement il vous excede
De merite et d'affection.

Je n'en puis estre refroidie
Ny rompre un cordage si dous,
Ny le rompre sans perfidie   15
Ny d'estre perfide pour vous.

Vos attentes sont toutes vaines
Le vous dire, est vous obliger,
Pour vous faire estre de vos peines
De vous et du temps mesnager.   20

2. A Phillis

Il y peut avoir quatre années
Qu'à Phillis j'ay voulu conter
Deux mille pieces couronnées,
Et plus haut j'eusse peu monter,
Deux ans apres elle me mande   5
Que por mille elle condecent,
Je trouvay la somme si grande
Je n'en voulus donner que cent,
Au bout de six, ou sept sepmaines
A cent escu elle revient,   10
Je dis qu'elle perdoit ses peines
S'elle en pretendoit plus de vingt,
L'autre jour elle fut contente
De venir pour six ducatons,
J'ay treuvay trop haute la vente   15
S'elle passoit quatre testons:
Ce matin elle est arrivee,
Gratis voulant s'abandonner,
Ou je l'ay plus chere trouvee
Que quand j'en voulus tant donner.   20

A.vi.1. 9 qui] chi *LR* (*u*)   mon] mont *LR* (*u*)   10 trop plain] trop plein *LR* (*c*):
tropple in *LR* (*u*)   11 Car] Et *LR*   excede *LR*, *Satyres*, 1616 : succede *Satyres*, 1614
13 n'en] ne *LR*   14 Ny] [catchword] Ni *LR* (*c*): In *LR* (*u*)   dous] doux *LR*,
Satyres, 1616   15–16 Ny . . . Ny] In . . . In *LR*   16 perfide] perfidi *LR*
17 toutes vaines] toutes en vain *LR*   18 vous] nous *LR*   19 estre de] espargner
LR (*c*) : Espargner *LR* (*u*)   vos] nos *LR* (*u*)   20 De] Du *LR*
   A.vi.2. A Phillis. *Les Satyres . . . du Sr Regnier*, 1614, f. 116 (*no text in LR*)

APPENDIX B

ALTERATIONS OF COPY-TEXT ACCIDENTALS

IN the following list, the works are identified only by their serial numbers, as given in the List of Contents, the text, and the critical apparatus. The readings of the lemma have been made on editorial judgement alone, except where otherwise specified. The rejected readings are those of the copy-texts, of which the sigla are not recorded here except in a few cases where clarity requires them. A few 'semi-substantive' or otherwise important alterations are recorded in the critical apparatus as well as in this list.

PUBLISHER'S PREFACES

To the Reader

15 Knowledge] Knowledg (*justifica-* *tion; see following note*)
allowed (*c*): allowred (*u*)

22 variety:] ~,

POEMS

No. 1
3 charitie,] ~ₐ
5 thus,] ~ₐ
6 Didymus.] ~ₐ

No. 2
4 morne,] ~ₐ

No. 4
4 ire,] ~ₐ
7 againe,] ~ₐ
9 come,] ~ₐ

No. 5
3 doome:] ~ₐ

No. 6
5 'tis] t'is

No. 7
1 præpare,] ~ₐ

No. 8
6 inshrin'd.] ~ₐ
8 men.] ~ₐ

No. 9
8 sheilds;] ~ₐ
11 too, [from]] ~ₐ
12 gaole] goale
14 againe.] ~ₐ
19 allay'd,] ~ₐ
24 Nativitie.] ~ₐ

No. 10
2 Miserie,] ~ₐ

No. 11
Dreame‸] ~.
17 Peere,] ~‸
19 more?] ~,
21 dy,] ~‸
25 and God] And god

No. 12
21 moist;] ~:

No. 13
Will] Wil
6 'cause] cause
10 sight:] ~,
11 Shakespear‸] ~.
14 morn;] ~,
16 scorn,] ~.
18 turn'd] turnd (*full line*)
    still] stil (*full line*)
19 dull] dul (*full line*)
    divided:] ~‸ (*full line*)

No. 14
6 (No . . . Harbinger)]
    omit parentheses (Harbinger,)
16 reflect:] ~,
26 known,] ~.
33 finde,] ~‸
34 twin'd,] ~‸
44 thought,] ~.
54 wake,] ~.

No. 15
8 nimbler (*c*): nimblea (*u*)
16 hand:] ~;

No. 17
5 buy?] ~,
9 Madam?] ~;
15 troth;] ~,

No. 21. *Inconsistent punctuation of*
    marginalia omitted
30 Fire] fire
45 *Sea's*] Sea's

No. 22
5–6 Indentation *Ed.*
6 Ass!] ~.

No. 27
11 Face,] ~‸

No. 29
5 ambitious:] ~;

No. 30
11 anguish;] ~‸

No. 32
2 flow'rs,] ~‸
12 new:] ~,
17 after-spring] after‸spring
21 strange;] ~,
36 dear,] ~‸

No. 33
3 agree;] ~,

No. 34
2 me,] ~;
14 dross,] ~‸

No. 35
10 turn!] ~.

No. 36
32 in,] ~‸

No. 38 *Division into octaves supplied*
15 words,] ~;
17 tale;] ~,

19 pleas'd:] ~,
25 fire:] ~,

No. 39
third,] ~₍
Leicester] Leceister
4 'Tis] Tis
  too *H17*: to *A11*
  guilt:] ~,
5 'tis] tis
9 Bathe, bathe *H17*: Bath, bath *A11*

No. 40
11 Surfet:] ~,
19 th'ave] t'have
23 dear:] ~,

No. 41
5 ayre,] ~;
10 Fruition;] ~.
15 Expectation] expectation

No. 42
4 ill.] ~:
8 Art:] ~;
12 Battery!] ~;
13 Persinda's *Cran2*: Persindaes *FA46*
14 (we know) *Cran2*: *omit parentheses*
  FA46
15 still:] ~,

No. 43
4 And] Aud
5 wise,] ~;
8 heart,] ~:
19 do.] ~,
31 wood₍] ~,

No. 44
14 Reason] reason
16 t'ensue;] ~:

21–2 fair, | compare;] ~; | ~.
23 o'th'] o'th
25–6 wit, | it;] ~; | ~:
34 before,] ~₍
36 breath;] ~,

No. 45
2 go,] ~₍ (*comma failed to print*)
10 part:] ~;
12 round;] ~₍
24 free.] ~:
33 too] to

No. 46
6 glaunce,] ~₍
11 Faire] faire
13 i'th'] ith'
16 grow;] ~,
19 wee;] ~, *H17, LR*
20 together! *LR*: ~. *H17*

No. 48
1 Deities] Dieties
17 my] шy (*u*)
18 Though] Toough (*u*)

No. 49
1 Decrees!] ~,
  exact,] ~₍
5 proportion₍] ~,
6 obedience:] ~.
13 desire;] ~.
16 fill;] ~,
27 die?] ~.

No. 50
5 faces:] ~;

No. 51
13 new;] ~,
17 'Tis] Tis

No. 52

33 odds,] ~∧

No. 53

3 (But . . . betrayed∧)] *omit parentheses*
(betrayed,)

4 rest∧] ~.

9 Desires;] ~,

13–14 lay, | Secure∧] ~∧ | ~,

16 stand,] ~.

19 confess∧] ~,

No. 54

1 pray thee *Σ*: prethee *FA46*

3 heart;] ~,

12 glory,] ~;

17 last! *Cran2*: ~; *FA46*

20 invite,] ~;

No. 55

4 relief,] ~;

17, 18 when 'tis] when't is

No. 56

2 air?] ~,

No. 59

5 Times] times

10–11 Folly, | dayes:] ~: | ~,

No. 60

24 'tis] tis

No. 61

28 thee,] ~∧

31 true,] ~∧

No. 62

7 love:] ~,

No. 63

14 fault:] ~,

21 stand:] ~,

23 out;] ~∧

No. 64

9 The] the

12 ore;] ~∧

13 Occasion's] Occasions

No. 65

18 too] to

No. 67

2 heart,] ~;

8 eyes;] ~.

10 Engineer:] ~;

33 march,] ~∧

No. 68

15 snatch:] ~.

16 souls,] ~∧

26 gaze∧] ~,

29 skin,] ~;

32 method∧] ~,

41 corse] coarse

No. 69

4 upon!] ~,

7 decided,] ~∧

18 now.] ~:

20–2 take: | grace;] ~; | ~:

No. 70

16 divine;] ~:

39 time,] ~;

No. 71

2 say;] ~∧

6 'Twas] T was
together;] ~,

10 Wenman *Cran6, EP53, Haz, Th*:
various disyllabic spellings Σ+
1648: Weniman *FA46*

12 Chillingworth *Harv7* (*Beaurline*):
　　Shillingworth *Σ*+*MD*: Shil-
　　lingsworth *EP53*, *FA46*: Sel-
　　lengworth *Cor*

15 Waller *Σ*+*Haz*, *Th* (Waler *Cor*):
　　Walter *FA46*: Wallett *Hunt*

20 call'd] calld (*full line*)
　　Plaies;] ~.

38 free;] ~,

57 Mathew *Cran6*, *Harv7*, *M3*:
　　Mathews *Σ*
　　on't!ʌ ... there?)] him) ... ~?ʌ

58-9 ear, | Court:] ~: | ~,

60 Carlile] Carleil
　　for't;] ~:

66 Queen;] ~,

89 troubles,] ~ʌ

90 Sid *Σ*+*FA48*: Cid *FA46*, *MD*

No. 72

18 high;] ~.

29 'Tis] Tis

30 whore; *FA46*: ~. *R&T*

No. 73

5 Sea-Captaineʌ] ~,

11 is,] ~;

No. 74

1 Timesʌ *FA46*: ~, *Mad*

No. 75

17-18 me, | Poetrie;] ~; | ~,

20-1 (I ... Jade;)] *omit parentheses*

No. 76

1 Dick,] ~ʌ

2 seen,] ~;

12 Forty *Σ*: Vorty *FA46* (*cf.* folk,
　　l. 11); *see note*

17 King,] ~ʌ

31 maid,] ~ʌ

31, 33 tale, | produce)] ~) | ~:

51 sight;] ~,

59 Katherine *H17*: Katherin *RP3*:
　　Katherne *FA46*: Kathrins *Ash3*

63 get;] ~,

74-5 bin, | purely;] ~; | ~,

81 Bride:] ~.

82-3 great; | eat,] ~, | ~;

84 deni'd.] ~:

87 obey:] ~,

103-4 dance, | glance;] ~; | ~:

116 away;] ~,

127 out, ... nowʌ] ~ʌ ... [out],

No. 77

3 You] you

4 understood:] ~,

13 high,] ~;

43 o'th] o'th

No. 78

3 Church Ceremonies] Chnrch Cere-
　　monis
　　done?] ~.

8 fire.] ~:

11 desire.] ~:

13 begun.] ~:

17 wore, —] ~,

18 ʌThe ... heretofore.] (~ ... ~)

22 carelesse] careles (*full line*)
　　mind, —] ~,

24 saw,] ~ʌ

30-2 happinesse, | eyes?] ~? | ~:

33 forbid!] ~,

38-9 Arts: | tame;] ~; | ~:

No. 80

1 above,] ~ʌ (*full line*)

3 willing;] ~ʌ (*full line*)

19 brown,] ~ˏ (*full line*)
22 place *MS.*: alace *LR*
23 knows:] ~ˏ (*full line*)

No. 82
29 'twas] twas

No. 83
8 misery,] ~;
12 Funeralˏ] ~,
13 allow'd] allowed (*u*)
14 Patches,] ~ˏ

No. 84 *Εἰ μὲν ἤν μαθεῖν*
5 δὲ] *omit accent*
7 δεῖ] *omit accent*

No. 84 *Scire si liceret* etc.
2 pulchrum] pulcrum

No. 84
7–8 it? | it. *MS.*: ~, | ~? *LR*

No. 85
2 Mart,] ~ˏ
4 fare,] ~.

No. 86
5 Thirty] 30

8 Insew] In Sew
13 with-out] whith=out
15 summe] sume
18 Summer] suṁer

No. 87
4 itˏ] ~.
6 Love] love
7 defiesˏ] ~,

No. 88
1 confirm'd] confirmd
11 softe-skinn'd] softe skinnd
18 Ev'ry] Eury
21 I'le] Ile
23 hange] hang

No. 91
8 deny? *OV*: ~. *LR*
14 field? *OV*: ~. *LR*
15 right;]~ˏ

No. 92
10 inspire,] ~;
12 quintessence] quintescence (*u*)
17 less;] ~,
29 agree? You] ~, you

LETTERS

No. 1
6 But] but

No. 2
18 robb'd] robd (*full line*)

No. 3
14 Madam] Maddame (*justification*)

No. 4
22 Don Alonzo] *Don Alonzo*

31 Lucinda's] Lucinda'es
36 Revells,] ~ˏ
39 —.] ~ˏ
43 miles,] ~ˏ
46 Servant.] ~,

No. 6
15 longerˏ] ~.

No. 7
16 Servant.] ~,

No. 8
8 me,] ~;
11 storm,] ~;

No. 9
6 tearmes.] ~;
    gaming] gaminng
13 free'd] fre'ed
18 finde,] ~; (*cf. l. 2*)
29 Their] their
43 Our] our
45 fatuis;] ~,
47 Burgers,] ~;
52 To] to

No. 10
15 was,] ~ₐ
16 Wesell,] ~.
18 Mast] Wast; *see note*
21 this,] ~.
27 gettings;] ~.
29 And] and
32 countrey:] ~,
39 who ₐ] ~,
63 affords.] ~,

No. 11
16 London] london
17 Where] where
18 Where] where
20 In] in
22 This] this
25 And] and
27 revived;] ~.
36 Holland] holland
38 And] and
40 In] in
43 Yet] yet

44 enough] enought
45 and] And
47 And] and
49 For] for
50–1 confes (though . . . sinn)] ~
    (, ~ . . . ~,)
51 And] and
56 Hollander] hollander
58 That] that
63 Lastly,] ~ₐ (*torn*)
68 Mai] mai
76 My] my

No. 12
5 in[to]
    Onely] onely
6 Bamber[g.]
7 garrison,] ~ₐ
8 t[he]
10 Indeed] indeed
11 There] there
    wor[th]
    reading;] ~,
12 idle[.]
    we receivd] wereceivd
13 Bambe[rg]
14 composition,] ~.
16 We] we
19 servan[t]
22 com[m]ing
23 assista[nc]e

No. 14
12 Kenings-hoff] Renings-hoff
13 Witzberg,] ~.
14 October,] Octob.
21 The] the
23 This] this

27 thousand,] ~.

29 On] on

30 But] but

37 beseidge] beseidg

38 He] he

43 action,] ~ₐ

56 His] his

No. 15

12 not,] ~ₐ

52 quiet mediocrity *FA48, Haz, Th*:
    quiet-mediocrity *FA46*

64 forgot,] ~;

84 them,] ~;

No. 16

7 The] the

8 Our] our

13 guard] gaurd

15 river,] ~.

19 Spaniards] spaniards

26 At] at

27 Hollanders] hollanders
    Fra[nc]fort (*minim wanting*)

28 The] the

35 Cyphre] Chyphre

39 Two] two

41 ones,] ~ₐ

43 If] if

46 thoug[ht] (*torn*)

47 se[rvant] (*torn*)

No. 17

7 For] for

8 Releive] Releiu (*edge of paper*)
    league] leaug (*edge of paper*)

10 Friday] friday

11 resistance,] ~ₐ

14 My] my

18 September] Septemb.

No. 18

11 beyond] beyoud

No. 19

2 France] france

5 changed,] ~.

6 The] the

7 eys,] ~.

9 Donawart,] ~ₐ

10 From] from

12 His] his

15 lowd;] ~,

16 Lordship,] ~ₐ

24 Lordship;] L.ˢᵖ·

26 repeated] reapeated (*cipher*)

28 monarchy)] ~,

38 [present] me,] ~.

47 Howsoever] howsoeuer

50 freindship] freinship (*cipher*)

51 And] and

56 First] first

57 another,] ~.
    represented] repreₐsented (*cipher*)

59 him,] ~ₐ

61 heere,] ~.

68 And] and

73 Besides] besides

79 Your] yʳ

81 it,] ~.

87 Besides] besides

88 us,] ~;

93 fortunat,] ~ₐ (*edge of paper*)

No. 20

3 aforehand,] ~ₐ (*full line*)

No. 22

6–7 ₐwhich . . . (I] (~ . . . ₐ~

8–9 own: . . . all, and] ~, . . . ~: And

12 satisfied] satified

No. 23

35 her₍ₐ₎ . . . bring,] ~, . . . ~;

53 suitable] sutable (*full line*)

56 do, since (as] ~ₐ (~ ₐ~

67 have that,] ~, ~ₐ

75 riches,] ~;

83 Wiston *Ed.*: Westenn *MS.*

No. 24

12 B.] Bₐ

15 new ones] new-ones

No. 25

12 That] that

No. 27

3 [for] me,] ~;

No. 28

1 Princesse)] ~ₐ

No. 30

5 Love] love

No. 32

6 Welchₐ] ~,

11 full] ful (*full line*)

No. 34

7 thought;] ~ₐ

No. 36

7–8 Army, . . . Scotchmanₐ] ~;
. . . ~,

17 *English*] English

18 [ ]] ( )

No. 37

17 Lord [ ]] ~ ( )

No. 38

11 Moon:] ~;

22 Imaginary *Σ*: *new paragraph* LR

39 Sun:] ~;

No. 40

9 Wee] wee

3000] 3000[1]

13 When] when

19 them] thim

21 Twede,] ~.

22 They] they

24 And] and

35 Wee] wee

36 On] on
undiscovered,] ~ₐ

38 Camp,] ~.
That] that

39 for.] ~ₐ

42 Lesley.] ~:

45 English] english

46 greivances;] ~ₐ

49 The] the
unravel[l] *MS.* (*torn*)

51 Plurisies,] Pluriseis.

53 The] the

55 is,] ~ₐ

57 That] that

63 By] by

No. 42

3 Honor,] ~ₐ (*full line*)

25 Ships,] ~ₐ

No. 43

9 Warwickshire;] ~,

10 Intelligence,] ~.

10–11 is, theₐ] ~ₐ ~,

14 My] my

15 himself₍ₐ₎] ~;

18 Scotch] Scocth
22 Answer,] ~.

No. 44
33 pull'd] pulld (*full line*)

No. 45
5 misfortune;] ~,

No. 46
4 Generall_Λ] ~.
10 lesse$_\Lambda$] ~,
13 paiing] paing
14 and th[e] *MS. (effaced)*
15 If] if
17 that$_\Lambda$] ~,

No. 47
16 purpose;] ~,

No. 48
13 different:] ~,
17 Tooth-aches;] ~,
21 it$_\Lambda$] ~,

No. 49
3–4 or (to] (or to

No. 50
16 Epidemical *LR* (*Errata*): Epedemical *LR* (*Text*); *see note*
24 seen$_\Lambda$] ~.
28 Friends,] ~$_\Lambda$
32 just, . . . mean$_\Lambda$] ~$_\Lambda$ . . . ~,
33 *Saturday*] Saturday

No. 51(*a*)
3 Sir] *Sir*
11 'Tis] *no paragraph*
   Love] love
12 fires;] ~$_\Lambda$
15 blind: ~,

18 way; . . . dream;] ~, . . . ~:
20 Love seeds] Love-seeds
25 new language *Σ*: new-language
   FA46
30 Who] who
32 long journey] long-journey
35 sinned?)] *omit parenthesis*
   for (as] (for as

No. 51(*b*)
8 ['tis] nothing;] ~:
13 marriage] mariage
15–16 Steed; . . . besides,] ~: . . . ~:
18 Marriage] *new paragraph*
20 That] *new paragraph*
22 blessing?] ~.
24 new language] new-language
   new waies] new-waies
26 marry;] ~,
31 first broacht] first-broacht
33 beaten road-way] beaten-road-way
34 A] a
   well-wayed] well wayed
36 fall.] ~:
37 'Tis] Tis (*full line*)
   long journey] long-journey
40 Thus (Jack)] ~, ~,
42 saith,] ~$_\Lambda$

No. 52
25 abstinence;] ~$_\Lambda$
38 still;] ~,
54 Antipathy:] ~;

No. 53
11 off] of
16 Partridges:] ~;
18 too;] ~.
28 surfet.] ~:

No. 55

3 inthrall] in thrall

4 would I chouse *interpolated super-script MS.*

choyce] cloyce

5 electe] elcte

7 sunder.] ~,

9 love:] ~ₐ

11 Parragons,] ~ₐ

beheld,] ~ₐ

12 freedom,] ~ₐ

13 minde.] ~ₐ

17 preeminence,] ~ₐ

18 silence;] ~ₐ

19 admiration.] ~ₐ

21 Admiration:] ~ₐ

23 resolved] resoulued

24 affection;] ~,

Desyre (Loves fyrebrand)] desyre loues fyrebrand

26 gracious] gracioues

27 loyall, secret, trew, faithfull,] *omit commas*

29 kindle] kendle

30 entertainment,] ~ₐ

32 answere,] ~ₐ

34 entertainement.] ~ₐ

37 too] to

longe,] ~ₐ

person,] ~ₐ

38 actions,] ~ₐ

39 blessednes,] ~ₐ

41 J S] JS

To Mr. Henry German, *etc.*

7 selfe.] ~,

8 government,] goverm.ᵗ

9 (att any tyme, much *FA46*: ₐatt any tyme (much *Cran*

15–16 *that ... what*] (that) ... (what)

19 ₐfor ... partₐ] (for ... part)

28–9 may. [*new paragraph*] In *Σ*: may in *Cran, Ltr41*

48 best? . . . Love.) *FA46*: best, . . . Loveₐ) *Cran*

50 Justice;] ~,

53 strangely] strangly

57 still;] ~,

62 leaves] leavs

68 (that is, pleasing)] (that is) pleasing

70 themselves,] ~:

70–1 faith) . . . accepted.] faith, . . . accepted)

75 King] king

90 For] for

93 her,] ~ₐ

95 her . . . her] hir . . . hir

99 her] hir

101 Queene,] ~ₐ

103 Kings] kings

107 whether] whither

108 King] king

114 whether] whither

118 whether] whither

119 King] king

120 habet:] ~,

122 whether] whither

124 pull'd] puld

126–8 Raignes; but . . . on,] Raignes (but . . . on)

130–1 present: . . . is)] present) . . . is:

134 'Tis] Tis

ACCOUNT

The Epistle.
12 uselesse;] ~:
26 it?] ~.
28 themselves₍ₐ₎ are,] ~, ~₍ₐ₎

A Discourse *etc.*
9 men,] ~₍ₐ₎ (*broken comma*)
12 Succeeders *Σ*: Succeders *FA46*
18 Since] since
24 dispute:] ~₍ₐ₎
33 falsely] falsly (*full line*)
56 3480;] ~.
57 of:] ~,
63 *Grecian*] Grecian
65 Brutus;] ~,
76 *the* [Stars]] the
83 of [*a*]] *of*
90 Juno,] ~₍ₐ₎
  Magna Mater,] magna, (*see critical apparatus*)
98 Conscience (the] ~) the
99 Prometheus] Promotheus

105 Parallel;] ~,
114 appear'd] appeard (*full line*)
144 weakest,] ~₍ₐ₎
165 Banquets₍ₐ₎] ~,
181 grossly] grosly (*full line*)
205 general,] ~:
217 power₍ₐ₎] ~,
218 *Romans*] Romans
261 seeing:] ~₍ₐ₎
265 For] *no paragraph*
266 which₍ₐ₎] ~,
270 foundation,] ~:
313 it,] ~;
318 disorder'd,] ~;
329 communicable *FA58, Haz, Th:* communicable *FA46*
  quo,] ~₍ₐ₎
341 (it may be)] *parentheses supplied*
360 Load-stone;] ~,

APPENDIX A

A.i.2
1 to't,] ~₍ₐ₎
25 scrutinous] scrutimous

A.i.3
1 cold,] ~₍ₐ₎
3 men,] ~.
6 all.] ~₍ₐ₎
14 mistress₍ₐ₎] ~,
17 won't] w'ont
19 Fooll,] ~.
22 E'en] 'Ene
  fast.] ~₍ₐ₎
23 gave,] ~₍ₐ₎
24 ever Crave,] ~, ~₍ₐ₎

A.i.4
Sir₍ₐ₎] ~,
13 right;] ~,
21 inside's] insid's

A.i.6
12 too;] ~₍ₐ₎
16 thee;] ~₍ₐ₎
19 adore,] ~₍ₐ₎
20 thee!] ~?

A.i.9
1 ornaments;] ~,
18 Stars;] ~,

A.i.10
22 'Gainst] Gainst

A.ii.3

13 merit,] ~ₐ

28 guifts,] ~ₐ

33 pride,] ~ₐ

39 'Twas] Twas

A.iii.3

7 verses;] ~,

9 you;] ~,

11 obligation.] ~,

A.iv.1

5 distressed] disstresed

A.iv.3

18 proportionabe *MS.*

33 (which] ₐ~

40 come;] ~,

44 her,] ~.

48 a very] avery

74 (and] ₐ~

80 undertaken,] ~.

95 (for] ₐ~

106 together,] ~ₐ

124 a letter] aletter
        outside,] ~.

140 Contrarye.] ~-

142 service. His] service, his

151 Suckling,] Sucking_ₐ

154 the] the the

157 exceptions.] ~ₐ

168 subjec *MS.*

A.iv.4

2 se *MS.*

14 him.] ~,

A.iv.6

3–4 thankes. Lett] thankes lett

5 sister. Impute] sister impute

6 tyme, . . . letter,] ~ₐ . . . ~ₐ

A.v.1

8 Sheep.] ~?

11 Face_ₐ] ~,

A.v.2

2 undone:] ~ₐ

3 there] theire

4 Helicon!] ~ₐ

7 art:] ~,

8 *London*] London

9 pritty,] ~ₐ

10 Citty.] ~ₐ

11 Th'art] T'hart

12 meate;] ~ₐ

13 troth,] ~ₐ

14 froth.] ~ₐ

15 takest now,] ~, ~ₐ

16 purged, . . . badd,] ~ₐ . . . ~ₐ

A.v.3

8 Poetry.] ~:

A.v.4

2 thing_ₐ] ~,

4 horse, . . . heart!] ~ₐ . . . ~,

7 back_ₐ] ~,

9 witty;] ~,

A.v.5

9 swears,] ~;

21 fashion,] ~:

27 remorse,] ~;

35 Highlandlers *W & D*

41 hee'l] heel (*cf. l. 10*)

A.v.6

9 arparrell *VB*

39 knocks,] ~.

A.v.7

3 swore,] ~ₐ (*full line*)

6 Bravado;] ~,

18 Troop a;] ~,

19 way,] ~ₐ (*full line*)

27 ask'd *MSS.*: aks'd *MusD*

COMMENTARY

POEMS

JUVENILE RELIGIOUS AND
CHRISTMAS-SEASONAL POEMS

On the inclusion of these eleven poems in the canon, see Introduction, pp. c–cli.

1. Upon St. Thomas his unbeliefe (p. 9)

Cf. the similar use of St. Thomas in 'Faith and Doubt' and of a triad of personifications ('Love, Reason, Hate') in 'A Barley-break'.

3. Upon Christ his birth (pp. 9–10)

The development of metaphor in this poem and 'Upon Stephen stoned' is similar to that in George Herbert's 'Sepulchre'.

6. Upon Innocents day (p. 10)

Both the explicit didacticism of the rhetorical questions and the integral use of 'milk' bear interesting comparison with Crashaw's 'To the Infant Martyrs'.

7. Upon Newyeares day (p. 11)

Cf. 'A Pedler of Small-wares' and 'To Mr. W. M. Against Absence', ll. 1–6.

ll. 3–4. *fitt for Ladyes dresses,* etc. Cf. 'a woman . . . drest up with a little more fancie' (*Account of Religion,* ll. 161–2).

8. Upon the Epiphanie Or starr that appear'd to the wisemen (p. 11)

l. 4. *afarr.* Most of these early poems are regular at least in having a fixed number of syllables, and 'farr' is likely to be an inadvertent error (cf. 'Upon Christmas', l. 11).

l. 5. *summum bonum.* Cf. 'A New-Years Gift', l. 15, and Letter No. 9, ll. 49–50.

9. Upon Christmas (pp. 11–12)

A facsimile of the manuscript of this poem is given *ante* p. xcix. This poem extols and 'acts out' the traditional Anglican celebration of Christmas (and of Sundays and holidays generally) as 'a time of Charitie, and gladnesse', in opposition to the 'poison-beareing slaunder' of Puritans, who 'by new-fond lights Inspir'd' attempt with 'Plough-day writs' to abolish 'these sacred rites' as 'profane'. A similar view is briefly expressed in *An Account of Religion*, where Suckling refers to 'our Sabbaths' as 'good mens delight, not their trouble' (l. 199).

l. 4. *Elysiums.* Cf. 'Sonnet III', esp. l. 19; *Aglaura* v(t). i. 71, v(c). i. 178–80; and *An Account of Religion*, ll. 95 and 154. Suckling also develops a pastoral Elysium elsewhere, though without using the term (e.g. in 'His Dream' and *The Goblins*, III. vii. 98–112).

l. 11. *too, from.* Without the emendation this line is defective in both sense and metre; the omission may have been deliberate, prompted by an apparent confusion in 'too from' in the copy.

l. 13. *Invoke the Gods of sports.* Generally appropriate for the context, but perhaps also in allusion to the anti-Puritan Declaration of Sports, which was extended to the whole country in May 1618. It provided that 'Our good people be not disturbed . . . from any lawfull Recreation; Such as dauncing, either men or women, Archerie for men, leaping, vaulting, or any such harme-lesse Recreation, nor from having of May-Games, Whitson Ales, and Morris-dances, and the setting up of May-poles and other sports therewith used' (*The Kings Maiesties Declaration to His Subiects Concerning lawfull Sports to be used*, 1618, p. 7).

l. 24. *Christ Nativitie.* An uninflected genitive, like 'heart blood'; for another possible example see 'Parson self' in 'A Ballade. Upon a Wedding', l. 74, text and note.

10. [Faith and Doubt] (p. 12)

l. 4. *Virgin-wombe.* Cf. 'Virgin-Love' in Letter No. 27, l. 5.

ll. 9–12. *Each Man is Thomas heere*, etc. Cf. 'Upon St. Thomas his unbeliefe'.

11. A Dreame (pp. 12–13)

This poem is a slight example of the religious version of a well-established secular genre, on which see the headnote to 'His Dream' immediately below. A facsimile of the manuscript is given in the Introduction, *ante* p. xcix. The poem could not have been written before 1617, when George Villiers was created Duke of Buckingham, by which title he is referred to in ll. 17–18, and it could not have been written much later than *c.* 1632, the approximate date of *The Sad One*, in which ll. 17–18 are used in an adapted form (see note). The intensity of feeling expressed here suggests that the poem does not long post-date the impeachment in 1624 of Suckling's uncle, the Earl of Middlesex, in which his enemy Buckingham had a prominent hand (see Prestwich, *Cranfield*, ch. x, and R. H. Tawney, *Business and Politics under James I*, 1958, pp. 231–63). On Suckling's strong feelings about his uncle's impeachment, see Letters No. 14, ll. 42–8, and No. 15 throughout.

l. 7. *'Twixt Hope and Feare*, etc. The expression of extremes in these terms is very common in Suckling; e.g. 'Joyes are our hopes stript of their feares' and 'How is religion fool'd betwixt our loves, And feares?' (*Aglaura*, v(t). i. 133, 168–9).

l. 10. *That span-long tyme* etc. A Biblical and proverbial commonplace: see Ps. 39:5 and Tilley L 251.

ll. 11–12. *noe Lyes (Though guilded o're)*. Cf. 'His Dream', l. 10, and 'To my Lady E. C. at her going out of England', l. 3.

ll. 15–16. *noe bribes (alasse) Could mee repreive*, etc. Cf. Letter No. 11, ll. 31–3.

ll. 17–18. *noe lustfull Peere, Noe smooth-fac'd Buckingham, was Favourite heere.* Cf. *The Sad One*, IV. iv. 5–6: 'There were no Kings then, nor no lustful Peers, No smooth-fac'd Favorites, nor no Cuckolds sure'; and 'smooth fac'd youth' in *The Goblins*, IV. ii. 43.

SECULAR POEMS (*c.* 1626–1632)

12. His Dream (p. 15)

This poem belongs to a well-established tradition that probably had its formal source in Ovid, *Amores*, I. v, although there are significant anticipations in Greek poetry (see, for example, *Anacreontea*, 37, in *Elegy and Iambus*, ed. J. M. Edmonds, 1931, ii. 69 [*Anacreontea* separately paginated]). The best-known examples approximately contemporary with Suckling are Donne's '[Image and Dream]' (*Elegies and Songs and Sonnets*, ed. Helen Gardner, 1965, p. 58 ['Elegy X. The Dreame' in Grierson's edition]) and 'The Dreame' (ed. Gardner, pp. 79–80). For two close parallels to the poem as a whole in Suckling's works see 'Against Fruition II', ll. 9–12, and *The Goblins*, III. vii. 98–112.

ll. 4–10. *a world of blest felicitie*, etc. Cf. *The Sad One*, IV. iv. 1–6 (the lines following in *The Sad One* are adapted from 'A Dreame', q.v., n. on ll. 17–18).

ll. 8–10. *that eye-pleasing Fruit that caus'd the jar* etc. Cf. 'Upon two Sisters', ll. 5–8.

l. 10. *though gilded ore.* Cf. 'A Dreame', l. 12, text and note.

ll. 13–14. *snow New faln from heaven.* Cf. 'new-faln snow' in 'A Ballade. Upon a Wedding', l. 116.

ll. 15–18. *Whose scent so chaf'd the neighbor air,* etc. Cf. 'Upon my Lady Carliles walking in Hampton-Court garden', ll. 7–9, and *The Sad One,* IV. i. 5–11.

l. 16. *surely.* The reading of *LR* (*Text*), 'softly', may have been caught from its occurrence in l. 12; the reading of the *Errata* may not have the authority of copy, but it is intrinsically more likely to be original.

13. A Supplement of an imperfect Copy of Verses of Mr. Will. Shakespears, By the Author (p. 16)

This poem might better be titled 'Variations on Verses' etc. and the marginal note 'Thus far Shakespear' deleted, because even the first two stanzas differ greatly from the originals in *Lucrèce* and the fourth is loosely based on the third in the source (the relevant stanzas from the description of the sleeping Lucrece—ll. 386–406—are given below from the 1594 quarto, sig. D2^{r+v}). Suckling's version lacks the fifth line of Shakespeare's rhyme royal, perhaps owing to a memorial corruption of which there are other suggestions, but the resulting stanza is that of *Venus and Adonis,* perhaps deliberately. Dr. Brinsley Nicholson suggested that Suckling's model was a 'trial' for *Lucrece,* in which Shakespeare used the *Venus and Adonis* stanza and 'commenced not at the beginning but at the central point of importance and interest . . . but . . . after writing about a stanza and a half, threw it aside and took to the seven-line stanza' (*The Shakespere Allusion-Book,* ed. John Munro *et al.,* 1901, i. 406). Unless *FA46*'s copy was defective or a compositor contributed the corruption in ll. 21–2, this may represent a draft rather than a finished poem.

> Her lillie hand, her rosie cheeke lies under,
> Coosning the pillow of a lawfull kisse:
> Who therefore angrie seemes to part in sunder,
> Swelling on either side to want his blisse.
> Betweene whose hils her head intombed is: 390
>   Where like a vertuous Monument shee lies,
>   To be admir'd of lewd unhallowed eyes.

> Without the bed her other faire hand was,
> On the greene coverlet whose perfect white
> Showed like an Aprill dazie on the grasse,   395
> With pearlie swet resembling dew of night.
> Her eyes like Marigolds had sheath'd their light,
>   And canopied in darkenesse sweetly lay,
>   Till they might open to adorne the day.

Her haire like golden threeds playd with her breath,   400
O modest wantons, wanton modestie!
Showing lifes triumph in the map of death,
And deaths dim looke in lifes mortalitie.
Each in her sleepe themselves so beautifie,
　　As if betweene them twaine there were no strife,   405
　　But that life liv'd in death, and death in life.

l. 1. *One of her hands, one of her cheeks lay under.* Suckling's first line is less close to the 1594 quarto text than to that of *England's Parnassus*, 1600, p. 396, which has 'Her Lilly hand her rosie cheekes lie under' (noted by C. M. Ingleby in *The Shakespere Allusion-Book*, i. 405; full reference above).

ll. 21–2. *But these, as rude, her breath put by; some guided* | *Wiselyer* etc. The reading of *FA46*, '. . . by still; some | Wiselyer', is defective in both rhyme and metre, which may be due either to scribal error (and editorial compensation) or to Suckling's original as an unfinished poem. One suggested emendation, 'put by; still glided', corrects these defects at the expense of sense and grammar (see *Gentleman's Magazine*, 1884, xxii. 472), which the present emendation avoids.

14. Love's Representation (pp. 17–18)

The subject, development, and tone of this poem have much in common with 'His Dream', as with some of the general parallels cited there. Parts of Marvell's 'Definition of Love' seem reminiscent of some lines in this poem (see, e.g., ll. 29–40).

l. 6. *Harbinger.* In *Aglaura*, by contrast, 'I feele anger, Revenges harbenger Chalking up all within, and thrusting out Of doores, the tame and softer passions' (II. iii. 95–7).

ll. 13–16. *Then first these thoughts I bid him show*, etc. Cf. 'Detraction execrated', ll. 13–16.

l. 33. *beamy Fetters.* Cf. 'A Supplement of an imperfect Copy', l. 19.

l. 50. *that Loves form that's now in fashion.* Presumably *libertin* love, as distinct from the speaker's 'Platoniques' (*Aglaura*, II. iii. 23; much of the dialogue of the scene is concerned with the contrast, but the opposite attitude is taken). For a full discussion of the contrast, and of French influences generally, see F. O. Henderson, 'Traditions of *Précieux* and *Libertin* in Suckling's Poetry', *ELH*, 1937, iv. 274–98.

ll. 53–4. *with this motion he did make, It heav'd.* The alteration of 'this' (*Text*) to 'the' (*Errata*) makes clear that the press-reader found the lines, as composed, awkward; and, though the compositor could have misread 'heav[']d' for his copy's 'heave' and himself supplied the comma after 'make' (l. 53), the lines make good sense without emendation, and 'the' is a doubtful nicety.

15. [A Barley-break] (pp. 18–19)

This poem is almost certainly to be dated *c.* 1626, for the variant text (f. 42ᵛ) falls between poems dated 1625 and 1626 in a manuscript miscellany in which the dated poems, mostly of the early 1620s, were copied in closely approximate, though not strict, chronological order (see L. A. Beaurline, 'The Canon of Sir John Suckling's Poems', *SP*, 1960, lvii. 514). It is subscribed 'dedit Francis Kneuett', who presumably supplied the copy to the collector or scribe (on Knevett, see n. on l. 19 of 'The Invocation'), and, interestingly, the same manuscript contains a harsh attack on Suckling's uncle, the Earl of Middlesex, for 'wantinge goodnes' (f. 27). The poem is stylistically similar to the juvenile poems, especially in the use of a triad of personifications like that in 'Upon St. Thomas his unbeliefe'. Suckling similarly personifies 'Love', 'Fancy', and 'Reason', perhaps also in allusion to the game of barley-break, in 'To his Rival I', ll. 12–14.

'In the country game of barley-break the two couples at either end of the field attempt to change partners without being caught by the couple in the middle (called hell). The couple in the middle must hold hands while chasing the others, and if they catch any one member of an opposing couple before they meet as partners, that pair must take their place in hell' (*The Poems of Sir Philip Sidney*, ed. W. A. Ringler, 1962, p. 495). The game was a literary as well as literal favourite of the period. Sidney, for example, narrates a playing at length in '[Lamon]', ll. 207–416 (*Poems*, ed. Ringler, pp. 247–56); 'W. N.''s (i.e. Nicholas Breton's) *Barley-breake, or, A Warning for Wantons*, 1607 (STC 18336), is a humourous pastoral narrative in heroic quatrains designed 'to cause mirth, as an Arbour iest' (sig. A2); and Middleton and Rowley allude to the game strikingly in *The Changeling*, III. iii. 165 and V. iii. 153–4.

16. A Candle (p. 19)

Like the three poems that follow, this poem is both a riddle and a kind of Character. Its subject, the clandestine uses of the candle, and its expression by double entendre are frequent in the 'facetious' verse of Suckling's day, as Jonson's reference to 'poesies of the candle' in *The Alchemist*, V. v. 41, attests. See, e.g., *The Riddles of Heraclitus and Democritus*, 1598, sig. C2; W[illiam] B[asse], *A Helpe to Discourse*, 1619, pp. 203–4 (also in later editions); and *Witts Recreations*, 1640, sig. Aa1ᵛ. This poem is very close to that in *A Helpe to Discourse* and may be a paraphrase of it:

> All day like one that's in disgrace,
> He resteth in some secret place,
> And seldome peepeth forth his head
> Until day-light be fully fled;
> When in the Maids or Goodwifes hand,
> The Gallant first hath grace to stand.

> Whence to a hole they him apply,
> Wherein he will both live and dy.

'A Candle' is printed with a tune in *Wit and Mirth: or Pills to Purge Melancholy*, 1706, 1707, 1709, and 1720.

l. 8. *Where by its good will it would dye.* Cf. 'the Waters will' in 'Upon Sir John Laurence's bringing Water', ll. 5–6.

17. A Pedler of Small-wares (pp. 19–20)

Together with the dubious 'Love and Debt alike troublesom' (q.v. in Commentary), 'A Pedler of Small-wares' ascribed to 'J. S.' is listed among manuscripts of Matthew Wilson, Esq., in *HMC 3rd Report*, p. 296. The figure of a pedlar and his pack is also used in 'Upon Newyeares day' and the doubtful 'To Mr. W. M. Against Absence'. Several of the lines (1–3, 14, 16) in this primarily iambic-pentameter poem seem to have the same four-stress rhythm as the much later written 'The Wits'. In the stanza headings the 'L' doubtless stands for 'Lady', but the single initials following hardly afford an adequate basis for convincing identification.

l. 10. *there's no Waste about ye.* The modernized spelling in *Haz* and *Th* suppresses the pun, which Suckling also uses in *The Sad One*, III. iii. 32–6, possibly after Shakespeare (*2 Henry IV*, I. ii. 138–9), though it is obvious enough to require no 'source'.

l. 20. *they.* The 'trick', 'artifice', or 'dodge' properly belongs to pedlars ('they'), not to the ladies ('you' *LR*), and the speaker charitably hopes that they will succeed where he has failed.

18. A Soldier (pp. 20–1)

This youthful Character owes much to the traditional Petrarchan analogy between war and love (of which Suckling's fullest development occurs in 'Loves Siege'), and it is possible that it owes something directly to what is probably the formal source of the analogy, Ovid's *Amores*, I. ix; with Suckling's last stanza, cf. Ovid's concluding distich: 'inde vides agilem nocturnaque bella gerentem. | qui nolet fieri desidiosus, amet!'

19. A Barber (p. 21)

The reference to 'great *Swedens* force' (l. 8) dates this poem before 6 November 1632, when Gustavus Adolphus died, but it was probably written somewhat earlier (see dated parallels below). As in the three preceding poems, the wit in this depends prominently on puns and plurisignation.

l. 2. *A Shaver too, sometimes no mad one though.* Cf. 'their Monks and friers, . . . the maddest shavers in the world', Letter No. 11 (5 May 1630), ll. 53–5.

l. 4. *trade against the haire.* A turn on a proverbial phrase (Tilley H 18), 'it goes against the Hair'.

l. 5. *I keep a state.* Cf. Letter No. 7 (Winter 1631/2, written while Suckling was in Germany with the English Ambassador to Gustavus Adolphus), ll. 6–7.

l. 9. *Witel.* Whitehall.

l. 15. *a pleasing Glass, that's made to lye.* Cf. *Aglaura*, v(t). iii. 5–6, and *Brennoralt*, IV. i. 20–1; and the 'false Opticks' of *Aglaura*, I. iv. 76 (on which see note), and v(t). i. 93, and Letter No. 23, ll. 50–2.

l. 18. *I with a Powder send him strait away.* A turn on a proverbial phrase (Tilley P 533), 'to send (come) with a Powder'.

20. Perjury [disdain'd] (pp. 21–2)

This poem is condensed and quoted from almost without alteration in *Aglaura*, IV. iv. 111–15 (see notes below), and there is a close general parallel in Letter No. 2 (to Mary Cranfield, 1629–35), ll. 6–11. Like many of these early poems, this one is in heroic couplets, but ll. 2, 3, and 6 are octosyllabic (cf. 'Upon A. M.').

Title. *LR*'s title, 'Perjury excus'd', expresses the opposite of the sense of the poem and is an unlikely if possible misreading of '. . . refus'd', the most obvious emendation. The title, like many others especially in *LR*, is probably unauthorial, and 'disdain'd' is stronger than 'refus'd' and more apt in application to both the speaker and 'Flora'.

l. 3. *Flora.* This pseudonym is used elsewhere only in 'Loves World', ll. 13–14.

ll. 5–6. *I am no Monster sure*, etc. This couplet is used with modifications in *Aglaura*, IV. iv. 111–12.

ll. 7–10. *And I have bound my self with oaths*, etc. With modifications these lines recur in 'Sonnet I', ll. 3–7.

ll. 13–14. *Oh no, 'tis equally impossible that I Should love again, or you love Perjury.* Used with minor alterations in *Aglaura*, IV. iv. 114–15.

21. Loves World (pp. 22–4)

This poem extends its amatory treatment of the correspondencies between macrocosm and microcosm to unusual length; and, although it has a dramatic dimension, it is almost a pastiche of metaphysical and proverbial commonplaces. Cf. the similar structural use of the four elements in 'Detraction execrated'.

l. 13. *My Flora was my Sun*, etc. Suckling uses this pseudonym elsewhere only in 'Perjury disdain'd' (l. 3).

ll. 23–4. *that 't would so fall* etc. Cf. the 'Song', 'No, no, faire Heretique, it needs must bee', ll. 7–8.

ll. 35–6. *A fire that's starv'd when fed*, etc. Cf. 'To his Rival II', ll. 5–8, where the phrasing is very close; the proverbial idea occurs frequently in Suckling's plays and poems.

ll. 49–50. This truncated stanza probably stood so in the copy; cf. 'The Wits', ll. 89–94, and 'The Expostulation II', which wants a line in the first stanza.

22. The Metamorphosis (p. 25)

Suckling makes more formally accomplished use of Cupid in Poems Nos. 47–55; given the differences of subject, this poem has more in common with the religious juvenile poems.

l. 4. *Jove himself into a Golden Rain.* Jupiter as a 'shower of gold' in 'some *Danae's* lap' also figures in *The Sad One*, III. ii. 13–20.

ll. 5–6. *These shapes were tolerable, but by th' Mass* etc. This epigrammatic closing couplet is very similar in phrasing and tone to the closing couplet of the following poem, and still more like ll. 19–20 of *'Lutea Allison'*, with which it also shares an oath. 'May him impenitent to th' gallows bring' ('Upon L. M. weeping', l. 10) shares synalœpha and the full accentuation of a four-syllable word with l. 5 here and ll. 19–20 of *'Lutea Allison'* ('lose't', l. 19; 'inexpiable', l. 20).

23. To B. C. (p. 25)

This poem of course fuses the traditional blindness of Cupid with the proverb explicitly referred to in l. 6 (Tilley B 452); Suckling uses the same idea, but only implying the proverb, in *Aglaura*, v(t). i. 97–9.

ll. 5–6. *But I despair*; etc. See 'The Metamorphosis', ll. 5–6, text and note.

24. Lutea Allison: Si sola es, nulla es (pp. 25–6)

'Allison', or 'Alison' (now Liesborn), was a Roman fortress built by Drusus near what was in Suckling's time the town of Wesel in the Spanish Netherlands (it is now in Germany), and this poem is perhaps approximately datable in 1629–30, when Suckling was in the Low Countries (he refers to Wesel, though not the Fortress, in a holograph letter, No. 10, written at Brussels on 3 May 1630; for his travels on the continent at this time, see Introduction, pp. xxxi–xxxiii).

Title. '*Lutea Allison*', in which the 'Allison' is apparently used metonymically, means the 'fort of clay' or 'loam'; 'lutea' has some of the connotations of emptiness and sterility of, for example, 'Mens empty hearts' and 'Their hearts, as well as inn's, are made of clay' ('Upon Christ his birth', ll. 6, 8). 'Si sola es, nulla es' is impersonally paraphrased in l. 14. There is a general similarity between this poem and Letter No. 53, and perhaps a particular one in Suckling's contrast between 'that which . . . is but preparing it self for loam, and a green-sickness' and 'blown roses' that 'can satisfie the sence, and do the end of their Creation' (ll. 7–9, 4–5).

l. 1. *Diana-like*. Cf. '*Diana's* Nunnerie' in *Aglaura*, II. i. 65, etc., and '*Diana's* grove' in l. 19 of I. i., where there are faint resemblances to this poem.

ll. 11–13. *to love, to wed*, etc. See note on title.

l. 12. *Hymens rites*. *FA46*'s 'rights' is misleading; cf. '*Hymens* Revels' in 'Upon my Lord Brohalls Wedding', l. 2.

l. 18. *skill to reap those sweets*. Cf. 'Womans Constancy', ll. 24–5.

ll. 19–20. *But not to lose't at all*, etc. This couplet is strikingly similar to 'The Metamorphosis', ll. 5–6 (and see note).

l. 22. *The world would have its end before its time*. Cf. 'Against Fruition I', ll. 15–16.

25. Upon the first sight of my Lady Seimor (p. 26)

'Lady Seimor' may have been Katherine, daughter of Sir Robert Lee, of Billesley, Warwickshire, which was in the same district as the Earl of Middlesex's estate at Milcote, where Suckling was a frequent visitor. She married Francis Seymour, first Baron Seymour of Trowbridge (1590?–1664), sometime before 1636 (see *DNB*, s.v. 'Seymour, Francis', and G.E.C., *Complete Peerage*, xi. 641).

l. 2. *Planet-strook*. The phrase is also used in *Aglaura*, IV. iii. 54 (on which see note), and a parallel phrase, 'Wonder strikes me dumb', in *The Sad One*, IV. i. 20. Tilley lists uses of this and similar phrases (P 389).

l. 6. *more then man*. Cf. 'a last Producer, that must be more then man' in *An Account of Religion*, ll. 17–18.

ll. 7–9. *An apparition of so sweet a Creature*, etc. Cf. *The Goblins*, IV. vi. 5–8, which also echo 'To a Lady that forbidd to love before Company' (ll. 11–13).

26. *Non est mortale quod opto*: Upon Mrs. A. L. (pp. 26–7)

Whereas Suckling's poem is Platonic, Carew addresses presumably the same lady in 'To A. L. Persuasions to love' (*Poems*, ed. Rhodes Dunlap, 1949, p. 4).

Title. Helios rebukes Phaethon, 'sors tua mortalis; non est mortale quod optas', in Ovid, *Metamorphoses*, ii. 55. In the modified form of this title, the phrase evolved into 'a pious aspiration, and in this form became extremely popular with English bookowners in the 17th century as a motto to be inscribed on a fly-leaf or title-page'; see *The Book Collector*, 1960, ix. 327–9, where J. C. T. Oates lists various occurrences of this use, the earliest dated of which is *c.* 1625.

ll. 3–4. *For I am sure thou art no Mortal creature*, etc. Cf. *The Goblins*, III. vii. 73–81, esp. 'She cannot be lesse than a goddesse' and 'such a creature Mine eyes did never yet behold' (ll. 73, 80–1).

ll. 5–6. *Thy piety is such, that heaven by merit, If ever any did, thou shouldst inherit.* Suckling is 'not so ill a Protestant as to beleeve in merit' (Letter No. 20, Autumn 1633, l. 16), that is, 'the quality, in actions or persons, of being entitled to reward from god' (*OED*), but he was familiar with the traditional doctrine, which was repudiated by most Protestant theologians.

ll. 7–8. *hadst thou bin Tempted as Eve*, etc. Cf. 'Upon A. M.', ll. 13–16, and 'Upon my Lady Carliles walking', ll. 30–1.

ll. 9–10. *sure Dame Nature Meant thee the pattern* etc. These lines are very close in sense to 'Upon A. M.', ll. 11–12. Suckling similarly personifies Nature in 'A Pedler of Small-wares', l. 10; '*Lutea Allison*', l. 10; 'Upon A. M.', l. 11; 'Upon two Sisters', l. 12; and Letters No. 9, ll. 21–3, and 38, ll. 40–1.

l. 11. *flowing Wit.* Cf. 'A Prologue of the Author's', ll. 9–10.

27. Upon A. M. (p. 27)

The imagery of battle and siege (ll. 1–9) is very characteristic of Suckling (cf. 'Loves Siege', text and Commentary), and this poem has, except for that, much in common with the preceding poem, which may have been written at about the same time. Antagonistic views—Platonic and anti-Platonic—superficially appear to be involved in 'Yeeld not' (l. 1, MSS.) and 'Yeeld all' (*LR*), but both 'versions' favour 'sweet reluctant amorous delay' and the first implies the eventual fruition that 'all' makes explicit in the second. 'Yeeld not [*now*, as it were]' is subtler and more likely authorial, 'all' possibly being an independent or entailed editorial alteration (see *Text* below). Distinct versions—conveying the same general sense—are, however, represented in the alternative final quatrains, of which the one in the present text (*L* and *LR*) is more characteristic in its concreteness and in its use of Biblical history and theological doctrine (cf. '*Non est mortale quod opto*', text and notes).

Text. The superior and more characteristic closing quatrain of *L* and *LR* argues that they are witnesses of a later version of this poem than *Don* (in which, however, the closing quatrain could be unauthorial). *LR*'s differences from *L* (and *Don* in ll. 1–12) could be 'intermediate' authorial or, more likely, editorial readings: *LR* increases ll. 1–2 from eight to ten syllables with a redundant 'sport and [toy]' in l. 2 and a 'withall' in l. 1 that contributes something to the sense of 'all' but nothing to 'not' (perhaps the reason for 'all'); and it increases l. 11 from nine to eleven syllables (as all three witnesses have in l. 12) by the interpolation of a superfluous 'never'. Its reading in l. 10 (see note below) perpetuates the military imagery but destroys the sense and syntax of ll. 10–12. It seems likely that ll. 1–2, 11–12, and 15–16 were meant to be metrically anomalous (as all are in *L*), or at any rate that they were left so in Suckling's original; cf. 'Perjury disdain'd' (ll. 2, 3, and 6), text and Commentary.

l. 10. *And frown as much as if you meant to mar.* The divergence of all three witnesses (*L*'s 'sometymes' for *Don*'s 'as much', and *LR*'s version of the entire line, which is consonant in its imagery but is unsyntactical) suggests that the line was octosyllabic ('And frown as if you meant to mar') in the original, as ll. 1–2 and 15–16 are in the present text (see headnote).

ll. 11–12. *That Face, which Nature sure intended* etc. Cf. 'Sure nature intended I should be alone' in *Aglaura*, I. iii. 52. Suckling frequently personifies Nature, as here (cf. 'Dame Nature' in *'Non est mortale quod opto'*, l. 9, and see note). These two lines are syllabically anomalous—the first has nine syllables, the second eleven—but they counterbalance in a primarily decasyllabic poem.

l. 13. *thy Grandame Eve.* Cf. *'Non est mortale quod opto'*, ll. 7–8, and 'Upon my Lady Carliles walking', ll. 30–1.

ll. 14–15. *Rather want faith to save thee, then believe Too soon.* Cf. *To Mr. Henry German*, ll. 69–70, and *An Account of Religion*, ll. 92–3.

l. 16. *Men most enjoy, when least they doe.* Cf. 'Against Fruition I', ll. 23–30.

28. Upon Sir John Laurence's bringing Water over the hills to my Lord Middlesex his House at Wiston
(p. 28)

This poem was written in early September 1630 (as Herbert Berry first discovered; see Berry, p. 63, n. 1). It obviously concerns an event of great local importance, for on 2 September 1630 Lawrence himself wrote from Pet-worth: 'The water will this night come againe in the pipes to Wistone [Sussex], it is allready led into the brewhowse where it runs bravely into the furnace, and there is a brewing made with that water. It is allmost come to the stables where it shall fall into a leaden troughe by the stable dore, for the horses to drinke of the pure fountayne; and thence by a pipe shall bee convayed into a pond to washe the horses. I have been at Arundell where I can make the daynty spring which runs out of the bottome of the well to mount up to the castle in abundance without any great charge'; and on 10 September: 'I have obayed your Injunction of love, and now at last through many difficultyes brought to perfection your waterworke, which runs delicately into every office' (Cranfield Papers, uncatalogued portions; see also Prestwich, *Cranfield*, pp. 520–1).

Title. . . . Wiston. LR's 'Witten', i.e. Whitton, Middlesex, where Suckling was born (see Introduction, p. xxvii), is surely editorial, probably involving substitution for the copy's correct reading (here supplied). The Earl of Middlesex had no house at Whitton, and the waterworks were built at Wiston, Sussex (see headnote above), from which Suckling addressed his letter to Sir George Southcot (No. 23). Cf. 'A Prologue of the Author's' following.

ll. 1–2. *And is the Water come?* etc. These lines derive their force from the proverbial phrase, 'If the mountain will not come to Mahomet, let Mahomet go to the mountain' (Tilley M 1213), and the major stress of l. 1 should accordingly fall on the first syllable of 'Water'.

l. 4. *Light bodies only naturally ascend.* Cf. reference to the water's 'mounting up' in the quotation given in the headnote.

l. 5. *How comes this then to pass?* This phrase appears to be intentionally ambiguous, 'this' meaning both 'this "Water"' and 'this [event]', implicitly a miracle (cf. 'The Miracle', esp. ll. 7–8).

ll. 6–7. *the Waters will: Then 'twas the Waters love.* Cf. 'A Candle', l. 8.

l. 8. *For Love will creep where well it cannot go.* This proverb (Tilley K 49) is also used in 'To his Rival II', ll. 1–2; and cf. *The Sad One*, I. i. 34 and *Aglaura*, I. ii. 13–15. An adverbial 'well' may be only expletive, but a substantive 'well' also makes—partly punning—sense in the context; cf. the quotation given in the headnote.

29. A Prologue of the Author's to a Masque at Wiston (p. 28)

The 'curious River' and the further development of the metaphor of flowing water associate this poem closely with 'Upon Sir John Laurence's bringing Water' preceding, and it was very likely written at about the same time (early September 1630). Menna Prestwich remarks that 'the prologue with its praise of rustic amusements must have had a sad ring for Middlesex [Suckling's uncle], reduced to watching a homespun masque after the splendid stagings of Inigo Jones' (*Cranfield*, p. 521).

Title. This title may be entirely editorial or partly authorial ('A Prologue to a Masque [at Wiston]', perhaps), but 'Witten' (*LR*) is almost certainly editorial and 'Wiston' correct, for the reasons given in the note on the title of the preceding poem (so Mrs. Prestwich agrees in *Cranfield*, p. 521, n. 2).

ll. 9–10. *Our wits . . . cannot flow.* Cf. 'flowing Wit' in '*Non est mortale quod opto*', l. 11.

30. To my Lady E. C. at her going out of England
(p. 29)

This poem is even more a pastiche of proverbs and commonplaces than 'Loves World', and it owes much of its mood and expression to *Hamlet* (with ll. 1–10 cf. I. ii. 76–86, II. i. 78–80, and III. i. 50–4, but most of the apparent influence is less explicit). If it was addressed to Suckling's cousin, Elizabeth Cranfield, as seems likely, it is terminally datable shortly after 13 April 1631, when a marriage licence was issued to her and Edmund Lord Sheffield, who in 1646 became second Earl of Mulgrave (G.E.C., *Complete Peerage*, ix. 39). If it had been addressed to 'M[ary] C[ranfield]', as one is tempted to suppose it may actually have been (see Introduction, pp. xxxi–xxxii, and Letters Nos. 1–8, text and Commentary), it would perhaps be terminally datable in the latter part of 1633, when she was urged to 'sale not tomorrow' (see letter in Appendix A.iv, No. 2).

l. 3. *gilded phrase.* Cf. 'A Dreame', l. 12, text and note.

ll. 7–8. *Such loud expressions* etc. Cf. *Aglaura*, III. ii. 98. Proverbial (Tilley S 664; cf. G 449) and of some antiquity, as in Seneca's *Hippolytus*, l. 607, 'curae leves loquuntur, ingentes stupent', which was 'a favourite tag of Jacobean dramatists' (R. A. Foakes, ed. *The Revenger's Tragedy*, 1966, n. on I. iv. 23).

l. 9. *The shallow Rivers rore*, etc. Proverbial (Tilley W 123, 130).

l. 14. *'tis the fire rak'd up* etc. Proverbial (Tilley F 264).

ll. 15–16. *wine . . . which is good does never need a signe.* Proverbial (Tilley W 462).

31. A Song to a Lute (pp. 29–30)

This poem parodies the third stanza of a song by Ben Jonson first printed in *The Devil is an Ass*, 1631 (II. vi. 104–13, written 1616), and subsequently in *The Under-Wood*, 1641 (No. 4, 'Her Triumph,' in 'A Celebration of Charis'). It bears interesting comparison with other parodies by Shirley and the Duke of Newcastle (see Commentary on *The Sad One*, IV. iv. 22–31, ii. 250–1), and an indelicate one, 'To all curious Criticks and Admirers of Meeter', printed as the Earl of Rochester's in *Poems on Several Occasions*, 1680, p. 104 (see facsimile, ed. James Thorpe, 1950). Crocodiles, foxes, peacocks, and (loosely) doves were proverbial for their offices in the poem (see Tilley C 831, D 573, F 629, P 157).

Suckling could have seen Jonson's poem in manuscript, but the style of this poem tends to confirm the suggestion that he saw it first in the printed text and wrote his parody in 1631 or 1632.

Text. Slightly different texts appear in the poems of *The Last Remains*, 1659, and *The Sad One*, which is bibliographically part of the same collection. They may be of independent derivation, but the similarity of their accidentals and

their particular differences suggest that the first is an edited transcription
of the same copy used for the second (see critical apparatus); certainly the
text in the play has greater intrinsic authority (see note on l. 4), and the play
greater authority, in general, than the poems.

l. 4. *ruder winds.* 'Waves' was probably suggested as an apparently designed
contrast with the 'wanton blasts' of l. 2; 'winds' is confirmed by Letter No. 9
(18 November 1629), ll. 2–4: 'the winde . . . crosses him continually that
crosses the Seas' (cf. Tilley W 412 and 698, cited in ii.   ). Carew uses
'ruder winds' in contrast with the 'winds' of 'Lovers sighs' in 'On sight of
a Gentlewomans face in the water', ll. 5, 15 (*Poems*, ed. Rhodes Dunlap,
1949, p. 102).

l. 5. *Crocodiles weeping.* Cf. *The Sad One*, IV. vi. 1.

32. Upon my Lady Carliles walking in Hampton-Court garden (pp. 30–2)

Lucy Hay, Countess of Carlisle (1599–1660), was much admired for her
beauty and wit by the courtiers of Charles I, including Thomas Carew (Suckling's interlocutor here), who wrote two New Year's poems to her as
'Lucinda', but not Suckling, who gives her the character of a 'sorry Lady
Muse' in 'The Wits' (ll. 60–4) and of an elegant trollop here. The manuscript
text of this poem, which supplies the final stanza wanting in *FA46* (perhaps
omitted deliberately because it is indecent and libellous), contains variant
readings intrinsically as valid as the readings of *FA46* and is subscribed
'T: C:', probably a conjectural attribution, but it is possible that the
manuscript incorporates alterations or suggested revisions made by Carew.
The stylistic homogeneity of the poem, its parallels with Suckling's other
works, and even the final stanza of the manuscript, which gives the last word
and laugh to Suckling, argue that Suckling wrote not only the speeches of
'J. S.', alternating with 'Thom''s speeches written by Carew (as the names of
actual persons in the dialogue might suggest), but the entire poem, of which
the manuscript perhaps gives an earlier version (see note on ll. 7–8). The
'dialogue' presents two views of Lady Carlisle that fuse in a single cynical
one in the last stanza, and the poem has a formal parallel in 'Upon my Lord
Brohalls Wedding', where, in a reversal of roles, Suckling has the favourable
last word at the expense of the cynical 'J'.

Text. The variants in *RP19* have the effect of making the two texts distinct,
if very similar, versions of this poem; both may be entirely authorial, the
manuscript's earlier, or (doubtfully) the manuscript text may incorporate
alterations by Thomas Carew. Most of the variants give an almost equally
good sense. *FA46* has rather better readings in ll. 6 ('And didst not') and
37 ('stops') but a possible corruption in l. 33 ('There is'; 'For there's', MS.);

in ll. 7–8, 16–17, 22–3, and 26, widely divergent readings of equal intrinsic authority require special consideration (see notes below). Except for the stanza wanting in *FA46*, both witnesses, unemended, present sound individual texts, and to incorporate variants from each would destroy the integrity of both by conflation.

ll. 7–9. *She threw rare perfumes all about Such as bean-blossoms newly out, Or chafed spices give* [. . . *perfumes ev'ry where Such as Arabian gumtrees beare.* . . . MS.]. With the *FA46* version cf. *Aglaura*, I. v. 37: 'Perfum'd by breath sweet as the beanes first blossomes. Rare!'; with the manuscript's, cf. 'His Dream', ll. 13–17 ('Arabick spices', etc.), and *The Sad One*, IV. i. 7 ('Arabick spices', etc.), which are closely related to each other. The implication of these parallels is that *FA46* has the later version of the poem.

ll. 16–17. *was to bring This unknown after after-spring* [*came to bring Newes of this unknowne after-spring* MS.]. *FA46*'s reading (in which 'unknown after' modifies 'after-spring') is the harder and better of the alternative readings; the manuscript's 'came to bring Newes' is an unanticipated and gratuitous intrusion of the image of a herald.

ll. 22–3. *way* | . . . *Bay* [*wayes* | . . . *Bayes* MS.]. Suckling elsewhere uses the plural, 'Bayes' (e.g. twice in 'The Wits', ll. 19 and 87, and in 'Sonnet III', l. 29), and 'ways' would complement the 'Thoughts' preceding it in the same line; but 'way' gives a stronger sense: 'I had my Thoughts, but [they were] not your way.'

l. 26. *masks and hoods* [*silkes and lawn* MS.]. *FA46*'s reading is subtler as expressing the first stage of a progressive discovery: first the face, then 'I was undoing *all* she wore'; and l. 33, 'For there's great danger in that *face*', also supports 'masks and hoods.'

l. 30. *Eve.* Cf. '*Non est mortale quod opto*', l. 8, and 'Upon A. M.', l. 13.

l. 33. *For there's* [MS.: There is *FA46*]. I have adopted the manuscript's reading on the supposition that 'There is' represents an editorial correction of a defective transcription ('There great danger', etc.), but *FA46*'s reading is not much inferior and may well be authorial.

33. Upon T. C. having the P. (p. 32)

'T. C.' is undoubtedly Thomas Carew, and this poem has striking parallels in Letter No. 50, 'To T. C.' (see esp. ll. 6–12). The double entendre expressed through fused metaphors of warfare and of fire and water occur in very similar form in Letter No. 49, 'The Wine-drinkers to the Water-drinkers' (see ll. 22–7). The treatment of fire and water is of course based on proverbial ideas (see Tilley F 246 and 260, and W 110).

Title. The expansion of 'P.' is obviously 'Pox' (as in Hazlitt and Thompson), but the initial may not be an editorial euphemism ('pox' is used in Letter No. 50, first printed in the same collection): used with 'T. C.' it has a certain wit that is lost in the expansion.

l. 3. *fire and water never could agree.* Proverbial (Tilley F 246); also used in *The Sad One*, IV. i. 44–5.

l. 12. *For evermore the water runs away.* Cf. 'On King Richard the third', ll. 6–7.

34. Love's Burning-glass (p. 32)

The central metaphor of a magnifying glass is used in the same way in condensed form in Letter No. 51(*a*), ll. 11–13. There are echoes in this poem of the dubious poem, 'The guiltless Inconstant', and a poem wrongly printed as Suckling's in *LR*, 'Upon Platonic Love', that seem to be more than fortuitous, but they should probably be taken as evidence of imitation rather than of authorship.

l. 10. *By how much I had rather burn then wink.* Cf. 'To Mr. W. M. Against Absence', l. 18.

35. The Miracle (p. 33)

Suckling develops the central metaphor in much the same way in *Aglaura*, IV. v. 21–31.

ll. 7–8. *Wonder of Love that canst fulfill, Inverting nature thus, thy will.* Cf. 'Upon Sir John Laurence's bringing Water', esp. ll. 5–8; 'A Prologue of the Author's', ll. 11–12; and Letter No. 30, ll. 5–6: 'and (though you are a Miracle your self) yet do not I believe that you can work any'. The poem is very close to the letter, for the miracle-worker is Love, or Cupid, addressed in apostrophe; 'thy will' is his, and 'it self' (l. 10) is the lady, Love's miracle in her nature and her effect upon the speaker.

l. 9. *another.* Besides being unmetrical (the acephalous last line suggests that this should be, too), *LR*'s 'one another' destroys the sense of the paradox: herself freezing, she causes the speaker to burn.

36. The deformed Mistress (pp. 33–4)

This poem belongs to the well-established and popular genre of the 'praise of ugliness' or 'The Paradoxical Encomium', in which Donne achieved rather more wit and individuality in 'The Anagram' than Suckling does here (see *Elegies and Songs and Sonnets*, ed. Helen Gardner, 1965, pp. 21–2, 138–9, and H. K. Miller, 'The Paradoxical Encomium', *MP*, 1955, liii. 145–78). An abundant source is MS. 1083/16 (Phillipps 9549) in the Rosenbach Collection, Philadelphia: 'Miscellanies or a Collection of Divers Witty and pleasant Epigrams, Adages, poems, Epitaphes &c.: for the recreation of the overtravelled sences: 1630: Robert Bishop.' Besides many poems by Carew, Sir John Harington, Herrick, and William Herbert, third Earl of Pembroke, this miscellany contains a number of such works, including, e.g. 'Women: Shee [*sic*] is loathsome, filthy, ugly and deform'd' (which is very similar to this poem), pp. 9–10, and 'In praise of a Gentle woman: Her haire but thin, in all they are but three', p. 32. Some of the materials of this poem are in effect reworked in the following poem, 'Upon L. M. weeping'.

ll. 3–4. *creature/feature.* A common rhyme for any poet, but Suckling uses it in lines with the same metre and cadence in '*Non est mortale quod opto*', ll. 3–4.

l. 11. *furrows.* Cf. 'No briny tear hath furrowed her smooth cheek' in 'Detraction execrated', l. 18.

l. 14. *With pimples embroder'd, for those I love.* 'Embroder'd' has less the sense associated directly with needlework than the extension, 'ornamented', 'set forth floridly'. The line in *WI* is metrically conventional, that in *LR* a four-stress line (cf. l. 25; 'A Pedler of Small-wares', ll. 1–3, 14, and 16; and 'The Wits' throughout).

l. 30. *timpanie.* Cf. 'To his much honoured, the Lord Lepington', l. 16, and Donne's 'The Anagram', l. 50.

ll. 31–2. *But soft, where am I now!* etc. Cf. 'Loves World', ll. 67–8.

37. Upon L. M. weeping (pp. 34–5)

This and the following two poems belong to the genre of the 'curse' or 'imprecation', which is of Roman origin; according to Puttenham, in a chapter devoted to the subject (I. xxix; quoted by Helen Gardner, reference cited below), 'They were called *Dirae*, such as *Virgill* made against *Battarus*, and *Ovide* against *Ibis*' (*The Arte of English Poesie*, ed. G. D. Willcock and A. Walker, 1936, p. 58). The genre is very similar to the 'Anathema', the religious formula for consigning to damnation. These poems may owe something to Donne's 'The Curse', but they share with it chiefly the form and ('Detraction execrated' most explicitly) the 'stock medieval theme, cursing that bugbear of the courtly lover the *losengour* or tale-bearer' (Donne's *Elegies and Songs and Sonnets*, ed. Helen Gardner, 1965, p. 163; cf. p. xxxvii). This poem, in particular, reworks many of the materials (in ll. 3–8 especially) of 'The deformed Mistress' preceding, but there are pronounced similarities of style as well as theme in all four.

ll. 1–2. *Whoever was the cause* etc. Cf. Donne's 'The Curse', ll. 1–2: 'Who ever guesses, thinks, or dreames he knowes Who is my mistris, wither by this curse.'

l. 6. *Since our first parents taught us how to sin.* Cf. 'Upon A. M.', l. 13: 'Take no corruption from thy Grandame *Eve*'.

ll. 9–14. *And in this fit* etc. Cf. 'Detraction execrated', ll. 33–6.

l. 10. *May him impenitent to th' gallows bring*. For the metre and contraction, cf. 'The Metamorphosis', l. 5, and note.

ll. 11–14. *Then might he for one tear* etc. Cf. 'On King Richard the third', esp. ll. 11–14.

ll. 13–14. *venter/enter* etc. Cf. *The Goblins*, I. iv. 52–3.

38. Detraction execrated (pp. 35–6)

This 'imprecation' is closely related to the following poem and the two preceding poems (on the genre, see headnote to 'Upon L. M. weeping') and it also has a prominent structural affinity with 'Loves World' in systematically exploiting the four elements (in stanzas 2–4) as the latter more extensively does the macrocosmic correspondencies.

ll. 1–4. *Thou vermin Slander*, etc. Akin to the 'monster jealousie' in *Brennoralt*, IV. vii. 68–73.

ll. 13–16. *Our thoughts . . . Were cloth'd in words, and Maidens blush* etc. Cf. 'Love's Representation', esp. ll. 13–16 and 29–36.

l. 21. *We shortned days to moments by Loves art*. Cf. ll. 38–40 (and note) and *Aglaura*, III. ii. 48–54.

ll. 22–4. *Whilst our two souls in amorous extasie* etc. Cf. Donne, 'The Exstasie', ll. 15–20.

ll. 33–6. *Curst be th' officious Tongue* etc. The anathema proper of the lover's 'imprecation'; cf. 'Upon L. M. weeping', ll. 9–14, and see headnote in Commentary.

ll. 38–40. *those hours Joy shortned to a dram: Each minute I will lengthen to a day, And in one year outlive Methusalem*. Cf. *Aglaura*, III. ii. 48–54, 142–4; and Donne's 'The Computation' and Cowley's more extended imitation of it, 'Love and Life', esp. ll. 5–6: 'So though my *Life* be short, yet I may prove | The great *Methusalem* of *Love*.'

39. On King Richard the third, who lies buried under Leicester bridge (p. 36)

Suckling's authorship of this 'imprecation', the genre to which the two preceding poems also belong (see headnote on 'Upon L. M. weeping'), is discussed in the Introduction, pp. civ–cv. Suckling refers to Richard III as 'the worst of our Kings' in *To Mr. Henry German* (see ll. 45–7).

ll. 1–2. *watry Canop' . . . streaming vapours*. In *The Goblins*, III. vii. 99–100, the 'Canopie' is the sky, 'Studded with twinckling Gems'.

l. 2. *streaming vapours*. Cf. 'Detraction execrated', l. 26.

ll. 4–5. *'Tis now too late to wash away thy guilt: Thou still art bloudy Richard.* Cf. *Macbeth*, II. ii. 46–56, esp. ll. 54–6: 'If he do *bleed*, I'll *gild* the faces of the grooms withal, For it must seem their *guilt*.'

ll. 6–7. *The water should . . . Turne quite Egyptian.* That is, 'treacherous and cowardly', like 'This foul Egyptian [that] hath betrayed me' in *Antony and Cleopatra*, IV. xii. 10; and perhaps, if 'Egyptian' has something of the sense 'gypsy', 'sleightfully deceitful', as in 'gypsies knots' that 'with ease Are fast and loose, as they that hold them please' ('Upon my Lord Brohalls Wedding', ll. 27–8).

SECULAR POEMS (*c.* 1632–1637)
40. Against Fruition [I] (pp. 37–8)

There are answers to this poem by Edmund Waller and Henry Bold (q.v. in Appendix A.i, Nos. 1–2).

Text. Three texts are derivative and without authority: *DonD* (from *Waller*), *P* (from *FA46*), and *SW* (from *Ash4*). *P*'s conflated reading in l. 20 may be fortuitous, and *DonD* apparently derives from one of the first two editions rather than from the much enlarged and extensively corrected third edition of *Waller*, 1645, since its 'thou *not* awak't' is plainly an attempted compensation for the earlier editions' 'thou awak't' (the third edition reads 'thou wert awak'd'; on the issues and editions of *Waller* see B. Chew, 'The First Edition of Waller's Poems', *The Bibliographer*, 1902, i. 296–303). The distribution of their readings in complex variations suggests that *RP16* and *Waller*, which have Waller's 'Answer', and *FA46* along with *Ash4* and *Cran2*, sharing a common ancestor, which lack the 'Answer', represent two independent lines of descent from a hypothetical original, an inference with which only the variant in l. 16 conflicts (see note). *Cran2* is of special interest as a scribal fair-copy found among family papers (see Introduction, p. ciii).

ll. 11–12. *By eating to a Surfet*: etc. Cf. 'Against Fruition II', ll. 5–6; 'Against Absence', ll. 35–6; and Letter No. 52, ll. 24–5.

ll. 13–16. *Urge not 'tis necessary, alas!* etc. Cf. '*Lutea Allison*', ll. 9–14.

l. 16. *then.* The distribution of 'then' and 'there' conflicts with the lines of descent of the witnesses suggested above, but the alteration from one to the other could easily arise either deliberately or from misreading; 'then' stresses the logical connection and seems to be confirmed by 'So' in the following line.

l. 20. *sights once seen.* *P* (from *FA46*) may share 'Scenes' with *DonD* and *Waller* either by conflation or, fortuitously, by sophistication. 'Scenes' is an obvious 'improvement' suggested by the metaphors of literary kinds, but it destroys the variety of 'Romances', natural scenes ('sights'), and 'Plays' apparently intended. Cf. 'Prospects' in l. 25 and 'A Ballade. Upon a Wedding', l. 4: 'Such sights again cannot be found'.

41. Against Fruition [II] (pp. 38–9)

This poem is adapted in an extended discussion of the 'Platonics' in *Aglaura*, I. v. 1–59 (individual parallels in which are not given in the notes below); there is an answer to it by Henry Bold (q.v. in Appendix A.i, No. 3).

ll. 5–6. *Love's a Camelion*, etc. Cf. *Aglaura*, I. iv. 52–4 and II. ii. 20–3. Air was the chameleon's proverbial diet (see Tilley M 226).

ll. 11–12. *Like waking in a morning*, etc. Cf. 'His Dream', 'Love's Representation', ll. 10–11, and Letter No. 51(*a*), l. 18.

ll. 15–16. *That monster Expectation* etc. Cf. 'Against Fruition I', ll. 23–4; *Aglaura*, II. ii. 30–2, and III. ii. 108–9 ('That monster, Expectation, will devoure | All that is within our hope or power'); and Letter No. 51(*b*), ll. 18–20.

l. 24. *By still denying what we still do crave.* Cf. 'To his Rival II', ll. 13–14.

ll. 25–6. *In keeping us in hopes* etc. Cf. *The Goblins*, 'Epilogue', ll. 7–8.

42. To Mr. Davenant for Absence (p. 39)

This is an answer to the dubious poem (printed in 1673 as Davenant's), 'To Mr. W. M. Against Absence', which is very possibly also by Suckling (see Introduction, pp. cxi–cxiii); since this poem fairly closely follows the imagery of that, individual parallels are not noted below. The military imagery used here (esp. ll. 5–16) is very characteristic of Suckling; cf. 'Loves Siege' and other parallels noted in the Commentary. The manuscript text is of special interest as a scribal fair copy found among family papers (see Introduction, p. ciii).

ll. 2–3. *wounded Deer . . . shift the place.* Proverbial as 'the stricken Deer withdraws himself to die' (Tilley D 189). Cf. *Aglaura*, III. ii. 13–15.

l. 14. *So does . . . the Canon. FA46*'s reading, 'do', is clearly an editorial alteration, for Suckling frequently employs collective plurals with singular verbs; cf. Letter No. 16, ll. 16–17: 'the canon plays upon them night and day from the towne'.

ll. 17–20. *Love is a fit*, etc. Cf. *The Sad One*, III. iv. 34–7.

l. 18. *Ill dyet onely makes it last.* Cf. 'Against Absence', l. 35.

43. Against Absence (pp. 39–40)

Text. Cran2 alone has no unique readings (it is otherwise of special interest in being a scribal fair copy found among family papers: see Introduction, p. ciii); *FA46* has two (in ll. 21 and 22, the first probably a sophistication, the second either that or a corruption), *Ash3* three, and *RP11* sixteen. There are only three shared variants: presence or absence of title, 'whiles/whilst' in l. 9, and 'held/holds' in l. 18. The first two suggest common derivation for *Ash3* and *Cran2*, and *FA46* and *RP11*, the third (which is probably a conflation or a fortuitous agreement, however) common derivation for *FA46* and *Ash3*, and *Cran2* and *RP11*. Because it has no unique readings and none of its disputed readings is wrong, *Cran2* may be regarded as the textual ancestor of the others; but I have retained *FA46* as copy-text for its accidentals, and because the evidence of the texts of the other poems in the same manuscript argues that the group was not the copy used for *FA46* and is therefore to be treated as collateral.

ll. 6–10. *A finger burnt's as great a pain*; etc. Proverbial (Tilley F 230, 240, 277). Cf. *Aglaura*, II. ii. 18–19 and v(c). iii. 165 ('selfe same physick') and *Brennoralt*, III. iv. 71–4.

ll. 17–18. *Absence were good if't were but sence That onely held th'Intelligence.* Cf. Donne, 'A Valediction: forbidding Mourning', ll. 13–16: 'Dull sublunary lovers love | (Whose soule is sense) cannot admit | Absence, because it doth remove | Those things which elemented it' (Suckling seems to draw on this stanza in *Aglaura*, I. iv. 60–1).

l. 18. *held.* The subjunctive 'held' expresses a condition contrary to fact, as it is plainly meant to do (cf. 'But love is love, and magick too', l. 20). The indicative 'holds' is doubtless unauthoritative and could have arisen fortuitously in more than one witness, owing to the syntactical ambiguity of 'That', which is (as with 'held') a defining relative pronoun but might be taken for a non-defining, especially since there was no clear differentiation of function between 'that' and 'which' in the earlier seventeenth century (indeed, the 'rules' of grammar and syntax invoked here had no seventeenth-century currency, but there were understood conventions of practice and norms of signification that may reasonably be described in terms of them).

l. 20. *But love is love, and magick too.* This line is also used in *Aglaura* (III. ii. 101).

ll. 29–32. *Beauty like mans old enemy's known* etc. Cf. 'Love's Sanctuary', esp. ll. 13–18.

l. 32. *pathlesse Grove.* Cf. 'The careless Lover', l. 31.

ll. 33–6. *Return then back*, etc. Cf. 'To Mr. Davenant for Absence', ll. 17–18, and *Aglaura*, I. iv. 57–64.

44. [To his Rival I] (pp. 41–2)

It is possible that the 'Rival' is Thomas Carew, since in 'To his Rival II' the lady is given the pseudonym 'Desdemona', which is used elsewhere and in the same way only in the undatable letter (No. 50) 'To T. C.' (of course, despite the stylistic similarities, these could be independent or completely

imaginary addresses to *a* rival). The identity of the lady is even more conjectural, but perhaps it is the 'A. L.' of Suckling's '*Non est mortale quod opto*:
Upon Mrs. A. L.' and Carew's 'To A. L. Perswasions to love'.

Title. From the first line of the poem it would appear that this is to be
regarded as a companion-piece to the poem that was titled 'To his Rival' in
FA46 ('To his Rival II' in the present edition).

ll. 5–6. *unto't/foot.* In 'Song' ('Why so pale and wan fond Lover'), ll. 9–10,
Suckling rhymes 'doo't/mute', and in 'A Ballade. Upon a Wedding', ll. 124–5,
'to't/do't'.

ll. 12–14. *And Love shall onely have his scope* etc. These lines may allude to the
game on which 'A Barley-break' is based (see poem and Commentary; there
the participants are 'Love, Reason, Hate').

ll. 19–20. *Mean time we two will teach our hearts* etc. Cf. *Aglaura*, II. iii. 72–3,
where the double sense of 'burdens' (also as 'refrains' or 'choruses') and 'parts'
(also as 'the melody assigned to a particular voice') has been eliminated in the
adaptation.

l. 20. *Lovers.* Suckling nowhere else uses 'Loves' as a disyllable, and as mono-
syllable here it is both metrically anomalous and inferior in sense to the
emendation, which may have been the reading of the printer's copy from
which 'r' was a compositor's omission.

ll. 21–42. *Thou first shalt sigh,* etc. These lines, with alterations, are used in
Aglaura, IV. iv. 73–85.

ll. 27–8. *that hand, that eye,* etc. A very similar couplet is used in 'Upon two
Sisters', ll. 21–2.

45. To his Rival [II] (pp. 42–3)

For the possible identities of the lady and the 'Rival' see headnote to 'To
his Rival I'.

ll. 1–2. *Love . . . must creep where't cannot go.* Proverbial (Tilley K 49); also
used in 'Upon Sir John Laurence's bringing Water', l. 8; cf. *Aglaura*, I. ii.
13–15, and *The Sad One*, I. i. 32–5.

ll. 5–8. *It will not be amisse t'enquire* etc. Cf. 'Song' ('No, no, faire Heretique,
it needs must bee'), ll. 14–18.

ll. 11–12. *For thou and I, like Clocks,* etc. Cf. 'Sonnet II', ll. 21–4, and 'Loves
Clock' (text and Commentary).

ll. 13–14. *She then by still denying* etc. Cf. 'Against Fruition II', l. 24.

ll. 17–18. *Where sparks and fire* etc. Cf. 'The guiltless Inconstant', ll. 3–4.

l. 28. *the common way.* Cf. *Aglaura*, III. ii. 142, and 'Song' ('If you refuse me
once, and think again', wrongly printed as Suckling's), l. 12.

ll. 29–36. *But ev'ry smile* etc. Cf. 'To a Lady that forbidd to love before Company', ll. 1–8.

ll. 37–8. *She shall not like the thing we do* etc. Cf. *Aglaura*, IV. iv. 47–8.

l. 44. *Desdemona*. Elsewhere used as pseudonym only in Letter No. 50, l. 32.

46. To a Lady that forbidd to love before Company (pp. 43–4)

As Hazlitt notes, disagreeing, 'Cibber, in his "Lives of the Poets", considers these as Suckling's best lines' (i. 53, n. 1), which is the more surprising given the unusual corruptness of the printed text, certainly the only one that Cibber can have seen. In some of its imagery this poem is closely related to 'To his Rival II' preceding, but there is nothing directly to suggest that the same lady (if a real one) is involved.

Text. Since both the accidentals and the substantives of *H17* are generally more authoritative than those of *LR*, I have used the manuscript as copy-text for this poem. *LR* may give the text of an early draft (see, for example, the variants in ll. 3, 4, 12, and 19), but most of its variants would appear to be plain corruptions, some inadvertent and some perhaps editorial.

ll. 1–8. *What noe more favours*, etc. Cf. 'To his Rival II', ll. 29–36.

l. 8. *a love that none but eyes can hear*. Cf. Shakespeare, *Son.* 23, ll. 13–14: 'O, learn to read what silent love hath writ! | To hear with eyes belongs to love's fine wit.'

l. 10. *Deare must I love you*, etc. Cf. *Aglaura*, IV. iv. 47–8.

l. 11. *Bee not so nice*. Cf. 'Loves World', l. 66, and 'A Ballade. Upon a Wedding', ll. 50–1.

ll. 11–13. *sooner shall they Trace . . . By prints they leave i'th' Ayre*. Cf. *The Goblins*, IV. vi. 5–8, and *An Account of Religion*, ll. 34–6.

l. 12. *featherd Travellers*. Suckling uses *LR*'s 'feather'd Choristers' in *The Goblins*, III. vii. 107 (cf. Henry King's 'each feather'd Chorister doth sing' in 'St. Valentine's Day', l. 1, *Poems of Henry King*, ed. Margaret Crum, 1965, p. 187), but what is apparently a common periphrasis lays superfluous emphasis on singing; it is strictly the notion of birds as 'Travellers' that is wanted here.

ll. 14–15. *the last starre . . . fledd from heaven to us*. I am unable to explain the particular significance of 'us', but it is very unlikely to be an inadvertent or editorial alteration, as 'earth', if not an earlier reading, is. Cf. 'Farewel to Love', ll. 11–12.

47. The Invocation (pp. 44–5)

I suspect that the title of this poem is editorial and to be accounted for by its placing as the first poem in *The Last Remains*, 1659, because 'The Expostulation' (the title of the two following poems—one so titled by the present editor—to which it is very similar) would seem better to describe its actual subject and treatment.

ll. 1–15. *Ye juster Powers* etc. These lines are used in condensed form in *Aglaura*, IV. v. 61–7.

l. 6. *It is but just, and Love needs must.* Cf. 'The Expostulation I', ll. 5–6.

l. 12. *leave.* LR's 'have' is very likely the result of misreading; 'leave one breast to hate' is the reading in *Aglaura*, IV. v. 65.

l. 19. *Death [can] heal I'm sure.* Cf. Tilley D 141, 'Death is a plaster for all ills', for which the sole entry is Ralph Knevet, *Rhodon and Iris*, 1631, II. ii, sig. D3ᵛ ('A Barley-break' is subscribed 'dedit Francis Kneuett').

l. 21. *love.* The speaker has just complained because he 'must live And *thus* survive' (ll. 13–14), observing that '*Cupid* can cure, Death heal I'm sure' (ll. 18–19); 'some end' (l. 22), which continues the parallelism and applies very well to 'die' and 'love' but not to 'live', demands the present emendation.

48. The Expostulation [I] (pp. 45–6)

This poem is closely related to those preceding and following. It is of special interest as being the only canonical poem, except for the translation, 'Disdain', in which Suckling employs a woman as fictional speaker ('Then let me love my *Coridon*', l. 13).

ll. 5–6. *It is as natural, as just,* etc. Cf. 'The Invocation', l. 6.

l. 18. *Though I be martyr'd in that fire.* Cf. 'Upon my Lord Brohalls Wedding', ll. 7–8.

l. 24. *Or clip Loves wings, or quench Loves flame.* Cf. 'The constant Lover', l. 5; and 'Then crowne my joyes, or cure my paine; Give me more love, or more disdaine' in Carew's 'Mediocritie in love rejected' (ll. 13–14), with which this and the preceding and following poems have much thematically and otherwise in common (Rhodes Dunlap cites other antecedents to, and parallels with, Carew's poem in *Poems of Thomas Carew*, 1949, p. 220).

49. [The Expostulation II] (pp. 46–7)

This poem is no more a 'Song' (its almost certainly editorial title in *LR*) than the two preceding poems to which it is very similar, and I have accordingly supplied a title that more helpfully describes its contents. The poem is either defective, unfinished, or very free of form for a poem so apparently formal in design: the first stanza wants a line of the stanza-pattern, and the rhymes and metre do not correspond from stanza to stanza. The apparently intended norm is shown by the second and third stanzas, which both rhyme *abbaacc* and have five feet in ll. 1, 2, and 7, two in l. 3, four in l. 4, and three in ll. 5–6; but it is interesting to note that the last stanza has the same rhyme scheme as Donne's 'The Good-morrow', from which ll. 21–3 are adapted. The poem must be regarded as unfinished in *form*, but there are no deficiencies in sense; it probably is as finished as it was ever likely to be and should not be thought of as a draft. For close parallels in theme and argument, cf. 'Loving and Beloved'.

ll. 21–3. *But thus to throng and overlade a soul* etc. Cf. Donne, 'The Good-morrow', ll. 8–11 (and see headnote).

50. Sonnet I (pp. 47–8)

The appearance together in *FA46* of 'Sonnets I, II, and III' suggests both that they may have constituted a group in the printer's copy (like the juvenile religious poems and the Cranfield variant texts of others, on which see Introduction, pp. xcix–ciii) and that the titles have at least the authority of that copy if not Suckling's own; moreover, there is some kind of external confirmation of the authority of many of *FA46*'s titles, and a number of poems have been left untitled, leading to the inference that few, if any, of its titles were supplied by the printer.

There is a musical setting of this poem by William Lawes in *A31* (an autograph collection), *Dx4*, *Dx42*, and *Select Ayres and Dialogues*, 1659, p. 14, and another by John Goodgroome in *Select Ayres and Dialogues for One, Two, and Three Voyces*, 1659, 1669 (entitled *The Treasury of Musick: Containing Ayres and Dialogues*), and *The Musical Companion, in Two Books*, 1673.

Text. None of the witnesses has more than three unique readings, and *FA46* and *Dx4* have none at all (*A31*, the William Lawes autograph collection, may be thought to have some special authority, but its sole unique reading, 'yet' for 'still' in l. 9, is surely in error, probably having been carried over from the preceding line). The distribution of shared readings does not enable the construction of a single most likely stemma, but the want of unique readings in *Dx4* and *FA46*, and the presence of only one in the presumptively authoritative *A31*, leaves the text significantly in doubt only in l. 14 (see note).

ll. 3–7. *There was a time* etc. Cf. 'Perjury disdain'd', ll. 7–10, where a nearly identical passage is used.

ll. 9–14. *and I have still desires*, etc. This stanza may owe something to 'The fervency of his affection' (Appendix A.i, No. 8), the antecedent to the doubtful poem, 'The guiltless Inconstant' (q.v. in Commentary); cf., especially, ll. 4–6: 'If Cupids mercy grant not my desire; | Whoe onely for this blessed favour cries, | Harden my heart, or else putt out those eyes.'

l. 14. *Whether my heart be faulty, or her eyes.* Cf. Letter No. 15, l. 63: 'that that heretofore made the faulty and the innocent alike guilty'. It is possible that *A31* and *Dx4* have an early and the remaining witnesses a revised reading, but certainly the reading of *FA46* is superior as excluding the stronger moral and legal connotations of 'guilty', which are extraneous here.

ll. 20–1. *Sure Beauties Empires,* etc. 'States have their conversions and periods as well as natural bodies' is given as a 'sentence' by Tilley (S 832), who cites *Jacula Prudentum*, 1651, as the first recorded occurrence (see *The Works of George Herbert,* ed. F. E. Hutchinson, 1945, p. 361: No. 1166).

51. Sonnet II (pp. 48–9)

On the title and arrangement of this poem in *FA46* see headnote on 'Sonnet I'. There are two seventeenth-century musical settings, one by William Webb (*Select Musicall Ayres, and Dialogues,* 1652; *Select Musicall Ayres and Dialogues, in Three Bookes,* 1653; and *Select Ayres and Dialogues,* 1659), and another by Nicholas Lanier [?] (*Dx4,* subscribed 'Lanere', and *Dx42*).

Text. Only *P, SMA, WI55* ('pleasant' for 'Pheasant' in l. 20), *WI62a* (title), and *WI62b* contain unique readings, and the few remaining and trivial shared variants do not make general genealogical study possible or necessary, although their distribution does establish the lack of authority of *P, SMA, WI62a* (which follows *WI55* except in correcting two obvious errors), and *WI62b* (which generally agrees with *FA46* but is very corrupt and possibly printed from a memorial transcription). The authorial reading is at no place in doubt.

l. 4. *little know-not-whats, in faces.* Cf. Letter No. 48, ll. 20–3 ('certaine *ie ne scay quoys*', etc.), and *Aglaura,* I. v. 36.

l. 8. *'Tis love in love that makes the sport.* Cf. *Aglaura,* I. v. 8–10.

ll. 17–20. *'Tis not the meat,* etc. Similar ideas are expressed in the same terms ('meat', 'Pheasant', etc.) in *The Goblins,* IV. iii. 4–9.

ll. 21–4. *What in our watches,* etc. Suckling frequently uses the watch and its works as metaphors. Cf. 'Loves Clock' and Commentary.

52. Sonnet III (pp. 49–50)

On the title and arrangement of this poem in *FA46* see headnote on 'Sonnet I'. As Thompson points out (p. 364), this poem was very likely inspired by the beginning of Donne's 'Loves Deitie'.

l. 5. *Chaplets.* This word occurs in collocation with 'Elizium' (l. 19) in *Aglaura,* v(t). i. 170–1.

ll. 15–18. *What posture can we think him in, That here unlov'd agen* etc. Cf. *Aglaura,* II. iii. 99–100.

ll. 19–21. *Or how can that Elizium be* etc. Cf. *Aglaura*, v(c). i. 178–80; Suckling frequently refers to Elysium (see note on l. 4 of 'Upon Christmas').

ll. 23–8. *And Sophonisba must* etc. Sophonisba is also referred to in Letter No. 44, l. 5 (see note). Philoclea, Pirocles, and Amphialus figure in Sidney's *Arcadia*; their significance here is self-explanatory.

ll. 29–32. *Some Bayes (perchance) . . . The noble Martyrs here.* Cf. *Brennoralt*, III. iv. 70–4.

53. [Love's Sanctuary] (pp. 50–1)

The text of this poem in *A23* may represent an early draft of the poem, since the two additional stanzas found there, though anticlimactic and variously at odds with the preceding four stanzas (the whole of the LR and the present text), are by themselves not uncharacteristic of Suckling and contain images and figures that he uses prominently elsewhere (see note on ll. 24+[25–36]).

Title. In *LR* this poem shared with 'The Expostulation II' (present edition) the almost certainly editorial, inappropriate, and unhelpful title, 'Song'; 'Love's Sanctuary', based on the semi-technical metaphor from hunting that figures climactically in the poem (see ll. 23–4 and note), is more usefully descriptive, and I have supplied it as title. With the hunting imagery used here, cf. that in 'To Mr. Davenant for Absence' and the dubious poem 'To Mr. W. M. Against Absence'.

ll. 1–3. *The crafty Boy* etc. Cf. *The Goblins*, III. vii. 68–72, 93–6.

l. 10. *by force.* Certainly the correct reading, used in contrast with 'all that beguiles'. The unsyntactical and senseless reading of *LR* (*Text*), 'sweet', was obviously repeated (by either the compositor or the scribe of the copy) from its occurrence in l. 8, the reading of the *Errata*, 'sweetly', being an editorial 'improvement' of a copy error.

ll. 13–18. *And then he brings me, where his ambush lay,* etc. Cf. 'Against Absence', ll. 29–32, and *Aglaura*, I. iii. 8–13.

ll. 23–4. *If other eyes invite the Boy to tarry, I'll flie to hers as to a Sanctuary.* 'Sanctuary' is here used in its semi-technical sense, 'privilege of forest', or the close season (*OED*). The last two lines in *LR* and the present text express a wish for the reversal of roles of hunter and hunted (or at any rate respite for the quarry), and make better sense and have more dramatic force than the reading of *A23*, which is either earlier or sophisticated but in any case pointlessly and weakly shifts the emphasis from the speaker to Cupid.

ll. 24+[25–36]. *Alas god knows I feard* etc. These additional stanzas found only in *A23* contain images and figures that Suckling uses elsewhere, notably 'forraine face' (as 'foreign aid' in 'Upon my Lord Brohalls Wedding', l. 31) and 'eys language' (cf. 'To a Lady', l. 8, and 'Loves Siege', l. 8), but, if they are authorial, they must represent an early draft of the poem, because they seriously disunify the dialectic of the whole. The imperfect rhyme of the first stanza ('face/go') is suggestive, but most telling are the oath 'god knows' and the abandonment of Cupid, the (here) gratuitous substitution of the very loosely integrated terms of parley for those of the hunt, the pointless return from the historical-present tense of stanzas 2–4 to the past tense of stanza one, and finally the redundancy—as well as the inconsistency—of the matter and manner of these two stanzas.

54. [Loves Feast] (pp. 51–2)

Text. The three texts present the characteristic ambiguity, but there are only six substantive or semi-substantive variants, none of much consequence, and the text is not seriously in doubt. *FA46* alone has a title and reads the probably editorial 'prethee' in l. 1; *Cran2*, which is of special interest as a scribal fair copy found among family papers (see Introduction, p. ciii), reads 'does' for 'doth' in l. 17; and *Ash3* reads 'well' and 'his' for 'will' and 'its' in l. 4, and 'att' for 'sit' in l. 13.

Title. The absence of an extant musical setting and of a title in the two variant texts suggests that 'Song' is unauthorial; the poem's contents are more helpfully described as 'Loves Feast', which I have supplied.

ll. 9–10. *And like old Hawks* etc. Images drawn from falconry abound in Suckling; cf., e.g., 'Upon my Lord Brohalls Wedding', ll. 36–40; Letter No. 23 (which also contains a close parallel with the following poem), ll. 37–43; *Aglaura*, IV. i. 13–15; and *Brennoralt*, IV. iii. 2–5.

ll. 16-20. *And oh! when once that course is past*, etc. Cf. *Aglaura*, IV. iv. 49–52.

55. [Loves Offence] (pp. 52–3)

For a condensed approximate paraphrase of the entire poem, see *The Goblins*, IV. ii. 25–32.

l. 6. *For wounds unsearcht but ranckle more.* Proverbial (Tilley D 358); cf. Letter No. 23, ll. 80–1.

ll. 11–12. *So, neither speaking doth become The Lovers state, nor being dumb.* Cf. 'Song' ('Why so pale and wan fond Lover'), ll. 6–10.

56. [Disdain] (pp. 53–4)

Suckling uses a woman as fictional speaker only in this translation and in 'The Expostulation I'. This and the following three poems share the ballad stanza (rhyming *abab* with the exception of 'The constant Lover' [*abcb*]); strong similarities of rhythm, cadence, syntax, and sense; and the use of feminine endings and acephalous lines (the rhythm of 'The constant Lover' might better be described as partly catalectic trochaics). The authorship of this, the following, and a dubious translation is discussed in the Introduction, pp. xcii–xciii.

In *LR* 'Disdain'—title supplied in the present edition—is editorially headed 'English'd thus by the Author' and follows a corrupt text (which exists in two states) of the French original (see Appendix A.vi, No. 1: text, critical apparatus, and Commentary), suggesting setting either by a compositor unfamiliar with French or from not very legible copy, perhaps authorial foul papers, or both. Text and translation in turn follow 'Profer'd Love rejected', which suggests that all three with or (probably) without 'A Phillis', the French original of 'Profer'd Love rejected', were grouped together, perhaps in a leaflet like those found among the Cranfield Papers (on which see Introduction, pp. xcix–ciii).

l. 3. *all your proffer'd services.* Cf. the title of the following poem, 'Profer'd Love rejected'.

l. 19. *rack your brain.* Cf. 'What Rack can Fancy find so high' in 'Loving and Beloved', l. 13, and the 'rack of doubt' in *Aglaura*, IV. i. 30.

57. Profer'd Love rejected (pp. 54–5)

This poem is a translation of a French original, 'A Phillis', which is printed in Appendix A.vi, No. 2. Another translation was printed as Charles Cotton's in *Poems on Several Occasions*, 1689, pp. 165–6 (it was not, however, included in *Cotton's Poems*, ed. John Beresford, 1923, or ed. John Buxton, 1958):

Epigramme de Monsieur des-Portes

Some four years ago I made *Phillis* an offer,
    Provided she would be my Wh-re,
Of two thousand good Crowns to put in her Coffer,
    And I think should have given her more.

About two years after, a Message she sent me,
    She was for a thousand my own,
But unless for an hundred she now would content me,
    I sent her word I would have none.

She fell to my price six or seven weeks after,
    And then for a hundred would doe;
I then told her in vain she talk'd of the matter,
    Than twenty no farther I'd goe.

T'other day for six Ducatoons she was willing,
    Which I thought a great deal too dear,
And told her unless it would come for two shilling,
    She must seek a Chapman elsewhere.

This Morning she's come, and would fain buckle *gratis*,
    But she's grown so fulsome a Wh-re,
That now methinks nothing a far dearer rate is,
    Than all that I offer'd before.

This poem has much stylistically in common with the preceding poem (with which it was probably grouped in the printer's copy) and the following two poems (see headnote on 'Disdain' and, on the authorship, Introduction, p. xcii). A text of the French original was not included with it in *LR* as one was with 'Disdain', and it was probably wanting in the printer's copy; but, given the posthumous publication of the book and the nature of the copy from which it was printed (see Introduction, pp. lxxxvi–lxxxix), I cannot see much reason to accept F. O. Henderson's suggestion that Suckling, while acknowledging 'Disdain' as a translation, intended to imply that 'Profer'd Love rejected' was an entirely original poem (see 'Traditions of *Précieux* and *Libertin* in Suckling's Poetry', *ELH*, 1937, iv. 285).

Title. The probably editorial title may have been suggested by the 'proffer'd services' of 'Disdain', l. 3, but 'proffered service' is also something of a formula (cf. Letter No. 55, l. 30).

58. [The constant Lover] (pp. 55–6)

This and the following poem, which are stylistically similar to the two preceding poems, were first printed in *Wit and Drollery*, 1656, as 'A Song by Sir John Suckling' and 'The Answer by the same Author', the title of the first accurately describing at least one certain aspect of the poem, for there is a musical setting by Henry Lawes in *HL* and (incompletely) *Dx4*. The evidence for the date of the poems is slim, but they may have been written *c.* 1635–7 (see headnote on 'The Answer'). On the intimate relationship between this poem and 'The Answer', and the authorship of the latter, see Introduction, pp. xci–xcii.

Mr. Beaurline suggests with great probability that 'The constant Lover' is based on the proverb, 'After three Days men grow weary of a wench, a guest, and weather rainy (rain)' (Tilley D 114: *c.* 1594); the proverb also reinforces the originality of 'hold' (*Σ*) and the lack of authority of 'prove' (*LR*) in l. 4. There may also be a more than analogical relationship between this poem and Donne's 'Farewell to Love'; compare, for example, ll. 11–15:

        But, from late faire
    His highnesse sitting in a golden Chaire [i.e., Love],
      Is not lesse cared for after three dayes
  By children, then the thing which lovers so
  Blindly admire, and with such worship wooe . . . .

And it is of interest that, literally translating Terence's '[Hui!] universum triduum!' (*Eunuchus*, II. i. 18), 'Three whole days together' (l. 2) reverses Terence's irony, where the phrase quoted is used by Parmeno to rebuke his master Phædria, who cannot bear to absent himself from his mistress for two days, as she has commanded, but is trying to 'steel' himself by contemplating 'vel totum triduum'.

The 'lexical economy' and rhetorical and incremental repetition in this dramatic song are noteworthy: 'Out upon it' and 'a pox upon't'; 'I have lov'd', 'am like to love', 'Such a constant Lover', 'Love with me had made no stay'; 'Three whole days', 'love three more', and 'whole wide world'; and 'very very Face' and 'dozen dozen in her place', for example. Partly on the basis of these well-established characteristics, I am inclined to think that the repeated 'shall' (l. 6) and 'Had it any been but she' (l. 13), which, though 'the same' as l. 12, is emphatically not the same by virtue of a difference of context, are the original readings (see notes).

Text. It is ironical that what is probably Suckling's best-known poem has been known almost exclusively from the corrupt text in *LR*. The poem is short and easily memorized, and perhaps as many texts represent memorial transcriptions—or contain memorial contamination—as were made directly from copy. Unique variants are found only in *LR* (three, one [l. 14] shared with *O2* [*c*]), and (with one each) *Eg9*, *F339*, *Harv7*, and *W&D*; in their texts of 'The Answer', *O2* and *OD* contain one unique variant each. Except for *W&D*, the ancestor of *O2*, these represent terminal states. The texts without unique variants are *AC84*, *Dx4*, *O2*, and *HL*. Of these, *AC84* follows *Wind-D* (of which it is a later edition) in seven unique variants, including interpolated lines; *Dx4* is apparently the textual model of *F339*, which differs from it only in minor conflicting readings in ll. 5 and 9; and *O2* (*u*)—which (as *c*) has been generally altered to agree with *LR*—is a direct descendant of *W&D*, from which it differs only in reading 'wings' with *Σ* against *W&D*'s 'wing' in l. 5 (that *O2* is sophisticated is manifest in its divergence from copy in Poems Nos. 80 and 90–3, which are derived from *LR*). *Harv7* is an unreliable witness owing to its obvious sophistication: its readings distribute almost at random with those of other witnesses, it has a unique line (11) in place of the other witnesses' (in which there are only minor variations), and in 'The Answer' it interpolates an entire stanza (l. 12+). The distribution of readings shared by two or multiple witnesses further suggests a close relationship between—and probably shared derivation and individually weakened authority for—*OD* and *Wind-D*, and *Dx4* (which shares the musical setting with *HL*, to which it does not otherwise seem to be closely related) and *Eg9*, which appears to be both corrupt and sophisticated (see critical apparatus).

HL, the Henry Lawes autograph manuscript, is an important if problematical witness. E. F. Hart, who also comments explicitly on the *HL* text of this poem (see note on l. 13), concluded on the basis of a collation of *HL*'s texts with those of 'contemporary literary editions' that 'Lawes took uncommon pains to transcribe them correctly' and attempted a 'scrupulous fidelity to his poet's text. The variants one finds in his texts almost always bear the stamp of being from poets' earlier drafts' ('Caroline Lyrics and Contemporary Song-Books', *The Library*, 1953, 5th ser. viii. 92). Hart's general findings cannot establish the absolute textual authority of *HL*'s text of this poem, but its readings plainly deserve serious consideration. *LR* and *HL* alone have the euphemistic 'the spite' for 'a pox' in *Σ* (-*AC84*, *OD*, *Wind-D*), and, since *LR*'s unique readings are almost certainly corruptions, it would appear that *LR* is a descendent, perhaps memorial and only partial, of *HL*; if it is not, the two may derive from a euphemized common ancestor. *LR* has little or no substantive authority except for its headings (see note on *Title* below), and I have retained it as copy-text solely for its accidentals, especially of punctuation.

Title. In the following poem, 'The Answer', or some title containing 'Answer', has the support of a majority of witnesses and is in any case an obvious and helpful title. 'Sir J. S.' and 'Sir Toby Matthews', the unique headings of the two poems in *LR*, are perhaps authorial, but I think that they should probably be regarded as speech headings rather than as titles (see Introduction, pp. xci–xcii). '[A] Song' has the (partly derivative) support of four witnesses (and cf. 'Sonetto' in *Eg9*) and is countenanced by the existence of a musical setting, but it seems doubtfully authorial and I have been reluctant to allow this unhelpful title to proliferate. I have therefore supplied a title—one commonly supplied in anthologies—by analogy with 'The careless Lover', which has much in common with these two poems.

ll. 1–4. *Out upon it,* etc. Cf. *Aglaura,* II. ii. 1–4.

l. 6. *shall.* The weight of support for 'can' does not correspond with the number of witnesses (see note on *Text* above), and it seems more likely to be a sophistication than 'shall' an inadvertent repetition (of 'shall' in l. 5); 'shall', which implicitly includes 'can', appropriately emphasizes the element of time in the endless futility of the quest.

l. 13. *Had it any been but she.* Of the two witnesses that share the attractive variant, 'Had it not been she alone', *Harv7* is apparently sophisticated and therefore an unreliable authority, and *HL* of high general authority as a collection (see note on *Text*); the authority here, then, is divided. I agree with E. F. Hart, who is 'not prepared to argue that "Had it not been she alone" is an improvement on the pointedness of "Had it any been but she" ' (op. cit. above, p. 107), but I feel still more strongly that a reading shared by all but two of the witnesses is most unlikely to be a general inadvertency, and that the various 'pointedness' of the line commends it as authorial. The rhetorical —and metrical—effect of the line, repeated, is quite different from that of its first use; and, as a 'bold' repetition, it is even less likely to be a sophistication (as is not true of the 'obvious' line of *Harv7* and *HL*) than a dittographic error repeated in several witnesses.

l. 14. *very very*. *LR*'s unique omission of one 'very' is almost certainly inadvertent; cf. *AC84* and *Wind-D* in l. 14 of 'The Answer' (critical apparatus), and, for another example of the same intensifying repetition, 'What would you say to me now, an I were your very very Rosalind?' (*As You Like It*, IV. i. 63–4).

59. [The Answer] (pp. 56–7)

For the general relationship between this and 'The constant Lover', see the headnote on the latter, and for Suckling's authorship, see the Introduction, pp. xci–xcii. Some kind of familiarity between Suckling and Mathew seems likely from the presence in the uncatalogued portions of the Cranfield Papers of letters from Mathew to Suckling's uncle, the Earl of Middlesex, one of which (unfortunately undated) begins, 'I was comaunded to send theise inclosed, to your iudicious ey: with this direction, that your lordship be pleased, to correct the ignorance, and oversight, therein', etc. Whether Suckling or Mathew wrote this poem, it should probably be dated before late 1637, when Mathew was rather harshly disparaged in 'The Wits' (ll. 57–64), because a friendly relationship seems to underlie the comparatively good-natured rebuke. And, since Suckling had been no admirer of Lady Carlisle for some time, it is possible that 'The constant Lover' and 'The Answer' were written before 1636, when Mathew's Character of her—explicitly mentioned in 'The Wits'—was first circulating (see David Mathew, *Sir Toby Mathew*, 1950, p. 80; 'The Wits', ll. 60–4; and 'Upon my Lady Carliles walking in Hampton-Court garden').

Text. The textual evidence for the relationships between the witnesses supports the inferences made from the evidence of 'The constant Lover' (on which see note on *Text*).

l. 8. *more Fool then Lover*. Cf. 'The careless Lover', l. 39: 'He makes not Love, but plays the Fool.'

l. 9. *Yet you needs must*. The authority is fairly evenly divided, but, without altering the character of the censorious Speaker, 'Yet you needs must' expresses the ironical disproportion more forcefully than 'But I grant you'.

60. The careless Lover (pp. 57–9)

l. 6 etc. [refrain line] *know*. 'Knows' would appear to be a misguided editorial alteration presumably made for the sake of the grammar and sense; the rhyme 'forgo it' demands 'know it', and the subjunctive 'know' seems otherwise superior to the indicative 'knows'.

ll. 15–18. *When I am hungry* etc. These lines, with alterations, are also used in 'Song' ('Honest Lover whosoever'), ll. 33–6.

ll. 24–5. *And when 'tis nam'd anothers health*, etc. These lines, with alterations, are also used in 'A Ballade. Upon a Wedding', ll. 100–1.

ll. 30–1. *the fall Of fountains or a pathless grove.* Cf. 'Against Absence', ll. 31–2: 'The ayre of some wild o'regrown wood Or pathlesse Grove is the Boyes food'; and *The Sad One*, IV. iv. 7–12.

l. 39. *He makes not Love, but plays the Fool.* Cf. 'The Answer', l. 8: 'more Fool then Lover'.

61. Song (pp. 59–60)

Title. There is no extant musical setting, and the title is probably editorial, having been suggested by the presence of a refrain. 'The perfect Lover' (see l. 42) would be more helpful.

ll. 3–4. *one wav'ring thought, if thy flame* etc. Cf. 'Song' ('No, no, faire Heretique'), ll. 14–18, and *The Goblins*, V. v. 226.

ll. 33–6. *If when thy stomack calls to eat*, etc. These lines, with alterations, are also used in 'The careless Lover', ll. 15–18.

62. Loving and Beloved (pp. 60–1)

This and the following poem are companion-pieces, as the similarity of their first lines readily suggests.

l. 13. *What Rack can Fancy find so high.* Cf. 'Disdain', l. 19, and *Aglaura*, IV. i. 30.

ll. 19, 21. *God of desire, . . . take thy brands back, and thy fire.* Cf. Letter No. 55, l. 24.

l. 25. *Loves Triumph, must be Honours Funeral.* Cf. *The Sad One*, IV. i. 48–50, and the proverb, 'When Love puts in friendship is gone' (Tilley L 549: 1576).

63. [Womans Constancy] (pp. 61–2)

This and the preceding poem are companion-pieces, as the similarity of their first lines readily suggests.

Text. For the substantive alterations in *FA48* see Introduction, pp. xcvi–xcvii, and note on l. 15.

ll. 9–10. *what we call Their sympathy, is but love to jett in general.* Jet is a form of coal that 'has the property of attracting light bodies when electrified by rubbing' (*OED sb*[1]. I, citing Jonson, *Every Man in his Humour* [1616], III. iii. 24–5: 'Your lustre too'll . . . Draw courtship to you, as a iet doth strawes').

l. 15. *the loadstone yet was never brought* [neere the Loadstone it was *etc. FA48*]. Thompson suggested that 'what Suckling wrote was, *It is because to th' load-*

stone yet 'twas never brought, and that a misprint in the first edition brought about the subsequent introduction of *near'* (p. 366), but *FA48*'s reading is plainly corrupt. Despite the movement of the women implied by 'womens hearts like straws do move' (l. 8), they are predominantly passive (as 'iron' and 'flowers') until aroused to 'lightness' by the proximity of men ('jett', 'loadstone', 'Bee'). The figure of the 'loadstone' is anticipated by 'sympathy' (l. 10), with which it is used elsewhere; cf. *To Mr. Henry German*, ll. 109–10, and *An Account of Religion*, ll. 359–60.

ll. 16–20. *If where a gentle Bee hath fall'n* etc. Cf. *Aglaura*, IV. iv. 28–30, where 'my thoughts like bees' etc. immediately follows a clock conceit closely related to 'Loves Clock' following.

ll. 21–5. *For still the flowers ready stand:* etc. Cf. *Aglaura*, V(t). iii. 87–92, and V(c). ii. 80–5.

64. [Loves Clock] (pp. 62–3)

The clock and its work are a favourite conceit of Suckling's; cf., for example, 'Sonnet II', ll. 21–4, and *Aglaura*, II. i. 66–8 and 'Epilogue(t)', ll. 6–8 (and see note below).

ll. 7–8. *Hope is the main spring* etc. These lines, with alterations, are also used in *Aglaura*, IV. iv. 26–8, which are immediately followed by 'my thoughts like bees' (ll. 28–30), with which cf. ll. 16–25 of 'Womans Constancy' preceding.

65. Song (pp. 63–4)

In this poem Suckling develops the paradoxes latent in a declaration that opens one of his letters to the historical 'Aglaura' (No. 26; see Introduction, pp. xxxix–xlii): 'But that I know I love you more then ever any did any, and that I hate myself because I can love you no more', etc. And his treatment of the extremes of love here bears interesting comparison with Carew's 'Mediocritie in love rejected' ('Give me more love, or more disdaine'), which also has much in common with 'The Expostulation I'.

'Song' was first printed in *Aglaura*, 1638, where it is—more than a musical interlude—a dramatic and thematic lyric (IV. iv. 4–23; see Commentary, ii. 271). In *FA46* it was printed with the *Poems, &c.*—evidently from the text in *Ag*, since only the accidentals differ—as well as in *Aglaura*. An early musical setting by Henry Lawes occurs in MSS. *Dx4*, *Dx42*, and *HL*, and in the printed song-books *SMA*, *SMA53*, and *Select Ayres and Dialogues for One, Two, and Three Voyces*, 1659, 1669 (entitled *The Treasury of Musick*).

Text. Of the six substantive variants, the omission of 'Song' by *HL* and *SMA* is insignificant, and four others are unique omissions or corruptions, but it is distinctly odd to find an error, 'I would' for ' 'Twould', in *Aglaura*, 1638, of which Suckling himself arranged the publication (though it need not necessarily have been seen through the press by him; see Commentary, ii. 257). 'I would . . . full' exclusively emphasizes the suggestion of physical impotence, while the context demands ' 'Twould . . . fall [= 'happen', at least in part]'; and there is support for ' 'Twould' in 'Loves World', ll. 21–4, esp. 'that 't would so fall There would appear no hope at all'. 'I' for 'T' is an easy error, by misreading or anticipation (the following line begins with 'I'), but however it came about it suggests that Suckling proof-read *Aglaura*, 1638, casually if at all (also see note immediately following).

Arrangement of lines in stanzas. The prosody of the two stanzas does not absolutely correspond: the second has a slant-rhyme in l. 13, and in ll. 16–17 reverses the arrangement of trimeter followed by dimeter in ll. 6–7. In *Ag*, *FA46* (both *Poems, &c.* and *Aglaura*), and *R* the indentations of lines in the two stanzas are not symmetrical, but they also don't correspond with the prosody: they deeply indent ll. 2, 3, 6, and 8, in the first stanza, but deeply indent ll. 12, 13, 15, and 16, and shallowly indent ll. 19–20, in the second. Most of these anomalies are probably due to the custom of giving the words of the first stanza of a song with the music and those of subsequent stanzas in their poetical form. With the support of *Aglaura*, 1648, I have made the first stanza symmetrical with the second, but I have also eliminated the indentation of l. 15, in which *Ag48* follows the other texts: l. 15, like l. 5, belongs at the left margin with ll. 4 and 14 to emphasize the rhyming of the pairs.

ll. 7–8. *'Twould then so fall*, etc. Cf. 'Loves World', ll. 23–4.

ll. 9–10. *Love that can flow*, etc. Cf. Letter No. 50, ll. 6–7, and Tilley F 378, 380–1.

ll. 17–18. *For that's a flame would die*, etc. Cf. 'Song' ('Honest Lover Whosoever'), ll. 1–4, and *The Goblins*, v. v. 226.

66. Song (p. 64)

This poem was first printed in *Aglaura*, 1638; in *FA46* it was printed with the *Poems, &c.*—evidently from the text in *Ag*, since only the accidentals differ—as well as in *Aglaura* (IV. ii. 14–28). Immediately after its occurrence in the play, Orsames refers to it as 'A little foolish counsell (Madam) I gave a friend of mine foure or five yeares agoe', which Willa McClung Evans interpreted to mean that 'the musical setting . . . would appear to have been written several years previous to the performance of the play and was already familiar to the audience' (*Henry Lawes, Musician and Friend of Poets*, 1941, p. 141), and L. A. Beaurline has used as grounds to suggest that this poem is 'the only mature literary work that appears to belong to a year earlier than 1637', Orsames's lines perhaps being 'Suckling's way of apologizing for using an older piece of his verse' ('The Canon of Sir John Suckling's Poems', *SP*, 1960, lvii. 515). An assertion by a character in a play is rather doubtful evidence for dating a poem, but 'Song', despite a literary maturity considerably less in evidence in poems known to have been written *c.* 1630–2, may indeed have been written earlier than one would suppose on stylistic grounds, which would suggest approximate contemporaneity with *Aglaura* (1637). The poem has been criticized in detail by Beaurline in ' "Why so Pale and Wan": An Essay in Critical Method' (*University of Texas Studies in Literature and Language*, 1963, iv. 553–63).

The enduring popularity of this 'song' is attested by at least five musical settings. The earliest setting, by William Lawes, which is given in MS. *Dx4*, was probably written for the first performance of *Aglaura* in 1637; the music is reproduced by Murray Lefkowitz in *William Lawes*, 1960, pp. 201–2. An anonymous setting is given in MS. *W3*; one by Lewis Ramondon in *Wit and Mirth: or Pills to Purge Melancholy*, 1707, 1712; one by T. A. Arne in *Clio and Euterpe or British Harmony* 1759, i. 86; and an anonymous one in '[Song] The *Words* by Sir John Suckling' [London, *c.* 1745], single-sheet folio.

H. E. Berthon suggested that a poem beginning, 'Pourquoi perdez-vous la parole', printed in *Les Satyres et Autre Oevvres Folastres du S*^r *Regnier*, 1614 and later editions, was Suckling's source for this poem (*MLR*, 1911, vi. 221–3), but it is certainly not the 'source' in the same way as 'Desdain' and 'A Phillis', which were printed in the same volume and freely translated by Suckling as 'Disdain' and 'Profer'd Love rejected', are sources. An answer to this poem, perhaps by John Egerton, second Earl of Bridgewater, is printed in Appendix A.i (No. 5), and the following Latin translation is given in Henry Bold's *Latine Songs, with their English: and Poems*, 1685, pp. 115, 117:

CANT. XXVIII.

I.

Cur palleas Amasie?
Cur quæso palleas?
Si non rubente facie,
Squallente valeas?
Cur quæso palleas?

II.

Cur stupias mi suavio,
Cur quæso taceas?
Si præstes nil eloquio,
Silentio valeas?
Cur quæso taceas[?]

III.

Hinc hinc! (ah pudet) nil aget,
    Hoc non movebit,
Suapte si non redamet,
    Nil prevalebit,
    Dæmon habebit.

Bold also wrote a poor imitation of the poem (see *Poems, Lyrique, Macaroni-que, Heroique,* 1664, p. 16), and still another occurs, with music, in the John Gamble commonplace-book (*Dx42*):

Stay wilde sinner;
    Cease thy suite:
if thy Fayre meanes Cannot winn her;
    thou wiltt never bringe her toott.
    tis nott all thy wiles Can doott;
if of her selfe shee will nott loveinge bee,
Faith lett her goe; shees not a wench For me.

hence lett her goe
    there are more
who now perhaps would gladly doe
    thou maist Chuse off halfe a score
    while Conffin'd in midst of store
tis meerly dotage, and will madness prove
pox where they doe nott like, they Cannott Love

67. [Loves Siege] (pp. 65-6)

H. E. Berthon suggested—in *MLR*, 1911, vi. 221-2—that Suckling based this poem on a French original beginning 'Amour Héraut de la beauté' in *Les Satyres et Autre Oevvres du Sr Regnier* (1617), a collection that provided the models for Suckling's translations, 'Disdain' and 'Proffer'd Love rejected', and also contained a poem suggested by M. Berthon as the source of 'Song' ('Why so pale and wan fond Lover?', q.v. in Commentary). Suckling's own experience of actual sieges during his membership in the Embassy of Sir Henry Vane to Gustavus Adolphus may have contributed to his fondness for the sometime Petrarchan conceit of the amorous 'siege' (cf., for example, Letter No. 16, esp. ll. 13-21), which he also uses prominently elsewhere (in *Aglaura*, in lines apparently adapted from lines in the poem or otherwise closely parallel with them). See, for example, 'A Soldier'; 'Upon A. M.', ll. 1-6; 'To Mr. Davenant for Absence', ll. 5-16; 'Upon my Lord Brohalls Wedding', ll. 29-35; *Aglaura*, I. vi. 18-25, and II. ii. 10-15 and 43-5; *The Goblins*, IV. iii. 30-1; and *Brennoralt*, III. i. 28-31 and III. iii. 1-10; there are many others. A musical setting of this poem is given, together with the words of the first stanza (as in *FA46*), in *Dx4*.

l. 8. *The language of her eyes.* Cf. 'To a Lady', l. 8, and 'eys language' in the first of two additional stanzas in the *A23* text of 'Love's Sanctuary' (critical apparatus, l. 24+).

l. 35. *That Giant* [Honour]. Carew also personifies 'The Gyant, Honour' in 'A Rapture', l. 3, as Donne does the 'Giant . . . Disdaine' and 'th'enchantresse Honor' in 'The Dampe', ll. 11-12.

68. Farewel to Love (pp. 66–8)

The tone, prosody, and imagery of this poem differ considerably from those in Donne's 'Farewell to Love', but, in addition to the shared theme, there is a general similarity of dialectical development, including a moderate use of 'conceited' language, that seems more than fortuitous, most overtly, perhaps, in ll. 11–20 and 37 (on which see note below). For this poem Suckling also drew on Donne's 'Ecclogue 1613', undoubtedly in ll. 11–15 and less certainly and more freely *passim* (cf. note on ll. 41–5).

l. 6. *my dear nothings.* Cf. 'prettie little harmlesse nothings' in *Aglaura*, III. ii. 147.

ll. 11–20. *As he whose quicker eye* etc. There is a general similarity of purport between these lines and ll. 31–4 of Donne's 'Farewell to Love': 'Since so, my minde | Shall not desire what no man else can finde, | I'll no more dote and runne | To pursue things which had, indammage me.' But there is a closer and more obvious resemblance between ll. 11–15 and Donne's 'Epithalamion 1613', ll. 204–5, which Suckling appears to have adapted: 'As he that sees a starre fall, runs apace, | And findes a gellie in the place.' Also cf. *Aglaura*, II. iii. 82–4: '. . . shee is false; | False as a falling Star, or Glow-wormes fire: | This Devill Beautie is compounded strangely.'

ll. 23–4. *Each wanton eye Enflam'd before.* Cf. 'The guiltless Inconstant', l. 5: 'Each wanton eye now kindleth my desire.'

l. 31. *Gum.* This emendation first appeared in *FA58*; it was also adopted, before Hazlitt, by the Rev. Alfred Inigo Suckling in *Selections*.

l. 33. *heart* [hair, 't *Th*: hair *Haz*]. *FA46*'s reading is awkward, and Thompson's emendation is prosodically superior to Hazlitt's, but it is questionable whether 'the right reading is obvious' (p. 373), partly because there is no strict parallel in Suckling for the strained rhyme and wrenched contraction of the emendation: 'doo't?/mute?', in 'Song' ('Why so pale and wan fond Lover?'), is weak, and the closest parallels occur within lines—'place, 't may be', in 'On New-years day 1640', l. 34, and 'deaths-head 'twill' in this poem, l. 27. Like Hazlitt and Thompson I take 'part' (l. 32) to be 'the parting of the hair', a sense that—with 'Gum'—obtains whether we read 'heart' or 'hair, ['t]' and is supported by the fact that this is a detail in a speculation upon 'What manner of deaths-*head* 'twill be' and by 'The Locks, that curl'd o're each eare be' (l. 36; *OED* notes 'part' in this sense as of nineteenth-century American origin, and 1698 as the earliest occurrence of 'parting' itself; but 'part' should probably be understood in a more general sense, related by context to 'The Locks'). 'Gum . . . hangs down the hair' is cosmetically accurate, but it is also both redundant and not much less idiomatically odd than 'hangs down the heart'. The latter, paraphrasable as 'Makes the beholding lover despondent', seems to me the 'right' if difficult reading, and, like the earlier stanzas individually, and generally the whole poem, it makes explicit the effect of women upon the unwary as well as upon the wise.

l. 37. *Master-worms.* A nonce-coinage by analogy from 'master-keys' (cf. 'Locks', l. 36, and 'holes', l. 40), possibly suggested by 'worme-seed' in Donne's 'Farewell to Love', l. 40 (see headnote and note on ll. 11–20). On the collocation of 'worms' and 'dust' see note below.

ll. 41–5. *A quick corse . . . Dust.* The collocation of '[Master-]worms' (l. 36), 'ev'ry woman' (l. 42), and 'Dust' (l. 45), indeed the general development and other particulars of the entire poem, suggest a partial source in Donne's 'Ecclogue 1613' (from which Suckling adapted ll. 11–15; see note), especially ll. 149–59, the stanza on 'Her Apparrelling':

> Thus thou descend'st to our infirmitie,
>> Who can the Sun in water see.
>> Soe dost thou, when in silke and gold,
> Thou cloudst thy selfe; since wee which doe behold,
>> Are dust, and wormes, 'tis just
> Our objects be the fruits of wormes and dust;
> Let every Jewell be a glorious starre,
> Yet starres are not so pure, as their spheares are.
> And though thou stoope, to'appeare to us in part,
> Still in that Picture thou intirely art,
> Which thy inflaming eyes have made within his loving heart.'

ll. 46–7. *They . . . These.* There is an elliptical change in number between stanzas 9 and 10: 'ev'ry woman' (l. 42) becomes 'They', i.e. 'women' (l. 46), and 'mine eye' (l. 42) becomes 'These', i.e. 'eyes' (l. 47).

69. Upon two Sisters (pp. 68–9)

The title of this poem may not be authorial in its present tepid form and is fairly obviously suggested in l. 13 (the omitted l. 6 may have been more explicit), but it readily implies a relationship with Letter No. 24, 'For the two Excellent Sisters', that has the support of historical inference. Letters Nos. 24 and 43 provide the major canonical evidence for the identification

of Suckling's 'Aglaura' with Mary Bulkeley, of Beaumaris, Anglesey, to whom
Letters Nos. 25–34, and perhaps 35, were probably addressed (see Introduction, pp. xxxix–xlii, and Commentary). Suckling's acquaintance with her seems
to belong to the years 1635–9, and their intimate relationship to the last two
or three years of that period. The inferential identification of the 'two
Sisters' in this poem is based partly on the aptness of association with Mary
Bulkeley and her sister Anne and partly on its stylistic similarity to Suckling's later work of more certain date (cf., for example, the close parallel
between ll. 1–8 of this poem with ll. 1–6 of 'A Summons to Town' following).
If this poem does indeed refer to Mary and Anne Bulkeley, the printer's copy
may have been provided by Sir John Mennes, who was associated with both
Suckling and the Bulkeleys and may well have provided the copy for the
letters to Mary Bulkeley (see Introduction, p. lxxxiv, and Mennes's letter
to 'Faire Mrs. Anne and Mrs. Mary', Appendix A.iv.6).

ll. 1–8. *Beleev't yong Man*, etc. Cf. 'A Summons to Town', ll. 1–6.

ll. 5–7. *Had the three Goddesses been just as fair*, etc. Cf. 'His Dream', ll. 5–10.

l. 6. [Wanting in all editions.] Hazlitt's conjectural emendation, 'As … and
Aglaura are', is probably right in associating this poem with Suckling's
'Aglaura' (see headnote), but so prosaic a line as 'As Anne and Mary Bulkeley,
past compare' (which I proffer only hypothetically) would more nearly
account for the printer's omission of the entire line (almost certainly because it
included personal names) and better correspond with Suckling's rhyme-words
for 'fair'—'chair' in 'The Wits' (l. 9), 'clear' in 'Loves World' (l. 62), and
'compare' in 'To his Rival I' (l. 22) and 'A Ballade. Upon a Wedding' (l. 3).

ll. 21–2. *This lip, this hand*, etc. Cf. 'The guiltless Inconstant', ll. 11–12.

SECULAR POEMS (1637–1641)

70. [A Summons to Town] (pp. 70–1)

The addressee of this poem, Suckling's only verse epistle, was first identified by the Rev. Alfred Suckling (*Selections*, p. 100 n.) as the 'ever memor-
able' John Hales, fellow of Eton College and something of a 'Socinian' (l. 9);
'though the Oxford rationalists, of whom Falkland, Hales, and Chillingworth
are the best known, may not themselves have been antitrinitarian in theology,
their latitudinarianism may be regarded as a step in the direction of Arianism
and Socinianism' (H. John McLachlan, *Socinianism in Seventeenth-Century England*, 1951, p. 55). Hales, the subject of ll. 95–8 of 'The Wits', was the
protagonist in a debate that may have been an historical catalyst to the
composition of that poem (see Commentary).

ll. 1–6. *Whether these lines* etc. Cf. 'Upon two Sisters', ll. 1–8.

l. 9. *Socinus*. Fausto Paolo Sozzini (1539–1604), an Italian theologian who 'in

1579 passed to Poland where he spent the rest of his life and did much to spread moderate Unitarian doctrines among the upper classes' (*Oxford Dictionary of the Christian Church*, 1963, s.v. 'Socinus'). Suckling himself was something of a 'Socinian' (see *An Account of Religion*, text and Commentary).

l. 10. *Jack Bond*. 'Jack Bond' may be the interlocutor in the dialogue, 'Upon my Lord Brohalls Wedding', which immediately preceded this poem in *FA46*, and also the addressee of Letter No. 52 (see Commentary on both works). A Mrs. Bond, wife of Thomas Bond and perhaps Jack Bond's mother, was one of Aubrey's sources of information about Suckling (*Brief Lives*, ii. 240), and a 'Warrant to John Bond, who is employed as Captain General for the expedition towards the island of Madagascar or St. Lawrence, near the East Indies' is catalogued in *CSPD 1638–9*, p. 623.

l. 14. *Oracles are not yet ceas't*. Cf. Letter No. 38, 'An Answer to a Gentleman', ll. 29–30: 'consider withall that Prophecies are ceas'd'. The cessation of the oracles at the birth of Christ was a matter of common informed belief and not infrequent poetical reference (prominently in Spenser and Milton) in the seventeenth century. The ultimate source of the idea was Plutarch's *De defectu oraculorum*, ch. xvii, which was well known through Philemon Holland's English translation, *Of the Oracles that have ceased to give Answere*, in *The Philosophie, commonlie called, The Morals*, 1603 (esp. pp. 1331–2), and frequent subsequent quotation of Holland by English authors (see C. A. Patrides, 'The Cessation of the Oracles: The History of a Legend', *MLR*, 1965, lx. 500–7).

71. [The Wits] (pp. 71–6)

'The Wits' is one of Suckling's two relatively major and best known poems, and, like the other, 'A Ballade. Upon a Wedding', it introduced a much-imitated minor genre—'the trial for the bays'—into English poetry. It is not original in pointing up the common odds between literary merit and monetary reward, but the wit of expression is very much Suckling's own. 'The Wits' is also important as a fictional-narrative work of literary criticism, expressing Suckling's and many of his contemporaries' views on the proper decorum of lyric poetry; compare, for example, Dudley Lord North's essay, 'Concerning petty Poetry', with which Suckling was probably familiar and apparently sympathetic (cited and discussed in the Commentary on Appendix A.iii.3, pp. 342–3). The rhythm and stanza-form are also unusual for the period: the four-stressed primarily anapestic verse resembles the Old English alliterative metre, and the stanza-form, as James W. Flosdorf has pointed out, is a version of the bob and wheel, consisting of *frons* and *cauda* quatrains joined together as octaves by a one-word bob of one or two syllables (see 'The Poetry of Sir John Suckling: A Study of his Versification, Rhetoric, and Themes', unpubl. diss., University of Rochester, New York, 1960, pp. 54–5).

'The Wits' was written in the late summer of 1637, and there is evidence that it was sung to the King during his hunting expedition to the New Forest in late August and early September of that year (see Introduction, pp. xliv and cii–ciii). On the supposition that Suckling would not have ridiculed Ben Jonson immediately after his death, on 6 August, P. H. Gray has argued that the poem was written before that date (*SP*, 1939, xxxvi. 60–76), but Suckling's long-standing hostility to Jonson and his attacks upon him during his declining years of theatrical failure and illness make the supposition questionable. On the other hand, Suckling's award of the last—mock-angry—word of a participant to his friend Davenant (ll. 103–10) may be pointed, since after a fierce rivalry, which may have begun covertly before Jonson's death, Davenant received the laureate's pension—though not the title—in 1638 (the status of the laureateship in 1637 and its relation to 'The Wits' is discussed by A. R. Benham in *MLQ*, 1945, vi. 21–7). There is no certain evidence of the poem's having been written either before or after 6 August.

There were also other possible historical stimuli to the writing of this 'trial for the bays', least directly in Suckling's extensive personal experiences with litigation and more directly in his reported participation in 'a trial of Skill' in 'Mr. [John] Hales's Chamber at Eaton', in which 'the Judges chose by agreement out of this Learned and Ingenious Assembly, unanimously gave the Preference to Shakespeare' over the Greek and Roman poets (see *Letters and Essays on Several Subjects*, ed. Charles Gildon, 1694, pp. 85–6; Nicholas Rowe's account of the 'trial' is given in full in the present edition, ii. viii). But formal literary antecedents are less uncertain hypothetical sources of 'The Wits' than general experience and anecdotes related long after the events.

Arguing that 'The Wits' was *not* modelled on Trajano Boccalini's *Ragguagli di Parnaso*, P. H. Gray concluded that it belongs 'in theme, though not in form to a more literary tradition than the ballad, to a particular genre of English satire coming down almost continuously from Skelton' (op. cit. above). Still more to the point, Apollo prominently figured in this kind of situation not many years before 'The Wits' was written in 'The Sacrifice of Apollo' (1619), in which Drayton celebrated the familiar gatherings of 'the Tribe of Ben' in the Devil Tavern's 'Apollo Room', for which Jonson himself supplied the name and wrote his 'Leges Conviviales' in 1624 (see *Works*, ed. Herford and Simpson, ix. 294–6). It is surely significant in this connection that Suckling has Apollo himself rebuke Jonson (ll. 25–7). Mr. Beaurline has called my attention to and enlarged upon J. W. Ebsworth's suggestion that 'The Wits' may have been written partly in reaction against 'On the Time-Poets', first printed in *Choyce Drollery*, 1656 (ed. Ebsworth, 1876: poem, p. 5; p. 405 n). In this 'poem', actually an extract from *William Hemminge's Elegy on Randolph's Finger*, c. 1630–2 (ed. G. C. Moore Smith, 1923), the speaker wishes that 'the great Appollo pleased wth Benn/[might] make the odd Number of the Muses ten' (ll. 51–2): and there may have been specific hints in 'he that wrote so byg'

(l. 105; cf. 'The Wits', ll. 13–14) and the importuning—of Puritans—by 'Poettes [that] had noe monye', etc. (ll. 138 ff.; cf. 'The Wits', ll. 115–18). And there are other possible promptings in such 'trials of wit' as the one to which John Taylor the Water-Poet challenged William Fenner on 7 October 1614 (see *Elegy*, ed. Moore Smith, p. 26, n. on l. 107).

But Dr. Johnson is right to speak of 'some stanzas . . . on the choice of a laureate' as belonging to 'a mode of satire . . . first introduced by Suckling' (*Lives of the English Poets*, ed. George Birkbeck Hill, 1905, i. 15), for the fully realized form is clearly Suckling's own invention. 'The Wits' initiated a genre in which, since 1637, 'perhaps every generation of poets has been teazed' (Dr. Johnson), and was followed by many later seventeenth-, eighteenth-, and nineteenth-century imitations, including, for example, poems by (or attributed to) John Wilmot, Earl of Rochester; John Sheffield, first Duke of Buckingham and Normanby; Leigh Hunt; and James Russell Lowell; as well as such anonymous poems as 'The Session of the Poets', 1668 (see George DeForest Lord, ed., *Poems on Affairs of State*, i (1963), 327–37); 'The Session of Lovers', 1687 (*Poems on Affairs of State*, 1703, ii. 156, and various B.M. and Bodl. MSS.); 'The Session of Ladies', 1688 (B.M. and Bodl. MSS.); and *The Trial of Skill: Or, A New Session of the Poets*, 1704, folio (on the genre and the poems that belong to it see Hugh Macdonald, *A Journal from Parnassus*, 1937).

The Participants in the Sessions. A suggestive introduction to some of the historical participants in this fictional literary sessions is Aubrey's description of Lord Falkland's life in the country: 'My lord much lived at Tue, which is a pleasant seat, and about 12 miles from Oxford; his lordship was acquainted with the best witts of that University, and his house was like a Colledge, full of learned men. Mr. William Chillingworth, of Trinity College (afterwards D.D.), was his most intimate and beloved favourite, and was most commonly with my lord; next I may reckon (if not equall) Mr. John Earles of Merton College (who wrote the Characters). . . . For learned gentlemen of the country, his acquaintance was . . . Sir Francis Wenman, of Caswell, in Witney parish; Mr. [George] Sandys, the traveller and translator (who was uncle to my lady Wenman); Ben. Johnson (vide Johnsonus [sic] Virbius, where he haz verses, and 'twas his lordship, Charles Gattaker told me, that gave the name to it); Edmund Waller, esq.; Mr. Thomas Hobbes, and all the excellent of that peaceable time' (*Brief Lives*, i. 151). All the persons named in 'The Wits' and listed below may be found in the *DNB*, and there are full biographical studies of many. Two persons mentioned or alluded to have not been identified: 'Selwin' (ll. 15 and n., 54–6) and 'he That makes God speak so bigge in's Poetry' (ll. 13–14 and n.). The others, with the lines that concern them, are:

15	Berkeley, John, first Baron Berkeley of Stratton (d. 1678)
15, 49–54	Berkeley, Sir William (d. 1677)

33–40	Carew, Thomas (1594 or 1595–1640)
98–102	Cary, Lucius, second Viscount Falkland (1610?–43)
12	Chillingworth, William (1602–44)
41–8, 104	Davenant, Sir William (1606–68)
12	Digby, Sir Kenelm (1603–65)
89–92	Godolphin, Sidney (1610–43)
95–8	Hales, John (1584–1656)
65–72	Henrietta Maria, the Queen (1609–69)
17–32	Jonson, Ben (1572–1637)
57–64	Mathew, Sir Toby (1577–1655)
13	May, Thomas ('Lucans Translator'; 1595–1650)
81–8	Montagu, Walter (1603?–77)
93–4	Murray, William, first Earl of Dysart (1600?–51)
16	Porter, Endymion (1587–1644)
11	Sandys, George (1578–1644)
9	Selden, John (1584–1654)
73–80	Suckling, Sir John (1609–41)
11	Townshend, Aurelian (*fl.* 1601–43)
16	Vaughan, Sir John (1603–74)
15	Waller, Edmund (1606–87)
10	Wenman, Sir Francis (*post* 1596–? *fl.* 1615–40)

Text. There are nine important mid seventeenth-century variant texts (*P*, a tenth, is fragmentary and obviously derivative). Seven are fully substantive (*FA46* and MSS.); *FA48*, primarily from *FA46* but containing variant readings of non-compositorial origin, is partly substantive (see Introduction, p. xcvii); *MD*, though from *FA48*, contains a few interesting but probably editorial departures from its model. None of the manuscripts is holograph or has external evidence of authority, though one, *Cran6*, has close family associations (see Introduction, pp. cii–ciii). All these texts are described, with bibliographical annotations, by L. A. Beaurline in 'An Editorial Experiment: Suckling's *A Sessions of the Poets*', a detailed, thoughtful, and provocative study of the variant texts and their inferential genetic relationships (*SB*, 1963, xvi. 43–60). Beaurline and I differ chiefly in details of method and choice of copy-text; between the ten substantive readings in which our texts differ, there is in most cases little to choose. It therefore seems superfluous to set out detailed alternatives to his tables and diagrams, and I have confined myself to a summary of my conclusions from a study of the evidence and to comments on a few individual problems.

A most important kind of directional evidence is the graphic pattern manifested or implied in the extant variant texts. The original pattern must have involved a division into octaves (ll. 89–94 a sestain by default), with the two quatrains of each joined by a single word placed between quatrains, because such a pattern alone will account for the variant patterns and the common omission of words inferentially intended to be suspended. With slight variations, *Harv7* and *M3* (numbered in octaves) have the original pattern. *Cor* and *Cran6* are uniformly divided into octaves without suspended words between quatrains (*Cor* has an erroneous grouping of octaves and sestain thus: ll. 89–96, 97–104, 105–10; see present text). *FA46* and *Hunt* are mixed, having about half octaves-with-suspensions and half separate quatrains (so numbered in *Hunt*, which erroneously groups ll. 93–4 with 95–8). *EP53* is uniformly divided into quatrains and has no suspended words.

Of the fifteen words apparently intended to be suspended, *M3* has all but one, omitting 'Then' at l. 92+. *Harv7* omits none of the words but fails to suspend at ll. 28+, 36+, and 114+. *FA46* has suspended words at ll. 4+ through 44+, and 98+ (seven); it omits the words of ll. 52+, 92+, and 106+. *Hunt* has suspended words at ll. 12+ through 60+ (seven), omitting the word at l. 92+. Of the manuscripts that have no suspended words, *EP53* omits none of the words; *Cor* omits two words (ll. 12+ and 36+); and *Cran6* has unique variants at ll. 52+ and 92+.

As purely physical evidence of the mechanical workings of scribes and compositors, these differences have special value: they suggest probable close genetic relationships, through a shared intermediate ancestor, between *Cor* and *Cran6*; *EP53*, *FA46*, and *Hunt*; and *Harv7* and *M3*. *Harv7* and *M3* would seem most faithfully to reflect the graphic characteristics of the hypothetical 'original', and the relationships suggested by the graphic pattern are supported by most of the other textual evidence. That all seven fully substantive texts are terminal is demonstrated by the unique variants they contain, in the following numbers (of a total of 146): *Cor* (25), *Cran6* (52), *EP53* (16), *FA46* (17), *Harv7* (14), *Hunt* (11), and *M3* (11). Though Beaurline's counts (in 'Experiment', p. 48) are substantially higher (because I excluded accidental and semi-substantive variants and treated the vagaries of the graphic pattern as a separate class), we statistically agree on the relative divergence of *Cran6* and *M3* and disagree insignificantly over *Cor*, *EP53*, and *Harv7*; we disagree more substantially only over *FA46* and *Hunt*. Since nearly all the unique variants are directional and manifestly corrupt, all extant witnesses must be regarded as descendants of a lost original.

Just as the number of unique variants is prima facie evidence of relative textual reliability, so to a lesser extent is the number of times in which a witness reads with the majority, when all textual states are terminal. In the total number of twenty-four variants in which two or three witnesses agree against the rest, the witnesses agree with the majority—in order of decreasing number—as follows: *M3* (21), *FA46* (19), *EP53* (18), *Hunt* (16), *Cor* (14), *Harv7* (14), and *Cran6* (12). On the other hand, the graphic pattern, a collective variant of great directional significance, substantially alters the relative authority apparent in the witnesses between the two extremes. The genetic hypothesis that seems to me best to account for the textual evidence would be expressed, in terms of Greg's formularies (in *The Calculus of Variants*), as '(x) *A*ᶜ {[*Cran6 Cor*] *M3*} {*Harv7* [*FA46* (*EP53 Hunt*)]}'; which means that *M3* and *Harv7* stand closest to the hypothetical 'original' on separate lines of descent, with *Cran6* and *Cor* sharing an intermediate ancestor below but in the same line of descent as *M3*, and with *FA46* standing alone on the line of descent below *Harv7*, and *EP53* and *Hunt* sharing an intermediate ancestor that stands below the immediate ancestor of *FA46*.

The position of *M3* in relation to the original is in no doubt, owing to its general substantive superiority over all the other witnesses. The position of *Harv7* is due partly to its authoritative graphic pattern and title (see note below), partly to the fact that where it differs from *M3* it tends to agree with *FA46*, *EP53*, or *Hunt*, or all three. At the same time, the distribution of its readings is so varied as to suggest contamination, and there is some evidence of sophistication (as in supplying 'Sʳ:' as an interlineal word in l. 56+ and in its 'correction' in l. 114, discussed below); its position is rather less assured than *M3*'s, and its hypothetically high position in its line of descent should not be regarded as evidence of authority equal to that of *M3*.

Of the seventeen variants—recorded in the critical apparatus—in which two witnesses share one reading and the rest another, twelve in general support the hypothesis suggested above; the five that do not would appear to be coincidental groupings (in four of these, *Harv7* agrees twice with *FA46*, once with *EP53*, and once with *Hunt*). Of the seven variants—recorded in the critical apparatus—in which three witnesses share one reading, the other four another, one fully supports the hypothesis (*Σ*: *Cor*, *Cran6*, *M3*); five variants support it in part (*Σ*: *Cran6*, *FA46*, *Harv7*; *Σ*: *Cor*+*Cran6* once with *Harv7* and once with *Hunt*; and *Σ*: *Harv7*+*M3* once with *Cor* and once with *Cran6*); and one variant is in conflict (*Σ*: *Cor*, *Harv7*, *Hunt*).

In substantive readings of relative importance, eight complex variants, in each of which there are three variant readings, must be resolved as cruxes; at the same time they test the hypothesis. These variants are to be found in the title and in ll. 16, 29, 53, 88, the suspended word at l. 92+, the placing of ll. 93–4, and l. 114. The variant in l. 114—'writ in great' *Σ*+*Harv7(u)*: 'writ[t]en great' *Cran6*, *Harv7(c)*: 'writ' *Hunt*—is a good example of a case where statistical distribution can lead to erroneous genealogical inferences and consequent editorial conclusions at the same time as the evidence leaves no doubt whatever of the authoritative reading, 'writ in great': six of seven witnesses confirm both 'writ' and 'great', which necessarily entails the authority of 'in'; the number of *Cran6*'s unique variants weakens its over-all authority, and only *Harv7*'s 'corrected' reading ('writen')—the uncorrected reading, 'writ in', being likely to reflect the copy—'supports' *Cran6*'s reading. Here the implications of the textual evidence support the probability of an otherwise well-founded inference (see note on l. 114 below).

The distribution of readings in ll. 16 ('and . . . with', etc.) and 53 ('sullenly', etc.) are perfectly consistent with the hypothesis, and the resolution that both the hypothesis and the critical demands of context would suggest is the same. The varied placing of ll. 93–4 supports the hypothesis to a slightly lesser extent. These lines were inferentially intended to form a single (anomalous) stanza with ll. 89–92; the pattern is clearly discernible in *Cor, Cran6, Harv7,* and *M3,* in all of which the couplet is attached more closely to the preceding than to the following quatrain (*Cor* alone makes an octave of ll. 89–96 and continues conspicuously to misdivide thereafter). *EP53* (in quatrains) ambiguously places the lines as a couplet midway between two quatrains, and *FA46* and *Hunt* apparently reflect the characteristics of the intermediate ancestor of all three by placing ll. 93–4 closer to the following than to the preceding quatrain (in *Hunt* ll. 93–8 are numbered as a stanza). The variants in ll. 29 and 92+ are of intermediate directionality. In l. 29, five witnesses read 'thought it not' and two (*Cor* and *Cran6*) read 'did not think'; the added 'so' in *Hunt* and *M3* would appear to be unoriginal, because no other witness has it and it could easily have arisen independently by anticipation of the following line, 'To discontent *so* ancient a wit'. In l. 92+ the omission of the suspended word in *FA46, Hunt,* and *M3* is negative evidence; the uniqueness of 'Next' in the unreliable *Cran6,* and the presence of 'Then' in the not closely related *Cor, EP53,* and *Harv7,* support the authority of 'Then', though the distribution is genetically neutral. The same kind of textual situation obtains with the title: *Cor, Cran6,* and *EP53* have none; *FA46* has 'A Sessions of the Poets'; and *Harv7, Hunt,* and *M3* have the almost certainly authoritative 'The Wits'.

Finally, the most difficult of these variants is that in l. 88, where *EP53, Hunt,* and *FA46* (which, according to the hypothesis, constitute a 'subfamily') read 'silence'; *Cor* and *Cran6* (hypothetically sharing an ancestor), along with *Harv7* (not closely related to them), read 'silent'; and *M3* reads 'silene'. Beaurline: '*Silent* may be the original reading because it involves more complicated grammar; but did M [*M3*] mean to put a *t* instead of an *e* or did his copy read *silence* and he left out the *c*? It cannot be determined either way. The probabilities favour *silent* as the harder reading' ('Experiment', p. 54). In my view, a 'c' is more likely to have been omitted than a perfectly clear 'e' to have been miswritten for 't'; I am also not persuaded that an adjective modifying a conventionally elliptical 'he' is the harder reading. I have preferred 'silence', chiefly because of the apparent directionality of 'silene' but also on the literary grounds that a personified silence's 'confessing' for a 'modest Mounsier' seems less likely than 'silent' to be corrupt or sophisticated.

In 'The Wits', as commonly, the most vexed variants for an editor are those of least significance for a critical reader. These are variants of the order of, for example, *in's/i'th'/in th'/in the* (l. 74) and *it was/that 'twas/that it was* (l. 107).

From the six such variants, in ll. 58, 59, 74, 80, 92, and 107, the reading of the present text has been chosen in accordance with the demands of context and parallel usages in this poem and elsewhere in Suckling's works, in the light of the genealogical implications of the other textual evidence (the variant in l. 107 is discussed in a note).

Beaurline based his text on *Harv7*, because 'as a messy and careless copy' it 'is less likely to have deliberate improvements by a scribe than a highly professional transcript', which the 'generally cleaned up' *M3* more nearly resembles, and because in its accidentals it 'agrees more with Suckling's known habits . . . by a ratio of forty-eight to twenty-one' ('Experiment', p. 56). His differs from the present text in ten substantive or semi-substantive readings (noted in the critical apparatus), in ll. 17, 29, 35, 46, 47, 68, 76, 88, 105, and 114. Of course, all manuscripts contain more 'authorial' (because older) spellings than contemporary printed texts, and invariably more scribal eccentricities alien to the author, as well. Like those of *Aglaura*, 1638, which was published by Suckling himself, the accidentals of *FA46* are those of comparatively sound contemporary currency and require little emendation; moreover, the punctuation, though probably by coincidence, manifests an authorial characteristic in its use of parentheses (none of the manuscripts has adequate punctuation, and Beaurline's is mainly that of *FA46*).

FA46 is a seventeenth-century-printer's text containing a number of errors, but it seems to me that its accidentals are closer to a text that the author would have acknowledged as authoritative than those of a careless transcript, and I have accordingly adopted it as copy-text. I have of course incorporated the presumably authorial graphic pattern and emended the readings wherever the textual evidence shows *FA46* to be in error.

Title. The title in *FA46*, 'A Sessions of the Poets', is unique, inaccurate (some of the participants are not 'poets'), readily suggested by 'A Sessions', 'Apollo', and 'The Laurel', in ll. 1–3, and therefore almost certainly editorial. Of the other six substantive texts, three have 'The Wits' and three want a title. The distribution is not strictly genealogical (though both *Cor* and *Cran6*, which apparently share an ancestor, omit), and omissions are more likely to arise fortuitously than identical titles are. Since *Harv7* and *M3*, the texts inferentially closest to the hypothetical original, and *Hunt* have 'The Wits', that title seems almost certainly authorial. Moreover, the poem is referred to in a letter nearly contemporary with its first public appearance as a 'Ballad made of the Wits' (George Garrard to the Earl of Strafford; see Introduction, p. xliv); 'A Sessions of Wit' in *Merry Drollery*, 1661, whose text is from *FA48*, supports 'The Wits' as a circulating title; and it is suggestive that Davenant's play, *The Wits*, was printed in 1636, the year before the poem was written.

Arrangement of Stanzas and Suspensions. To complete a pattern defective in *FA46*, interlinear words at ll. 60+, 76+, 84+, and 114+ have been transposed from the following lines, and, at ll. 52+, 68+, 92+, and 106+, supplied from other witnesses. The sense of the poem argues for a structure based on octaves, and the graphic pattern of a number of the witnesses proves that octaves with single words suspended between their quatrains in a form of bob and wheel was the original design (see detailed comments in the note on *Text* above). Herbert Berry suggests that Suckling 'must have bent himself to a rigid pattern of this kind because of the demands of the music he had in mind' (*Sir John Suckling's Poems and Letters from Manuscript*, 1960, p. 38). Although *FA46*'s omissions of suspended words suggest either defective copy or compositorial inattention to copy, it is interesting that the pattern of suspensions is abandoned on p. 8 (sig. A4ᵛ; it is resumed only once, on p. 10, sig. A5ᵛ): on p. 9 a quatrain was omitted, almost certainly deliberately, that would have unbalanced the pattern (see note on ll. 68+–72).

l. 1. *Sessions*. All the substantive witnesses read 'Sessions' except *Cran6* and *FA46*, which has a supporting 'Sessions' in its unique and probably editorial title. Cf. *Brennoralt*, I. iii. 23–4 ('A Candidate or so, 'gainst the next Sessions'). *Session* denotes only 'a sitting', but *Sessions* 'a trial'.

l. 9. *Selden*. The persons referred to by surname are identified in an alphabetical list above.

l. 10. *Wenman*. Thompson, citing Aubrey, first identified 'Weniman' (*FA46*), or 'Wainman' (*FA48*), as Sir Francis Wenman 'of Caswell, in Witney parish' (p. 359; see note on the participants above). Sir Francis was the son of Sir Richard, first Viscount Wenman (1573–1640), and younger brother of Sir Richard, the second Viscount (1596–1665).

l. 13. *Lucans Translator*. Thomas May.

ll. 13–14. *he That makes God speak so bigge in's Poetry*. Cf. 'Rounce Roble hoble, he that wrote so byg'—referring to Richard Stanyhurst (1547–1618) —in *William Hemminge's Elegy on Randolph's Finger* (l. 105), possibly a partial source of 'The Wits' (see headnote). No satisfactory identification of the person referred to here has been proposed. Hazlitt suggested Francis Quarles, and A. R. Benham proposed George Wither or Phineas Fletcher (*MLQ*, 1945, vi. 23).

l. 15. *Selwin*. Thompson: 'This person . . . has left no traces which make identification certain—probably one of the Selwyns of Matson, near Gloucester, and an ancestor of Horace Walpole's witty friend, George Selwyn' (p. 361).

Berkeleys both the brothers. First identified as William and John Berkeley by R. C. Bald (see *MLN*, 1943, lviii. 550–1; cf. ll. 49–53). The odd spelling 'Bartlet[t]', is found in five of the seven fully substantive witnesses, suggesting that it was a predominant contemporary if not authorial spelling.

l. 17. *good old Ben*. Ben Jonson died on 6 August 1637, at about the same time 'The Wits' was written (see headnote).

l. 20. *his were call'd Works, where others were but Plaies.* Jonson's 'presumption' (cf. l. 26) in publishing a collection of his plays, as no one had ever done before, aroused the indignation of many lesser playwrights and poets, and for years after the Folio *Workes of Beniamin Jonson*, 1616, was the object of punning deprecation. In 'To Ben Jonson' (*c.* 1631?), Carew refers to 'Thy labour'd workes' (l. 45); and Peter Whalley, in the life prefixed to his edition of *Jonson's Works*, 1756, i. xlv, notes the epigram, 'Pray tell me, Ben, where does the myst'ry lurk? | What others call a Play you call a work?', with the reply, 'The author's friend thus for the author says; | Ben's plays are works, when others works are plays.'

l. 32. *made him mine host of his own new Inne.* A pointed reference to Jonson's play, *The New Inn*, which failed so badly on its first production in January 1628/9 that it was not heard to the conclusion, prompting the bitter 'Ode to Himself' and an extraordinary description on the title-page of the 1631 Octavo: 'A Comœdy. As it was neuer acted, but most negligently play'd, by some, the Kings Seruants. And more squeamishly beheld, and censured by others, the Kings Subiects. 1629. Now, at last, set at liberty to the Readers. . . .'

ll. 35–6. *His Muse was hard bound, and th'issue of 's brain | Was seldom brought forth but with trouble and pain.* Cf. Dudley Lord North, 'Concerning petty Poetry', in *A Forest of Varieties*, 1645, p. 5: 'Strong lines may be drawne on with Cartropes, but the fairest have generally an easie birth. It is rare for any thing to be well and hardly performed' (for Suckling's association with North and this essay, see Appendix A.iii.3, text and Commentary). Whether or not Suckling influenced or was influenced by North, the parallel supports 'hard bound' and clarifies the range of meaning in the passage.

l. 39. *that his Grace* [the disgrace *Cor*]. The manuscript corruption would appear to be an error of auditory origin, suggesting memorial or dictated transcription. *Cor* is one of the most corrupt of the substantive witnesses (see note on *Text* above).

l. 40. *Cup-bearers* [Sewers *Cran6*] *place.* An example of scribal trivialization: Carew had become Sewer in Ordinary to Charles I probably in 1630 (see *Poems*, ed. Rhodes Dunlap, 1949, p. xxxv).

ll. 41–8. *Will. Davenant . . . travelling in France, . . . There was not one Laureat without a nose.* Davenant had 'gott a terrible Clap of a black handsome wench that lay in Axe-yard, Westminster . . . which cost him his nose, with which mischance many witts were too cruelly bold' (Aubrey, *Brief Lives*, i. 205–6), among them Suckling, here, and Richard Brome in *The Court Beggar*, 1640 (see the chapter on 'Suckling's New Strain of Wit' and Brome's satirical treatment of both Suckling and Davenant in R. J. Kaufmann, *Richard Brome: Caroline Playwright*, 1961, pp. 151–68). 'Travelling in France' may be either an extension or itself a current euphemism for the contraction of syphilis by the usual means (cf. the certainly current euphemism for syphilis, 'French crown, goods or gout', q.v. in *A Dictionary of Slang and Unconventional English*, ed. Eric Partridge, 5th ed., 1961). Davenant's lost nose became virtually his biographical emblem (see Alfred Harbage, *Sir William Davenant*, 1935, pp. 44–7).

l. 50. *But first they would see how his snow would sell.* R. C. Bald suggests that this may refer, if not to a contemporary joke intelligible even then only in Court circles, 'to the frigidity, or purity, of *The Lost Lady*, which . . . had probably been read and discussed among Berkeley's friends, but had yet to stand the test of actual performance' (*MLN*, 1943, lviii. 551).

l. 53. *Sullenly.* On the distributional evidence, 'Sullenly', also the 'strongest' of the alternatives, is probably original (see note on *Text* above).

ll. 57–8. *Toby Mathew . . . Was busily whispering some-body i'th'ear.* ' 'Twas his Custom always to be whispering in Company' (Anthony Wood, *Athenæ Oxonienses*, ed. Phillip Bliss, iii (1817), 403, n. 6).

ll. 60–4. *But Sir, you may thank my Lady Carlile for't; For Had not her Character furnisht you out* etc. Mathew's 'Character of the Most Excellent Lady, Lucy Countess of Carliele', first printed in *A Collection of Letters, Made by Sr Tobie Mathews K^t*, 1660, was circulating in 1636. Suckling, who may at one time have been on friendly terms with Mathew, though never with Lady Carlisle, appears to have interpreted the Character as a gesture of sycophantic self-seeking (on Suckling's relationship with Mathew—who is either the fictional speaker or the author of 'The Answer' to 'The constant Lover'—see 'The Answer', text and Commentary; and for Lady Carlisle see 'Upon my Lady Carliles walking in Hampton-Court garden', text and Commentary).

ll. 68+–72. *This Made a dispute;* etc. This quatrain is found in every substantive text except *FA46* (the 'manuscript' accidentals in *FA48* perhaps suggest high genuine or putative authority for the source of *FA48*'s non-editorial alterations). It was probably omitted deliberately from the first edition of *Fragmenta Aurea* because it was indecently insulting to the Queen, and it may have been excised by the 'correctors of the press' at the time of licensing and restored surreptitiously in the second edition, 1648 (all that was required for a 'new licence' to reprint was 'the presenting of two printed copies of the book to be reprinted'; see W. W. Greg, *Some Aspects and Problems of London Publishing between 1550 and 1650*, 1956, p. 13).

l. 72. *fooling.* 'A certain clownish kind of raillery' as practiced by '*un mauvais buffon*' (Lisideius in Dryden's *Essay of Dramatic Poesy*), but the word also has a secondary sexual sense, which complements that of 'gratify' (l. 70). Cf. *Aglaura*, II. v. 20–3: 'let's goe on the Queens side and foole a little', etc.

ll. 81, 84. *Wat Montague . . . his own Pastoral. The Shepheard's Paradise*, first printed in 1659 but acted before Charles I by the Queen and her Maids of Honour on 8 January 1632/3.

l. 88. *silence* [silent *Cor*, *Cran6*, *Harv7*: silene *M3*]. The textual evidence is ambiguous; I have retained *FA46*'s 'silence' on the apparent directional suggestion of *M3*'s 'silene', and because a personified silence's 'confessing' for a 'modest Mounsier' seems to me less likely than 'silent' to be corrupt or sophisticated.

l. 93. *Murrey*. Probably William Murray, Gentleman of the Bedchamber and later first Earl of Dysart, to whom Suckling refers in Letter No. 19, ll. 11 and 18, where the name is spelt with an 'e', as here. In Bodl. MS. Malone 13, a poem beginning 'Come hether the merryest of all the land | to day the Beare att the Bridge foote is bayted', subscribed 'W Murrey' (f. 38ᵛ), is followed by an answer, subscribed 'Peter Apsley', which begins 'Though Murray bee vndoubtedly his Countryes Cheifest Witt' (f. 41). Both poems are printed with the same ascriptions in *Wit Restor'd*, 1658, pp. 16 ff.

l. 96. *keep such a coil*. A proverbial phrase (Tilley C 505: 1571).

l. 103. *an Alderman*. Almost certainly a 'typical' rather than particular Alderman as an appropriately ironical choice for the crown of wit (cf. the Alderman of Letters Nos. 36–7).

ll. 107–8. *that 'twas the best signe | Of good store of wit to have good store of coyn* [that the best signe | Of good store of wit's to have good store of coyn *FA46*]. In *FA46* 'wit's' is plainly an unauthoritative syntactical compensation for an omission in its source of '[i]twas', which is found in all the other substantive witnesses; the 'that' in *FA46* (l. 107) may have stood in its copy, but it could also have been editorially supplied, as an obvious metrical justification, to a defective copy-line that read '[He] Openly declared the best signe'.

'He that is wise is rich' is of course proverbial (Tilley W 534: *c.* 1525), and an idea of doubtless greater antiquity than Ovid's 'Ingenium quondam fuerat pretiosius auro; | at nunc barbaries grandis habere nihil' (*Amores*, III. viii. 3–4). As Herford and Simpson note (*Works*, ix. 544), Ovid is the source of the following lines by Jonson, which Suckling echoes in this passage: 'The time was once, when wit drown'd wealth: but now, | Your onely barbarisme is t'haue wit, and want. | No matter now in vertue who excells, | He, that hath coine, hath all perfection else' (*Poetaster*, I. ii. 253–6). The same idea is expressed in *The Goblins*, I. iii. 60–1 and IV. iv. 60–2.

l. 107. *that 'twas*. A vexed, because ambiguous, if trivial variant. Because of other variants in the line of its text (see critical apparatus), *FA46* affords only partial evidence in support of 'that' as original; but the only evidence against 'that' comes from *Cor* and *Cran6*, which have reduced authority (see note on *Text*), and *EP53*, which alone does not have it of those witnesses to which it is closely related. *M3* and *Harv7*, the two texts inferentially closest to the lost original, along with *Hunt*, support ''twas', and here phonetic and metrical 'difficulty' support its originality: the contraction initiates the utterance of a *sententia* in indirect discourse which 'that 'twas' does, and 'that it was' does not, appropriately emphasize.

l. 114. *writ in great*. The evidence establishing this as the original reading is discussed in the note on *Text* above; 'writ in great' is a contemporary idiom that Suckling also uses in Letter No. 23, ll. 59–60 (see *OED*, s.v. 'Great').

l. 115. *clear'd* [cheer'd *EP53, Hunt, FA48, Haz, Th*]. Cf. *The Sad One*, IV. vi. 10: 'Brother, clear up'.

72. To his much honoured, the Lord Lepington, upon his Translation of Malvezzi his Romulus and Tarquin (pp. 76–7)

Henry Carey, Lord Lepington and later second Earl of Monmouth (12 April 1639), was related to Suckling by his marriage to Suckling's cousin, Martha Cranfield, to whom Letter No. 22 is addressed (q.v., text and Commentary). In 1635 Suckling seems to have taken some part in the arrangements for the marriage of their daughter, Anne, and he was on close terms with the family for most of his life (see Introduction, 'Life' *passim*).

In the first edition of Lord Lepington's ₁translation (1637), no commendatory poems were included, but in the second (1638) Suckling's poem was accompanied by others written by Thomas Carew, William Davenant, Aurelian Townshend, and Sir Francis Wortley. The imprimatur is dated 22 January 1637.

73. To my Friend Will. Davenant; upon his Poem of Madagascar (p. 78)

The imprimatur of this book is dated 26 February 1637. *Madagascar* had a good deal to do with the grant to Davenant of the pension and status of laureate on 16 December 1638, and, as Alfred Harbage describes it, 'in a sense this is a "state" poem. Prince Rupert, whom Davenant had entertained in his *Triumphs of the Prince D'Amour*, had remained in England, and his presence had suggested a project whereby he was to sail forth and conquer Madagascar. . . . Davenant had viewed this gallant design not practically but poetically, and at its height he had composed the heroic verses in which his disembodied spirit hovers over the island and views the glories of Rupert during its conquest' (*Sir William Davenant*, 1935, pp. 64–5). The poem of the title is accompanied in the volume by a number of other poems, to the Queen, to court dignitaries, to his personal friends, and to his patrons, Endymion Porter and Henry Jermyn.

There is a close parallel to this poem in the Epilogue to the tragi-comic version of *Aglaura*, written at approximately the same time.

74. On his other Poems (p. 78)

ll. 3–4. *since the great Lord of it (Donne)* etc. Cf. Carew's 'Elegie upon the death of Dr. John Donne', ll. 47–50 and, especially, 95–6: 'Here lies a King, that rul'd as hee thought fit | The universall Monarchy of wit.'

75. An Answer to some Verses made in his praise (pp. 78–9)

Two books are known to have been dedicated to Suckling, and several commendatory poems were addressed to him posthumously (see Introduction, p. xlv, and Appendix A.ii.1–3 and A.iii.1, 3), but this poem readily associates itself with none of them, and it is perhaps as likely that it is a literary exercise as that it is an actual reply to lost commendatory verses. It is, of course, generically akin, as the recipient's quasi-public utterance, to the commendatory poem; it is also idiomatically similar to (especially Suckling's) prologues and epilogues to the plays (see note on ll. 9–10 below). The parallels in the plays suggest that the poem belongs to the mid 1630s.

l. 5. *Blind Homer's Muse.* Cf. *The Goblins*, IV. v. 20–2.

ll. 9–10. *Gods and Kings/things.* Cf. *Aglaura*, v(c), 'Prologue to the Court', ll. 21–2.

ll. 11–12. *But you of Nothing;* etc. The force of 'Nothing' is greater than might be recognized in passing: see ' "Nothing is but what is not": Solutions to the Problem of Nothing' in Rosalie L. Colie, *Paradoxia Epidemica*, 1966, pp. 219–51.

l. 16. *He shews himself most Poet, that most feigns.* A hyperbolic and mildly ironical extension of the traditional notion that 'Painters (Travelers) and poets have leave to lie' (Tilley P 28: 1586) and, paradoxically, of Sidney's assertion, in *An Apology for Poetry*, that 'the poet nothing affirmeth' (cf. l. 11), in refutation of the view of poets as liars.

l. 19. *Barbed Steed.* There are 'barbed steeds' in *Richard II*, III. ii. 117, and *Richard III*, I. i. 10, as doubtless in countless extra-Shakespearian places.

l. 21. *Bat Jewels Jade.* The common and customarily pejorative 'jade' is also used by Suckling in *Aglaura*, I. iv. 16–20, and 'Bat Jewel' is probably akin, as rustic type, to 'lusty Roger' and 'little George' (cf. 'A Ballade. Upon a Wedding', ll. 22–3).

76. A Ballade. Upon a Wedding (pp. 79–84)

Like 'The Wits', the other of Suckling's two relatively major poems, 'A Ballade' also initiated a minor genre, that of the 'rusticated epithalamion', a gently burlesqued version of the traditional pastoral epithalamion in which a realistically rural speaker describes a real city wedding in a narrative drama-tic-monologue that employs images of farm and field and expresses attitudes rooted in country matters (Suckling's speaker may be regarded as a West Country man, on the suggestion of several variants; see l. 12, text, critical apparatus, and note). 'A Ballade' has the effect of simultaneously burlesquing a formal wedding and the formal epithalamion. Though none could strictly be regarded as a source, several works might have afforded suggestions for 'A Ballade', notably the epistolary genre of 'the letter of the rustic wooer' inaugurated by Nicholas Breton, and Breton's 'A Letter to laugh at, after the old fashion of loue, to a Maide' and 'Roger, to Margery his sweete-heart' with 'Her answere' (*A Poste with a Packet of Madde Letters, The first part*, 1605, sigg. F2r+v and G2r+v; Letters Nos. 51–3 belong to genres inaugurated or employed by Breton, who may be directly echoed in two of them: see head-note on No. 51(*a*)). Closer in time to the date of 'A Ballade' (see below) is Thomas Randolph's 'The milk-maids Epithalamium' (*Poems*, ed. G. Thorn-Drury, 1929, pp. 117–18); it was first printed in 1638, but Randolph's poems circulated widely in manuscript both before and after his death on 17 March 1634/5.

The prosody of Suckling's modified ballad-stanza (sestains of 2–1–2–1 iambic-tetrameter and trimeter lines, rhyming *aabccb*) closely accords with the diction and the identity of the speaker, but it is doubtful whether the stanza itself is of his invention. Carew uses—with very different effect—a similar verse-form in 'An Hymeneall Song on the Nuptials of the Lady Anne Wentworth, and the Lord Lovelace', which consists of four loose units of three linked tercets each, the first two rhymed and metred like Suckling's, the third a triplet. 'A Ballade' may also be related to Carew's poem in occasion (see below).

'A Ballade' was certainly written before mid 1639, and quite possibly in mid 1638 in connection with the marriage of John Lord Lovelace, as Herbert Berry has persuasively argued (see *Sir John Suckling's Poems and Letters from Manuscript*, 1960, pp. 11–18). It therefore antedates, by approximately a year and a half, the marriage between Roger Boyle, Lord Broghill, and Lady Margaret Howard on 27 January 1640/1, with which it has been commonly associated since the eighteenth century and in connection with which Suck-ling did write 'Upon my Lord Brohalls Wedding'. Lord Broghill's wedding was first suggested as occasion in the *Memoir* accompanying *A Collection of State Letters of the Right Honourable Roger Boyle*, 1742 (p. 49), by his early biographer and sometime chaplain, Thomas Morrice, who was 'born eight years after the wedding and ordained only five years before Orrery died' (Berry, pp. 15–16), and who, according to the preface to the *Memoir*, 'regards neither dates, nor order of time, but jumbles circumstances together as they occurred to his remembrance' (*Collection*, p. viii). This association can scarcely be regarded as authoritative.

The pair of lampoons, 'Upon Sir John Suckling's hundred horse' and 'Sir John Suckling's Answer', which were written between January and June 1639, provide a *terminus ad quem* for 'A Ballade' that dissociates it from Lord Brog-hill's wedding: they employ the stanza of 'A Ballade' and paraphrase its first line ('I tell thee Jack thou'st given the King' and 'I tell thee foole who e're thou be') in a mocking attack upon Suckling's preparations for the First Bishop's War that must postdate 'A Ballade' itself. A *terminus a quo* of 1637 or after is strongly suggested by the stylistic evidence. The 'depersonaliza-tion' and quasi-dramatic manner—quite different from the first-person poeti-cal Characters, 'A Barber', 'A Soldier', etc., of early composition—readily associate it with the years of Suckling's completed plays (1637-40) and 'Upon my Lord Brohalls Wedding' (1641); the fluency of diction and prosody is characteristic of his relatively mature manner in datable poems and in the plays other than the early *The Sad One*; and the closest extended parallel passages are to be found in *The Goblins* (*c.* 1639) and *Brennoralt* (*c.* 1640).

The stylistic evidence also supports the evidence, less certain than the lampoons' but very persuasive, that 'A Ballade' was written to celebrate, in its whimsical way, the wedding of John Lord Lovelace and Lady Anne Went-worth on 11 July 1638 (*Allegations for Marriage Licences Issued by the Bishop of London*, ed. J. L. Chester and G. J. Armytage, 1887, p. 236). In *The Works of Richard Lovelace*, 1864 (p. xxxii), Hazlitt approached this association by conjecturally identifying the 'Dick' of the 'Ballade' with Richard Lovelace, and in 1868 he suggested it, having found in *H17*—the chief external evidence —the title 'On the Marriage of the Lord Louelace' (see *N&Q*, 4th ser. ii. 599; in his first edition of *Suckling's Works*, 1874, he rejected Lord Lovelace's wedding in favour of Lord Broghill's: see i. 42, n. 1). In his edition of *The Poems of Richard Lovelace*, 1930, C. H. Wilkinson concluded that 'it is far more probable that it ["A Ballade"] was not written for any wedding and that its connexion with Richard Lovelace is merely based on an inaccurate guess' (pp. xxiii–xxiv).

The identification of 'Dick' as Richard Lovelace is certainly questionable, but the association of 'A Ballade' with Lord Lovelace is less so. The title in Harleian MS. 6917 gains authority from the manuscript's generally careful preparation and from its containing poems chiefly of the late 1630s; it is supported by the same association in *An Antidote Against Melancholy*, 1661, where 'Sir John Sucklins Ballad on the Ld. L. Wedding' occurs as an index-entry (sig. A2^v, No. 16), suggesting at the least a widely recognized con-nection (the text of 'A Ballade' in *An Antidote* follows *FA48*, but the title there reflects the influence of *Wits Recreations Refined*, or *Recreations for Ingenious Head-peeces*, 1650, 1654: 'A Ballade: A Discourse between two Country-men'). The rest of the evidence for the association—discussed in detail by Berry (pp. 11-18)—is inferential and consists in points of consonance between 'A Ballade' and Lord Lovelace's wedding. It is not certain that 'A Ballade' was written specifically for Lord Lovelace's wedding, but the poem takes on an added dimension of historical charm in its perhaps having celebrated an elaborate wedding of members of the peerage by means of a poetical *reductio ad rusticum*.

The early and lasting popularity of 'A Ballade' is attested by its frequent reprinting in the seventeenth century as well as by numerous imitations. Norman Ault notes its occurrence in seventeen poetical miscellanies printed between 1650 and 1713 (see *Seventeenth Century Lyrics*, 2nd ed., 1950, p. 500, note on p. 158), and some of the imitations are to be found in: R[obert] B[aron], *Pocula Castalia*, 1650, p. 66; *Wits Interpreter*, 1655, p. 171; R. Fletcher, *Ex Otio Negotium*, 1656, p. 226; *An Antidote Against Melancholy*, 1661, pp. 49, 50; *Merry Drollery*, 1661, pp. 45 and 46, and 1670, p. 317; *Rump Songs*, second part, 1662, pp. 189–92; [John Raymund], *Folly in Print, or A Book of Rhymes*, 1667, p. 116; *The New Academy of Complements*, 1669, p. 239; *Wit at a Venture: or, Clio's Privy-Garden*, 1674, p. 59; N[athaniel] T[hompson], *A Choice Collection of 120 Loyal Songs*, 1684, pp. 130, 243 (also in later editions); *Pills to Purge Melancholy*, 1699, p. 81; *Poems on Affairs of State*, 1704, iii. 57; *Wit and Mirth, or Pills to Purge Melancholy*, 1714, pp. 183, 243, and 1720, pp. 282, 381; and *The Bath Teazers, or a Comical Description of the Diversions of the Bath* [London, 1715?], single-sheet folio. Another imitation, 'The Chequer Inn', which appears in numerous manuscript miscellanies, has been printed as an unauthenticated poem by Marvell, though it has also been attributed to Henry Savile (see *Marvell's Poems and Letters*, ed. H. M. Margoliouth, 1952, i. 312; *Poems on Affairs of State*, vol. i, ed. George DeForest Lord, 1963, pp. 252–61; and *Andrew Marvell: Complete Poetry*, ed. Lord, 1968, pp. xxxi–xxxii).

'A Ballade' was also sung. There is a tune in *Dx42*, and John Murray Gibbon prints another 'tune which was favoured by many other ballad writers during the Great Rebellion' to which 'A Ballade' was sung (see *The Melody and the Lyric from Chaucer to the Cavaliers*, 1930, pp. 184–5). Whether this or other tunes were first written for 'A Ballade' is uncertain, but 'A Ballade' was the poem with which the tunes were popularly associated, for many other poems are specified to be sung 'to the tune of I tell thee Dick'; see, for example, *Folly in Print*, pp. 8 and 116, and *A Choice Collection,* pp. 130 and 243 (both cited in full above). Another tune is printed in *Wit and Mirth: or Pills to Purge Melancholy*, 1699, 1705, 1707, 1714, and still another in *A Comicall Parly between two Countrymen on sight of a Wedding* [London, 1720?], single-sheet folio.

Text. Of the texts of 'A Ballade' printed in seventeen printed miscellanies noted by Norman Ault (see above), all are derivative, most of them from editions of *Fragmenta Aurea*. The text in *MD* is of interest in indicating the various provenance of that collection ('The Wits' is from *FA48*, 'A Ballade' from *RP3*), but it has no authority. The manuscript texts in *B*, *F92*, and Bodleian Eng. Misc. c. 292, ff. 108–9ᵛ (eighteenth century) are also derivative. Four substantive texts of the entire poem survive, in *Ash3*, *FA46*, *H17*, and

RP3; there is a fragment of a fifth in *Dx42* (ll. 1–4 only); and *FA48*, which contains non-compositorial departures from *FA46*, is partly substantive. *Ash3* contains two texts, (*a*), f. 292, and (*b*), f. 51, a copy of (*a*). Berry has printed an annotated transcription of *H17* (pp. 11–25), but the evidence of the other manuscripts is here used in the construction of a critical text for the first time.

All four substantive texts are terminal, as is proved by the presence or absence, and the placing, of individual stanzas, which also constitute partial proof of the derivation of *Ash3*(*b*) from *Ash3*(*a*) and *MD* from *RP3*. *FA46* alone contains all twenty-two stanzas; *Ash3* omits eight (9, 14–19, and 21), *H17* three (9, 11, and 17), and *RP3* (followed by *MD*) one (16). Additional evidence is to be found in the presence of other unique variants in all four: *FA46* contains seventeen, *Ash3* in effect twenty-four (shared by *Ash3*[*a*+*b*]); *Ash3*(*b*) contains four directional unique variants, and *Ash3*(*a*) three variants susceptible of easy conjectural correction: 'A' for 'Our' (l. 16), 'dooing' for 'going' (l. 25), and 'y^f' for 'that' (presumably as 'y^t', l. 63). *H17* contains nineteen, and *RP3* in effect seventeen (all shared by *MD*, which has unique variants in ll. 11, 'the' for 'our', and 14, 'mine' for 'thine'). The unique variants are, intrinsically, about equally corrupt; none has prima facie authority.

Three of the substantive witnesses contain what are certainly inadvertent transpositions of stanzas. *Ash3* has st. 8, and *H17* st. 17, after l. 72 (st. 12); both stanzas begin with 'Her', as do 10–12 (st. 9, beginning with 'He', is wanting in both), and homœography is a common cause of accidental omission. The inferentially authorial sequence of *descriptive* stanzas (7–8, 10–12; 9 is a rhetorical interjection on the bride and groom together) is 'Her fingers', 'Her feet', 'Her cheeks', 'Her mouth', 'Her lips'; the placing of 'fingers' and 'feet' first and in juxtaposition is not so inevitable as that of 'cheeks', 'mouth', and 'lips', and it is possible that one of the first two stanzas was deliberately displaced in *Ash3* and *H17*. But, inadvertent or deliberate, replacement is more or less inevitable after l. 72, since the descriptive sequence is terminated in that stanza, ll. 72–8 (st. 13) shifting the perspective from the bride's physical attributes to her effect 'upon the parson and others who saw her. In *FA46* the transposition of stanzas 11 and 12 could be deliberate, but it too is probably due to homœography. But the misplacing of st. 14 after l. 96 (st. 16) in *FA46* is not to be accounted for so simply, since the first and last three lines within the stanza are also transposed. The displaced stanza is the first on sig. C4^v(o), the two stanzas that should have followed it being the last on sig. C4(i). It might be supposed that the transposition of tercets in the first stanza on C4^v(o) represents an attempt to compensate for a stanza omitted on the preceding page of the inner forme, which had already gone to press, but if this were so the catchword on C4 should be 'Passion' instead of 'The'; it would therefore appear that the error stood in the compositor's copy.

In l. 82, it should be noted, 'Kitchin's great' in *FA46*—'Kitchin great' *Σ*—is a syntactical compensation necessitated by the transposition of tercets.

FA48 generally follows *FA46*, from which it departs in eight places. In ll. 38 and 46 it contains unique, probably sophisticated, variants. In ll. 3, 107, and 127–8, and in the correct placing and order of ll. 79–84 (st. 14), it agrees with *Σ* against *FA46*; and in l. 120 it has a pair of related 'mixed' variants (see critical apparatus). Since *FA48* follows *FA46* in the transposition of stanzas 11 and 12, and contains variants shared with other witnesses in lines that *Ash3* omits, it would appear that its alterations derive from a source closely related to *H17*, which omits st. 11 (*RP3* has this and st. 12 in the correct order).

The evidence of the variants in the four fully substantive witnesses in general supports the descent of *FA46* and *RP3*, and *Ash3* and *H17*, from intermediate ancestors on separate lines of descent from the hypothetical original; or, in Greg's formulary, '(*x*) *A*ᶜ (*FA46 RP3*) (*Ash3 H17*)'. In addition to the omissions and transpositions of stanzas (the omission of st. 9 in both *Ash3* and *H17* suggests shared derivation and supports this genealogy), there are twenty-seven verbal variants more complex than those in which a single witness reads at odds with the rest: seventeen support the genealogy suggested, three are compatible with it though equivocal (ll. 33, 73, and 74), one—in which all four substantive witnesses diverge—is neutral (title; see note), and six are ostensibly incompatible (ll. 1, 28, 37, 60, and 120 [two]); all are recorded in the critical apparatus, and the incompatible and equivocal readings are discussed in the notes. The genealogy suggested does not assure the validity of my choices between variants, but the choices are based on directional evidence that is consistent with it, and the immediately relevant evidence—including considerations of context—in each case dictates the particular choice. I have retained *FA46* as copy-text for its generally careful printer's accidentals.

Title. Since the substantive witnesses are apparently collateral and none of the variant titles has the support of more than one witness, Suckling's own title (if any) is conjectural. *H17*'s title is doubtful despite the support for the association with John Lord Lovelace in an index-entry in *An Antidote Against Melancholy*, 1661 (see headnote), and its text is without special authority. Many of Suckling's poems are untitled in the early texts, and a number in *FA46* and especially *LR* seem to have editorially supplied titles; the almost certainly authorial titles are distinctly laconic (cf. especially 'A Dreame', 'The Miracle', 'Against Absence', and 'The Wits'), identifying subject or occasion and taking no account of verse-form (there is rarely much occasion for them to do so). It might seem, therefore, that 'The Wedding', which closely parallels 'The Wits', is most likely to be authorial; but 'Upon a Wedding' in *FA46*'s title has the support of a number of authorial titles beginning with 'Upon' (cf. especially the juvenile religious poems), and there are no negative parallels to discount the formally descriptive 'A Ballade', which describes not only the verse-form of the poem but also its 'rustication' of the traditionally formal and elevated epithalamion (see headnote).

ll. 1–6. *I tell thee Dick, where I have been,* etc. The nature of the variants here suggests convergent 'conventionalization' or 'trivialization' resulting from failure to distinguish between poet and rustic as speaker. In what I take to be the authorial reading (*FA46*'s and the present text's), ' I tell thee Dick' (*Dx42, FA46, H17*) is more appropriately forceful and dramatic than 'Ile' by being a strong asseveration rather than a simple declaration. The syntax of 'Where I have been' etc. (*Ash3, FA46, RP3*)—with 'that' elliptically implicit before 'Where'—is more complex, idiomatic, and colloquial; and, having an interruptive and intensifying exclamation involving an apposition ('Oh things') within an apposition ('Where', l. 2), it is also more dramatically verisimilar than the reading of *Dx42* and *H17*, in which the explicit 'that', replacing 'where', makes 'I have been' rather than 'Such sights' the substantival clause and 'Such sights again' etc. an independent clause.

ll. 2, 3, 4. *things/things/sights.* The overall textual evidence suggests that *FA46* and *RP3*, and *Ash3* and *H17*, respectively, share independent ancestors (see note on *Text*), which reduces *FA46* and *RP3* to a single inferential authority; but it is plain that the readings of *Dx42* (which omits 'sights', and, though containing only four lines, represents a lost ancestor) and *Ash3* (which omits 'things') could not be original, because the remaining variants (having both 'things' and 'sights') could not have arisen from them independently. *H17*'s 'sights/sights/things' is more probably sophisticated, on the suggestion of '[sights] have seen' (l. 2), than the reading of *FA46* and *RP3*, which is stronger: it expresses collective tangible particulars in 'things', 'seen', and 'beyond compare', avoids the redundancy of 'sights . . . seen' and the weakness of 'things . . . found', and climactically emphasizes spectacularity in 'sights . . . found' (which implicitly includes the 'things').

l. 12. *Forty.* 'Vorty', a phonetic West Country spelling, is unique in *FA46* and probably an interpretative alteration, as 'Volk' (l. 11) and the 'West Country men' of its title almost certainly are in *An Antidote Against Melancholy*, 1661, in which the 'Vorty' of its ultimate source, *FA48*, is apparently thus editorially complemented.

l. 19. *Course-a-Park.* 'A country game, in which a girl called out one of the other sex to choose her' (*OED*).

ll. 22–4. *lusty Roger . . . little George . . . Vincent of the Crown.* Type-appellations, the second in general currency as a proverb, 'As good as George of Green' (Tilley G 83: 1590), and the first perhaps so, too; cf. the following stanza from 'The Hampshire Mayd, or the Wenches Progress', in [John Raymund], *Folly in Print*, 1667, p. 16 (Suckling may, however, be the source of the use here, since the same collection contains an imitation of 'A Ballade'):

> The Carryer came up with me
> A well trust, lusty Roger,
> As broad i'th' back
> As any Puck,
> I'm sure he was no dodger.

l. 28. *Yet* [But *Ash3, RP3*]. The distribution is at odds with the genetic relationships suggested in the note on *Text*, but 'But' is probably a coincidental dittographic error, since l. 25, the first line in the stanza, begins with 'But'. The sense 'for all that, nevertheless', which 'Yet' precisely conveys and 'But', especially when it has just been used, does not, would seem to be demanded by the context.

l. 32. *Whitson-ale*. An 'ale', or country 'festival of merrymaking at which much ale was drunk' (*OED*), held at Whitsuntide.

l. 33. *Could* [Can *RP3*: Did *Ash3*]. 'Can' is plainly corrupt, as incompatible with 'yet' in the same line, but it supports 'Could' as a more probable source of variation than 'Did', which is also inappropriately less assertive than 'Could'. The two divergent readings here may well be misguided attempts at 'elegant variation' (another 'could' is used in the following line).

l. 37. *fingers were* [finger was *Ash3, FA46*]. The singular would appear to be an editorial trivialization prompted by attentive but unreflective literal-mindedness; the emphasis upon a single finger's size, with its uncontrolled implications, is distracting and slightly grotesque.

ll. 46–8. *she dances such a way! No Sun upon an Easter day* etc. The superstition that the sun 'danced' in celebration of the Resurrection persisted at least until the nineteenth century (see *N&Q*, 3rd ser., 1864, v. 394, 448; 6th ser., 1884, ix. 390, 456).

l. 50. *so*. The difference in sense between *RP3* and *FA46* is one of nuance, and, though 'so' is as likely to be an editorial metrical justification as its absence is to be an inadvertent omission, the over-all regularity in the number of syllables per line in 'A Ballade' supports 'so' as probably authorial.

ll. 52–4. *And then she lookt* etc. Cf. *The Goblins*, IV. iii. 25–6.

ll. 58–9. *For streaks of red* etc. Cf. *Brennoralt*, IV. vi. 16–17.

l. 60. *The* [That *H17, RP3*]. The distribution is at odds with the genetic relationships suggested in the note on *Text* above, and the equivocal variants make the original reading uncertain. If 'The' were in error, it could (though improbably here) have resulted from anticipation of the 'the' later in the line. I have preferred 'The' chiefly because 'That' seems unnecessarily demonstrative. The source of confusion is probably a paleographically ambiguous abbreviation, either 'yᵉ' or 'yᵗ' (in l. 63, *Ash3*[*a*]'s 'yᶠ' is corrected to 'yᵗ' in *Ash3*[*b*], for example).

ll. 61–6, 67–72 (stanzas 11–12). [Order of stanzas.] The descriptive sequence of the three stanzas beginning with l. 55 in the present text is 'cheeks', 'mouth', 'lips', which is supported both by the weight of textual authority and by the climactic effect and transitional sense of 'I durst no more upon her gaze, Then on the Sun in July' (l. 72). *FA46*'s probably erroneous placing could be either 'editorial' ('Lips' before 'Mouth'), irresponsibly mechanical, or due to copy. The homœographic mis-setting of one stanza in place of another beginning with the same word is an easy error; but, since both stanzas are present, the hypothetical error must have been recognized, and, since the transposition of a few lines of type is easy, a compositor's error would probably have been corrected. It seems likely, therefore, that *FA46*'s order is either editorial or scribal, probably the latter; it is noteworthy that ll. 61–6 are wanting in *H17*.

l. 71. *her*. The weight of textual authority, as well as the climactic and transitional effect, leaves 'her' in little doubt; 'them' would appear to be a misguided editorial conventionalization ('them' pronominally agrees with 'eyes'), perhaps partly prompted by the traditional Petrarchan comparison between eyes and sun.

l. 73. *should be*. The 'had . . . bin' in the following line (*Σ*) suggests the strong possibility of convergent variation by dittography in *Ash3* and *RP3* in this line, which could not have occurred with *FA46*'s and *H17*'s shared 'be'. The repetition of 'had . . . bin' in successive lines is somewhat awkward here and seems contrary to the required sense, which is that, if this kind of wishing were a sin in general, the parson himself would have been guilty of it on that particular occasion. *FA46*'s 'should' seems superior to *H17*'s 'might' as denoting simple potentiality rather than power or capability, and 'might' is further weakened by *H17*'s unique 'might not doe' for 'had not done' in l. 128.

l. 74. *Parson self*. The emendation in the present text, involving the relatively archaic and probably (and appropriately) dialectal use of the uninflected genitive (cf. 'Christ Nativitie' in 'Upon Christmas', l. 24), would account, as hypothetically original reading, for all the variants as attempts at conventionalization through obvious alterations.

ll. 79–84. [Placing of and arrangement of lines within the stanza.] This stanza effects the transition from the description of the bride to an account of the wedding festivities, and its placing and internal transposition in *FA46* are manifestly in error, the possible cause of which is discussed in the note on *Text* above.

ll. 100–1. *And when 'twas nam'd anothers health*, etc. With alterations these lines are used in 'The careless Lover', ll. 24–5.

l. 115. *in he came*. The pair of 'hyparchetypal' variants here would seem to be directional, the 'he came in' of *Ash3* and *H17* probably being a syntactical conventionalization; the construction in the reading of the present text ($+\Sigma$) is parallel with 'there she lay'.

l. 116. *new-faln snow melting away*. Cf. 'His Dream', ll. 13–14, and *Brennoralt*, IV. vi. 11–12.

l. 120. *Good b'w'y*. The modern 'Good-bye', a contraction of 'God be with you' in use in that form as early as 1573 (*OED*), explains some of the confusion here. The variants in the substantive witnesses suggest that 'Good' and 'b'w'y'' (variously spelt but clearly representing the contraction) are original, *H17*'s (like *Ash3[b]*'s) 'God' and *Ash3(a)*'s and *FA46*'s 'Boy' being sophisticated, though the latter could be simply a different but misleading phonetic spelling of the same contraction; cf. Webster, *The White Devil* (ed. John Russell Brown, 2nd ed., 1966), I. ii. 75: 'Sir God boy you.' The possibility that 'Good Boy!' is meant to represent a misunderstanding by the rustic speaker seems to me to demand more subtlety of the poem than it manifests elsewhere. And, despite the poem's earthy rustication, the hearty invitational commendation of 'Good Boy!' seems a little less appropriate for the bride than 'Go[o]d b'w'y'', which more gently conveys something of the same effect as well as others, and also contributes to the effect of 'Bridget' and 'Nell' in the last stanza.

77. On New-years day 1640. To the King (pp. 84–6)

It seems probable that this poem was written in late 1640 to be sung to the King on 1 January 1640/1, for 'at court the new-year gifts were always given on that day' even though England continued to follow the Julian calendar, in changing the year-number in March, until 1752 (see W. W. Greg, 'Old Style—New Style' in *Joseph Quincy Adams: Memorial Studies*, Washington, D.C., 1948, pp. 563–9). Although Suckling uses a refrain in 'Songs' that were probably never intended to be sung, it seems likely that this poem was indeed sung to the King, as 'The Wits' was in 1637 (see Commentary). If it was sung, the third stanza, especially 'Like those in Musick we create' (l. 22), acquires an added dimension of presentational depth and force.

ll. 1–5. *Awake (great Sir) the Sun shines heer*, etc. Cf. Letter No. 15, ll. 56–7.

l. 34. *such strange Rapes*. Cf. the use of 'such gentle rape' in *Aglaura*, I. iii. 22.

78. Upon my Lord Brohalls Wedding (pp. 86–7)

The marriage of Roger Boyle, Baron Broghill, the younger son of the first Earl of Cork, to Lady Margaret Howard, took place on 27 January 1640/1, only a few months before Suckling's flight to France. 'A Ballade. Upon a Wedding' (q.v. in Commentary) has been mistakenly believed also to have been associated with this wedding. The dialogue of the poem is, of course, a rhetorical fiction, but, since the poem is occasional in referring to a real marriage, it is natural to attempt to identify 'S''s—that is, presumably, Suckling's—interlocutor. Thompson took for granted that Jack Bond, whose full name is mentioned in 'A Summons to Town' (l. 10, q.v., text and Commentary), is the 'B' here as well as the 'Jack' of Letter No. 52, 'A disswasion from Love' (pp. 368, 401); but it seems distinctly odd that the sometime suitor of 'Mistris [presumably Lady Margaret] Howard' (Letter, l. 53) should not know 'who's gone mad to day' (poem, l. 4), although the letter could ante-date the poem by several years, or the unawareness could be part of the pose.

Herbert Berry has suggested that 'B' is, 'apparently, Jack Barry, a fellow officer in the King's army. Barry had stood as Broghill's second in a duel less than a year before over . . . Frances Harrison, one of the Queen's maids of honor, who had been Broghill's fiancée' (p. 15 and note). He adds that Suckling 'found the episode suitable for at least an echo in the poem' (in ll. 29–32) and suggests that Barry may also be the 'Jack' of Letter No. 52. 'Brohall our gallant friend' (l. 7) is not inconsistent with Barry as interlocutor (though, historically at least, a close friend might be expected to know of the wedding), but the cynical Jack Bond seems to me equally likely: in 'A Summons to Town'—which follows this poem in *FA46*—'*Jack Bond* swears' that '*Socinus* and the Schoolmen . . . do but fool men' (ll. 9–10). And the use of 'bonds' in l. 27 takes on additional significance as a pun on the surname of a once 'interested party'.

Speech-prefixes. The text in *FA46* has only the first three speech-prefixes (at ll. 1, 4, and 5); the rest have been editorially supplied. The poem is manifestly intended to continue as a dialogue, in terms of which alone the alternations of attitude in the rest of the poem make total sense. The dialectical antagonism of the poem seems to consist in 'S''s enthusiastic advocacy of conventional love and marriage, especially in relation to these two lovers, which is partly expressed in a description of the ceremonies of this particular marriage ('S''s mildly ironical observation on the weakness of lovers' law in ll. 24–6 is, in its amused indulgence, consonant with his more directly favourable comments), and 'B''s cynical interruptive commentary on amorous human nature in general.

The supplied speech-prefixes seem to me obvious enough to require no discussion except for 'B' supplied for ll. 27–8 and 'S' for ll. 29–40, for which there are two entertainable alternatives: (1) 'S' for ll. 27–8, 'B' for ll. 29–32, and 'S' for ll. 33–40 (*Haz* and *Th*); and (2) 'B' for ll. 27–32 and 'S' for ll. 33–40. There are two sources of ambiguity in this section, the question in ll. 29–32 (present text, question treated as rhetorical) or 29–30 (*FA46*, question direct, though still 'rhetorical'), and the typographical break between ll. 28 and 29. The first suggested alternative is untenable in giving to 'S' lines (27–8) that are, in their laconic and cynical sententiousness, consonant with all of 'B''s earlier comments but not with 'S''s. Nor is there much to support the assignment of ll. 29–32 to 'B'. *FA46*'s question-mark at the end of l. 30 (which is, in any case, as likely to be editorial and interpretative as the punctuation of the present text) suggests a direct question for which ll. 31–2 furnish the reasons for asking; but (1) the colon punctuating l. 32 in *FA46* suggests continuing utterance by the same speaker (certainly not 'B', since ll. 33–40 constitute the counter-argument); (2) there is—as nowhere else in the poem —a verse-paragraph break between ll. 28 and 29; and (3) 'fair Nymph', which is generally inconsonant with 'B''s comments, cannot be regarded as (appropriately for 'B') ironic, because there is nothing in 'S''s previous remarks to provide a basis for its use as such. Lines 29–32, which read at least as defensibly as unequivocal praise of the bride as ironical disparagement, seem to me to make the best sense if they are treated as a rhetorical question (self-answered in 'The Gods forbid!', l. 33) implicitly refuting 'B''s cynical generalization in ll. 27–8 and anticipating direct refutation, partly in the same metaphorical terms, in ll. 34–40.

ll. 5–11. *Dull Heretick*, etc. Cf. 'Song' ('No, No, faire Heretique') and *Brennoralt*, III. iv. 70–4.

l. 8. *Martyrs to the fire*. Cf. 'The Expostulation I', l. 18.

ll. 27–8. *The bonds . . . (like gypsies knots) . . . are fast and loose*. Proverbial (Tilley P 401 [1578]; cf. F 78 [1639]); and 'bonds' may pun on a surname (see headnote). *Fast and Loose* is 'an old cheating game that used to be practiced at fairs. A belt was folded, and the player was asked to prick it with a skewer, so as to pin it *fast* to the table; having so done, the adversary took the two ends, and *loosed* it or drew it away, showing that it had not been pierced at all' (Brewer's *Dictionary of Phrase and Fable*, 1965).

ll. 29–32. *But was the fair Nymphs praise* etc. On the interpretation of these lines as rhetorical question see note on *Speech-prefixes* above.

l. 32. *But enterr'd breaches made by others eyes*. Cf. *Aglaura*, I. vi. 20–5.

ll. 36–40. *To Hawkes (good Jack) and hearts* etc. Cf. Letter No. 23, ll. 37–43; *Aglaura*, IV. i. 13–17; and *Brennoralt*, IV. iv. 1–5.

DUBIA

The only authority for Suckling's authorship of the first six dubious poems (Nos. 79–84) is their inclusion in *LR* (q.v. in Introduction, pp. lxxxvi–xciv). The next three, 'To Mr. W. M. Against Absence', 'A New-years Gift', and 'Gnomics' (Nos. 85–7), were found, though without ascription, among family papers that include texts of poems certainly by Suckling (see Introduction, 'Dubious Works', pp. cxii–cxiv). 'Inconstancie in Woman' (No. 88) has a manuscript attribution to Suckling; 'To Celia, An Ode' (No. 89) is ascribed to Suckling in an eighteenth-century printed miscellany; and 'In Brennoralt' (No. 90) is associated with Suckling through the title of his play (on these see Introduction, 'Dubious Works', pp. cx–cxi).

79. Love turn'd to Hatred (p. 88)

The text of this poem in *A4* is anonymous; that in *RP14* is headed 'Capt. Tyrell. of Mrs Winchcombe' and is followed by 'An Answere to ye former Paper by Mr Womack' (q.v. in Appendix A.i.6).

Text. The variants are both insufficient in number and too equivocal to suggest a genealogical formula other than that of the independent derivation of all three from a common ancestor, though the certainly correct unique reading of *RP14* in l. 8 (see note) might appear to suggest an intermediate ancestor shared by *LR* and *A4*.

l. 8. *should.* An equivocal variant, since the 'shall' of *LR* and *A4* could be due to dittography (cf. 'shall be' in l. 9) as well as to copy, and 'should' could be an editorial correction. Certainly 'should' is wanted, on the assumption that at no time would 'ghosts' have been 'welcom . . . at midnight'.

80. Love and Debt alike troublesom (pp. 88–9)

Together with the canonical 'A Pedler of Small-wares', this poem, ascribed to 'J. S.', is listed in *HMC 3rd Report*, p. 296, among the manuscripts of Matthew Wilson, Esq. (they were sold in 1916 to the late G. D. Smith, Esq., of New York, but I have been unable to discover their present whereabouts); the texts, which have the same titles as the poems in *LR*, could have been *LR*'s source, but it is equally likely that they were transcribed from *LR*.

The text of this poem in *A23*, where it is accompanied by a perhaps traditional tune, is anonymous and very corrupt. These doggerel fourteeners seem on stylistic grounds unlikely to be by Suckling, but they could be a very early composition of his (see Introduction, *The Last Remains*, 1659, p. xciii). The theme and attitudes expressed are not uncharacteristic, and the quasi-proverbial and epigrammatic earthiness of the last two lines is very much in his idiom. There is a parallel treatment of the theme of the *beatus vir* and 'the golden times of Innocence' in *The Sad One*, IV. iv. 1–20 (a passage in which Suckling paraphrases a couplet from the juvenile poem 'A Dreame'), but the commonplaceness of the ideas and the differences of style allow this to be taken as no compelling evidence of Suckling's authorship.

ll. 1–2. *This one request I make to him* etc. Cf. the openings of 'The Invocation' and 'The Expostulation I and II'.

l. 9. *Though Crœsus compassed great wealth.* 'As rich as Crœsus' was of course proverbial (Tilley C 832: 1577).

ll. 13–14. *Our Merchant he in goods is rich*, etc. Cf. *Aglaura*, IV. iv. 58–63.

l. 18. *vex't*. The emendation suggested by the rhyme-word, '[be]twixt' (l. 17), has paleographical support in the possibility of scribal ambiguity in a secretary-hand original between 'vext' and 'vexe' (the spelling in 'To Mr. W. M. Against Absence', l. 10, for example), and makes at least as good sense as 'vex' in emphasizing cause rather than effect.

l. 24. *As good stuff under Flanel lies, as under Silken clothes*. Cf. *Aglaura*, II. ii. 68–9, and *The Goblins*, IV. iii. 1–14 (an extended comparison between 'Country wenches' and 'Towne-Ladies').

81. Song (pp. 89–90)

This Caroline ballad-stanza version of the matter of Donne's darker lyric, 'The Message', is ascribed to Lady Alice Egerton in *RP1*, a folio manuscript of 'POEMS SONGS a PASTORALL and a PLAY by the Rᵗ Honᵇˡᵉ Lady JANE CAVENDISH and Lady ELIZABETH BRACKLEY' (title-page; on this manuscript see *PMLA*, 1931, xlvi. 802–38), where it is followed by 'An answeare to my Lady Alice Edgertons Songe of I prethy send mee back my Hart' (q.v. in Appendix A.i, No. 7). There is a conflicting ascription of at least equal prima facie authority to Dr. Henry Hughes in Henry Lawes's *Ayres and Dialogues . . . Third Book*, 1658 (p. 6), a book in which most of the verses were supplied by Hughes, as L. A. Beaurline notes ('The Canon of Sir John Suckling's Poems', *SP*, 1960, lvii. 499–500). The text in the Henry Lawes autograph collection, *HL*, is without ascription, but Hughes supplied the lyrics for thirty-five of the songs, a number second only to Carew's thirty-eight (see *The Library*, 5th ser., 1953, viii. 91–2, and on Hughes, Beaurline, 'Canon', p. 499, n. 10).

Its inclusion in *LR* is the only authority for Suckling's authorship of this poem, but the association with Henry Lawes, who wrote music for 'The constant Lover' and 'Song' ('No, no, faire Heretique'), and Lady Elizabeth Brackley, suggests means by which a copy might have been found among Suckling's papers presumably used as copy for *LR* (see Introduction, pp. lxxxvi–xciv). Lady Elizabeth Brackley, *née* Elizabeth Cranfield, daughter of James Cranfield, second Earl of Middlesex, was related to Suckling, and Lady Alice Egerton and Henry Lawes in turn were associated at least in connection with the first production in 1634 of Milton's *Mask presented at Ludlow Castle* (*Comus*), in which both acted and for which Lawes wrote the music for the songs. When *Comus* was first printed, anonymously, in 1637, it contained a dedication by Henry Lawes to Lady Elizabeth Brackley's husband-to-be, John Egerton, Viscount Brackley, second Earl of Bridgewater (1649), who may have written a poem in answer to 'Song' ('Why so pale and wan'; see Appendix A.i.5, text and Commentary).

Text. A number of the seventeenth-century texts of this poem are plainly derivative (as noted in the critical apparatus), but conflation in the remaining witnesses, much of it probably due to memorial transcription, makes possible the construction of a number of alternative stemmata, all tentative and none of editorial value. The text in *LR* is very corrupt, but I have retained it as copy-text because it is the source for the association with Suckling and for its generally satisfactory printer's accidentals, rejecting its readings where the textual evidence shows them probably to be in error. Something of a case could be made for the rejected readings in ll. 4 ('have'), 6, 12, and 16, but not, I think, a very strong one.

82. The guiltless Inconstant (pp. 90–1)

On the authority of *Ros2*, *Ros4*, and *TCD*, this poem was written in answer to or was at least inspired by a six-line poem by John Gill, 'The fervency of his affection' (q.v. in Appendix A.i, No. 8). It was posthumously printed as Carew's in 1640 (see *Poems*, ed. Rhodes Dunlap, 1949, p. 283), but Carew's authorship, like Suckling's, is supported solely by inclusion in a posthumous collection. Citing several close parallels in works certainly by Suckling (see notes on ll. 5, 11–12, 17–18), L. A. Beaurline concluded that this poem 'is either Suckling's work or a very close imitation of him' ('The Canon of Sir John Suckling's Poems', *SP*, 1960, lvii. 505; cf. p. 501), but it is equally possible that Suckling was imitating passages in a poem by someone else, in which both he and Carew shared an interest and of which they had copies (on the printer's copy for *LR* see Introduction, pp. lxxxvi–xciv; cf. Suckling's 'Love's Burning-glass' and Carew's 'The Tinder'). The poem is almost certainly by Walton Poole, to whom it is ascribed in five of nine substantive witnesses (two of which were unknown to Beaurline): *A33*, *Eg27* (subscribed 'W. P'; headed 'The Sparke. T. C.' in a later addition), *F7*, *Ros4*, and *TCD* (*Ros4* has heretofore been known only indirectly through C. L. Powell's discussion of an otherwise unidentified manuscript 'in the possession of Mr. Bertram Dobell' that 'has not been previously examined'; see *MLR*, 1916, xi. 288). *M6* and *Ros2* are anonymous.

In a study of variant texts of another poem by Poole, ' "If Shadows be a Picture's Excellence": an Experiment in Critical Bibliography' (*PMLA*, 1948, lxiii. 831–57), Edwin Wolf II tentatively identifies Poole as 'the second son of Sir Henry Poole, of Okesey, co. Wilts.', about whom he is able to add a few other details (see pp. 835–6 and genealogical chart *post* 836). Of his subject-poem he remarks that, 'because of its almost ubiquitous appearance in MS. commonplace-books of about 1620 to 1660, it may have been the most widely circulated single poem of the period' (p. 834), and the very obscurity of the author lends some support to ascriptions of poems to him in manuscript miscellanies (other poems attributed to him are noted on p. 835), as the early date of the range does to the possibility of Suckling's having imitated, rather than written, 'The guiltless Inconstant'.

Text. On the evidence of their agreement with substantive witnesses in all but their own unique readings, two of the eleven texts of this poem are derivative, *West-D* from *F7*, and *M6b* from *M6a* (*M6b* corrects two unique obvious errors in *M6a*, 'some of' for 'some' [*Σ*], l. 17, and 'sparkling' for 'sparkle' [*Σ*], l. 32). All the substantive witnesses contain two or more unique readings (those of *F7* and *M6a*, of course, shared with their derivatives), which are neither intrinsically authoritative nor often likely to prompt conjectural restoration of the probably original reading, and therefore represent terminal states. Because of probable conflation, the absolute genealogical relationship of the states is uncertain, but the distribution of variants (noted in the critical apparatus) suggests that two independent lines of descent from a hypothetical common original are represented by five and four witnesses, respectively, one by *A33*, *F7*, *Ros2*, *Ros4*, and *TCD* (*A33*, *F7*, and *Ros2*, and *Ros4* and *TCD*, representing separate subordinate lines of descent), and the other by *Eg27* and *M6*, and *Car* and *LR* (the two pairs representing separate subordinate lines). In terms of Greg's formularies, the relationships would be represented thus: '(*x*) *A*ᶜ {[(*A33 F7*) *Ros2*] [*Ros4 TCD*]} {[*Eg27 M6*] [*Car LR*]}'. The distribution of variants in ll. 15 ('first/chief'), 19 (two), and 29 ('broke/crackt') supports this genealogy, but variants in ll. 15 ('may/I/do') and, especially, 30 ('faces/beauties') are in conflict (the variants in l. 15 could be editorially convergent and those in l. 30 conflated, however). The textual closeness of *Car* and *LR* supports the historical inference that Suckling and Carew shared an interest in this poem. Choice of a copy-text on the basis of the most authorial accidentals is impossible here, and, of the two printed texts, which alone have adequate punctuation, *LR* is superior to *Car*, for which reason I have adopted it as copy-text.

Title. This poem quite likely had no authorial title. The only title supported by more than one witness is 'The Sparke' (*Poems of Thomas Carew*, 1640), but 'The Sparke. T. C.' heading the text in *Eg 27* was added some time after the original transcription of the poem, to which the subscription 'W. P.' belongs (in this miscellany a space is normally left between the last line of one poem and the title of the next, but here there is no space, and a single rule—used nowhere else—separates the preceding poem from 'The Sparke. T. C.'). In *Ros4* 'The answer to it' refers to the antecedent poem mentioned at the beginning of the headnote.

ll. 3–4. *Since like to tinder* etc. Cf. 'To his Rival II', ll. 17–18.

l. 5. *Each wanton eye* etc. Cf. 'Farewel to Love', ll. 23–4.

ll. 11–12. *This for her shape I love*, etc. Cf. 'Upon two Sisters', ll. 21–2.

l. 14. *I chuse there by the kernel, not the rind.* Cf. Tilley K 18 ('He has lost the Kernel and leaps at the shell', 1639) and N 360 ('Sweet is the Nut but bitter [hard] is the shell', 1578).

ll. 17–18. *And like to Merchants* etc. Cf. *Aglaura*, IV. iv. 58–63.

ll. 23–30. *And as a Looking glass* etc. Cf. Donne, 'The Broken Heart', ll. 29–30: 'And now as broken glasses show A hundred lesser faces'.

83. [To the Lady Desmond] (p. 92)

This neither uncharacteristic nor very characteristic poem evidently cir-culated fairly widely in manuscript (and probably by recitation) in circles with which Suckling was familiar, and a copy possibly found among the papers provided for the printer of *LR* may account for its being included as his. The texts in *A11* and *F24* are anonymous; the one in *A Forest of Varieties*, by Dudley Lord North, with whom Suckling is known to have been associated in literary matters (see Introduction, p. xlvi, and Appendix A.iii.3), is said to be 'Of another Author'; and the text in *M3* is subscribed 'P. Apsley', presumably the 'Peter Apsley' to whom another poem in the same manu-script miscellany, and also in *Wit Restor'd*, 1658, is attributed (see note on 'The Wits', l. 93). Peter Apsley, heir of Sir Allen Apsley, lieutenant of the Tower (1569?–1630), was born in Ireland in 1606; he matriculated at Christ Church, Oxford, on 19 November 1621, aged 15, and took his B.A. on 13 Feb-ruary 1622/3 (Foster, *Alumni Oxonienses*, i. 29); he was also a captain in Lord Goring's regiment during the First Bishops' War (*CSPD 1639*, pp. 142, 202), in which Suckling commanded his celebrated troop of horse (see Introduction, pp. xlvii–xlviii). His father, who, 'coming up to court to seek his fortune, . . . lost all at play', served—as Suckling apparently did—in 1627 in the expedi-tion to the Ile de Ré, when he 'caught a fever, followed by a consumption, of which he died 24 May 1630' (*DNB*). The text attributed to Apsley is of high intrinsic authority (see note on *Text*), and, though there is insufficient evidence to make his authorship certain, his claim is stronger than Suck-ling's.

The 'Lady Desmond' of the title helps date the poem approximately, if she is—indeed the only eligible candidate—Lady Bridget Stanhope (born *c.* 1615), daughter and co-heiress of Sir John Stanhope, of Sudbury, Suffolk; she married George Feilding, Earl of Desmond (by reversion, 1622, and possession, 1628), on 17 April 1630—and was suing him for divorce in the High Commission Court in 1635 (G.E.C., *Complete Peerage*, iv. 258).

Text. All the witnesses except *M3* contain unique readings: there are four and seven, respectively, in *A11* and *F24*, and one each in *LR* ('not' for 'no', l. 14) and *North* ('one on' for 'on one', l. 3). Four shared variants link *A11* and *F24* (ll. 7–8 omitted; *A11* also omits 9–10); *LR* and *North* ('which' for 'that', l. 4); and *A11* and *North* (which omit 'Madam' before l. 1, though *A11* incorporates it in l. 2, and share 'bee . . . will' in place of 'were . . . would', ll. 13–14, which could have arisen fortuitously as editorial intensification). There is not really sufficient evidence for convincing genealogical inferences, but the textual evidence in general suggests that *A11* and *F24*, and *LR* and

North, share intermediate ancestors on separate lines of descent from a common hypothetical original, and that *M3* either stands closest to the original on *A11+F24*'s line of descent or is itself the textual (though not necessarily bibliographical) ancestor of the other four witnesses. None of the variants conflicts with the hypothesis that *M3* stands nearest the original, and, while I have retained *LR* as copy-text for its generally adequate accidentals, the substantives of the present text are those of *M3*.

ll. 12–13. *For if to every common Funeral* etc. Cf. *Aglaura*, v(t). i. 175–80.

84. [Foreknowledge] (p. 93)

The Greek and Latin poems, which I have not been able to trace, may be the products of a school exercise. It is natural to suppose, but uncertain, that the Greek is the original poem, the other two being successive translations.

The Fane commonplace-book, in which the anonymous variant text occurs, was compiled between 1655 and 1665, when the opening and closing letters from the compiler, Mildmay Fane, second Earl of Westmorland, to his son Henry Fane were dated (ff. 1, 131). The book consists of transcriptions of family letters (ff. 2–24ᵛ), including several from Mary, Countess of Westmorland to her son Sir Francis Fane, and Characters of continental countries and miscellaneous entries (ff. 26–131). The variant text occurs in the Character of England (f. 79), as does an anecdote about 'Jack Suckling', clearly the poet (f. 81ᵛ; see Introduction, pp. lxv–lxvi). Three of the Countess's letters are of particular interest in being addressed to her son (1) at Westmorland House in Great St. Bartholomew's, where a house of Suckling's uncle, the Earl of Middlesex, was also located (ff. 13ᵛ–14, dated 25 January 1628); (2) in Leyden, Holland (ff. 14–15, dated 15 September 1630); and (3) with Sir Henry Vane's embassy to Gustavus Adolphus in Germany (ff. 15ᵛ–18). The anecdote and Suckling's known presence at about the same time in the places to which the three letters are addressed certainly support the likelihood of his acquaintance with Fane. And it is perhaps tempting to suppose that Fane's mother's advice what to do 'when any of yoͬ acquaintances hinders you in these good courses already layd before you' and her urging 'good guides' (ff. 14ᵛ, 15ᵛ) allude to Suckling.

Mildmay Fane, himself both multilingual and a poet, may have been the author of one or more members of this 'trilogy' as well as perhaps of 'Gnomics' (q.v. in Commentary, p. 299).

85. To Mr. W. M. Against Absence (p. 94)

Of all the dubious poems, this one, to which Suckling wrote an answer ('To Mr. Davenant for Absence'), has the strongest claim to his authorship on internal evidence and to some extent on external evidence, but Davenant has a strong counter-claim in the printing of the poem as his in *Works*, 1673, and the title there, which is at odds with Suckling's possible authorship (see discussion in Introduction, pp. cxi–cxiii).

Text. In the eleven substantive variants in the texts of this poem ('doth/does', in l. 10, is purely morphological), the readings of *Cran2* are either equal or superior to those of *Dav*, which, however, supplies a title that would seem to be authoritative as well as helpfully descriptive, whoever wrote the poem. The variants in ll. 1, 12, 13–14, and 15 are especially significant. In *Dav*, 'thou', in l. 1, simplifies the sense and syntax by altering an extended relative clause (ll. 2–6), which 'validates' the metaphorical use of 'Pedlar', to a rhetorically weaker direct assertion, making 'Thou know'st' (l. 7) a separate declaration instead of—as in *Cran2*, despite the period in l. 6—the main subject and predicate of the first sentence; syntactical complexity of the same kind occurs in 'The Expostulation II', where, after 'Unjust Decrees', a defining clause constitutes the remainder of a six-line stanza, the major construction resuming with 'Let it suffice' in the second (l. 7). In l. 12, it is possible that 'between' compensates for a 'but' omitted in a defective line, by the expansion and alteration, presumably for the sake of euphony, of ''twixt'; at any rate, 'but' is clearly stronger in sense, rhythm, and emphasis, especially with ''twixt', than the line without it. Lines 13–14 have the look, especially in *Dav* but to a lesser extent in *Cran2*, of tetrameter lines expanded to meet the demands of the metrical pattern, which may, either in a defective original or at an earlier stage of composition, have read, 'Takes not the object from your Eye | But makes you abler to descry' (cf. the metrically anomalous lines in 'Perjury disdain'd', ll. 2, 3, and 6, and 'Upon A. M.', text, ll. 1–2, 11–12, and 15–16, and note on *Text*). Nevertheless, though mildly redundant, 'too-strong' and 'fit [and]' contribute intensity to the expression of the same general sense, as 'It does not take the [object]' and 'rather [makes you abler]' do not; and it is worth noting that the former are more characteristic of Suckling, the latter, with their metrical smoothness and prosodic consonance, of Davenant. In l. 15, *Dav*'s 'wandring weake' has only alliteration, 'fleeing' (l. 9), and general aptness to justify its two adjectives ('weake' is especially weak), whereas *Cran2* brings the tenor of the entire poem into a single adjective, 'loving', and its modified quasi-compound, 'smal Philosopher' (see note on l. 15 below).

A comparison of the entire poem with other poems by Suckling and Davenant generally supports Suckling's rather than Davenant's authorship, and a comparison of the two texts suggests that *Dav* is a sophisticated version of either a draft or a defective original, and *Cran2* the finished poem.

Title. In 'To Mr. W. M. Against Absence', 'W. M.' is presumably Walter Montagu, who figures in 'The Wits', ll. 81–8 (q.v., text and note).

ll. 1–6. *Pedlar in love, that with the common Art Of traffiquers* etc. Cf. 'Upon

Newyeares day', l. 4; 'A Pedler of Small-wares'; *Aglaura*, IV. v. 10–18; and Davenant's 'On the Death of the Lady Marquesse of Winchester', ll. 1–6 (*Madagascar*, 1638, p. 92):

> In care, lest some advent'rous Lover may
> (T'increase his love) cast his owne Stock away;
> I (that finde, th'use of griefe is to grow wise)
> Forbid all traffique now 'tweene Hearts, and Eyes:
> Our remnant-love, let us discreetly save,
> Since not augment; for Love, lies in the Grave.

ll. 3–6. *Thinking thy passions (false as their false ware)* etc. Cf. Letter No. 50 ('To T. C.'), esp. ll. 12–16: 'The care thou hast of me, that I should traffick right, draws me by way of Gratitude to perswade thee to bottle up some of that ['Horseley Air'], and send it hither to Town; thy returns will be quicker then those to the Indies, nor need'st thou fear a vent, since the disease is Epidemical.'

ll. 7–10. *Thou know'st the deere being shot*, etc. Cf. 'To Mr. Davenant for Absence' (an answer to this poem), ll. 1–4; 'Loves Offence', esp. ll. 1–6; *Aglaura*, I. iv. 39–40 and III. ii. 13–15; *The Goblins*, V. i. 1–5; and *Brennoralt*, I. ii. 32–4.

ll. 12–14. *a thin cloud 'twixt the Sun and you*, etc. Cf. 'To Mr. Davenant for Absence', ll. 5–16, esp. ll. 9–10: 'Who parts the object from the sence, Wisely cuts off intelligence'; Letter No. 1, ll. 7–10 ('daylight through courtaines', etc.); Letter No. 52, ll. 8–9 ('for Absence doth in a kind remove the cause (removing the object)'); and *The Sad One*, II. i. 13–16 ('The Cloud that interpos'd betwixt my Hopes before', etc.).

ll. 13–14. *Eye/descry*. Suckling uses 'descry' six times in the poems, rhyming it with 'eye' in 'Upon my Lady Carliles walking in Hampton-Court garden', ll. 26–7.

l. 15. *smal Philosopher*. The use of 'smal' here, as virtually part of a compound on the analogy of, for example, 'small-wares' (cf. 'A Pedler of Small-wares'), is similar to that in 'the small Poets' of 'The Wits', l. 115.

ll. 15–16. *Philosopher/to fly from her*. Suckling rhymes 'Philosophie' with 'sure't cannot be' in 'Upon Sir John Laurence's bringing Water', ll. 1–2, and with 'deifie' in *Aglaura*, 'Prologue to the Court' (alternative fifth act), ll. 11–12; but there are closer parallels in Davenant's 'Chronologer/him freed by her' (*Jeffereidos, or the Captivity of Jeffery*, II. 99–100) and 'Theater/skilfull Eare' ('To Endimion Porter, upon his recovery from a long Sicknesse', ll. 21–2).

l. 18. *For that's a kind of seeing when you winke*. A turn on a number of proverbs, the closest being perhaps Tilley W 500 (1566): 'Although I Wink I am not blind.' Cf. 'Love's Burning-glass', ll. 9–10: 'And now I bless my Love, when I do think | By how much I had rather burn then wink' (N.B. rhyme-words and use of 'do').

86. [A New-years Gift] (pp. 94–5)

The basis for the association of this doubtful poem with Suckling is discussed in the Introduction, p. cxiii.

l. 2. *The Eagles youth, renew'th Againe*. *Aquilæ senecta* (Erasmus, *Adagia*, 355c) and the eagle's renewal of youth are proverbial (Tilley E 5).

ll. 5–6. *Five thousand Sixe Hundred Thirty yeare* etc. The date and year of the creation of the world was much speculated upon in the Renaissance, and estimates ranged from the traditional 3760 B.C. of the Jewish calendar to well beyond 5200 B.C.; but, because of the tradition that the world would end on or before its 6,000th year, most estimates fell within a century of 4000 B.C., and the date calculated by Archbishop James Ussher (1581–1656), 4004 B.C., gained the widest acceptance (see C. A. Patrides, 'Renaissance Estimates of the Year of Creation', *HLQ*, 1962–3, xxvi. 315–22). On the basis of Archbishop Ussher's calculations, this poem would be datable in 1626/7.

l. 15. *satisfactus*. 'An act of reparation for an injury committed. In Christian theology it is usually applied to the payment of a penalty due to God on account of sin' (*Oxford Dictionary of the Christian Church*, 1957, s.v. 'Satisfaction'), here used loosely, as 'summe Duty *rather*' makes explicit.

ll. 21–4. *Long may you wish* etc. This quatrain is similar, in metre, cadence, phrase, and emphasis upon the relationship between the present and the hereafter, to the last four lines of 'On King Richard the third'.

87. [Gnomics] (p. 95)

This pastiche of proverbial commonplaces, which slightly resembles 'To my Lady E. C. at her going out of England', was found among the Cranfield Papers (see Introduction, pp. cxiii–cxiv). The initial-letter-acrostic 'RACHEL FANE' leaves the poem of uncertain authorship, but the lady's brother, Mildmay Fane, second Earl of Westmorland, is a strong contender, as a writer well known for epigrams, acrostics, anagrams, and the like; the poem is not in his *Otia Sacra*, 1648, but his—untraced—manuscript 'Fugitive Poetry' contains other poems. Baptized 28 January 1612/13, Rachael Fane married, as her second husband, Lionel Cranfield, third Earl of Middlesex, in 1655, and the poem could be thus accidentally and remotely associated with Suckling, though he had some connection with the Fane family otherwise (see Commentary on 'Foreknowledge', p. 296). I am indebted to Mr. Bruce Haber for noticing the acrostic name while checking the proofs, and to Professor W. R. Elton and the Henry E. Huntington Library for providing me almost instantaneously with a microfilm copy of the very rare *Otia Sacra*.

l. 6. *good*. Current, if uncommon, in seventeenth-century usage (*OED*, *Good*, *v.*).

88. Inconstancie in Woman (pp. 96–7)

Suckling's authorship of this not very coherent but popular variation on the theme of 'The Indifferent' (cf. Donne's) is supported only by a single, apparently conjectural attribution of uncertain date (see Introduction, p. cxi). There are musical settings in *Dx4*, *Dx42*, *HL*, *MDC*, *SMA52* (and later editions), and *Inconstancy in Woman. A New Song* [by John Webber, *c.* 1770]. An answer is given in Appendix A.i.10.

Text. Of the fourteen variant texts of this poem, four are demonstrably derivative, *F308* and *Wind-D* from *AC*, and *H39* and *MDC* from *SMA52* (all share otherwise unique variants with their sources and contain unique variants of their own). The distribution of variants in the remaining texts is almost random, except that *SMA52* quite consistently agrees with *HL*. The probably authoritative reading is in serious doubt only in ll. 3 ('This', etc.) and 9 ('ones', etc.; see notes), and in the alternative 'I'le'/'I' in ll. 9, 12, and 13 (discussed below). Since there is little to choose between the major variants, and the only alternative procedure is the exercise of a doubtful eclecticism, I have retained all the substantives of the copy-text, on the supposition that *HL*, and *SMA52* for the most part, represent what E. F. Hart has called the 'true version' of the song ('Caroline Lyrics and Contemporary Song-Books', *The Library*, 5th ser., 1953, viii. 105; besides these two texts, Hart knew only *F62*, through *N&Q*, etc., but by the measure of the other texts collated here his conclusion is still sound).

In the second stanza, the variations between 'I'le' and 'I' distribute as follows:

9 I'le *F62*, *HL*, *MDC*, *SMA52*: I *Σ*
12 I'le *Σ*: I *AC*, *F308*, *F339*, *Wind-D*, *WI*
13 I'le *Dx42*, *F62*, *H69*, *HL*: I *Σ*

In l. 17, *AC* (with its derivatives *F308* and *Wind-D*) alone reads 'I', which weakens the authority of its support for 'I' in ll. 9, 12, and 13. The major authority for 'I'le' in all three cases is *HL*, since *SMA52* abandons it in l. 13 (*MDC* is derivative, and *Dx42*, *F62*, and *H69* are conflated). In ll. 9 and 12 the majority have the most obvious and ostensibly 'correct' reading, a simple declarative reservation following 'Yet still' (etc.; see critical apparatus), *v.* an assertion of will and futurity, in l. 9; and the future (and doubtless correct) 'I'le' in l. 12, following 'soe' (l. 11). Similarly, in l. 13 the majority's 'I' eliminates the slightly awkward ululation of 'musicall I'le longe'. Alternatives of relative difficulty and ease prove nothing, but by the usual rule the former is more likely to be authoritative, and so it seems to be here (see notes on ll. 3 and 9 below); there is, moreover, slight support for 'I'le' in all three cases as more consonant with the decisive 'Then' (l. 7), which concludes the 'present' deliberation of ll. 1–6.

l. 3. *This*. 'This' could be a dittographic error (cf. 'Love this', l. 2) in some but probably not all witnesses, and it is both a less likely error and a less conventional reading than 'To', which also begins the following line.

l. 9. *ones*. This reading has the support of only two witnesses (neither very authoritative) besides the copy-text, and it may not be 'original'. Nevertheless, 'Ladyes' (l. 7) suggests it, and clarity of sense (ill-served by the ambiguous 'faire one') supports it, as differentiating the class of the 'faire ones' (or sex) from the member, 'the fatt and softe-skinn'd dame', who is not necessarily a beauty but a woman, despite the 'please myne Eye' of l. 10 (this is not a very coherent poem).

89. To Celia, an Ode (p. 97)

On the doubtful eighteenth-century ascription of this poem to Suckling see Introduction, pp. cix–cx.

90. In Brennoralt (p. 97)

On the doubtful association of this poem with Suckling see Introduction, p. cx.

l. 1. *they tell*. The manuscript variant 'shee tells' is a plausible sophistication: without an antecedent for 'they', one would expect 'thy love' to be the chief witness of her own chastity, but this is a quasi-dramatic poem addressed to a 'young Souldier' (l. 2), and 'Take no friends word' (l. 5) demands a complement, which 'they tell' is.

l. 11. *Goddess't*. Probably a nonce-coinage, on the analogy of the less uncommon nonce-use of *woman*, 'to make like a woman in weakness or subservience', as transitive verb (*OED*, s.v. *Woman*, *v*).

POEMS WRONGLY PRINTED AS SUCKLING'S IN
THE LAST REMAINS, 1659

91. Song (p. 98)

The sole authority for the association of this poem with Suckling is its inclusion in *LR*; a copy of the poem may have been found among the papers that his sister made available to the printer (see Introduction, pp. lxxxviii–xciv). That it is, however, Lord Herbert of Cherbury's is attested by its inclusion both in *A37*, a collection that contains corrections and the subscription 'The Verses of Ed. L. Herbert of Cherbery and Castle Island; 1630' in Lord Herbert's own hand, and, augmented by three stanzas (q.v, below), in *Occasional Verses*, 1665, which has a dedication by Sir Henry Herbert. Lord Herbert's brother, to Lord Herbert's grandson Edward, the third Lord (see *Poems*, ed. G. C. Moore Smith, 1923, pp. xxiii–xxvi; as Moore Smith notes, the manuscript collection is not quite accurately dated, since it contains Lord Herbert's 'Elegy on Doctor Dunn', who died on 31 March 1631).

In *LR* 'Song' is printed as the first three stanzas of a longer poem, the rest consisting of 'Upon Platonic Love'. This error in the printed text probably originated in the physical characteristics of the copy, in which the second poem, untitled, followed 'Song' without indication that it is a separate poem, an error not especially easy of detection, since (1) there is some similarity in the stanza forms of the two (and different stanza-forms could in any case be found in the same poem, as in a number of George Herbert's poems); and (2) the sense seems curiously incomplete in eighteen lines. Lord Herbert himself must have felt this apparent deficiency, since the following three stanzas, which are metrically homogeneous but not otherwise closely integrated with the first three, complete the poem in *Occasional Verses*:

> Give me then so much love, that we may burn
>   Past all return,   [20]
> Who 'midst your beauties, flames, and spirit lives,
>   So great a light must find
>   As to be blind
> To all but what their fire gives.

> Then give me so much love, as in one point   [25]
>   Fix'd and conjoynt
> May make us equal in our flames arise,
>   As we shall never start
>   Until we dart
> Lightning upon the envious eyes.   [30]

> Then give me so much love, that we may move
>   Like starrs of love,
> And glad and happy times to Lovers bring;
>   While glorious in one sphere
>   We still appear,   [35]
> And keep an everlasting Spring.

Text. There are seven substantive variants in the three texts of this poem, in the title (see note below) and ll. 4, 6, 8, 13, and 15 (two). *OV* shares the reading of *LR* against *A37* in ll. 4 and 8, and that of *A37* against *LR* in the title and in ll. 6, 13, and 15. Of *LR*'s four unique readings in the body of the poem, 'Nor is that right' (l. 15) for 'You are deceiv'd' (which also occurs in l. 3, in a similar context) suggests conjectural reconstruction rather than deliberate alteration, as does 'that' for 'who' (l. 15); and so, though it is something of an improvement, does 'By every one that hath a heart' for 'Or such wherein you have no part' (l. 6), in alternative lines that are respectively characteristic of Suckling and Lord Herbert. *LR*'s 'think't' for 'think it is' (l. 13) looks rather like a paleographical than a memorial defect or editorial alteration, since it is both cacophonous and metrically anomalous (copy: 'thinke too soon'?). Of the two readings shared by *LR* and *OV*, 'Whom' for

'When' in *A37* (l. 8) is an improvement that could have been made by anyone at any stage of transmission accidentally as well as deliberately; 'got and born' for 'freely borne' (l. 4), with its emphasis on procreation and on action and specific detail rather than on attitude and abstraction, is distinctly charac- teristic of Suckling. It is possible that Suckling, as friendly editorial critic, was the source of this reading (see the general remarks on possible collabora- tion and correction in the Introduction, p. xlvi), but the textual evidence more strongly favours the hypothesis that the *LR* text represents a patched- up memorial reconstruction of a version of the poem in which Lord Herbert had already made the alterations in ll. 4 and 8.

The 'integrity' of *LR*'s text, which represents a distinct if corrupt version of the poem, seemed worth preserving, and I have retained its substantives and altered the punctuation in only three lines (in ll. 8 and 14, where a question-mark is demanded, and in l. 15, where the sense is confounded by an absence of punctuation after 'right').

Title. *LR*'s 'Song' could have been supplied by either Suckling or the printer to a text without a title. 'Ditty' is certainly authoritative: the two texts associated with Lord Herbert contain it, and it is a favourite of his, being the sole title of four of his poems and occurring in the titles of three others.

92. [Upon Platonic Love] (pp. 99–100)

In *LR* this 'anti-Platonic' poem was printed as a continuation of the 'Song' by Lord Herbert of Cherbury (q.v. in Commentary above). Except for the general thematic congeniality of its argument, its inclusion in *LR* is the only 'evidence' for Suckling's authorship. It is subscribed 'S^r: R: E:' in *A11* and was included in *A10*, a manuscript collection of 'Some English and Scotts amorous Poems of S^r: Robert Ayton' (f. 1^r) compiled by Ayton's nephew, Sir John Ayton. This collection was evidently intended for publication, but the address to the 'Courteous Reader' (f. 1^v) implicitly acknowledges the doubtful provenance of the copy, for Ayton had 'neither publisht in print, nor kept coppyes of anything he writt, either in Lattin or English', and some of the poems 'were formerly printed in other mens names, and pray the[e] to Correct any faults that may [have] escapt in the press or other ways, farewell'. The date of the collection is uncertain, but it is natural to suppose that it was compiled well before Sir John's death in 1676 and probably well after Sir Robert's death in 1638, since Sir John had been in exile with Charles II, returning to England with him in 1660 (the conjectural date of the collec- tion has some bearing on the corrupt and apparently conflated text of this poem in *A10*, since it may well have been influenced by that in *LR*).

As 'Vpon Platonick Love: To Mistress Cicely Crofts, Maide of Honor', this poem has been accepted as Ayton's by his most recent editor, Charles B. Gullans (see critical apparatus), who discusses the variant texts of the poem in some detail (text, pp. 195–7, and notes, pp. 316–18; cf. his comments on Sir John Ayton, pp. 100–2). On the basis of its association with Mrs. Cicely Crofts in the titles of *A11* and *H17*, Gullans tentatively dates the poem as not earlier than 1630 and perhaps as late as 1633 (p. 261), suggesting that it probably postdates the production, on 8 January 1632–3, of Walter Montagu's pastoral play, *The Shepherd's Paradise*, whose Neoplatonic conception of love Ayton in effect ridicules here (as Suckling does in fact in 'The Wits', ll. 81–8). Mrs. Crofts had herself acted in the production, and the poem was almost certainly written during or after 1630, by which time she had become a Maid of Honour, and well before 29 June 1636, when she married Thomas Killigrew the elder (see Gullans, pp. 317–18).

Text. As Gullans implies in acknowledging the exercise of his own judgement 'more freely [on this] than on the text of any other poem' (p. 316), the lines of transmission are impossible to reconstruct from the extant variant texts. Oral-aural transmission and memorial transcription would seem to account for a number of the variants (e.g. *LR*'s readings in ll. 3, 20, 25, and 35), and convergent variation doubtless for some of the widespread contamination in and almost random agreements between the witnesses. All the witnesses contain or manifest unique variants (*LR*'s shared with its direct descendant *O2*) that are apparently corrupt, and none has any but intrinsic authority. The provenance of *A10*, the only text demonstrably associated with the author (posthumously and indirectly, through his nephew) is unknown (see headnote), and it contains more unique and obviously corrupt readings than any other text; the sources of 'corrections' (*A10x*) introduced by Sir John Ayton after the original transcription are equally uncertain.

The evidence of complex variants suggests possibly shared derivation and accordingly weakened individual authority for *A11* and *H17* (title; ll. 5, 11, and 21), but conflicting variations make even this relationship doubtful. No genealogical hypothesis will account for more than a few variations, but all except one or two of the unique readings are manifestly inferior to the alternatives and presumably corrupt, and there are at least reasonable grounds for choosing between most of the complex variants, a majority of which are as likely to represent convergent variation as direct transmission. The accidentals of none of the texts have special authority, and I have retained *LR* as copy-text for its generally satisfactory if somewhat heavy printer's accidentals. In choosing between substantive variants, I have, like Gullans, exercised my own judgement, which in most cases is supported by what seems to me to be the weight of general textual authority. In the eight places where our texts differ, Gullans generally favours the scribal readings of his copy-text (*A10*: ll. 5, 13, 27–8 [twice altered, the second time to restore the original reading]) or Sir John Ayton's alterations (*A10x*: ll. 7, 25, 35 [two variants: order of phrases and a reading]); his title is a hybrid, mine a single one of little authority adopted for convenience.

Title. It is questionable whether any title has much authority: *A10*, *F25*, and *LR* have no title, and the one in *A10x* and *L*—adopted in the present text chiefly for its economical descriptiveness and convenience—is of later addition. There is support for the inclusion of 'Mistress Cicely Crofts' in Gullans's hybrid title on the basis of probable historical associations (see headnote), but the possibility of shared derivation makes the dual textual authority of *A11* and *H17* somewhat questionable (see note on *Text*).

ll. 27–8. *Our . . . us . . . we/Our.* In *A10* the alteration from singular to plural and then back to singular (*A10x*[2]) demonstrates an ambiguity of design that is, I think, apparent rather than real. As the preceding stanza was concessive and confessional ('I must needs confess', etc.), this one is assertive and declarative: 'I hold that perfect joy makes all *our* parts As joyful as *our* hearts'; the following two lines offer the empirical evidence of the universal human experience of the senses in validation of the view held. These 'senses' are not only the speaker's, but everyone's, and therefore hers, too. The general assertion more persuasively develops the argument than a continued personal confession would, and it is, moreover, an essential preparation for the speaker's assertion in the following stanza that she 'may descend' to his 'end' (the senses, as both limit and object), while he, though he 'faine would tune my fancy to your Key', 'cannot reach to that abstracted way'. The argument here as of the whole poem generally is based on the same Neoplatonic conceptions as Donne's 'The Exstasie' (q.v. in Appendix D, 'The Ecstacy', in *Elegies and Songs and Sonnets*, ed. Helen Gardner, 1965, pp. 259–65).

l. 35. *they can their joys no more extend.* Authority for the order of the three phrases 'they can', 'their joys', 'no more' is hopelessly divided (perhaps slightly stronger for the reading of the present text) and the order itself of almost no critical consequence, though it might be observed that '. . . they can extend' (*F25*, *LR*) would closely parallel 'they did end' (l. 36, all witnesses), but so, in another way, does '. . . no more extend'; and that 'they can . . . extend' also loosely parallels 'let our souls begin' as 'their joys' does 'where', which affords limited critical support to the witnesses' authority for the present reading.

93. Song (pp. 101–2)

This poem is absurdly attributed to Donne in *Ros4*. The sole authority for its association with Suckling is its presence in *LR*, in which it may have been included because a copy was perhaps found among Suckling's papers (see Introduction, pp. lxxxvi–xciv). It was published as his own by Owen Felltham (1620?–68) in *Lusoria*, 1661, where it is preceded by the following note: 'This ensuing Copy the late Printer hath been pleased to honour, by mistaking it among those of the most ingenious and too early lost, Sir John Suckling' (p. 20, No. xxxii). I see no reason to doubt Felltham's claim, despite the apparent influence of *LR* on the *Lusoria* text and the inferiority of the latter's unique readings, which are probably due to the exercise of Felltham's failing judgement on a poem written many years earlier and of which he may not even have kept a copy.

Text. Of the nine texts of this poem, three are entirely derivative: *O2* from *LR*, with which it is identical (except in reading 'on' in l. 1); and *RD7* from *Lu*, and *A25* from *Ros4* (both share otherwise unique readings with their originals—*RD7* also has *Lu*'s prefatory note—and contain unique readings of their own); the poem is ascribed to Donne in *Ros4* and was probably on that account taken into *A25*, 'a manuscript first intended as a Donne collection' (see Margaret Crum, ed. *Poems of Henry King*, 1965, p. 58). *Lu* is apparently in part derived from *LR*, with which (along with their derivatives, *RD7* and *O2*) it shares six otherwise unique readings (ll. 1, 7, 17 [two], 18, and 24). Of the remaining witnesses, *EP5* contains directional unique variants that are unoriginal, and *Ros4* (which has a unique title) shares unoriginal readings with *A25*; *Harv6* contains no unique readings, and *H18*'s title alone is unique.

Despite the association of *Lu* with the author of the poem, the apparent influence of *LR* upon it and its aberrant readings in ll. 8, 14, 18–19, 20, and 24 give it the status of a derivative and corrupt text, nor do its printer's accidentals give it special authority. Except for the titles in *H18*, *LR*, and *Ros4* (discussed below), the internal textual evidence suggests that *Harv6* should be regarded as the archetype: its substantives seem to be original, and its punctuation is sparing and sound. The other texts hypothetically derive from it in four lines of descent: (1) *H18–Ros4–A25*; (2) *EP5* alone; (3) *LR–O2*; (4) *Lu–RD7* (the original readings—those of *Σ*—of *Lu* in ll. 1, 7, and 17 theoretically preclude its direct exclusive descent from *LR*). On this hypothesis I have of course adopted *Harv6* as copy-text, from which I have departed only in adopting the title, 'Song', from *LR*.

Title. Six of the nine texts, including the one published by the author, have no title, and all three of the titles in the texts that have them are different, leading to the general conclusion that there was no authorial title. The titles of *H18* and *Ros4* are stock miscellany-titles, and may be regarded as directional, since the substantives of *Ros4* ('To his loue') are identical with those of *H18* ('To his Mistrisse')—and *Harv6*—except where, with its descendant *A25*, it introduces unique readings (ll. 8 and 11; its 'whilst', shared with *LR* and *O2* against *Σ* 'while', is an insignificant formal variant). I have adopted 'Song', which has no authority, as a title of convenience with the sanction of tradition; except for tradition, 'To his Mistrisse' has equal claim.

l. 20. *Promont*. Despite the use of 'Palace' in *Lusoria*, there is support for the rather unusual 'Promont' as the original authorial reading in Felltham's use of the word elsewhere, notably in *Lusoria*, p. 21 (No. xxiv), and *Resolves*, 1661, 2nd Cent., p. 352 (No. lxxvi).

LETTERS

No. 1 (p. 107)

The occasion of this letter was Suckling's departure to join Lord Wimbledon's regiment in Holland (see Introduction, p. xxxi). Letter No. 9 was written shortly after his arrival. For the relationship between Suckling and Mary Cranfield, see Introduction, pp. xxxi–xxxii. Although they seem to have carried on a protracted youthful love affair, or at least to have been very close friends, there is evidence in two previously unprinted letters to her from the poet's sister Martha (q.v. in Appendix A.iv, Nos. 1–2) that something of an estrangement had developed well before Mary's death in late 1635.

ll. 9–10. *Let it suffice, that those countryes which I am now to visit,* etc. Aubrey asserts that 'by 18 he had well travelled France and Italie, and part of Germany, and . . . Spaine' and had 'returned into England an extraordinary accomplished gentleman' (ii. 240), but these lines seem to imply that Suckling was about to visit the Low Countries, and perhaps even the Continent, for the first time.

Nos. 2–8 [1629–1635 (?)] (pp. 107–12)

Comparison with Suckling's holograph letter to Mary Cranfield (No. 1), and place references, internal similarities of phrasing, subject, and tone, and their grouping in *Fragmenta Aurea* (Nos. 2 [followed, however, by No. 52], 3, and 4 occur together as do Nos. 5–8, both groups followed by letters closely associated with the Cranfield family), suggest that the following letters, especially Nos. 4–7, were also written to her; but the subject matter makes it impossible to assign to more than three or four a date less approximate than the limits of a three-to-five-year period. The contents suggest that Letters Nos. 5–7 were written from abroad, probably Germany, in 1631–2, and 2–4 and 8 at home in England, either in August 1630–September 1631 or after 10 April 1632 (see Introduction, pp. xxxi–xxxiii).

No. 2 (pp. 107–8)

ll. 1–3. *Fortune and Love have ever been so incompatible,* etc. Cf. Letters No. 3, ll. 10–14, and No. 29, ll. 1–3.

ll. 6–11. *for though you have left behind you, faces whose beauties might well excuse perjury in others,* etc. Cf. 'Perjury disdain'd'.

ll. 8–14. *since to the making that no sin,* etc. Cf. Letters No. 3, ll. 1–9, and No. 6, ll. 10–14.

ll. 11–15. *So that now a gallerie* etc. Cf. Letter No. 29, ll. 15–19, and, for another reference to Van Dyck, Letter No. 48, ll. 18–23. Van Dyck painted the portrait of Suckling used as frontispiece to this edition (*c.* 1638), and, though he did not come to England until 1632, his work was well known there, and James I had employed him in 1620–1.

ll. 18–24. *You* (*Madam*) *have my heart already*, etc. Cf. Letter No. 8, esp. ll. 13–17.

No. 3 (pp. 108–9)

ll. 1–9. *Though* (*Madam*) *I have ever hitherto beleeved play* etc. Cf. Letter No. 2, ll. 8–14. Suckling uses 'Protestant' both to express the limitations of his own judgement (since Protestants rejected the doctrine of infallible authority) and, in the sense of 'devoted champion', as Herrick uses it in 'To Anthea, who may command him any thing': 'Bid me to live and I will live | Thy Protestant to be'. Cf. the use of 'Protestant' in Letters No. 9, l. 13, and No. 20, l. 16, and of 'Catholiques' in No. 2, l. 14.

ll. 12–16. *so just a quarrel . . . to Fortune* etc. Cf. Letter No. 2, ll. 1–3.

No. 4 (pp. 109–10)

It might at first appear that the salutation of Suckling as risen from the dead alludes to the rumours of his death in the Second Bishops' War (see Introduction, p. lii), and that this letter should therefore be dated in late 1640, but from the opening lines and ll. 15–18 and 32–5 it is plain that he had been about a week in London after an apparently extended stay at Milcote (see also note on l. 3).

l. 3. *Milcot.* Thompson: 'Milcote, in the Alcester division of Barlichway hundred, co. Warwick, is about three miles S.S.W. of Stratford-on-Avon, and forms part of the parish of Weston-on-Avon in Gloucester diocese' (pp. 402–3). From its earliest days Milcote had belonged to the Greville family. Pressed by debt, Sir Edward Greville sold the whole of the estates surrounding Milcote to the Earl of Middlesex on 9 May 1623 (see Charles J. Phillips, *A History of the Sackville Family* [1930], ii. 378). It seems likely that family visits were made there earlier in the 1630s, but it first 'from 1635 . . . replaced Wiston as Middlesex's country home'; in 1636 the Earl 'dictated retirement to Milcote to recuperate after the disaster of the Exchequer fine' (see Prestwich, *Cranfield*, pp. 523, 517).

blessed shades. Cf. 'Elizium, a place of blessed shades' in *Account*, ll. 154–5, and 'Elysiums' in 'Upon Christmas', l. 4, 'Sonnet III', l. 19, and *Account*, l. 95.

No. 5 (pp. 110–11)

This letter is datable by the reference to the 'losse of all' the Imperialists' companies (ll. 10–11) in the Battle of Breitenfeld, on 7 September, in which approximately 20,000 out of 35,000 men were lost (see Roberts, ii. 535–7). Suckling had arrived in Hamburg with Sir Henry Vane's embassy to Gustavus on 5 October, and almost immediately he wrote to the Earl of Middlesex a full account that is now lost but is referred to in Letter No. 12, ll. 2–5 (see Commentary and Berry, p. 63).

l. 7. *so great a goodnesse as yours.* Cf. Letter No. 1, ll. 5–6.

l. 10. *at.* *FA46*'s 'all' may be an anticipation of an occurrence later in the line, but it probably represents a misreading of 'at' ('al' is Suckling's predominant spelling in the early letters).

No. 6 (p. 111)

This letter is undatable, but 'at this distance' (l. 4) suggests that it may have been written from abroad, probably Germany, which would date it in the Autumn of 1631 or the Winter of 1631–2.

ll. 11–14. *superstition hath ever been fuller of Ceremony* etc. Cf. Letters No. 2, ll. 8–14, and No. 3, ll. 1–9.

No. 7 (pp. 111–12)

This letter is not certainly datable, but Suckling's description of the place and its women is very similar to that in Letter No. 18 [December 1631], ll. 11–16, and it may have been written from the same place at approximately the same time; and only in this letter (l. 13) and in No. 19 (l. 96) does Suckling use 'peremptory', for him something of a 'state' word.

ll. 4–7. *all our dayes are (as the Women here) alike:* etc. Cf. Letter No. 9, ll. 2–3.

l. 6. *Such great State do Beauty and the Sun keep.* Cf. 'A Barber', l. 5.

ll. 11–12. *Books . . . (Feasts heretofore).* Cf. *Aglaura*, Epilogue (c), ll. 1–2, and *Goblins*, Prologue, ll. 3–8.

No. 8 (p. 112)

There is nothing in this letter that makes the addressee certain. It contains none of the warm protestations of affection and devotion of some of the other letters, but the acknowledgement of obligation for 'favours' (ll. 7, 8, 13), apparently more narrowly and directly obliging than the favour shown a petitionary suitor by a tolerant lady, suggests a reasonably close relationship. If this letter is to Mary Cranfield, it would appear from its cooler tone and its placing as the last of this group of letters in *Fragmenta Aurea* that it was written after Suckling's return from Germany in April 1632, perhaps at about the time that Mary's brother-in-law wrote to her that Suckling was going from Bath to the Spring Garden to bowl (see Introduction, p. xxxii).

ll. 5–17. *A strange proud return you may think I make you* etc. Cf. Letter No. 2, ll. 18–24.

ll. 10–11. *cloud is breaking . . . storm.* Cf. Letter No. 24, ll. 20–3.

No. 9 (pp. 112–14)

This letter was written shortly after Suckling's arrival in Holland ostensibly to join Lord Wimbledon's regiment in the Dutch service (see Introduction, p. xxxi; and, for the letter's discovery and printing, see Introduction, p. civ and n. 3). A letter to Mary Cranfield (No. 1) was written from Gravesend on 30 October, immediately before his departure. Hazlitt conjectured that 'Will' was Davenant (ii. 173–4, n. 1), an identification that has been generally accepted, although there is no real evidence to show that Suckling and Davenant were acquainted at this time. The true addressee is identifiable from a holograph letter (No. 11) written a few months later and fully addressed to William Wallis (see Berry, p. 51); the two letters are stylistically very similar, and there are striking particular parallels, the force of one depending upon an antecedent in a letter written earlier (Nos. 9, ll. 51–2, and 11, ll. 8–13).

l. 2–3. *the winde . . . bad.* Cf. Letter No. 7, ll. 4–6.

l. 2, 4. *the winde . . . crosses him.* Cf. 'A Song to a Lute', l. 4.

ll. 9–11. *That soe much Rope . . . they should be pumpt.* Variations very similar to these on a recorded proverb, 'He that is born to be hanged (drowned) shall never be drowned (hanged)' (Tilley B 139), and on an apparently proverbial simile, also occur in juxtaposition in *The Tempest*, I. i. 49–51 (see also I. i. 31–6), the second in the form 'though the ship were . . . as leaky as an unstanched wench'.

l. 12. *Purgatorie.* Cf. Letter No. 11, l. 64.

l. 13. *Protestant.* Cf. Letters Nos. 3, l. 8, and 20, l. 16.

l. 16. *Mr. Brett.* Arthur Brett, the Earl of Middlesex's brother-in-law, through his second wife, Anne Brett, is also mentioned in Letter No. 11, l. 76 (on his identity see Berry, p. 51).

l. 19. *Infidells.* Cf. Letter No. 11, l. 19.

ll. 35–6. *more then the quantity of a graine of Mustard-seede in faith,* etc. After Matt. 17:20.

ll. 46–8. *they chuse . . . as we doe our Maiors, . . . by their . . . little witts,* etc. Cf. Letter No. 11, ll. 15–17.

ll. 49–50 *summum bonum.* Cf. 'Upon the Epiphanie', l. 5.

ll. 51–2. *not a man here but would doe that which Judas did, for halfe the money.* Cf. Letter No. 11, ll. 8–13.

No. 10 (pp. 114–16)

Suckling had evidently remained in Holland, first in Lord Wimbledon's service and later as a student at Leyden University, until a few days before this letter was written from Brussels, the capital city of the Spanish Netherlands (see Introduction, pp. xxxi–xxxiii; Letter No. 11, ll. 7–13; and Berry, p. 54).

l. 14. *The Prince of Orange.* Frederick Henry, Prince of Orange, had taken Wesel on 19 August 1629, shortly before Suckling's arrival in Holland.

ll. 17–18. *Linge . . . Mast* etc. i.e. Lingen and the Maas district ('The 'Wast' of Suckling's holograph, as the historical circumstances indicate, is plainly a mistake for 'Mast'); the Dutch did not finally capture Maastricht, its chief city, until 1632 (see *CSPV 1629–32*, pp. 629, 631, 633).

l. 19. *The Archduchesse.* Isabella Clara, who governed the Spanish Netherlands.

l. 27. *Shertogenbosck and Fernanbuc.* s'Hertogenbosch (the Dutch name for Bois-le-Duc) was taken by the Dutch on 7 September 1629, as Pernambuco, a Spanish seaport in Brazil, was in February 1630.

l. 46. *Henry Vandenberg.* Count Henry van den Berg had commanded the forces of the Spanish Netherlands during the hostilities of 1629.

l. 47. *Francisco di Sapata.* As Berry points out (p. 58, n. 41), Don Francesco Zappata had been in England the previous summer (*CSPV 1629–32*, pp. 148, 161, 168).

ll. 51–5. *Granendonc . . . Bolduc.* Grobindonck had been governor of Bois-le-Duc when it was taken by the Dutch in 1629. 'The necessities that pressed them to yeeld were of powder and men; all things els having bin yet in good aboundance with them' (Sir Dudley Carleton to Viscount Dorchester, 12 September 1629: P.R.O., S.P. 84/140, f. 42ʳ, an uncalendared document discovered by Berry).

No. 11 (pp. 116–18)

A facsimile of the first page of this letter is given in the Introduction, between pp. xcviii–xcix.

Suckling had evidently just arrived in the Spanish Netherlands from Holland, where he had been from November 1629 through April 1630; cf. the letter antecedent to this (No. 9), and see Introduction, pp. xxxi–xxxiii.

ll. 9–13. *the greatest part of them* etc. Cf. Letter No. 9, ll. 50–2.

ll. 15–17. *it is as rare a thing to see . . . as in London to see a Lord Maior have store of witt.* Cf. Letter No. 9, ll. 46–8.

l. 19. *infidells.* Cf. Letter No. 9, l. 19.

ll. 38–40. *Sir Randal Cranfeild . . . Sir Robert Harlo* etc. Sir Randall Cranfield, the Earl of Middlesex's brother, had obtained a patent for himself, and after him his son, Vincent, as 'Master and worker of the monies of gold and silver within the Tower of London', but Sir Robert Harley, by procuring a patent for the same office, 'couzened' him of his position. The Cranfields complained of Harley's machinations in a petition dated 30 May 1628 (see *HMC 4th Report*, p. 17, and Berry, p. 61, nn. 49–50). Vincent Cranfield was a lifelong friend of Suckling's and apparently a man of scarcely less remarkable prodigality (see Introduction, pp. xlviii–l).

ll. 49–51. *For their honoring the Lady Mary above al*, etc. The irreverant wit of this line partly depends upon its allusion to the Earl of Middlesex's daughter, 'the Lady Mary' Cranfield, on whose relations with Suckling see Introduction, pp. xxxi–xxxii.

l. 55. *They are the maddest shavers in the world.* Cf. a similar use of this pun in 'A Barber', l. 2: (1) one who shaves with a razor; (2) wag.

l. 64. *Purgatory.* Cf. Letter No. 9, l. 12.

l. 72. *the yong Ladyes.* The young ladies living at home would have been Middlesex's daughters, Mary, Elizabeth, Frances, and perhaps Susanna Cranfield. Martha Cranfield had married in 1620.

l. 76. *Mr. Brett.* See Letter No. 9, l. 16 and note.

No. 12 (pp. 118–19)

This letter was written a few days after Suckling's arrival in Germany as a member of the party of Sir Henry Vane, Charles I's Ambassador to Gustavus Adolphus (see Introduction, p. xxxiii, and Berry, pp. 63–4). It is clear from ll. 2–5 that Suckling had already given a full account of the Battle of Breitenfeld in a letter, now lost, that was probably written immediately upon his arrival in Germany. Letter No. 5, to Mary Cranfield, was also written soon after his arrival and may have accompanied the lost letter to the Earl of Middlesex.

ll. 5, 8, 13. *Rostac . . . Micleberg . . . Witzberg.* Rostock, Mecklenburg, and Würzburg.

ll. 16–17. *We are now upon our journey to the Camp.* According to Sir Henry Vane's dispatch of 9 November 1630, the party left Hamburg for Gustavus's camp on 11 October, the day after this letter was dated (P.R.O., S.P. 81/37, f. 118; see Berry, p. 63, n. 4).

l. 23. *Tilley.* John Tserclaes von Tilly, the Imperialist General defeated by Gustavus at Breitenfeld in September 1630.

No. 13 (p. 119)

This letter was clearly written in October 1631, during the journey of Vane's party from Hamburg to Gustavus Adolphus's camp at Würzburg, which lasted from 11 October to 5 November (see Berry, p. 80). Suckling's description of the 'March' here (ll. 5–8) corresponds closely with that given in Letter No. 14, ll. 6–9, which was written on 9 November after the party's arrival in Würzburg. It is possible that it was addressed to the Earl of Middlesex, for, though Suckling normally addresses him formally as 'Right honorable' (but 'My Lord' in Letters Nos. 15, 40, and 43), '[there is] none to whom he owes more obligation then to your Lordship' seems especially characteristic of his attitude toward the Earl. On the other hand, Suckling's 'negligence' (l. 4) implies that he had not previously written to 'my Noble Lord', whereas he had written to the Earl of Middlesex twice since his arrival in Germany earlier in the same month (see Letter No. 12, text and Commentary). If, as is probable, the Earl of Middlesex is not the addressee, identification can only be conjectural; a strong candidate is perhaps Suckling's cousin by marriage, Henry Carey, Lord Lepington, to whose wife, Martha, Suckling inferentially wrote Letter No. 22 in 1635 and to whom he addressed a commendatory poem in 1638 (No. 72).

During the journey, Vane's party was forced to stop in Braunschweig for four days because of Imperialist action, and it is probable that the letter mentioned in ll. 2–3 reached Suckling and that this reply was written there (see Vane's reports of 18 and 19 October, and 9 November, P.R.O., S.P. 81/37, ff. 88, 93–5, 118; and Berry, p. 66, n. 17).

l. 7. *Sheets have been the hardest to come by.* Cf. 'the miserye of liing in straw' (Letter No. 16, ll. 9–10).

No. 14 (pp. 119–21)

For a detailed account of the historical circumstances of this letter's composition and narration, see Berry, pp. 66–72 (text, notes to transcription, and map).

ll. 8–10. *at length wee are arrived at Wirtzberg, where the Embassador had Audience on Sunday last.* Vane's party arrived at Würzburg on Saturday, 5 November, and his audience with Gustavus was held on the next day (see his dispatch of 9 November, P.R.O., S.P. 81/37, f. 118; and Gardiner, vii. 189).

l. 12. *Erford, Kenings-hoff, and Sweinsford.* Erfurt, Königshofen, Schweinfurt.

l. 14. *the Castle.* Marienburg, 'the powerful fortress on the other side of the River Main' (Berry, p. 66).

20–1. *Prage was taken by the Heyre of Wallesten* etc. A confused report. Prague was actually taken, on 5 November, by the Saxons under Arnim, not by the heir, Max von Waldstein (see Berry, p. 69).

l. 21. *Duke of Sax*. John George, Elector of Saxony. In abbreviating, Suckling evidently miswrote 'Di' for 'D.', the usual abbreviation (the title is given as 'D. of Saxe' in P.R.O., S.P. 81/37, f. 98, which was also written in October 1631).

l. 22. *Nodimberg*. Nuremberg.

ll. 22–3. *200000 rextallars and . . . 150000*. £50,000 and £37,500, respectively. A *reichsthaler* was worth 5s. (P.R.O., S.P. 81/37, f. 264, cited by Berry, p. 69, n. 26).

l. 28. *Coronell Hebron*. Sir John Hepburn, a Scottish officer in Gustavus's army.

l. 30. *Rotenberg and Wintzem*. Rothenburg and Windsheim.

ll. 34–5. *my Lord Marquis*. James, third Marquis and first Duke of Hamilton, who had received a commission in 1630 to raise an army for the Swedish service (Roberts, ii. 414–15). He is mentioned again in Letter No. 19, l. 6.

ll. 52–6. *The gentleman that shal present these lettres . . . is Mr. Gifford*. Gifford carried both Suckling's letter to the Earl of Middlesex and 'the duplicate of my [Vane's] dispatch of the 12th November' to the King (P.R.O., S.P. 81/37, f. 126). Suckling had evidently known Gifford for some time, for Gifford had also been a volunteer in Lord Wimbledon's regiment in Holland (see Introduction, p. xxxiii), and a Captain 'Gifforde' had also accompanied the expedition to the Ile de Ré in 1627 (Folger MS. V. a. 275, f. 59). Letter No. 18 appears to have been written to him after Suckling had received news of his safe arrival in England.

No. 15 (pp. 121–3)

Suckling's uncle, the Earl of Middlesex, is almost certainly the addressee of this epistolary Character. Lucius Cary, second Viscount Falkland (1633), was suggested by Thompson, but he is 'a very unlikely choice', as Berry notes, 'since Falkland did not hold any considerable position from which to retire until after Suckling's death' (p. 82, n. 74). Suckling's uncle as the addressee, and the approximate date of this Character as 9–29 November 1631, were first proposed in Berry's dissertation ('A Life of Sir John Suckling', University of Nebraska, 1953); for his more recent discussion, see Berry, pp. 80–2. There is strong support for this as the correct date in Suckling's reference to a Character that he had determined to enclose but refrained from sending because of 'the Consideration, that I am troublesome enough in this way of intelligence' in his letter to the Earl of 29 November 1631 (No. 16, ll. 35–9), and in his expression, in brief, of very similar sentiments in his letter of 9 November 1631 (No. 14, ll. 42–8).

Menna Prestwich has recently suggested that the Character, 'certainly meant for Middlesex', was 'probably written in 1637' (*Cranfield*, p. 548), on several grounds. 'A reference to the Exchequer case [1632–5] can be read between the lines' (p. 548); at the conclusion of the case, Middlesex was held responsible for arrears to the crown of £24,000 and also fined £12,000 (pp. 497–505). In 1636 an active Court interest in reform led to Middlesex's 'being sounded for his views, and in the New Year of 1637 more definite approaches were made' (p. 547), the first on 20 January 1636/7 by the Earl of Dorset, and another, shortly after, by the Marquis of Hamilton—with whom Suckling had been associated in Germany (see Letters Nos. 14, ll. 34–42, and 19, ll. 53–65; Hamilton's letter does not survive, but Middlesex's draft of a reply to him is dated 2 February 1636/7). 'In November 1637 a committee to consider Household retrenchment was appointed on which there sat Lord Keeper Coventry, the Earl of Dorset, and the third Marquis of Hamilton, all favourable to Middlesex' (p. 547), and Middlesex himself 'jumped at the chance of returning to office and hurled memoranda at Hamilton' (p. 549); he 'continued to hope and to write advice as late as 1641', but he was never returned to office.

Between ll. 2 and 37–42, especially, might well be read a 'reference to the Exchequer case', which forced Middlesex to sell some of his lands; ll. 20–2 could allude to the solicitations by Dorset and Hamilton of 1636/7; and Suckling's description of the 'reformed' Court (ll. 48–80) suggests his immediate presence there. The possibility that this Character was written in 1637 cannot be lightly dismissed. Nevertheless, the details of the Character are applicable to the general circumstances of Middlesex's retirement from public life after his impeachment in 1624 (on which see Prestwich, *Cranfield*, chs. x–xiii, and R. H. Tawney, *Business and Politics under James I*, 1958, pp. 231–74); the reference to the Court—which in November 1631 Suckling had not long since left—as 'there' rather than 'here' (l. 50) suggests Suckling's absence from it; and Letters Nos. 14 and 16 strongly support Berry's and the present dating. 'While all the world is thus in action, pardon me (my lord) if I must hope your Lordshipp will not long be idle. Since you cannot now sett downe with satisfaction of your owne conscience, The Christian world never more needing able men than at this present', etc. (Letter No. 14, 9 November 1631, ll. 42–6), is in effect a hastily written condensation of the thoughtful and detailed Character, which could well have been written before Suckling's arrival in Germany (certainly Letter No. 16 does not suggest that Suckling had much leisure for formal composition during November 1631). 1631 seems to me the most likely date, but it is not impossible that a Character much later finished—as in 1637—could have been based on an earlier version written in 1631.

ll. 7–9. *that great soul of yours, like a Spider* etc. Cf. Bacon: 'if it [the wit and minde of man] worke upon itselfe, as the Spider worketh his webbe, then it is endlesse, and brings forth indeed Copwebs of learning, admirable for the finesse of thread and works, but of no substance and profite' (*Advancement of Learning*, 1605, I. iv. 5; ed. W. A. Wright, 1868, p. 32). It was indeed 'ironic in view of the enmity that had existed between Cranfield and Bacon that Suckling chose to use Bacon's metaphor' (Prestwich, *Cranfield*, p. 522).

l. 25. *Oleoes.* Highly spiced stews, served (1670) as a second course (see *OED*, where Suckling's use is the earliest dated occurrence). Cf. *Brennoralt*, II. iii. 25–7: 'Liberty and publique good are like great Oleos, Must have the uper end still of our tables, Though they are but for shew'. Under no circumstances would 'aloes' (Hazlitt's emendation) provoke appetite.

ll. 56–7. *upon the appearing of the Sunne*, etc. Cf. 'Upon New-years day 1640', ll. 1–5.

l. 67. *it is as winds are.* Cf. Letter No. 9, ll. 2–4.

No. 16 (pp. 123–4)

ll. 5–6. *In my last you had . . . most certaine news. For Francefurt was taken* etc. Gustavus's army entered Frankfurt on 17 November. Suckling may have written a letter, now lost, in which he gave an early, unconfirmed report of Frankfurt's capture, but he is probably referring to what he had reported in Letter No. 14 (ll. 23–6) of Gustavus's remarks to Sir Henry Vane (see Berry, pp. 72–6).

l. 9. *liing in straw.* Cf. Letter No. 13, l. 7.

ll. 13, 15, 17. *Nodimberg . . . Mentz . . . Colen.* Nuremberg, Mainz, and Cologne.

l. 16. *the canon plays.* Cf. 'so does (we know) the Canon too' ('To Mr. Davenant for Absence', l. 14).

ll. 35–9. *a Character*, etc. The Character is probably Letter No. 15 (q.v. text and Commentary).

ll. 38–9. *smootherd that motion as soone as it was borne.* With minor alterations this phrase is used in *The Sad One*, I. i. 39–42.

No. 17 (p. 125)

Suckling miswrote 'September' for 'December' in the date of this letter, owing undoubtedly to 'hast' (l. 17), but the day is probably correct (see Berry, p. 77, and, for the historical circumstances in general, pp. 76–80). Vane sent his messenger, Cole, with a dispatch 'of great importance, and required speed' either on 3 or 4 December, probably early on the 4th, when Suckling dated his letter (see P.R.O., S.P. 81/37, f. 183).

l. 16. *Maidenburg.* 'Apparently Marienberg' (Berry, p. 79, n. 67).

No. 18 (pp. 125–6)

This letter was probably written to Mr. Gifford, who had carried Sir Henry Vane's dispatch of 12 November to England, after Suckling received news of his safe arrival (see Letter No. 14, ll. 52–6; Berry discovered the uncalendared State Papers cited below and first commented on Gifford's, Holme's, and Cole's courier services). It could not have been written before 7 December 1631, for on that date Gustavus first crossed the Rhine (Roberts, ii. 557). The overcoming of Tilly, at Breitenfeld, and the crossing of the Main took place still earlier. If Gifford had left Würzburg on 12 or 13 November, there would have been ample time for Suckling to receive a report of his arrival in England by the second week in December, during or shortly after which this letter was probably written. On 7 December Vane's courier, Peter Holme, was sent to London with a dispatch, the reply to which was sent to Vane on 19 December by a courier named Cole (see P.R.O., S.P. 81/37, ff. 183, 259ʳ, and Berry, p. 77). Gifford remained in England until 31 December or shortly after (on S.P. 81/37, f. 262ᵛ, is the notation, 'To Mʳ. Comptroller [Vane] the 31. of December. 1631 by Mr. Gifford').

This letter may have been addressed to Gifford at the Earl of Middlesex's House in Great St. Bartholomew's, London, and perhaps arrived after Gifford had left, being kept with the other letters from Suckling that were eventually given to Humphrey Moseley for *Fragmenta Aurea* (see Introduction, pp. lxxxiv–lxxxv).

ll. 13–16. *Northern Beauties*, etc. Cf. Letter No. 7, ll. 4–7.

No. 19 (pp. 126–9)

Portions of this letter written in a simple numerical cipher in the original were hastily deciphered between the lines by the recipient, who made two not very important errors, 'shewed' for 'seemd' (l. 9) and 'really' for reality' (l. 45). A diplomatic transcription including cipher and interlinear deciphering is given, with detailed commentary and notes, in Berry, pp. 82–93; in the present edition, ciphered portions are indicated, by italics, in the critical apparatus.

Suckling left Frankfurt for England with Vane's dispatch of 30 March and, having written briefly to Vane from Dover, arrived at Court on Tuesday, 10 April; his extended audience with the King, to which he was personally conducted by the Lord Treasurer, took place on Thursday or Friday, 12 or 13 April (see Berry, pp. 83–5).

l. 5. *lookinge asquint.* Cf. *The Sad One*, I. i. 59.

l. 8. *my Lord Treasurer.* Richard Lord Weston (created Earl of Portland in 1633), who had won the Lord Chancellorship from Suckling's father in 1621.

l. 9. *Donawart.* Donauwörth.

ll. 9–10. [my Lord Treasurer] *seemd . . . Somethinge coole if not cold! Perchance his garb.* Cf. *The Sad One*, III. iii. 8–15.

l. 11. *Maxfeild, Murrey.* James Maxwell and William Murray, both Gentlemen of the Bedchamber.

l. 16. *Sir Isaack Wake.* The English Ambassador to France.

l. 42. *blanks.* 'A document, "paper", or "form", with spaces left blank to be filled up at the pleasure of the person to whom it is given' (*OED* 6). Here the word clearly refers to papers authorizing Vane to enter into negotiations on the King's behalf.

l. 56. *my Lord Marquis.* James, third Marquis and first Duke of Hamilton, who commanded an army of volunteers in the Swedish army. Suckling mentions going to sup with him in Letter No. 14, ll. 34–42.

l. 64. *Jacob Ashley.* Berry notes that Astley had been 'with Vane for a time during the winter. He carried a dispatch back to London in March and with Vane's son carried this letter to Germany' (p. 91, n. 118).

l. 69. *Sharneses.* Baron Hercule de Charnacé, one of the two French Ambassadors at Frankfurt.

l. 70. *they thinke you all much a Spaniard.* Cf. *The Sad One*, IV. ii. 19–22. As Berry suggests (p. 92, n. 120), it would appear that Suckling intended to write 'Swede', not 'Spaniard', meaning that Vane—an Imperialist to the protestants in Germany—is thought an arch-protestant by those in England with Spanish-Imperialist sympathies.

l. 72. *my Lady Dane.* 'L. Dane', in the original; she is probably 'the Lady Deane who had a son in Vane's service', as Berry notes (p. 92, n. 121; see *CSPD 1631–33*, p. 133).

No. 20 (p. 129)

Anne Willoughby was the nineteen-year-old heiress of Sir Henry Willoughby, of Risley, Derbyshire. Suckling unsuccessfully courted her in 1633 and again in 1634 (see Introduction, pp. xxxv–xxxviii, and Berry, pp. 94–7). This letter is datable by the apparent reference to it (as refused by his daughter 'about a yeare agoe', ll. 59–60) in Sir Henry Willoughby's letter of 31 October 1634 to Charles I, in which Suckling's conduct of his suit is thoroughly condemned (see this letter in Appendix A.iv, No. 3).

l. 8. *quarrel . . . starres.* Cf. *Aglaura*, I. iii. 16–17, and Letter No. 27, ll. 6–8.

l. 16. *Protestant . . . merit.* Cf. '*Non est mortale quod opto*', ll. 5–6, and Letters Nos. 3, ll. 7–9, and 9, ll. 13–14.

No. 21 (p. 130)

Sir Kenelm Digby (1603–65) was 'held to be the most accomplished cavalier of his time', and 'such a goodly handsome person, gigantique and great voice, and had so gracefull elocution and noble addresse, etc., that had he been drop't out of the clowdes in any part of the world, he would have made himselfe respected'. He was 'well versed in all kinds of learning', and in the eyes of his contemporaries there were few physical or intellectual attributes that he lacked (see Aubrey, i. 224–7). But on this occasion his malicious gossip seems to have been at least partly responsible for Suckling's attempt to take his revenge for a beating he had received from Sir Kenelm's brother, Sir John Digby, Suckling's rival for Anne Willoughby's hand. This letter was evidently written after Suckling had assaulted Sir John Digby and his party outside Blackfriars, and Suckling's is the only claim that he was the victor in the encounter (see Introduction, p. xxxvii). Although Digby is not one of the major participants in 'The Wits', written three years after this letter, he is mentioned without rancour by Suckling in a catalogue of those present ('The Wits', l. 12).

No. 22 (p. 130)

Martha Lady Carey, Suckling's first cousin, was the eldest daughter of Lionel Cranfield, first Earl of Middlesex, by his first wife, Elizabeth Sheppard. In 1620 she married Henry Carey, Lord Lepington, who became second Earl of Monmouth on 12 April 1639 (see G.E.C., *Complete Peerage*, ix. 59). The date, subject, and addressee of this letter are identifiable, because it is apparently the one referred to in a letter from Lady Carey to her father, dated 15 May [1635], which is given in Appendix A.iv (No. 4); the date is further discussed in the Commentary on that letter.

ll. 12–13. *the Uncle is no less satisfied then the Nephew.* Cf. Appendix A.iv, No. 4, ll. 8–9: 'this daye he [Suckling] writes to me, that your lordship approves of it'.

l. 16. *Pluto's Court . . . the God of Moneys.* Strict mythological propriety demands 'Plutus', but confusion between this pair of gods was common in the Renaissance, and 'Pluto's' is very likely authorial as well as the reading of the printer's copy. Cf. Webster's *The Duchess of Malfi*, III. ii. 283, 'Pluto, the god of riches', and for a discussion and other examples see T. S. Dorsch's detailed note on IV. iii. 101 ('Dearer than Pluto's mine, richer than gold') in the New Arden edition of *Julius Caesar*.

l. 17. *Loves.* 'Love' is perhaps a compositor's corruption accompanying a misunderstanding of 'Moneys' (l. 16) as the ordinary plural rather than the possessive singular; but Pluto's' (l. 16) suggests that the latter was intended, and 'Money[']s' demands 'Love[']s'.

No. 23 (pp. 131–3)

A copy of this letter among the Cranfield Papers (uncatalogued portions) is dated and addressed as in the present text (this information is wanting in the printed text) and endorsed, in the hand of the Earl of Middlesex, 'The

Coppy of Sr In Suckline his lettr to Sr Georg SowthCot'. The relationship between the two texts is discussed in the Introduction, pp. ci–cii, and the circumstances of Martha Suckling's unhappy first marriage on pp. xxxviii–xxxix. That the Earl of Middlesex acted as a kind of referee in the Southcot marital disputes is clear from a letter, partly prompted by Suckling's letter, that Southcot wrote to the Earl on 18 November 1635; it is given in Appendix A.iv (No. 5).

ll. 38–43. *a young woman is a Hawk* etc. Cf. 'Upon my Lord Brohalls Wedding', ll. 36–40; *Aglaura*, IV. i. 13–15; and *Brennoralt*, IV. iv. 2–5.

ll. 49–50. *Doubts and fears are of all the sharpest passions*, etc. Cf. *Brennoralt*, I. iii. 86, and *The Sad One*, I. i. 72–3.

ll. 50–2. *through these false Opticks 'tis, that all you see is like evening shaddows*, etc. Cf. *Aglaura*, I. iv. 76, and v(t). i. 93 ('false Opticks'); and Letter No. 36, ll. 5–8 ('evening shaddows'). The development of metaphor in all three is very similar.

l. 56. *the wise man*. 'Solomon' (*FA46*) may be Suckling's second thought (though Solomon says nothing of the kind) but it is so obviously suggested by the exclusive 'the' that it seems more likely to be a sophistication.

ll. 60–75. *yet is there difference of Lunacy* etc. Cf. *Brennoralt*, III. iv. 19–22.

ll. 66–7. *Money in your hands is like the Conjurers Divel*, etc. Cf. *Aglaura*, II. ii. 30–2, and *The Goblins*, IV. i. 26–30; and see Tilley D 319. The 'hand' of *FA46* is here, like 'finger was' in 'A Ballade. Upon a Wedding' (l. 37), probably a literal-minded sophistication.

ll. 68–70. *The rich Talent that God hath given*, etc. The turn on the parable of the talents (Matt. 25: 14–30) makes Southcot a peculiarly domestic 'unprofitable servant'.

l. 70. *ill Spirits*. Southcot refers to these, and this letter otherwise, in his letter to the Earl of Middlesex (see headnote above).

ll. 80–1. *yet it is some part of a cure to have searcht the wound*. Cf. 'Loves Offence', l. 6, and see Tilley D 358 and W 930.

No. 24 (pp. 133–4)

This letter provides the earliest evidence for Suckling's association with the Bulkeley family of Beaumaris, Anglesey. One of the 'Two Excellent Sisters' (presumably Mary Bulkeley and Anne [Bulkeley] Fawkenor) was almost certainly the 'Aglaura' and 'Dear Princesse' addressed by Suckling in the following eleven letters. The tentative date of this letter was first suggested by Thompson (p. 406); the time of year is clear from the last paragraph of the letter. The evidence for the identification of Mary Bulkeley as 'Aglaura' is discussed in the Introduction, pp. xxxix–xlii, and in Berry, p. 104.

l. 6. *my Lord of C.* Thompson suggested James Hay, first Earl of Carlisle (the husband of the Countess unkindly treated in 'Upon my Lady Carliles walking in Hampton-court garden' and 'The Wits', ll. 60–4): 'Lord Carlisle had much experience in foreign embassies. He died in 1636, which suits well with the possible allusion to the Duchess of Buckingham's second marriage, and indicates the date of the letter as 1635–36' (p. 406). But Robert Dormer, Earl of Carnarvon (d. 1643), would also seem a strong candidate: it was in his company that Suckling landed at Dieppe after his flight in May 1641 (see Introduction, pp. lvii–lviii); he, too, had been in the Second Bishops' War, and he had, moreover, close connections with Wales (*DNB*).

l. 8. *your Cozen Dutchesse.* Probably Katherine Manners, widow of George Villiers, first Duke of Buckingham (see Introduction, p. xli). She was related to the 'Two Excellent Sisters' through the marriage of her niece, Dorothy Hill, to their brother, Richard Bulkeley. Suckling might almost have said '*our* Cozen Dutchesse', for he too was in a manner related to her: the mothers of the Duke of Buckingham and Anne Brett, the second wife of the Earl of Middlesex, were sisters.

l. 12. *B. W. . . . the Lady of the Isle.* Hazlitt: '*B. W.*' may represent 'the inverted initials of one of the same [Bulkeley] family' (ii. 200, n. 1); Thompson: the 'allusion to the Lady of the Isle is doubtless to the widowed Lady Bulkeley [Mary's mother]' (p. 406). There is insufficient evidence to support either assertion.

ll. 21–2. *Mistris Thomasses bleak Mountains.* Thompson: 'Mistress Thomas may reasonably be identified with Blanch, daughter of Robert Coytmor, of Coytmor (? Coed Mawr) Carnarvonshire, who married Thomas Bulkeley, brother of the second Sir Richard, and was therefore aunt by marriage to the two sisters' (p. 406). A 'Mistress *T.*' is mentioned in Letter No. 48, l. 20.

Nos. 25–34 (pp. 134–9)

These ten letters—all probably but not with absolute certainty—to Mary Bulkeley, Suckling's 'Aglaura', cannot be precisely dated, but it appears that all the letters to her in *FA46* were printed in chronological order except No. 24 ('For the Two Excellent Sisters'). Two letters (Nos. 34 and 35) were probably written to Mary after their affair was terminated, probably in October 1639, shortly before her marriage; but only the limits of a four-year period—1635/6 to Summer 1639—may confidently be assigned to the other letters, with the possible exception of No. 33 (q.v., text and Commentary). It may be, as Berry suggests (p. 104), that the affair belongs primarily to the years 1638 and 1639, but there is no evidence to show when the earlier friendship developed into love. The inclusive dates and the general circumstances of the affair are further discussed in the Introduction, pp. xxxix–xlii, and in the Commentary on individual letters below.

No. 25 (pp. 134–5)

ll. 9–10. *make love feed on doubts*, etc. Cf. 'To his Rival II', ll. 41–2.

ll. 14–15. *There needs no new Approaches* etc. Cf. 'Loves Siege' and other parallels cited in the Commentary for that poem.

No. 26 (p. 135)

ll. 2–4. *But that I know I love you more* etc. The same idea is expanded in 'Song' ('No, no, faire Heretique').

No. 27 (pp. 135–6)

ll. 5–9. *Virgin-Love* etc. Cf. 'Virgin-wombe' in 'Faith and Doubt', l. 4, and the expression of similar sentiments in the doubtful letter, No. 55, ll. 7–19.

No. 29 (pp. 136–7)

There are striking similarities of sentiment and expression between this letter and Letter No. 2.

ll. 16–19. *Variety of Beauty and of Faces* etc. Cf. 'Upon two Sisters', ll. 19–20.

No. 32 (p. 138)

l. 4. [*B*]. Hazlitt suggested Baron-Hill, the seat of the Bulkeley family (ii. 198); Thompson added that it might have stood for either Baron-Hill or Beaumaris, where Baron-Hill was located (p. 405).

l. 6. *Welch man.* Suckling elsewhere uses 'man' generically, without article, for the 'male human being', most closely in 'There never yet was honest man | That ever drove the trade of love' ('Loving and Beloved', ll. 1–2), but there is no strict parallel for the use here. The effect of *FA46*'s comma is to make 'man' an odd and gratuitous vocative. Hazlitt's emendation (and, except for the spelling, the reading of the present text) makes better sense than Thompson's, which would seem to demand an additional alteration from singular to plural.

No. 33 (p. 139)

This letter expresses anxiety and clearly suggests vicissitude in the relationship between Suckling and the 'Princess' brought about by his 'extravagant wishes', her resulting 'fears', and his responding 'restlessness'. The letter following was written, as its contents make clear, shortly after Suckling had paid a visit to her; this letter may have been written not long before the visit, perhaps in the late summer of 1639.

No. 34 (p. 139)

One cannot be certain, but it is possible that this letter expresses a kind of fulfilment of both Letters No. 33, to which Suckling could have received an unfavourable reply, and No. 43, written in September 1639, in which he expressed his intention to go to Wales to 'kisse Mrs. Buckleys hands'. Mary Bulkeley was married in late 1639 (see Introduction, p. xlii), and one can conjecture that his 'Abruptnesse' and his having perhaps 'sinn'd farther then we think of' was in part prompted by news of her forthcoming marriage. But the letter is so general that only an abrupt and inamicable parting between Suckling and the 'Fair Princesse' is certain.

No. 35 (p. 139)

Suckling's assumed role of Mountferrat—the knight brought to disgrace and ruin by a woman in Fletcher, Field, and Massinger's *Knight of Malta* —suggests that Mary Bulkeley had already married, as the lady had who failed to requite the knight's love in the play. If that inference is correct, this letter must have been written in the last months of 1639 or very early in 1640, because Mary had married in late 1639 (see Introduction, p. xlii).

Nos. 36–7 (pp. 140–2)

These two letters were probably written in Summer or Autumn 1638, not long after the Covenant had been accepted by the Scots (see note on l. 29 below). The military preparations to which Suckling refers did not begin in earnest until shortly before June (Charles announced preparations for war on 20 June).

Thompson suggested that the second letter may be a cynical reply from a Scottish lord who was genuinely a Covenanter (p. 415); and it is possible that the first letter was written by Suckling to a Royalist Scottish lord, though Suckling was never an alderman, and at least to that extent an element of 'depersonalization' is involved here. But there is little room for doubt, I think, that these two letters employ imaginary correspondents to a single rhetorical end, because the reply damns the Covenanters' cause no less than the original enquiry (Thompson also thought this interpretation the more likely). 'Alderman [   ]' and 'Lord *M.*' may have replaced the names of actual persons, but there is insufficient evidence to identify them.

No. 36 (pp. 140–1)

ll. 5–8. *Distance . . . evening shadow*. Cf. Letter No. 23, ll. 50–2.

l. 12. *St. Michael-Mounts Mens security*. Thompson: 'Some proverb or local custom may be alluded to. But possibly Suckling is merely referring to the heavenly protection, which, according to tradition, was vouchsafed to the "guarded mount", as to its parent monastery off the Norman coast' (p. 414).

l. 14. *Witheringtons and Howards Estates.* The first lay in Northumberland, the second in Cumberland.

l. 29. *this New Covenant.* 'In effect it was a restatement of the Confession of 1580 buttressed by a protest against all that had been done to alter true religion in Scotland' (C. V. Wedgwood, *The King's Peace, 1637–1641,* 1955, p. 198). The Covenant was read to and accepted by two or three hundred ministers assembled in Glasgow on 27 February 1637/8; by 2 March it had been accepted by the nobility, gentry, clergy, and people (see Gardiner, viii. 344–6).

No. 38. An Answer to a Gentleman in Norfolk that sent to enquire after the Scotish business
(pp. 142–4)

A 'Copy of a letter to a gent. in Norfolk concerning the Scottish business' was No. 11 among 'Mr. Vassall's papers seized 27th Sept. 1639', according to a note made by Secretary of State Sir Francis Windebank on that date (*CSPD 1639*, p. 526; No. 16 was *An Account of Religion*). Internal and other evidence confirm the date of this letter as April 1639, which is given in the title of *D*. The 'alteration and irresolution about the Levies' lasted no longer than the first reports of Sir Alexander Leslie's strength, estimated in a report of 19 April at nearly 10,000 and shortly afterward at 30,000. The 'Doctors of State' had not yet given the Scottish affair a name, and it was only 'perchance' that they believed it to be rebellion. Presumably they would have been more certain had the abortive encounter of 3 June—described in Letter No. 40 —already taken place. The want of factual material implies that little was certainly known. The letter was probably written while the King's party was at York (from approximately 1 to 19 April), preparing for the march to the North (see Introduction, p. xlvii, and Berry, p. 98).

The 'letter' was perhaps written—if to a particular person—to Charles Suckling of Woodton, Norfolk, who had inherited the family's lands there. Suckling at some time—probably before 1639—had perhaps written a letter to his second son, Charles Suckling of Bracondale, to persuade him to marry (No. 53). But it is most likely that this 'letter' is 'a short political tract couched in the form of a letter to an imaginary correspondent' (Thompson, p. 415), as apparently wide circulation, suggested by the variant texts, confirms.

Text. All seven witnesses are collateral, *Ash3* and *LR* having the fewest unique variants (seven and eight) and *Ash8* and *C* the most (nineteen and sixteen). The distribution of variants suggests that independent lines of descent from a hypothetical original are represented respectively by (1) *LR* and, descending from an intermediate ancestor, *Ash8* and *C*; and (2) *Ash3*, with *Eg27*, *D*, and *T8* (the last two sharing a subordinate ancestor) descending from an intermediate ancestor below *Ash3*'s. These relationships would be represented in terms of Greg's formularies as: (*x*) *A*ᶜ {LR [*Ash8 C*]} {*Ash3* [*Eg27* (*D T8*)]}. There are some conflicting variations, but the close relationship between *Ash8* and *C*, and *D* and *T8*, is reasonably certain, and *Ash3* and *LR* are generally reliable witnesses. Authority is divided between the hypothetical major lines of descent in ll. 19, 21, 27 (twice), 30, 31 (twice), 34–5, and 36; but the sense is seriously affected only in ll. 27, 30, and 36, which are discussed below.

Title. The reference to Norfolk is omitted in *LR*, but four manuscripts have it, three (*T8, C, lost MS.*) reading 'in', and the fourth (*Ash8*) 'of', 'Norfolk'. The reference to the county may have been deliberately omitted to avoid possible association with a particular addressee.

ll. 16–18. *A King or no King . . . Pretences speciously conscionable* etc. Possibly a deliberate reflection of Charles's proclamation of 27 February: 'We have now thought it . . . necessary . . . to inform all our loving Subjects . . . what froward and perverse Returns they [the Covenanters] have made to us, notwithstanding all their specious Pretences. . . . So the question is not now, Whether a Service-Book is to be received or not? Nor whether Episcopal Government shall be continued, or Presbyterial admitted? But whether we are their King or not?' (Rushworth, *Historical Collections*, 1659, ii. 830 ff.). The phrase 'A King and no King' was no doubt suggested by the title of Beaumont and Fletcher's play, *A King and No King*.

ll. 17–21. *In great Mutinies and Insurrections* etc. Cf. *Brennoralt*, III. ii. 73–5.

ll. 26–7. *Nemo cogitur credere invitus.* Probably quoted *memoriter* from Cassiodorus, *Variarum*, ii. 27: 'Religionem imperare non possumus, quia nemo cogitur, ut credat invitus.'

l. 27. *Liberty.* 'that Liberty' (the rejected reading) adversely alters the sense from a clear distinction between liberty of thought and liberty of action to a cloudy one between conscience and conscientious action, which can hardly have been intended.

ll. 29–30. *consider withall that Prophecies are ceas'd.* Cf. 'A Summons to Town', ll. 11–14, 'Oracles are not yet ceas'd', etc., and Commentary.

l. 34. *that they should order Religion.* This is a reflection of the passage in Cassiodorus partly quoted by Suckling (see note on ll. 26–7).

ll. 34–5. *in the world.* This phrase, an unlikely editorial interpolation, limits the sense of 'order' to 'regulate', 'manage' (cf. *Account of Religion*, l. 7: 'a great Disposer and Orderer of things'), and makes its range of application more finite.

ll. 35–8. *Lesly himself* etc. Sir Alexander Leslie, later first Earl of Leven, entered the army of Gustavus Adolphus in 1605 and fought with distinction under the Swedish King for nearly thirty years. In May 1630 he had returned to England to assist the Marquis of Hamilton in training a troop of English soldiers for service in Germany. He was with the English contingent at the recovery of Magdeburg from the Imperialists in January 1632. If Suckling did not personally know Leslie when he was in Germany, he undoubtedly heard about him from Sir Henry Vane, the Marquis of Hamilton, and others. Even in Germany Leslie took an active interest in developments in Scotland: he subscribed himself and caused 'a great number of our commanders in Germany subscryve our covenant' (Robert Baillie, *Letters and Journals, 1637–1662*, 1841–2, i. 111). Neither Leslie nor Suckling had a hand in the tract, *A Coppy of Generall Lesley's Letter to Sir John Suckling, with Sir John Sucklings Answer to his Letter*, 1641.

l. 36. *here*. 'here', i.e. 'this side of the Channel, *v.* abroad', makes better sense than 'there', i.e. 'Scotland', which is, given the subject of the letter, an obvious if not very thoughtful alteration.

ll. 42–4. *The great and wise Husbandman* etc. Cf. Ps. 80: 12–13.

No. 39 (p. 144)

After 3 June the people would no longer 'think what we would do if we were let loose' (ll. 14–15), because on that day the English forces retreated without a battle before the numerically superior Scots (see Introduction, p. xlviii). The letter must have been written, therefore, before this date. There is no evidence by which the addressee might be identified. For the historical circumstances, see Berry, pp. 97–8.

ll. 2–7. *We are at length arrived at that River*, etc. In *1 Henry IV*, III. i. 96–100, the Trent; here, the Tweed.

l. 5. *scantlet*. The word is 'cantle' in Suckling's source (see preceding note).

ll. 13–14. *Tower-Lyons in their Cages*. Cf. *Aglaura*, IV. i. 18–19, text and note.

No. 40 (pp. 145–6)

Suckling's description of the 'battle', which took place on Monday, 3 June, is corroborated by other accounts (see Introduction, p. xlviii, n. 2). For the historical circumstances, see Berry, pp. 97–103.

l. 42. *This daie being Wensdaie*. Suckling's letter was dated 6 June, which was Thursday, and it was written at one o'clock in the morning (see l. 54).

l. 65. *my lady Carey*. Suckling's cousin, Martha Lady Carey (in fact, Lady Monmouth since 12 April 1639), to whom Letter No. 22 was apparently written.

No. 41 (pp. 146-7)

This letter was written between 6 June (the date of Letter No. 40) and 17 June—after the cessation of hostilities, but before the signing of the Treaty of Berwick on the 18th. It is probably to be dated after 11 June, the date of the conference between the Scots and English commissioners to which Suckling seems to allude in ll. 11–13 (see Berry, p. 103, n. 22).

No. 42 (pp. 147-8)

The Treaty of Berwick 'now on foot' (l. 4) was signed on 18 June (see Berry, p. 103, n. 22). Thompson quotes the Earl of Clarendon's comment on it: 'An Agreement was made, if that can be call'd an Agreement in which no body meant what others believ'd he did' (*History*, i (1701), part I, 123).

ll. 18–21. *Necessity, not good nature* etc. Cf. *Brennoralt*, I. iii. 65–9.

No. 43 (pp. 148-9)

The news of the Dutch and Spanish fleets in the Downs is that of the latter part of 1639, and this letter is precisely datable by Suckling's reference to St. George's Feast 'on Munday next' (l. 23), which had been postponed until 7 October in 1639 because of the preparations for the First Bishops' War during the time that it was normally held (see *CSPD 1639–40*, p. 19; this letter was first dated by Berry, q.v. for the historical circumstances, pp. 104–7).

ll. 5–6. *D. Cadimans* etc. Probably Dr. Thomas Cadiman, one of the royal physicians; Davenant wrote a poem 'To Doctor *Cademan* Physitian to the Queene' (*Madagascar; with Other Poems*, 1638, p. 84).

ll. 9–12. *The noise and fame of this fleet* etc. For a full account of the activities of the Dutch and Spanish fleets see Gardiner, ix. 60–8.

l. 21. *Roben Lesley.* Sir Alexander Leslie (see note on Letter No. 38, ll. 35–8) was sometimes referred to as 'Robin' by the Marquis of Hamilton and others (see the index entries for Leslie in *HMC Hamilton Report*).

l. 24. *I intend to kisse Mrs. Buckleys hands.* 'Milcote was just off one of the principal routes to North Wales, that through Shrewsbury and Chester' (Berry, p. 104), and Suckling would have been on his way to Anglesey to see Mary Bulkeley, his 'Aglaura' and 'Dear Princess' (see Introduction, pp. xxxix–xlii, and Letters Nos. 24–35, text and Commentary).

No. 44 (pp. 149-50)

Sir George Southcot committed suicide in October 1639. Lady Southcot, Suckling's sister, later married William Clagett, of Isleworth, Middlesex, at an unknown date. Aubrey first identified Lady Southcot as the addressee of this letter (ii. 244), and Berry the date of Southcot's suicide.

l. 5. *Sophonisba.* Suckling refers to her also in 'Sonnet III', ll. 23–5. She was the daughter of Hasdrubal and the wife of Masinissa, and committed suicide as an act of love and devotion to her husband.

ll. 15–18. *Nothing (Madam) has worse Mine than counterfet sorrow*, etc. As Beaurline suggests, Suckling may here be echoing a passage in a letter of Balzac, in which 'Olympa' is urged not to grieve or counterfeit grief for the loss of a bad husband: 'Yet you seeme with him to have lost all, and doe so cunningly counterfeit the afflicted, I can hardly beleeve what I see', etc. (Letter xv, 'To Olympa from Balzac, 22 July 1622', *The Letters of Mounsieur de Balzac*, trans. William Tyrwhit, 1634 and 1638, p. 265).

ll. 24–5. *whether it were with his garters or his Cloak-bag strings.* Proverbial, in part, as 'He may go hang himself in his own Garters' (Tilley G 42), which is also a commonplace expression in Jacobean drama, as Irving Ribner notes of Tourneur's *The Atheist's Tragedy*, II. v. 137 (Revels edition, 1964, p. 55), citing *1 Henry IV*, II. iv. 49–50; in the latter scene there is also a reference to Falstaff as 'that stuffed cloak-bag of guts' (l. 497).

ll. 26–30. *The Spanish Princesse Leonina* etc. Suckling's account is very close to that in *New Epistles of Mounsieur de Balzack, Translated out of French, into English, by Sr Rich: Baker Kt.... The Third Part*, 1638 (p. 27): 'You should alledge unto her the Princesse *Leonina*, so highly esteemed of the Court of *Spaine*, and the prime ornament of this last age. Knowing that her husbands quirry was come, to relate unto her the particulars of his death, & hearing that his Secretary was to come the morrow after, shee sent the quirry word, to forbeare comming to see her, till the Secretary were come, that so sher might not be obliged to shed teares twice.'

ll. 36–9. *a line of Mr. Shakespears*, etc. *Julius Caesar*, V. iii. 89.

No. 45 (pp. 150–1)

After the death of Henry Grey, seventh Earl of Kent, on 21 November 1639, Edward Nicholas wrote on 12 December in possibly indelicate mock-sympathy that 'the Countess Dowager of Kent doth soe much lament the death of her husband that Mr. Selden cannot comfort her' (P.R.O., S.P. 16/435, No. 64, catalogued in *CSPD 1639–40*, p. 158), and it seems not unlikely that this was the occasion of the illness Suckling mentions, and that John Selden was the addressee of the letter. Elizabeth Lady Kent was the daughter and co-heiress of Gilbert Talbot, seventh Earl of Shrewsbury, and an 'ingeniose woman' according to Aubrey (ii. 220); Suckling probably knew her well, for the houses of the Earl and Countess, Whitefriars, in London, and another in Wrest, Bedfordshire, were gathering-places for the court wits. John Selden (1584–1654), the great jurist and orientalist and one of Suckling's 'Wits' (l. 9), was solicitor and steward to the Earl and Lady Kent, whom he is thought to have married after the Earl's death and whose estate he inherited upon her own death on 7 December 1651. As in Nicholas's remark, there are hints of irony in this letter (see 'conversation' and ll. 7–13 generally), and Selden could be its putative rather than real addressee.

ll. 9–13. *And though such excellence cannot change* etc. The wish that Lady Kent may go on living is expressed in terms of the 'conversation' between mortals and God or the angels on earth (Old Testament) and that in Heaven (New Testament), to which the way was opened by Christ.

No. 46 (p. 151)

After Conway arrived at Hull on 17 April 1640 he wrote to the Earl of Northumberland that he had found 'few troops and fewer captains', adding, 'divers troops are on their way, but I saw only one captain with his troop'; he recommended that Northumberland would 'do well to send them [the captains] out of London' (*CSPD 1640*, p. 43). On 20 April he wrote to order Captain Porter to repair with his troop of horse to Newcastle (*CSPD 1640*, p. 53), and his letter to Suckling was probably of approximately the same date (see Introduction, pp. l–li, and Berry, p. 108, who argues that the letter 'must belong to mid-April or mid-May, more likely the former'). Sir John Mennes, who was commissioned on the same day as Suckling, arrived at Newcastle with his troop on 29 April (ibid., p. 83). For an account of the historical circumstances, see Berry, pp. 107–9. A facsimile of this letter is given in the Introduction, between pp. xcviii and xcix.

l. 15. *manners*. In the manuscript Suckling wrote a 'g' (or less probably a 'y'), perhaps originally intending either 'goodness' or 'good manners' but changing his mind (cf. Berry, p. 109, n. 37).

No. 47 (p. 152)

The Earl of Newcastle was appointed governor to the Prince (to which office Suckling refers in ll. 6–8) on 4 June 1638 and, if this letter was correctly dated 'January 8th', it could only have been written in 1639, 1640, or 1641, as Berry points out in arguing that Suckling wrote it 'in 1641, in connection with the opening stage of the army plot' (see pp. 110–15). A generally late date for the letter is supported by its orthography, and in the manuscript volume in which it is bound it falls between letters dated 29 September 1639 and 5 February 1640 (i.e. 1641).

ll. 21–2. *the noblest Planett of our Orb in Conjunction* etc. Cf. *Aglaura*, II. v. 12–16.

LETTERS OF UNCERTAIN DATE AND ADDRESSEE

No. 48 (p. 153)

Thompson (p. 418) suggests that this letter may have been addressed to the same persons as Letter No. 24, 'For the Two Excellent Sisters', but most of the references are too obscure to be identified; it seems to be a reply to a letter written in hieroglyphs or cipher, in which drawings were included.

ll. 2–3. *as was wisely said of a Neece of Queen Gorbodukes*. In *Ferrex and Porrex*, or *Gorboduc*, the King is Gorboduc, the Queen Videna, but the alteration to 'King' in the Errata is surely without the authority of copy, unless 'Queen' was, oddly, compositorial. Cf. *Twelfth Night*, IV. ii. 12–15: 'for as the old hermit of Prague . . . very wittily said to a niece of King Gorboduc "That that is is"'.

l. 7. *Secretary Cook*. Sir John Coke, Secretary of State from 1625 to 1639.

ll. 11–12. *what Beaumont said* etc. Francis Beaumont, 'The Examination of his Mistress' Perfections', ll. 21–3; Thompson notes that, 'as usual, Suckling quotes *memoriter*' (pp. 418–19).

ll. 18–23. *Vandike* etc. Cf. the reference to Van Dyck (who painted the portrait of Suckling used as frontispiece to this edition) in Letter No. 2, ll. 11–13.

l. 20. *Mistresse T*. See Letter No. 24, ll. 21–2, text and Commentary.

l. 21. *certaine je ne scay quoys*. Cf. 'Sonnet II', l. 4 ('know-not-whats'), and *Aglaura*, I. v. 36. It is most unlikely that 'certaine' was also intended to be French, though the spelling in *LR*, 'certaine', probably stood in Suckling's original and misled scribe or compositor or both; Suckling uses the word eight times in the holograph letters (all dated 1631 or before), always employing the terminal *e*.

No. 49 (pp. 153–4)

l. 13. *the Bear at the Bridge-foot*. 'A celebrated tavern at the Southwark end of old London Bridge, on the west side of High Street. It was pulled down in December 1761, when the houses on the bridge were removed and the bridge widened' (Henry B. Wheatley, *London Past and Present*, 1891, i. 135–6). It was much frequented by the court wits (see note on 'The Wits', ll. 93–4).

l. 14. *Colonel Young*. Perhaps Jack Young, who accompanied Suckling and Davenant on a journey to Bath (see Introduction, pp. xlii–xliii).

l. 17. *Captain Puffe of Barton*. Thompson suggests that this evident nickname may be an inaccurate allusion to 'goodman Puff of Barson' in *2 Henry IV*, v. iii. 93–4. There is a reference to a 'Capt. Pouffie [Povey?]' in *CSPD 1638–9*, p. 623.

l. 19. *Monsieur de Granville*. Perhaps Sir John Granville, who was on the expedition to the Ile de Ré with Suckling in 1627 (see Introduction, pp. xxx–xxxi).

ll. 22–7. *For the Waters* etc. The passage of waters is similarly interfused with the tactics of battle in 'Upon T. C. having the P.' (q.v. text and Commentary).

No. 50 (pp. 154–5)

l. 2. *drive that trade*. Cf. 'Loving and Beloved', l. 2, and *Aglaura*, III. ii. 89. See also note on 'Jack Bond' ('The Wits', Commentary, l. 10).

ll. 6–7. *flowing as much with Love as thou hast ebbed*. Cf. 'Song' ('No, no, faire Heretique'), ll. 9–10, and Tilley F 378, 380–1.

ll. 8–9. *Horseley Air . . . Waters of the Bath*. Carew had evidently gone from Bath to West Horseley, where his friend Carew Ralegh lived (see *Poems of Thomas Carew*, ed. Rhodes Dunlap, 1949, p. xxxviii; cf. note on l. 22).

l. 16. *Epidemical*. The Errata correction is doubtless editorial, and a graphic form resembling the reading of the *LR* text probably stood in the copy (Suckling's *i*'s frequently look like secretary *e*'s in the holograph letters because the dot is joined to the following letter).

l. 22. *The disease of the Stomach, and the word of disgrace*. '= "raw"+"lie", or "Rawlie" (Ralegh)' (*Carew's Poems*, p. 288; see note on ll. 8–9 above); Dunlap also notes that the same rebus is quoted of Sir Walter Ralegh by Aubrey (ii. 182).

l. 29. *Duke of B*. i.e., Buckingham, something of a political arch-villain for Suckling (see 'A Dreame', text, esp. l. 18, and Commentary).

No. 51(*a*) (pp. 155–6)

The following letter parallels this one very closely, and the two were printed in parallel columns in *FA46*, an arrangement that has little to recommend it, since the two are not parallel line-for-line or even, consistently, paragraph-for-paragraph (parallels between the two letters are not recorded in the notes). The 'Tom' addressed is traditionally Thomas Carew, almost certainly the intended rhetorical or real correspondent (No. 51[*b*], 'An Answer', has traditionally been attributed to him). These two letters constitute a unified two-part exercise in an epistolary genre inaugurated by Nicholas Breton, in *A Poste with a Packet of Madde Letters*, 1602 (and many later and enlarged editions), that of 'the misogynist letter dissuading a friend from marriage' (see Jean Robertson, *The Art of Letter Writing*, 1942, pp. 26, 68–9). Directly relevant are Breton's 'A Letter of counsell to a friend' with 'His Answere', which Suckling may echo in both of these letters (see note on ll. 9–10), and 'A disswading from marriage' with 'The Answere' (*A Poste . . . The first part*, 1605, sigg. C2ᵛ–4 and E2ʳ⁺ᵛ).

ll. 1–4. *Bedlam.* Cf. Letter No. 52, ll. 54–7.

ll. 9–10. *to fall into a Quagmire* etc. Here and in ll. 32–3, and in the following letter, ll. 32–9, Suckling may be echoing Nicholas Breton (see headnote): 'so shalt thou haue a hand ouer these humors, yᵗ would haue a head, ouer thy heart: and be maister of thy sences, by the vertue of thy spirit: otherwise, Will hauing gotten the bit in his teeth, will run away with the bridle: and Reason, being cast off, may neuer sit well againe in the saddle: but why do I vse these perswasions for the remoue of thy passions? If thou be soundly in, thou wilt hardly get out: but if thou be ouer shoes, thou maist be saued frō drowning' ('A Letter', sig. C3); and 'hee that is maister of himselfe, shal not neede to his mistresse; and therefore he that cannot ride, let him leaue the saddle' ('His Answere', sig. C3ᵛ). Cf. *Aglaura*, I. iv. 35–40.

ll. 11–12. *Love is of the nature of a burning-glasse.* Cf. 'Love's Burning-glass'.

ll. 23–4. *Thou now perchance hast vowed . . . to any one face*, etc. Cf. 'Perjury disdain'd', ll. 7–10, and 'Sonnet I', ll. 3–5.

No. 51(*b*) (pp. 157–8)

See the headnote on Letter No. 51(*a*). 'An Answer' has traditionally been attributed to Thomas Carew (inferentially the 'Tom' of No. 51[*a*]), but it seems very likely that it too is by Suckling (see 'Printed Sources' in the Introduction, p. lxxxvi) and parallels cited below; parallels with the preceding letter are not noted).

ll. 9–10. *kept fixt to its first object.* Cf. 'my Virgin-Love has staid for such an object to fixe upon' (Letter No. 27, ll. 5–6).

l. 12. *Recipe.* Cf. Suckling's use of 'Recipez', etc., in Letter No. 52, ll. 8–10.

ll. 19–20. *ravishing Realities which out-doe what Fancy or expectation can frame unto themselves.* Cf. 'Against Fruition II', ll. 15, 23; 'Love's Representation', ll. 10, 38; 'Loving and Beloved', l. 13; 'To his Rival I', l. 10; and 'Upon two Sisters', ll. 12–14.

l. 25. *an excesse of joy, which oftentimes strikes dumb.* Cf. 'Against Fruition I', ll. 27–8.

ll. 34–6. *A well-wayed horse* etc. Cf. Letter No. 53, ll. 11–13; and see note on Letter No. 51(*a*), ll. 9–10.

l. 42. *2da Sect. cuniculorum.* An imaginary reference.

No. 52 (pp. 158–9)

Were it not for the references to actual persons (e.g. the 'Mistris Howard' of l. 53 is presumably Lady Margaret Howard), one might suppose this to be an entirely fictional exercise in an epistolary genre inaugurated by Nicholas Breton (see headnote on Letter No. 51[*a*]). 'Jack' here and 'B' in 'Upon my Lord Brohalls Wedding' have traditionally been identified as the 'Jack Bond' of 'A Summons to Town' (l. 10, q.v., text and Commentary), but it seems odd that the same person should be in love with 'Mistris Howard' here yet be in ignorance of her marriage as 'B' is in 'Upon my Lord Brohalls Wedding' (perhaps much later, however). Berry (p. 15) has suggested that the addressee may be Jack Barry, a close friend of Roger Boyle, Lord Broghill, who married Lady Margaret Howard in 1641 (see Commentary on 'Upon my Lord Brohalls Wedding'). This letter cannot be dated more certainly than 1640 or earlier.

ll. 8–9. *Absence . . . (removing the object)*. Cf. 'To Mr. Davenant for Absence', esp. ll. 9–10.

l. 10. *Recipez*. Cf. Letter No. 51(*b*), ll. 11–12.

l. 20. *the cryed-up Beauties*. Cf. *The Goblins*, III. vii. 8–9.

ll. 24–5. *these Agues are easier cured with Surfets than abstinence*. Cf. 'To Mr. Davenant for Absence', ll. 17–20; 'Against Absence', ll. 35–6; and *Aglaura*, I. iv. 53–9.

ll. 27–8. *That . . . ado*. These lines, which I have been unable to trace, may indeed be by 'an old Author', but both the metre and the idea sound suspiciously like Suckling.

ll. 36–7. *smothered fires . . . breathed out*. Proverbial (Tilley F 265); cf. Letter No. 55, ll. 19–25.

ll. 42–3. *though in the Scripture . . . Wine*. Thompson quotes 1 Esdras 4: 14 ff.: 'O sirs, is not the king great, and men are many, and wine is strong? who is it then that ruleth them, or hath the lordship over them? are they not women?' (p. 408). The idea is, in general, proverbial (Tilley W 474, 696).

ll. 47–8. *a last remedy . . . worse than the disease*. A turn on the familiar proverb (Tilley D 357).

l. 55. *my Lord of Dorset*. Presumably Edward Sackville, the fourth Earl, to whom Suckling addressed *An Account of Religion* (1637), but the reference is chiefly illustrative.

ll. 54–7. *Bedlam*. Cf. Letter No. 51(*a*), ll. 1–4.

ll. 54–7. *it is in love as in Antipathy: The Capers* etc. Beaurline suggests that 'Antipathy' may be in error for 'Antipasto', in which capers are commonly found. *Antepast* 'Something taken before a meal to whet the appetite; a foretaste' was in use in England as early as 1590 (*OED*), and Suckling may have written some such unrecorded variant form as 'Antipastry' or more likely 'Antipasty', which could have been either misread or not understood and editorially 'corrected'. Cf. the use of 'great Oleoes' that 'rather make a shew then provoke Appetite' in Letter No. 15, ll. 25–6.

No. 53 (pp. 160–1)

'Honest Charles' may be a fictional addressee, for this letter clearly belongs to a well-established literary genre, that of 'A Letter of perswading to marriage' (sigg. E4^{r+v} in Nicholas Breton's *A Post withe a Packet of Madde Letters. The first part*, 1605; for Breton's inauguration of the genre to which Letters Nos. 51–2 belong, see headnote on No. 51[*a*]). Charles Suckling of Bracondale was the second son of the poet's uncle, Charles Suckling of Woodton, Norfolk; baptized in 1607 and married in 1644, he died of the plague on 15 July 1666. His wife was Mary, daughter and heiress of Thomas Aldrich of Mangreen, by whom he had three sons and five daughters, four of whom survived their father (Joseph Muskett, *Suffolk Manorial Families*, ii (1908), 203, and the monumental inscription, quoted in Francis Blomefield, *History of Norfolk*, v (1806), 460–1).

l. 10. *to love widdows is as tolerable an humour.* Cf. Letter No. 51(*a*).

ll. 12–13. *Colts that are un-way'd*, etc. Cf. Letter No. 51(*b*), ll. 34–6.

l. 25. *Women are like Melons.* Cf. Letter No. 23, ll. 31–3.

No. 54 (p. 161)

There is nothing specific enough in this letter to identify addressee or occasion, and it seems very likely that it is a literary exercise in the genre of the railing letter.

No. 55 (pp. 161–2)

The grounds for the tenuous association with Suckling and the less uncertain one with Sir John Mennes of this stylistically uncharacteristic letter are discussed under 'Dubious Works' in the Introduction, p. cxiv. The loose parallels are certainly insufficient to constitute much evidence of Suckling's authorship, and the letter appears to be a literary exercise in the form of a 'declaration of love' (cf. note on l. 36). If the letter were written by Suckling to Mary Bulkeley, his 'Aglaura' and 'Dear Princess', it was probably written between 1636 and 1638. Cf. the letter from Sir John Mennes in Appendix A.iv (No. 6). The sentiments of ll. 1–13 have a general consonance with Letter No. 27, ll. 1–12, but the style is quite different. There are also loose parallels in 'smoothered long in silence' (ll. 19–20: cf. Letter No. 52, ll. 35–7, text and Commentary) and the not very compact extension of the metaphor that culminates in 'Desyre (Loves fyrebrand)' (l. 24), with which compare 'Loving and Beloved', ll. 19–21.

l. 30. *proffered service.* Cf. the title 'Profer'd Love rejected' (quite possibly editorial, however, since the phrase is apparently a formula) and 'Disdain', l. 3.

l. 36. *serious employments and zealous cogitations.* Something of a formula; cf. 'Thus feareing lest with my prolixitie I may molest[,] your more serious cogitations', etc., in a letter from William Bagot, at Oxford, to his father, Walter Bagot, written in 1622 (in Giles Dawson and Laetitia Kennedy-Skipton, *Elizabethan Handwriting, 1500–1650: A Manual,* 1966, pp. 102–3).

TO MR. HENRY GERMAN, IN THE BEGINNING OF PARLIAMENT, 1640 (pp. 163–7)

This epistolary tract was probably written at about the time of the opening of the Long Parliament on 3 November 1640, or perhaps a few weeks after (see note on ll. 104–5 below). Its nominal address to Henry Jermyn, one of Suckling's fellow conspirators in the Army Plot of 1641 (see Introduction, pp. liii–lvii), is given in both *FA46* and *T6. Ltr41—A Coppy of a Letter Found in the Privy Lodgeings at Whitehall,* 1641—is of special interest as perhaps having been published before Suckling's flight to France, but it is textually corrupt and was certainly not authorized (see Introduction, p. xcv, and note on *Text* below). The political positions advocated in this tract and in *Brennoralt* are very much the same, and there are several close parallels; see especially *Brennoralt,* I. iii. 65–99.

Text. For the associational authority and the over-all textual superiority of the Cranfield manuscript used as copy-text in this edition, see Introduction, p. ci. In order of the prima facie authority suggested by the number of their unique variants (given in parentheses), the witnesses are: *Cran* (3), *FA46* (13), *St* (16), *T6* (29), *Ltr41* (64), and *TC* (88). *Ltr43,* which has 31 unique variants, is derived from *Ltr41* (whose otherwise 'unique' variants are in fact shared with *Ltr43*) and has no authority. It would appear from three passages found in *Ltr41-St-TC* but wanting in *Cran-FA46-T6* (ll. 58+, 72+, and 85+) that these groups of witnesses respectively represent earlier and later versions of the work as well as comparatively inferior and superior lines of independent descent. All three passages sound authorial enough probably not to be non-authorial interpolations, but they are superfluous and digressive; and the first—'For as *Cato* said of the *Romans*', etc., which is several lines long and in itself not uncharacteristic—is both digressive and moderately at odds with the sense of the context. Other differences between the two versions are comparatively trivial, a few suggesting sophistication or trivialization, e.g. ll. 60 (see note), 99 ('Love' for 'Sex'), and 105 ('a thing'). Of the first group *St* is the most reliable witness, the others being very corrupt. The strict textual relationship of the witnesses of the other group is complicated by the 'ambiguity of three texts', but all three are comparatively reliable witnesses, and *Cran* is their virtual (but evidently not historical) ancestor.

ll. 29–30. *In goinge about to Shewe the King a cure nowe,* etc. Cf. 'Loves Offence', l. 6, and Letter No. 23, ll. 80–1 (and see Tilley D 358).

ll. 34–5. *Kings may bee mistaken and Counsellors corrupted, but true interest alone (saies Mounsieur de Rohan) cannot erre.* As Thompson notes, Suckling alludes to a tract by Henri, Prince de Léon and Duc de Rohan, that was translated into English by H[enry] H[unt] as *A Treatise of the Interest of the Princes and States of Christendome,* 1640: 'The *Prince* may deceive himselfe, his *Counsell* may be corrupted, but the interest alone can never faile' (p. 1).

ll. 40–1. *as the Scripture saies* etc. Cf. John 8: 44, and 1 John 3: 8.

ll. 45–8. *There was not amonge all our Princes* etc. See Suckling's youthful condemnation, 'On King Richard the third, who lies buried under Leicester bridge'.

l. 45. *Courter.* The distribution of the variant 'Courtier' suggests that it is a sophistication; *OED* lists no use in the sense 'a wooer' before the mid eighteenth century, and 'Courter' is plainly demanded.

l. 58+. *For as Cato said of the Romans,* etc. See comment in the remarks on *Text* above.

ll. 59, 62–3. *neither the persons of the Scottish . . . not much risen in value.* Cf. Letter No. 41, l. 4.

l. 60. *a considerable number.* The entire sentence is elliptical and awkward, and *FA46*'s unique omission seems as likely to represent editorial rejection of an unsatisfactory reading (probably that of the present copy-text) as inadvertency. The intended sense would seem to be that 'the persons are not a considerable number, but the things they undertake are considerable'. The rejected reading, 'considerable', applies better to 'things' than to 'persons', but reasonably well to both, and, as obvious, is more likely to be unauthoritative than 'a considerable number', which applies better to 'persons' than to 'things'.

ll. 65–6. *since as Cumenes said,* etc. I have been unable to identify the specific passage; as Thompson notes, 'the quotation is probably a free rendering of a maxim' (p. 412).

ll. 104–5. *some servants which hee thinkes somewhat hardly torne from him of late.* The Earl of Strafford was sequestered from the House of Lords on 11 November; the Secretary of State, Sir Francis Windebank, was forced to flee the country on 10 December, as was Sir John Finch, the Lord Keeper, on the 23rd; Archbishop Laud was impeached on the 18th (Gardiner, iv. 235, 243, 247).

Suckling may have written this tract before the flight of Windebank and Finch but probably after Strafford's arrest.

ll. 105–6. *which is of soe tender a nature*, etc. Suckling's definition of a king's obligation to his ministers is put in more Machiavellian terms in *The Goblins*, III. i. 40–2.

ll. 109–13. *As Iron in particular sympathie stickes to the Load stone*, etc. Cf. 'Womans Constancy', ll. 11–15, and *An Account of Religion*, ll. 359–61.

AN ACCOUNT OF RELIGION BY REASON (pp. 168–80)

Parson Robert Davenant told Aubrey that 'that tract about Socinianisme was writt on the table in the parlour of the parsonage at West Kington' (ii. 244), but the preliminary 'Epistle' was signed, if not the *Account* written or at least completed, at Bath on 2 September 1637 (for further details, see Introduction, pp. xliii–xliv). The addressee of the *Account* was the father-in-law of Frances Lady Dorset, who probably provided much of the copy for *Fragmenta Aurea*, 1646 (see Introduction, pp. lxxxiv–lxxxv). That the Account was in circulation very soon after its composition is attested by the fact that a copy was No. 16 among 'Mr. Vassall's papers seized 27th Sept. 1639', according to a note made by Secretary of State Sir Francis Windebank on that date (*CSPD 1639*, p. 526; No. 11 was a 'Copy of a letter to a gent. in Norfolk concerning the Scottish business', Letter No. 38 in the present edition).

'Socinianism' was both a flexible body of contemporary Biblical–Unitarian doctrine, formalized in sixteenth-century Italy chiefly by Faustus Socinus, and a catchword 'used to cover different kinds of unorthodox religious opinion. In an age when nice discrimination between heresies could hardly be expected, "Socinians" were all who departed radically from the orthodox Christian scheme of redemption or found difficulty with the metaphysical notions enshrined in Catholic doctrinal formulae, or even allowed to reason its legitimate place in religion' (H. John McLachlan, *Socinianism in Seventeenth-Century England*, 1951, p. 3). It 'may be regarded as a blend of Italian rationalism with Polish anabaptist tendencies', and 'its two leading characteristics are . . . its scrupulous and vigorous biblicism and its acknowledgement of the rights of reason in religion' (McLachlan, pp. 5, 11). Many of the ideas that Suckling develops in the *Account* have broad origins in Renaissance humanism, but he owes much in particular to the belief—first propounded by Philo Judæus and revived at the Renaissance by Pico della Mirandola and others —that the wisdom of Greece, Egypt, and other enlightened nations was derived from God's revelation to Moses. H. John McLachlan remarks that the *Account* is of special interest 'as an early attempt at a comparative study of religions' (p. 65, n. 2).

Text. The relationship between the witnesses is uncertain because of the 'ambiguity of three texts'. Individually, *S* (for a description of which see

Introduction, pp. ciii–civ) is generally reliable through about l. 104; the remaining major portion of the text was apparently copied in haste and contains a great many errors (probably also owing to haste it appears to contain a few authorial readings that were altered in the more thoughtfully transmitted *FA46* and *AS*). *AS* is a generally sound text copied in the secretary hand of a professional scribe; it is punctuated with care and contains only about thirty-two unique substantive readings, against nearly eighty in *FA46*, some of them corruptions, others obviously due to editorial interference.

The presence of unique readings in all three witnesses and the distribution of readings generally argue that none is derived from either of the others. The three are probably independent, despite slight evidence that *AS* and *S* derive from a common exemplar (see critical apparatus and text of the 'Discourse', ll. 1, 53, 58, 59, 76, 78, 267, 272, 299, 337, and 370); the same evidence can be used to support editorial treatment of copy in *FA46*, because nearly all these 'superior' readings correspond with manifest or apparent errors in the manuscripts. Most of *FA46*'s unique readings—notably in its omissions—are unauthoritative, as are the unique readings of *AS* and *S* (all three differ significantly only in ll. 65, 76, 85, 90, 130, 175, 216, 337, and 344, and *S* appears to have the original reading in ll. 76, 175, and 337; in the others corruption is multiple or originality of reading otherwise uncertain).

FA46 has been used as copy-text for its accidentals of spelling and punctuation, which, while not Suckling's own, are those of good contemporary practice and require less clarifying alteration than those of *AS*—for its substantives the 'best' text. Besides the 'superior' readings commented on above, there is evidence of editing in *FA46* especially in the correction of Suckling's quotation from Manilius in the 'Epistle' (see note on l. 23) and in the alteration of the title of the 'Discourse' proper (see note). Most of the effects of this editing are unauthoritative and unacceptable, and I have rejected *FA46*'s unique readings in favour of those shared by the manuscripts with three kinds of exception: I have retained (1) two almost certainly authoritative readings (ll. 60 and 267; see notes); (2) a few probably unauthoritative readings required or desirable as editorial emendations (notably in ll. 1, 53, 58, 59, 65, 271, 299, and 363); and (3) a few readings of comparative indifference (notably 'hath' in *FA46* for 'has' in the manuscripts; in a number of instances all three texts agree in one or the other).

l. 4. *Socinianisme.* See headnote.

l. 23. *Neque enim decipitur ratio neque decipit unquam. Astronomicon*, ii. 131. *FA46*'s 'Nam neque ... nec' corresponds with the source, but the manuscripts are probably right in sharing a quotation made *memoriter* (as Thompson comments, 'the greater number of references to classical and other authors in the pamphlet are made *memoriter*, and apparently in most cases at second hand', p. 421).

l. 29. *my Lord of Middlesex.* Suckling's uncle, Lionel Cranfield, the first Earl.

Title. A Discourse written by Sir John Suckling, Knight, to the Earl of Dorset.
From this title at the head of the 'Discourse' proper *FA46* omits 'written'
and 'to the Earl of Dorset', but this information has been incorporated in the
Account's title-page.

ll. 23–4. *That there is then a God, will not be so much the dispute.* Cf. *To Mr. Henry
German*, ll. 15–16.

ll. 35–6. *left not so much as footsteps to trace them by.* Cf. 'To a Lady that forbidd
to love before Company', ll. 11–12.

l. 42. *Olympicks.* If one may judge from the parallels, the building of Rome and
the reign of Salmonassar, specific events (Olympics) rather than the periods
reckoned from them (Olympiads) were intended, but 'Olympiades', though
wrong, could be authorial, 'Olympicks' in the manuscripts representing
either editorial correction or misreading; it seems more likely, however,
that in *FA46* it was taken into this line on the suggestion of l. 55.

l. 55. *about the eightieth Olympiad, in the year of the world 3480.* The 'eightieth
Olympiad', 456 B.C. (see note on l. 42 above), is at odds with 'the year of the
world 3480', i.e. 520 B.C. (calculated from the traditional year of the Creation
as 4000 B.C.).

l. 60. *divers others, Orators and Poets. AS* has 'other', *S* 'others' with the *s* deleted;
FA46 and *S* (before 'correction') are almost certainly right.

ll. 75–6. *darknes was before night. AS*'s thoughtless 'might' confirms *S*'s 'night';
FA46's 'light' is an obvious and not very thoughtful sophistication (cf.
Gen. 1: 2–5).

l. 162. *drest up with a little more fancie.* Cf. 'Upon Newyeares day', ll. 3–4.

l. 175. *incertain.* An adjective rather than a noun is clearly wanted, and
S's 'incertain[e]' is probably authorial (Suckling spells 'inconcernd' in
Letter No. 40, l. 40; and one of the press-variants in *The Sad One*, 1659, I. i. 71,
sig. E5ᵛ, is 'incertain' (*u*), 'uncertain' (*c*); cf. l. 337, critical apparatus and
note).

ll. 259–64. *But it may be urged as more abstruse*, etc. Cf. *Aglaura*, III. ii. 50–4.

l. 267. *Heathen.* Despite 'Heathens' in all three witnesses in ll. 154, 164, 222,
and 280, *FA46*'s collective singular is probably authorial: cf. 'The Soldier'
and Letter No. 14, ll. 15 and 40.

l. 271. *unpurified.* The manuscripts' 'purified' may be authorial, but there is
confusion of referent here: 'unpurified' modifies 'the soul' (l. 270) and expresses
a similar idea more clearly; 'purified' must be taken to modify 'him' (i.e.
'God', l. 270), presumably in allusion to Exod. 33: 20, or, more close to the
whole passage (cf. 'the soul of the soul', l. 259), 'Who sees Gods face, that is
selfe life must dye' (Donne's 'Good Friday, 1613. Riding Westward', l. 17);
with which cf. *The Goblins*, IV. ii. 38: 'It is the soule of vertue, and the life of

life'. Finally, cf. ll. 273–4: 'Arts and Sciences . . . cleanse us not enough to come to God'.

l. 337. *increated.* The manuscripts' similar reading argues that *FA46* errs by omission; *AS*'s 'intreated' is plainly a thoughtless misreading.

ll. 346–55. *There is a hidden Original of waters in the earth,* etc. This extended metaphor is also used in *Aglaura,* II. iii. 8–11.

ll. 359–60. *these things of which we make sympathy the cause, as in the Load-stone.* Cf. 'Womans Constancy', ll. 9–15, and *To Mr. Henry German,* ll. 109–13.

ll. 363–6. *stranger for me . . . then if a Clown.* *FA46*'s 'stranger' is very likely an editorial improvement of the manuscripts' 'as strange', which probably survived inadvertently (Suckling does not elsewhere use 'as' with 'than' in comparisons).

ll. 366–7. *a Watch* etc. One of Suckling's favourite metaphors. See 'Loves Clock' and Commentary for other uses.

APPENDIX A. POEMS AND LETTERS CLOSELY ASSOCIATED WITH SUCKLING

I. ANSWERS AND AN ANTECEDENT TO THE FOLLOWING POEMS BY OR ASCRIBED TO SUCKLING

1. In Answer of Sir John Sucklins Verses (pp. 181–3)

Text. It is clear from *RP16*'s unintelligible conjecture in l. 38, as well as from the distribution of its readings in the 'Con' passages, that it is a text not derived from but collateral with *Waller.* On the derivation of *DonD* from the first or second edition of *Waller* see the Commentary on 'Against Fruition I'.

5. Answer [to 'Song. Why so pale and wan fond Lover?'] (p. 186)

This poem was first printed by G. F. Sensabaugh in *MLN,* 1937, lii. 410–11, and again by George R. Price in *N&Q,* 1951, cxciv. 559–60. Both writers tentatively assigned it to John Egerton, second Earl of Bridgewater, on the strength of a transcription in his hand in the Bridgewater copy of *Aglaura,* 1638, now in the Huntington Library (signed 'J. Brackley' on the title-page). This was the only text known to either. Price added that Bridgewater's authorship 'must remain . . . a strong presumption, unless they [the verses] can be shown to occur elsewhere', as they do in *F24,* but without ascription. There is no foundation for a firm assignment to anyone, but in this connection it is of interest that Bridgewater's wife may have written the answer to 'Song' ('I prethee send me back my heart') that is printed below (A.i.7).

7. An answeare to my Lady Alice Edgertons Songe etc. (pp. 187–8)

RP1 is a folio manuscript of 'POEMS SONGS a PASTORALL and a PLAY by the R^t Honble Lady JANE CAVENDISH and Lady ELIZABETH BRACKLEY' (see Commentary on 'Song' ['I prethee send me back my heart']). There is a manuscript text of an answer to 'Song' ('Why so pale and wan fond Lover?') in the hand of Elizabeth Brackley's husband, John Egerton, second Earl of Bridgewater, and it is possible that both answers are by the same person, though there is little evidence for the confident assignment of authorship for either poem.

8. The fervency of his affection (p. 188)

Suckling may imitate this poem in stanza 2 of 'Sonnet I'; cf., especially, the last two lines (13–14): 'Oh! some kind power unriddle where it lies, | Whether my heart be faulty, or her eyes?' See also the Commentary on 'The guiltless Inconstant'.

9. Occasioned partly by the Verses above, etc. (pp. 188–9)

North's letter to Suckling (Appendix A.iii.2, q.v., text and Commentary) demonstrates a sympathetic and direct association between the two men in literary matters, but North's address of his answer to 'The incomparable Lady Carlile' makes equally plain that whatever attitudes they may have shared did not extend to persons (see 'Upon my Lady Carliles walking in Hampton-Court garden', text and Commentary).

II. COMMENDATORY POEMS AND AN EPITAPH

3. Epitaph upon Sir John Suckling (pp. 191–2)

I have been unable to identify the person to whom this epitaph is attributed, but there are two other poems similarly subscribed in the same manuscript (B.M. Harleian 6918): 'Loues Contentment', beginning 'Come my Clarinda, wee'll consume | our Ioyes noe more, at this low rate' (f. 92^{r+v}, 'J: Paulin'); and 'A competent wish', beginning 'Graunt me my kinder fates, euen when you please | a little wealth, but let it come with ease' (ff. 92^v-3, 'James Paulin').

III. DEDICATIONS, ETC.

1. To the Right Worshipfull Sir John Suckling Knight (p. 192)

ll. 3–4. *since you have honoured the Muses with a famous Poeme.* In the general sense of 'Poem', which was commonly used of plays (cf., e.g., Webster's dedications in *The Duchess of Malfi* and *The White Devil*), the 'famous Poeme' could be *Aglaura*, if this dedication postdated the licence, but it would seem rather more likely to refer to 'The Wits', which was written and sung to the King a few months before *Ovid de Ponto* was licensed, was indeed famous, and involved Apollo as judge in a 'trial for the bays'.

2. To the Right Worthy of his Honours etc. (p. 193)

l. 6. *the Stages [trial], that gave it some partiall allowance.* Covent Garden had been produced in or about February 1632/3 (see G. E. Bentley, *The Jacobean and Caroline Stage*, iii (1956), 932–4).

l. 7. *Serpit humi tutus nimium, timidusque procellæ.* 'Too cautious, and afraid of the storm, it creeps along the ground' (Horace, *Ars Poetica*, l. 28).

ll. 12–13. *the publication of your late worthy labour.* Suckling's *Aglaura* was probably printed a few weeks before it was licensed, on 18 April 1638.

3. For Sir John Suckling etc. (p. 193)

I am grateful to Miss Margaret Crum of the Bodleian Library for calling this letter to my attention. Beaurline discovered it independently and has published it together with the 'preface concerning Poetry' to which it primarily applies; that is, 'Concerning petty Poetry, made more generall in addresse then at first. Preludium to the first Verses' (*Forest*, pp. 1–6; see Beaurline, 'Dudley North's Criticism of Metaphysical Poetry', *HLQ*, 1962, xxv. 299–313). 'Concerning petty Poetry' (*c.* 1610–12, probably in a form less 'generall in addresse') is the first of three prefaces, the second being a note in justification of love as a subject for lyric verse, the third an 'Advertisement upon the first Verses' (written in 1638) concerning physical and spiritual love. On the grounds that at the end of the third preface 'North uses the word "conversion" in the sense of converting his muse to a higher type of love', a sense similar to that of its use in this letter (ll. 3, 6), Beaurline suggests that the third preface was sent to Suckling along with the first preface and 'The Corona', a sequence of devotional verses also of recent composition (p. 303, n. 7). This letter was presumably written between 17 November 1638 and 19 March 1638/9, the dates of the letters preceding and following this in *A Forest of Varieties*.

The critical views expressed in 'that peece which you honored with your pretended conversion' are, as Beaurline points out, perfectly consonant with those one might infer 'natural, easy Suckling' to have held, and North's solicitation, here, of 'some further vertue of operation from you' and 'friendly correction', though perhaps simply a gesture of courtesy and respect, prompt one to suppose that Suckling may have had a hand in the final version of the preface or 'The Corona', or both. Consonance of attitude, however, is insufficient proof of historical influence, much less of revision or 'correction', and a few close parallels of idea, phrase, or figure afford but weak additional evidence, especially when the direction of transmission is ambiguous (in the one comparatively striking parallel cited, in the Commentary on 'The Wits', ll. 35–6, Suckling could have been influenced by North, whose preface may have been in circulation in 1637 before the poem was composed; see Beaurline, p. 301).

ll. 3, 6. *conversion.* As Beaurline notes (op. cit. above, p. 303, n. 7), North is probably 'punning on the word—a favorite device—first meaning mere approval, second the technical meaning used in logic, and third the religious meaning'. In l. 6 it appears also to have much the same sense as 'friendly correction' (l. 9).

IV. LETTERS

1. (p. 194)

On the historical context of this letter and its association with Suckling, see Introduction, pp. xxxi–xxxiii. The addressee may be inferred from the explicit address of the following letter, which also involves Phillip Willoughby and appears to have been written at about the same time.

2. (pp. 194–5)

The approximate date and the writer of this letter as one of two of Suckling's sisters, may be conjecturally inferred from the date and subscription of the preceding letter. Both apparently concern attempts by Suckling's sisters to promote the amorous interests of Phillip Willoughby with Mary Cranfield (on the connection with Suckling see Introduction, pp. xxxi–xxxiii).

l. 12. *my Lady Shefeald.* Mary Cranfield's sister, Elizabeth (see 'To my Lady E. C. at her going out of England', text and Commentary).

More-park. Moor Park, near Rickmansworth, Herts., the seat of Henry Carey, Lord Lepington, husband of Mary Cranfield's sister, Martha (there is a letter from her partly concerning Suckling in Appendix A.iv.4).

ll. 14–15. *in a lyne yett try what may be done for stay at least for coming.* The apparent sense is that, before coming to London, the addressee should at least try, by a letter, to delay Willoughby's departure ('to morrow after dinner').

3. (pp. 195–9)

For the general biographical context of this letter and other details concerning the courtship, see Introduction, pp. xxxv–xxxviii.

4. (p. 199–200)

Henry Carey, Lord Lepington (second Earl of Monmouth, 1639) and Lady Carey had two sons and eight daughters (*CSPD 1639*, p. 36). Three of the daughters married, according to the will of one of them, Lady Elizabeth Carey (see Fairfax Harrison, *The Devon Carys*, New York, 1920, i. 388), but only Anne was married before 1662, when a grant was made of Kenilworth Castle, Warwickshire, to her sisters, Ladies Elizabeth, Mary, and Martha Carey (*Calendar of Treasury Books, 1660–67*, p. 361). Martha married John, first Earl of Middleton in Scotland on 16 December 1667 (Sir James Balfour Paul, ed., *The Scots Peerage*, vi. 185), and Mary became the second wife of William Feilding, third Earl of Denbigh, shortly after 7 April 1673, when their licence was issued (*Calendar of Marriage Licence Allegations in the Registry of the Bishop of London*, ed. R. M. Glencross, ii (1940), 29).

Anne Carey married James Hamilton, first Earl of Clanbrassil (1644), shortly after 23 September 1641, when their marriage licence was issued (*Allegations for Marriage Licences Issued by the Bishop of London*, ed. Joseph L. Chester and George J. Armytage, 1887, ii. 261). The exact date of the marriage cannot be established because the parish registers of marriages before 1653, for Rickmansworth, Herts., where they were married, are missing (see *Hertfordshire Parish Registers. Marriages*, ed. Thomas M. Blagg, 1914, iii [i]). The important point for the dating of this letter, however, is that the marriage articles were dated 12 and 13 November 1635 (see John Lodge, *The Peerage of Ireland*, revised and enlarged by Mervyn Archdall, 1789, iii. 5), which makes it virtually certain that Anne Carey is the subject and 1635 the year of this correspondence.

ll. 8–9. *this daye he writes to me, that your lordship approves of it* etc. See Letter No. 22, ll. 12–13: 'the Uncle is no less satisfied then the Nephew'.

l. 17. *Moore.* Moor Park, the seat of Lord and Lady Carey, near Rickmansworth, Herts.

5. (p. 200)

For the historical context of this letter see Introduction, pp. xxxviii–xxxix.

l. 4. *your neece my wife.* Suckling's sister, Martha, who had married Southcot only a few months before, on 2 July 1635.

6. (p. 201)

On the basis of the known associations of both Mennes and Suckling with the Bulkeley family, it is tempting to suppose, though there is no evidence to show, that Suckling is alluded to in 'our' (l. 2). For the associations, the basis for the identification of the addressees of this letter, and the general historical context, see Introduction, pp. xxxix–xlii.

l. 5. *Mrs. Rose and your littell sister.* The sister is presumably Margaret Bulkeley (see Introduction, pp. xl–xli); I am unable to suggest more exact identification for 'Mrs. Rose'.

V. LAMPOONS

1. Upon Aglaura in Folio [I] (pp. 201–2)

On the extravagant folio printing of *Aglaura* which this and the following two lampoons ridicule, see Introduction, p. xlv. This lampoon was printed in *The Weeding of the Covent-Garden*, 1658, sig. A2 (*Brome*), one of *Five New Playes*, 1659, which was published five or six years after Brome's death; but there is some support for Brome's authorship in *EP53*, which is subscribed 'R:[W:]' (only the 'R:' belongs to the original transcription; 'W:' has been written in an area from which the original second initial and all but the left half of the 'c' and the loop of the 'k', in 'cook[e]s', l. 42, were defaced). Furthermore, there is the support of contemporary literary history, in general, in Brome's active and vociferous involvement in 'the "second war of the theaters" being waged between the courtiers and the professional dramatists' in 1638 (when *Aglaura* was published) and after, and his apparent identity as 'the spokesman for this anti-cavalier faction which, as a group, had to resent the fact that the amateur court dramatists were giving their plays away and also wooing the jaded Caroline audiences away from professional competitors by the expensive novelty of elaborate scenery and costume' (R. J. Kaufmann, *Richard Brome: Cavalier Playwright*, 1961, p. 151; on the production of *Aglaura*, see Introduction, pp. xliv–xlv; and ii. 261–2). More specifically, Brome ridiculed lavish court productions (implicitly, that of *Aglaura*) in the prologue to *The Antipodes*, 1640 (produced in 1638), and directly satirized Suckling and Davenant in *The Court Beggar* in 1640 (see Kaufmann's chapter on 'Suckling's New Strain of Wit', pp. 151–68).

Text. All the texts except *MusD* have directional unique variants, proving them collateral: *Brome* has five, *EP53* two (and two defaced words), *F60* eight, *H17* one, and *PB* twelve. Two pairs of texts inferentially shared intermediate ancestors: *F60* and *PB* (see complex variants in ll. 33 and 39), and *H17* and *MusD* (see complex variants in title and ll. 15, 23, 30, 40, and 42). *H17* (a manuscript dating from the early 1640s at the latest) could not be the strict historical descendant of *MusD* (1655), but it is, in effect, virtually a 'textual' descendant, differing from it only in a unique variant in l. 2 and in omitting l. 20. Except for the somewhat doubtful directionality of the variants in ll. 23, 30, 40, and 42, *MusD* could be regarded as the textual ancestor of the rest; but the readings in ll. 23 and, especially, 40, suggest that *H17* and *MusD* represent one line of descent and the remaining witnesses another. If *MusD* is not taken as the textual ancestor of the other witnesses, two genealogical patterns will account for a majority of the variants (except for some in *Brome*, which appears to be conflated): (1) *H17* and *MusD* share an intermediate ancestor on one line of descent from the hypothetical original, and *EP53* and *Brome*, and *F60* and *PB*, respectively, share intermediate ancestors on the other; or (2) on the second line of descent, *EP53* descends alone from the intermediate ancestor from which the subordinate ancestor of *Brome*, along with the ancestor of *F60* and *PB*, descends. By either hypothesis readings of the pattern *H17, MusD: Σ* must be chosen on the basis of apparent directionality or critical superiority, and four are of some importance. In l. 23, 'should' is demanded by 'would' in the following line, but 'doe' —which ought to be accompanied by 'will'—could be an archetypal inaccuracy. For the title, and the variants in ll. 40 and 42, see notes.

Title. In *Brome*, *F60*, and *PB*, 'printed' literally differentiates between printed and manuscript folios (*R* is in fact a folio manuscript of *Aglaura*), and the poem doubtless refers to the folio of *Aglaura* printed in 1638; but the title in *H17* and *MusD* sufficiently identifies the subject and has the additional merit of more accurately characterizing the poem, which treats *Aglaura* more in terms of character and personification than as a literal book, that is 'Aglaura in Folio' rather than '*Aglaura* in Folio'.

l. 28. *the great bed at Ware.* This celebrated, elaborately carved oak bed, measuring over ten feet square and seven feet high, was housed at the Saracen's Head Inn at Ware at the end of the sixteenth century (it is now in the Victoria and Albert Museum in London). Shakespeare (in *Twelfth Night*, III. ii. 43) and Jonson (*The Silent Woman*, v. i. 64) also refer to it.

l. 38. *London measure.* The term is explained in the passage to which Brome alludes, in the Prologue to *Aglaura* (as tragedy), ll. 14–16: 'As in all bargaines else, Men ever get | All they can in; will have London measure, | A handfull over in their very pleasure.'

l. 40. *more.* *Brome*'s and *F60*'s 'more' best explains the variants ('much' in

H17 and *MusD*, 'most' in *PB*, and 'nere' in *EP53*) and would seem to be original. In particular, *EP53*'s 'nere', whether a plain (and easy) misreading or an editorial accommodation prompted by 'sportted' (in *EP53* alone), must have originated in 'more'.

l. 42. *looks.* 'Cooks' is attractive, in the implication that the pages of *Aglaura* are only fit for wrapping pies (a sally that could be due to misreading, since 'l' and 'C' may be very much alike in italic hand), but 'looks' is certainly the original reading: it complements and resolves the paradox that 'those leaves be fair | To the judicious, which more spotted are' (i.e. fairer to the mind than to the eye; ll. 39–40).

2. [Upon Aglaura in Folio II] (p. 203)

If the initials of the subscription are really the author's, Thomas May (1595–1650) is a not unlikely candidate for the authorship of this poem: he was an admirer of Ben Jonson, whom Suckling had lampooned in 'The Wits' in 1637; at one time a professional playwright out of need, like Brome; an anti-royalist (he was secretary to Parliament in 1646 and published a *History of the Parliament of England* in 1647); and a translator of Latin classics (*Lucan's Pharsalia*, *Virgil's Georgics*, and *Selected Epigrams of Martial*) and writer of plays on mythical and Roman historical subjects (*Antigone, Cleopatra, Julia Agrippina*). But proof beyond the subscription and general congeniality is wanting, and references to 'Pactolus', 'Helicon', and 'Homers Illiads' (the last in a proverbial phrase) are grammar-school commonplaces.

l. 4. *Pactolus streames and Helicon.* The point seems to be geographical distance: the river Pactolus (whose sands Midas turned to gold) was in Lydia, rising in Mt. Tmolus; Mt. Helicon, sacred to the muses, was in Bœotia.

ll. 4–5. *Helicon! Well.* 'Helicon | well', in *EP53*, is ambiguous, suggesting that a periphrasis for the fountains of Aganippe or Hippocrene was intended; but 'Pactolus streames' and 'Helicon' are differentiated in italic hand from the secretary hand of most of the poem as 'well' is not.

l. 18. *With Homers Illiads in a Nutt.* A copy of the *Iliad* small enough to fit in a nutshell is referred to by Pliny in his *Natural History*, VII. xxi (an English translation by Philemon Holland was published in 1601), and in Stephen Gosson's *The School of Abuse*, 1579, occurs another use of a phrase probably as current in the seventeenth century as 'the truth in a nutshell' more recently: 'the whole world is drawen in a mappe; Homers Iliades in a nutte shell' (repr. for the Shakespeare Society, 1841, p. 3).

4–5. Upon Sir John Suckling's hundred horse and Sir John Suckling's Answer (pp. 204–6)

The contemporary and persisting popularity of this pair of lampoons is attested by the survival of sixteen variant texts (fourteen for the 'Answer'), ranging in date from very soon after the events referred to, of January–June 1639 (*Eg9* has '1639' in the title), to the early 1670s (many poems in *H39* were taken from *The New Academy of Complements*, 1669). The termini of composition are clearly ascertainable from the explicit reference to the 'hundred horse' Suckling engaged himself, towards the end of January 1638, to provide for the King, and negatively from the fact that no reference is made to the precipitate retreat of the King's forces, including Suckling, before the Scots at Kelso on 3 June 1639 (see Introduction, pp. xlvii–xlviii), which is fully exploited in the two lampoons following, both of which allude to the Treaty of Berwick (18 June) and the hostilities preceding it.

Since the two poems are found as a pair in all but two of sixteen instances, it seems probable that they were composed at about the same time and very early became a unified fictional exchange of topical insults, even though they may not have been written by the same person or originally conceived as two parts of a single poem. 'Upon Sir John Suckling's hundred horse' uses generally accurate and telling biographical detail and allusion—e.g. to the notorious episode in Blackfriars' Alley (see Introduction, pp. xxxvii–xxxviii)—to good effect in a poem that is something of a second-person Character, in which Suckling's extravagance, wit, reputed cowardice, amorous gallantry, and inveterate propensity for gaming, figure by turns. 'Suckling's Answer', which is 'confessional' but not biographically circumstantial, is almost equally ungenerous to the Scots Covenanters, the King's party, and Suckling himself. The use in these poems of the same comparatively unusual version of the ballad stanza Suckling used in 'A Ballade. Upon a Wedding', and the mimicing of 'A Ballade's' first line ('I tell thee Dick, where I have been'), are of interest as formal means of mockery, and they are incidentally important in providing a terminal date for 'A Ballade' that dissociates it from its traditional connection with a wedding that took place in January 1640/1 (see 'A Ballade' in Commentary).

These two poems were twice printed in the seventeenth century, in *Wit and Drollery*, 1656, and *Le Prince d'Amour*, 1660. Hazlitt was the first to print the 'Answer'—without the first poem—in recent times, in *Works*, 1874, i. 107; 1892, i. 83–4; and R. G. Howarth the first to print 'Upon Sir John Suckling's hundred horse', in *Minor Poets of the Seventeenth Century*, 1931, and rev. ed., 1953, p. 242. Hazlitt took his text from Bodleian MS. Ashmole 36–7 (*Ash3[a]*), and Howarth took his texts from 'manuscripts in the Bodleian Library and the British Museum'. Texts of both poems have been more recently printed by C. I. A. Ritchie from Durham University Library MS. Mickleton and Spearman 9 (*Du*) in *The Durham Philobiblion*, 1955, ii (pt. i). 3–6.

No one has solved the problem of authorship for either poem, but Sir John Mennes has traditionally been regarded as the author of the first, and Suckling, ambiguously, as the author of the second, despite Hazlitt's comment on the lines that 'it is very doubtful, on the whole, whether they were really from Suckling's pen' ('Life', 1892, i. xli, n. 2). Reprinting Hazlitt's text, still without the original poem (which Hazlitt had not mentioned), Thompson remarked of the poem only that 'it seems to have been written in answer to some satirical doggerel by Sir John Mennes on Suckling's preparations for the Scottish war' (p. 378). This suggestion is probably due to Aubrey: 'I want the scoffing ballad that Sir John Menis made against him [Suckling], upon his fine troope and his running away. To which Sir John Suckling replyed in another ballad:—"I prithee, foole, who ere thou bee" ' (*Brief Lives*, ii. 245, n. 2); or to Anthony Wood (*Athenae Oxonienses*, ed. Phillip Bliss, iii (1815), 925–6). Suckling certainly cannot have written the 'Answer', which condemns him no less than the poem it answers; and, despite Aubrey's attribution, it seems scarcely more likely that Sir John Mennes, whose conjectural associations with Suckling were so various (see 'Life'), wrote 'Upon Sir John Suckling's hundred horse'. Aubrey's own attribution very likely has no more substance than the appearance of the two poems in Mennes's and James Smith's *Wit and Drollery*, 1656 (pp. 44–7), in which the texts hardly show the care of an author's hand (though used as copy-text here, *W&D* has a stanza out of order as well as numerous smaller errors). Mennes's and Smith's text of 'Upon Sir John Sucklings most warlike preparations', together with the paucity of variant texts and Aubrey's attribution, gives their *Musarum Deliciae*, 1655, somewhat less questionable associational authority for Mennes's possible authorship of that poem.

Text. In the sixteen texts of 'Upon Sir John Suckling's Hundred Horse' and the fourteen of 'Suckling's Answer' contamination and conflation are rampant, and it is obvious that memorial transcription and oral-aural transmission were common in the various recordings of the text. Eleven of the texts contain directional unique variants in one poem or the other, or both, and must be regarded as terminal states; these, with the numbers of their unique variants, are: *Ash3(a)* (8), *Ash3(b)* (6), *Du* (10), *Dx42* (2; only one line of 'Answer'), *EP53* (2; omits 'Answer'), *F60* (1), *H17* (7), *H69* (3), *Hunt* (2), *T4* (6), *W&D* (4). The normal supposition, that texts without unique variants are ancestral, holds here for three of the five remaining witnesses: *W* is apparently derived from *Eg9*, and *H39* is certainly derived from *PD*; *T4* (which contains unique variants) is apparently derived from *C*. The distribution of readings in complex variations, as may be seen from those—all the major conflicting variations—recorded in the critical apparatus, suggests persistent relationships between various witnesses as follows. Perhaps sharing one line of descent from the hypothetical original are *Dx42*, *F60*, *H69*, *PD* (and *H39*), and *W&D*; in addition, *F60* and *W&D*, and *Dx42* and *H69*, appear to share hypothetical intermediate ancestors. Belonging to the other line of descent, that of the majority, *Eg9* (and *W*) and *C* (and *T4*) appear to be the most independent witnesses, with *EP53* and *H17* probably sharing an intermediate ancestor, and four others—*Ash3(a)*, *Ash3(b)*, *Du*, and *Hunt*—sharing another. But the many conflicts, and the nature of many of the variants, make this hypothetical division, as well as others that the distribution suggests, an unreliable foundation for choosing between variants.

Only a full record of the substantive variants could indicate the range and depth of textual confusion, and such a record would be disproportional to the present purpose of constructing a *generally* authoritative text of these poems. I have here adopted the expedient procedure of considering the reading of the majority of texts to be original—subject, however, to (1) the demand of the local context and the whole poem for a word or words communicating a consonant sense, and (2) the apparent over-all reliability, and tendency toward certain kinds of errors, of individual substantive texts. I have adopted *W&D* as copy-text because it has generally adequate seventeenth-century (printer's) accidentals of spelling and, especially, punctuation; it is far from a specially authoritative text, but so is each of the others, and *W&D* requires about as little emendation as any other text.

4. Upon Sir John Suckling's hundred horse (pp. 204–5)

On the pair of lampoons of which this is the first, see the notes preceding.

Title. The title adopted here is the most accurately descriptive of the titles, but it seems quite likely that the 'original' was no more detailed than 'Upon/ To Sir John Suckling'. Four witnesses (*Ash3[b]*, *Dx42*, *EP53*, *Hunt*) have no title. Three witnesses have titles added after the original transcription: *C* ('Verses agt Sr John Suckling who found 100 horse agt Scotland', different and later hand than text), *Du* ('A Satyr upon Sir John Suckling, the Poet', eighteenth-century or later hand), and *W* ('To Sr Jo: Suckling', probably middle or later seventeenth century). Titles contemporaneous with the texts of the poem are found in *Eg9* ('A libel by ye Scots, upon Sr Jhon Sucklin'), and *T4* ('Verses sent to Sr John Suckling'). The others are noted in the critical apparatus (cf. the title of 'Sir John Suckling's Answer' in critical apparatus).

l. 4. *a hundred horse*. See the Introduction, p. xlvii, for Suckling's offer to the King and the lavish equipage of his troop.

l. 11. *Two Tailors made seaven run away.* A turn on the proverb, 'Nine (Three) Tailors make a man' (Tilley T 23: *ante* 1600).

l. 14. *the [foe]*. The majority's 'thy' may be right, but the Scots were not Suckling's especial foe, and 'thy[selfe]' in the preceding line could have caused a dittographical or memorial error.

l. 24. *Black-Friers Alley.* A notorious episode in 1634, in which Suckling and a group of his men, in an attempted assault upon Sir John Digby, were apparently driven away by a considerably smaller number (cf. 'Two Tailors made seaven run away', l. 11, and see Introduction, p. xxxvii).

ll. 35–6. *from thy hands,* | *Were never made to fight.* A troublesome construction, as the more or less random distribution of the variant 'for [thy/those hands]' suggests (*H39* and *W* depart from their models, for example). I take it that the reading of the present text is original and the construction elliptical, 'which' (or 'that') being understood before 'Were'.

5. Sir John Suckling's Answer (pp. 205–6)

On the pair of lampoons of which this is the second, see the note preceding that on 'Upon Sir John Suckling's hundred horse'.

Title. In *Eg9*, '1639', though probably in the same hand as the title and text of the original transcription, is darker and of later addition. The full heading in *Du*—of eighteenth-century or later addition—is 'Sir John Sucklings Answer; see + Stanza 3ᵈ'.

l. 12. *hangs him in his Ears.* Tilley lists as proverbial, without defining, 'To hang one's Ears' (E 22: 1670); the tenor is obviously that the King's ears are constantly at the disposal of the Bishops.

l. 25. *Lashly.* Sir Alexander Leslie, Lord-General of the Scottish forces during the First Bishops' War in 1639 (see Letter No. 38, esp. note on ll. 35–8). Hazlitt: 'The spelling *Lashly* is preserved, as it may have been intentionally so written' (i. 83 n); despite the spelling variations in texts unknown to Hazlitt, I agree: the occurrence of 'sh', a phonetically odd spelling-variant, in seven witnesses supports the inference that 'Lashly' was intended.

l. 36. *'Tis but to cloak their knavery.* Cf. the proverb, 'The Hood (habit, cowl) makes not the monk' (Tilley H 856: 1561). It is of some interest that in three epistolary tracts, one written in April 1639, Suckling remarks on the Covenanters' use of religion as a pretence 'speciously conscionable' (see Letters Nos. 36, ll. 39–45; 37, ll. 38–43; and 38, ll. 23–29).

6. [Upon Sir John Sucklings Northern Discoverie] (pp. 207–8)

This and the following poem relate both to the preparations for the First Bishops' War in January–May 1639, as the preceding pair of poems does, and to the events of the war and its conclusion in the Treaty of Berwick, which was signed on 18 June 1639, as the other pair—apparently written earlier—does not (on this 'war' and the part of Suckling and his 'hundred horse' in it, see Introduction, pp. xlvii–xlviii). Though Suckling's personal cowardice is almost certainly exaggerated, there are elements of truth, distorted here for polemical purposes: the King's forces *were* guilty of an ignominious retreat before the Scots, and many, including Suckling by his own scarcely damning confession, were 'sick of Loosnesses . . . , which we ascribe to their violent drinking of Twede water', but which the poem predictably ascribes to other causes, in ll. 24–30 (see Suckling's letter describing the first encounter of the war, No. 40).

l. 17. *Barwick.* i.e. Berwick (see headnote).

l. 18. *in another ruff.* This phrase puns on contradictory senses of 'ruff'. *OED Ruff*, *sb.*⁶ 2: 'An exalted or elated state; elation, pride, vainglory'; *sb.*⁶ 4: 'Excitement, passion, fury, Freq. *in a ruff*'.

l. 21. *Jack of Lent.* A *Jack a Lent* was 'a figure of a man set up to be pelted; an ancient form of the sport of "Aunt Sally", practised during Lent. Hence *fig.* a butt for everyone to throw at' (*OED*).

l. 41. *Carpet Knight.* 'Originally, perhaps = *Knight of the Carpet* [one dubbed in time of peace upon the carpet, as opposed to one dubbed in the field]'; usually, as here, 'a contemptuous term for a knight whose achievements belong to "the carpet" (i.e. the lady's boudoir, or carpeted chamber) instead of to the field of battle; a stay-at-home soldier' (*OED*).

7. Upon Sir John Sucklings most warlike preparations etc. (pp. 208–9)

On the historical events distorted to Suckling's considerable personal disadvantage in this poem, see the headnote on 'Upon Sir John Sucklings Northern Discoverie'. Sir John Mennes is somewhat more likely to have been the author of this lampoon than of 'Upon Sir John Suckling's hundred horse' (see Commentary), on the grounds that the text in *Musarum Deliciae*, with which Mennes was associated, is both sound and, so far as I am aware, the only substantive text of the poem. Still, the positive evidence is not great, and Aubrey's remarks do not much contribute to it: 'Sir John Menis made a lampoon of it [i.e. "a troope of 100 very handsome young proper men"] (vide the old collection of lampoons): "The ladies opened the windows to see | So fine and goodly a sight-a"' (*Brief Lives*, ii. 242). If, as is likely, Aubrey's 'old collection' is *Musarum Deliciae*, his comment echoes rather than fortifies the associational authority; moreover, despite the reference to 'a hundred horse more' in l. 3, he may be confusing 'Upon Sir John Suckling's hundred horse' with this poem, which he quotes inaccurately and probably *memoriter* (ll. 9–10).

l. 35. *Tre Trip*, i.e. *Trey-trip* 'A game at dice, or with dice, in which success probably depended on the casting of a trey or three' (*OED*).

INDEX OF FIRST LINES AND TITLES

In the following list, first lines are in upper and lower case, titles in SMALL CAPITALS. ? indicates poems of uncertain authorship, ‡ poems wrongly printed as Suckling's in the seventeenth century, and * poems not by but closely associated with Suckling, such as answer poems, lampoons, and the like.

A a

PRINTED IN GREAT BRITAIN
AT THE UNIVERSITY PRESS, OXFORD
BY VIVIAN RIDLER
PRINTER TO THE UNIVERSITY